A Comparative Analysis of Systems of Education Law

Charles J. Russo · Leijun Ma
Editors

A Comparative Analysis of Systems of Education Law

教育科学出版社
ESPH Educational Science Publishing House

Springer

Editors
Charles J. Russo
University of Dayton
Dayton, OH, USA

Leijun Ma
Research Center for Education Legislation and Standards
The China National Academy of Educational Sciences
Beijing, China

ISBN 978-981-97-1051-5 ISBN 978-981-97-1052-2 (eBook)
https://doi.org/10.1007/978-981-97-1052-2

Jointly published with Educational Science Publishing House Limited
The print edition is not for sale in China (Mainland). Customers from China (Mainland) please order the print book from: Educational Science Publishing House Limited.

This Springer imprint is published by the registered company Springer Nature Singapore Pte Ltd.
The registered company address is: 152 Beach Road, #21-01/04 Gateway East, Singapore 189721, Singapore

Paper in this product is recyclable.

Preface

One

Education and law have been accompanied by the development of human society.

Education in a broad sense is not a unique phenomenon of human beings. Education was the instinctive behavior of the animal kingdom long before the emergence of human beings. Therefore, there has been education since the birth of human beings. Education has not only contributed to the emergence of human beings, but also promoted the progress of human society. Human upright walking has led to the contradiction between the narrow pelvis and the highly developed brain. The solution to this contradiction is that the human fetus must be born before the brain is mature, which makes the human newborn unable to survive on its own. The time it needs to be taken care of is far longer than other mammals. This phenomenon makes education play an essential role in human growth. In early human society, education mainly existed in different families, clans, or tribes, and the content of education also primarily focused on survival, labor, and behavior rules.

Since the beginning of human society, customary law, the original form of law, has maintained the order and operation of human society. In primitive society, human beings had to rely on certain rules to ensure their basic security, whether inside or outside the clan. At the same time, people can also rely on the provisions of customary law to predict the consequences of behavior to establish a relatively stable survival order.

The emergence of writing has also promoted the development of education and law. With its own words, the history of word of mouth has been passed on more reliably. We can also understand the changes in education and law in human society over thousands of years from a modern perspective. According to the findings of historical archaeology, the rudiments of ancient schools emerged in the two river basins, ancient Egypt, ancient India, ancient China, ancient Hebrew, ancient Greece, and other places in succession. Among them, the Egyptian court school built in 2500 BC is probably the oldest school recorded in human history (Midinsky 1950). However, these schools are basically targeted at specific minorities, and it is still difficult for ordinary people to receive education in this form of school education. In terms of law, around 3000 BC, the written law of cuneiform characters, represented by the Code of Hammurabi, was born in the two river basins, which fixed the content of the previous customary law in the form of words. This is a landmark event in the history of law.

In the development process of education and law, the two developed relatively independently in the early stage, but with the intentional or unintentional intersection and combination of the two, the education law was born—a law that takes the right of citizens to receive education as the object of protection. However, people's understanding of the right to education is also changing. The earliest education law can only protect the right to education of minorities. Before large-scale school education, formal education was often the privilege of some minorities. Although Plato proposed that all citizens' children should receive formal school education, he divided the natural materials of human beings into bronze, silver, and gold, and people of different materials should receive different education. Confucius also once put forward the concept of "education without discrimination," but "I have never denied instruction to anyone who, of his own accord, has given me so much as a bundle of the dried meat as a present." Only those who take out ten pieces of dried meat as a gift can have the opportunity to be Confucius' students.

The landmark event after the combination of law and education occurred in Europe after the eighteenth century. In 1763, Prussia promulgated the General Compulsory Education Law, in 1833, France promulgated the Guizot Education Law, and in 1833 and 1870, Britain promulgated the Factory Law and the Primary Education Law. These educational legislations have advantageously promoted the popularization of education and made school education from the privilege of a few to the right of all. Subsequently, the legislation to promote the popularization of education, especially the special compulsory education legislation, began to develop worldwide, and the right to education gradually evolved into an important human right with consensus worldwide.

Two

There is no classification of disciplines in the world. The development of human knowledge has promoted the classification and specialization of knowledge. In the statements of Socrates and Confucius, the contents of pedagogy and law are often integrated, so both modern pedagogy and law will invariably cite their ideas in the literature.

Although there was a rudiment of discipline classification in ancient Greece, the emergence of universities promoted discipline classification. Ancient Egypt, ancient India, and ancient China all had some rudiments of early universities. For example, in ancient China, Imperial College, Guozixue, Guozijian, and other educational institutions were set up as the highest educational institutions in the country. In the Middle Ages, a number of modern universities were established in Europe. The Roman law of the University of Bologna, the medicine of the University of Salerno, the theology of the University of Paris, and the mathematics and natural sciences of the University of Oxford all became the center of school teaching. The innovation of Berlin University in 1809 marked the birth of a university in the modern sense. The natural sciences, social sciences, and humanities were separated from each other and formed a relatively fixed discipline knowledge system within the university. The existence of disciplines also leads to the division of majors and the formation of learning societies in universities. Human knowledge systems are artificially cut off from each other and isolated into relatively independent knowledge frameworks.

However, since the beginning of the last century, many scholars have begun to question this rigid division of disciplines, and on this basis, gradually formed a cross-disciplinary field—namely cross-disciplinary. John Higham once described the interdisciplinary as "People living in the room, with the door closed, look out from the open window and have a pleasant conversation with their neighbors (Geng 2018)." As mentioned above, the research scope of education and law has gradually begun to intersect and overlap, forming the interdisciplinary of educational law.

Human knowledge continues in succession, questioning, and innovation. The same is true of education and law. For example, for equality, in different historical development periods, we often give different value judgments. Even in the contemporary era, we can have different judgments on equality from different perspectives. However, this does not prevent mankind from pursuing some common values. For example, education in all countries is pursuing high-quality development on the premise of equality. For example, in the application of education punishment, education and law often have different perspectives. Educators often emphasize that education punishment is an educational method and pay more attention to human differences. Jurists often emphasize that education punishment is a rule of conduct and pay more attention to human equality.

Three

The development of education is inseparable from the protection, prediction, and guidance of law. The role and reaction of education law on education is based on the fact that we must use the more rigid vision of law to examine. Why should we carry out education? What kind of education should be carried out? And how we carry out education. In the end, we still need to return to the question of what the human rights of people in education are—the origin of educational law. In response to this question, different countries often put forward different solutions in their legislation, and these solutions are not solidified. Even within a country, there may be differences in the legislation of different regions, and there may be differences in the legislation of a fixed region in different development periods.

Therefore, there are not only differences in core concepts, logical starting points, analytical frameworks, and other dimensions between pedagogy and jurisprudence in the study of educational jurisprudence, but also differences in the aspects of educational jurisprudence due to differences in time and space. This is the source of the brilliance of our blue planet. The idea of diversity is that we can think more from the perspective of a third party and see the problems we haven't seen before. This is also the "habitual illusion" put forward in the field of security—it is difficult for a person to see the problems of familiar things around him. The mutual exchange between different countries, cultures, and systems can not only make us familiar with each other, but also can certainly eliminate the stereotyped, rigid, and even wrong impression between each other.

This book attempts to invite scholars from different countries to pay close attention to the comparative study of education legal systems in different countries, giving us a space to view the differences in education laws from a multidimensional perspective. Some of the countries were boasting that they had the world's best school system—perhaps because it was the one they knew best (Schleicher 2018). There is no specific educational legal system that is the best for all countries in the world, but there must be an educational legal system that is most suitable for each country. Even from the vertical perspective of a country's historical development, there is no unique and best legal system of education, because the legal system of education is constantly changing with the development of society and education, so that the law should not only adapt to the development of education, but also act as a driving force for the development of education.

This attempt to compile books will certainly prompt us to constantly reflect on the development of our education legislation. Of course, this mutual reference is absolutely not a copy, because the education laws of all countries are not only faced with common educational challenges, but also rooted in the educational background formed by the country's politics, economy, and culture. Just as the formation and evolution of the two major legal systems, the civil law system and the case law system, each country can choose according to its own actual situation, whether to take the written law or the case law as its main source of law. However, this does not hinder the reference, reference, and even integration between the civil law system and the case law system. Therefore, the education legal system and education legal system of various countries can be used for reference.

First of all, we have some common values of educational legislation. For example, Article 26 of the Universal Declaration of Human Rights states that everyone has the right to education. For example, Article 7 states that all are equal before the law and are entitled without any discrimination to equal protection of the law (The United Nations 1948). These common values of human society provide the basis for the protection of citizens' right to education and the equality of the right to education at the conceptual level and the level of international law.

Secondly, countries face more or less common educational challenges in their development. Although different countries have different levels of economic development and different social and cultural backgrounds, we are likely to face some common challenges at present and in the future. For example, the informatization and digitalization of education may have a profound impact on the educational system, educational content, school functions, teacher functions, teaching evaluation, etc., of schools in various countries. For example, the knowledge that can only be learned in school in the past can be mastered by students through the Internet, Muke, flipped class, and other forms. Under this teaching mode, how does the school provide support and guarantee for students' learning? What role should teachers play in students' learning? These problems also need specific education legal systems to respond and guide.

Thirdly, the design and implementation of specific education laws also have broad reference space. For the same educational legal phenomenon, different countries often provide different solutions, and diversified solutions also provide more possibilities for educational legislation. For example, even countries with the same civil law system often have different schemes in the presentation of written law. For example, Russia, France, and other countries have provided a model of a complete education code, that is, to regulate education legislation relatively completely by formulating a unified "education code." Japan, on the other hand, regulates some of the most fundamental legal issues of education by formulating the "Basic Law of Education," and on this basis, formulates some special separate legislation to regulate specific legal issues in the field of education. In China, efforts are being made to compile a unified education code based on the existing separate education legislation. In the USA, which is classified as a case law system, it also plays a special role in education legislation through the compilation of education laws in the "American Code."

This diversified legislative scheme of educational legal system will have a far-reaching impact in the future, both in the research of educational law and in the legislative practice of various countries.

Four

The development of education in the world today is facing severe challenges. This kind of challenge comes from the problems that people have paid attention to and have not yet discovered. For the problems that have been concerned and need to be responded to by legislation, we can formulate laws through the legislature and propose solutions at the legislative level. But the most challenging thing is that the law should not only solve the problems that actually occur at present, but also predict the problems that may occur in the future.

The predictive function of education law is shown in two aspects. First of all, people can predict the possible consequences of their actions through educational laws, so that the current subject of educational legal relations can avoid bearing the losses caused by illegal costs. At the same time, the education law also needs to predict what kind of education phenomenon will appear in the future and regulate what kind of legal consequences this kind of legal phenomenon will produce, so as to avoid unexpected results.

Our humanity and planet Earth are under threat. The pandemic has only served to prove our fragility and our interconnectedness. Now urgent action, taken together, is needed to change course and reimagine our futures (UNESCO 2021).

The threats that mankind faces are not only from nature, but also from wars, conflicts, and disputes caused by various reasons. We realize that the development of science and technology has continuously reduced our perceived distance on the earth. It only takes more than ten hours to travel from the USA to China on the other side of the earth, and the application of the Internet has enabled us to learn, discuss, and even play almost simultaneously. The connection, communication, and dependence between countries are also unprecedented. The production shortage of electronic chips in one country may lead to the paralysis of global electronics, automobile, and other industries. More and more products we buy in supermarkets are from different countries in the world. In this context, it is impossible for any country in the world to develop independently of other countries. Therefore, how to abandon the thinking of zero-sum game and pay attention to the coordinated development of the community of human destiny is also a problem that education and law need to pay attention to and deal with.

Education is an effective way to guide people to reasonably understand the conflict of interest itself, objectively view the differences in the world, and solve various conflicts by non-violent means. As pointed out in the "Reimagining our futures together: a new social contract for education" issued by UNESCO, We face a dual challenge of making good on the unfulfilled promise to ensure the right to quality education for every child, youth, and adult and fully realizing the transformational potential of education as a route for sustainable collective futures. To do this, we need a new social contract for education that can repair injustices while transforming the future (UNESCO 2021).

It is also worth considering what role education will play in the future social development. Since Confucius and Socrates, educators have recognized the double purpose of education: to impart the meaning and significance of the past and to prepare young people for the challenges of the future (Schleicher 2018).

Education has promoted the progress of human science and technology and the improvement of living conditions, and the progress of science and technology has made the scope, depth, and difficulty of students' learning content in school unprecedented. In many countries, the pressure and burden of learning not only offset the happiness brought by technological progress, but also forced some schools to equate the cultivation of students with the manufacture of machines. This makes us reflect, is the purpose of education to improve or reduce human happiness? How to deal with the competition among students, families, and even countries caused by utilitarian education?

Education law may not solve these problems from the root, but these problems are the problems that education law research has to face.

Leijun Ma
Deputy Director of Research Center for
Education Legislation and Standards
The China National Academy
of Educational Sciences
Beijing, China

References

Midinsky (1950) World history of education, life, reading and new knowledge joint bookstore, Beijing, 11

Geng Y (2018) Transdisciplinarity center of American research university and the development of university innovation—analysis from the perspective of institutional innovation. Comp Educ Res (9):24–28

Schleicher A (2018) World class how to build a 21st-century school system. https://www.oecd-ilibrary.org/docserver/9789264300002-en.pdf?expires=1672543261&id=id&accname=guest&checksum=D7E74DA7849075603BF867C7DFED045E, 18p

The United Nations (1948) Universal Declaration of Human Rights. https://www.un.org/en/about-us/universal-declaration-of-human-rights. Accessed 31 Mar 2022

UNESCO (2021) International Commission on the Futures of Education, Reimagining our futures together: a new social contract for education. https://unesdoc.unesco.org/ark:/48223/pf0000379707?posInSet=1&queryId=09ce3804-31d6-4c5c-884a-d3ed127fc836. Accessed 31 Mar 2022

Contents

The Right to Education in Argentina

Pablo A. Iannello

1 Introduction

The current Argentinean legal system grants the right to education the status of a fundamental right. As it has been recognized in the Constitution, as well as, international statues, including human rights treaties; right to education has been considered a pillar of democratic society since the return of democracy in 1983. The relation between education and democratic society has been stressed many times by the Argentinean Courts.

The right to education is also considered as a measure of positive action for granting equality of opportunity. In the recent years some Courts decisions have adopted some sort of priority view, recognizing that lower income sectors may have to attend school at the earliest stage possible so that both parents may generate an income (Ronconi 2014).

P. A. Iannello (✉)
Law and Tech Program, UADE, Buenos Aires, Argentina
e-mail: copyright@esph.com.cn

Law and Economics, Intellectual Property, Legal Theory and Comparative Legal Systems, UADE, Buenos Aires, Argentina

Law and Economics, Intellectual Property, Legal Theory and Comparative Legal Systems, UdeSA—Universidad de San Andrés, Victoria, Argentina

Law and Economics, Intellectual Property, Legal Theory and Comparative Legal Systems, UTDT, Buenos Aires, Argentina

UBA, Lagos, Nigeria

University of Dayton School of Law, Dayton, USA

C. J. Russo and L. Ma (eds.), *A Comparative Analysis of Systems of Education Law*,
https://doi.org/10.1007/978-981-97-1052-2_1

A proper view of education as a fundamental right, as well as a human right in Argentina, can only be explained as a part of the incorporation of human rights treaties as part of the Argentinean Constitution amendment occurred in 1994 which granted several human rights treaties the same status than the Local Constitution (Ronconi 2014).

Among the treaties incorporated in 1994 after the constitutional amendment, some of them are particularly relevant granting the right to education such as: the Universal Convention on Human Rights; the Convention on the Rights of the Child of 1989; the International Covenant on Civil and Political Rights of 1966; the American Convention on Human Rights signed in 1969; the Convention on the Elimination of All Forms of Discrimination against Women of 1979 and the Convention on the Rights of Persons with Disabilities of 2006.[1]

These treaties jointly with the provision of the article 14 on the Constitution[2] allow to see the right of education in a twofold way: education as adequacy and education as equality of opportunity.

As it is well known, the Universal Declaration of Human Rights, signed in 1948, promoted the consideration of education as a human right. In congruence with its great importance, the United Nations proclaimed January 24th as the International Day of Education, with the aim of commemorating and enforcing this right on all people.[3]

Education is considered an essential service and a social right that allows the growth and cognitive development of individuals Education allows improve the skills of each member of society. In a way education is a fundamental good that defines a person's life prospect. Since education facilitates access to knowledge as well as socialization more education is usually a way of obtaining a better socio economic position (Brandon 2016).

---

[1] *Universal Convention on Human Rights*, Art 26 (December 10th, 1948) Accessed for the last time December 26th, 2022: http://www.infoleg.gob.ar/?page_id=1003; *Convention on the Rights of the Child*, Art 29 and 30 (November 20th, 1989) Accessed for the last time January 2nd, 2023: https://www.un.org/es/events/childrenday/pdf/derechos.pdf; *International Covenant on Civil and Political Rights*, Art 18 and 20 (December 16th, 1966) Accessed for the last time December 14th, 2022: https://www.argentina.gob.ar/sites/default/files/derechoshumanos_publicaciones_colecciondebolsillo_06_derechos_civiles_politicos.pdf; *American Convention on Human Rights*, Art 12 and 26 (November 22nd, 1969) Accessed for the last time December 8th, 2022: https://www.argentina.gob.ar/sites/default/files/derechoshumanos_publicaciones_colecciondebolsillo_10_convencion_americana_ddhh.pdf; *Convention on the Elimination of All Forms of Discrimination against Women* (December 18th, 1979) Accessed for the last time November 29th, 2022: http://servicios.infoleg.gob.ar/infolegInternet/anexos/25000-29999/26305/norma.htm; *Convention on the Rights of Persons with Disabilities* (December 13th, 2006) Accessed for the last time November 15th, 2022: https://www.argentina.gob.ar/normativa/nacional/ley-26378-141317/texto.

[2] *Argentina National Constitution*, Art 14 (May 1st, 1853) Accessed for the last time November 3rd, 2022: http://servicios.infoleg.gob.ar/infolegInternet/anexos/0-4999/804/norma.htm.

[3] *United Nations General Assembly* (December 3rd, 2018) Resolution 73/25, adopted during the 73rd regular session of the United Nations. Accessed for the last time January 10th, 2023: https://documents-dds-ny.un.org/doc/UNDOC/GEN/N18/412/83/PDF/N1841283.pdf?OpenElement.

Granting access education at all stages, brings each person the possibility of a future with equal opportunities and with possibilities of choice in various aspects, since it allows to analyze the information received from their environment and obtain their own conclusions. It allows hundreds of people to get out of poverty and marginalization. Education should be egalitarian, inclusive and of good quality for all (Colombo and Luzzi 2022).

As the Universal Declaration of Human Rights states, "*Everyone has the right to education. Education shall be free, at least for elementary and fundamental instruction. Elementary instruction shall be compulsory. Technical and vocational education shall be made generally available and higher education shall be equally accessible to all based on merit*". (Declaration of Human Right. Art 26, 1948).[4]

Despite the socioeconomic advantage that access to education may generate, it is also accepted that an adequate education, in turn, makes it possible to encourage and inculcate respect for others, to understand fundamental freedoms and to adequately develop the human personality (Rodino 2015).

Nowadays Argentina faces significant challenges in granting right to education. After the pandemic suffered worldwide, several problems were exposed. Among those with vital relevance can be mentioned the disparity in the technological gap, as well as the role of educational institutions as foster homes that supplement the roles of parents (Alvarez et al. 2020).

The structural difference has always been a stone in the road of developing educational policies in the region preventing equality of opportunity to become real. The pandemic has stressed that gap because exposed the socioeconomic differences in accessing technology (Alvarez et al. 2020).

Justice and national authorities should oversee setting a limit and enforcing people's rights, sanctioning, and taking measures in case of deprivation or violation of the right to education. As Habermas has pointed out normative explanations should not be detached from social reality.

In Argentina there is a significant gap between the rights as recognized in the books and their implementation. A proper description of reality is the base for the efficacy in the legal system. The right to education has not always kept that dialectical structure (Jover 2001).

This chapter is structure as follows: Section 1 provides a quick overview of the evolution of right to Education in Argentina from a Historical point of view; Section 2 explain the main features of the current Argentinean educational system; Section 3 provides an overview of different case laws in which Courts have addressed education as a right; Section 4 depicts some challenges for the right to education, lastly some concluding remarks are offered.

---

[4] *Universal Convention on Human Rights*, Art 26 (December 10th, 1948) Accessed for the last time December 26th, 2022. http://www.infoleg.gob.ar/?page_id=1003.

2 Evolution of Legal Rules in Education

The Argentinean educational system in Argentina has been shaped because of certain events which have defined and shaped the educational system to reach its current structure Those events may be summarized in three pillars discussion of jurisdictional issues, cultural, religious and gender diversity, and equality of opportunity as a matter of democracy. The following paragraphs offer a short overview of this historical picture.

(a) **The origins in the XIX century**

The legal roots of the right of Education in Argentina can be easily found in the Constitution of 1853/1860 which contained an expressed right to education in the article 14 by stating that *"all inhabitants of the Nation have the right to teach and learn"* (Argentinian Constitution—Art. 14, 1853).[5]

This is not a minor detail, since it shows that Argentina granted education an expressed constitutional status since its origin as a country. On the other hand, it shows a very progressist perspective if it is considered that the Argentinean Constitution mirrored the US Constitution where no explicit provision is contained about the right to education at the Constitutional Level.[6]

Enlightenment and liberalism were the mainstream way of thinking by the time the Constitution was enacted, and they dominated political, economic and philosophical discourses. Thus, the right to learned and teach should be understood as part of the bundles of rights that and individual was supposed to be granted with in order to access knowledge without interference of State. This perspective was also consistent with the idea of the minimal state. So, from this liberal perspective education was conceived as a tool for allowing individuals a proper understanding of the world relieving him from the obscurantism of the "ancient regime" (Peters 2019).

During this classical liberalism era education also played a major role in Argentina, since it allowed to transform the wild lands and their inhabitants into western the western world As such, the creation and implementation of the educational system and institutions were considered as an expression of discipline and control of society. These would allow the propagation of western values to a new citizenry which in its beginnings was constituted through absolute power (Peters 2019).

---

[5] **Art. 14**—Todos los habitantes de la Nación gozan de los siguientes derechos conforme a las leyes que reglamenten su ejercicio; a saber: de trabajar y ejercer toda industria lícita; de navegar y comerciar; de peticionar a las autoridades; de entrar, permanecer, transitar y salir del territorio argentino; de publicar sus ideas por la prensa sin censura previa; de usar y disponer de su propiedad; de asociarse con fines útiles; de profesar libremente su culto; de enseñar y aprender.

[6] The Court refused to examine the system with strict scrutiny since there is no fundamental right to education in the Constitution and since the system did not systematically discriminate against all poor people in Texas (San *Antonio Independent School District v. Rodriguez*), 411 U.S. 1 (1973).

Besides the content of the art. 14, the Argentinean Constitution of 1853 also mandates the provinces, based on art 5,[7] to enact their own constitutions, which must be consistent with the basic civil and political rights recognized in the federal Constitution As a result, Provinces also recognized the right to education. This is an important feature that has shaped the legal framework of education until today since it determines the possibility of concurrent jurisdiction on educational matters. This structure was modified with the constitutional amendment of 1994 as it will be developed later this chapter.[8]

Education was then understood as a mechanism of social control which is aligned with the obligation of the "minimal state" spread in XIX century of securing access to only to primary school. On the other hand, the possibility of education was even considered a privilege of the highest social sectors, precisely of the country's elite. We can even affirm that education in principle was not considered as a right of society. (De Singlau 2018).

The educational system during this period was shaped by Domingo Faustino Sarmiento, a former president of Argentina but also a men of literacy and politics. Sarmiento embraced the ideas of liberalism and enlightenment as apply for setting the foundational basis of the right to Education in Argentina, It was Sarmiento who dictated the first "Organic Law of Public Education" which imposed the obligation to attend primary education and the creation of various educational establishments. (Villavicencio 2010).

As a man of his time Sarmiento saw education as a tool to promote civilization understood as the world of enlightenment and liberalism. In order to achieve that view basic education was supposed to be available to everyone. That was the only way to oppose the "Barbarie" and transform Argentina into a civilize European nation.[9]

In 1884 a cornerstone of the Argentinean education system was enacted: the 1420 Act. Its principals' goals were to achieve free, compulsory, gradual, secular, and egalitarian primary education for boys and girls. This last aspect was not something normal in the world where women were relegated from all areas of society. The statue established the obligation for the state to recognize compulsory free and gradual education for the entire population and the training of teachers and the obligation of parents to enroll and take their children to school under sanction. Parents, in turn, were empowered to inspect and form part of a National Education Council, which oversaw enforcing the rights of children and the general administration of schools (Finnegan and Pagano 2007).

[7] **Art. 5**—Cada provincia dictará para sí una Constitución bajo el sistema representativo republicano, de acuerdo con los principios, declaraciones y garantías de la Constitución Nacional; y que asegure su administración de justicia, su régimen municipal, y la educación primaria. Bajo de estas condiciones el Gobierno federal, garante a cada provincia el goce y ejercicio de sus instituciones.

[8] *Argentina National Constitution*, Art 14 (May 1st, 1853) Accessed for the last time November 3rd, 2022: http://servicios.infoleg.gob.ar/infolegInternet/anexos/0-4999/804/norma.htm.

[9] The idea of Barbarie should be framed in the Argentinean intellectual history as a concept of what it was known as generación del 37. The concept referred to the local iliterated people that lived in the provinces as opposed to the well instructed and rich people of Buenos Aires.

However, implementation was not quite straight forward. Members of the conservative party, that governed Argentina between 1880 and 1916, were reluctant to the idea of implementing a popular education, since they considered that false expectations were generated about the social ascent through education and that clearly, they were going to be frustrated. After an arduous analysis and testing of the facts, they went on to observe it with the passage of time from a positive posture and national progress, thus guaranteeing this fundamental right (Finnegan and Pagano 2007).

Some years later, the Law 1.420[10] was supplemented with the enactment of the law 4874 which was enacted in 1905, known as the "Láinez Act", since it was promoted by the Senator of the province of Buenos Aires, Manuel Láinez. The main objective of the Láinez act was to amend the poor performance of the States in reducing analphabetism allowing provinces to require aid to the federal State for the creation of rural primary schools, but also allowed the federal state to decide the creation of primary school, without previous request of the provinces. From a constitutional perspective this is a significant change since it meant two overlapping educational systems coexist the one promoted by the provinces in accordance with art 14 and 5 of the Constitution and the one promoted by the Federal State (Scioscioli 2017).

(b) **The emergence of Social constitutionalism movement and its implications in education law**

At the beginning of the XXth Century Argentina faced a huge wave of immigration. Immigrant were mainly illiterate so that represented a challenge for a brand new and still fragile educational system. However, immigration came to the new world with a novel political and economic ideas such us socialism and anarchism whose impact on educational law happened to be clear in the years to come. The main outcome was the emergence of Social Constitutionalism.

This movement known is based on the enlargement of fundamental rights granted by the constitution, including social and economic rights. In other words, social constitutionalism demands an active participation of the State in the economic life of the community (Herrera 2014).

Therefore, it was expected that the state played a more active role on education, since education was no longer a tool to achieve the liberal standards on XIX century, but to promote social mobility.

Some commentators have used the Hohfeldian right's structure to explain the right of education. This approach is quite useful because the shift from the liberal view to the social constitutional view implied a shift from a claim based right to education to an immunity granting equal access to education.

A clear example of the impact of social constitutionalism in education law was the enactment of the law 12.558.[11] The aim of this legislation was the implementation of the "fosters home schools for under the joint supervision of the ministry of education

[10] Accessed for the last time December 10th 2022: http://www.saij.gob.ar/1420-nacional-ley-educacion-lns0002601-1884-06-26/123456789-0abc-defg-g10-62000scanyel.

[11] Accessed for the las time 16th, 2022: https://www.argentina.gob.ar/normativa/nacional/ley-12558-233063/texto.

and the Ministry of health". This law was landmark since considered education from a broader perspective including access to food for and health care for children within the time they attend mandatory schooling.

Another, significant reception of social Constitutionalism took place during the precedency of Juan Domingo Perón, The First Five-Year Plan (1947–1952) during Perón's presidency conceived education as a tool to realize the purposes of expanding social rights for children including education.

It is worth to notice that, despite the positive distributive impact during this period, it was also the time for nationalism which also affected education. An example of this nationalist view that was the presidential Decree No. 26944/47,[12] which stated a mandatory provision of teaching the national values to all students. (Decreto No. 26.944/47, 1947).

Another major event during Perón Presidency was the amendment of the Constitution which took place in 1949. The new basic rule contained very detailed provisions about education understood as part of cultural rights. The 1949 Constitution developed right to education with significant level of detail which was reserved for lower norms.[13]

---

[12] Accessed for the last time December 10th, 2022: http://www.bnm.me.gov.ar/giga1/normas/3534.pdf.

[13] *Argentina National Constitution*. Reform 1949. Art. 5—Cada provincia dictará para sí una Constitución bajo el sistema representativo republicano, de acuerdo con los principios, declaraciones y garantías de la Constitución Nacional; y que asegure su administración de justicia, su régimen municipal, la educación primaria y la cooperación requerida por el Gobierno Federal a fin de hacer cumplir esta Constitución y las leyes de la Nación que en su consecuencia se dicten. Con estas condiciones, el Gobierno Federal garantiza a cada provincia el goce y ejercicio de sus instituciones; Art. 37—La educación y la instrucción corresponden a la familia y a los establecimientos particulares y oficiales que colaboren con ella, conforme a lo que establezcan las leyes. Para ese fin, el Estado creará escuelas de primera enseñanza, secundaria, técnico-profesionales, universidades y academias. (1) La enseñanza tenderá al desarrollo del vigor físico de los jóvenes, al perfeccionamiento de sus facultades intelectuales y de sus potencias sociales, a su capacitación profesional, así como a la formación del carácter y el cultivo integral de todas las virtudes personales, familiares y cívicas. (2) La enseñanza primaria elemental es obligatoria y será gratuita en las escuelas del Estado. La enseñanza primaria en las escuelas rurales tenderá a inculcar en el niño el amor a la vida del campo, a orientarlo hacia la capacitación profesional en las faenas rurales y a formar la mujer para las tareas domésticas campesinas. El Estado creará, con ese fin, los institutos necesarios para preparar un magisterio especializado. (3) La orientación profesional de los jóvenes, concebida como un complemento de la acción de instruir y educar, es una función social que el Estado ampara y fomenta mediante instituciones que guíen a los jóvenes hacia las actividades para las que posean naturales aptitudes y capacidad, con el fin de que la adecuada elección profesional redunde en beneficio suyo y de la sociedad. (4) El Estado encomienda a las universidades la enseñanza en el grado superior, que prepare a la juventud para el cultivo de las ciencias al servicio de los fines espirituales y del engrandecimiento de la Nación y para el ejercicio de las profesiones y de las artes técnicas en función del bien de la colectividad. Las universidades tienen el derecho de gobernarse con autonomía, dentro de los límites establecidos por una ley especial que reglamentará su organización y funcionamiento; Art 14—De la educación y la cultura La educación y la instrucción corresponde a la familia y a los establecimientos particulares y oficiales que colaboren con ella. Para ese fin, el Estado creará escuelas de primera enseñanza, secundarias, técnico profesionales, universidades y academias.

The 1949 Constitution was declared void after the *coup of* 1955, that took down Perón from the presidency and the 1853 version of the constitution was restored. However, a new section (art. 14bis) was included, which endures until the current version of the Argentinean constitution. This section contains the second-generation rights in Argentinean Constitution.

In the following years a significant debate about how to regulate education took place at the University level. The core of the discussion was whether Catholic education should be imposed, or religion had to be removed from the curriculum at the University level. The reason why this debate initiated after Perón was removed had to do with the high role that the catholic church and some catholic movement had played against Peron. They saw the opportunity to promote the ideas about what was called "educación libre" based on the idea that each university had the possibility to decide whether to include religious studies as mandatory courses in their curriculum. (Micheletti 2018).

(c) **The transformation in the 1990s**

In 1991, the enactment of the law No. 24.049[14] on the Transfer of Establishments Middle and Higher Non-University Level constituted the beginning of a significant transformation in the Education. The origins of this new piece of legislation had no direct relation with education. The reasons behind that law were mainly to solve a problem of budget deficit at the Federal public spending system. Argentina was under a severe international debt restructuration. In order to success in that process federal stated had to reduce spending's. Education was among the target areas to reduce the deficit. Although this goal is highly debatable, this was achieved by transferring all administrative and financial responsibilities of the group of the schools financed by the federal government to the provinces (Ministerio de Educación 2003).

In 1993, the Federal Education Law No. 24,195[15] was enacted establishing a 10-year compulsory schooling period that extends from the last year of the Initial Level to the ninth year of General Basic Education. This law generated great resistance, mainly regarding changes in the academic structure, since the extension of the schooling stage, once again, played hard on the most vulnerable sectors. People with lower socioeconomic level, would face higher difficulties to finish their compulsory studies. The law also equated public education with private education and collaborated with socio-educational differentiation. For many authors this also created an advantage for those facing the possibilities of access to elite education, which lead to increase the differences in society (Feldfeber and Ivanier 2003).

The most significant event in the 90s was the amendment of the Argentinean Constitution which had a great impact in education. The new version of the Argentinean Supreme Law contained three important features related with the right to education. Firstly, it incorporated several human rights treaties granting the constitutional hierarchy. Among the treaties included it was the convention for children´s

[14] Accessed for the last time December 16th, 2022: https://www.argentina.gob.ar/normativa/nacional/ley-24049-448/texto.

[15] Accessed for the last time December 10th, 2022: https://www.argentina.gob.ar/normativa/nacional/ley-24195-17009/texto.

rights, as is was previously mentioned education became a human right. Secondly art. 75 Inc. 17[16] recognized the right of respecting cultural heritage native people. So, in the provinces in which locals live they have a right to receive an education which respect their cultural background including their original languages. Last and more important, art 75 Inc. 19[17] of the Constitution recognized education as a form of achieving an egalitarian society.

In 1995, Law 24,521[18] on higher education was passed. It introduced innovations in the educational system at the university level, it was highly criticized and led to the filing of hundreds of judicial appeals by the university community for considering that its view of education was merely commercial instead as a right for an equal society (Finnegan and Pagano 2007).

Regarding the granting of university degrees, the law established the simultaneous and automatic granting of the academic degree and the professional qualification without distinction between public and private education (Law 24,521—Educación Superior 1995).

The same statute created the National Commission for University Evaluation and Accreditation (CONEAU)[19] which is in charge of the supervision of university degrees including a mechanism for evaluation and accreditation regime of university

---

[16] *Argentina National Constitution* Art 75. Inc 17. Reconocer la preexistencia étnica y cultural de los pueblos indígenas argentinos. Garantizar el respeto a su identidad y el derecho a una educación bilingüe e intercultural; reconocer la personería Jurídica de sus comunidades, y la posesión y propiedad comunitarias de las tierras que tradicionalmente ocupan; y regular la entrega de otras aptas y suficientes para el desarrollo humano; ninguna de ellas será enajenable, transmisible ni susceptible de gravámenes o embargos. Asegurar su participación en la gestión referida a sus recursos naturales y a los demás intereses que los afecten. Las provincias pueden ejercer concurrentemente estas atribuciones.

[17] *Argentina National Constitution* Art 75. Inc 19. Proveer lo conducente al desarrollo humano, al progreso económico con justicia social, a la productividad de la economía nacional, a la generación de empleo, a la formación profesional de los trabajadores, a la defensa del valor de la moneda, a la investigación y al desarrollo científico y tecnológico, su difusión y aprovechamiento.

Proveer al crecimiento armónico de la Nación y al poblamiento de su territorio; promover políticas diferenciadas que tiendan a equilibrar el desigual desarrollo relativo de provincias y regiones. Para estas iniciativas, el Senado será Cámara de origen. Sancionar leyes de organización y de base de la educación que consoliden la unidad nacional respetando las particularidades provinciales y locales; que aseguren la responsabilidad indelegable del Estado, la participación de la familia y la sociedad, la promoción de los valores democráticos y la igualdad de oportunidades y posibilidades sin discriminación alguna; y que garanticen los principios de gratuidad y equidad de la educación pública estatal y la autonomía y autarquía de las universidades nacionales.

Dictar leyes que protejan la identidad y pluralidad cultural, la libre creación y circulación de las obras del autor; el patrimonio artístico y los espacios culturales y audiovisuales.

[18] Accessed for the last time December 3rd, 2022: http://servicios.infoleg.gob.ar/infolegInternet/anexos/25000-29999/25394/texact.htm#:~:text=Proh%C3%ADbase%20a%20las%20institucio nes%20de,que%20alienten%20formas%20de%20mercantilizaci%C3%B3n.

[19] CONEAU is composed of twelve members of recognized academic and scientific hierarchy, with experience in university management. They perform their functions in their personal capacity, with independence of judgment and without assuming the representation of any institution. The members of CONEAU are appointed by the National Executive Power.

degrees, which was an absolute novelty in the Argentine university legislation, establishing the mandatory nature of the internal evaluation or permanent self-evaluation of the university institutions and their periodic external evaluation. With respect to postgraduate programs, only specialization, master's and doctoral programs are subject to periodic accreditation. This regulation also created a Council of Universities, with the objective of creating a certain degree of university coordination (Finnegan and Pagano 2007).

3 Current Structure of Education Law in Argentina

Nowadays, the legal framework of Argentina is the result of different political views about education. As it was previously explained after the amendment of the Constitution in 1994 of International human rights treaties will be considered as having Constitutional Hierarchy. This clarification is essential to understand the current legal framework of education in Argentina, since courts will usually appeal to the human rights discourse for solving educational matters.

Jurisdiction over educational matters remains concurrent at National, Provincial, and county level. Each level will have the obligation to enforce the rights and impart obligations to the citizenry.

The basis for considering access to education as a human right is granted by the 1990 Convention on the Rights of the Child Article 27[20] which stablishes that "parents or others responsible for the child have the primary responsibility to secure, within their abilities and financial capacities, such conditions of life as are necessary for the child's development. States Parties, in accordance with national conditions and within their means, shall take appropriate measures to assist parents and others responsible for the child to implement this right and, where necessary, shall provide material assistance and support programs, particularly regarding nutrition, clothing and housing" (Convention on the Rights of the Child 1989) i.e., parents shall be

[20] Convention on the Rights of the Child 1989. Art 27—Los Estados Partes reconocen la importante función que desempeñan los medios de comunicación y velarán por que el niño tenga acceso a información y material procedentes de diversas fuentes nacionales e internacionales, en especial la información y el material que tengan por finalidad promover su bienestar social, espiritual y moral y su salud física y mental. Con tal objeto, los Estados Partes: (a) Alentarán a los medios de comunicación a difundir información y materiales de interés social y cultural para el niño, de conformidad con el espíritu del artículo 29; (b) Promoverán la cooperación internacional en la producción, el intercambio y la difusión de esa información y esos materiales procedentes de diversas fuentes culturales, nacionales e internacionales; (c) Alentarán la producción y difusión de libros para niños; (d) Alentarán a los medios de comunicación a que tengan particularmente en cuenta las necesidades lingüísticas del niño perteneciente a un grupo minoritario o que sea indígena; (e) Promoverán la elaboración de directrices apropiadas para proteger al niño contra toda información y material perjudicial para su bienestar, teniendo en cuenta las disposiciones de los artículos 13 y 18.

responsible for the fulfillment of the rights and needs of children and in case of impossibility of such fulfillment the State shall be present (Feldfeber and Ivanier 2003).

On the other hand, the right to learn and teach, enshrined for the first time in the Argentine National Constitution sanctioned in 1853, remains to be one of the pillars of education law.

Section 17 of Article 75 established the obligation of the National Congress to "Recognize the ethnic and cultural pre-existence of the Argentine indigenous peoples. To guarantee respect for their identity and the right to a bilingual and intercultural education".

On the other hand, subsection 19 of article 75 determined the need to "Sanction laws of organization and basis of education that consolidate national unity while respecting provincial and local particularities; that ensure the non-delegable responsibility of the State, the participation of the family and society, the promotion of democratic values and equality of opportunities and possibilities without any discrimination whatsoever; and that guarantee the principles of free and equitable public state education and the autonomy and autarchy of the national universities".

The National Education System is the organized set of educational services and actions regulated by the State that make possible the exercise of the right to education. It is made up of the educational services of state and private management, cooperative management, and social management, of all the jurisdictions of the country, covering the different levels, cycles, and modalities of education". We can see how it includes not only public education, but also the support and containment of private educational entities. It seeks to obtain certain coherence and unification of the structures throughout the country. It is also stated in our Preamble as one of the objectives of article 5,[21] which is to promote the general welfare of society.

The Federal State is the one who guarantees the financing of the Education System, which a percentage of the national budget must always be destined to education, without exception. The National Education Law contemplates the need and obligation to guarantee access to education at all levels and modalities through state management, including National Universities (Ley de Educación 26,206—Art 16, 2006).

Today the right to education in the Argentine Republic is specifically regulated, at the statutory level by the National Education Law No. 26,206, which was passed by the Congress in 2006, with the aim of establishing bases and guidelines to rebuild and recover education. It seeks to achieve a fairer and more equitable society. Education is a fundamental State policy to reaffirm national sovereignty and identity and constitutes a national priority. This law does not affect the autonomy of the provinces in educational matters (Ley de Educación 26,206—Art 6, 2006).

[21] *Argentina National Constitution* 1949. Art. 5—Cada provincia dictará para sí una Constitución bajo el sistema representativo republicano, de acuerdo con los principios, declaraciones y garantías de la Constitución Nacional; y que asegure su administración de justicia, su régimen municipal, la educación primaria y la cooperación requerida por el Gobierno Federal a fin de hacer cumplir esta Constitución y las leyes de la Nación que en su consecuencia se dicten. Con estas condiciones, el Gobierno Federal garantiza a cada provincia el goce y ejercicio de sus instituciones.

This law also seeks to continue with the exercise of a democratic citizenship that allows respecting and guaranteeing the fundamental rights and freedoms of the whole society. Education must be recognized as integral, of quality and permanent for all the inhabitants of the Nation at national and provincial level (Ley de Educación 26,206—Art 4, 2006).

The State must guarantee the living conditions of all citizens that allow them to access and exercise the right to education. The dissatisfaction of basic needs related to housing, food, health, and work does not allow to face a series of rights and causes us to be in front of an institutional conflict. There is dissatisfaction of fundamental human rights (Ley de Educación 26,206—Art 12, 2006).

The National Education System has 4 educational levels: Initial Education which constitutes a pedagogical unit and comprises children from forty-five (45) days up to and including five (5) years of age, the last year being compulsory; Primary Education, is compulsory and constitutes a pedagogical and organizational unit intended for the training of children from six (6) years of age until 12 years old; and Secondary Education, usually runs from 13 year old until 17 constitutes a pedagogical and organizational unit intended for adolescents and young people who have completed the Primary Education level.. Education remains mandatory since four years old until the end of secondary school (Ley de Educación 26,206—Art 17, 2006).

At the higher education level three educational structures coexist until the end of the transition stage towards the implementation of the new National Education and Higher Education Law, which comprises Universities and University Institutes, state or private authorized, in accordance with the denomination established in Law No. 24,521 and Higher Education Institutes of national, provincial or Autonomous City of Buenos Aires jurisdiction, state or privately managed (Law 26,206—Ley de Educación Nacional, 2006).

On the other hand, our law provides for eight modalities, which each jurisdiction shall be free to choose: Technical Professional Education, Artistic Education, Special Education, Permanent Education for Young People and Adults, Rural Education, Intercultural Bilingual Education, Education in Contexts of Deprivation of Liberty and Home and Hospital Education (Ley de Educación 26,206—Art 17, 2006).

Education shall be public and universal at all levels. To allow access to all children and thus encourage continuity in the school system, providing support not only to students but also to families in general. By recognizing the right of access to public education, our legislation seeks to promote social inclusion, equity and equal opportunities that allow the country's progress and the insertion of all social strata in the system.

The enforcement authority of Law 26,206 will be the Ministry of Education of the Nation. Its function will be to dictate general executive orders on equivalence of curricula and curricular designs of the jurisdictions, in accordance with the provisions of Article 85 of the National Education Law and to grant national validity to degrees and certifications of studies, on revalidation, equivalence and recognition of degrees issued and studies carried out abroad; and to coordinate and manage international technical and financial cooperation and promote integration, particularly with the Mercosur countries (Ley de Educación 26,206—Art 85, 2006).

The highest educational authority of the jurisdiction to which the educational institution belongs must process before the Directorate of National Validity of Degrees and Studies the validity of all degrees and certificates issued at all educational levels. The relevance of such validity is linked to the unification of the National Educational System to guarantee that all educational offers comply with the minimum and indispensable requirements throughout the national territory.

4 Conflicts in the Right to Education and the Role of Courts

From a "law in the books" perspective Argentinean educational system is quite well designed and grounded. However, application also named as "law in the practice" is far from being perfect.

Children are obliged to attend an educational establishment from the age of 5 and must continue until the completion of their secondary education. The National State promotes various institutional and pedagogical alternatives to promote and encourage education and carefully observes the fulfillment of all requirements (Ley de Educación 26,206—Art 16, 2006).

The lack of access to vacancies at all levels is a recurrent problem that requires immediate regulation by the national government. They must take measures to guarantee access, permanence, and graduation from education. Another conflict facing our country is the lack of concrete figures (Teregi 2009).

The functioning of the institutions must be supervised, avoiding abuse or misappropriation of the budget destined to the growth and development of education.

In recent years, through the implementation of public policies, certain incentives have been put in place to encourage the most vulnerable sectors of society to study, such as education programs, scholarships, family allowances linked to school financial aid. These policies seek to provide better structural conditions for education. (Resolución 29/2023—Ministerio de Educación 2023).

Inequality and fragmentation of the educational system is another of the major conflicts we encounter. In the 2000s, the country suffered a great economic crisis which, therefore, increased social inequalities and poverty levels grew exponentially, resulting in great social instability. This context generated a negative impact on education. Today this situation is repeated and has been deepened by the Covid-19 pandemic, we can observe great differences regarding education in the various sectors of society (Barrera Buteler 2020).

Inequalities in this area lead individuals to the courts seeking to defend the right to education and equal access to this right. Equality is widely recognized in constitutional matters. Only those classifications that are reasonable will be allowed. There must be certain functionality with the purpose sought in the case of allowing categorization and the State is the one who must justify the different treatment(Vernor 2019).

In a leading case from the year 2000 "González de Delgado, Cristina y otros c. Universidad Nac. de Córdoba a/Amparo"(CSJN 323/2659, s.f.) the Supreme Court reached a decision applying the balancing test between the right of freedom of association and the right of equality in educational matters. In this case, the fathers, and mothers of regular students at the Monserrat National School, which is part of the National University of Córdoba, filed an amparo challenging Resolution 2/97 of the Superior Council of the University, which would transform the school into a coeducational institution. Until then, only men were allowed to enter the school, excluding women. The parents claimed their right to choose the education of their children, who at that time were in their first and second year. The Court resolved the issue by arguing the legitimacy of Ordinance 2/97 of the Higher Council of the University.

In the joint vote, no mention is made of the equality issue raised in the case. In his arguments, the Court argued that the plaintiffs have not shown what would be the compelling public interest that would make it advisable to exclude the young women from the benefits of the education provided by the Monserrat. The Court considered as suspect classification in any discrimination based on gender as far as access to education is concern (Ronconi 2015).

In the Court view there were no arguments to exclude women from admission to Monserrat School, as also recognize the concept of structural inequality that this group has suffered making an specific claim that the impossibility of entering the school perpetuates this situation structural inequality (Saba 2019).

More recent case law about education can be categorized in two main areas.

On the one side those cases containing a tension between religion content in public schools, and on the other side, cases related with granting equal access to the initial stages of education. The first group of cases have been more common in the provinces, which tend to be more conservative, and religion still play a role in education. The latter group cases have occurred mainly in the Capital city and in the suburbs, since they are the most populated areas. It's also the region where poverty ratios are significantly high.

In the following lines I will present a brief of some leading cases on each of the topics previously mentioned. The cases selected aim to show how many of the points stated in the previous section are not just a historical reflection of education law but the living law about how courts understand the right to education.

1. *The case "Asociación Civil Asamblea Permanente por los Derechos Humanos c/ Dirección General de Escuelas s/ Amparo.* (CSJN 4956/2015, 2022)

In 2022 the Argentinean Supreme Court rule a case in which the plaintiff where seeking for the unconstitutionality of an administrative resolution of the "Dirección General de Espuelas de Mendoza". The administrative rule mandated to celebrate the "Día del Patrón Santiago" and "Día de la Virgen de Cuyo" in all schools of the Province of Mendoza.

The plaintiff went on appeal to the Supreme Court because of the affection of arts 14, 5 and 121 of the Argentinean Constitution. Its main argument was that the Defendant had breached the state duty of State neutrality in public school related to religious matters and that those celebrations also affected the right to no discriminations since it granted relevance only to catholic festivities. The court rejected the plaintiff request. The main arguments for the rejection were:

(a) The celebrations invoked; despite the fact they may have a religion origin are more related with the culture of the people of Mendoza than with any religious significance. So, the province of Mendoza did not impose any religious activity since those festivities are related with historical events of the province despite any relation with the roman catholic religion.
(b) Federal State set the basis for education in the Argentinean territory. However, the provinces enjoy a significant autonomy for regulating primary educations in their own districts.
(c) These kinds of celebrations do not affect the right to privacy since there is no evidence that either students or faculty that may decide not to celebrate may be discriminated in any way.

2. *The case N. B. C. V. Gobierno de la Ciudad de Buenos Aires*

In 2020 the Superior Court of the City of Buenos Aires had to decide a petition about whether the denial of a place in a public school for his two years old son was a violation to the Constitutional right to education as well as a violation to human rights treaties with constitutional hierarchy. For the majority of the Court, there were no violation on the plaintiff rights.

(a) In the Court view the Federal Constitution as well as the Constitution of the City of Buenos Aires mandates the State to grant access to education from elementary school (4 years old) until the end of high school. There is no interpretation nor in the Constitutional text nor in inferior norms that allow an interpretation upon which local states must grant access to education prior to the four's years old.
(b) It is true that the Federal Constitution in article 14 as well as art. 17 of the Local Constitution recognize grants a right of education. However, it is also true that for the cases in which education is not mandatory—below 4 years old, or after finishing high school—the legal system adopts a prioritizing view by which the less advantages are given priority to those with more social and economic advantages in getting a place in the non-mandatory educational system.
(c) Since neither the Federal Constitution nor the local Constitution contain a criterion for priority it has been interpreted that it should be given priority to those with lower incomes a poorer social condition.
(d) It is no possible to grant a subsidy to attend public education to the plaintiff because of denial of a place in a public school, since that may constitute a privilege without justification.

The afforded mentioned cases reflect two areas in which that the case law has been a great tool to shape the scope of right of education.

On the one side the relation between education and religion. The ongoing view accepts a clear right to a secular education. However, as it was stated, this limit does not imply that the catholic roots of the Argentinean society can be invoked as part of the cultural heritage taught in public school.

On the other side, an a much more contemporary problem the scope and limits of right to education in term of access from and egalitarian and prioritizing perspective. This last approach has left open a significant question which is priority of what (Correas 2008). Case law on this matter is consistent with the idea that a priority place should be given to those with fewer resources. However, a proper measure of those resources is measure it is still pending. Last but not least, education legislation still needs a further development in terms of policy goals to determine the kind of outcome searched: improving welfare, improving opportunities, leveling access to opportunities etc.

5 The Path Forward on the Right to Education in Argentina

There is a general agreement that education is an essential tool for socialization and progress aligning common values of a specific political community (Mcmillan 2010).

In many Latin American countries, including Argentina, economic and social crisis have slowed down and jeopardize access to education for children, especially those in the early stages.

Despite being a Constitutional right recognized since the second half of the XIX century it was only after regaining democracy in 1983 that Argentina embraced a Human Right based approach on education. As it was pointed out, the most important milestone of this approach it the view of education as an entitlement.

In many ways the content of local Statues remains unclear on how to peruse education not only as an induvial value, that is the economic valued added to each individual for being educated, but also as subject oriented equality of opportunities (Hemelsoet 2012).

Although Argentina has subscribed most second and third generation human right treaties including those that recognized education as a human right, the country is still facing significant challenges to implement this view. Economic restrictions can be named among the principal causes against a more comprehensive achievement to educational goals.

In a context of structural State deficit both at Federal and Province level, education is usually not on the top priority on the political agenda.

A reason that might explain this is institutional myopia. Since the benefits of a good education policy are middle or long term. Politicians tends to implement policy that can show result before the next electoral period. As long as macroeconomic instability persists it is hard to believe that the landscape will change. Since policy makers are constraint by short term public policy agenda and perverse incentives in terms of immediate results that can be shown in electoral campaigns leaving education as a forgotten issue (North 1993).

The lack of proper educational policy was exposed during the COVID-19 pandemic. The restrictions imposed prevented students from attending in person to classes. At that stage those with access to private education could afford the technological means to continue online instructions from home. However, those students, of lower income and depending completely on public school where more severely affected than those attending private institution (Ortigoza 2021).

This situation has exposed a severe inequality in the structure of financing education in Argentina. Despite a proper reception of education as a human right in statues and in case law, efficacy an implementation remains as the biggest challenges in Argentinean education law.

6 Concluding Remarks

The reception of education as a right in Argentina was the result of the enlightment ideas spread in the XIX century. According with this view. Education was a cornerstone for the consolidation of the country in late XIX century. Education was understood a tool for incorporate locals in the "civilization".

The liberal view entered a crisis in the first half of XXth century with the social Constitutionalism. During this period education was view as a tool for securing ascending social mobility. Also, during this period, a strong nationalism entered at school as a compulsory requirement by the State.

The amendment of the Argentinean Constitution in 1994 had a great impact in education since it granted the status of human rights. However, it took several years until the content begun to be applied by courts in an effective way.

Event with a significant effort made by the judiciary for recognizing the right to education on an equality of opportunity basis there still are significant challenges to be face specially from the policy making point of view.

Lack of long-term policies and the problem of institutional myopia remain as the main problems for an improvement in the quality of Argentinean education.

References

26.944/47, D. N. (1947) Obtenido de http://www.bnm.me.gov.ar/giga1/normas/3534.pdf. Accessed 21 Mar 2022

Alvarez M et al (2020) Segregación educativa en tiempos de pandemia: balance de las acciones iniciales durante el aislamiento social por el Covid-19 en Argentina. Revista Internacional de Educación para la Justicia Social 9:25–43

Argentinian Constitution—Art. 14 (1853) Argentina

Brandon N (2016)Distributing educational opportunities: positionality, equality and responsibility. Int J Child Rights 24:575–598

Barrera Buteler GE (2020) El derecho argentino frente a la pandemia y postpandemia COVID. In: Colección de Estudios Críticos de la Facultad de Derecho de la Universidad Nacional de Córdoba

Colombo and Luzzi (2022) Una mirada integral del derecho a la educación. (Diciembre de 1948). Declaration of Human Right. Art 26

Convention on the Rights of the Child (20 de Noviembre de 1989)

Correas IM (2008) Los Derechos Humanos y la Constitución Argentina reformada. Consideraciones en ocasión de un aniversario. Persona y Derecho, p 71–103

CSJN 323/2659 (s.f.) http://www.saij.gob.ar/corte-suprema-justicia-nacion-federal-ciudad-autonoma-buenos-aires-gonzalez-delgado-cristina-otros-universidad-nacional-cordoba-recurso-hecho-fa00000224-2000-09-19/123456789-422-0000-0ots-eupmocsollaf. Accessed 20 May 2022

De Singlau F (2018) Educación y desigualdad. Desarrollo progresivo del derecho a la educación y su situación en Argentina. Revista Omnia 1:63–86

Decreto Nº 26.944/47 (4 de Septiembre de 1947) Fines de la Educación. Boletin Official, Buenos Aires, Argentina

Feldfeber M and Ivanier A (2003)La descentralización educativa en Argentina el proceso de transferencia de las instituciones de formación docente. Revista mexicana de investigación educativa, p 421–445

Finnegan F and Pagano A (2007) El derecho a la educación en Argentina. Flape, Buenos Aires

Hemelsoet E (2012)A right to education for all: the meaning of equal educational opportunities. Int J Child Rights 20:523–540

Herrera C (2014) En los origenes del constitucionalismo social argentino: discursos en torno a la constitución en torno a la constitución de 1949. Historia Constitucional:391–414

https://cijur.mpba.gov.ar/files/articles/3971/CSJN_Asoc._Dchos_Humanos_FALLO_CSJ_004956_2015_RH001.pdf. Accessed 26 Sep 2022

Jover (2001)What does the right to education mean? A look at an international debate from legal, ethical, and pedagogical points of view. Stud Philos Educ 3:213–223

Law 1420. Educación común (8 de Julio de 1884)

Law 12,558—Art 2 (30 de Septiembre de 1938) Instituciones Complementarias de la educación común

Law 24521—Educación Superior (20 de Julio de 1995)

Law 26206—Ley de Educación Nacional (27 de Diciembre de 2006)

Ley de Educación 26,206—Art 4–17 (Diciembre de 14 de 2006) Argentina

Mcmillan L (2010) What's in a right? Two variations for interpreting the right to education. International review of education. Int Rev Educ:531–545

Micheletti MG (2018) laica o libre: las disputas por la creación de las universidades privadas (1955–1959). Lagos

Ministerio de Educación Cy (2003) Descentralización y estrategias en educación: Caso Argentina. Buenos Aires

North DC (1993)Toward a theory of institutional change. Political economy: institutions, competition and representation, p 61–69

Ortigoza MA (2021)América Latina. Entre la nueva realidad y las viejas desigualdades. Revista de Estudios Interdisciplinarios en Ciencias Sociales 23:129–140

Peters MA (2019) The enlightenment and its critics. Educ Philos Theory 51:886–894

Resolución 29/2023—Ministerio de Educación (2023) Argentina

Rodino AM (2015) La educación con enfoque de derechos humanos como práctica constructora de inclusión social. Revista IIDH 6:202–223

Ronconi (2014) La influencia del derecho internacional en el derecho de la educación: una mirada de las condiciones de gratuidad y laicidad. J Supranat Policies Educ

Ronconi L (2015) Derecho a la educación: el rol de los tribunales de justicia garantizadores del acceso a la educación en condiciones de igualdad. Revista Latinoamericana de Educación comparada:66–80

Saba R (2019) Mas allá de la igualdad formal ante la ley: ¿Qué le debe el Estado a los grupos desventajados? Siglo XXI Editores
Scioscioli S (2017) La educación basica como derecho fundamental: implicancias y alcances en el contexto de un estado federal. Eudeba.
Teregi F (2009) Las trayectorias escolares. Del problema al desafío de la política educativa. Ministerio de Educación
Vernor M (2019) El derecho a la educación: casos de exclusión y discriminación. Revista IIDH:268–308
Villavicencio S (2010)Sarmiento y la nación cívica. Groupe de recherche Amérique Latine Histoire et Mémoire de l'Université Paris-VIII 19:90

The Legal Framework of the Australian Education System

Joan Squelch

1 Introduction

On the 1st of January 1901, the *Commonwealth of Australia Constitution Act 1900*[1] came into force and established the Commonwealth of Australia, a federal system consisting of a central federal government and six regional governments (the states) according to which law-making powers are shared between the Commonwealth (federal) Government and state governments (Joseph and Castan 2019). In addition, two self-governing territories[2] also have their own law-making powers but are still subject to the authority of the Commonwealth Government.[3] Prior to this date, Australia was made up of six separate and independent British colonies.[4] The first colony established by Letters Patent in 1788 was New South Wales (NSW), which received all suitable and applicable English law that was in force at the time (Castles 1963). The establishment of the remaining colonies that likewise received English

[1] The *Commonwealth of Australia Constitution* is an imperial act of the UK parliament, the *Commonwealth of Australia Constitution Act 1900* (UK) that consists of nine sections including the *Australian Constitution*. The Constitution was, however, drafted by elected Australian colonial representatives at Constitutional Conventions in the 1890s and approved by voters in colonial referenda. See, Aroney et al. (2015).

[2] The Northern Territory (NT) once part of New South Wales (NSW) and South Australia was surrendered to the Commonwealth in 1911 and was granted self-government in 1978 under the *Northern Territory (Self-Government) Act 1978*. The Australian Capital Territory (ACT) was established in 1911 as the seat of government and acquired self-government in 1988 under the *Australian Capital Territory (Self-Government) Act 1988*.

[3] *Australian Constitution* s 122.

[4] New South Wales (1778), Tasmania (Van Diemen's Land) (1825), Western Australia (1829), South Australia (1836), Victoria (1851), and Queensland (1859). Apart from Western Australia, the colonies were at one time part of New South Wales.

J. Squelch (✉)
School of Law and Business, The University of Notre Dame Australia, Fremantle, Australia
e-mail: copyright@esph.com.cn

C. J. Russo and L. Ma (eds.), *A Comparative Analysis of Systems of Education Law*,
https://doi.org/10.1007/978-981-97-1052-2_2

law[5] followed and by the 1890s, all six British colonies had become self-governing, representative and responsible governments with their own constitution and each with their own legal system. It was during the colonial period that the first educational institutions were established. This chapter provides an overview of the legal foundations, nature and structure of the Australian education system.

2 The Legal Nature of the Australian School System

The first colonial schools were mainly denominational (religious) and independent schools until the respective colonial governments introduced government schools and a public education system in each of the colonies (Campbell and Proctor 2014). The NSW Board of National Education was created in 1848 and tasked with establishing government schools and a public education system that would operate alongside denominational schools (Government of NSW 2023a). The NSW Board of National Education opened its first school in 1848 and by 1851 operated 31 schools (Government of NSW 2023b). A Denominational School Board was appointed to manage government subsidies to church operated schools. The passing of the NSW Public Schools Act of 1866 saw the introduction of a consolidated Council of Education to manage and regulate government and denominational schools, and in 1880 the Public Instruction Act introduced the Department of Public Instruction and 'free, secular and compulsory' education (Government of NSW 2023c). Similarly, in the colony of Victoria that had inherited the denominational and government system from NSW, the Common Schools Act of 1862 created a single Board of Education to oversee a system of 'common and rural' schools. In 1872, the Board of Education was replaced by a Department of Education. Victoria was also the first colony to introduce 'free, secular and compulsory education' under the 1872 Education Act (State Library Victoria 2023).

Similar developments took place in the other colonies. In Western Australia (WA), for example, one-teacher schools for the children of settlers were operating in the 1830s (Fletcher 1979). The first General Board of Education was established in 1847 to establish and administer government schools in the colony. The first Catholic schools were established in 1843, which grew into a significant system of Catholic education. The General Board of Education provided subsidies to Catholic schools (Government of Western Australia 2023a), but following a campaign against government financial aid to church-controlled schools, the Assisted Schools Abolition Act of 1895 was passed to abolish aid (Fletcher 1979). In Queensland, the Education Act of 1860 established a Board of General Education that had authority to establish and administer schools vested in the Board as well as supervise schools controlled by churches (Government of Queensland 1984). The State Education Act of 1875 introduced compulsory education for Queensland children between the ages of 6 and

[5] The *Australia Courts Act 1828* (Imp) set the date of reception of English statutory law as 1828 for the colonies of New South Wales, Queensland, Tasmania, and Victoria.

12, and education was to be free and secular, which resulted in the withdrawal of financial assistance to church schools. The 1875 Act also established a Department of Public Instruction to administer the legislation (Government of Queensland 2023). Likewise, compulsory education was implemented in Tasmania in 1868 and in South Australia in 1875.

By 1908, following federation, all the colonies that joined together in the new federation had government education departments administering free, compulsory and secular education (Campbell and Proctor 2014). Children were able to attend government-aided schools, independent schools and denominational schools. This background to Australia and schooling sets the scene for the remainder of the section that provides an overview of the current legal framework of the Australian school system.

2.1 Sources of Law in Education

As stated in the introduction, Australia is a federal system with shared law-making powers between the central Commonwealth Government and state governments (Joseph and Castan 2019). In addition, two self-governing territories[6] also have their own law-making powers. Australia therefore has nine jurisdictions each with its own government comprising the executive, legislative and judicial branches. The High Court of Australia is the highest court in the country that has original and appellate jurisdiction and whose jurisdiction is final.[7] The two primary sources of education law are statutory law and common law derived from federal, state and territory jurisdictions.

2.1.1 Statutory Law

Statutory law (legislation) enacted by parliament includes primary legislation and an extensive body of subordinate legislation (delegated law) namely regulations. Law-making powers are shared between the Commonwealth and states. The Commonwealth Parliament, however, has limited law making powers as prescribed by the *Commonwealth of Australia Constitution Act* (hereafter the Australian Constitution). Section 51 of the Australian Constitution enumerates the concurrent matters on which both the Commonwealth Government and state governments, including the self-governing territories, can legislate. The states have the remaining or residual powers. Moreover, states have plenary law-making powers under their own state constitutions. Education is one example of a residual power of the states. However, over time the Commonwealth Government has extended its law-making powers

[6] See (n 3).

[7] *Australian Constitution* ch III.

to education through the indirect use of powers under Section 51 of the Constitution such as the corporations power and trade and commerce power. Therefore, all Australian jurisdictions have powers to make laws with respect to education.[8] Statutes pertaining to education includes the vast body of general statutory law, such as anti-discrimination legislation, as well as education-specific laws such as the School Education Act 1999 of Western Australia.

2.1.2 Common Law

Common law, or judge-made law, is a further primary source of law that has its roots in English law dating back centuries that was received by the colonies and which has continued to develop over time (Castles 1963). It is made up of an extensive collection of court decisions. The High Court of Australia has held that 'there is but one common law' in Australia; however, the separate jurisdiction of states is recognised and their appropriate application of common law principles.[9] The doctrine of precedent (*stare decisis*) is a central feature of the common law whereby lower courts follow the decisions and legal principles laid down by superior courts within the same jurisdiction when deciding on similar cases.[10]

2.2 Commonwealth Administration of Education

The Commonwealth Government does not have powers per se to legislate on education. However, the Commonwealth (federal) Government now plays a significant role in education, especially higher education, given education is of national importance. As highlighted in the Preamble to the Australian Education Act 2013 (Cth), which regulates school funding:

> Education is the foundation of a skilled workforce and a creative community. A strong and sustainable schooling system is critical for Australia's future prosperity. A good education prepares students for full participation in society, both in employment and in civic life. Education also has a role to play in overcoming social and economic disadvantage.

The Preamble further notes that:

> There is an ongoing and essential role for the Commonwealth in school education through its unique position to provide national policy leadership and facilitate national performance assessment and reporting. Transparency and accountability ensure public confidence in the education system and promote excellence in teaching and school leadership.

---

[8] The conflict between Commonwealth and state laws is dealt with by s 109 of the *Australian Constitution*, which provides that Commonwealth laws shall prevail to the extent of any inconsistency.

[9] *Lipohar v The Queen* 200 CLR 485, 500 [24].

[10] The High Court of Australia is the final court of appeal and is not bound by its own decisions.

Therefore, although states and territories are responsible for the provision and maintenance of schools, the Commonwealth Government plays an active role in setting national priorities and standards, curriculum development, allocating and administrating funds, quality assurance and education reform.

2.3 *State and Territory School Education and Legislation*

Since federation, the states and subsequently the territories have been responsible for the provision of education and maintaining their own education system. Although there are separate and distinct jurisdictions, school education across jurisdictions is underpinned by core principles,[11] in particular:

- the right of every child to education;
- the best interests of the child are paramount;
- the recognition and importance of diversity and non-discrimination;
- the involvement of parents in their children's education; and
- community engagement.

All state and territory jurisdictions have passed education legislation for the establishment and governance of education.[12] School education legislation in all jurisdictions provides for the establishment of a ministry of education (department of education) and the establishment of schools. The legislation also covers key matters such as access to education, school attendance, the governance and management of schools, educational instruction, curriculum, school funding, non-government school registration, and parent and community involvement.

2.3.1 The Administration of School Education

Centralised departments of education, with varying names, are established in all state and territory jurisdictions as part of the public sector to oversee education. Departments of education are generally responsible to the relevant Minister for education (political leader and public servant) for education. The responsible government Minister has the broad power to do all that is necessary for the purposes for school education, delivering educational programs and furthering the best interests of students.[13] A Minister also has the power to issue educational policies and guidelines relating to educational matters. Each education department has a head of department,

---

[11] See, e.g., *Education and Children Services Act 2019* (SA) s 7(4); *Education Act 2016* (Tas) s 4; *Education and Training Reform Act 2006* (Vic) s 1.2.1.

[12] *Education Act 2004* (ACT); *Education Act 1990* (NSW); *Education Act 2015* (NT); *Education (General Provisions) Act 2006* (Qld); *Education and Children Services Act 2019* (SA); *Education Act 2016* (Tas); *Education and Training Reform Act 2006* (Vic); *School Education Act 1999* (WA).

[13] See, e.g., *School Education Act 1999* (WA) s 216.

referred to as the Director General, Chief Executive or Secretary, who is responsible for the overall management of the department and who assists the Minister to administer education legislation. In Western Australia, for example, the Department of Education is established under Section 35 of the Public Sector Management Act 1994 and the School Education Act 1999. The Director General is the chief executive officer of the department and is appointed under Section 45 of the Public Sector Management Act 1994.[14] They are, inter alia, responsible for 'determining, implementing and monitoring the standard of educational instruction in government schools; and the standard of care provided to students in those schools'.[15] The Department of Education oversees and regulates the establishment and provision of government and non-government schools.

2.3.2 Types of Schools

The Australian school system offers a diverse range of primary and secondary schools.[16] Schools are categorised into three broad groups: government schools (public); independent schools (non-government) and Catholic systemic schools.

Government schools are established under the authority of the education minister pursuant to applicable education legislation. School education acts give ministers powers to establish government (public) schools,[17] which make up the largest number of schools in Australia.

Independent schools form an important part of the school system and an alternative to government schools in all jurisdictions. The independent (private) school sector includes a wide variety of denomination and non-denominational schools. Some schools are faith-based, others are based on a particular pedagogical foundation such as Montessori[18] schools, while others are aligned with a philosophical foundation such as the Steiner[19] schools. Independent schools are required to be registered with a department of education and comply with the requisite registration standards. It is an offence under education law to establish or conduct a non-government school unless it is registered. Registration standards cover matters such as curriculum, staff-student

[14] *School Education Act 1999* (WA) s 151.

[15] *School Education Act 1999* (WA) s 61(1).

[16] Primary education covers the first 7 to 8 years of schooling, secondary schooling is 4 to 5 years, with senior secondary being the final two years of schools. Primary schooling generally includes a pre-primary year of schooling.

[17] See, e.g., *School Education Act 1999* (WA) s 55.

[18] Montessori schools provide an approach to education based on the educational philosophy and pedagogy of 'Dr Maria Montessori, a physician, anthropologist and pedagogue': <https://montessori.org.au/about-montessori>.

[19] Steiner education is founded on the life and work of 'Rudolf Steiner an Austrian scientist, philosopher and artist who lived from 1861 to 1925': <https://www.steinereducation.edu.au/steiner-education/about-rudolf-steiner-and-the-growth-of-the-steiner-waldorf-education-movement/>.

ratios, hours of tuition, teacher registration, school discipline,[20] student safety, governance, premises and facilities, and financial resources. The Minister has the power to cancel a school's registration should they fail to comply with and meet the registration standards. The Minister or head of department has the power to inspect premises and prevent the operation of unregistered or non-complaint schools. Non-government schools may also combine to form a system.[21]

Catholic systemic schools are a collection of Catholic schools that are members of a cohesive, state-based school system which falls under the authority and governance of a single body. For example, Catholic schools in Western Australia that form part of a system are overseen by the Catholic Education Commission of Western Australia that is appointed by the Bishops of Western Australia to govern the system (Catholic Education Western Australia 2023). Furthermore, the Catholic school system operates under a system agreement with the WA Department of Education that authorises schools to operate with the system and avoids the need for each school applying for registration.

2.3.3 School Funding

School funding in Australia is a combination of Commonwealth and state/territory funding. School funding is primarily a needs-based model. Government schools receive the majority of their funding from the respective state or territory government, with additional financial support from the Commonwealth Government. Conversely, independent (non-government schools) are mainly funded by the Commonwealth Government, which is supplemented with additional funds from state and territory governments.

The Australian Education Act 2013 (Cth) is the principal legislation for granting, administering and reviewing[22] funds to schools. Section 3 of the Australian Education Act provides that: The objects of this Act are:

(a) to provide a Commonwealth needs-based funding model for school education that:

  (i) includes a base amount of funding for every student and loadings for students and schools who need extra support; and
  (ii) is affordable, simple, predictable and fair; and
  (iii) invests in evidence-based reforms that will improve student outcomes.

---

[20] Corporal punishment for instance is prohibited in government and non-government schools.

[21] See e.g., *Education Act 2016* (Tas) s 145 which states that eight or more registered non-government schools may form a system of non-government schools.

[22] The National School Resourcing Board is an independent body that reviews and provides 'independent oversight' of the Commonwealth funding model: <https://www.dese.gov.au/national-school-resourcing-board>. See *Australian Education Act 2013* (Cth) s 128.

Commonwealth funding under this legislation is directed to approved authorities of non-government schools, that is, the body corporate of a school approved by the relevant Minister. Additionally, financial assistance is also provided to states under Section 96 of the Australian Constitution (conditional grants) and to territories under Section 122 of the Australian Constitution. This financial assistance is therefore conditional upon the states and territories agreeing to certain conditions, or agreements relating to school education and/or 'nationally agreed to initiatives'.[23]

Government and non-government schools also raise funds through parent contributions and fund-raising activities. While non-government school charge compulsory school fees, public schools are intended to provide free basic education. However, for public school to operate and provide a high quality education and educational experience they have to raise funds. Public schools may therefore request 'voluntary contributions and payments' from parents (Government of Victoria 2023b). Voluntary contributions may be requested for various items and school activities including books, stationery, equipment, technology, educational and sporting activities, school excursions and additional elective subjects. Statutory limitations are generally placed on voluntary contributions, and parents (or carers) who are unable to make a voluntary contribution owing to financial hardship may receive assistance for a school. Moreover, students may not be excluded from activities, discriminated against or embarrassed if voluntary contributions cannot be paid.

2.3.4 Compulsory School Attendance

It is recognised that every child has a right to receive a school education that is accessible and meets the educational needs of all children. Compulsory education is legislated for in all jurisdictions. Children who have reached 'compulsory school-age' must be enrolled at and attend primary and secondary school. There are variations in compulsory school-ages across jurisdictions but generally all children between the ages of 5 and 6 must attend school and continue to do so until the age of 16 or 17.[24] Parents therefore have a legal duty to ensure their children enrol in and attend school and failing to do so may result in a fine unless an approved exemption from attendance applies. Notwithstanding distance education delivery, generally, a child is considered to be 'in attendance' if they meet the requirements in terms of being physically present on the premises at the times stipulated by the school.[25]

Parents have the option of sending their children to a government or non-government school, or they may choose to home-school their children. Parents (the home educator) who choose to home school their children must be registered with the

[23] *Australian Education Act 2013* (Cth) s 4 (Guide to the Act). Further operational and implementation details are contained within the *Australian Education Regulation 2013* (Cth).

[24] *Education Act 2004* (ACT) ss 9–10; *Education Act 1990* (NSW) ss 21B-22; *Education Act 2015* (NT) ss 38–40; *Education (General Provisions) Act 2006* (Qld) s 9, ss 176–177; *Education and Children Services Act 2019* (SA) s 60; *Education Act 2016* (Tas) s 4; *Education and Training Reform Act 2006* (Vic) s 2.1.1; *School Education Act 1999* (WA) s 9.

[25] See, e.g., *Education (General Provisions) Act 2006* (Qld) s 177.

relevant department of education and comply with any registration requirements such as ensuring their children receive a high-quality education and providing an annual progress report on their children's education.[26] Home education may be provided by parents or a registered teacher. Home educators who are registered are responsible for the child's educational program and are required to follow an approved education program. A home education program may include part-time attendance as a school. Home educators and the progress of children are monitored, and the head of the education department may cancel the home educator's registration if a child has not made satisfactory educational progress.

2.3.5 Admission to Schools

In keeping with compulsory education, a school aged child is entitled to enrol in the designated government school in their neighbourhood. If the child does not reside in the neighbourhood, a school may enrol the child if there is capacity to do so. A school, however, may refuse to enrol a student, usually with the relevant Minister's approval, if it is in the interest of ensuring the safety of the student and other students.

Children with disabilities likewise have a right to education and to enrol in their local school. It is unlawful for a school to discriminate against a student on the basis of their disability by refusing to or failing to accept a student's application for admission or by denying a student access.[27] Therefore, children with a disability who meet the basic admission requirements to attend school have the right to attend school 'on the same basis' as children who do not have a disability. The Australian Disability Standards for Education 2005 (Cth) (Disability Standards) sets out the legal obligations of government and non-government schools in relation to students with disabilities and attendance. Section 4.1 of the Disability Standards requires that a school (education provider):

> must take reasonable steps to ensure that the prospective student is able to seek admission to, or apply for enrolment in, the institution on the same basis as a prospective student without a disability, and without experiencing discrimination.

Schools enrolling students with disabilities are required to ensure that students have the necessary support and are provided with reasonable accommodations or adjustments to ensure that they can participate on the same basis as other students. Adjustments are described as 'a measure or action (or a group of measures or actions) taken by an education provider that has the effect of assisting a student with a disability', which includes making adjustments in relation to a school admission or enrolment and in relation to participation in a course or program.[28] An adjustment is 'reasonable' if it balances the parties of all affected' taking into account various

[26] See, e.g., *School Education Act 1999* (WA) ss 47–48; *Education Act 1990* (NSW) ss 72–73; *Education (General Provisions) Act 2006* (Qld) s 217.

[27] *Disability Discrimination Act 1992* (Cth) s 22.

[28] *Australian Disability Standards for Education 2005* (Cth) s 3.3. The Disability Standards are subordinate legislation made under s 31 of the *Disability Discrimination Act 1992* (Cth). It is

factors such as the nature of the student's disability, the effect of the adjustment on the student, the student's ability to participate in a course and the costs and benefits of making an adjustment.[29]

2.3.6 Secular Education

Education in government schools is secular[30] and schools may not promote any particular denomination or religious practices. However, government schools are not prohibited from providing general religious education or engaging in religious activities. General religious education covers different kinds of religious systems, beliefs and practices. Attendance and participation in religious education and activities is not mandatory and parents may choose not to allow their children to participate. Special religious instruction may also be offered with ministerial approval, and it must be delivered by accredited representatives of religious denominations or groups. Parental consent is required for students to participate in special education classes. Schools are required to provide alternative learning activities for students and to supervise students who do not participate in religious education classes. Although religion in government schools has been challenged on occasion, the courts have upheld the right of government school to offer religious education and to allow diverse religious activities.[31]

2.3.7 Curriculum Framework

A Minister or the head of an education department determines the curriculum framework according to which instruction in government schools is provided. The head of education is also responsible for determining and monitoring the standard of educational instruction in government schools.[32] In each jurisdiction, the determination

---

unlawful for a person to contravene a disability standard: *Disability Discrimination Act 1992* (Cth) s 32.

[29] *Disability Standards* s 3.4.

[30] See, e.g., *Education and Children Services Act 2019* (SA) s 7(4); *Education Act 2016* (Tas) s 125; *Education and Training Reform Act 2006* (Vic) s 2.2.10.

[31] *Aitken & Ors v The State of Victoria—Department of Education & Early Childhood Development* (Anti-Discrimination) [2012] VCAT 1547 affirmed the right of Victorian state schools to offer non-compulsory Special Religious Instruction as per the education legislation, and there was no finding of discrimination against students who did not attend SRI and who were provided with alternative instruction and learning activities. In *Williams v Commonwealth of Australia* (2012) 248 CLR 156 (School Chaplaincy Case) while it was held that the Commonwealth Government did not have authority to fund chaplaincy services in government schools (which was rectified by passing legislation granting spending authority), schools were nonetheless entitled to provide chaplaincy services to students and the school community on a voluntary basis.

[32] See, e.g., *Education (General Provisions) Act 2006* (Qld) s 21; *Education and Children Services Act 2019* (SA) s 8(1)(a); *School Education Act 1999* (WA) s 61.

and implementation of a curriculum framework in schools is subject to an independent statutory curriculum and assessment authority (or curriculum and standards authority) established under education legislation.[33] The curriculum assessment or standards authority regulates the school curriculum and assessment and, although its functions may vary between jurisdictions, they typically include setting standards for student achievement and assessment, developing criteria and standards for curriculum and assessments, issuing guidelines for the development of courses and assessment, evaluating and accrediting courses, developing external assessments, setting rules for the conduct of assessments and examinations, establishing minimum requirements for graduation from secondary schools, and conducting research and policy analysis.[34]

2.3.8 Teacher Registration

All jurisdictions require teachers to be registered before they commence teaching. Teacher registration authorities established under state and territory legislation are an independent regulatory authority that is responsible for registering and maintaining a register of all teachers.[35] The authorities are subject to the control of the relevant Minister. Teacher registration authorities manage teacher registration, facilitate the continuing development of the teaching profession and maintain community confidence in the teaching profession. Teacher registration boards are therefore also responsible for managing the professional conduct of teachers which involves inter alia determining professional standards, assessing information relevant to applications for registration such as criminal record checks, receiving complaints about teacher conduct, investigating teacher conduct, and managing disciplinary processes and hearings. Teacher registration authorities have the authority to imposes conditions on or cancel a teacher's registration.

---

[33] For example, the Victorian Curriculum and Assessment Authority established under the *Victorian Curriculum and Assessment Authority Act 2000* (Vic), and the Western Australia School Curriculum and Standards Authority established under the *School Curriculum and Standards Authority Act 1997* (WA).

[34] *Education and Training Reform Act 2006* (Vic) s 2.5.3; *School Curriculum and Standards Authority Act 1997* (WA) s 9; *Education (Queensland Curriculum and Assessment Authority) Act 2014* (Qld) pt 2, div 2; *Education Act 2016* (Tas) s 125(2).

[35] *ACT Teacher Quality Institute Act 2010* (Act); *Education Standards Authority Act 2013* (NSW); *Teacher Registration (Northern Territory) Act 2004* (NT); *Education (Queensland College of Teachers) Act 2005* (Qld); *Teachers Registration and Standards Act 2004* (SA): *Teachers Registration Act 2000* (TAS); *Victorian Institute of Teaching Act 2001* (Vic); *Teacher Registration Act 2012* (WA).

2.3.9 Managing Student Conduct

Principals and teachers have an important role to play in providing a safe and orderly school environment and managing student behaviour (Squelch 2015). In all jurisdictions relevant state and territory education legislation and regulations set out the disciplinary methods and procedures for managing student behaviour and misconduct, namely suspension and exclusion, for serious forms of misconduct such as physical violence, drug related offences and bullying. Disciplinary methods for less serious misconduct include supervised detention, time-out strategies aimed to re-enforce positive behaviour and, in some jurisdictions, school or community service. Corporal punishment is prohibited in government and non-government schools (Squelch and Russo 2020).

2.4 *Suspension and Exclusion*

Suspension (temporary removal) and exclusion (sometimes also referred to expulsion) from school are permitted for serious or persistent offences. The authority for managing suspension and exclusion is set out in education legislation, regulations and department policies.[36] For non-government schools, the grounds on which a student may be suspended or excluded from school, and the procedures to be followed, are based on the terms of the contract formed between the school and the parents (i.e. common law).

Students in government schools accused of serious misconduct and who may be suspended or excluded from school have a right to procedural fairness (or natural justice, a common law doctrine that has been incorporated into education legislation). This means that a student has a right to be informed of actions to be taken against them, the right to be heard (i.e. to respond to allegations) and the right to a fair and impartial decision based on relevant information. Although there are variations across the jurisdictions, in general, a student is entitled to be accompanied by a support person, usually a parent, to meetings and disciplinary hearings. The student and parent (or primary carer) are entitled to be provided with all the relevant information concerning the allegation of misconduct, the possible disciplinary consequences, the reasons for considering suspension or exclusion and the disciplinary process. The student must be given an opportunity to respond to the allegations and information provided. If a decision is taken to suspend a student, the student and parent must be given written notification of the decision to suspend. The notification generally sets out the reasons for the decision, the duration of the suspension and any arrangements for the student to complete school work during the suspension period (Squelch 2015). In terms of a

[36] *Education Act 2004* (ACT) s 36; *Education Act 2015* (NT) s 91; *Education (General Provisions) Act 2006* (Qld) ss 281–282; *Education and Children's Services Act 2019* (SA) s 76, s 77; *Education Act 2016* (Tas) s 130; *Education Training and Reform Act 2006* (Vic) s 2.2.19; *School Education Act 1999* (WA) s 90, s 92.

student being excluded, in some jurisdictions the principal has authority to exclude a student, but in most jurisdictions a disciplinary report and recommendation are made to the Minister for Education or delegate who has the final authority to exclude a student from school.[37] Students will usually have a right to appeal a decision if the school has not followed correct procedures.

Although it is still somewhat controversial as to whether students in non-government schools are entitled to natural justice, non-government schools nonetheless are required to have appropriate student management policies and processes in place that include provisions for due process as part of the requirements for registration (Squelch and Russo 2020).

2.5 *Physical Restraint of Students*

The physical restraint of students is one of the more controversial and risky issues for principals and teachers when managing student behaviour. Education legislation and policies do allow principals and teachers to use reasonable force or restraint on a student but only in emergency situations to protect the student concerned and the safety of others, or to prevent the destruction of property. What constitutes 'reasonable force' may be determined with reference to factors such as the student's age and size,[38] the nature of the behaviour, the likely response of the student, the purpose of the physical restraint, and the circumstances in which restraint is used.[39] In Western Australia, for instance, a member of staff in a government school may take such action, including physical contact with a student or a student's property, as is reasonable to manage a student, re-establish order and to prevent or retain a person for placing others at risk or damaging property.[40] Likewise in Victoria, a staff member in a government school 'may take any reasonable action that is immediately required to restrain a student of the school from acts or behaviour that are dangerous to the

[37] See. e.g., *Education Act 2004* (ACT) s 36; *Education Act 2015* (NT) ss 92–93; *Education Act 1990* (NSW) s 35(3); *Education (General Provisions) Act 2006* (Qld) ss 291–295; *Education and Children's Services Act 2019* (SA) s 77; *Education Act 2016* (Tas) s 134; *School Education Act 1999* (WA) s 94.

[38] In *Ayling v Director-General Department of Education and Training* [2009] WAIRComm 413 (26 June 2009) 33 it was held that the force used by a male deputy school principal on a female student was unreasonable in the circumstances. It was held that 'superior physical strength [was used] to subdue a much smaller female student for the purpose of preventing her from leaving the school grounds…in circumstances where there was no risk to the safety of any person or property'. The student at that stage had not been charged with any wrong doing.

[39] *Barry Landweher v Director General, Department of Education and Training* [2017] WAIRC 00233 (26 April 2017) [42]. In this case the teacher's physical contact with a student was held to be unreasonable as the degree of physical contact of pushing the student and then grabbing the student by the shirt, was neither necessary nor reasonable to manage the student. It was noted that 'the teacher should attempt to de-escalate the situation and end the restraint as soon as possible, when the teacher has determined the student is no longer presenting a risk' [100].

[40] *School Education Regulations 2000* (WA) reg 38.

member of staff, the student or any other person'.[41] Physical restraint of a student is therefore used as a last resort and is not to be used if it places a member of staff at risk. It is also not used to merely discipline students.

2.5.1 The Care and Safety of Students

Education authorities, principals and teachers have a duty to maintain safe school environments and to protect students against foreseeable risks that may cause injury. The failure to do so may give rise to an action for negligence. The tort of negligence protects a person from being harmed by another person who does not take reasonable care. Negligence is described as 'conduct by one person that wrongfully and unreasonably causes adverse effects on another' (Davis 2012). For liability to arise in negligence the following elements must be met: the student is owed a duty of care, the duty of care was breached, the breach of the duty of care caused the harm or injury, and the plaintiff's injury is one that is compensable (Jackson and Varnham 2007).

It is well established under the common law tort of negligence that school authorities owe a duty of care to students. In the oft cited statement in *Commonwealth v Introvigne* it was held that

> A school authority owes to its pupils a duty to ensure that reasonable care is taken of them whilst they are on the school premises during hours when the school is open for attendance. … It proceeds on the footing that the duty is not discharged by merely appointing competent teaching staff and leaving it to the staff to take appropriate steps for the care of the children. It is a duty to ensure that reasonable steps are taken for the safety of the children, a duty the performance of which cannot be delegated.[42]

A school authority can then be held liable for negligence if the duty of care owed to students is breached and that breach causes harm or injury to the student. As flagged in the quote above, the duty of care is that which is reasonable in the circumstances and to take appropriate measures or precautions to avoid harm or injury. The duty of care extends beyond the school gates to include school activities and school excursions that take place outside the school.

A breach of duty arises when the school authority, including a principal or teacher, fails to meet the requisite standard of care. The standard of care that is owed is based on an objective test and is taken to be that of an ordinary, careful person of normal intelligence and disposition (Mendelson 2007). The objective test is one of reasonableness and reasonable foreseeability (Mendelson 2007). In *Richards v Victoria* it was noted that the duty of care is not 'a duty of insurance against harm but

---

[41] *Education and Training Reform Regulations 2017* (Vic) reg 25.

[42] *Commonwealth v Introvigne* (1982) 150 CLR 258, 269–270 (education authority held liable of the injury sustained by a student during a playground incident before school commenced). See also *Geyer v Downes* (1977) 138 CLR 91.

a duty to take reasonable care to avoid harm being suffered'.[43] For instance in *The Trustees of the Roman Catholic Church for the Archdiocese of Sydney v Kondrajian* it was stated that:

> the mere fact that a serious injury or even death may occur while children are playing a game at school will not automatically result in a finding of breach of duty of care ... It remains for the plaintiff to show that the school or teacher involved did not take such reasonable precautions for the safety of the child as would have prevented harm.[44]

Civil liability legislation generally provides a person will not have breached their duty of care unless the risk [of harm] was foreseeable, the risk was not insignificant and a reasonable person in that circumstances would have taken appropriate precautions.[45] When determining whether 'a reasonable person would have taken precautions against a risk of harm', the following aspects are considered: the probability of harm, the likely seriousness of the harm, the burden of taking precautions and the social utility or benefit of the activity that creates the risk.[46] In a school context, factors to consider when determining a breach of duty may include the age of the child, the nature of the activity, the location and environment, the condition of equipment, and importantly, the level of supervision required and provided.[47] If it is established that there was a breach of duty of care, and that the breach of duty was a direct cause of the harm or injury then the injured person may be entitled to monetary damages. Civil liability legislation requires that the negligence or fault of the person (the *tortfeasor*) 'was a necessary condition of the occurrence of the harm'.[48]

---

[43] *Richards v State of Victoria* (1969) VR 136, 138.

[44] *The Trustees of the Roman Catholic Church for the Archdiocese of Sydney v Kondrajian* [2001] NSWCA 308, [62].

[45] See, e.g., *Civil Liability Act 2002* (WA) s 5B.

[46] Ibid s 5B(2).

[47] See, e.g., *Kretschmar v The State of Queensland* (1989) ATR 80–272 (education authority not liable for injury sustained by a primary school student while playing a boisterous game as part of a class activity); *Vandescheur v State of New South Wales* [1999] NSWCA] 212 (education authority not liable for student injured in a playground game of cricket) and *Trustees of the Roman Catholic Church for the Diocese of Canberra and Goulburn (as St Anthony's Primary School) v Hadba* [2005] HCA 31 (school authority not liable for injury sustained by a child while playing on a flying fox). In these cases, while it was recognised that the games carried some risk and students could get injured, students had been adequately instructed and supervised.

[48] See, e.g., *Civil Liability Act 2002* (WA) s 5C. If the injury or harm suffered is too remote from the negligent conduct, then there is no liability for negligence. For example, in *Australian Capital Territory Schools Authority v El Sheik* [2000] FCA 931, Wilcox J held that the respondent had failed to establish a 'causal connection between the alleged breach of duty—the failure to provide supervisors in a ratio of 1:50 pupils—and the injury suffered by him' [22] and that the 'Authority is liable to pay damages, only if it can be established that [the] injuries were sustained as a result of a breach by the Authority of its duty of care to him' [27].

2.5.2 School Governance

School education legislation generally requires government[49] and non-government schools to have a school council (or board), unless exempted, that is responsible for school governance matters. Legislation distinguishes governance from day-to-day management. School councils are responsible for guiding and monitoring the strategic direction of a school and advising the principal on strategic matters. The day-to-day management or operational matters of the school is the responsibility of the school principal and senior executive and administrative staff. For example, Section 132(a) of the WA School Education Act states that 'a council cannot intervene in the control or management of a school'. Similarly, Section 81(3)(a) of the Queensland Education (General Provisions) Act 2006 states that a school council may not interfere with management by the school's principal of day-to-day operations of the school and its curriculum.

As a governance structure, school councils have an important role to play in promoting effective schools, creating a positive school culture, promoting quality education and forging positive relations between the school, parents and community. The composition, powers and functions of school councils are found in legation and common law. They are representative bodies whose membership is drawn from teachers, parents (who make up the majority of members), community members and students. The school principal; is usually an ex officio member. The common functions of a school board are broadly to develop the vision and strategic plan for the school, approve and monitor the school budget, review and approve curricula, develop and review policies, ensure compliance with policies, review the school performance, raise funds, manage the hire, licence and shared use of school facilities, and promote the school in the community.[50] Powers of school councils may include entering into contracts, employing staff and charging fees for goods and services. These powers may vary between jurisdictions.

In relation to non-government schools, the effective operation of school boards (or council) is a requirement for registration. Generally, a department head may approve the establishment of a non-government school if they are satisfied that there is a properly constituted and functioning governing body that is also separate from the day-to-day management of the school by the principal.[51]

2.5.3 Parent and Community Involvement

In addition to school councils, parent and community involvement is essential for promoting and supporting vibrant school communities. Parents are the child's first

[49] *School Education Act 1999* (WA) s 125.

[50] See, e.g., *Education (General Provisions) Act 2006* (Qld) s 81; *Education and Children's Services Act 2019* (SA) s 41; *Education Act 2016* (Tas) s 113; *Education and Training Reform Act 2006* (Vic) s 2.3.4; *School Education Act 1999* (WA) s 128.

[51] See, e.g., *School Education Act 1999* (WA) s 160.

educator, and they are responsible for their children's education. The NSW Education Act 1990 for instance states that 'the education of a child is primarily the responsibility of the child's parents'[52] and the Education Act of Tasmania acknowledges that 'a child's parents are the first and most important educators of the child'.[53] Similarly, Queensland legislation provides that parents, teachers and school communities should work collaboratively to achieve the 'best educational outcomes for children'.[54] It is also well documented in research that parent involvement in their children's education is a major contributing factor to school success (Wages 2016). Therefore it is important and necessary to involve parents in the school and their children's education. This is also recognised in education legislation, for instance, that a 'State should work with parents to achieve the best outcomes for young people'.[55]

To this end, schools may establish parent and community associations that work in partnership with the school and community to support the school and promote the interests and development of the school. These associations organise and engage in a wide range of activities including fund raising activities to further improve school amenities and resources. Associations are generally referred to as a Parents and Citizens Association (P&C) or a Parents and Friends Association (P&F), the latter is more often associated with non-government schools. Associations are not-for-profit organisations established under legislation and operate in accordance with an approved constitution that is consistent with education legislation.[56]

3 The Higher Education System

The Australian higher education system is complex and is made up of universities[57] and a wide range of other public and private higher education providers, many of which offer specialist education services (Universities Australia 2023)All higher education providers must be registered with the Tertiary Education and Quality Standards Agency (TEQSA) (discussed below) and are listed on a national register.

---

[52] *Education Act 1990* (NSW) s 4(b).

[53] *Education Act 2016* (Tas) s 4(1)(d).

[54] *Education (General Provisions) Act 2006* (Qld) s 7(d).

[55] *Education (General Provisions) Act 2006* (Qld) s 7(e)(iii).

[56] See, e.g., *Education (General Provisions) Act 2006* (Qld) s 118; *School Education Act 1999* (WA) s 142. Subject to ministerial approval, associations may also be required to be incorporated under relevant state legislation such as the *Associations Incorporation Act 2015* (WA) in Western Australia. In Queensland P&Cs are specifically excluded from incorporation under the *Associations Incorporation Act 1981* (Qld).

[57] There are currently 41 universities in Australia: 38 public universities and 3 private universities. This includes the University of Divinity that is constituted by the *University of Divinity Act 1910* (Vic). In 2021 the University of Divinity was registered with the Tertiary Education and Quality Standards Agency (TEQSA) as a higher education provider.

3.1 *University Administration and Regulation*

Universities, the focus of this section, are established by an Act of Parliament of a state or territory.[58] The first Australian universities were established during the colonial period, the first being the University of Sydney in 1850 followed by the University of Melbourne in 1853, the University of Adelaide in 1874 and the University of Tasmania in 1890. The first universities to be established following federation were the University of Queensland established in 1909 and the University of Western Australia in 1912 (Squelch 2015). The second half the twentieth century saw an exponential growth in universities in Australia.[59]

Universities are regulated by Commonwealth (federal) and state or territory laws. As with school education, the Commonwealth Government does not have the constitutional power to legislate directly on higher education; this is a state matter. However, the Commonwealth exercises extensive control over higher education by passing laws that regulate higher education under different heads of law-making powers under Section 51 of the Australia Constitution, such as the corporations power, taxation power and trade and commerce power. This is particularly evident in the areas of university funding, registration of institutions and quality assurance.[60] The primary Commonwealth education legislation is the Higher Education Support Act 2003 (Cth) and the Education Services for Overseas Students Act 2000 (Cth). Universities are also subject to a plethora of general Commonwealth legislation that regulates matters such as employment, industrial relations, discrimination, health and safety, consumer protection, privacy, intellectual property and more recently modern slavery.

3.1.1 University Funding

University funding is regulated by the Higher Education Support Act 2003 (Cth). Public universities receive most of their funding from the Commonwealth Government, while private universities receive limited government funding. Funding is provided through a complex system of research and teaching grants, and student fees. The Commonwealth Grant Scheme (CGS) is the major source of funding that is payable to institutions as 'a benefit to students'.[61] The CGS subsidises student fees via a Commonwealth Supported Place (CSP), which is essentially a subsidised enrolment. The CSP is made up of the Commonwealth contribution and the student's contribution. Students do not have to pay back the subsidised part of the tuition fees, but they are responsible for the student contribution. Students are able to pay the

---

[58] The exception is the Australian National University (ANU) located in the capital city Canberra that was established by the Commonwealth Government under the *Australian National University Act 1946* (Cth).

[59] Ibid 8–9.

[60] Ibid.

[61] *Higher Education Support Act 2003* (Cth) Part 2–2.

student contribution by accessing HECS-HELP, which is a Commonwealth Government loan to help cover the cost of the student contribution for a course of study.[62] Not all enrolments in universities are a CSP. If a student is not eligible for a CSP, then students are enrolled as full-fee paying students, who in turn can access a FEE-HELP loan to pay tuition fees for units of study.[63] Student loans are repaid as a debt through the Australian Taxation Office either as a voluntary repayment or a compulsory repayment. A compulsory repayment is made once a student commences employment, and their earnings meet the annual compulsory repayment threshold (Australian Government 2023b).

3.1.2 Higher Education Standards and Quality Assurance

The Commonwealth Government has extended its regulatory control over universities in relation to accreditation and quality assurance. All higher education providers, including universities, are required to be accredited by and registered with the Tertiary Education and Quality Standards Agency (TEQSA). TEQSA was established in 2011 by the Tertiary Education Quality Standards Agency Act 2011 (Cth) as an independent body to administer the TEQSA Act and oversee the accreditation and registration of higher education providers. The aim of the TEQSA Act is to ensure that students receive a consistently high quality and standard of education. Some of the key objectives stated in the TEQSA Act are therefore to provide for national consistency in the regulation of higher education; to regulate higher education using a standards-based quality framework; and to promote a higher education system that is appropriate to meet Australia's social and economic needs for a highly educated and skilled population.[64] To achieve these objectives, TEQSA is granted extensive regulatory powers and functions under the TEQSA Act. Most importantly, TEQSA is empowered to register entities as authorised higher education providers, to accredit courses of study, to investigate compliance with the TEQSA Act, to protect academic integrity and to 'advise and make recommendations to the Minister on matters relating to the quality or regulation of higher education providers'.[65]

The Higher Education Standards Framework (Threshold Standards) is also established as a legislative instrument under Section 58(1) of the TEQSA Act, which is monitored and reviewed by TEQSA.[66] The Threshold Standards set out a comprehensive list of quality assurance standards that must be met and maintained by higher education providers. The Standards cover: student participation and engagement; the learning environment; teaching; research and research training; institutional quality assurance; governance and accountability and representation, information

---

[62] *Higher Education Support Act 2003* (Cth) s 87.1.

[63] *Higher Education Support Act 2003* (Cth) s 101.1.

[64] *Tertiary Education Quality Standards Agency Act 2011* (Cth) s 3.

[65] *Tertiary Education Quality Standards Agency Act 2011* (Cth) s 134.

[66] *Higher Education Standards Framework (Threshold Standards) 2021* (which replaced the *Higher Education Standards Framework (Threshold Standards) 2015*).

and information management. TEQSA has authority to review and monitor a university's performance against the Standards, and to investigate and enforce compliance. TEQSA's approach to compliance is to 'promote a culture of effective self-assurance'; however TEQSA will adopt 'a multi-faceted approach that escalates enforcement actions to assure compliance where this is necessary' (TEQSA 2018). Enforcement actions available to TEQSA cover a range of administrative sanctions and civil penalties.[67] Administrative sanctions include cancelling the education provider's registration, reducing the period of registration, and imposing conditions on education programs.[68] A relevant court can order the payment of a civil penalty for breaching the Act, and issue an injunction restraining a person from contravening a provision of the Act or requiring a person to comply with a provision of the Act.[69]

3.1.3 University Governance

Although universities operate in an increasingly external bureaucratic and regulatory environment, they nonetheless still have much autonomy and authority over their governance and management of all areas of the institution. As noted, universities are constituted by a state or territory Act of Parliament which sets out the establishment, structure, powers and functions of governing bodies of the university. Universities are a body corporate with perpetual succession.

The principal governing authority of a university is referred to variously as the Council[70] or Senate.[71] The governing authority consists of the Chancellor of the University, who is the head of the university, the Vice-Chancellor, appointed members and elected members from staff, students and the community. The university governing authority appoints the Vice-Chancellor who is the chief executive officer of the university. The powers and duties of a Vice-Chancellor are generally prescribed by university statutes and regulations. The university governing authority is responsible for the overall control of university operations, its strategic direction and financial matters. A governing authority has the power to make statutes, regulations and by-laws subject to the enabling university act regulating all matters concerning the university. Statutes for instance may control matters such as the use of the common seal of the university, awarding degrees, appointment of staff, enrolment of students, fees and scholarship, student residences and facilities.[72]

---

[67] *Tertiary Education Quality Standards Agency Act 2011* (Cth) s 97.

[68] *Tertiary Education Quality Standards Agency Act 2011* (Cth) ss 99–101.

[69] *Tertiary Education Quality Standards Agency Act 2011* (Cth) s 97, s 117 and s 127.

[70] See, e.g., *Curtin University Act 1966* (WA) s 8; *Edith Cowan University Act 1984* (WA) s 8.

[71] See, e.g., *University of Western Australia Act 1911* (WA) s 5; *Murdoch University Act 1973* (WA) s 12; *University of Queensland Act 1998* (Qld) s 7.

[72] See, e.g., *University of Western Australia Act 1911* (WA) s 31; *Curtin University Act 1966* (WA) s 34; *Murdoch University Act 1973* (WA) s 24; *Edith Cowan University Act 1984* (WA) s 26; *University of Notre Dame Australia Act 1989* (WA) s 20.

The academic governing body referred to as the Academic Board or Academic Council is usually a standing committee of the university governing authority and advises it on academic matters. An academic governing body is mainly responsible for academic leadership, implementing policies, promoting and maintaining university standards in teaching and research, and overseeing the development of academic activities.[73] Membership of academic governing bodies is made up of elected members from academic and professional staff, and students. It may also include co-opted members. An academic governing body generally has oversight of a wide range of policies relating to academic programs and courses, academic standards, learning and teaching, research, student admissions, examinations, academic integrity, student conduct, student well-being and quality assurance. An academic governing body may also establish standing committees that have specific areas of responsibility within the university.

3.1.4 Student Representation

Students have an important role to play in university governance in terms of representing students' rights and interests. According to Tyrrell and Varnham, the 'student voice' and active student participation in university governance are crucial for developing and promoting meaningful partnerships and increasing student engagement, satisfaction and successful academic outcomes (Tyrrell and Varnham 2015). As explained by the authors, the 'student voice' and student participation are valuable for enhancing genuine democratic decision-making, developing students' leadership skills and preparing students for 'citizenship of a democratic society'.[74] University acts and statutes generally make provision for undergraduate and postgraduate students to be elected representatives on a university council[75] and academic board. Student-lead organisations and associations[76] also make a valuable contribution to promoting the objects and culture of a university by organising and delivering a range of academic, social and cultural activities and events for students. Student organisations and associations also help to provide various services to promote and support student health and well-being.

---

[73] See, e.g., *Murdoch University Act 1973* (WA) s 21; *Edith Cowan University Act 1984* (WA) s 18.

[74] Ibid 27.

[75] See, e.g., *University of Western Australia Act 1911* (WA) s 8(1)(g); *Curtin University Act 1966* (WA) s 9(1)(d); *Murdoch University Act 1973* (WA) s 12(1)(e); *Edith Cowan University Act 1984* (WA) s 9(1)(f).

[76] See, e.g., The establishment of Student Guilds whose primary function it is to represent the common interest of students: *University of Western Australia Act 1911* (WA) s 28; *Curtin University Act 1966* (WA) s 44; *Murdoch University Act 1973* (WA) s 20; *Edith Cowan University Act 1984* (WA) s 41.

3.1.5 Student Services and Amenities Fees

Universities are permitted to charge a fee for non-academic student services and amenities (SSA).[77] These services include providing child care services, financial advice, employment and career advice, legal services, recreational activities, sporting facilities and food services.[78] The SSA fee is index each year. Students 'studying on a part-time basis cannot be charged more than 75% of the maximum amount that students studying on a full-time basis are charged' (Australian Government 2023c). Universities may choose not to charge the fee and they may charge different amounts for different categories of students. Students who meet the eligibility requirements for fee assistance can obtain financial assistance and defer payment through the SA-HELP government loan scheme (Australian Government 2023a).

3.1.6 International Students

International students make up a large cohort of university students. According to Universities Australia, the international student market is Australia's fourth largest export market and in 2019–2020 was worth AUD37.5 billion to the Australian economy (Universities Australia 2023). The international student market was significantly impacted by COVID 19 from which universities continue to recover.

Universities that provide educational services to overseas (international) students (within or outside of Australia) on a student visa are regulated by the Education Services for Overseas Students Act 2000 (the ESOS Act) and the National Code of Practice for Registration Authorities and Providers of Education and Training to Overseas Students 2018.[79] The National Code is a legislative instrument and its purpose is to 'provide nationally consistent standards for the registration and conduct of registered providers and the conduct of persons who deliver educational services on behalf of registered providers'.[80]

The ESOS Act sets out the legal framework for delivering education services to overseas students. A university must be registered in order to provide services to overseas students.[81] A breach of the ESOS Act may result in universities incurring substantial penalties including conditions being attached to their registration, and suspension or cancellation of their provider registration.[82] A primary aim of the ESOS Act is to 'provide financial and tuition assurance to overseas students for courses for

[77] *Higher Education Support Act 2003* (Cth) s 19–37(5), amended by the *Higher Education Legislation Amendment (Student Services and Amenities) Act 2011* (Cth).

[78] *Higher Education Support Act 2003* (Cth) s 19–38(4).

[79] The National Code is a legislative instrument made under the *Education Services for Overseas Students Act 2000* (Cth) s 33.

[80] *ESOS Act* s 34.

[81] *ESOS Act* s 8.

[82] *ESOS Act* pt 6.

which they have paid'.[83] To this end, the ESOS Assurance Fund is established under the ESOS Act to protect the interests of students and to ensure that they are provided with alternative course or for their course money to be refunded if a provider (e.g., a university) cannot provide the course for which the student has paid.[84] The ESOS Act also aims to ensure compliance with Australia's immigration laws. Providers are required to collect and report on information relevant for the administration and compliance of student visas.[85]

The Office of the Commonwealth Ombudsman for Overseas Students (Ombudsman) has an important role to play in supporting overseas students. The Ombudsman has the authority to investigate complaints from overseas students about private education providers, such as a private university. Complains may be about refusing a student admission to a course, fees and refunds, course attendance or the cancellation of enrolment (Commonwealth Ombudsman 2023). Complaints relating to the quality of the course or teaching, resources and facilities are not investigated.[86] Overseas students who have complaints about a public education provider (e.g., a university) may lodge a complaint with the relevant state or territory ombudsman (Ombudsman Western Australia 2021).

3.1.7 The University as an Employer

University employment relations and conditions of employment are governed by Commonwealth and state legislation, and common law. In addition, universities may have their own internal statues, policies and guidelines that regulate the employment context.

The Fair Work Act 2009 (Cth) (FWA), a federal law, is the primary legislative framework for employment relations in most workplaces in Australia including universities.[87] For the purpose of the FWA, a university is a 'national system employer'[88] and therefore is bound by the FWA and must comply with the minimum National Employment Standards (NES).[89] The NES apply to the employment of all national system employees 'which cannot be displaced'. The NES set

---

[83] *ESOS Act* s 4A.

[84] *ESOS Act* ss 45–46.

[85] *ESOS Act* s 4A; s 175.

[86] Ibid.

[87] The FWA covers those employed in a constitutional corporation, the private sector, and employers and employees where states have transferred their industrial relations powers to the Commonwealth system. The public sector and local government employees in a state are generally not covered by the FWA. The FWA does not yet cover non-constitutional corporations in Western Australia.

[88] *Fair Work Act 2009* (Cth) s 14. Universities have been categorised as 'trading corporations' and therefore a 'constitutional corporation' for the purpose of the FWA. Although universities are different to other kinds of commercial corporations insofar as their primary purpose is the provision of education, universities have been held to engage in sufficient trading activities from which substantial profits are derived: *Quickenden v O'Connor* (2001) 109 FCR 243.

[89] *Fair Work Act 2009* (Cth) s 61.

minimum standards for maximum weekly hours of work, flexible working arrangements, conversion of causal employment, parental leave entitlements, annual leave, personal/careers/compassionate leave, community service leave, long service leave, public holidays, termination and redundancy payments, and the requirement of the Fair Work Ombudsman to issue a Fair Work Information Statement on FWA entitlements.[90]

A central feature of the FWA is the provision for modern awards and enterprise agreements. Awards are industry or occupational based agreements that are made by the Fair Work Commission[91] that contain basic terms and conditions of employment together with the NES for that particular industry or group.[92] Most national system employees are governed by a modern award.

An enterprise agreement is made at an 'enterprise' level and contains the terms and conditions of employment that apply to a particular employer and employees covered by the enterprise agreement.[93] Enterprise agreements must comply with the NES entitlements; they cannot be excluded or reduced. Most universities operate according to an enterprise agreement, which are negotiated between university management and employee representative bodies, bargaining entities, such as the National Tertiary Education Union. An enterprise agreement cannot be made with a single employee. An enterprise agreement must be lodged and approved by the Fair Work Commission,[94] and once it is implemented it applies to all university employees irrespective of an employee's membership of a union or employee representative body. An enterprise agreement generally does not apply to senior management employees, who are employed on the basis of a separate contract. Enterprise agreements are generally very detailed and contain provisions relating to the following matters: categories of work, job classifications, recruitment, hours of work and workloads, remuneration and entitlements, leave entitlements, work flexibility, staff development, redeployment and termination of employment. Notably, university enterprise agreements also generally include detailed provisions on work performance management, grievance procedures and dispute resolution procedures.

In addition to the FWA scheme, the common law also applies to employment relations. There is no legal requirement to have a written contract of employment. Whether a contract is in writing or by oral agreement, employers and employees have common law duties and obligations. For an employer, a primary obligation is

---

[90] *Fair Work Act 2009* (Cth) pt 2–2.

[91] *Fair Work Act 2009* (Cth) s 132. The Fair Work Commission can also vary and revoke awards. The Fair Work Commission is the national workplace tribunal for Australia. In Western Australia, the Western Australian Industrial Relations Commission that is established under the *Industrial Relations Act 1979* (WA) deals with industrial matters concerning employers and employees within the state system and who do not come under the national fair work system (i.e. employers who are constitutional corporations and their employees).

[92] *Fair Work Act 2009* (Cth) pt 2–3. An example of an award is the Higher Education Industry—Academic Staff—Award 2020. However, this award does not apply to university employees who are covered by an enterprise agreement.

[93] *Fair Work Act 2009* (Cth) s 172.

[94] *Fair Work Act 2009* (Cth) s 54, s 186.

the duty of care an employer owes to its employees. The duty of care is codified in federal and state work health and safety legislation.[95] For employees, common law duties include the duty of care and skill, duty of good faith and a duty to obey lawful instructions or directions.[96]

4 Emerging Issues

This section discusses selected continuing and emerging issues in education and related law in Australia.

4.1 Diversity and Non-discrimination Schools

Valuing diversity and protecting students against discrimination are two key principles underpinning education. In recent times, the protection of transgender students against discrimination has come to the fore. Transgender discrimination whether direct or indirect is unlawful. However, state and territory laws are patchy on dealing with transgender discrimination in schools especially non-government schools. The Commonwealth Sex Discrimination Act 1984 makes it unlawful to discriminate against a person because of their sex, gender identity, sexual orientation and intersex status. Section 21 of the Sex Discrimination Act states specifically that it is unlawful for an education authority to discriminate against a person on these grounds by refusing to accept a student's application for admission, by denying access or limiting access to a benefit provided by the education authority, by expelling a student or subjecting to the student to 'any other detriment'. Education institutions that are authorised single-sex institutions are exempt, that is, 'conduct solely for students of a different sex from the sex of the applicant'. In addition to this federal law, state and territory have anti-discrimination or equal opportunity legislation that prohibits discrimination on the ground of sex; however, jurisdictions vary as to protections for transgender, intersex, and binary gender identities. Currently, for example, the Western Australian Equal Opportunity Act 1984 only protects transgender people who have been issued with a certificate under the Gender Assignment Act 2000, which prescribes how people can legally change their gender. However, the Western Australian Law Reform Commission's Review of the Equal Opportunity Act 1894

[95] See e.g., *Work Health and Safety Act 2011* (Cth) pt 2.

[96] *Sheikholeslami v University of NSW (No.3)* [2008] FMCA 35 in which a direction to undertake the assigned undergraduate teaching was not unreasonable or disproportionate nor beyond the terms of employment [86]. *Miller v University of New South Wales* [2001] AIRC 1055 which held that a direction to an academic staff member to undertake additional teaching duties was reasonable [35].

has made recommendations to provide anti-discrimination protection for transgender people without the need for a certificate from the Gender Reassignment Board, and to strengthen protections for gender-diverse staff and students in religious schools (The Law Reform Commission of Western Australia 2022).

4.2 *School Safety and Discipline*

Schools have a duty to provide safe school environments. All schools are required to develop and implement student behaviour policies and procedures that are aimed at promoting safe, orderly and disciplined learning environments. The issue of student safety and discipline is therefore an ongoing issue that continues to present challenges for principals and teachers. Some of the more serious challenges schools face involve disruptive behaviour in class that impedes learning, cyberbullying, anti-social behaviour and violence against staff and students, damage to property and drug offences. Adding to this is the increasing problem of 'vaping' or the use of e-cigarettes by students and the impact this has on students' health and school performance (AMA New South Wales 2023). In most jurisdictions it is illegal to sell e-cigarettes to, or buy e-cigarettes for, any person aged under 18 years whether or not the e-cigarettes contain nicotine.[97] In Western Australia it is illegal to sell e-cigarettes that contain nicotine to anyone (Government of Western Australia 2023b). Smoking and vaping ought to be banned in all schools and there is a need for greater awareness training on what e-cigarettes are, the dangers of vaping and the laws that regulate vaping.

4.3 *Parental Behaviour in Schools*

Parents have a crucial role to play in the education of their children. Education legislation therefore makes provisions for the formal and informal involvement of parents in schools via school councils and parent associations as explained above. However, a troubling issue facing schools is the disruptive, damaging and often violent behaviour of parents on school property. There are reports of parents disrupting classes, threatening, abusing and intimidating staff, destroying property and assaulting teachers. Patents have also turned to social media to disparage and discredit schools, and to

---

[97] See, e.g., *Tobacco Control Act 1987* (Vic) s 12; *Tobacco Products Control Act 2006* (WA) s 6, s 7.

defame staff. In the Queensland case of *Brose v Baluskas & Ors*[98] the school principal was awarded damages[99] for defamatory statements[100] made on social media by a group of parents.

Such behaviour by parents undermines the school and school culture, causes reputational damage, causes harm and distress, detracts from teaching, negatively impacts on students, results in staff absenteeism, and wastes time and resources. As stated in the Victorian Policy on School Community Safety Orders:

> When parents and carers behave aggressively towards staff or members of the school community, it can have a significant impact on the physical and mental health, safety and wellbeing of the staff, students and other members of the school community who experience it. (Government of Victoria 2023a)

School principals do have authority to control and manage school premises so that schools are safe and orderly places. A principal of a government school in Western Australia may, for example, make orders in relation to school premises to maintain good order, to ensure the safety and welfare of persons and to prevent or minimise damage to property.[101] A school principal is also authorised to order a person who is not a student to leave the school's premises[102] and they may make an order to prohibit persons from entering school premises if they are likely to cause harm or damage.[103] In Victoria, recent changes to education legislation authorise government school principals to issue 'School Community Safety Orders' to manage the school safety.[104] Orders can be issued against persons, other than staff and students, to prohibit or restrain certain behaviour on school premises. Orders, however, can only be issued once all other alternatives have been considered (Government of Victoria 2023a). Similarly, in South Australia a person may be issued with a 'barring notice' and be barred from school premises if they behave in an offensive or threatening manner, use abuse, threatening or insulting language, trespass or commit an offence in relation to the premises.[105] In NSW, school principals can use the historic Inclosed Lands Protection Act 1901 (NSW) to control access to school property. Principals may take action for trespass against a person, including a parent, who remains on

---

[98] *Brose v Baluskas & Ors (No 6)* [2020] QDC 15 (28 February 2020). In *Ryan v Premachandran* [2009] NSWSC 1186 (6 November 2009) a Sydney School Principal was awarded some AUD80,000 in damages for defamatory statements made by a parent in an email sent to several other parents.

[99] The School Principal was awarded AUD182,500, most of which was settled out of court, with two parents being ordered by the court to pay $3000 each.

[100] *Brose v Baluskas & Ors (No 6)* [2020] QDC 15 (28 February 2020), [137], [181], [238], for examples of imputations made.

[101] *School Education Regulations 2000* (WA) reg 70(2).

[102] Ibid reg 75.

[103] Ibid reg 7.78(1) and (2), subject to exceptions in reg 79 that includes students and teachers.

[104] *Education and Training Reform Act 2006* (Vic) pt 2.1A.

[105] *Education and Children's Services Act 2019* (SA) s 93.

the school premises after they have been asked to leave the school,[106] or if they are behaving in an offensive manner on school property and refuse to leave when asked.[107]

4.4 Teacher Shortages

One of the major current issues facing school education is the shortage of teachers. This poses a significant threat to the quality of education, teacher and student well-being, community confidence in the education system and international standing. The problem of teacher shortages is attributed to a range of factors notably unsustainable workloads and teacher burnout, uncompetitive wages, lack of respect for the teaching profession, the lack of permanent positions, safety in schools and student behaviour, teacher training and declining graduate numbers (Rafferty 2022). In August 2022, federal, state and territory ministers commenced a series of meetings to address the issues and to draft a National Action Plan (Australian Government 2022). Addressing teacher shortages is complex but proposed strategies include enhancing the status of the teaching profession, improving working conditions, increasing teacher salaries, providing greater job security by reducing casual positions and increasing tenure, reducing administrative workloads, increasing time for teaching preparation and providing incentives to encourage students to become teachers.

4.5 Modern Slavery

Modern slavery has increasingly gained global attention and growing concerns about the widespread occurrence and impact of modern slavery. Modern slavery refers to 'situations of exploitation that a person cannot refuse or leave because of threats, violence, coercion, deception, and/or abuse of power' (International Labour Office 2017). It covers practices such as forced labour, slavery, human trafficking, debt bondage and forced marriage. The International Labour Organisation estimated that in 2016 there were some 40 million people, predominantly women and children, who were victims of modern slavery of which 25 million people were in forced labour and 15 million in forced marriage (International Labour Office 2017). In Australia, the Commonwealth Modern Slavery Act 2018 (Cth) (MSA) came into force on 1 January 2019. The MSA applies to business and entities with an annual consolidated revenue of at least AUD100 million. Importantly, it established a national Modern Slavery Reporting scheme. Businesses and entities that are bound by the MSA are required

[106] *Inclosed Lands Protection Act 1901* (NSW) s 4.

[107] *Inclosed Lands Protection Act 1901* (NSW) s 4A.

to submit and register a Modern Slavery Statement that address potential risks in relation to supply chains. Entities that are not mandated to submit statements may opt to register a statement. The MSA has implications for educational institutions in relation to supply chains that extend to the procurement of school uniforms, furniture, equipment, catering, cleaning and travel, to mention a few. Universities and some of the larger private educational entities that fall within the scope of the MSA are therefore required to submit a Modern Slavery Statement. For example, Modern Slavery Statements have been registered by The Roman Catholic Trust Corporation for the Diocese of Cairns (Queensland), which is a body corporate, serving 30 Catholic schools and colleges, and The Anglican School Corporation (Sydney, NSW) that likewise controls a number of schools.

5 Conclusion

The Australian education system operates within a federal structure of government and is therefore governed by a combination of federal and state or territory laws, and the common law. The higher educator sector is mainly governed by federal education laws alongside a wide range of general laws that govern aspects such as industrial relation, workplace safety, privacy and more recently modern slavery. The school education system is the responsibility of each state and territory. Each jurisdiction has its own ministry and department of education that oversees the establishment of schools and the delivery of education. Schools are governed by federal and state or territory laws, but mostly by state and territory education legislation.

References

According to Universities Australia there are about 170 higher education providers in Australia. https://www.universitiesaustralia.edu.au/policy-submissions/teaching-learning-funding/australian-higher-education/. Accessed 11 Mar 2023

AMA New South Wales. 'Unpacking vaping in schools'. https://www.amansw.com.au/unpacking-vaping-in-schools-2/. Accessed 11 Mar 2023

Aroney N et al (2015) The constitution of the commonwealth of Australia: history, principle and interpretation. Cambridge University Press, London, p 95

Australian Government (2022) Department of Education. Teacher workforce strategies (Issues paper, 2022). https://ministers.education.gov.au/sites/default/files/documents/Teacher%20Workforce%20Shortages%20-%20Issues%20paper.pdf. Accessed 11 Mar 2023

Australian Government (2023a) 'SA-HELP'. Study Assist. https://www.studyassist.gov.au/help-loans/sa-help. Accessed 11 Mar 2023

Australian Government (2023b) 'Loan repayment'. Study Assist. https://www.studyassist.gov.au/paying-back-your-loan/loan-repayment. Accessed 11 Mar 2023

Australian Government (2023c) Student support and amenities fee. https://www.dese.gov.au/higher-education-loan-program/approved-hep-information/student-services-and-amenities-fee. Accessed 11 Mar 2023

Campbell C, Proctor H (2014) A history of Australian schooling. Allen & Unwin, Canberra, p 102

Castles A (1963) The reception and status of English law in Australia. Adelaide Law Rev 2(1):1
Catholic Education Western Australia (CEWA). https://www.cewa.edu.au/. Accessed 11 Mar 2023
Commonwealth Ombudsman (2023) Overseas students. https://www.ombudsman.gov.au/How-we-can-help/overseas-students. Accessed 11 Mar 2023
Davis J (2012) Connecting with Tort law. Oxford University Press, London, p 369
Fletcher L (1979) 'Schooling for Young colonists'. In: Neal WD (ed) Education in western Australia. University of Western Australia Press, Canberra, p 9–25
Government of NSW (2023a) 'Early history'. History of New South Wales government schools. https://education.nsw.gov.au/about-us/our-people-and-structure/history-of-government-schools/government-schools/early-history. Accessed 11 Mar 2023
Government of NSW (2023b) 'National system'. History of New South Wales government schools. https://education.nsw.gov.au/about-us/our-people-and-structure/history-of-government-schools/government-schools/national-system. Accessed 11 Mar 2023
Government of NSW (2023c) 'Public schools act 1866'. History of New South Wales government schools. https://education.nsw.gov.au/about-us/our-people-and-structure/history-of-government-schools/government-schools/public-schools-act-1866. Accessed 11 Mar 2023
Government of Queensland (1984) 'A brief history'. History of education in Queensland. https://education.qld.gov.au/about-us/history/brief-history. Accessed 11 Mar 2023
Government of Victoria (2023a) Department of Education and Training. 'School community safety orders'. School operations. https://www2.education.vic.gov.au/pal/school-community-safety-orders/policy. Accessed 11 Mar 2023
Government of Victoria (2023b) Education. 'School operations'. Parent payments. https://www2.education.vic.gov.au/pal/parent-payment/policy. Accessed 11 Mar 2023
Government of Western Australia (2023a) Education and school information. https://www.wa.gov.au/organisation/state-records-office-of-western-australia/education-and-school-information. Accessed 11 Mar 2023
Government of Western Australia (2023b) Department of Health. Electronic cigarettes in Western Australia. https://ww2.health.wa.gov.au/Articles/A_E/Electronic-cigarettes-in-Western-Australia. Accessed 11 Mar 2023
International Labour Office (ILO) (2017) Global estimates of modern slavery: forced labour and forced marriage. https://www.ilo.org/wcmsp5/groups/public/---dgreports/--dcomm/documents/publication/wcms_575479.pdf. Accessed 11 Mar 2023
Jackson J, Varnham S (2007) Law for educators. Lexis Nexis Butterworths, Chatswood, p 188
Joseph S, Castan M (2019) Federal constitutional law: a contemporary view. LawBook Co, Canberra, p 80
Mendelson D (2007) The new law of Torts. Oxford University Press, London, pp 314–315
Montessori schools provide an approach to education based on the educational philosophy and pedagogy of 'Dr Maria Montessori, a physician, anthropologist and pedagogue'. https://montessori.org.au/about-montessori. Accessed 11 Mar 2023
Ombudsman Western Australia. Annual report 2020–21. https://www.ombudsman.wa.gov.au/Publications/Annual_Reports.htm. Accessed 11 Mar 2023
Rafferty S (2022) 'Queensland teacher shortage reaching "crisis" point with 270 vacant teaching posts'. ABC News. https://www.abc.net.au/news/2022-03-31/queensland-teacher-shortage-takes-hold/100951138. Accessed 31 Mar 2022
Squelch J (2015) 'The legal framework of higher education'. In: Varnham S, Kamvounias P, Squelch J (eds) Higher education and the law. The Federation Press, vol 7
Squelch J, Russo CJ (2020) A comparative analysis of school discipline and procedural fairness in private schools in Australia and the United States. Int J Law Educ 23:5

State Library Victoria (2023) 'School and education history in Victoria'. https://guides.slv.vic.gov.au/education. Accessed 11 Mar 2023
Steiner education is founded on the life and work of 'Rudolf Steiner an Austrian scientist, philosopher and artist who lived from 1861–1925'. https://www.steinereducation.edu.au/steiner-education/about-rudolf-steiner-and-the-growth-of-the-steiner-waldorf-education-movement/. Accessed 11 Mar 2023
TEQSA (2018) 'TEQSA's approach to compliance and enforcement'. https://www.teqsa.gov.au/latest-news/publications/teqsas-approach-compliance-and-enforcement. Accessed 22 May 2018
The law reform commission of Western Australia, review of the equal opportunity act 1984 (WA) (Final Report No 111, May 2022). https://www.wa.gov.au/system/files/2022-08/LRC-Project-111-Final-Report_0.pdf. Accessed 11 Mar 2023
The national school resourcing board is an independent body that reviews and provides 'independent oversight' of the commonwealth funding model. https://www.dese.gov.au/national-school-resourcing-board. Accessed 11 Mar 2023
Tyrrell J, Varnham S (2015) The student voice in university decision-making. In: Varnham S, Kamvounias P, Squelch J (eds) Higher education and the law. The Federation Press, Canberra, p 26–27
Universities Australia (2023) 'International'. https://www.universitiesaustralia.edu.au/policy-submissions/international/. Accessed 11 Mar 2023
Wages M (2016) Parent involvement: collaboration is the key for every child's success. Rowman & Littlefield, Canberra (缺少页码)

Education Federalism in Brazil: Contradictions, Challenges, and Possibilities

Nina Ranieri

1 Introduction

In the three decades of validity of the Federal Constitution of 1988 (FC) Brazil lived the longest democratic period in its history, in addition to expressive changes in the social area. In the field of education, there was considerable progress in the educational levels of the population in general and of young people in particular, when compared to previous periods. If in the 1980s the net enrollment rate in primary and secondary education was 80.1% and 14.3%, respectively, in 2000 it reached 94.3% and 33% (Brasil 2022). In 2019, according to data from the National Household Sample Survey—PNAD, we reached a rate of 99.7% in primary education (practically universal) and 89.2% in secondary education (Brasil 2017). The positive change is fundamentally due to five conditions promoted by the Federal Constitution 1988: valorization of social rights and impulse towards their universalization; decentralization of competencies and charges among the federated entities; new parameters for resource allocation, among which the Fund for the Maintenance and Development of Basic Education and the Valorization of Education Professionals—FUNDEB stand out, the existence of channels for social participation and control of the public sphere.

The adaptation of the legal Country to the real Country, however, is by no means complete. School exclusion and dropout, as well as inadequate levels of learning and poor results in the international comparison, prove that recurring problems in Brazilian education—such as inequities in access and permanence in school, quality of teaching, and funding—are not conjunctural. The numbers are known: in 2019, 1.1 million school-age children and adolescents aged 15 to 17 were out of school; in November 2020, because of the pandemic, more than 5 million children and adolescents, between 6 and 17 years old, were not attending school. Of these, more

N. Ranieri (✉)
University of São Paulo Law School—FD/USP, São Paulo, Brazil
e-mail: copyright@esph.com.cn

UNESCO Chair on the Right to Education, FD/USP, São Paulo, Brazil

C. J. Russo and L. Ma (eds.), *A Comparative Analysis of Systems of Education Law*,
https://doi.org/10.1007/978-981-97-1052-2_3

than 40% were children aged 6 to 10 years, a range in which education was practically universal before the pandemic. In addition, the low learning rates presented in reading and mathematics, related to problems of access and permanence, accentuated the regional and social inequalities and limitations on productivity gains (Brasil 2019a).

The causes are diverse, they concern internal and external factors to the school. From them, the complex division of competencies, educational charges, and incomes among the entities of the Federation stands out, object of this article aims to present the Brazilian educational system from the perspective of federalism, pointing out its contradictions, challenges, and possibilities (UNICEF 2022).

2 Education Federalism in Brazil—A General View

Educational charges in Brazil are shared by the Federal Constitution among the federated entities—Union, States and Municipalities, which have their own education systems under national legal regulation, through the National Educational Bases and Guidelines Law—LDB (Law 9.394/1996). At the federal level, the body in charge of the elaboration and execution of public policies is the Ministry of Education, assisted by the National Board of Education—CNE, which has normative and advisory competences. In the States and Municipalities, the same functions are carried out by the respective Education Departments and Councils.

Such educational federalism has ineffective centralizing characteristics, particularly when considering the diversity of its territory and population and the heterogeneity of federated entities. These have negative consequences for the execution of educational charges by most federated entities, since the main executors of obligations and policies (States, Federal District and Municipalities) do not have legislative competences or adequate income for their responsibilities, which results in different conditions of offers due to fiscal difficulties, administrative and school management incapacity, and permanent dependence on the Union, especially in the Municipalities. Furthermore, the federal redistributive and supplementary function is inefficient and does not consider local and regional socioeconomic differences. There are also difficulties in relation to the practice of collaboration and disconnection among the more than 5500 education systems.

According to the FC, the provision of public, compulsory and universal basic education is the responsibility of all federated entities (Union, States, Federal District and Municipalities), at different levels (art. 211). Municipalities are primarily responsible for day care centers and preschools and, together with the States and the Federal District, for elementary education. States and the Federal District are primarily responsible for secondary education. The Union, to which was not assigned any level of priority action, is responsible for supplementary and redistributive action at all levels of education and, in particular, in higher education. The detailing of competencies is provided by the National Educational Bases and Guidelines Law—LDB (Law no. 9.394/1996). Every 10 years, the National Education Plan—PNE, secured by law, establishes educational objectives and goals to be achieved by the federated entities, within the scope of their respective competences (currently, the PNE established by Law 13.005/14 is in force). To support the financial costs of compulsory education, the Constitution establishes that the States, the Federal District and the Municipalities must invest 25% of their tax revenues in education and the Union, 18%.

To ensure the universalization of quality public education, the Federal Constitution established in its art. 208, Paragraph 2 that: "The non-offering of compulsory education by the Public Power, or its irregular offer, is the responsibility of the competent authority." Important consequences can be drawn from this provision: all entities of the Federation are committed to guaranteeing the provision of free and compulsory basic education from 4 (four) to 17 (seventeen) years of age, including its free offer for all those who they did not have access to it at the proper age (FC, art. 208, I); the meaning of "regular offer"—for the purpose of not holding the competent authority responsible—goes beyond the quantitative aspects (existence of vacancies in sufficient number to meet demand); it also includes the quality of education, thanks to the provision of art. 206, I and VII of the FC: "Article 206. Teaching will be based on the following principles: I – equal conditions of access and permanence in school; (...) VII – guarantee of standards of quality;".

The same conclusion can be drawn from art. 214, III of the FC, which lists, among the objectives of the integrated action of the public authorities, in the different federative spheres, the improvement of the quality of education. Law 13,005/14, in turn, when defining the PNE guidelines, adds to the demand for quality improvement (art. 2, IV), the overcoming of regional inequalities (art. 2, III). The concept of regular provision of compulsory education (basic education from 4 to 17 years of age), therefore, encompasses universalization and quality. The art. 211, Paragraph 7 of the FC, in turn, determines that the minimum quality standard will consider the adequate conditions of offer and will have as a reference the Cost of Quality Education per Student (CAQ), to be agreed in a collaboration regime by means of a complementary law.

The cooperation regime comprises the States, Municipalities, and the federal government, with the objective of ensuring the universalization, quality, and equity of compulsory education (FC, art. 211, Paragraph 4), through the execution of a set of common obligations and exclusive obligations for the federal government. In the latter case, the obligations are intended to provide technical and financial assistance to the States, the Federal District, and the Municipalities for the development of their education systems and the priority attendance of compulsory education.

The adoption of collaboration regimes among federated entities is typical of contemporary federalism, in which the sharing of decisions and responsibilities, in the implementation of public policies, requires the coordination of actions by the level of government. In the field of education, the Brazilian Union, States, and Municipalities have been finding it difficult to carry out joint tasks; the progress obtained was due to the greater or lesser managerial or technical, and financial capacity of the federated entities (Abrucio 2010). The conclusion is reinforced by the way in which the distribution of legislative competencies among federated entities takes place. The Union reserves the right to legislate on guidelines and bases for national education (FC, art. 22, XXIV); and competence concurrent with that of the States and the Federal District to legislate on education through general norms (FC, art. 24, IX). The competence of States and Municipalities, in this scenario, is quite restricted since it remains.

In greater the competencies of the Union, the greater the tendency noted in contemporary constitutionalism to extend the competition space of federated entities, in a compensatory way, especially in fiscal and administrative matters, even if legislative centralization is maintained (Kincaid 2020). This is not what happens in Brazil, since the States, the Federal District, and the Municipalities legislate only in relation to what is not included in the federal sphere. Due to the strong legislative centralization, the problem, as already indicated in the introduction, is that there is no correspondence between the ownership of legislative, and enforcement competences, except for the Union. In other words, the Union legislates for States and Municipalities. What is verified, therefore, is the determination, by the Union, of municipal and state educational charges, including in the financial plan, without considering the possibility of policies for local realities. Considering that, of the 5570 Brazilian municipalities, 25.0% have less than 20,000 inhabitants and 45% have less than 10,000 inhabitants, it is easy to notice the difficulties (Brasil 2013).

Recently, Constitutional Amendment 108/2020, when defining the objectives of educational collaboration between the federated entities in art. 211, aimed at confronting these problems, determined the edition of infraconstitutional rules of coordination, awaiting consideration in the Chamber of Deputies (Brasil 2019b).

Universalization is ensured by free education (FC, art. 208, I), census of elementary school students (FC, art. 208, Paragraph 2), survey of demand for early childhood education, and active search for children in early childhood (art. 208, IV), as a strategy to guarantee the right the education. Quality, in turn, in view of current legislation, comprises the infrastructure, human and input conditions that allow the development of relevant and adapted educational processes, such as quality of food and health of students, the school environment, infrastructure and basic inputs, educational content and processes, results and public funding. But how to guarantee, in each of the more than 5500 municipalities, adequate conditions for the regular provision of elementary education, for example? From a financial point of view, resources come from the three spheres of government and from FUNDEB, as explained below.

The Constitution guaranteed resources for the maintenance and development of education through the linking of tax revenue, in the form of articles 167, IV and 212. In art. 68 of the LDB, the sources of funds are detailed: I—revenue from taxes of the Union, the States, the Federal District, and the Municipalities; II—revenue from constitutional transfers and other transfers; III—income from education salary and other social contributions; IV—revenue from tax incentives; V—other resources provided for by law." The education salary, social contribution provided for in Paragraph 5 of art. 212, provides other resources to finance programs, projects and actions aimed at financing public basic education.

Additionally, the Fund for Maintenance and Development of Basic Education and Valorization of Education Professionals—FUNDEB, composed of municipal, state and federal tax funds, guarantees the redistribution of resources for all levels of compulsory education, according to the number of students enrolled in each public school system, of which at least 60% must be applied to teachers' remuneration. The Fund's monetary resources vary according to the annual collection, guaranteeing a minimum amount per student and a national floor for teachers' remuneration established by the federal government.[1] Whenever those minimum values are not reached, the federal government guarantees them, through three different types of complementation (Annual Value per Student; Total Annual Value per Student; Annual Value per Student Result/Performance) (Brasil 2021).

According to art. 41 of Law 14.113/2020, amended in part by Law no. 14,276/2021, the implementation of said complementation will occur gradually, in the period from 2021 to 2026, until reaching the entire percentage established in art. 5 of the aforementioned Law (23%), and in 2021, according to the aforementioned provision, the value of the complementation will be 12% (twelve percent) of the total revenues of the Funds, of which 10% (ten percent) refer to the complementation in the VAAF modality and 2% (two percent) referring to complementation in the VAAT modality. Finally, Law No. 12,858/2013, which provides for the allocation to the areas of education and health of a portion of the profit sharing or financial compensation for the exploration of oil and natural gas, determines the application of 75% of the revenues earned by all the federal entities, as a proportion of gross domestic product, pursuant to art. 214, VI of the FC.

In 2020, through Constitutional Amendment 108, the FUNDEB (since then called NEW FUNDEB) became a permanent financing instrument. The NEW FUNDEB increases the Union's contribution (from 10 to 23% until 2026) and promotes improvements in the redistribution of financial resources regarding the socioeconomic level of the students and the entities availability of resources. These measures are intended to address fiscal disparities in the country.

3 Major Legal Developments

Despite the advances in the educational area introduced by the 1988 Constitution, namely compulsory education extended to the entire population, regardless of age, and the financing of basic education through FUNDEB, different conditions of offer and permanent dependence on the Union on the part of States and Municipalities, as well as fiscal difficulties and incapacity of technical execution of charges on the part of the federated entities, especially the Municipalities, have prevented or hindered

[1] In this case, it is a value below which the Union, the States, the Federal District and the Municipalities will not be able to set the initial salaries of the public teaching careers, for the workday of 40 hours per week.

the overcoming of the main educational obstacles at the national level mentioned in the introduction to this article.

Among the causes internal to the school are the different conditions of offer, in which the inadequacy of school facilities for teaching, the precarious training of teachers and the devaluation of the teaching career, inefficient school management, the absence of national parameters of quality of education provision. Among the external causes, in terms of public educational management, the mismanagement of public resources, the lack of systemic planning of public policies, discontinuity of programs, disarticulation between the spheres of government prevail. Some of the actions to face them are included in the document *Educação Já 2022* (Education Immediately), prepared by the non-governmental organization *Todos pela Educação* (All for Education), from which the following proposals are extracted (Todos pela Educação 2022).

First, in view of the immediate effects of the Covid-19 pandemic on Basic Education, the expansion of school dropout must be faced. Initiatives in this direction must necessarily be intersectoral in nature. More immediately, it is essential that, in an integrated way, public bodies (such as the Education and Social Assistance Departments) actively seek out children and young people, with identification, registration, control and monitoring of those who are out of school or at risk of dropping out at this time. In addition, welcoming actions and emotional support for students must be carried out. In the educational aspect, the recomposition of learning and the promotion of digital inclusion are imperative at this moment. All these actions are the responsibility of States and Municipalities. The federal government and the National Congress have the task of seeking to advance impact measures on a national scale, in order to strengthen policies implemented locally and support federative entities, with an emphasis on reducing asymmetries between them. Norms and guidelines for education networks, offering free tools and systems and financial support for carrying out actions are some examples of what should be done at the national level.

Secondly, there is an urgent need to modernize and improve school management in the municipalities. To this end, it is necessary to have directors and pedagogical coordinators selected in a technical and judicious way, to give them administrative and pedagogical autonomy to manage the schools and to guarantee support and follow-up by the Education Departments.

Research conducted by Abrucio (2010) shows that, in the 1990s, the results of decentralization in the provision of basic education, promoted by municipalization, were not homogeneous. Financial dependence, scarcity of resources, low administrative capacity, difficulties in formulating and implementing government programs produced national disparities with negative results in political, administrative and financial terms. Additionally, decentralization took place in a pulverized way, with little coordination among federated entities promoting, in the early 2000s, the establishment of what the author calls "compartmentalized federalism". In 2017, in 4900 municipalities, all with a population of up to 50,000 inhabitants, representing 33% of the national population, identical conclusions were presented, regarding the inability of efficient management by most municipalities (Grin and Abrucio 2017).

Secondly, it is necessary to improve collaboration between States and Municipalities, through national law, as happened, at the national level, with the former FUNDEB and the institution of a minimum wage for professionals in the public teaching profession of basic education (Law at the. 11,738/2008), through FUNDEB resources. Although these two cases are not about collaboration of education systems, but about successful forms of intergovernmental coordination, it is worth noting that in both cases the coordination took place through a federal norm of national validity, with induction of assumption of obligations through the redistribution of resources between spheres of government and conditional assistance to the Municipalities.

Another example always remembered is that of the State of Ceará, which in 2009 instituted an incentive system, through tax rewards, in the area of education, according to Quality Index, calculated annually, as follows: 4.5% due to the Education Quality Index (IQE); 0.5% according to the Environmental Quality Index (IQM); and 1.25% according to the Health Quality Index (IQS). The Education Quality Index, specifically, considers data from the Ceará Basic Education Assessment System (SPAECE), to which all municipalities are submitted, using as criteria indicators that portray the objectives of the state policy for education and its evolution (Todos Pela Educação 2021).

The inclusion of the financial dimension in the concept of quality of education was decisive in these cases, as recognized by the jurisprudence of the Federal Supreme Court—STF, in Original Civil Actions—ACOs nos. 648, 660, 669 and 700, filed by the states of Bahia, Amazonas, Sergipe and Rio Grande do Norte. In them, the federal government demanded the complementary transfer of amounts from the Basic Education Maintenance and Development Fund—FUNDEB, due per student enrolled in elementary school, based on the national average and not in face of the state values (Brasil 2018a). In addition, the Court has recognized, on other occasions, that the allegation of reservation of the possible in the face of social rights to health and education is not admissible (RE 431.773/SP, Rapporteur Justice Marco Aurélio; AI 674.764-AgR/PI, Rapporteur Justice Dias Toffoli) (Brasil 2018b). Such recognition, however, is not enough. At the federal level, the implementation of more distributive and quality-inducing financing involves regulating and implementing the redistributive and quality-inducing mechanisms approved by the NEW FUNDEB. The approval of NEW FUNDEB will allow, over the next few years, Brazil to reduce the critical educational underfunding that persists, especially in the poorest municipalities.

Other measures, such as the creation of policies to induce the improvement of the management of state and municipal education secretariats, combined with the improvement of the administrative and budgetary management of the MEC in order to make the coordination of the national system more efficient would already be a great step in facing the problems related to educational governance. Among them: improving the organization of functions and responsibilities within the Ministry of Education, and its municipalities; developing a Human Resources policy aimed at strengthening the technical staff of the Ministry of Education, and its municipalities; updating the technological park of federal education management; creating a support program to improve the management of state and municipal Education Departments.

Also at the federal level, strengthening the governance of Education involves regulating and implementing the National Education System to encourage the agreement of educational policies and the collaboration of entities in the management of Brazilian Education. For state governments, it is imperative to exercise the role of coordinating the educational policy in their state, strengthening the collaboration regime with the municipalities to improve the offer of Education. These are necessary actions to face the great challenges that Brazilian Education already had before 2020 and that were accentuated by the Covid-19 pandemic, due to the closure of schools, particularly affecting students in a situation of greater vulnerability.

4 Outlook of Future Developments

Due to inequalities, in the Brazilian territory, in the offer and quality of education, the burning issue of Brazilian education in this third decade of the twenty first century is the legal institution of the National Education System—SNE, in collaboration regime, through integrated actions of the public powers of the different federative spheres for the accomplishment of the goals, guidelines and strategies of the PNE, foreseen in the art. 214 of the FC (via Constitutional Amendment no. 59/2009) and in art. 13, of the PNE.

In fact, Brazil already has several national instruments for the organization of compulsory education. This is what proves the validity of national legislation (constitutional norms, the LDB and other general education norms), the edition of the National Education Plans—PNE (the current one, defined by Law 13.005/2014), the existence of the National Education Council—CNE, the institution of a national salary floor for teachers (Law no. 11,738/2008), of the National Curricular Common Base—BNCC (prepared by the federal government based on article 210 of the FC, article 9, V, and article 35-A of the LDB, and in the PNE). In addition, the country has initiatives for educational improvement nationwide, such as the Basic Education Development Index—IDEB, the National School Feeding Program—PNAE (Law no. 11,947/2009), the National Program for Access to Technical Education and Employment—PRONATEC (Law no. 12,513), among others.

Despite these instruments and initiatives, the big problem is the different administrative and fiscal conditions of States and Municipalities, something that the future National Education System—an instrument perceived, in the educational area, as adequate, although insufficient, to overcome educational ills—cannot resolve. Training, qualifying, demanding learning outcomes, rewarding good learning outcomes, and inducing sustainable development in the various education systems, through federal policies with a local scope, are demonstrably more effective and efficient than the unconstitutional assumption of elementary education by the Union.

As already mentioned, to date the National Education System has not been created by law. Starting from the assumptions that there is no subordination among the education systems and that only when it legislates on guidelines and bases does the

Union exercise an ordering function of national scope, it is concluded that the national system is not hierarchically superior to the others, but, above all, an instrument of coordination. In this sense, it is expected that it will mitigate the negative effects of Brazilian educational federalism through the definition of agreement instances and rationalization mechanisms for the use of education resources; encouraging the creation of regional education centers and other forms of educational association. In addition, it should promote the quality of basic education at all stages and modalities, improving school flow and learning.

5 Conclusion

The tension between the division of powers and the unity of power in the Federal States is inherent to their nature. Tuning the degree of tension between central power and peripheral units, in terms of decentralization and control, becomes, consequently, crucial for achieving educational goals.

Brazilian educational federalism, in many aspects, is inadequate to the dimensions of the country, to the heterogeneity and diversity of States and Municipalities, and to the need to offer quality basic education. Its contradictions are revealed in the lack of correspondence between the ownership of charges and legislative competencies, in the inadequate tax regime, in the inability to manage most of the federated entities, in the standardized and unique political-administrative autonomy for all Municipalities—which in everything contrasts with the factual inequality existing among the more than 5000 municipalities.

When the current Federal Constitution was drafted, the debate on educational federalism in the 1987/1988 Constituent Assembly did not consider the historical construction of political institutions in the country, so that the municipalization of education was made reductionist and unrealistic way, without taking into account the financial and administrative conditions of more the Brazilian municipalities. Therefore, the problem to be faced today is not between centralization and decentralization, but about which decentralization for which goals. Overcoming such impasses is not a simple task, but it is urgent. The Constitution itself indicates the different paths to be explored: collaboration, cooperation, and coordination. There are no other possible solutions to reconcile asymmetries, different offer conditions and permanent dependence on the Union, conditions inherent to large Federal States.

The Federal Constitution of 1988 has ample capacity to adapt, thanks to its reform conditions. This means, in addition to absorbing the pressures of the majority conflict, inherent to democracies, it can promote the improvement of the incremental implementation of public policies, in view of the demands of society, as occurred, for example, with the creation of the former FUNDEF.

What is the role of law in relation to these challenges? Studies in educational law are gaining renewed importance today, not only because of the legal system's ability to guarantee distributive rights and demand their implementation, but above all because of its ability to understand and bring together the educational and legal fields.

From this point of view, research on federative arrangements in a broad perspective, incorporating the organizational aspect to the purposes of state action, constitutes an urgent research agenda for the guarantee of educational rights.

References

Abrucio F (2010) A Dinâmica Federativa da Educação Brasileira: Diagnóstico e Propostas de Aperfeiçoamento, "in" Educação e Federalismo no Brasil: combater as desigualdades, garantir a diversidade/organizado por Romualdo Portela de Oliveira e Wagner Santana. UNESCO, Brasília, p 64

Brasil (2013) Brazilian Institute of Geography and Statistics. IBGE. https://agenciadenoticias.ibge.gov.br/agencia-sala-de-imprensa/2013-agencia-de-noticias/releases/31461-ibge-divulga-estimativa-da-populacao-dos-municipios-para-2021

Brasil (2017) National research for continuous household sample—continuous PNAD. Education 2017. Brazilian Institute of Geography and Statistics—IBGE. https://sidra.ibge.gov.br/tabela/7138. Accessed on 5 Jan 2022

Brasil (2018a) Original civil actions 648, 660, 669 and 700, filed, respectively, by the States of Bahia, Amazonas, Sergipe and Rio Grande do Norte. Rel. Min. Marco Aurélio. http://www.stf.jus.br/arquivo/cms/noticiaNoticiaStf/anexo/ACO648EF.pdf. Accessed on 9 Dec 2018

Brasil (2018b). Supreme court. http://portal.stf.jus.br/processos/detalhe.asp?incidente=2543670. Accessed on 9 Dec 2018

Brasil (2019a) Basic education evaluation system—SAEB. https://download.inep.gov.br/educacao_basica/saeb/2020/documentos/Apresentacao_Resultados_Amostrais_Saeb_2019.pdf

Brasil (2019b) Bill (PLP) 235/2019, approved in the Senate and pending in the Chamber of Deputies, since 03/17/2022. Available in: https://www.camara.leg.br/proposicoesWeb/fichadetramitacao?idProposicao=2318217. Accessed on 8 Dec 2022

Brasil (2021) FUNDEB regulation by law no. 14.113/2020, amended by Law no. 14,276, of 12/27/2021. Available at https://www.planalto.gov.br/ccivil_03/_ato2019-2022/2021/lei/L14276.htm Accessed on 1 May 2022

Brasil (2022) Brazilian Institute of Geography and Statistics—IBGE. https://seriesestatisticas.ibge.gov.br/series.aspx?vcodigo=SEE17 Accessed on 1 May 2022

Grin EJ, Abrucio F (2017) O que dizer das capacidades estatais dos municípios Brasileiros em um contexto de descentralização de políticas. In: XIII Congreso Nacional de Ciencia Política—La política en entredicho. Volatilidad global, desigualdades persistentes y gobernabilidad democrática. Organização: Sociedad Argentina de Análisis Político y la Universidad Torcuato Di Tella, Buenos Aires, 2 al 5 de agosto de 2017. Available in: https://www.researchgate.net/profile/Eduardo_Grin/publication/31891. Accessed in 28 Aug 2022

Kincaid J (2020) Why centralization and decentralization in Federation?—Dynamic de/centralization in federations: comparative conclusions. Publius: The Journal of Federalism 49/1. https://dardanelli.net/research/ Cf. also, "Powers in balance" "in" FAPESP Research, July 2018, Year 19, no 269, p 80

Todos Pela Educação (2021) Education that works—the case of Sobral (CE). Building effective school management in all schools. Todos pela Educação. São Paulo. Available at: https://educacaoquedacerto.todospelaeducacao.org.br/wp-content/uploads/2021/11/educacaoquedacerto-todospelaeducacao-sobral-digital.pdf. Accessed on 8 Dec 2022

Todos Pela Educação (2022) Educação Já 2022. Available at: https://todospelaeducacao.org.br/wordpress/wp-content/uploads/2022/04/educacaoja2022-abril02-todospelaeducacao.pdf?utm_source=download&utm_id=documento. Accessed on 1 May 2022

UNICEF (2022) Scenario of school exclusion in Brazil. https://www.unicef.org/brazil/media/14026/file/cenario-da-exclusao-escolar-no-Brasil.pdf. Accessed on 1 May 2022

China's Education Legal System

Leijun Ma

1 Background of China's Education Legal System

In China's thousands of years of development history, the Chinese legal system, which is different from the "continental legal system" and the "common law system", has been formed. The Chinese legal system not only had an important impact on the development of ancient China, but also on the legislation of some countries in East Asia and Southeast Asia. After the defeat of several wars and economic decline in the middle and late nineteenth century, the Government of the Qing dynasty government began to reconstruct the legal system in the early twentieth century with the "continental law system" as a model. After the establishment of New China in 1949, the legislative model of the former Soviet Union also had a significant impact on China. In 1978, China began implementing the policy of reform and opening up, which greatly promoted the development of China's economy, society, and the rule of law. So far, China has formed a legal system with the Constitution as the commander, the law as the backbone, administrative regulations and local regulations as important components, and the Constitution, civil law and commercial law, administrative law, economic law, social law, criminal law, litigation and non-litigation procedural law and other legal departments.

At present, there are nearly 530,000 schools of all levels and types in China, with over 290 million students enrolled. The level of education popularization at all levels has reached or exceeded the average level of middle-income countries, with preschool education and compulsory education reaching the world average level of high-income countries, and higher education entering the stage of popularization. The average length of education for the working-age population is 10.9 years. 200,000

L. Ma (✉)
China National Academy of Education Sciences, Beijing, China
e-mail: copyright@esph.com.cn

C. J. Russo and L. Ma (eds.), *A Comparative Analysis of Systems of Education Law*,
https://doi.org/10.1007/978-981-97-1052-2_4

dropouts from compulsory education all returned to school for education, which historically solved the long-standing problem of dropping out of school.[1]

In recent years, China has highlighted the priority of education development and put forward that education is a "national priority". It has made remarkable progress in promoting the popularization of higher education, strengthening the construction of modern vocational education system, starting the construction of the Double First Class University Plan, deepening the reform of the examination and enrollment system, promoting the reform of education evaluation, and deepening the classified management of private education. Since the promulgation of China's first education law, the Degree Regulations, in 1980, China has successively promulgated laws in the field of education, such as the Education Law, Teachers' Law, Compulsory Education Law, Higher Education Law, Vocational Education Law, Private Education Promotion Law, and Family Education Promotion Law. In addition, the National People's Congress is currently reviewing the "Preschool Education Law" and is expected to complete the legislative process in the near future. These educational legislations have greatly promoted the development of education.

2 Composition of China's Education Legal System

2.1 China's Education Administration System

The Constitution, Education Law, and other education laws of the People's Republic of China have made clear legal provisions for the education administrative system. The Constitution stipulates that the State Council leads and manages educational work, and local governments at or above the county level shall manage the education affairs within their respective administrative regions in accordance with the law. Article 14 of the Education Law stipulates: "The State Council and local people's governments at all levels shall lead and manage education work based on the principle of hierarchical management and division of responsibilities. Secondary and lower education shall be managed by local people's governments under the leadership of the State Council. Higher education shall be managed by the State Council and the people's governments of provinces, autonomous regions, and municipalities directly under the Central Government".

In accordance with the State Council's institutional reform plan approved at the first session of the 11th National People's Congress and the Notice of the State Council on Institutional Structure, the Ministry of Education was established as a component department of the Ministries of the People's Republic of China. At present, there are 27 functional departments and bureaus of the Ministry of Education, including the General Office, Department of Policies and Regulations, Department

[1] The Propaganda Department of the CPC Central Committee held a press conference on the results of education reform and development. http://www.scio.gov.cn/xwfbh/xwbfbh/wqfbh/47673/49089/index.htm#1.

of Development Planning, Department of Comprehensive Reforms, Department of Personnel, Department of Finance, Department of Basic Education, Department of Supervision of After-School Tutoring Institutions, Department of Vocational and Adult Education, Department of Higher Education, Office of National Education Inspection, Department of Minority Education, Department of Teacher Education, Department of Physical Health and Arts Education, etc.[2] The Ministry of Education has a total of 18 responsibilities, which mainly include: researching and formulating guidelines and policies for educational work, drafting laws and regulations on education, researching and proposing education reform and development strategies and the national education development plan, and overall management of education funds of the department, etc.[3] In addition, the Ministry of Education also has 32 directly affiliated units such as China National Academy of Education Sciences, National Academy of Education Administration, etc.[4]

Local education institutions are institutions where local people's governments at all levels organize, lead, and manage educational undertakings, mainly referring to local governments at all levels and their education administrative departments. Local education administrative departments are divided into three levels: province, city, and county, under the unified leadership of the government at the same level, and under the guidance of higher education administrative departments.

2.2 *The Sources of Education Law in China*

The education legal system in China consists of education laws, administrative regulations, and departmental regulations. With the development of the times and the need for education reform, since the promulgation of the National Medium and Long Term Education Reform and Development Plan Outline (2010–2020) in 2010, China has further supplemented and adjusted the existing education legal system. At this point, China has basically formed an education legal system with complete departments, sound systems, standardized content, and good results. More importantly, China's education legal system is based on China's basic national conditions, fully absorbing and drawing on international education and education legislation concepts and experiences to form an education legal system.

The specific sources of China's education legal system will be explained separately below.

---

[2] http://en.moe.gov.cn/about_moe/departments/.

[3] http://en.moe.gov.cn/about_moe/what_we_do/.

[4] http://en.moe.gov.cn/about_moe/affiliated_institutions/.

2.2.1 Constitution

The Constitution of China stipulates the fundamental social, economic and political system of contemporary China, various basic principles, guidelines and policies, the basic rights and obligations of citizens, the composition, functions and powers, and responsibilities of major state organs, which involve the most fundamental and important aspects of all fields of social life. The Constitution is formulated and revised by the National People's Congress, the highest authority in China. The status of the Constitution determines that its formulation and revision procedures are extremely strict. The Constitution has the highest legal effect, and all laws, administrative regulations, and local regulations shall not conflict with the Constitution. In China, the National People's Congress supervises the implementation of the Constitution, the Standing Committee of the National People's Congress interprets and supervises the implementation of the Constitution, and holds accountable any violations of the Constitution.

In the Constitution, the specific provisions on education mainly include:

The basic principles for the development of education by the state are stipulated, namely: "The state develops socialist education and improves the scientific and cultural level of the people throughout the country. The state establishes various schools, popularizes primary and compulsory education, develops secondary education, vocational education, and higher education, and develops preschool education", etc. (Article 19); The state strengthens the construction of spiritual civilization by popularizing ideal education, moral education, cultural education, disciplinary education, and legal education, and by formulating and implementing various rules and conventions among people of different ranges in urban and rural areas (Article 24); The state trains young people, adolescents, and children to develop in an all-round way in morality, intelligence, physique, and other aspects (Article 46).

The right to education of citizens is stipulated, namely: "Citizens of the People's Republic of China have the right and obligation to receive education" (Article 46, paragraph 1).

The educational obligation of parents is stipulated, namely: "Parents have the obligation to raise and educate underage children" (Article 49, Paragraph 3).

The principles of national management education are stipulated, namely: the State Council "leads and manages education, science, culture, health, sports, and family planning work" (Article 89, Paragraph 7); "Local people's governments at or above the county level shall manage the education, culture, health, and sports undertakings of their respective administrative regions within the limits of their authority as prescribed by law..." (Article 107); "The organs of self-government of China's national autonomous areas independently administer local education, science, culture, public health and sports..." (Article 119).

2.2.2 Education Law

In the Chinese education legal system, the effectiveness of education laws is weaker than the Constitution. Education laws stipulate the basic national education system, which are the prerequisite and basis for the formulation of education administrative regulations, local education regulations, and departmental rules. At present, China has promulgated eight special education laws, including the Education Law, the Compulsory Education Law, the Higher Education Law, Regulations on Academic Degrees, the Vocational Education Law, the Teachers' Law, the Private Education Promotion Law, and the Law on Standard Spoken and Written Chinese Language. In addition to the above laws, China has also formulated laws closely related to education, such as the Law on the Promotion of Family Education, the Law on the Protection of Minors, and the Law on the Prevention of Juvenile Delinquency.

2.2.3 Education Administrative Regulations

Education administrative regulations refer to normative education documents formulated by the highest administrative organ of the country, the State Council, which have a legal status and effectiveness second only to the Constitution and laws. The decisions and orders issued by the State Council, which are normative, also belong to the sources of law. For example, the Regulations on Teacher Qualifications, the Regulations on School Health, the Regulations on School Physical Education, the Interim Measures for the Implementation of the Regulations of the People's Republic of China on Academic Degrees, and the Interim Provisions of the State Council on Studying Abroad at One's Own Expense. At present, the number of educational administrative regulations in China far exceeds the number of education laws formulated by the National People's Congress and its Standing Committee.

The administrative regulations formulated by the State Council shall not conflict with the Constitution and laws. Therefore, the Standing Committee of the National People's Congress has the power to revoke administrative regulations, decisions, and orders formulated by the State Council that contradict the Constitution and laws. According to the Provisional Regulations on the Procedure for Formulating Administrative Regulations issued by the General Office of the State Council, educational administrative regulations generally have three forms, namely regulations, orders, and rules. The comprehensive and systematic regulations on a certain aspect of educational administrative work are called "regulations", the regulations on a particular aspect of administrative work are called "orders", and the specific provisions for educational administrative work are called the "rules".

2.2.4 Local Education Regulations

Local education regulations are normative education legal documents formulated by certain local state power organs in accordance with the specific situation and actual needs of education development in their respective administrative regions, which have legal effects within their respective administrative regions. According to the provisions of the Constitution and the Organization Law and Legislative Law of Local People's Congresses and Local People's Governments revised in 1986, the people's congresses and standing committees of provinces, autonomous regions, municipalities directly under the central government, cities where provincial people's governments are located, and larger cities approved by the State Council have the power to formulate local regulations. Local education regulations are effective only if they do not conflict with the Constitution, laws, and administrative regulations.

The "Regulations on the Prevention and Handling of Personal Injury Accidents among Primary and Secondary School Students in Beijing" passed at the 6th meeting of the 12th Standing Committee of the Beijing Municipal People's Congress belong to this type of regulation.

2.2.5 Education Regulations in China's National Autonomous Areas

Regional ethnic autonomy is a fundamental political system in China. The people's congresses in China's national autonomous areas have the right to formulate regulations on autonomy and separate regulations on education in accordance with the political, economic and cultural characteristics of the local ethnic groups, but they shall not take effect until they are submitted to the standing committees of the national or provincial people's congresses for approval. Autonomous regulations are comprehensive regulations with a wide range of contents. The separate regulations on education are normative documents related to a certain aspect of educational affairs, generally using names such as "regulations", "orders", "alternative regulations", and "alternative measures". The regulations on ethnic autonomous education are only valid within the autonomous region. For example, on November 28, 2002, the 31st Meeting of the Standing Committee of the Ninth People's Congress of Xinjiang passed the "Several Provisions of the Xinjiang on the Implementation of the Teachers' Law of the PRC".

2.2.6 Rules of the Education Department

The rules of the education department are administrative legal normative documents, which are normative educational legal documents formulated by the State Council of the People's Republic of China within the scope of authority. The matters stipulated in the departmental educational rules should belong to the implementation of laws or the administrative regulations, decisions and orders of the State Council. For example, the Measures for Handling Student Injury Accidents issued by the Ministry of Education are educational rules.

In the vertical structure of the education legal system, the principle of constitutional supremacy, the principle that education laws are superior to education regulations, the principle that education regulations are superior to education rules, and the principle that national education regulations are superior to local education regulations should be followed in determining the legal effect of laws and regulations.

2.3 *Main Education Laws*

2.3.1 Education Law of the PRC[5]

The Education Law is the most important law in the education legal system. The Education Law comprehensively regulates the nature, policies, and basic systems of education, the basic principles of educational activities, clarifies the basic norms of educational activities, and provides a legal basis for the formulation of other special education laws. It also lays the foundation for establishing an education legal system in line with China's national conditions. The formulation of the Education Law not only opened up a new stage of China's education legal system construction, but also has milestone significance in the history of education development. It marks the beginning of China's education development being fully integrated into the legal track.

The Education Law was formulated in 1995 and was revised three times in 2009, 2015, and 2021. Its content is very rich, with the characteristics of combining comprehensiveness and pertinence, standardization and guidance, principles and operability. As the Basic Law of Education, the Education Law not only comprehensively regulates and adjusts various educational relationships, but also highlights the prominent issues in educational reform and development at that time and makes targeted provisions; At the same time, forward-looking development directions have been proposed based on the trend of education development. The Education Law mainly formulates basic norms on major issues related to education as a whole, such as the status of education, educational policies, basic principles of education, basic systems, guarantee of educational investment and conditions, the legal status of schools, the relationship between education and society, external exchanges and cooperation in education, and legal responsibilities, providing a legislative basis for the formulation of other education laws and regulations, The specific issues related to various levels and types of education are formulated by other special education laws and education administrative regulations.

[5] http://en.moe.gov.cn/documents/laws_policies/201506/t20150626_191385.html.

2.3.2 Compulsory Education Law of the PRC[6]

The compulsory education system is one of the important education systems in the country, which is of great significance for the development of citizens themselves. At the same time, compulsory education is also a fundamental project for cultivating qualified talents and improving the quality of the entire nation. Ensuring that school-age children and adolescents receive compulsory education is an important manifestation of the country's guarantee of citizens' equal right to education, and it is also an important responsibility of the government.

The Compulsory Education Law was enacted in 1986, which established the compulsory education system in the form of national laws and provided a clear legal guarantee and basis for the implementation of compulsory education; The implementation of the compulsory education system has established the concept that all people must accept compulsory education in accordance with the law, which is the beginning of truly moving towards the rule of law in education. The revised Compulsory Education Law in 2006 highlights the characteristics of compulsory education in the new era, with specific and clear legal norms, strong pertinence and operability, providing comprehensive legal protection for the implementation of compulsory education in the new era.

2.3.3 Teachers' Law of the PRC[7]

The Teachers' Law is a law formulated around the important subject of educational activities—teachers, and is also a very important law in the education legal system. The Teachers' Law was promulgated in 1993, before the Education Law, and was amended in 2009. The drafting of the Teachers' Law has been ongoing for 8 years. In the mid-1980s, China's reform and opening up continued to deepen, and economic development provided more opportunities for personal development. Due to the relatively lagging education reform and development at that time, the country's investment in education was insufficient, teacher salaries were low, and the instability of the teacher team had become a prominent issue affecting the quality of education and the development of the education industry. Solving the problem of teachers, improving their treatment and quality, and building a high-quality teaching team are urgent requirements for promoting education development, adapting to the needs of reform and opening up and the realization of socialist modernization. It has become an urgent task for education reform. With the development of national legal construction, ensuring the construction of the teaching staff in accordance with the law and establishing a targeted teacher system have become important tasks in educational legislation.

---

6 http://en.moe.gov.cn/documents/laws_policies/201506/t20150626_191391.html.

7 https://flk.npc.gov.cn/detail2.html?MmM5MDlmZGQ2NzhiZjE3OTAxNjc4YmY2Yzc5OTA0ZmI%3D.

The main content of the Teachers' Law includes the rights and obligations of teachers, the qualifications and appointment of teachers, the cultivation and training of teachers, the assessment and treatment of teachers, rewards for teachers, and related legal responsibilities.

2.3.4 Vocational Education Law of the PRC[8]

The Vocational Education Law was formulated in 1996 and revised in 2022, a special law specifically regulating vocational education. Vocational education is an important component of Chinese education. Vocational education, as a form of education to cultivate various practical and skilled talents, is of great significance for China's economic development and the improvement of labor quality. The Vocational Education Law stipulates that vocational education is a type of education that holds equal importance to general education, and the state promotes the coordinated development of vocational education and general education. The Vocational Education Law also stipulates the basic principles of vocational school education and training, the system of educational certificates, training certificates, and vocational qualification certificates, the management system of vocational education, the level of vocational school education, the investment and guarantee conditions of vocational education funds, and the responsibility of enterprises for the development of vocational education.

2.3.5 Higher Education Law of the PRC[9]

The Higher Education Law was formulated in 1998 and revised in 2015. It is a special law that comprehensively regulates higher education. Higher education is an important component of Chinese education and the most important stage for cultivating high-level specialized talents. Standardizing higher education in accordance with the law is of great significance in ensuring the development of higher education and promoting higher education reform in accordance with the law. The Higher Education Law, based on the basic principles of the Education Law and the characteristics of higher education, stipulates the tasks, training objectives, management system, educational forms, levels, years of study, enrollment methods, admission conditions, academic qualifications and degree systems of higher education. It also stipulates the basic conditions and procedures for the establishment of higher education institutions, as well as the internal management system and autonomy of higher education institutions, the rights and obligations of teachers and students, as well as the guarantee of funding and conditions for higher education.

---

8 http://en.moe.gov.cn/documents/laws_policies/201506/t20150626_191390.html.

9 http://en.moe.gov.cn/documents/laws_policies/201506/t20150626_191386.html.

2.3.6 Private Education Promotion Law of the PRC[10]

The Private Education Promotion Law was formulated in 2002 and revised in 2016. It is a law in the education legal system that specifically regulates private education. Since the reform and opening up, private education in China has developed rapidly, playing a positive role in promoting the reform of the school system, promoting education development, increasing citizens' educational opportunities, and ensuring citizens' right to choose education.

The "Private Education Promotion Law" first clarifies the scope of application of private education in the "General Provisions": "Social organizations or individuals outside of state institutions who use non-state financial funds to organize activities of schools and other educational institutions for society shall be subject to this law." The main characteristics of private education, such as the main body of education, the sources of funds, and the enrollment targets, have been clarified. At the same time, the public welfare nature of private education has been clarified: "Private education belongs to public welfare undertakings and is an integral part of socialist education." The revised "Private Education Promotion Law" in 2016 stipulates the classification management of non-profit and for-profit private schools, providing a guarantee for the standardized development of private education.

2.3.7 Regulations on Academic Degrees of the PRC[11]

The Regulations on Academic Degrees were formulated in 1980 and amended in 2004 to promote the growth of Chinese scientific professionals, the improvement of academic levels in various disciplines, and the development of education and science, and meet the needs of modernization construction. The degree is divided into three levels: bachelor's, master's, and doctoral. Foreign students studying in China and foreign scholars engaged in research work in China may apply for degrees from the degree awarding unit. For those who have the academic level specified in this regulation, corresponding degrees shall be awarded.

2.3.8 Law on the Standard Spoken and Written Chinese Language of the PRC[12]

The Law on the Standard Spoken and Written Chinese Language was formulated in 2000 in accordance with the Constitution in order to promote the normalization, standardization and healthy development of the common language of the state, make the common language of the state play a better role in social life, and promote

[10] http://en.moe.gov.cn/documents/laws_policies/201506/t20150626_191387.html.

[11] Regulations on Academic Degrees of the People's Republic of China http://en.moe.gov.cn/documents/laws_policies/201506/t20150626_191392.html.

[12] http://en.moe.gov.cn/documents/laws_policies/201506/t20150626_191388.html.

economic and cultural exchanges among ethnic groups and regions. This law establishes the legal status of Putonghua and standardises Chinese characters as the "national common language and writing system", which mainly includes the use, management and supervision of the national common language and writing system.

2.4 Judicial Precedents

China belongs to the continental legal system, so legislation holds the most core and important position in the education legal system. Compared to countries with case law systems, judicial precedents not only lack legal validity in China's judicial practice, but also appear relatively weak in China's educational law research. However, with the trend of mutual learning and integration between the continental legal system and the case law system in recent years, the Chinese education law community has increasingly attached importance to the research on educational judicial precedents. This research not only promotes the development of the theoretical system of education law itself, but also promotes education legislation and justice. China's Supreme People's Court has also successively issued some guiding cases in recent years, requiring that "people's courts at all levels should refer to similar cases when trying them" (Ma 2016).

China's education law also attaches great importance to case study. For example, Professor Zhan Zhongle from Peking University once presided over the selection and research of the "Top Ten Administrative Dispute Cases for Promoting the Rule of Law in Education", which effectively promoted the improvement of the theoretical system of education law and the relevant legal regulations of education legislation. One of the most representative cases is Liu Yanwen v. Peking University. In 1999, Liu Yanwen, a doctoral student at Peking University, sued Peking University for not obtaining a doctoral degree certificate and graduation certificate. The debate in this case involves whether the internal affairs of higher education institutions can be litigated, and whether the refusal of Peking University to issue Liu Yanwen's degree certificate and graduation certificate is legitimate, etc. After this case, it has to some extent promoted the process of improving the internal governance system of Chinese universities, and there has been a clearer division of academic and administrative power in universities.

3 Main Legal Developments

Since 2011, the center of China's education legislation has gradually shifted from legislation to revision and interpretation, in order to better adapt to the development of the times and meet the needs of the people (Shen 2018). This is mainly reflected in significant revisions to existing education laws such as the Compulsory Education Law, Education Law, Higher Education Law, Vocational Education Law, and

Private Education Promotion Law. At the same time, the revision of laws such as the Teachers' Law and the Degree Regulations is also being promoted through the legislative process. Furthermore, it is worth noting that educational judicial precedents have significantly impacted education legislation and justice.

3.1 Revision of the Compulsory Education Law

China officially formulated the Compulsory Education Law in 1986, which significantly promoted the development of compulsory education in China. However, with the realization of China's "two basic" goals (basically popularizing nine-year compulsory education and basically eliminating illiteracy among Young adult people) at the beginning of this century, compulsory education has shifted from a low-level popularization focusing on school opportunities to a high-level popularization stage that improves education quality and promotes balanced development. Compulsory education is facing new development opportunities and many new problems and challenges. Therefore, revising the Compulsory Education Law has become a hot topic of concern for all sectors of society (Sun 2006). On June 29, 2006, the 22nd Session of the Standing Committee of the Tenth National People's Congress adopted the newly revised the Compulsory Education Law of the PRC.

The revision of the Compulsory Education Law mainly focuses on the following aspects: first, it emphasizes the public welfare, unity and mandatory principles of compulsory education, and exempts students from tuition and miscellaneous fees at the compulsory educational stage; The second is to promote the balanced development of compulsory education, solve the problem of unbalanced development between the east and the west, between urban and rural areas and between schools in the process of China's compulsory education development, and give students at the compulsory educational stage fair learning opportunities and conditions; The third is to clarify the mechanism for ensuring the funding of compulsory education by governments at all levels, stipulate that compulsory education should be included in the national financial guarantee, shared by the State Council and local people's governments at all levels, and implement a new mechanism for ensuring funding through provincial coordination; The fourth is to establish a management system for compulsory education, which is led by the State Council, planned by the people's governments of provinces, autonomous regions, and municipalities directly under the central government, and mainly managed by county-level people's governments; The fifth is to propose the concept of quality education, requiring schools to comprehensively promote the comprehensive development of students; The Sixth is to make new regulations on improving the status and treatment of teachers in the compulsory educational stage, and made it clear that the average salary of teachers should not be lower than the average salary of local civil servants. The revision of the Compulsory Education Law this time significantly reflects the trend of China's compulsory education from "having access to education" to "having access to good education".

3.2 *Education Law Package Revision*

The Education Law Package Revision is an innovation in China's education legislation. On July 27, 2012, the Ministry of Education submitted the "Revised Proposal for the Education Law Package (Draft)" to the State Council for review, requesting that the revised proposals for the Education Law, Higher Education Law, and the Private Education Promotion Law be submitted to the National People's Congress for revision. On December 26, 2015, the Standing Committee of the National People's Congress passed a decision on revising the Education Law and the Higher Education Law. On November 7, 2016, the National People's Congress passed a decision on revising the "Private Education Promotion Law". The comprehensive revision of education laws has played a significant role in accelerating the process of education legislation and improving its efficiency. In addition, the Education Law was once again revised by the National People's Congress on April 29, 2021.

The revision of the Education Law first reflects the two major concepts of improving quality and promoting fairness. It puts forward that "the state guarantees the priority development of education", and pays special attention to protecting the right of minority students and vulnerable groups to receive education; Secondly, the concepts of building a "modern national education system", "lifelong education system", and "modernization of education" were proposed, which adapted to the new trend of education development and improved China's education system; Once again, the Education Law has redefined the public welfare nature of education, removing the previous law's provision that "no organization or individual may establish schools or other educational institutions for profit." Finally, the revision of the Education Law has strengthened the provisions on legal responsibility in education, providing detailed legal responsibilities for behaviors such as cheating in national exams.

The revision of the Higher Education Law mainly focuses on the following contents: first, improving the policies and tasks of higher education, stipulating that higher education must serve the people and be combined with productive labor, and emphasizing that the task of higher education is to cultivate high-level professionals with a sense of social responsibility, innovative spirit and practical ability; The second is to strengthen the role of academic committees in higher education institutions and enhance their status and role in universities; The third is to decentralize the examination and approval power of higher education, and delegate the licensing power for establishing higher education institutions and other higher education institutions that implement education below the junior college level to the provincial people's government; The fourth is to improve the investment mechanism for higher education, clarify that higher education implements a mechanism that focuses on the investment of the organizers, the educated share the training costs reasonably, and higher education institutions raise funds through multiple channels.

The revision of the "Private Education Promotion Law" mainly focuses on the following contents: firstly, implementing classified management of private schools, dividing them into two categories: non-profit private schools and for-profit private schools. The organizers of non-profit private schools shall not receive educational benefits, while the organizers of profit private schools can obtain educational benefits. The remaining balance of non-profit private schools is used for educational purposes, while the remaining balance of profit private schools shall be handled in accordance with relevant laws and administrative regulations such as the Company Law. The second is to increase support measures for private schools. It is specially stipulated that non-profit private schools can also adopt supportive measures such as government subsidies, fund rewards, donation incentives, etc. Article 47 of the new "Private Education Promotion Law" stipulates that private schools enjoy tax preferential policies stipulated by the state: among them, non-profit private schools enjoy the same tax preferential policies as public schools to promote the development of non-profit private schools.

3.3 Revision of the Vocational Education Law

On April 20, 2022, the Standing Committee of the National People's Congress passed the revision of the Vocational Education Law. This revision mainly focuses on the following aspects: firstly, it emphasizes the equal importance of vocational education and general education. The new law stipulates that vocational education is a type of education with equal importance to general education, and vocational school students have equal opportunities with ordinary school students at the same level in terms of enrollment, employment, career development, etc. Discrimination policies are prohibited (Zhou and Anlei 2017). The second is to promote the integration of vocational education and the general education system. The new law focuses on establishing and improving a modern vocational education system that serves lifelong learning for the whole nation. It stipulates that higher vocational school education is implemented by higher vocational schools and ordinary institutions of higher learning at the junior college, undergraduate and higher education levels, and supports vocational enlightenment, vocational cognition, vocational experience, etc. in ordinary primary and secondary schools. The third is to clarify the important role of enterprises in vocational education. The new law stipulates that enterprises should play an important role in running schools, promote their deep participation in vocational education, and encourage them to hold high-quality vocational education.

4 Typical Cases of Educational Disputes

4.1 Liu Yanwen v. Peking University

The plaintiff Liu Yanwen is a doctoral student majoring in Electronic, Ionic, and Vacuum Physics in the Department of Radio Electronics, Peking University, Grade 92. On April 27, 1994, Liu Yanwen passed the written exam arranged by Peking

University, and on May 10 of that year, he passed the comprehensive doctoral examination with a good score. Afterwards, Liu Yanwen entered the preparation stage for his doctoral thesis defense. On December 22, 1995, Liu Yanwen filed an application for thesis defense and submitted his doctoral dissertation "Research on Photocathodes with High Current Density Driven by Ultrashort Pulse Laser" to the university. The relevant departments of the university arranged and hired experts of the discipline to review and peer review the thesis. The peer reviewers believe that the paper meets the level of a doctoral thesis and agree to defend it; The reviewer's opinion is "agree to arrange the thesis defense". In 1996, the overall opinion of academic review and peer review of Peking University paper was "reaching the level of a doctoral thesis and can be defended." On January 10, 1996, the thesis defense committee of Liu Yanwen's department held a thesis defense meeting. After the defense, Liu Yanwen passed the defense with a total of 7 votes. The thesis defense committee made a decision to "grant Liu Yanwen a doctoral degree and recommend that Liu Yanwen make necessary revisions to the thesis." On January 19, 1996, the degree evaluation committee of Liu Yanwen's department discussed the doctoral degree. 13 members were supposed to be present, and 13 members were actually present. 12 people agreed to grant Liu Yanwen a doctoral degree, and 1 person did not agree to grant Liu Yanwen a doctoral degree. The voting result was that it was recommended to grant Liu Yanwen a doctoral degree. On January 24, 1996, the Academic Degrees Evaluation Committee of Peking University held its 41st meeting. Among the 21 members who were supposed to attend, 16 were actually present. There were 6 who agreed to confer the degree of Dr. Liu Yanwen, 7 who did not agree to confer the degree of Dr. Liu Yanwen, and 3 who abstained. The voting result was that the Academic Degrees Evaluation Committee of Peking University did not approve the conferment of the degree of Dr. Liu Yanwen. Afterwards, Peking University awarded Liu Yanwen a graduate certificate. Liu Yanwen filed a lawsuit with the court, requesting the court to order the defendant Peking University to issue him with a doctoral degree certificate. After trial, the court held that after Liu Yanwen obtained the status of pursuing a doctoral degree student status at Peking University as a graduate student in September 1992, he studied the prescribed courses according to the training plan and requirements formulated by Peking University, took the examinations of the courses and passed the examination, and also completed and passed the graduation thesis defense, and passed the moral and physical examination. In accordance with Article 33 of the former National Education Commission's "Regulations on the Management of Graduate Student Status", Liu Yanwen meets the graduation qualifications for obtaining a doctoral degree, and Peking University shall issue him with a doctoral degree certificate. The academic degree committee of the university did not listen to Liu Yanwen's defense opinions before making a decision not to approve the award of Dr. Liu Yanwen's degree; After making the decision, it was not actually delivered to Liu Yanwen, which affected Liu Yanwen's exercise of the right to appeal or file a lawsuit with relevant departments. The decision should be revoked. Peking University did not issue a doctoral diploma to Liu Yanwen due to its doctoral degree not being approved by the university's degree evaluation committee, and instead issued a graduation certificate, which had no legal basis, and the court did not support it. Based on this, the court ruled to revoke the decision made by the Peking University Degree Evaluation Committee not to grant Dr. Liu Yanwen's degree, and ordered the Peking University Degree Evaluation Committee to review and make a new decision on whether to approve the granting of Dr. Liu Yanwen's degree within 3 months after the judgment came into effect.

Peking University is dissatisfied with the judgment and has filed an appeal. The First Intermediate People's Court of Beijing Municipality ruled to revoke the judgment of the Haidian District People's Court and remand it for retrial. In December 2000, the Haidian District People's Court rejected Liu Yanwen's lawsuit request on the grounds of "exceeding the statute of limitations".

The Liu Yanwen case has attracted great attention in China's judicial practice and legal theory research. The focus of this case mainly lies in whether the judiciary can intervene in the internal affairs of the university, and what the basis and standards for intervening in the internal affairs of the university are. After the Liu Yanwen case, there have been several lawsuits against universities in China due to reasons such as student dismissal, and failure to obtain graduation and degree certificates. Among these cases, the courts in China basically take the form of review, that is, whether the university meets the relevant requirements of Procedural justice when dealing with relevant affairs, and whether there is obvious unfairness to conduct judicial review. In judging purely academic disputes, Chinese courts still respect the basic principles of university autonomy and Academic freedom and do not intervene in principle.

4.2 *Qi Yuling v. Chen Xiaoqi*

In 1990, Qi Yuling and Chen Xiaoqi were junior high school students at the 8th Middle School in Tengzhou City, Shandong Province, and both participated in the preliminary examination of the secondary technical school. Chen Xiaoqi failed the preliminary examination and lost her qualification to continue taking the unified admission exam. After passing the preliminary examination, Qi Yuling also exceeded the admission score line for commissioned trainees in the unified enrollment examination that year. Shandong Jining Commercial School issued an admission notice to Qi Yuling, handed over by Tengzhou No. 8 Middle School. Chen Xiaoqi took Qi Yuling's admission letter from Tengzhou No. 8 Middle School and, under the planning of her father Chen Kezheng, used improper means to study at Jining Business School under Qi Yuling's name until graduation. After graduation, Chen Xiaoqi still used Qi Yuling's name and worked at Bank of China Tengzhou Branch. Qi Yuling found that Chen Xiaoqi was taking her name, and filed a civil lawsuit with the Intermediate People's Court of Zaozhuang City, Shandong Province.

Due to Chen Xiaoqi's infringement of Qi Yuling's right to name and education, Qi Yuling did not receive higher education and had to undergo further studies. Therefore, according to Article 46 of the Constitution and the reply of the Supreme People's

Court, the High People's Court of Shandong Province determined that Chen Xiaoqi had violated Qi Yuling's right to education under the Constitution. Thus, it was ordered that Chen Xiaoqi and others, as well as the unit, bear corresponding civil legal responsibilities.

The "Qi Yuling Case" is known as the "First Judicial Case of the Chinese Constitution", which is the first judicial case in which a Chinese court has made judgments based on the Constitution in a civil case. It is particularly noteworthy that when the Education Law was revised in 2021, it added the legal responsibility and remedies for "impersonation of enrollment", further improving the scope and procedures for protecting citizens' right to education.

4.3 Meng Mu Tang Incident

In September 2004, the full-time private school "Meng Mu Tang" was opened in Songjiang, Shanghai. The teaching content mainly focused on the reading of scriptures, such as "The Book of Changes", "Tao Te Ching", "The Analects of Confucius", and other traditional Chinese classics; English starts from A Midsummer Night's Dream; Mathematics is reorganized and arranged by external teachers based on the concept of scripture reading education; Physical education classes mainly focus on self-cultivation exercises such as yoga and Tai Chi. On July 17, 2006, the Education Bureau of Songjiang District, Shanghai issued a notice, pointing out that "Mengmu Hall" is an illegal educational institution, engaged in illegal educational activities, and should immediately stop illegal acts. On the 24th, a spokesperson for the Shanghai Municipal Education Commission explained three main reasons: the school has not been approved by the education administrative department and has not obtained a school license; The requirement of "reading classics education" is not in line with the multi-disciplinary and comprehensive development of compulsory education, which violates multiple provisions of the Compulsory Education Law; Unauthorized collection of high tuition fees without approval from the pricing department. It is also illegal for parents not to send their school-age children to educational institutions approved by the state for compulsory education in accordance with the regulations.

This incident has attracted great attention from the education and legal sectors, and has been selected by relevant institutions as one of the top ten constitutional examples in China in 2006. The focus of this case is whether the guardian of a compulsory education child can choose a form of education outside of school for the child based on the right to family education. According to the relevant provisions of the Compulsory Education Law, compulsory education is compulsory in China, that is, the parents or other legal guardians of compulsory school-age children and adolescents should ensure that they enter school on time and complete compulsory education according to law. At the same time, schools that carry out compulsory education must comply with the educational standards set by the state. The Education Law also stipulates that the establishment, change, and termination of schools and other educational institutions shall go through the procedures of examination, approval, registration, or filing in accordance with relevant national regulations. The Private Education Promotion Law of China provides legal protection for the legal status of private schools and training institutions, but their operation must comply with relevant registration and approval procedures. In this case, Meng Mu Tang did not have the corresponding educational qualifications without the review and approval of relevant institutions. Meanwhile, China's Compulsory Education Law has not yet allowed home education for children of compulsory education age. However, with the popularization of compulsory education in China, there is still some debate in the academic community on whether legislation can allow compulsory education for school-age children and adolescents to receive home education.

5 Trends in China's Education Legal System

As mentioned earlier, China's education legal system has been basically established. However, China's social and economic development is developing at an unprecedented pace, which has forced education legislation to face several new problems and tasks. At the same time, we should also recognize the guiding role of educational legislation in the development of education, view the development of education from a forward-looking perspective, and predict the future development trend of educational legislation. In the future, China's education legal system may exhibit the following development trends in terms of concept, form, and content:

5.1 Codification Trend

In China, the trend of codifying education laws is directly related to the overall trend of education legislation. On May 28, 2020, the National People's Congress adopted the Civil Code. The successful formulation of the Civil code has drawn further attention in the legal field. Can codification be adopted in other legislative fields? In 2017, scholars in China proposed the idea of formulating the Education Code and pointed out that it would be a huge, complex, and highly challenging task (Sun and Ma 2017). In 2021, the National People's Congress included the Education Code, the Administrative Code, and the Environmental Code in the country's legislative plan. On the one hand, the codification of China's education law is due to the fact that there are still some gaps in the existing education legislation. However, filling the gap in education legislation in the form of existing separate education legislation may be a lengthy process. On the other hand, the codification of education law can effectively solve the problem of systematic logic and legislative conflicts between current education legislation, thereby promoting the standardization, logicality, and applicability of the education legal system. The compilation work of improving the Education Code is not a simple process of compiling existing education laws and regulations, but a process of following the legislative purpose of the new Education

Code, based on the legislative concept of the new Education Code, adopting a new legislative model of the Education Code, following the legislative logic of the new Education Code, constructing a new legislative framework of the Education Code, and filling in the legislative content of the new Education Code. The codification of education law and the study of education law are interrelated, interdependent, and mutually reinforcing. The process of codification of education law may promote the transformation of basic concepts, system frameworks, and even research paradigms in education law, providing a new space for the development of education law (Ma 2020).

5.2 *Fairness Trends*

Education equity is an important means to prevent the intergenerational transmission of poverty, reflecting the value pursuit of social fairness and justice. At present, the right to education of Chinese citizens has been basically protected. However, how to ensure that citizens of different social classes, ethnic groups, and regions can promote their maximum development through education, and provide equal opportunities and conditions for children from different family backgrounds to receive education, especially to promote the opportunity for children from economically disadvantaged families to change their social and economic status through education, It is a particularly important focus for future education legislation. But as Edgar Bodenheimer pointed out: "Justice has a Protean face, which is changeable and can take on different shapes at any time and have very different faces (Bodenheimer 1999)." From different educational subjects or different social cultures, we may have different interpretations of fairness. For example, China's education legislation prohibits the establishment of key schools and key classes in the compulsory educational stage. Is there any contradiction between this provision and the cultivation of innovative top talents? And what kind of impact will this contradiction have on educational equity? However, in any case, educational fairness plays an important role in China's education legislation in the future.

5.3 *High Quality Trends*

As mentioned earlier, the Chinese people's demand for education has shifted from "being able to attend school" to "being able to study well", and their demand for educational quality is increasing day by day. This demand requires education legislation to make corresponding adjustments to the original legislative contents such as the system and mechanisms of education management, the allocation and use of education funds, the cultivation and construction of teaching staff, and the evaluation and monitoring of learning achievements, so as to meet the needs of education reform and development. This high-quality development is guided by the people's satisfaction with the demand for high-quality education, continuously improving the degree and level of high-quality education development, shifting from scale expansion to structural upgrading, and from extension-based development to connotation-based development, achieving a more fair, balanced, coordinated, comprehensive, innovative, high-quality, sustainable, and safer development of education (Haimin and Hongjun 2021). For example, China's education legislation still adopts a prohibition on "home education" at the compulsory educational stage, which is based on the background that China's compulsory education has just been popularized. However, with the development of education, people, for example, have diversified demands for education. How to respond these diversified educational needs in education development and legislation? Education legislation must focus on high-quality education, enhance the happiness index of the people through the high-quality development of education, and promote the comprehensive development of the country's politics, economy, technology, culture and other fields.

5.4 Procedural Trends

In the past, China's education legislation was often referred to as "soft law" by researchers in the legal field. The key reason was that the previous education legislation was often declaratory legislation, with poor implementation and low illegal costs, which resulted in many cases in which the relevant education legal subjects people intentionally violated the education legislation, but it was difficult to hold them legally responsible based on education legislation. The lack of practice in judicial disputes and conflicts of interest in "soft law" results in a lack of accuracy in the assumed behavior patterns and legal responsibilities of educational law (Wang 2019). Therefore, how to improve the implementation of education legislation, increase the procedural provisions of education legislation, and enable the substantive rights of relevant legal subjects to be protected in a procedural way is the trend that China's education legislation needs to pay attention to in the future. In fact, from the revision of the Compulsory Education Law in 2006 to the revision of the Education Law in 2021, this trend of emphasizing procedural legislation has been reflected, and it is becoming increasingly evident in education legislation. Education legislation has gradually "grown teeth", increasing the cost of illegality, thereby enhancing the authority and enforcement of education legislation, and more fully exerting the various functions and roles of education law.

5.5 Digital Trends

British scholars Anthony Seldon and Oladimeji Abidoye proposed in their book "The Fourth Education Revolution" that personalized education, with artificial intelligence, augmented reality, and virtual reality as the main contents, constituted the fourth education revolution (Anthony and Abidoye 2019). The fourth educational revolution may have disruptive changes in our educational concepts, content, facilities, methods, and evaluation. It is particularly noteworthy that this digital trend may play a greater role in promoting educational equity. China has begun to attempt to use distance education to transmit some high-quality educational resources to remote and poorly educated areas. The COVID-19, which began at the end of 2019, accelerated the arrival of this transformation to a certain extent. During the epidemic, Chinese schools used online education to teach students, which not only gave play to the advantages of using digital education to disseminate high-quality educational resources, but also emerged teaching obstacles caused by personnel quality and hardware conditions. However, in any case, education legislation must give sufficient attention, anticipate the impact of information technologies such as artificial intelligence on education in advance, and provide necessary guidance and regulation.

6 Conclusion

For nearly two hundred years since the failure of the Opium War in the mid-nineteenth century, China has been searching for a development path that is suitable for China's national conditions and in line with the actual situation. Among them, prioritizing the development of education, making it the engine that leads the development of the country and society, promotes all-round progress in politics, economy, technology, culture, and other fields, and enhances people's rights and happiness, is an important experience. Since China implemented reform and opening up in the late 1970s, it has always been the goal of China's education rule of law to guide, promote and guarantee the development of education through education legislation, and safeguard citizens' basic rights to equal access to high-quality education.

As the world's largest developing country, having a large population and insufficient economic development are the basic national conditions of China. The contradiction between the growing need for a better life for the people and insufficient development has become the main contradiction in Chinese society. This determines that China's education legislation must be based on China's basic national conditions, fully absorb and draw on the relevant experience of international education development and education legislation, and form a model of education rule of law construction with Chinese characteristics. However, compared to the rapid development of education in China, the legal system of education in China still needs to be improved as soon as possible. The most prominent issue in China's education legal system currently is that there are still many legislative gaps in the horizontal structure, and the supporting implementation system or subordinate support system for each law in the vertical structure still needs to be improved (Qin and Kunpeng 2016). In order to meet the above needs, research on educational law should critically inherit traditional research methods and draw on advanced experience from different disciplines and theories, so that the research on the positioning of educational law can accurately reveal the changes in the external environment of educational law, deeply understand the interdisciplinary nature of educational law, and scientifically predict the future development direction of educational law (Lao 2022). In this process, how to better play the fundamental, stable, and long-term guarantee role of the rule of law, promote education reform and development through rule of law thinking and methods, comprehensively improve the level of rule of law in education, enhance citizens' awareness of the rule of law, promote understanding and exchange between countries with different cultural backgrounds, and jointly create harmony, happiness, and development for humanity, is a problem that should be paid attention to in the future construction of China's education rule of law system, It should also be a concern for the development of the rule of law in international education.

References

Anthony S, Abidoye O (2019) Fourth educational revolution. Mechanical Industry Publishing, Beijing, IV

Bodenheimer (1999) Jurisprudence—philosophy of law and legal methods. China University of Political Science and Law Press, Beijing, p 252

Lao K (2022) Departmental legal positioning and codification of education law. Educ Res 7:17–30

Liu H, Hongjun Z (2021) High quality: transition Korea of China's basic education development path. Educ Res 4:11–24

Ma L (2016) Case study in the field of educational law. Educ Sci Forum 7:4–7

Ma L (2020) On the codification of China's education law. Educ Res 485(6):145–152

Qin H, Kunpeng G (2016) Thoughts on improving China's educational legal system. J Beijing Normal Univ (Social Sci Edn) 254(2):5–12

Shen S (2018) From educational legal system to educational legal system—the road of building educational legal system. East China Normal University Press, Shanghai, p P27

Sun X (2006) Revision of the compulsory education law: background, process, and major breakthroughs. Res Educ Dev 15:11–17

Sun X, Ma L (2017) Education jurisprudence. Education Science Press, Beijing, p 27

Wang D (2019) Exploration of education soft law. Educator 28:40–43

Zhou H, Anlei J (2017) Private education will achieve multiple positive effects. Chinese J Educ 3:1–3

The Costa Rican System of Education Law

Dennis P. Petri and Emily Arias González

1 Introduction

Costa Rica is proud to have more teachers than soldiers and has always prized education as a pillar of its democracy. At the turn of the twentieth century, Costa Rica was the undisputed pioneer of education in Latin America. Yet despite its significant contributions to economic growth and upward social mobility, the nation's education system seems to have stagnated since the 1980s. In particular, it has proven difficult to implement educational reforms that meet the needs of a changing modern society.

In this chapter, we first review the Costa Rican system of education from a legal perspective. We briefly trace the system's historical origins, its constitutional foundations, and the main legal norms that govern it, as well as describe its organizational structure. We also discuss the ways by which the system is financed and detail its main structural challenges.

In the section that follows, we take an in-depth look at the major legal developments for Costa Rica's education system since its inception. We start by discussing the evolution of the system, exploring its developmental trajectory via three distinct stages that correspond to distinct philosophies of education, identifying a key challenge: namely, that with each transition, existing norms are not reformed wholesale and thus are perpetuated as the ensuing stage unfolds. To interrogate this problem, we proceed by exploring the tensions inherent in, and indeed between,

D. P. Petri (✉)
Faculty of Social Sciences, Latin American University of Science and Technology, San Jose, Costa Rica
e-mail: dpetrix316@ulacit.ed.cr

E. A. González
Faculty of Social Sciences, Latin American University of Science and Technology, San Jose, Costa Rica

C. J. Russo and L. Ma (eds.), *A Comparative Analysis of Systems of Education Law*,
https://doi.org/10.1007/978-981-97-1052-2_5

two competing pedagogical models, which we term the Social-Democratic Pedagogical Model (SDPM) and the Neoliberal Adjustment Model (NAM) respectively. Particularly, we show that when the latter model came to replace the former, elements of the SPDM still remained; and that, similarly, when moves were made to return to the former, elements of the NAM endured. We then further exemplify the tensions between contrasting models of pedagogy by exploring the phenomenon of second-cycle examinations, which have long been controversial, as well as the centuries-old debate concerning the role of religious instruction in the Costa Rican education system.

In the final section of this chapter, we discuss a selection of emerging issues regarding the future development of education in Costa Rica, namely: the scarcity of resources; the challenges posed by so-called high school dropouts; the disparities between public and private education; the gender gap in educational equality, access, achievement, and progress; and the difficulties to reform the education system because of bureaucratic resistance.

2 Nature of the Legal System

2.1 History

In the wake of the 1948 Civil War, the Constitutional Assembly that drafted Costa Rica's 1949 Constitution, which still endures today, had two main preoccupations: the first was to ensure that, from that moment on, the democratic process would be respected; and the second was to guarantee the permanency of the liberal social security and universal education standards—which truly reflect what would later become known as the second generation of human rights—that were implemented in the 1940's in the case of social security and as far back as 1886 in the case of education (see Castro Vega 2007).

In Costa Rican political culture, these dual preoccupations have always been viewed as interrelated. To safeguard the democratic process, a political system was implemented based on a strict separation of powers (both among the three constitutional powers and within the executive), along with an independent electoral tribunal, progressive human rights standards, and all kinds of measures to prevent power concentration in the hands of one political institution (Petri 2023). In addition, Costa Rica took the unprecedented step in 1948 of abolishing its standing army. Consequently, the country has remained an electoral democracy since 1953 and has not been plagued by military coups, unlike so many others in the region.

The abolition of the military gave rise to a popular foundational myth: that Costa Rica had always been a country of peace and that monies which would otherwise be spent on defense were now to be dedicated to social matters (education, healthcare, and economic development) (Huhn 2008). Former president Oscar Arias famously referred to this myth in his acceptance speech for the Nobel Peace Prize in 1987, which he received for his contribution to the peace agreements in Central America, stating that: "because our country is a country of teachers, we closed the army camps [...] Our children go with books under their arms, not with rifles on their shoulders." Across the nation, former army barracks were transformed for use as schools and, as alluded to in our introduction above, Costa Ricans take pride in the fact that their educational workforce outnumbers their military personnel.

Notwithstanding the idealism palpable in this particular vision of their education system,[1] it is undeniable that Costa Rica has achieved significant socio-economic improvements, boasting a human development index superior to 0.8 (UNDP 2022). In terms of education, the country possesses a youth literacy rate of 99%, a primary school completion rate of 105%, and a lower secondary school completion rate of 69.2%. Government expenditure on education has consistently stood at more than one fifth of total expenditure for decades now (World Bank 2022). These are major accomplishments, considering that, in 1883, some 85% of the population was illiterate and primary school enrolment was a mere 43% (Salazar Mora 1980, p. 250).

2.2 *Constitutional and Legal Foundations*

The 1949 Constitution, which confirmed the reforms implemented decades previously, issued an unequivocal mandate to the country's political institutions to promote education; indeed, the chapter on education in the Constitution is fourteen articles long.[2] Besides guaranteeing access to universal and mandatory education (Art. 78), it also created a substantial budgetary commitment (a minimum of 8% of the GDP). The provisions of the Constitution institutionalized education policy in such a way that it remained independent of the government in office; they created four public universities, which would not only have budgetary autonomy and academic freedom but also their own jurisdiction of their campuses, which is an unusually broad interpretation of "university autonomy" (Arts. 84–85); and they also allowed for a non-public (private) education system which would be subject to inspection by the state (Arts. 79–80).

Finally, the Constitution's preoccupation with equal opportunity can be gleaned from its provisions to support "destitute schoolchildren" (Art. 82) and to promote education for adults (Art. 83) (see Araya Pochet 2005, pp. 197–206). In August 1949, Costa Rica also implemented the so-called "bachillerato por madurez" system, allowing those adults who, for whatever reason, fail to graduate from high school, to pursue a university education, subject to an assessment that takes into consideration their work and life experience.

---

[1] There is no empirical evidence that the reduction of military spending leads to the investment in development. There are many countries that have high military spending while at the same time high development levels. Also, many technological innovations are developed in military institutions.

[2] This is much more than in most Western constitutions, some of which do not even mention education.

Although the 1949 Constitution explicitly prioritized the educational system, "a concern for education [is] a true constant in the history of Costa Rica" (Dabène 1992, p. 80). Several public, private, and Church-led education efforts had already been implemented over the course of the nineteenth century, but the 1886 "Fundamental Law of Common Education" was the real game-changer: from that moment on, primary education in Costa Rica was free of charge and mandatory for all. Illiteracy dropped to 50% by 1927 as a result, and government spending on education multiplied sixfold as the next three decades unfolded. By the turn of the twentieth century, Costa Rica had become the unrivaled leader of education in Latin America. Throughout the 1900s, the Costa Rican commitment to education remained paramount and represented a serious contribution towards upward social mobility in the nation.

Finally, we must note that in the constitutional framework exposed above, the Costa Rican education system is regulated by an extensive collection of laws and regulations of which the Education Code (1944, numbering some four hundred and twenty-four pages), the Organic Law of the Ministry of Public Education (1965, fifty pages), and the Basic Education Law (1957, twenty-one pages), are some of the most important. These laws continue to be reviewed and updated frequently.

2.3 *Organizational Structure*

The Costa Rican education system, like other Latin American countries, was shaped by the legacy of Spanish colonial rule. Following independence, the nation continued to conform to European education trends and was heavily influenced by both the Enlightenment and the French Revolution (Robles 2017). Currently, the country's education system follows the classic French-Napoleonic model and is based on four levels of education: pre-school, primary, secondary, and university education (Art. 77 of the Constitution).

Inspired by the humanist ideal, the system is comprehensive. The curriculum at primary and secondary level, which is normally completed in twelve years, offers a wide range of classes that cover arts, sciences, and physical education. No specializations are offered at any level of primary and secondary education. According to the "Consejo Superior de Educación" (Education Counsel) of Costa Rica, preschooling in the country focuses on developing children's interests and potential, in such a way that best matches their emotional, cognitive, expressive, linguistic, and motor skills. Children's subsequent schooling, or "General Basic Education", is then divided into three cycles. The first and second cycles correspond broadly to primary school in the USA and the third cycle to middle and high school. During the General Basic Education stages, schooling is organized by subjects; the three cycles, in total, last for nine academic years, with terminal assessments taking place at the end of each cycle. These assessments are graded from 1 to 100, while the minimum pass score varies with each stage. At the middle/high school stage, which we term the third cycle, three pathways are available to students, namely: academic, technical, and artistic, with the academic pathway lasting two years and the technical pathway three; the minimum pass score at this stage is 70. At the end of their years in General Basic Education, students may then progress to university level, where minimum pass scores and duration of degree programs vary according to the institution and course of study.

In 2018, an important reform has been to lower the mandatory age for educational instruction to four years old. According to Silvia Castro, a leading education expert in the country, this is especially significant in reducing learning delays for children raised in households with low literacy and education levels. According to Castro, lowering the mandatory age for educational instruction further still would make a huge difference (Teletica Radio 2021).

In terms of administration, the Costa Rican system is highly centralized. School boards exist, but these have little influence, and schoolteachers are paid directly by the Ministry of Public Education (MEP), which runs the overall system. With the 1949 Constitution, Public Education was granted its own government department; before, it was part of the Ministry of Finance, Public Education, War and Navy (UNESCO 2006). The MEP divides the country into regions, so as to respond to geographical, cultural and economic differences as well as to the needs of national development; these comprise seven provincial directorates and twenty regional directorates of education, according to decrees no. 23489 and no. 23490 (July 29, 1994). Each regional directorate is subdivided again, into smaller local units called school circuits, which correspond to the educational services run by the MEP. These circuits are overseen by a supervisory director, who is the immediate superior of all the school and college principals operating in the local area.

Despite this centralized system, local government does exercise a limited administrative function. Boards of education and administrative boards exist, which are the responsibility of local authorities. These promote education in their respective regions. Board of education members are appointed by government officials who supervise education in the district; requirements for their appointment and removal are determined centrally. For middle/high school (the "third cycle"), and also for alternative educational institutions, administrative boards are appointed in the same manner as the boards of education; local governments define the rules regarding the appointment of the members of these administrative boards. School boards and parent associations are then designated as support bodies to the educational and administrative boards, respectively; but in many cases, the latter are auxiliary to the former. External public relations are carried out by the boards of education, administrative boards, school boards, and parent-teacher associations, along with a number of other minor administrative functions. Teacher training is centralized, however: the National Center for Didactics (CENADI) is the body of the MEP that was created to provide direct support for teaching and learning, including the collaboration of parents and the wider community. The Research and Improvement Center for Technical Education (CIPET) oversees training and continuing professional development for teachers in service of the MEP.

In terms of financing, the Costa Rican government uses the program budgeting technique to allocate annual resources to public institutions. This allows to distinguish with sufficient clarity the distribution corresponding to each ministerial program, varying according to its objectives and goals. In the case of the MEP, most of the resources allocated to the education sector (state universities and university colleges, among others), are channeled through this budgetary process. The allocation of resources is done in accordance with the laws that stipulate pre-established amounts and percentages; practice indicates that the MEP acts more as a middleman for such resources and funds, since the budgetary requests, monetary amounts, and so forth, pertain to the institutions themselves. Current expenses are the most significant item in the MEP budget, with a constant percentage running at close to 98% of the total. In accordance with the provisions of Article 36 of the Financial Administration Law, the MEP must submit to the Ministry of Finance no later than 1 June of each year the budgetary proposals for the upcoming fiscal year, which must take into consideration the objectives, goals, and monetary ceilings previously established by the treasury. Within the budgets of central government institutions, monies are otherwise allocated to satisfy the various needs of the education system. These funds are used for: maintenance; construction and reconstruction of education infrastructure; purchase of materials, furniture, plant and equipment; support for the school library program; and granting scholarships.

Finally, as far as the legislative framework is concerned, the education system of Costa Rica was first set out in the Fundamental Law of Education, which was approved in 1957, and this regulation continues to provide the backbone of the country's education system today. The Superior Council of Education is the governing body of this system; it has the power to make decisions regarding the national curriculum. Following the Fernandez Act of 2002, however, the education system has been reformed in order to provide equal opportunities for all students, with policies that guarantee the free exchange of special education and compensatory services in the public and private sectors and that reconsider curriculum structure, akin with the various factors affecting the development of the education system more widely. These include the implementation of the behavioral and organizational aspects of the curriculum, the prioritization of results, and the development of a more "socio-critical" approach to education policy.

2.4 Challenges

Notwithstanding its significant achievements, in terms of almost total literacy and primary school enrolment, the quality of the Costa Rican education system is generally considered to have stagnated since the 1980s (Martinez and Loria 2018).

For example, failure rates for university graduates taking the Bar examinations have increased, as too have poor scores of teacher trainees at assessment stage, and the standards for some university programs are quite basic. As a consequence, for the past ten years only 28% of the population aged over twenty-five years have gone on to secure employment in the services sector of the economy. This percentage is low when compared to the average of 44% for countries belonging to the Organization for Economic Cooperation and Development (OECD), a club which Costa Rica joined in 2021 (Informa-TICO 2019). Costa Rica's relatively low rate of service sector employment is largely attributable to the fact that many young people enter the labor market without having finished high school, while others do not manage to complete their university studies. The growth of university students over the last twenty years, especially at private universities, clearly has not brought about better study and employment opportunities for the majority. Almost two thirds of the 1,341 university programs are concentrated in a few areas of study: education, economic sciences, health sciences, and social sciences. A mere 37% of university education courses currently cover STEM subjects like technology, engineering, or mathematics.

An urgent priority for Costa Rica, then, is to guarantee minimum standards in the university sector, particularly among private providers, according to a 2017 report by the OECD. The same report found that existing legislative proposals would not be sufficient to secure this end, in that they did not propose clear mechanisms to address the many poor-quality unaccredited programs offered by private universities. A vital element for this challenge is the need to obtain better, more substantial data. Reliable performance data sets are not available, because institutions are not presently required to report key institutional/system performance indicators (for example: time to complete degree studies; student retention rates; graduation success rates for low-income students; post-graduation pathways). Specific information, such as that concerning the household income of students, or the number of part-time students, is often unavailable. The relative absence of data regarding university education in Costa Rica is surprising and separates the country not only from OECD member states but moreover from other nations in the region. Chile, Peru, and Colombia have all established increasingly robust, public-facing information systems which help to inform policymakers' decisions, as well as to guide prospective students and their parents.

Among the proposals generated by these reports regarding the advancement of the education system are the following: (a) appoint a minister of education who is or has been an educator; (b) submit the directorships of regional education offices for public tender, so as to ensure recruitment of top candidates for the positions; (c) require teachers to hold an academic degree from accredited universities; (d) monitor the performance, level of knowledge, and continuing professional development of educators; (e) guarantee, at government level, the construction and maintenance of the necessary infrastructure through localized studies, in addition to promoting continuous training for educators which embraces policies of inclusion; and (f) promote comprehensive follow-ups programs for spelling, reading, research, and other matters, without perpetuating the present overreliance on numerical evaluation which leads to impaired or staggered progress rates (OECD 2017).

3 Major Legal Developments

3.1 Phases of the Education System

According to Toruño (2015), the evolution of the modern Costa Rican public education system can be divided roughly into three phases. Each phase corresponds to a new pedagogical concept and the consequent introduction of new legislation and policies. However, each phase never completely eliminates pre-existing rules and practices, which are thus passed down to the new phases. Where contradictions arise, between the remnants of older visions of education and the newer models, these are often addressed through litigation, rather than through reevaluating and amending previous practices.

The first phase can be identified as "municipal-ecclesiastic." During this period, education was organized locally under the influence of religious conservatism and was primarily geared towards the needs of an agrarian economy (Molina 2007).

In the late 1800s, this first phase was succeeded by the "centralized-secular" phase, during which a centralized organization was established to teach basic knowledge and skills (namely mathematics and Spanish, to promote social and economic interactions at the time). Notwithstanding its secularizing impulse, the Concordat of 1852 continued to give the Catholic Church a significant share of power over the education system in Costa Rica. As a result, the centralized system was also used to transmit patriarchal-religious values and was implemented chiefly in primary education, mainly in the first, second and third grades (Camacho 2005).

As with elsewhere in Europe and Latin America, the nineteenth century gave rise to a salient opposition of liberal (secular) and conservative (Catholic) views on education. Some analysts have interpreted the role Catholic Church as a hindrance to education (see Dabène 1992; Salazar Mora 1980), pointing to the fact that the Catholic Church called for the boycott of public schools due to the attempts of liberals to secularize education; but at the same, one must not ignore the importance of the numerous educational initiatives that were led by the Church since colonial times. In any event, a consensus was reached between the liberal and conservative factions in 1882 when the Church granted full support for public education, in exchange for the inclusion of mandatory religious education classes in the curriculum (Robles 2017).

The third phase of the education system's development was that of the establishment of the "university-pedagogical" vision, which started in the 1940s. It was carried out through various reforms that allowed for the implementation of modern educational institutions, such as the University of Costa Rica which was initially organized according to the following law-based schools: the School of Law, the School of Pharmacy, the School of Agriculture, and the School of Fine Arts. From 1942 to 1960, various new schools were also established. In 1973, the National University was established, following by the Distance State University in 1977. October 1942 also saw the founding of the national organization for Costa Rican educators, known as ANDE, which has conferred various benefits upon students and teachers for more than sixty-five years now.

3.2 Competing Pedagogical Models

From an ideological standpoint, the concept of education in Costa Rica can be divided into two different visions: the Social Democratic model and the Fundamental Law of Education (Dengo 2011). The former is the framework that was approved in 1957; it continues to be used to this day.

During the university-pedagogical phase, or third phase, the so-called Social Democratic Pedagogical Model (SDPM), which had been created in 1948, remained the dominant vision for education in Costa Rica until 1985. The SDPM provided a framework for the development of a society that valued the contribution of each of its citizens (Toruño 2015). The goal of this model was to create a society that was committed to the establishment of a culture of "productive social development". The development of the SDPM in Costa Rica was informed by the 1949 Constitution and the 1957 Fundamental Law of Education, to which we have alluded previously. Created in the wake of the Civil War, the SDPM emphasized the need to establish a culture that promoted the importance of education, which would help Costa Rica to develop a strong and sustainable relationship with its citizens.

To this end, a key mechanism of the SDPM was the establishment of a collective mentality within society. This mentality, it was theorized, could then be used to legitimize the dominant group through the creation of the new citizen. The concept of productive social development also formed an integral part of the scheme's wealth distribution policy. It was responsible for ensuring that the country's citizens received the necessary resources to maintain their level of social development. According to Miranda (2010), education in the SDPM was conceptualized as a political and cultural unit that would form the skeleton of a society which valued every citizen equally but would also develop a qualified reserve labor army. Hence, the SDPM was explicitly linked to the abolition of the army. This is built on the popular belief that the education system was a vital part of the nation's development (Toruño 2015).

Through this narrative, the public could easily understand the importance of education which, although culturally laudable, would also help to strengthen the political standing of the National Liberation Party, Costa Rica's dominant political party during the second half of the twentieth century. Indeed, as Dabène has noted, the establishment of the SDPM can also be viewed of an integral part of the National Liberation Party's strategy to maintain its political dominance in the country at the time (Dabène 1992).

During the 1970s, the development of the SDPM in Costa Rica was affected by various factors that influenced social democracy and education in the country. Budgetary reforms resulted in a real-term reduction in the funds allocated for education and also led to the establishment of a system that allowed the private sector to participate in education (Toruño 2015). Other factors affecting the development of the education system during the 1970s was the increasing number of school days each week and a noticeable lack of proper educational infrastructure. Finally, an important factor during this decade was the attempt to increase the role of local governments in education administration, as part of a broader policy of decentralization; however, political and social resistance prevented this initiative from being realized.

The Costa Rican education system then underwent further changes in the period from 1978 to 1982, largely due to economic factors, such as the failure of the import substitute model in the 1980s, the drop in the price of agricultural export products, and the increase in interest rates at the international level, all of which caused investment in education to decrease until the 1990s (Molina 2018).

Within this context, in 1986, a new pedagogical perspective emerged: the Neoliberal Adjustment Model (NAM), which reemphasized economic development and increased monetary resources for teaching. Although the NAM did not completely replace the SDPM, it brought about significant changes, which we shall now explore.

In his first presidency (1986–1990), Dr. Óscar Arias Sánchez appointed as Minister for Education the philosopher Francisco Antonio Pacheco. Although Pacheco's administrative work is generally considered to have been outstanding, he did not garner the necessary support to bring the various reforms he envisaged to full fruition. However, he significantly developed contemporary ICT instruction in the country through modifying the "Computer Education Program", which had been created by the previous administration. To achieve this, an agreement was established between the MEP and the Omar Dengo Foundation (FOD), which, it is worth noting, represented a major contribution, since to this day, information computer technology has proven to be an invaluable resource for the education of children and young people in Costa Rica. ICT education, as such, quickly became so prominent in the nation's education system that many state and private universities were offering degree courses in information technology as early as the 1990s.

One the most striking reforms of the era, which endures today, was the resuscitation of the Baccalaureate, or "bachillerato", which is a set of examinations taken by secondary students wishing to pursue a degree. According to the Organization of Ibero-American States (1997), the return of the Baccalaureate represented a policy stance that viewed assessment "not as an end, but [rather] as a means to reactivate the educational lifeblood of the country, involving students, parents, authorities, and indeed the entire community, to this commitment" (p. 6). The Baccalaureate program was then consolidated in the 1990s, incorporating new curricular approaches.

Despite the efforts of diverse political bodies and economic organs, the NAM of pedagogy ultimately failed to replace the SDMP. However, it succeeded in implementing a different type of education system. Despite its name, educational reforms under the Neoliberal Adjustment Model did not extend to privatizing a large portion of institutions or establishing a curricular system based on conservative currents of opinion, but instead focused on developing education programs that were designed to meet the varying needs of the country's distinct regions.

At this juncture, we must note that the reflections above reveal a number of key tenets underpinning the development of the Costa Rican education system during the years 1950–1980. These include: the concept of universal access to education; the tailoring of study courses to meet the requirements of different local areas; and the implementation of new study and examination programs.

Yet other factors, such as cultural differences and political persuasions, must also be considered. A study of the various writings of Leonardo Garnier during his time as Education Minister (2006–2014), for instance, clearly shows his desire to implement a curriculum that restores some of the key tenets of the SDPM, in opposition to the NAM. Some of the reforms carried out under Garnier's leadership were based on principles of citizenship, aesthetics, and ethics. In elementary school, the curriculum was changed to include topics such as relationships and sexuality. The latter met with considerable controversy, as conservatives rejected it.

In addition to numerous reforms, Garnier also decided to analyze the educational policies, the study of which reveals his attitudes to be at odds with the prevailing educational model at the time. Garnier's columns in La Nación, for example, center around the development of new study programs (Toruño 2015). Furthermore, the concept of "education for harmonious coexistence," which was also presented by Garnier, breaks with the traditional conservative vision of education; it focused on adapting education in schools to meet the needs of different regions. He also highlighted the importance of catering to multiple learning styles, which he linked to the development of a better society. The inclusion of such concepts in the education policy framework would eventually allow Costa Rica to return to the SDPM.

Consequently, during these restorative reforms, various changes were implemented at the primary and secondary levels. These included changes to the Spanish language curriculum, the introduction of plastic arts into primary education, and the development of a pluricultural curriculum. Citizenship and social skills were also introduced, with an emphasis on communicating effectively and efficiently, developing a consensus, and making decisions. Such programs also included opportunities to participate in a variety of social and political activities and addressed how to respond to diversity and difference. In addition to these changes, the education system also adopted four pillars for teaching and learning: Know, Enjoy, Express, and Explain. Although an in-depth exploration of these so-called four pillars is not considered relevant for the purposes of this study, they do serve as useful illustrations of the new curriculum and can be used in extra-curricular and citizenship settings, as well as for traditional subjects (Toruño 2015).

Over the past decade, investment has increased for infrastructure projects such as the construction of new schools and the renovation of public facilities like libraries. From a SDPM standpoint, we might therefore deduce that the Costa Rican education system is progressive; but a different analysis, one which considers the remnants of the Neoliberal Adjustment Model reforms that still endure today, would arrive at different conclusions. Our premise, then, is that the decision to restore the SDPM constituted a statement of the hegemonic project of education in Costa Rica, rather than a truly progressive philosophy.

As a final aside, we would note that the process of implementing such a hegemonic project is complex, due to the various actors operating within the relevant domain. These actors include both the power groups that defend the model and the groups that act against it, where the latter include pressure groups, who wish to maintain a certain status quo, and progressive groups, who have an alternative agenda (Toruño 2015).

3.3 High School Protests

In 2019, the education sector was rocked by Kenneth Sánchez, the controversial leader of MEDSE (Movimiento Estudiantil de Secundaria), a protest group that was behind the historic high school students' strikes and blockades unleashed against the government, which led to the resignation of the minister of education in July of the same year.

Sánchez, an 18-year-old activist, indeed had a remarkable impact; he was able to take advantage of new technology and resources for mobilization in a most efficient way, by filming and disseminating on social media instances of police violence, for example. For the same reasons, young people of Sánchez's generation often attract criticism, and perhaps delegitimization, due to the suspicions, founded or not, of manipulation by political groups. Officially, the student marches were declared as a denunciation of the FARO exam (Fortalecimiento de Aprendizajes para la Renovación de Oportunidades), which they claimed unfairly judged whether a student was qualified to access university study.[3] However, workers then joined the demonstrations; these included taxi and truck drivers. Suspicions of instrumentalization by unions to promote other parallel agendas, soon emerged. The student marches were characterized by police repression, which increased demonstrators' resentment of the then minister of education, Edgar Mora. He resigned from his post in July 2019 (Petri 2020).

Beyond the opposition to the FARO exam, which essentially is a type of baccalaureate exam, one trend in the Costa Rican education system has been the gradual erosion of examinations, inspired by new pedagogical philosophies. Furthermore, it has become increasingly difficult for students to fail a year, as this is considered to be discriminatory. The controversy around second-cycle examinations has led to many strikes since 2018. Shortly after assuming office, president Rodrigo Chaves urged the national Education Council to order the complete elimination of second-cycle examinations, which it did on 9 June 2022.

Notwithstanding the arguably legitimate reasons for these changes, at least according to the insights of some education experts, they have made the Costa Rican education system less competitive internationally, as studies by the OECD indicate (Schleicher 2017). This issue does not only apply to high schools, but also to university education, as is evident when considering the high failure rates of graduated university students in professional exams for lawyers and medical personnel, or the poor grades of teacher training graduates in teachers for assessment (Schleicher 2017).

[3] MEDSE had other demands as well like ending the dual education project that would allow students to also work as apprentices in private companies, better infrastructure. and the resignation of the minister of education Edgar Mora.

3.4 Religious Education and Religious Accommodation

The place of religious instruction continues to be controversial. Because Costa Rica is officially a Catholic state, there are concerns that the education system is subordinate to the Catholic Church. In 1994, the UN Human Rights Committee raised this question in its annual report, alleging the Teaching Career Law grants the National Episcopal Conference undue influence over public religious instruction (HRC 1994; Scolnicov 2011, p. 69). Although religious education remains mandatory in public schools, it was decoupled from the influence of the Catholic Church in 2010 when a ruling by the Constitutional Chamber ordered that the Church should no longer have the authority to approve the candidacies of 1400 teachers of religious studies. It also ordered that alternative religion classes should be offered to cater to non-Catholic students (Murillo 2019). Both rulings have not fully materialized, however, mainly because of a lack of qualified teachers (Cerdas 2021).

Further examples also confirm that the influence of the Catholic Church is no longer quite so prominent. In 2018, the Ministry of Education adopted a sexual education curriculum, ignoring the loud protests of the Catholic bishops and other conservative religious groups (ACI Prensa 2018).

At times, issues related to the accommodation of the beliefs of religious minorities arise. There have been several cases of restrictions on the observance of religious law related to the refusal of a school to allow a Seventh-Day Adventist student to reschedule an exam originally scheduled for a Saturday in 2010 and the denial of a high school director of a request for leave to celebrate a Jewish holiday in 2012. More recent anti-Semitic incidents in public schools were quickly addressed (Radio Jai 2017; Sala Constitucional 2017). Such issues, although they are often corrected after talks between religious leaders and public officials, do reveal a worrying lack of religious literacy among education officials, in our opinion, however (Petri 2022).

4 Outlook of Future Developments and Emerging Issues in Education Law

4.1 Resource Scarcity

As explored in the previous section, the education system has undergone multiple reforms that are aimed at improving the quality of teaching and learning. Although these changes have succeeded in ameliorating some aspects of the system, a number of trends remain which challenge its future evolution.

One key factor is that, as the private sector has repeatedly complained, the education system would seem to fail to deliver the workforce it needs. Private sector employers, according to an OECD report, are often forced to retrain the graduates they recruit (OECD 2017). Promising initiatives, such as financial education, promoted by the country's banks and financial institutions as part of their corporate social responsibility, have only been introduced as pilot schemes in a handful of schools (OECD 2017).

An important challenge for the nation's education system is that of consolidating a high-quality teaching profession to address the graduate skill gaps. In Costa Rica, the gap between the theory and practice of education is stark. According to studies, over 40% of teachers of English and 30% of mathematics teachers do not know how to teach their curriculum (OECD 2017). Despite the improvement in teacher training courses, teachers still receive little feedback and support regarding their pedagogical practice and subject knowledge. Currently, an evaluation system is used as a tool for ensuring the continuing professional development of teachers, but this has been accused of flimsiness and of lacking a basic understanding of the day-to-day challenges for teachers. A further point of note is that only nineteen of the existing two hundred and sixty teacher training programs are actually accredited (OECD 2017), which means that the vast majority of so-called qualified teachers are unprepared to deliver the curriculum.

Teacher numbers are also an issue, especially in rural areas. Raising salaries has been one attempt to address the shortfall (Martinez and Loria 2018). Salaries constitute the main item of education expenditure, with a growing trend at the per capita level (Martinez and Loria 2018). Notwithstanding the resources allocated to the sector, and in spite of the reforms that have been carried out, the country does not have an evaluation system to link salaries to student results or to quality standards for teaching staff, which has been denounced by the periodic *Estado de la Educación* (Martinez 2012) think tank reports. In the same vein, such reports identified a lack of selectivity in MEP teacher hiring processes; the Ministry's recruitment system dates to 1970 (Martinez 2012) and proposes that applicants have a university degree, accrue years of experience, and undertake training courses. However, currently the nation's teachers require other skills, in addition to certification.

4.2 School Dropouts and Equality of Access

As alluded to in an earlier section of this chapter, Costa Rica was among the first countries in the region to send students to primary school. Today, almost all students go on to make the transition to secondary school; the challenge, then, is in ensuring that all students encounter a positive learning environment and are equipped with the necessary skills to succeed in their studies, so that they go on to graduate with a complete General Basic Education (high school). According to the OECD, around 30% of students leave high school by age 15 (OECD 2017) and this same 30% tends to lack basic mathematical, literacy and science skills. Sadly, during the first stage of the COVID-19 pandemic, it was reported that some eight thousand primary school students left the education system and did not return (Castro 2021a, b).

So-called "high school dropouts" are a major issue. Several social groups have succeeded in raising awareness about this issue (Infobae 2011), but so far none of the reforms they advocate have been implemented. "Dropouts" choose to leave education to work, so that they can provide for their family. To date, many programs have sought to counteract the phenomenon; for example, presidents Óscar Arias and Laura Chinchilla proposed in 2006 and 2010 respectively a plan called "Avancemos", which focused on scholarships and monies for resources like school supplies, clothing, and food (Infobae 2011). This plan helped to reduce dropout rates by 2% over three years but still did not solve the issue, which remains somewhat intractable (Infobae 2011).

To palliate the ongoing problem of school dropouts and equality of access to education, Costa Rica has introduced a new economic growth strategy that explicitly focuses on improving the quality of teaching and learning to promote upward social mobility. It sets targets for higher levels of performance and achievement by the country's teachers and schools respectively. This is supported by a strong central government strategy that aims to improve the quality of the education system overall.

Between 2018 and 2021, the education system was paralyzed for long periods of time; important strikes occurred in 2018, followed by the MEDSE strikes in 2019, and then the COVID19 lockdowns and school closures in 2020 and 2021. The latter disproportionately affected children from rural and poorer areas, who did not have access to computers or internet connections.

4.3 The Divide Between Public and Private Education

The divide between public and private education is also growing, the latter being preferred by the social classes that are economically better-off (Seevers 2014). Overall, private schools tend to have a better reputation than public schools, because they are perceived to have higher quality educational resources and teaching staff. This situation has created an intense debate about whether students who attend private schools receive a better education (Gimenez and Castro 2017). It is important to point out, however, that, the differences between public and private schools are not as important as they seem: not all private education institutions have more resources or better teachers than public institutions. The main difference lies in the fact that students of public and private institutions have very different socioeconomic characteristics, leading to a selection bias (Gimenez and Castro 2017). As a result, on average, students from private schools belong to families with more economic resources and higher educational levels. For this reason, the social and cultural capital of the family, available educational facilities in the home, and the external effects associated with having students belonging to these environments as classmates are likely to be the real explanations of the better results of students from private schools (Gimenez and Castro 2017).

The situation is radically different for university education. More than 58% of the population considers that public universities offer better education than private universities. Less than a quarter (24%) prefers private universities. In particular, the University of Costa Rica, a public university is considered the best a superior university and has more students in the country and the candidates for jobs that have a degree from this university are preferred by most employers (Denton 2014).

It is important to note that different mechanisms and institutions regulate the private education sector, whereby individual institutions have a high degree of self-regulatory freedom. Public resources are still involved, however, since private universities receive tax exemptions from the Costa Rican state and pay a reduced value added tax rate of 2%, instead of the 13% that corresponds, on average, to other settings (Blanco and Chacon 2020).

Finally, access to private schooling remains unequal and its results correspond to the economic differences of the families concerned. Most students who complete their studies in private educational institutions go on to gain better jobs, nationally and internationally, which allows them to send their own children to these same schools, perpetuating the self-selectivity and economic privilege inherent in the private school system (Blanco and Chacon 2020).

4.4 Gender Disparities

In Costa Rican society, gender disparities persist; but in terms of educational achievements, statistics are more favorable for girls than for boys. For example, the lower secondary completion rate is 71% for females, against 67.5% for males (World Bank 2022). This gap widens even more in the case of university education.

Although these figures suggest that girls overwhelmingly outperform boys academically, the Ministry of Public Education continues to implement several initiatives to address "the gender achievement gap." It could be argued that these initiatives have been so successful that they are no longer necessary; or perhaps they should focus more on keeping boys from dropping out of school instead.

Various amendments to the official curriculum have been suggested; however, these changes have not yet been realized, as there are still various issues that first need to be resolved (Vargas 2021). Gender equality in education is not a new concern in Costa Rica, however, since proposals regarding the issue first date back to the 1980s. Despite the various initiatives that have been launched to improve the status of women in the country, the progress that has been made has arguably not been widely felt.

Until 2014, official policies on gender equality in education were established by the Ministry of Public Education. This reflects how far the country has gone in addressing this matter, but it suggests, we would hold, that the Ministry does not have a strong stance on the issue of gender equality in education, since issues remain prevalent on the ground (Vargas 2021). In 2000, the Ministry of Public Education and the International Network of Women in Education (INAMU) collaborated to create a strategic plan that aimed to establish a culture of gender equity in the country's education system; the plan was then consolidated in 2001 (Araya Umaña 2008). Actions were designed to help to create the necessary conditions for the advancement of gender equality through the country's education system. After a long, protracted struggle, the Commission for the Development of Gender Equity in Education succeeded in securing legislation to implement sex and relationship education programs throughout Costa Rica. Furthermore, from 2012 to 2013, a committee known as "Schools for Change" was established, which explored the role of gender disparity in early childhood education.

In 2014, the MEP established a number of initiatives aimed at reinforcing gender equality in Costa Rica (Vargas 2021). These included promoting gender equality, educating from a gender-informed perspective, explicitly valuing and practicing non-discrimination, and using a gender-conscious approach in structural and administration matters. The introduction of these equality-based educational policies has rightly been regarded as a key component in the country's efforts to improve the lives of Costa Rican women.

4.5 *Bureaucratic Resistance to Reform*

Because of the significant levels of bureaucratic resistance, political and legal reforms in Costa Rica tend to take a lot of time to materialize. In the education sector specifically, bureaucratic resistance to reform is particularly strong and has slowed down many reform processes, to a large degree because of the presence of very powerful teachers' unions, which have been closely connected to the National Liberation Party which has been the dominant political party since the 1948 Revolution.

For example, the bureaucratic processes within the Ministry of Public Education were affecting the selection of beneficiaries of computers and tablets with Internet access for students who do not have technological resources to receive virtual classes. In this sense, the suspension of the school year for more than a month and a half would not be used to improve the connectivity of students in public schools and colleges through the Connected Homes Plan, financed with resources from the National Telecommunications Fund (Fonatel). And it is that the MEP does not finish defining the students who would receive the resources, since it has not been able to access the database of the Mixed Institute of Social Assistance (IMAS) to identify the possible beneficiaries of a computer and a connection to the Internet (Castro 2021a, b). Due to these problems, there were frequent strikes by schoolteachers.

A frequently mentioned complaint is the large amount of paperwork education staff need to deliver around the evaluations of students, meetings with parents and other teachers, did active units, self-evaluations, individual student reports and additional administrative paperwork due to the lack of personnel. These problems are applicable to the public administration system more broadly, but are particularly acute within the education system.

In fact, Costa Rica, unlike other OECD countries, lacks a public authority leader with clear responsibility for the education sector public superior and the ability to plan strategically. Of the existing institutions, the National Council of Rectors (CONARE) operates solely as an instrument for the self-government of public universities, while the National Council of Private Higher University Education (CONESUP) deals exclusively with private universities (Schleicher 2017). There is no entity that has responsibility for the sector as a whole. There also is no platform where the actors can meet to ensure coherence between programs and institutions in terms of objectives, information or requirements of system-wide monitoring—upon which to allocate significantly public funds (Schleicher 2017). An implication of the former is that it is difficult to develop and implement new policies on topics such as student finance, the quality of university education, or to cover the needs of an economy that is changing quickly. As a result, a solid basis for the development of a competitive higher education sector is absent.

5 Conclusion

Despite the various education initiatives introduced over the past decade, it is concerning that the education system in Costa Rica remains regulated by a law that has not been updated since 1957. The Fundamental Law of Education, which was issued some sixty-five years ago, does not respond adequately to the needs and requirements of modern society. This is because the regulatory body established by the 1957 law has similarly undergone no reform since its inception.

In this way, Costa Rica continues to elaborate its educational goals and systemic reforms according to a framework for education that was conceptualized decades previously, when the reality of Costa Rica and the world at large differed greatly from our current context. There is no doubt that, at the time of its formulation, this legislation provided the necessary foundations for the Costa Rican system, underpinned by a Humanist philosophy of education. However, time passes; and changing times bring changing educational needs. Therefore, we would hold that Costa Rica should not base its current education system on the hopes of the past, but rather on a vision for the future, which should be socially co-constructed. In this respect, we would consider it imperative that society and the legislator collaborate in defining a new framework for education, which must gather in a single normative compendium the legal advances that have existed until now as decrees or regulations. This will reduce normative dispersion and will facilitate the incorporation of innovative approaches to education in Costa Rica.

The Costa Rican education system has undergone many changes. At the beginning of this chapter, we discussed the different models that have been adapted in the last centuries and how they have evolved into what they are today and what challenges the result of those models have brought to the educational system. We conclude that the system has always been focused on benefiting the population and targeting high standards for helping the economy and society. For example, back in the 1940s or 1950s, when the first universities were founded and the modern education legislation was adopted, the objective was to educate the population in order to provide opportunities to everybody. In the 1980s and 1990s, under a different economic development model, high school education was reoriented to support the needs of the economy.

Then in the 2000s and again today, several attempts were made to change the evaluation system and make it more accessible. The education system has always tried to adapt to the circumstances and the needs of the people, whether the needs of the labor markers or the imperative of promoting literacy. At the same time, the necessary reforms have only been implemented slowly.

The system is still evolving and needs work. To this day, Costa Rica still has one of the most successful education systems in Latin America. It has been proven from time to time that is has the capacity to show good results and prepare students for the labor market. It provides benefits to the whole population. Costa Rica continues to dedicate 7.6% of the country's Gross Domestic Product (GDP), in contrast to the average of the OECD countries of 5% (Barquero 2017).

At the same time, there are many inconsistencies in the system, like the accessibility gaps, gender gaps and administrative obstacles. Even though education is a long-term benefit to the country, it is important to provide opportunities for people to access education. For Costa Rica it is imperative that this happens, as it does not have an army. Indeed, education can bring about huge improvements to many areas of Costa Rica's international relations. These are aspects that could improve the results of education by miles, but the bureaucracy of the country still makes it hard to fix. As discussed, the education models from the 1940's or 1980's have proven difficult to reform. Like baccalaureate exams, old study plans for technical high schools, gender and class gaps, are still on the table. There are many opportunities for improvement.

References

ACI Prensa (2018). Costa Rica: Iglesia explica a candidatos presidenciales por qué se opone aguías sexuales. https://aciprensa.com/noticias/iglesia-en-costa-rica-expone-oposicion-sobre-guias-sexuales-a-candidatos-a-la-presidencia-44837. Accessed 25 Jan 2018

Araya Pochet C (2005) Historia del derecho constitucional costarricense. EUNED, San Jose

Araya Umaña S (2008) Contenidos y alcances de la equidad de género en las políticas educativas. In: Informe de investigación, Instituto de Investigación en Educación, Facultad de Educación, Universidad de Costa Rica. http://repositorio.inie.ucr.ac.cr/handle/123456789/304

Barquero K (2017) Costa Rica invierte en educación mas Que cualquier pais de OCDE. Periódico La República, 7 Aug 2017. https://www.larepublica.net/noticia/costa-rica-invierte-en-educacion-mas-que-cualquier-pais-de-ocde

Blanco L, Chacon MJ (2020) Diferencias entre la educación universitaria pública y privada costarricense: rendimientos y calificación del trabajo. Revista de Ciencias Econ 38(2):7–40. https://doi.org/10.15517/rce.v38i1.39039.

Camacho J (2005) Un siglo de educación costarricense: 1814–1914. EUCR, San José

Castro J (2021) Burocracia en el MEP frenaría selección de beneficiarios de equipos E internet para clases virtuales. La República, 21 June 2021. https://www.larepublica.net/noticia/burocracia-en-el-mep-frenaria-seleccion-de-beneficiarios-de-equipos-e-internet-para-clases-virtuales

Castro K (2021) País lucha contra una peligrosa amenaza pospandemia: la deserción escolar. CRHoy.com., 20 June 2021 https://www.crhoy.com/nacionales/pais-lucha-contra-una-peligrosa-amenaza-pospandemia-la-desercion-escolar/

Castro Vega Ó (2007) Fin de la Segunda República: Figures y la Constituyente del 49. EUNED, San José

Cerdas ED (2021) UNA: Ministerio de Educación solo imparte clases de religión católica pese a orden de Sala IV. La Nación, 10 Mar 2021. https://www.nacion.com/el-pais/educacion/una-ministerio-de-educacion-solo-imparte-clases-de/D7YT77KXRRB5RJ7QCYBE66NXLM/story/?fbclid=IwAR22eX5OKGq-JlUtmVLTu8RSYtQiRmmWPKTYVPxiZXVBy-11UNrc62zbCJE

Código de Educación (1944)

Dabène O (1992). *Costa Rica: Juicio a la Democracia.* San José: FLACSO-CEMCA

Dengo ME (2011) Educación costarricense. EUNED, San José

Denton C (2014) ¿Distingue el Mercado entre universidades? La República, 12 Nov 2014. https://www.larepublica.net/noticia/distingue_el_mercado_entre_universidades%20

Gimenez G, Castro G (2017) ¿Por qué los estudiantes de colegios públicos y privados de Costa Rica obtienen distintos resultados académicos? Perfiles Latinoamericanos 25:195–222. https://doi.org/10.18504/pl2549-009-2017

Huhn S (2008) A history of nonviolence: insecurity and the normative power of the imagined in Costa Rica. German Institute of Global and Area Studies (GIGA) Research Programme: Violence, Power and Security No. 84, August 2008

Human Rights Committee (1994) Concluding observations on the Costa Rica state report, UN Doc. A/49/40 vol.1: 31. http://hrlibrary.umn.edu/hrcommittee/hrc-annual94.htm

Infobae (2011) Costa Rica y su éxito contra la deserción escolar. Infobae, 18 April 2011. https://www.infobae.com/2011/04/18/1023257-costa-rica-y-su-exito-contra-la-desercion-escolar/

Informa-TICO (2019) Las grandes pegas del sistema educativo costarricense. Informa-Tico, 29 Aug 2019. https://www.informa-tico.com/29-08-2019/grandes-pegas-sistema-educativo-costarricense

Ley Fundamental de Educación (1957)

Ley Fundamental de Educación Común (1886)

Ley Orgánica del Ministerio de Educación Pública (1965)

Martinez B (2012) Cronología de la educación costarricense. Editorial Edin, San José

Martinez J, Loria M (2018) La educación pública costarricense: principales tendencias y desafíos. Academia de Centroamérica. https://www.academiaca.or.cr/serie-vision-para-el-desarrollo/la-educacion-publica-costarricense-principales-tendencias-y-desafios/

Miranda G (2010) La fundación del Partido Liberación Nacional y el origen del proyecto político educativo socialdemócrata en Costa Rica. Una aproximación hermenéutica crítica. Revista de Ciencias Sociales 130:185–213. https://hdl.handle.net/10669/25348

Molina I (2007) Educación y sociedad en Costa Rica: de 1821 al presente (una historia no autorizada). Diálogos Revista Electrónica de Historia 8(2):149–356. https://hdl.handle.net/10669/19201

Molina I (2018) El financiamiento educativo público en costa rica a largo plazo (1860–2016). Historia y memoria 16(24):168–198. https://doi.org/10.19053/20275137.n24.2022

Murillo Á (2019) Educación religiosa en escuelas públicas: una historia sin solución. Semanario Universidad, 11 June 2019 https://semanariouniversidad.com/pais/educacion-religiosa-en-escuelas-publicas-una-historia-sin-solucion/

OECD (2017) Análisis de la OCDE acerca de las políticas nacionales para educación: la educación en Rosta Rica. https://www.oecd.org/education/school/La-Educacion-en-Costa-Rica-Resumen-Ejecutivo.pdf

Petri DP (2020) Costa Rica: the school of protest/Costa Rica: La escuela de la protesta. Web series "Protesta: activismo en los tiempos de pandemia." Observatoire Politique de l'Amérique Latine et des Caraïbes (Sciences Po Paris) & Transparencia por Colombia. https://www.youtube.com/watch?v=g0klo3E9tlE&t=1s

Petri DP (2022) If it's not broken, don't fix it: review of religious policy in Costa Rica. Rhombus 2(1):16–42. https://platformforsocialtransformation.org/download/religiousfreedom/Petri-If-its-not-broken-dont-fix-it-review-of-religious-policy-in-Costa-Rica_2.pdf

Petri DP (2023) La separación de poderes costarricense. Divide y sobrevivirás: una evaluación de la resiliencia de la democracia costarricense. Derecho en Sociedad 17(2):133–151. https://revistas.ulacit.ac.cr/index.php/derecho-en-sociedad/article/view/177/140

Radio Jai (2017) Costa Rica: un estudiante judío demandó al Ministerio de Educación por prohibirle usar una kipá. Laicismo.org., 4 May 2017. https://laicismo.org/costa-rica-un-estudiante-judio-demando-al-ministerio-de-educacion-por-prohibirle-usar-una-kipa/161990
Robles A (2017) Vista de Sistema educativo costarricense: ¿Puerta o barrera para el pensamiento crítico? Revista Ensayos Pedagógicos XII(2):17–31. https://doi.org/10.15359/rep.12-2.1
Sala Constitucional de la Corte Suprema de Justicia (2017). Sentencia No. 09050
Salazar Mora Ó (1980) Le système politique au Costa Rica 1889-1919. Tesis doctoral, Université de Paris III
Schleicher A (2017) Educación en Costa Rica. OECD. https://www.rectoria.ucr.ac.cr/site/wp-content/uploads/2017/08/aspectos-destacados-2017.pdf
Scolnicov A (2011) The right to religious freedom in international law. Between group rights and individual rights. Routledge, London
Seevers M (2014) Solo 30% de costarricenses son profesionales. Universidad de Costa Rica, 23 Jan 2014. https://www.ucr.ac.cr/noticias/2014/01/23/solo-30-de-costarricenses-son-profesionales.html
Teletica Radio (2021) Lluvia de ideas para mejorar la Educación en Costa Rica. 26 May 2021 https://www.facebook.com/ulacitcostarica/posts/4174360439254016
Toruño C (2015) Reformas curriculares 2006–2014: del ajuste pedagógico neoliberal a la reinstauración del modelo pedagógico socialdemócrata. Revista Rupturas 5(2):21–48. https://revistas.uned.ac.cr/index.php/rupturas/article/view/881/789
United Nations Development Programme (UNDP) (2022) Human development index. Available at: https://hdr.undp.org/data-center/human-development-index#/indicies/HDI
United Nations Education, Scientific and Cultural Organization (UNESCO) (2006) Costa Rican education system. International Bureau of Education. https://www.ibe.unesco.org/sites/default/files/Costa_Rica.pdf
Vargas Y (2021) La igualdad y la equidad de género en la educación secundaria costarricense: Criterios para un diseño de evaluación. Rev Actual Investig Educ 21(3). https://doi.org/10.15517/aie.v21i3.48154
World Bank (2022) World Bank open data. Available at: https://data.worldbank.org/

Trends and Practices in English Education Law

Javier García Oliva and Helen Hall

1 Introduction

In common with many other nations, education in England has been a political trophy since at least the nineteenth century, with all elements of the ideological spectrum keen to snatch it from their rivals, and demonstrate that their camp is best equipped to guard both its present and future. Long before the inception of modern Human Rights Law, and the incorporation of guarantees to education within domestic law,[1] there was widespread consensus that the welfare of society depended on all sections of the populace receiving an adequate and appropriate education (Benchimol 2016).

This concern stemmed historically from two dominant anxieties: (1) that young people should grow equipped to be economically productive members of their community, and (2) that future citizens should receive a moral formation in conformity with prevailing societal norms (Button and Sheetz Nguyen 2013). At first blush these preoccupations might seem quaintly Victorian, and far removed from the debates of the XXI century era, but these twin themes remain at the heart of contemporary clashes over the educational scene. The desire to provide the economy with a deep pool of skilled workers is openly stated (Hurley 2022). In contrast, the battle to capture and mould impressionable hearts and minds is often less overt, but nonetheless easy to discern in controversies over the Prevent Strategy in schools (Busher and Jermone 2020), or acceptable parameters and content for teaching about gender and sexuality (Ferguson 2019).

[1] European Convention on Human Rights ("ECHR"), Protocol 1, Art 2.

J. G. Oliva (✉)
University of Oxford, Oxford, England
e-mail: copyright@esph.com.cn

H. Hall
Nottingham Trent University, Nottingham, England

C. J. Russo and L. Ma (eds.), *A Comparative Analysis of Systems of Education Law*,
https://doi.org/10.1007/978-981-97-1052-2_6

Overlaying this, there is the pragmatic reality that manifesting an interest in the educational welfare of children and young people is likely to be a promising strategy with the electorate. Few people would contest the validity of this objective, and an image of championing the needs of children is class fodder for campaign managers and strategists: in fact, the stereotype of the baby-kissing politician exists for a reason. The consequence of this, from a legal perspective, is a scarred and bumpy landscape for analysists to navigate, as we are left with a hotchpotch of provisions which attest to generations of reforms, counter-reforms, fashions and fads. Sometimes new ministerial and parliamentary brooms have swept away previous structures, but accidentally left residual traces lurking in forgotten corners of the statute book. On other occasions, new schemes have been deliberately heaped up on top of the old, like a teetering pile of folders on a civil servant's desk. At no stage has anyone had the will, or frankly capacity, to rationalise the framework into a coherent whole with unifying aims. However, with this extended health warning in place, we shall attempt to provide an overview of the current legal system, before moving on to look at recent developments, and then projected plans, on our way to finally drawing the threads together in a conclusion.

2 Nature of the Legal System

As set out in our introduction, the United Kingdom at state level has treaty obligations in International Law which recognise the right to education. Two particularly important instruments in this regard are the European Convention on Human Rights ("ECHR")[2] and the United Nations Convention on the Rights of the Child ("UNCRC").[3] Nonetheless, it should be noted that in the United Kingdom, being a dualist state, the ECHR only becomes legally binding when it is incorporated into the corpus of national law.[4]

Alongside this black letter provisions, it is also critical that a commitment to free universal education for children from kindergarten age until an age of potential economic independence[5] is a longstanding part of the Constitutional Culture (García Oliva and Hall 2020) of modern Britain as a whole, including England. This was a key element of the post-war reconstruction which took place in the 1940s, and despite many points of disagreement, both right and left wing voices acknowledged the importance of equality of opportunity.[6] Nevertheless, it is also vital to appreciate that while the *offer* of free, full time education is an integral part of our Constitutional

[2] ECHR, Protocol 1, Art 2. See also Articles 8 and 9.

[3] United Nations Convention on the Rights of the Child, Art 28.

[4] Human Rights Act 1998.

[5] It would be inaccurate to assert adulthood, as although the Education Act 1944 raised the age of compulsory education from 14 to 15, the age of majority was 21 until the Family Law Reform Act 1969, when it was reduced to 18.

[6] Education Act 1944.

Culture, there is an equally strong expectation that parents must have a choice to decide whether or not they wish to avail themselves of this. The freedom to make alternative, private arrangement for the education of minors is profoundly ingrained.[7]

The sole requirement imposed in respect of children of compulsory school age be in receipt of an "efficient" and "full-time" education,[8] whist those vested with parental responsibility are at liberty to determine how this should be achieved.[9] In practical terms, there are essentially three options: (1) Home education; (2) Privately funded education in a school setting; and (3) State funded education. The legal arrangements for each framework are distinct, so we shall address them in turn.

2.1 Home Education

This is an area of English life which is lightly regulated, and beyond the overarching mandate that the education must be "full-time" and also "efficient", nothing concrete is specified. Clearly, the parameters are drawn in a way which precludes children being denied education in order to work in agriculture, the family business of any other industry. For instance, there are specific regulations which apply in respect of child performance, and these address educational provision, as well as welfare, in a more holistic sense.[10] Other than that, however, the lines are extremely blurred, because there is no set curriculum, list of subjects, knowledges or competences required. Neither are there specifications in respect of the adults imparting the education.

Teaching qualification or form of license are not compulsory, and home educators do not need to demonstrate a bare minimum level of educational attainment. As a result, strikingly, it would be entirely feasible for a parent, or other figure, to teach a child in a home-schooling setting without ever having passed a public examination of any kind. This is obviously concerning from an educational perspective, but it is also problematic as no legal regulation restricts the freedom of individuals to offer themselves as tutors. This huge degree of flexibility is a major potential risk in terms of safeguarding in relation to people seeking to groom, exploit and abuse children, and the fact that such young people may have fewer independent adults to whom disclosures may be made, renders their position even more acutely perilous.

The situation becomes still more disturbing when it is remembered that there is no duty imposed on local authorities or state officials to proactively and/or regularly assess the standard of education being offered to a child, unless they have some reason to be concerned for that individual's wellbeing. It is true that the Education Act declares that public authorities must identify children who are not registered

[7] García Oliva, "Obstacles to tackling Illegal Religious Schools in the Constitutional Culture of the United Kingdom", *Anuario de Derecho Eclesiástico del Estado*, 2023 (forthcoming).

[8] Education Act 1996 s7.

[9] Children Act 1989 s2.

[10] The Children (Performances) Regulations 1968, art 10.

and not receiving an adequate education, but this provision is vague in nature and gravely weakened by the caveat "in so far as possible."[11] It does not come close to mandating, or even *enabling*, regular checks to be carried out. Either a lack of economic resources on the part of a struggling public sector, or refusal on the part of families to cooperate may render such checks and intervention "not possible".

It must be emphasised that several factors lead to a worrying scenario: Parliament has remained ambiguous to impose any obligations on agents of the state to monitor home-schooling situations, no power of entry to a dwelling house is vested on local authority, and there is no right to demand that a child is subjected to an interview or written test. Indeed, the sole purpose of the exercise is to assess the quality of the education which has been arranged.[12] Predictably, this *laissez-faire* regime has generated considerable divergence of approach between local authorities. Given the acute ongoing economic crisis, and the twin forces of Brexit and a global pandemic, local government bodies in England have been in many cases unable to facilitate basic and fundamental services, e.g. keeping street lighting on during the hours of darkness,[13] being the reality on the ground that those which have not been made non-negotiable by law are being retrenched in order to conserve meagre funds. The truth is that child services are under acute strain, and the optional monitoring of home-schooling is in jeopardy of removal.

Another layer of complexity, and potential danger for minors, lies in the fact that children who never enter the state school system (as opposed to those who begin attending, but are subsequently withdrawn), are likely to be unknown to the local authority.[14] There is no duty imposed on parents to notify public authorities of their intention to home-school, if this is done from the time that the child reaches the age for compulsory education. This means that some children are in a practical sense invisible to the local educational authority, and it is clearly "not possible" to check on the progress of young people who are not identified. Department of Education guidance goes as far as to encourage parents to inform the local authority, and request the help and support which are on offer in their area, but there is no compulsion. Some (although of course by no means all) parents opt to home-school because of a distrust of state provision and intervention, and those in this category are highly unlikely to make any voluntary disclosures.

In contrast, where children have begun attending school, parents are required to write and give notice of their intention to withdraw a child and home-school, meaning that the possibility of oversight is greater (and if there are any wider welfare concerns, the school may already have flagged this to social services, which do have power to

---

[11] Education Act 1996, s.436A.

[12] Education Act 2002, s.175.

[13] "Councillor calls for street lights to be turned on in Lincoln" *The Lincolnite* (11/9/2022) https://thelincolnite.co.uk/2022/08/councillor-calls-for-street-lights-to-be-turned-on-in-lincoln/ (accessed 11/1/2023).

[14] Department for Education, "Elective Home Education" (01/04/20), paras 4.1–5.19.

demand to see and check on a child). Nevertheless, even in the best case-scenario, there is no guarantee of any inspection or safeguarding. This has been a significant factor in exacerbating the problem of "illegal schools", which are not licensed or regulated in any way.

Department of Education guidance makes clear that home schooling families may very properly use external tutors for some purposes (and it would clearly be detrimental to educational outcomes and the aims of the law, for example, to forbid home-schoolers paying for their children to attend an art class). They may also meet with other home-schooling families and share resources, which again is within the spirit of the law in relation to promoting a rounded and effective educational experience.

Notwithstanding, the government guidance explicitly warns in plain language that groups of five or more children being taught communally will be classified as learning within a school setting, and that operating an unregistered school may amount to a criminal offence. The Office for Standards in Education, Children's Services and Schools ("Ofsted") has power to enter, inspect and close down such underground schools.[15] Unfortunately, this is of limited use when the lack of monitoring in respect of the individual children attending them means that it is easy for communities minded to behave unlawfully to simply decamp and set up a similar unregulated school elsewhere. This is an endemic issue with some small subsections of the Jewish and Islamic communities in England. Public authorities are hampered in tackling this evil, but there is, undoubtedly, a lack of political will to seriously undermine the immense latitude allowed for parental choices in relation to the education and upbringing of children. In addition, the rest of the educational landscape needs to be seen in light of this ordering of priorities.

2.2 *Private Schools*

Private or independent schools are educational establishments not in receipt of direct financial support (although they are permitted to benefit indirectly via Charity Law, for example receiving significant tax concessions). Commentators like James, Kenway and Boden observe that this is politically controversial, and are justified in the point, although it must be noted that private schooling has a hugely significant place in English culture and imagination (Malcolm et al. 2022). It is seen as something aspirational, and for instance, the popularity of the *Harry Potter* franchise is linked to nostalgic ideas of English boarding schools. In some ways, they are the direct descendant of twentieth century children's novels featuring protagonists from socially disadvantaged backgrounds who break into this privileged world, overcome prejudice and find themselves beloved heroes and heroines (See for instance, the satirical, but fond, treatment of this genre by Neil Gaiman in the *Ocean at the End of the Lane*) (Gaiman 2013).

[15] Ibid paras 6.6 and 6.7.

The romance and perceived desirability of private schooling has such a deeply rooted place in English culture and imagination, that it is very difficult to imagine it being abolished via means of legal reform. Concerns about their role in perpetuating social inequality are met with the counter argument that they relieve pressure on the strained public sector. Furthermore, it would make little or no sense to permit such broad scope for parental action in respect of home-schooling, and simultaneously restrict families' ability to opt for fee-paying education.

Private institutions have a lot of freedom in relation to their curriculum, environment and ethos. It should be highlighted that even though many independent schools have a marked religious identity or tradition, state supported schools are also permitted to have a defined and marked faith character. As we shall discuss further, this is not uncontroversial, but is a long established part of the English educational system. The truth is that religious schools in the private sector generally draw less debate; the combined considerations that such institutions are not reliant on public funding, and that parents (whether paying or choosing to take advantage of a bursary scheme) are de facto paying customers. There is nothing oppressive or problematic about delivering a service that clients have requested, on the one hand, and businesses have a vested interest in cultivating, rather than alienating, those to whom they hope to sell their wares.

Of course, it might be questioned whether this model of parent as client and school as a provider is desirable from a child-centred perspective, given the vested interest that the school has in prioritising parental preferences over those of pupils should there be a clash. This is a valid point, but it can be seen as a natural and inevitable consequence of the wider balance between family autonomy and child autonomy (Gilmore and Bainham 2013).

Private schools are free to determine their curriculum, including in relation to religious studies, but must offer education on relationships and sex. Moreover, the environment, buildings and quality of teaching must satisfy minimum standards outlined in law, and this must be monitored by regular mandatory inspections.[16] The regime does permit institutions to determine which of the available inspectorates they wish to engage with, having a choice between Ofsted (which undertakes regular inspection of state funded schools as one part of its remit), the Independent Schools Inspectorate or the Schools Inspection Service (UK Government 2022a, b, c). All of these frameworks of oversight ensure that the standard of teaching is acceptable and that the social, physical and emotional needs of pupils are appropriately cared for. Despite the fact that in some ways the system operates on a quotidian basis by the application of "soft law", rather than with the constant menace of hard legal sanction, this does not mean it is ineffective. Obviously, Ofsted has the independence and rigor to be expected from a publicly funded entity, while the other two regulatory schemes not only have reporting powers to Government, they also have the influence

[16] Education (Independent School Standards) Regulations 2014.

of peer pressure and reputational capital.[17] It would clearly been damaging for both an inspecting body and all schools associated with it, were it found to have endorsed an institution which was seriously failing its pupils.

As a related issue while it is true that private schools have considerable freedom in which to determine their own curriculum, this cannot be divorced from the realities and demands of life in contemporary Western Europe. A school failing to equip students for tertiary education or the world of work is highly unlikely to pass through the fire of inspection unscathed, and a reasonable spread of subjects must be taught. Equally, there is no explicit legal requirement to deliver a minimum percentage of the teaching content in English, nor even to ensure that pupils taught primarily in another language gain fluency in English. This flexibility exists for good reasons, and it is possible to envisage a wide range of circumstances in which parents might wish a child to learn primarily in a non-English tongue, e.g. families from non-Anglophone jurisdictions, who reside in England for a brief time for work purposes, or a community wanting to set up a Cornish language primary school to follow on from a Cornish nursery framework (Movyans Skolyow Meythrin 2023). Yet the lack of specificity which is characteristic of England's legal model more generally does not render the borders of discretion infinitely plastic, and it would be very difficult to envisage a private school meeting the standards of any inspecting body if it did not demonstrate that pupils attained an acceptable level of fluency in written and oral English.

Nonetheless, academic rigor is not the only limitation placed upon the de facto operation of private schools. The concern for what Victorians might have termed moral upbringing remains present, as we shall discuss further below, although many of the values being inculcated have evolved. The contemporary law demands that within independent schools, Equality Law, as well as liberal democratic values and human dignity, must be respected (UK Government 2014).

As might be anticipated, there are also conditions about the suitability of teaching staff,[18] even though the specific qualifications demanded of professionals in state-maintained schools are not imposed by law in the private sphere (UK Government 2022a, b, c). The nature of premises and accommodation are also regulated, in order to ensure that the health, safety and wellbeing of students are not placed in jeopardy.

Two things in particular are worth noting before we move on. First, despite the fact that there are far more controls, both legal and practical, in place than we see for education in a home-schooling environment, there is still considerable scope given for both parental and educational freedom. Secondly, the more prescriptive elements of legislation in force relate not to academic considerations, but the aspects of school life geared to forming the inchoate worldviews of children and teenagers. Even in the private sector, there is a recognition that despite the generous deference to parental choice and family autonomy, the wider community has a vested interest in the education of children.

[17] Education and Skills Act 2008, s.106.

[18] Ibid, pp. 34–37.

2.3 State Funded Schools

As we have already touched upon, religion is not excluded from the publicly funded educational sector, and some so called "faith schools" are state maintained. Institutions with a defined religious alignment are commonly referred to as faith schools, and even governmental authorities sometimes use this label (UK Government 2023a, b). This is somewhat misleading, because it gives the erroneous impression that other schools have a secular, or least religiously neutral, nature, which is far from accurate. The principal difference between schools with a designated religious character (herein after referred to a "DRC Schools") and other state schools (which we shall label "Non-DRC Schools") is, as Vickers correctly observes, whether or not they can take advantage of legislative concessions within the Equality Law framework (Vickers 2011).

The divide between DRC and Non-DRC is distinct from a further division found in contemporary Education Law, namely that of governance arrangements. There are a range of different models operating within the state supported sector (UK Government 2023a, b). To give a brief overview, there are: Maintained Schools (community schools and foundation schools); Free Schools and Academies. Maintained schools are all funded and overseen by the local authority, and in the case of community schools this control is very direct, with the authority employing staff and overseeing pupil admissions. In contrast, foundation schools employ staff and have responsibility for admission.

Furthermore, where academies are concerned, funding and external oversight come directly from the Department for Education, via the Education and Skills Funding Agency. Academies enjoy far greater autonomy than maintained schools, they are not obliged to follow the National Curriculum (although given that pupils sit the same exams as the rest of the state sector, radical divergence at secondary level might be problematic), and they are free to set their own term times. Some schools, often with high rates of academic success, voluntarily choose to opt for academic status, and at the same time, any local authority school judged "inadequate" (effectively failing an inspection) will have no choice but to transition to academy status. Thus, these extremely autonomous state funded schools tended to be either high or low performing.

Academies are run by academy trusts, which are not for profit companies, and might be run as a single school or a cluster. Sometimes academies have "sponsors", and these can take the form of a range of legal persons: businesses, faith groups, universities, other schools or voluntary groups. Free Schools have essentially the same governance arrangements as academies, but are founded as new initiatives, in contrast to academies which will have converted from a previous incarnation as a different type of school (UK Government 2023a, b).

Even from this whistle-stop tour, it is very clear that England currently has a bewildering array of governance arrangements, and these are potentially significant for the educational experience of pupils who join them. For example, an obligation to follow the national curriculum versus freedom to locally determine the teaching program is not a minor distinction. Yet it is doubtful how far the public at large understands the range of models in place, or the implications for each one. This is problematic, in and of itself, given its negative implications for transparency and freedom of parental choice, but the presence of sponsors in the background of many academy contexts has heightened controversy still further.

The policy of academies has been championed by Conservative, Labour and Coalition Governments, and underpinned by a suspicion of local authority control, associating this model with stagnation claimed by policy-makers to come from a lack of competition or external drive for improvement. Instead, marketisation, or at least quasi-marketisation, was heralded as a magic bullet, but unfortunately, there is mounting evidence that what was touted as a miracle cure may well have been snake oil, at least for many communities. A small number of academies have performed well, and built vibrant educational communities in place of predecessor schools which had let down generations of children. Nonetheless, in sharp contrast, there have been a number of scandals around financial irregularities and disaster, sometimes stemming from misfeasance or incompetence, or on other occasions being the result from ambitious acquisitions of further schools into an academy cluster.[19] If this were not sufficient cause for concern, there is also mounting evidence that not everyone eagerly clamouring to run a school via an academy trust had the necessary expertise and understanding to perform effectively.

Another particularly unsuccessful feature of the academy model, driven by a combination of political policy translated into legal structures, and pragmatic considerations at a grassroots level, is that there is no effective way of de-transitioning, because once a school has jumped, or been plucked from, the local authority's grasp, there is no going back. Like an amoeba engulfing another cell, a school entering this model will see its reserves and buildings absorbed into the legal entity of the trust, and it cannot, therefore, reverse this legal phagocytosis.

Moreover, even if matters do become dire enough to be untenable, the prospect of seeking refuge with another, more successful academy trust are not always good. A school saddled with poorly maintained buildings and tatty equipment, combined with demoralised staff and alienated pupils, is not an especially attractive prospect to take on. When financial challenges with ongoing implications are added into the equation (e.g. private finance initiative contracts of long duration which have gone sour. These schemes are intended to relieve the taxpayer of finding capital upfront for major projects, but have the draw back of leaving the public purse making payments for decades, sometimes in a context of substandard service provision), it is easy to understand why other trusts would not rush to take on the "opportunity".

This backdrop of turbulence, complexity, and not infrequently dissatisfaction, in relation to the governance in schools, is a crucial consideration in relation to the discussion on which we are about to embark. We are moving to look at major legal developments, and shall focus, in particular, on the ideological controversies

---

[19] "Theft and Fraud in Academy Trust Accounts", *Times Educational Supplement* (3/3/2020) https://www.tes.com/magazine/archive/theft-and-fraud-revealed-academy-trusts-accounts (accessed 11/1/2023).

which are being felt in contemporary schools, reflecting fissures in society generally. However, their implications can only be fully understood if the degree of autonomy and instability inherent in the operation of contemporary educational structures is grasped. In other words, many legislative provisions are focused in guaranteeing a balance between the freedom of the quasi-market, on the one hand, and the societal interest in the developing ethics and worldview of young people, on the other, but it must be remembered that the governing bodies of schools will not necessarily, and automatically, reflect the will and desires of the local community, parents or pupils. This is very different from the literal market place of the private sector, and schools may find themselves in the control of academy trusts and sponsors not entirely of their choosing.

3 Major Legal Developments

English society has been rocked in recent years by anxiety over extremism, particularly in the forms of Islamic and Far Right extremism, as well as clashes over sexuality and gender identity. They will be dealt with towards the end of this analysis. These tensions have, in turned, spilled over into legal battles in the educational arena, and in both contexts, there is a struggle to influence the narrative being presented to future citizens. If the narrative is in the control of governing authorities of academy trusts who do not enjoy the support of school communities, then conflicts will inevitably be exacerbated. The language used to describe it may no longer be one of moral formation, but the essential project of moulding the worldview of young people around mainstream societies norms remains unchanged. Nonetheless, in order to fully understand this, we need to pause to consider the explicit ideological orientation of schools, and in particular the legal arrangements in place in respect of their defined religious character.

What makes "faith schools" so different? It must be stressed, once again, that the answer to this question is avowedly not the involvement of religion in collective school life. It is often counter-intuitive to people not familiar with the English paradigm to learn that all state schools are, in some sense, faith schools (Sandberg 2012). As Rivers explains, this a practical consequence of the structures of an established religion (Rivers 2010). It is striking that the Non-DRC schools are required by statute to hold a daily act of worship,[20] which is '*wholly or mainly of a broadly Christian character*',[21] a feature of the law which undermines any claim that England might have a secular educational framework.

Having said this, it is key to appreciate that the mandatory act of daily worship is interpreted in an expansive and inclusive manner. Most schools have some form of morning gathering which is partly administrative in nature, with reminders about rules about acceptable uses of footballs or the contents of lunchboxes. The "worship"

[20] *Education Act 1996*, c 56, s 390.

[21] Ibid at Sch 20.

element often takes the form of a short moral or philosophical reflection given by a teacher, and the "broadly Christian" character is frequently reflected in appeals to general principles which most people of good will would endorse, regardless of their spiritual orientation, e.g. showing kindness to other members of the community.

Similarly, non-DRC schools are required to provide religious education, but once again there is a parental right to withdraw pupils.[22] Every local authority is bound by legislation to establish a Standing Advisory Council on Religious Education (SACRE),[23] in order to regulate the content of religious education in state funded non-DRC schools.[24] Church of England representation is mandatory, but the arrangements specifically allow for the presence from other faith groups and quasi-faith groups (e.g. humanism). Although the non-statutory governmental guidance promoting the incorporation of multiple religious perspectives onto the SACRE technically has the status of "soft law", and is therefore non-binding, in the vast majority of areas it is accepted and seen as desirable (HM Government 2010). Working with grassroots faith groups to ensure that children gain an nuanced and accurate appreciation of the various beliefs in their surrounding district, as well as the wider world, is generally regarded as a positive project by public authorities.

Therefore, the key characteristic which renders DRC schools special is not their engagement with religion per se, but the manner within which this can happen. They may lawfully implement what would otherwise be unlawful discrimination of religious grounds when it comes to pupil admission, and give places preferentially to pupils from the designated believing community.[25] It must be acknowledged that this is not without limitation, as it may only be exercised if the school in question is oversubscribed.[26] This detail has critical implications on the ground for families hoping to send their child to such an institution, but at the same time, it is telling in relation to the principles underpinning the policy. The intention of the law as drafted was to allow religious believers to send their children into an education environment in line with their worldview, or at least to facilitate this. Moreover, the purpose of the statutory concession is not to enable schools to develop a monochrome religious and cultural environment, shielding pupils from wider English society, or transmit radically divergent views.

It is also fair to observe that the law *enables* DRC schools to discriminate with regard to pupil admission, but it does not require them to do so. Some institutions, for example, a considerable number run by the Church of England, have consciously opted to reject this policy, preferring instead to foster their particular ethos in an inclusive manner, whilst welcoming all perspective students on an equal basis (Romain 2013). Nevertheless, it would be disingenuous not to concede that many DRC schools do exercise their option to discriminate, and are able to do so effectively because over subscription is extremely common. One factor in this is, without doubt, that many

[22] School Standards and Framework Act 1998, s. 71.

[23] Education Act 1996, s. 390.

[24] Education Act 2002, s. 80.

[25] Equality Act 2010, Schedule 11.

[26] Schools Admission Code for 2007, paras 2.41–3.

publicly funded DRC schools have a reputation for academic success, high quality pastoral care and a wide spread of enrichment activities, making them a desirable prospect for both parents and students.[27] Given the disarray in some parts of the public sector, flagship schools are highly sought after.

As Johnes and Andrews argue, the reasons behind the impressive performance of these schools are complicated, but it is demonstrable that social factors play a key role (Johnes and Andrews 2017). A high percentage of pupils arrive having enjoyed numerous social, economic and cultural advantages in their upbringing and education beforehand, and therefore, have the dice weighed in their favour from the very outset as far as exam performance is concerned. This tends to create a cycle of self-seeding, whereby socially advantaged parents of younger pupils see data and hear anecdotes about the positive attributes of the school, opt to send their children there, and help to perpetuate its success. It is the equal and opposite effect to the downward cycle into which struggling schools, particularly academies, may fall.

The greatest focus for disquiet about this aspect of the educational framework relates to the exacerbation of social inequality, and the widening of the gap between different sections of English society. It is not primarily targeted at the DRC character of the schools, nor debates about their governance status (indeed, as noted above, it is common for both coveted and failing schools to function as academies). It must, of course, be conceded that Humanist and Secularist organisations campaign against state funded DRC institutions, but this (legitimately in democratic society) reflects their particular social and political agenda, whilst the preponderance of attacks are focused on the implications of sustaining structures of social marginalisation (Humanists UK 2023). Even though there are occasional expressions of frustration from parents about the effort sometimes required to engineer an admission (Penman 2010), and disquiet from faith communities around insincere expressions of belief and belonging, this is not a high profile or continual issue in public debates.[28]

It is vital to emphasise that religion in the public square is not a hot-button issue, tied to political identities and loyalties in England, in a comparable way to that of many other jurisdictions. Both the left and ring of the political landscape have believing and non-believing elements (Conservative Humanists 2023), and debates around the future of matters such as Church of England establishment are possible without drawing out profound seams of ire and bitterness (Bates 2022). Support for DRC schools has come from Governments of all political colours, in the same way that the academy horse has been backed by both major sides. Furthermore, the nature of the academy governance structure, with the possibility of conferring responsibility for running schools on different types of enterprise, has given a new dimension to education with a faith-based character. The truth is that the problems in finding organisations willing to take on failing academies in dire straits, outlined above, are sometimes solved by religious groups prepared to do this as part of their commitment

[27] Godfrey and Morris (2018).

[28] "Faking Faith to Get Children a Heysham School Place", *Lancaster Guardian* (08/11/2016) <https://www.lancasterguardia.uk/news/faking-faith-to-get-children-a-heysham-school-place-658130> (Accessed 11/1/2023).

to social engagement. This reality is potentially problematic for a range of reasons: vulnerable members of society should not have ideological environments imposed upon them as a price for reasonable education, and spiritual motivations for taking on schools in financial trouble can lead to over stretching resources to snapping point.[29] Nonetheless, Governments are frequently inclined to overlook such issues when an apparent resolution to intractable challenges, or even an acute crisis, are offered.

As England continues to emerge from the devastation of a pandemic, neither the Government nor the opposition parties are proposing to dismantle the academy system. The Labour Party has indicated that it wishes to tighten up regulation, addressing abuses, increasing oversight and clawing back the freedom over curriculum setting.[30] It has also indicated that it will not force schools within local authority control to transition to this governance model, but has made it clear that it will equally not end the academy system or interfere with high performing academies. Consequently, the patchwork quilt of governance structures will probably stay, should these policy statements come in the fullness of time to reach the statute book (which is, of course, by no means a certainty).

In summary, both DRC schools, and a mixed economy of governance, including academies, are relatively fixed and stable parts of the legal and political landscape, but this does not mean that there are not live and ongoing struggles, particularly around worldview and environment, as we have already indicated. These legal conflicts, as might be anticipated, reflect the fault lines in English society more generally, and the prevailing anxieties of the day. Policy considerations on transgender issues are more likely to result in litigation than questions directly arising from a school's religious ethos.

For example, conservative Christian parents Nigel and Sally Rowe threatened legal action against a Church of England primary school, which had opted to respect Equality Law and the gender identity of a transgender pupil (Dyer 2021). Their initial complaint was that their young son was confused by a classmate changing from a boy to a girl, and they feared that he would be disciplined for expressing this confusion at school. There was no evidence to support that this would have happened, however, and that their son's understandable curiosity about the world would meet with anything other than age-appropriate responses to questioning. Probably for this reasoning, the claim was not pursued. Nevertheless, they did subsequently successfully bring an action for judicial review, challenging the decision of the Department for Education not to intervene in the local authority's transgender uniform policy.[31] It should be noted that requiring a review of a policy does not equate to having demonstrated that it was substantially inappropriate, but this is not a central concern at present, because

[29] "DFE lets Harris and Oasis off the hook for £9.4 m academy sponsor contributions", *Schools Week* (11/12/2021), https://schoolsweek.co.uk/academy-sponsor-contributions-harris-dfe-write-off/ (accessed 11/1/2023).

[30] "Labour fleshes out schools policy with promise of "ambitious" new laws", *Schools Weeks* (28/9/2022), https://schoolsweek.co.uk/labour-fleshes-out-schools-policy-with-promise-of-ambitious-new-laws/ (accessed 11/1/2023).

[31] "Parents force review of schools trans guidance", *The Times* (24/9/2022) https://www.thetimes.co.uk/article/parents-force-review-of-school-trans-guidance-m35dvvf8p (accessed 11/1/23).

the key question here was that a conflict over gender and sexuality arose between Christian parents and a Church of England school, reflecting wider social fissures. Clashes over these questions are indeed witnessed within faith groups and political parties, and do not split participants along easily predictable lines.

Nonetheless, this is not to suggest that legal clashes never arise where battle lines are drawn cleanly between secular, civic values and a religious ideology. For instance, in a litigation over children spending time with a transgender parent, courts recognised a factual concern that the minors involved would be subject to discriminatory behaviour in their state funded school DRC school if the relationship continued.[32] However, as the Court of Appeal robustly outlined, such behaviour would have been unlawful, and it would have been serious for public authorities, including courts, to tolerate it unchallenged.

The handling of the case can partly be explained by the context in which it arose. It was a dispute between estranged parents over the upbringing of children, and as such as the primary objective of the court was to guarantee the welfare of those children.[33] The judge at first instance deemed that it was necessary to examine the factual backdrop as it was in reality, rather than as it ought to have been, and make decisions on the basis of what was likely to happen to those children in the future. In truth, no outcome of the dispute was going to be good, as the circumstances were tragic for all involved. The parents were from a conservative part of Ultra-Orthodox Judaism, and the biological father of the children was transgender and felt no longer able to hide this and continue living as male. He opted to transition and live as a woman, but this meant leaving his community and effectively cutting all ties. The mother argued that if her children were permitted to keep in contact with their father, they would be socially ostracised as a moral and spiritual risk to their peers and the wider community. The finding at first instance accepting this, and refusing the father's application to spend time with the children was deeply unsatisfactory, but the decision of the appellate court to simply sweep aside such anxieties was also troubling. The dilemma required the wisdom of Solomon to resolve, and perhaps English judges cannot be castigated too much for failing to meet such an unattainable standard. For the purposes of our current investigation, the core point is that the approach of both courts was inevitably very different to what would have been witnessed in a Public Law clash around education policy or the governance of a school directly. The likely outlook of the school community was merely one factual element in the wider best interests' decision, being taken in light of what was undoubtedly an agonising situation for all parties.

It is telling that we do not find large numbers of instances of either contemporary or historic cases of battles about alleged indoctrination accusation within DRC schools, and it is true that their *raison d'etre* is to provide education within a faith-based ethos, finding this reflected in the governance arrangements. This explains why, for example, as far as teacher recruitment is concerned, DRC schools are granted special accommodation in the application of Equality Laws. We should also note that the nature of

---

[32] *Re M* [2017] EWCA Civ 2164.

[33] Children Act 1989, s. 1.

this latitude depends upon the precise arrangements in place, meaning that we cannot entirely divorce the questions of governance and ideology. For instance, voluntary controlled and foundation schools may take faith into account during the appointment process for a head-teacher,[34] and also have the option of allocating up to one fifth of appointments as '*reserved teachers*'. This enables applicants during the recruitment process to be filtered according to their '*fitness and competence*' to deliver religious education in harmony with the faith-based character of the employing institution.[35]

Furthermore, the fitness of teaching staff is not measured exclusively on the basis of their knowledge of doctrine. In certain circumstances, staff at DRC schools undermining religious instruction by behaving in way that was incompatible with doctrine could legitimately face disciplinary action, and in the case of head-teachers and reserved teachers, even dismissal, if their actions were grave enough to undermine their '*fitness and competence*' to perform the role they have been appointed for. Furthermore, DRC which are voluntary aided enjoy even greater discretion: faith related considerations may be taken into consideration when appointing *all* teaching staff and are a possible ground for disciplinary action and dismissal.[36]

Therefore, we would not seek to deny that the legal machinery in place to guard the religious ethos of the school is weak or unimportant. Our observation is simply that in practical terms, the shape of the law is not producing clashes with aggrieved parents alarmed that teachers are intending to instil religious values or force elements of practice on pupils against their will. There may be problematic instances and cases, but we have not found evidence that DRC schools, regardless of their governance structure and levels of autonomy, are fostering oppressively religious environments in ways which are boiling over into litigation.

As stated earlier, we have already acknowledged the wider degree of flexibility given to DRC schools in relation to the nature and content of teaching. Religious education falls outside of the national curriculum, and as might be anticipated, DRC institutions deliver a program which aligns to their chosen ethos (UK Government 2023a, b). The freedom that institutions have to determine the structure for the delivery of other subjects varies according to the form of governance arrangements, but all come within the umbrella of state oversight.[37]

One flashpoint bucking the trend of relative harmony is the topic of evolution and creationism, but even here there have not been a plethora of challenges from concerned families. It has generally been third parties asserting that the State needs to take a more hard-line approach to the presentation of narratives in conflict with mainstream scientific understanding being given space within science lessons, as opposed to religious education (Turner 2016). Having said which, it would be unjust to give the impression that teaching of creationism or intelligent design is widespread in English schools, and that authorities have been supine while this has continue, as, in fairness, the debates have involved a small minority of institutions. This may

[34] *School Standards and Framework Act 1998*, c 31, s 60 (as amended).

[35] Ibid at s. 58.

[36] Ibid at s 60.

[37] Education Act 2005, s5 and Education and Inspectors Act 2006.

partly be because the shadow of the state inspectorate means that there are limits upon the nature of the material which can be conveyed, and it is also the case that the overwhelming majority of DRC would have no desire to promote such material, as it is not a mainstream position within the faith groups most commonly represented in defining ethos, e.g. Anglican, Roman Catholic. It is also fair to observe that belief in Darwinism or literal accounts of Scripture are not powerful social talismans in England. They are not indicative of voting choices on other issues, and not the source of high profile and bitter conflicts.

Of far more concern is the spectre of extremism. Safeguards against this are built into the legal framework, and schools seen to be presenting ideas which undermine individual liberty, the rule of law or democratic principles,[38] would be far more likely to bring down swift and decisive regulatory action.[39]

There have been instances where extremist groups have been feared to have infiltrated and misappropriated school authorities, and both the State and the wider society have responded decisively. The high profile "Trojan Horse" scandal is a particularly powerful instance of this, when authorities at a number of Birmingham schools were accused of attempting to introduce a hard-line Islamic ethos into state funded institutions, and (as the label implies) to do so without attracting undue attention and consequently, interference.[40] The legacy of this affair has been extremely divisive, with some factions claiming that it was no more than an Islamophobic hoax, and others warning of the dangers of so lightly dismissing worries over genuinely alarming developments. The truth, as it often the case, is probably less binary than either of these perspectives imply. There is evidence of some very inappropriate conduct on the part of some figures running these schools, but nothing to suggest an organised conspiracy on the scale implied. For our current purposes, however, the point is that there is vigilance about the worldview being presented in state-funded schools, and legal and political action will be mobilised if this is seen as potentially harming children and young people.

In addition to extremism, to which we have already alluded, the other area in which this will probably arise is gender/sexuality. Both themes are issues which stalk the imagination and fears of English society at present, and as such, these are the questions which generate clashes over the indoctrination of children, far more than creationism or prayer in assembly. By and large, public authorities are trying to hold a middle line, and courts, needless to say, must maintain the norms and neutrality of the legal framework. So, for instance, protests around Birmingham schools, sparked by concerns, stemming in large part from the dissemination of misinformation, about the nature and content of teaching on human relationships and gender, resulted in prohibition on assembly and demonstration within a designated

---

[38] Department for Education, "Promoting Fundamental British Values as part of SMSC in Schools: Departmental Advice for Maintained Schools", 2014.

[39] Ofsted "School Inspection Handbook" (1/07/2022) <https://www.gov.uk/government/publications/school-inspection-handbook-eif/school-inspection-handbook> (accessed 11/1/2023).

[40] "A History of the Trojan Horse Scandal", *The Week* (17/2/2022) https://www.theweek.co.uk/news/uk-news/955783/history-of-trojan-horse-scandal-true-story (accessed 11/1/2023).

area.[41] Nevertheless, there has been no decisive action from the national Government or Parliament effectively clarifying the parameters of what is both permitted and required within English state funded school on the subject of LGBTQ + inclusion, largely because there is not sufficient consensus within political parties. All sides of the debate are fearful that their opponents will go too far in influencing children and young people, so are vigilant, but no one faction is strong enough to force through its perspective.

It should be stressed that all schools have a specific duty to consult with parents in devising Relationships Education, but the Government has made it clear that there is no right of withdrawal from this aspect of the curriculum (UK Government 2022a, b, c). In theory, this is a field in which the needs of children have been clearly prioritised, by both executive and legislature,[42] over and above the desire to respect parental control of the material and narratives to which those are exposed.[43] Sex education is not offered to pupils until secondary school, and there is an option for parental withdrawal in respect of this aspect of the program, up until three terms before the young person turns sixteen, at which point the pupils themselves may elect to attend these classes, irrespective of parental wishes.

It should be noted that the duty to offer relationships education during primary years, and sex and relationships education at secondary stage, applies to DRC as well as non-DRC institutions, and to the independent sector. As a result, there is no escape from the provisions at an organisational level with the lawful school system. Some (alternative to concerns) have been expressed over school authorities communicating with parents in an attempt to orchestrate a mass opt out of sex education (Woode 2019).

In fairness, there is a broad political consensus that it is important for individual welfare and collective social needs that young people grow up understanding their bodies, the mechanics of human reproduction, the practicalities of sexual health (e.g., ways in which STIs may be transmitted, prevented and treated), as well as the dangers of abusive relationships. However, beyond this, the border of consensus ends, and ideological factions are keen to police what children and teenagers might learn in a school setting. Consequently, we are likely to keep witnessing ongoing conflict in this area for the foreseeable future.

---

[41] "LGBT School Exclusion Zone Decision Put Off", *BBC News* (18/10/2019) https://www.bbc.co.uk/news/uk-england-birmingham-50104211 (accessed 11/1/2023).

[42] Statutory guidance has been issued pursuant to Education Act 2002 s80A and Education Act 1996 s408.

[43] Department for Education, "Relationships Education, Relationships and Sex Education (RSE) and Health Education" (25/06/2019, updated 13/09/2021).

4 Outlook of Future Developments/Emerging Issues in Education Law

As we observed above, the leading opposition party has announced its intention to tighten up governance arrangements for academies, but essentially to continue with the current system of hybrid governance arrangements, should it be successful at the next election (and of course, should it find sufficient parliamentary time and agreement to implement its policy aims. The proposal is very much one of adjusting and improving the current model, as opposed to a legislative slash and burn tactic of removing one set of legal arrangements and replacing them with another. The truth is that both major political groupings are sufficiently invested in the academy project, and if they retreated and changed tactic, they would probably lose face and capital, in some instances literal as well as metaphorical).[44] Furthermore, at a time of ongoing fiscal strain, there is no readily available web of resources on which to draw in order to establish a new system. Local government, already staggering under economic and administrative burdens, is in no position to easily resume responsibility for schools now in receipt of central finances and independently managed.

Although there are ongoing concerns that government bail outs for academy trusts in financial crisis are costing the public purse dearly, there is an absence of practical options to otherwise address the situation.[45] Academies, like Private Finance Initiatives, were a means of public authorities deferring expenses until a later date, but did not come with any ready mechanism to extricate the state sector from debt or ongoing burdens should the arrangements become problematic in any way, shape or form. Under these circumstances, bailing out a vessel taking on water is preferable to allowing it to sink when there is no lifeboat on board, and precisely for these reasons, it is difficult to envisage major reform to the basic governance arrangements in place.

Nevertheless, based on the suggestions of the shadow Education Secretary, there may be a renegotiation of the relationship between governance structure and autonomy when it comes to curriculum setting and other academic decisions. Such approach would potentially, at least, allow for a greater degree of uniformity than we currently observe, and would perhaps mitigate some of the pockets of abuse in the present. Whilst the teaching of creationism is not high on the public and media agenda, no mainstream educationalists are advocating it as desirable, and a regime in which schools were required to follow a designated science curriculum, for example, might be an improvement.

[44] "It's all about the money: The REAL reason behind forced academisation", *Schools Week* (14/4/2016) https://schoolsweek.co.uk/its-all-about-the-money-the-real-reason-behind-forced-academisation/.

[45] "DFE lets Harris and Oasis off the hook for £9.4 m academy sponsor contributions", *Schools Week* (11/12/2021) https://schoolsweek.co.uk/academy-sponsor-contributions-harris-dfe-write-off/ (accessed 11/1/2023).

In terms of proposals from the Government, it is telling that: (1) Of the two historical elements of concern around education, the economy productivity and the developing worldview of future citizens, the latter is a source of far more urgent public concern, particularly in light of the twin issues of extremism and LBGTQ + issues; (2) The focus of discussion should be, in fact, on the latter.

For that reason, Prime Minister Rishi Sunak's announcement of plans for every pupil to study mathematics until the age of eighteen has come as surprise (Mitchell 2023). At least one commentator has opined that this proposal is slightly less useful than an initiative to provide a free cactus for every family in the nation. The stated intention behind the plan is to enable the future workforce to develop the skills that they need to maximise their employment opportunities, or productivity more generally. Significantly, more critics have suggested that this is a tactic to distract the political arena from a context of industrial strife, an acute cost of life crisis and a host of other problems to which there is no easy or immediate solution.

This is certainly good reason to fear that this is another example of education being a convenient political vehicle, especially in a tight corner. Sunak has no background as an educationalist, and no robust, objective evidence has been put forward to support the idea that obligatory maths until the age of eighteen would benefit the population as a whole.[46] Furthermore, worryingly, no bright line distinction appears to have been drawn between numeracy and financial literacy, and the reality is that many academic, but arts/humanities leaning pupils, will have attained the former long before reaching the age of sixteen, having mastered percentages, statistics and basic algebra to a level sufficient not only for their chosen career paths, but also to make informed choices about evidence on risk with regard to healthcare decisions or selecting a mortgage. They will no need more of this fundamental input, and will not gain from studying more mathematics, as opposed to devoting time to a pursuit that may benefit them to a much greater degree, and better match their aptitude, e.g. attaining greater fluency in a language.

Equally, there are other pupils for whom more basic skills are a struggle, but helping them effectively is a task which requires professional knowledge and an evidential approach, not a slick sound bite and a blanket policy. It is far from clear that labelling the input that they need as "mathematics" will do anything other than further demoralise and alienate them. Formulating the detail of educational policy and strategy requires expertise, dialogue and nuance, in ways that do not always fit neatly with political rallying calls.

In justice to the Prime Minister, the proposal has only recently been circulated, and there may be more subtly than first appears, but to date, this development has all of the hallmarks of an amendment to the education law framework rooted in political popularism and whims, rather than rational policy making. As observed at the outset of our discussion, a focus on the interests of children is perceived as a shrewd strategy to garner public sympathy and support.

Another possible motivation on the part of Sunak is to recall the policies of Margaret Thatcher, whose legacy still divides opinion starkly. To a considerable

[46] "Rishi Sunak: About Me", *UK Conservatives*. https://www.rishisunak.com/about-me.

number of right-wing conservatives, she is associated with a golden age, and her own background as a chemistry influenced an ideological prioritisation of science within the educational system (Guise 2014). There may be perhaps an element of a beleaguered politician seeking to associate himself with an era and ideology viewed by many of his supporters with nostalgia.

All things considered, the dimension of Education Law is, perhaps regrettably, strongly tied to politics, and ultimately, what the law requires to be taught in schools is a matter for a politically dominated Parliament.

5 Conclusion

The foregoing discussion demonstrates that some key, overarching themes within Education Law and reform have been reprised many times over the last two hundred years. The vulnerability of this area of the juridical framework to be treated as a political football is all too apparent, and the latest attempts to reform control of the curriculum alone the lines of what appears to be a Prime Ministerial whim, rather than the result of coherent, researched and coordinated policy, are undoubtedly problematic, but they are in no sense unusual if the legal landscape of the past two centuries is surveyed. Enactments detailing what will be taught, how and to whom, have been fashioned more by the tides of political fortune than the work of independent commissions or other more balanced advisors.

We are not suggesting that neutrality is achievable, or even aspirational when it comes to educational frameworks, but an evidence-based approach would be preferable to appeals to emotive rallying calls. Moreover, reasoned and transparent decision-making would at least enable public debate about Education Law to be centred on the benefits and drawbacks of identifiable policies. Any policies put forward are likely to reflect the two core concerns which have been driving the field of education law in England since at least the Victorian era: (1) How to equip future members of adult society to be economically productive; and (2) How to ensure that the worldview of young people is shaped in accordance with the prevailing values of the community of which they will form an active part. These values change radically over time, but it was disingenuous to pretend that any human society is not at pains to transmit its cultural ideas and beliefs. Whether these be the Anglicanism of the XIX century English establishment, or the equality and diversity of the XXI century, the motivation to pass on what are deemed positive modes of thinking and doing, can be discerned.

At the present moment, English society is profoundly divided over core values in two respects: (1) How best to confront extremism; and (2) Questions surrounding gender identity and humanity. These tensions make the challenge of shaping education policy around such values almost insurmountable, as there is a lack of consensus. For this reason, the current executive actors are anxious to push this element of educational strategy into the background, and attempt to focus instead on the economic productivity question. However, addressing this without a well defined and justified strategy will not be really beneficial for anyone involved, and it is unlikely that ignoring the strong feelings and raging conflicts over prevailing worldviews will be a sustainable tactic in the long-term.

References

A history of the Trojan horse scandal. The Week, 17 Feb 2022. https://www.theweek.co.uk/news/uk-news/955783/history-of-trojan-horse-scandal-true-story. Accessed 11 Jan 2023

Bates S (2022) The church of England: has it got a prayer? The European, 29 Aug 2022. https://www.theneweuropean.co.uk/the-church-of-england-future-justin-welby/. Accessed 11 Jan 2023

Benchimol A (2016) Intellectual politics and cultural conflict in the Romantic period: Scottish Whigs, English radical and the making of the British public sphere. Taylor & Francis, London, p 126

Busher J, Jermone L (2020) The prevent duty in education: impact, enactment and implications. Springer, London, pp 1–10

Button M, Sheetz Nguyen J (eds) (2013) Victorians and the case for charity: essays on responses to English poverty by the state, the church and the Literati. McFarland, London, p 14

Conservative Humanists. https://conservativehumanists.org.uk/. Accessed 11 Jan 2023

Councillor calls for street lights to be turned on in Lincoln. The Lincolnite, 11 Sep 2022. https://thelincolnite.co.uk/2022/08/councillor-calls-for-street-lights-to-be-turned-on-in-lincoln/. Accessed 11 Jan 2023

DFE lets Harris and Oasis off the hook for £9.4m academy sponsor contributions. Schools Week, 11 Dec 2021. https://schoolsweek.co.uk/academy-sponsor-contributions-harris-dfe-write-off/. Accessed 11 Jan 2023

Dyer O (2021) Isle of Wight parents suing over trans uniform row. Isle of Wight Radio, 15 Oct 2021. https://www.iwradio.co.uk/news/isle-of-wight-news/isle-of-wight-parents-suing-government-over-trans-uniform-row/. Accessed 11 Jan 2023

Faking faith to get children a Heysham school place. Lancaster Guardian, 8 Nov 2016. https://www.lancasterguardia.uk/news/faking-faith-to-get-children-a-heysham-school-place-658130. Accessed 11 Jan 2023

Ferguson D (2019) We can't give in: the Birmingham school on the frontline of anti-LGBT protests. The Guardian, 26 Nov 2019. https://www.theguardian.com/uk-news/2019/may/26/birmingham-anderton-park-primary-muslim-protests-lgbt-teaching-rights. Accessed 11 Jan 2023

Gaiman N (2013) The ocean at the end of the lane. Headline, London, p 90

Garcìa Oliva J, Hall H (2020) People's and sovereignty: constitutional law lessons from Greenland and Denmark. Public Law 3:331–349

Gilmore S, Bainham A (2013) Children: the modern law. Family Law, Bristol, p 85

Godfrey R, Morris A (2018) Explaining high attainment in faith schools: the impact of religious education and other examinations on pupils' GCSE point scores. British J Religious Educ YEAR 30(3):211–222

Guise G (2014) Margaret Thatcher's influence on British science. Notes Rec R Soc London 68(3):301–309

HM Government (2010) Religious education in English schools: non-statutory guidance. See especially, pp 19–25

Humanists UK (2023) Faith schools why not? https://humanists.uk/campaigns/schools-and-education/faith-schools/faith-schools-why-not/. Accessed 11 Jan 2023

Hurley J (2022) Schools failing to give pupils entrepreneurial skills. The Times, 5 July 2022. https://www.thetimes.co.uk/article/schools-failing-to-give-pupils-entrepreneurial-skills-67x355tjd. Accessed 11 Jan 2023

It's all about the money: the REAL reason behind forced academisation. Schools Week, 14 Apr 2016. https://schoolsweek.co.uk/its-all-about-the-money-the-real-reason-behind-forced-academisation/. Accessed 11 Jan 2023

Johnes R, Andrews J (2017) Faith schools do better chiefly because of their pupils backgrounds. London School of Economics, 11 Jan 2017. https://blogs.lse.ac.uk/religionglobalsociety/2017/01/faith-schools-do-better-chiefly-because-of-their-pupils-backgrounds/. Accessed 10 Nov 2022

Labour fleshes out schools policy with promise of "ambitious" new laws. Schools Weeks, 28 Sep 2022. https://schoolsweek.co.uk/labour-fleshes-out-schools-policy-with-promise-of-ambitious-new-laws/. Accessed 11 Jan 2023

LGBT school exclusion zone decision put off. BBC News, 18 Oct 2019. https://www.bbc.co.uk/news/uk-england-birmingham-50104211. Accessed 11 Jan 2023

Malcolm J et al (2022) The public cost of private schools: rising fees and luxury facilities raise questions about charitable status. The Conversation, 27 June 2022. https://theconversation.com/the-public-cost-of-private-schools-rising-fees-and-luxury-facilities-raise-questions-about-charitable-status-182060. Accessed 11 Jan 2023

Mitchell D (2023) More Maths: Rishi Sunak's calculation doesn't add up. The Guardian, 8 Jan 2023. https://www.theguardian.com/commentisfree/2023/jan/08/more-maths-rishi-sunaks-calculation-doesnt-add-up. Accessed 11 Jan 2023

Movyans Skolyow Meythrin (2023) https://movyansskolyowmeythrin.yolasite.com/. Accessed 11 Jan 2023

Ofsted (2022) School inspection handbook, 1 July 2022. https://www.gov.uk/government/publications/school-inspection-handbook-eif/school-inspection-handbook. Accessed 11 Jan 2023

Parents force review of schools trans guidance. The Times, 24 Sep 2022. https://www.thetimes.co.uk/article/parents-force-review-of-school-trans-guidance-m35dvvf8p. Accessed 11 Jan 2023

Penman A (2010) I faked religion to find a school. The Independent, 30 Sep 2010. https://www.independent.co.uk/news/education/schools/i-faked-religion-to-find-a-school-2093403.html. Accessed 11 Jan 2023

Rivers J (2010) The law of organized religions. OUP, Oxford, p 234

Romain J (2013) Faith schools cannot continue their immoral policy of discrimination. The Guardian, 2 Nov 2013. https://www.theguardian.com/commentisfree/belief/2013/sep/02/faith-schools-immoral-discrimination-london-oratory. Accessed 11 Jan 2023

Sandberg R (2012) Law and religion. CUP, Cambridge, p 152

Theft and fraud in academy trust accounts. Times Educational Supplement, 3 Mar 2020. https://www.tes.com/magazine/archive/theft-and-fraud-revealed-academy-trusts-accounts. Accessed 11 Jan 2023

Turner B (2016) The new Blackwell companion to the sociology of religion. Wiley, New Jersey, p 299

UK Government (2014) Guidance on promoting British values, 27 Nov 2014. https://www.gov.uk/government/news/guidance-on-promoting-british-values-in-schools-published. Accessed 11 Jan 2023

UK Government (2022a) What is a PGCE course? https://getintoteaching.education.gov.uk/what-is-a-pgce. Accessed 15 Nov 2022

UK Government (2022b) The education hub. https://educationhub.blog.gov.uk/2022/06/10/what-is-a-free-school-everything-you-need-to-know/. Accessed 11 Jan 2023

UK Government (2022c) Relationships education, relationships and sex education, (RSE) and health education: frequently asked questions. https://www.gov.uk/government/news/relationships-education-relationships-and-sex-education-rse-and-health-education-faqs (Date of consultation 15/11/2022)

UK Government (2023a) Types of school: faith schools. https://www.gov.uk/types-of-school/faith-schools. Accessed 11 Jan 2023

UK Government (2023b) Types of school: overview. https://www.gov.uk/types-of-school. Accessed 11 Jan 2023

Vickers L (2011) Religious discrimination in schools: the employment of teachers and the public sector duty. In: Hunter-Henin M (ed) Law, religion and freedoms in Europe: education in Europe. Ashgate, Surrey, pp 87–106

Woode D (2019) Charity criticises a faith school for encouraging parents to withdraw pupils from sex education lessons. Inews, 24 July 2019. https://www.inews.co.uk/news/charity-faith-school-sex-education-lessons-stamford-hill-london-318107. Accessed 11 Jan 2023

Education Law in India

Shaun Star and Arindam Bharadwaj

1 Introduction

The Indian civilisation has had a long tradition of education as some of the oldest institutions of higher learning such as Nalanda, Ujjain and Taxila, dating back to almost fifth century BC, were located within the Indian subcontinent (Mukherjee 2015). There was also a rich tradition of free residential education in *Gurukuls* (schools) within the households of the *Gurus* (teachers), where the students would live a humble life providing their services within the household of the *Guru,* and well-off students would voluntarily pay *Guru Dakshina* (equivalent to an honorarium) after the completion of their education, in the form of land or cattle etc. as a marker of respect for the teacher (Mukherjee 2015). These institutions of higher learning declined and disappeared in modern times over several thousands of years of history, with waves of military invasions, political conflicts and colonialism (Mukherjee 2015).

In 1757, when the East India Company embarked on its political career in India, there was no education system organised and supported by the state as communities had their own indigenous system of teaching and learning (Basu 1982). From the Battle of Plassey onwards, as the British started colonising and increasing their presence throughout India, they were soon faced with the question of what their policy towards indigenous Indian institutions and practices should be (Basu 1982). For a long time they believed that there should be as little interference as possible and supported the indigenous system of education; however, after passing the Charter Act of 1813, the East India Company became responsible for education policy in India and were required to set aside an annual sum for native education with the

S. Star (✉) · A. Bharadwaj
O.P. Jindal Global University, Sonipat, India
e-mail: sstar@jgu.edu.in

A. Bharadwaj
London School of Economics and Political Science, London, UK

C. J. Russo and L. Ma (eds.), *A Comparative Analysis of Systems of Education Law*,
https://doi.org/10.1007/978-981-97-1052-2_7

aim to promote both the Oriental culture and Western science (Whitehead 2005). This also gave the colonial missionaries the right for the first time to go to India to preach the gospel and establish schools (Whitehead 2005). Soon after the first war of independence broke out in 1857 which ended the East India Company's rule, the Crown and the British Government assumed direct control of India and for the next few decades British Education policy was enforced and administered by the provisional governments in British-ruled India (Whitehead 2005). Since its Independence, India has rigorously undertaken the dual task of expanding facilities of education and improving standards by attempting to advance elementary education for all and creating facilities of post-elementary education for all who have the capacity and the interest (Kabir 1957). While there have been several milestones that the Indian education system has achieved, there equally are several segments which requires more focus and improvement such as better representation of individuals from lower socio-economic backgrounds in institutions of higher education, improvement in the quality of teaching as well as teachers in elementary schools, and upscaling technological infrastructures across governmental institutions.

This chapter will first set out the structure of the key institutions and regulatory frameworks that ensures the smooth functioning of India's education system, including a discussion of where executive and legislative responsibilities lie in the context of India's federal model. Second, the major legal developments in the field of education will be discussed. This section includes several of the salient developments in education law and policy in India, including the evolution of the Indian Government's New Education Policies (NEPs), affirmative action policies and reservation, the progression of the fundamental right to education in India from judicial activism to Constitutional amendment, and significant nation-wide education policies such as the abolition of child-labour and the rolling-out of the Mid-day Meal Scheme. Finally, this chapter will explore outlooks for future developments within law in the field of education in India, focussing on key issues such as the risk of corruption, unethical conduct and other integrity issues in education and how such issues are being addressed, the challenge of providing access to *quality* education for all, and the internationalisation of education policy including the debate on the introduction of foreign education institutions (especially in higher education) in India. While education law is a complex and evolving area of law in India, this chapter provides an analysis of the most salient regulatory developments, challenges and opportunities effecting key stakeholders in education, most notably; governments, education institutions and students.

2 Nature of the Legal System

India is a Republican Democracy which attained its independence from the British Empire on 15 August 1947. The Constitution of India, which came into force on 26 January 1950, divides the Indian State into three branches namely—the executive, the legislature, and the judiciary (Srikrishna 2008). The Constitution of India, like many post-war constitutions, was based on the Westminster model with a Parliament comprising of bicameral legislative bodies—The Lower House, also known as the *Lok Sabha* and the Upper House, also known as the *Rajya Sabha*, at the Centre (Nariman 2006). The Executive at the Centre and in the states function under what is known as a cabinet system of government, i.e., a council of ministers collectively responsible to the legislature (Nariman 2006). Independent India maintained the British practice of a head of state in the office of the President who like the British crown 'reigns but does not rule' (Mirta 2017). Effective executive power rests with the Council of Minister, headed by the Prime Minister, who is chosen by the majority party or coalition in the *Lok Sabha* and is formally appointed by the President (Britannica 2007). The Government structure at the States closely resembles that of the Union. The Executive Branch is headed by the Governor, who is appointed by the President of India and who functions on the aid and advice of the Council of Ministers, headed by the Chief Minister (Britannica 2007). All States have a Legislative Assembly, also referred to as the *Vidhan Sabha* and a small number of States also have an upper house, called the *Vidhan Parishad* (Legislative Council) (Britannica 2007). The legal hierarchy places the Supreme Court of India at the apex, which serves as the highest Constitutional Court, final court of appeal in certain civil as well as criminal matters and also exercises extraordinary powers in certain cases.[1] Each State has its own High Court which is the final court of appeal in that jurisdiction and below it are District Courts in each district entrusted with the administration of justice.[2]

The Constitution, while distributing the legislative powers between the Union Parliament and the State legislature, enumerates various items of legislation under three lists enumerated under the Seventh Schedule of the Constitution—List I (Union List), List II (State List), List III (Concurrent List).[3] Education is mentioned under Entry 64–66 of List I and Entry 25 of List III. List I gives the Union Parliament the power to legislate on matters concerning institutions for scientific or technical education financed by the Government of India[4] and for institutions for professional training, special studies or research.[5] The Union Legislature is also responsible for the co-ordination and determination of standards in institutions for higher education or research and scientific and technical institutions.[6] List III gives both the Union Parliament and the State Legislature the power to enact laws concerning education

[1] Srikrishna 2008, 242.

[2] Id. at 243.

[3] Mahendra Pal Singh, *V.N. Shukla's Constitution of India*, 794 (Eastern Book Company, 13th edn., 2017).

[4] *See* Constitution of India, Schedule VII, List I, Entry 64: Institutions for scientific or technical education financed by the Government of India wholly or in part and declared by Parliament by law to be institutions of national importance.

[5] *See* Constitution of India, Schedule VII, List I, Entry 65: Union agencies and institutions for— (a) professional, vocational or technical training, including the training of police officers; or (b) the promotion of special studies or research; or (c) scientific or technical assistance in the investigation or detection of crime.

[6] Constitution of India, Schedule VII, List I, Entry 66.

including technical education and universities, subject to the entries of List I.[7] As a consequence, the Central Parliament has exclusive powers to legislate in certain aspects of education (as per List I) and the Central and State Parliaments share powers to make laws under other aspects of education (as per List III).

In addition to the powers to make laws in the field of education, the provision of free and compulsory education for all children up to the age of fourteen has been a directive principle for state policy since the inception of the Indian Constitution.[8] However, after a series of debates and landmark litigations, in 1993 the Supreme Court recognised free and compulsory elementary education as a fundamental right of every child in India flowing from the constitutional right to life and personal liberty.[9] To ensure sufficient and effective realisation of this right, the Union Parliament by way of 86th Constitutional Amendment in 2002 inserted Article 21-A[10] (Right to Education) providing for the fundamental right to free and compulsory education to all children between the age of six and fourteen (Star and Bharadwaj 2020, 2021). The Right of Children to Free and Compulsory Education Act, 2009 operationalised and provided the framework of legal rules which recognises and implements the fundamental right to elementary education in India (Alka Malvankar 2018). The Act lays down the modalities for the implementation of free and compulsory education for children between the ages of six and fourteen, guaranteed under Article 21A of the Constitution of India (Alka Malvankar 2018). The Constitution also provides all religious as well as linguistic minorities the right to establish and administer educational institutions of their choice.[11] This right conferred on certain minority groups is to ensure their equality with the majority groups and protect their interests (Jain 2005).

While the legislature is responsible for enacting laws within the bounds of their powers under the Constitution, it is the Ministry of Education (MoE) in the Central Government and other ministries in the State Governments that are responsible for the operationalisation of all educational legislation, and also draft rules and policies for its implementation. The MoE, formerly known as the Ministry of Human Resource Development (MHRD), was established by the Government of India (Allocation of Business) Rules, 1961 and currently functions through two main departments—the

---

[7] *See* Constitution of India, Schedule VII, List III, Entry 25: Education, including technical education, medical education and universities, subject to the provisions of entries 63, 64, 65 and 66 of List I; vocational and technical training of labour.

[8] *See* Constitution of India, Article 41: The State shall, within the limits of its economic capacity and development, make effective provision for securing the right to work, to education and to public assistance in cases of unemployment, old age, sickness and disablement, and in other cases of undeserved want. *Also see,* Constitution of India, Article 45 which states that the State shall endeavour to provide early childhood care and education for all children until they complete the age of six year, which was inserted in the Constitution by the Eighty-sixth Amendment Act 2002.

[9] Unni Krishnan, J. P. versus State of Andhra Pradesh, (1993) 1 SCC 645.

[10] Constitution of India, Article 21 A: Right to education—The State shall provide free and compulsory education to all children of the age of six to fourteen years in such manner as the State may, by law, determine.

[11] *See* Constitution of India, Article 30.

Department of School Education and Literacy which is responsible for the development of school education and literacy in the country and the Department of Higher Education which is responsible for one of the largest higher education systems of the world (Ministry of Education)[12]. The objectives of the MoE includes the formulation of the National Policy on Education and its implementation; expanding access and improving quality of educational institutions; providing financial help in the form of scholarships and subsidies to students from deprived sections of the community; and encouraging international cooperation and working closely with organisations such as UNESCO. The Education Departments in State Governments are broadly responsible for overseeing school education, teacher training, examination, youth welfare activities and implementing the National Policy on Education formulated by the Central Government.[13] In terms of the budgetary allocations, in 2021–22 the MoE was allocated 932.24 billion rupees (USD 12.4 billion), which constituted 2.67% of the Central Government's estimated expenditure for the financial year 2021–22.[14] While the National Policy on Education of 1968 recommended the spending on education be 6% of the Gross Domestic Product (GDP), the expenditure on education by both the Centre and the States as a proportion of the GDP has been approximately 3% between 2014–15 and 2018–19.[15]

The Indian School Education system is one of the largest in the world with more than 1.5 million schools, nearly 9.7 million teachers and approximately 265 million students of pre-primary to higher secondary level.[16] Schools are either owned by the Government (Central, State or Local Government Bodies) or by the private sector (individuals, trusts or societies) (British Council 2019). Those which are owned or aided by the Government are largely free for students or may charge nominal fees and those that are unaided support themselves mostly through student fees (British Council 2019). In 2017, approximately half of all schools were classified as government-run, 12% were considered government-aided and 32% were private-unaided schools (British Council 2019). The total number of higher education institutions was approximately 55,165 in 2019–20, including universities, colleges and some stand-alone institutions (Government of India 2019–20), with approximately 38.5 million students enrolled in total (Government of India 2019–20). Universities in India are typically established by separate legislation, or alternatively in accordance with existing regulations. The Central universities are established and incorporated by a Central legislation, while state universities are established and incorporated by a Provincial or State legislation, and private universities are established through a State/Central legislation using a sponsoring body registered under the Societies

---

[12] Ministry of Education, Government of India, Overview (https://www.education.gov.in/en/about-moe)

[13] Education Department, Government of NCT of Delhi (http://edudel.nic.in/directorate.html).

[14] PRS Legislative Research, *Demand for Grants 2021–22 Analysis: Education* (https://prsindia.org/budgets/parliament/demand-for-grants-2021-22-analysis-education).

[15] Id.

[16] Unified District Information System For Education Plus (UDISE+), Department of School Education and Literacy, Ministry of Education, Government of India 1, 9 (2019–20) <https://www.education.gov.in/sites/upload_files/mhrd/files/statistics-new/udise_201920.pdf>.

Registration Act or Companies Act or any other corresponding law in the applicable jurisdiction.[17] Some institutions, based on their performance, are also accredited with distinct statutes; for instance, some premier public higher education institutions have been declared as 'Institutes of National Importance' by the Central Parliament, providing them with more autonomy from the government, and some high performing institutions being declared by the Central Government as an 'Institution Deemed to be University'.[18]

The Department of School Education and Literacy has nine autonomous bodies, established by the Union Parliament, which aid and advise the MoE on various matters. These bodies are: (i) the Central Board of Secondary Education (CBSE); (ii) the Central Institute of Education Technology (CIET); (iii) the Central Tibetan Schools Administration (CTSA); (iv) the Kendriya Vidyalaya Sangathan (KVS); (v) the National Council of Education Research & Training (NCERT); (vi) the National Council for Teacher Education (NCTE); (vii) the National Institute of Open Schooling (NIOS); (viii) the Navodaya Vidyalaya Samiti (NVS); and (ix) the National Bal Bhavan.[19] CBSE is responsible for laying down school curriculum and conducting nation-wide examinations including higher secondary board exams, pre-medical, engineering entrance tests, and teachers eligibility/recruitment exams.[20] CIET's major aim is to promote the utilisation of educational technologies including radio, television, films, satellite communication and cyber media to widen educational opportunities and promote equity.[21] The CTSA is responsible for establishing, managing, and assisting schools that are focussed on the education of Tibetan children living in India while preserving and promoting their culture and heritage.[22] KVS was specifically established to cater to the educational needs of children of transferable Central Government employees, including Defence and Para-military personnel, by providing a common programme of education.[23] NCERT assists the Central and State Governments on policies and programmes for school education and also undertakes research in areas related to school education, prepares and publishes model textbooks, supplementary material, and educational kits.[24] NCTE's main objective is to achieve planned and coordinated development of the teacher education system throughout

[17] Department of Higher Education, Ministry of Education, Government of India, Overview (https://www.education.gov.in/en/institutions).

[18] Id.

[19] Department of School Education & Literacy, Ministry of Education, Government of India, Institutions (https://www.education.gov.in/en/autonomous_bodies).

[20] Central Board of Secondary Education, *CBSE@90*, 92 (SAUV Communications Pvt. Ltd. 2019).

[21] Central Institute of Educational Technology (CIET), About CIET (https://ciet.nic.in/).

[22] Central Tibetan School Administration (CTSA), Department of School Education & Literacy, Government of India (https://dsel.education.gov.in/ctsa).

[23] Kendriya Vidyalaya Sangathan (KVS), Ministry of Education, Government of India, Vision and Mission (https://kvsangathan.nic.in/).

[24] 'National Council of Educational Research & Training (NCERT), About us (https://ncert.nic.in/about-us.php?ln=).'

the country and maintain proper norms and standards of teacher education.[25] NIOS was established by the National Policy on Education 1986 which provides several vocational and life enrichment courses in addition to general academic programs.[26] The NVS runs schools and curriculums for children predominantly from the rural parts of India.[27]

The National Bal Bhavan caters to children between the age group of 5 to 16 years and aims to enhance the creative potentials of children in the fields of creative arts, performance, writing, and innovation by providing them opportunities and a common platform.[28]

The Department of Higher Education functions with six autonomous apex level bodies, established by Acts of the Union Parliament, which broadly are responsible for maintenance and coordination of all institutions of higher education in India. The six bodies include: (i) the All India Council of Technical Education (AICTE); (ii) the Council of Architecture (COA); (iii) the Indian Council of Historical Research (ICHR); (iv) the Indian Council of Philosophical Research (ICPR); (v) the Indian Council of Social Science Research (ICSSR); and (vi) the University Grants Commission (UGC).[29] The AICTE is responsible for the planning and coordination development of the technical education system in the country, regulating and maintaining norms as well as standards and promoting quality technical education across all institutions.[30] The COA, apart from regulating architectural education, also regulates the practice of the profession throughout India and maintains the register of architects.[31] The ICHR's primary aim is to promote historical research and encourage objective and scientific writing of history.[32] The ICPR reviews and regulates philosophical research and also sponsors projects and provides financial support and technical assistance to institutions.[33] The ICSSR promotes research in the field of social sciences and also provides grants for projects, fellowships, international collaborations, capacity building, and publication in order to promote research in the broad field of social science.[34] The UGC is the leading autonomous body under the Department of Higher Education which oversees the working of all universities and institutions of higher

---

[25] 'National Council for Teacher Education (NCTE), Objective (https://ncte.gov.in/Website/about.aspx).'

[26] 'National Institute of Open Schooling (NIOS), Objective (https://www.nios.ac.in/).'

[27] 'Navodaya Vidyalaya Samiti (NVA), Vision (https://navodaya.gov.in/nvs/en/Home1).'

[28] 'National Bal Bhavan, Overview (http://nationalbalbhavan.nic.in/aboutus/overview.html).'

[29] 'Department of Higher Education, Ministry of Education, Government of India, Apex Level Bodies (https://www.education.gov.in/en/apex-level-bodies).'

[30] 'All India Council for Technical Education (AICTE), Overview <https://www.aicte-india.org/about-us/overview>.'

[31] 'Council of Architecture (COA), About us <https://www.coa.gov.in/>.'

[32] 'Indian Council of Historical Research, Aims & Objectives <http://ichr.ac.in/content/innerpage/aims---objectives.php>.'

[33] 'Indian Council of Philosophical Research (ICPR), Aims and Objectives <http://icpr.in/about.html>.'

[34] 'Indian Council of Social Sciences Research (ICSSR), ICSSR at a Glance <https://icssr.org/icssr-glance>.'

learning and also determines the allocation of grants-in-aid from the public funds to these higher education institutions.[35] Apart of these six bodies, there are other autonomous regulatory bodies, established by Acts of Parliaments, which oversee education in other technical fields and do not fall within the preview of the MoE. For instance, the National Medical Commission, formerly known as the Medical Council of India, regulated the medical institutions and professionals across the country and is affiliated with the Ministry of Health and Family Welfare,[36], and the Bar Council of India, which regulates legal education and practice in India, is affiliated with the Department of Legal Affairs, Ministry of Law & Justice of the Union Government.[37]

3 Major Legal Developments

There are several major legal developments that have taken place as India's education system has evolved. This section sets out some of the most salient legal developments that have had a profound impact on education in India, including major policies such as the National Education Policy, the enactment of the Right to Education Act, reservation (quota) policies for certain disadvantaged groups, policy reform with respect to child labour and the establishment of the mid-day meal scheme.

As India changed progressively from a colonial, agrarian economy into a more globalised country run by democratic institutions, economic growth coupled with social justice was a key aim of the Government in this transition.[38] At Independence, India inherited large-scale illiteracy and lack of proper provision for education. The first post-independence census of 1951 indicated that only nine percent of women and 27% of men were literate (Kingdon 2007). At the time of Independence, there were 19 universities and 695 colleges with an overall enrolment of fewer than 270,000 students (Altbach 2022). The challenge of coping with the demands of expansion, a new world order and political and other pressures on higher education meant that some affirmative steps were required to be taken to strengthen both quality and quantity in the Indian education sector to meet the growing industrial and economical demands (Altbach 2022).

The Central Advisory Board of Education is the oldest and the most important advisory body of the Government of India on education, which was first established in 1920, dissolved in 1923, revived in 1935 and has been in existence ever since (Biswas and Agrawal 1986). Shortly after Independence, Maulana Abul Kalam Azad, India's first Education Minister, addressed the Board in 1948 and asked for the constitution and appointment of new commissions to assess the modern educational issues and

35 'University Grants Commission (UGC), Genesis <https://www.ugc.ac.in/page/Genesis.aspx>.'

36 '[1] See National Medical Commission, Introduction <https://www.nmc.org.in/aboutnmc/introduction/>.'

37 'See The Bar Council of India, About the Council <http://www.barcouncilofindia.org/about/about-the-bar-council-of-india/>.'

38 Subrata K. Mirta 2017, 176.

recommend measures (Biswas and Agrawal 1986). The Board instituted the University Education Commission (1948–49) which recommended the setting up of the University Grants Commission (UGC) and a Secondary Education Commission for reconstructing secondary education by introducing programmes and replacing the old system, which was constituted in 1953 and was led by A. Ramaswamy Mudaliar (Biswas and Agrawal 1986). Then came the Kothari Commission constituted in 1965 which had a peculiar international character as five of fifteen members were from other countries, including the USA, former USSR, France, Japan, and the UK, and it had approximately 20 international consultants (Vaidyanatha Ayyar 2017). The main idea behind having the international presence was to draw on the experience and perspectives of educationists from major parts of the world in order to establish an all-round developing system which was on par with international standards (Vaidyanatha Ayyar 2017).

3.1 *National Education Policies*

A significant policy development with respect to education in India was witnessed with the drafting and adoption of the National Policy on Education (NPE) in 1968. The NPE was informed by the comprehensive review of the prevailing education conditions by the Kothari Commission and it aimed at transforming India's education system at all levels, raising the quality of education at all stages, development of science and technology and expansion of education opportunities (Aggarwal 1993). The NPE of 1968 was also the first major policy document to recommend that the Government must fulfil the Directive Principle under the Indian Constitution seeking to provide free and compulsory education for all children up to the age of 14 (Aggarwal 1993), and to increase the investment in education up to six percent of the national income (Aggarwal 1993). Despite the policy's significant recommendations, it had a limited scope and effect at a national level primarily because education was then a State subject falling within the ambit of List II of Schedule 7 of the Constitution (Dewan and Mehendale 2015). It was only in 1976 that education became a concurrent subject falling within the ambit of List III through the 42nd Constitution Amendment, but despite this shift in responsibility to the Central Government, the implementation of education policy remained weak (Dewan and Mehendale 2015). In the mid-1980s the Ministry of Education, with the assistance of the National University of Educational Planning and Administration, prepared a status paper confronting the challenges in the education system which was tabled before the Lok Sabha and based on this report the new NPE was drafted and adopted by the Parliament in 1986 (Dewan and Mehendale 2015). This NPE of 1986, however, was revised and readopted in 1992 (Dewan and Mehendale 2015). Both the 1986 NPE and the revised version's main objectives were to establish a national system of education meant to serve national goals and produce young men and women of character and ability committed to national service and development (Dewan and Mehendale 2015). The policy also suggested the vocationalisation from secondary school and promotion of technical, computer and management education with a focus on innovation, research and development (Dewan and Mehendale 2015). It also emphasised the removal of disparities in educational opportunities by attending specific needs of underprivileged and vulnerable groups.[39]

The new National Education Policy (NEP) was announced by the Indian Government in 2020 and has been formulated after a long halt of 34 years. The NEP 2020 encompasses a wide range of recommendations for school education to higher education in order to transform Indian educational system into a 'new normal' by expanding and strengthening digital infrastructure (Kumar 2020). The policy aims to use technology to enhance learning experiences in physical classrooms and also reach out to those who are unable to join higher education institutions by using online portals (Kumar 2020). The policy proposed the establishment of a National Research Foundation for catalysing quality academic research in all fields of study and to build a robust research ecosystem in Indian universities (Kumar 2020).

3.2 *Reservation and Affirmative Action*

Most Constitutions of the modern world contain statements to the effect that there shall be no discrimination based on race, colour, and religion with additional provisions requiring preferential treatment for certain group, justified based on historic reasons (Zachariah 1972). India too established several Government employment quotas and educational benefits as positive discrimination/preferential treatment to help speed the social and economic elevation of specific groups from the lowest levels of the country's population (Zachariah 1972). There are groups of individuals who have belonged to certain castes for generations who have faced continued burden of social stigma and economic challenges in India (Mosse 2018). As a result, the Constitution of India includes provisions which allows the Government to take action against adverse discrimination towards individuals from the Schedule Castes (SCs), Scheduled Tribes (STs), and Other Backward Castes (OBCs). The Constitution also permits preferential treatment in the form of reservations in certain educational and professional sectors for their upliftment (Barooah et al. 2007). For a long time, individual state governments were appointing commissions and drawing out lists of backward castes for reservation in education institutions and public appointment; however, it was the Janata Party led Central Government in 1978 that appointed the All India Backward Classes Commission under the chairmanship of Bindhyeswara Prasad Mandal, which submitted its report in 1980 and its recommendations were

[39] J.C. Aggarwal 1993, 349.

accepted.[40] The Mandal Commission, after taking into consideration all the Backward Castes and various judgements of the Supreme Court of India which laid down that reservation of posts must be below 50%,[41] proposed the reservation to be pegged at a figure of 22.5% for SCs and STs and 27% for the OBCs (Maheshwari 1997). The Commission recommended that for the execution of this reservation policy, a roster system for each category of reserved seats or posts in jobs or educational institutions must be adopted, advertising the total number of seats and the number of reserved seats/posts for SC/ST/OBC candidates in each year of enrolment (Government of India 1980). In 1993, the federal government implemented the first stage of the Mandal Commission's recommendations (Khanna 2020) and later the proposal was formalised after Parliament passed the Central Educational Institutions (Reservation in Admission) Act, 2006 providing for 15, 7.5 and 27% reservation in Central institutions of higher education and research for members of the SC, ST and OBC communities respectively.[42]

With the implementation of the reservation policy set forth by the Mandal Commission, the proportion of students from backward castes was seen increasing, as by the late 1990s the SC proportion rose from 7 to 7.8% and the ST proportion rose from 1.6 to 2.7% (Weisskopf 2004). Moreover, by the end of the century, SC and ST student representation in higher educational institutions had reached roughly one-half and one-third of their representation in the population as a whole (Weisskopf 2004). The Indian Parliament passed the 103rd Constitution Amendment Act in 2019 which in effect created provisions for reservation in education institutions for individuals coming from economically weaker sections (EWS) of the society but who do not belong to the SC, ST or OBC community, as a result of a long-standing demand on behalf of poor and disadvantaged individuals who were not born into the SC, ST or OBC community (Deshpande 2019). While the improvement in the status of education of SC, ST and OBC, their improving rates of participation in education and the inequality between the scheduled population and non-scheduled population is impressive, still the absolute levels of educational status of the schedules population are far below the status of their counterparts and there still is a very long way to go (Tilak 2015).

3.3 *The Right to Education*

After Article 21A was inserted in the Indian Constitution recognising the fundamental right to education for every child between the ages of 6 and 14, the Right of Children

---

[40] Chalam (1990). *See* Article 46 the Constitution of India: The State shall promote with special care the educational and economic interests of the weaker sections of the people, and, in particular, of the Scheduled Castes and the Scheduled Tribes, and shall protect them from social injustice and all forms of exploitation.

[41] *See* Balaji v. State of Madras (AIR 1963 SC 649), reaffirmed in the case of Indra Sawhney v. Union of India (AIR 1993 SC 477).

[42] *See* Section 3 of the Central Educational Institutions (Reservation in Admission) Act, 2006.

to Free and Compulsory Education Act, 2009 (RTE Act) was passed by the Union legislature providing the legal rules and framework for the recognition and effective implementation of free and compulsory education for children between the ages of 6 and 14.[43] The RTE Act also made it mandatory for all private schools, except those for minority religions, to reserve up to 25% places in each school-class for students from economically weaker sections and disadvantaged social groups of the society.[44] Since education being on the concurrent list, the implementation and the associated financial burden of providing free education became a shared responsibility between the central and the respective state governments (Ray and Saini 2016). The Governments by the RTE Act were made liable for all direct and indirect costs of education, including those related to uniforms, textbooks, school admission and tuition fees (Ray and Saini 2016). Accordingly, the state legislatures enacted state-specific statutes for the effective implementation of the RTE Act, which requires the State Government or local authorities to have school established in a proximate area[45]; to undertake school mapping and identify all children in remote areas, children with disabilities and children from disadvantaged and weaker sections of the society[46]; requires both government-aided as well as private schools to provide reservation for the children of disadvantaged groups and children of weaker sections[47]; and requires all schools either owned or aided by the State Government or a local body to provide free education, textbooks, writing material and uniform to students and to provide children with disabilities with free special learning and support material.[48] A table consisting of all state legislations currently in force for the effective implementation of the RTE Act and for regulation primary education has been included as Appendix.

Since the enactment of the RTE Act, it has achieved many milestones but has also faced some criticisms. For instance, the RTE Act and its implementation across all Indian states has resulted in an increase of student enrolment in schools, as nationally between 2009 and 2016, the number of students in the upper primary level increased by 19.4% and only 3.3% of children between the age of 6–14 years living in rural areas were out of school in 2016 (Bhattacharjee 2019). One of the most far-reaching and important aspects of the RTE Act has been the reservation of 25% seats at entry for students from economically weaker sections and disadvantaged groups of the society and more than 3.3 million students have secured admission under this provision (Bhattacharjee 2019). RTE required some qualitative norms to be fulfilled by schools including 1:30 student ratio, ramps for students with disabilities, provision for drinking water, and availability of a playground; however, only 13% of all

---

[43] Alka Malvankar 2018, 2.

[44] Id. at 6.

[45] *See* Section 4 of The Assam Right of Children to Free and Compulsory Education Rules, 2011.

[46] *See* Section 9 of the Chhattisgarh Right of Children to Free and Compulsory Education Rules, 2010.

[47] *See* Section 14(h) of The Andhra Pradesh Right of Children to Free and Compulsory Education Rules, 2010 and Section 5 of The Arunachal Pradesh Right of Children to Free and Compulsory Education Act, 2009.

[48] *See* Section 5 of The Assam Right of Children to Free and Compulsory Education Rules, 2011 and Section 5 of The Bihar State Free and Compulsory Education of Children Rules, 2011.

schools in India have achieved full compliance with these RTE norms (Bhattacharjee 2019). Critics have also argues that the RTE Act enables the right to schooling but not education; as too much attention has been paid to infrastructure as opposed to learning, thereby causing disparities across location, economic category, social group and gender (Kumar et al. 2019). This disparity has been widened due to the spread of Covid-19 and national lock-down in India since March 2020 as millions of children had little or no access to education as a result of continued school closures and lack of access to technology (Star 2021).

3.4 *Abolition of Child Labour*

Child labour refers to the exploitation of children through any form of work that deprives children of their childhood, interferes with their ability to attend regular school, and is harmful to their overall development (Kaur and Byard 2021). Child labour for decades has been a global problem and since the launch of the International Programme on the Elimination of Child Labour by the International Labour Organisation (ILO) in 1992, addressing and eliminating the problem of child labour has been an important development priority (Mukhopadhaya et al. 2012). ILO's report in 2010 indicated some encouraging signs as the report indicated the number of child labourers globally aged between 5 and 14 years falling by 18% from 186 million in 2000 to 153 million by 2008 (Mukhopadhaya et al. 2012). The elimination of child labour has been intrinsically linked with the goal of increasing access to primary school education, the main idea being that there are significant net benefits that flow from higher earnings generated by children that move from work to school and complete at least their primary education before returning to the workforce (Mukhopadhaya et al. 2012).

The Indian Constitution since its inception has aimed to eliminate child labour in India as Article 24 provides for the fundamental right against exploitation for children below the age of fourteen years and states that no child can be employed to work in any factory or mine or engage in any hazardous employment.[49] Moreover, the 42nd amendment to the Constitution in 1976 made it a directive policy for the Indian State to enact policies which ensure that children are given opportunities and facilities to develop in a healthy manner and in conditions of freedom, dignity and that children are protected against exploitation and against moral and material abandonment.[50] For the effective realisation and the implementation of the constitutional provisions against child labour, the Union Parliament enacted the Child Labour (Prohibition and Regulation) Act, 1986 which aimed at banning employment of children (who have not completed their fourteenth year) in specified occupations, regulate conditions of work of children in employment where they are not prohibited from working

[49] *See* Constitution of India, Article 24.

[50] *See* Constitution of India, Article 39(f) inserted by the Constitution (Forty-second Amendment) Act, 1976 (w.e.f. 3-1-1977).

and to lay down penalties for violators.[51] The Indian Parliament recently introduced four labour codes which are set to codify and replace 29 separate labour legislations (Vanamali 2021); however, the 2020 Codes refer to the Child Labour (Prohibition and Regulation) Act of 1986 for associated purposes.[52]

After the enactment of the Child Labour (Prohibition and Regulation) Act, the Government of India initiated the National Child Labour Project (NCLP) under the Ministry of Labour & Employment in 1988 which established a National Authority for the Elimination of Child Labour, comprising of representatives from various key governmental departments.[53] The National Authority undertook the task of child labour elimination by adopting a three step strategy: (i) conduct surveys to identify working children and particularly those engages in hazardous occupations and processes; (ii) withdraw all working children, within the age group of 5 to 9 years and directly put them into the formal school system run the *Sarva Shiksha Abhiyan* (education for all scheme); (iii) withdraw working children between age group of 9 to 14 years from workplaces and enrol them in special schools run by the NCLP.[54] The schools, both run under the *Sarva Shiksha Abhiyan* and by the NCLP, provided students with educational as well as vocational training, nutritious mid-day meals, health check-up facilities, and a stipend to meet their basic expenses.[55] In 2017, an online portal named PENCiL (Platform for Effective Enforcement for No Child Labour) was started by the NCLP which registers complaints against any matter related to child labour and forwards it to the respective district nodal officer (DNO), who checks the veracity of the complaint and undertakes coordinated rescue measures (Katiyar 2019).

Though child labour, both globally and in India, had been gradually declining over the past years, the COVID-19 pandemic and nation-wide lockdowns threatened this development. The COVID-19 pandemic forced India's children out of schools and many children were clandestinely relocated to farms and factories to work.[56] In March 2020, when the nation-wide lockdowns were announced in India, there were around 2,743 interventions related to child labour, which dipped steeply to 446 in April but again started to increase as lockdown restrictions eased over time.[57] The usual reason for the rise was the need for additional household income, particularly significant in cases where the parents were either unemployed or were engaged in menial work.[58] The COVID-19 lockdowns coupled with their negative economic and employment consequences in many respects overrode India's concerted efforts

---

[51] *See* Statement of Objects and Reasons, The Child Labour (Prohibition and Regulation) Act, 1986.

[52] *See* Section 2(1)(a) and 25(4) of the Occupational Safety, Health and Working Conditions Code, 2020.

[53] Pundarik Mukhopadhaya et al. 2012, 653.

[54] Id.

[55] Id.

[56] Navpreet Kaur and Roger W. Byard 2021, 209.

[57] Id.

[58] Id.

to eradicate child labour and demonstrated the need for a more collaborative and proactive approach to bridge the gap.[59]

3.5 *Mid-day Meal Scheme*

For many years school feeding programs have been used as a policy instrument to incentivise school participation around the globe. Such policies have also been associated with various benefits including improved health, higher productivity, better cognitive ability, and reduced child labour (Kaur 2021). India's school feeding program, known as the Mid-day Meal Scheme (MDMS), is the largest school feeding program in the world covering over 113.6 million beneficiaries (Kaur 2021). The National Programme for Nutrition Support to Primary education, also known as MDMS, was launched by the Indian Government in 1995 with the aim of universalisation of primary education by increasing enrolment, reducing drop-outs, increasing daily attendance, and increasing the level of nutrition amongst students of primary classes by providing free cooked lunch (Kaur 2021). The Central Government bears the cost of providing raw grains and the state governments are responsible for financing the expenditure of cooking and for providing cooked meals in primary schools (Ramachandran 2019). Initially raw food grains were provided by the school authorities to children directly; however, after the intervention by the Supreme Court, the State Governments and local authorities were directed to provide a hot cooked mid-day meal containing 300 kcal energy and 12 g of protein per day for a minimum of 200 days a year to all children studying in all government, local body and government-aided primary schools.[60] The Court also ordered States and Union Territories to ensure the monitoring of the MDMS programme and emphasised for the adequate participation of community-based organisations, people's representatives, non-governmental organisations and parents themselves for ensuring that the food is prepared according to the norms and reaches the children.[61]

Several studies have shown that the MDMS, with the regularity of funds and flow of food grains up to the school level in both urban and rural areas, has improved regular attendance in classrooms, increased retention rates with reduced drop-out rates, and has also shown improvements in the scholastic performances by children (Rameshwar Sarma et al. 1995). Importantly, mid-day meals have also been proved to a cost-effective and one of the most viable means of increasing enrolment in primary schools (Jayaraman and Simroth 2015). Studies also suggest that eating lunch at school, for both social and nutritional reasons, is an activity that children genuinely enjoy and hence in addition to providing parents with an incentive to send

---

[59] Id. at 212–213.

[60] Prema Ramachandran (2019), 543–544. *See* PUCL versus Union of India and others, Writ Petition [Civil] 196 of 2001.

[61] Id. at 544.

their children to school, the mid-day meals give the children themselves an incentive to go to school and engage in activities there (Jayaraman and Simroth 2015).

4 Outlook for Future Development

The Indian education system has achieved many accolades, from having one of the largest primary education systems in the world to having generated several Nobel laureates and leading scholars in various disciplines. However, its grandeur is hugely affected by certain practices which impair the quality of education and confidence in the system (Tierney and Sabharwal 2016).

4.1 Integrity, Corruption and Ethics in Education

One challenge facing the delivery of access to quality education in India is the threat of corruption, fraud, and other integrity issues which threaten to undermine the quality of, an confidence in, the education system. The Indian education system garnered worldwide attention when a major cheating scandal was exposed. This scandal, known as the *Vyapam* (Madhya Pradesh Vyavsayik Pariksha Mandal) scam, involved thousands of individuals who took medical examinations on behalf of other students (Tierney and Sabharwal 2016). The scam involved the corruption of contractual teachers and police constables, among many others, and the manipulation of the premedical test that determines admission to medical colleges (Editorial 2015). This ruined the educational prospects and careers of thousands of innocent young people and eroded the faith of citizens in public institutions and the government (Editorial 2015). More than 500 people have been charge by the Central Bureau of Investigation (CBI), including some high profile businessmen and senior government officials, and the prosecution is underway (Naveen 2021).

4.2 Access to Quality Education

While India has done remarkably well in ensuring access to education, despite its significant population, there are still challenges in delivering quality education to the masses. In terms of school education, several studies have shown a dismal state of affairs in government schools where there is not just a shortage of teaching staff in some areas, but those who teach often lack accountability, widening the enormous quality gap between private and government schools.[62] Moreover, in government schools the number of teaching staff is significantly lower (per student) and rampant

[62] Alka Malvankar 2018 , 5.

absenteeism among teachers is a common feature, which results in either no active teaching or nominal teaching activities taking place.[63] Approximately 4.6 million teachers teach in government elementary schools in India and about 20% of them lack adequate professional qualifications, and many more lack the required skills, knowledge and attitude to ensure effective learning.[64] Focus on teachers, teacher education and training is an essential task which needs to be undertaken so that pupils coming from diverse learning environments and socio-economic backgrounds can reach the adequate levels of competency and knowledge.[65]

With the spread of the COVID-19 virus, India faced widespread lockdowns from March 2020 for almost two years, and while the majority of schools and colleges transitioned to online delivery of classes as well as assessments to avoid the disruption of educational services, the digital platform still remains an uncharted territory for the majority of students from lower-middle or lower socio-economic segments of the society (Mahapatra and Sharma 2020; Eri et. al. 2021). Children with disabilities found themselves in a more disadvantaged position with the suspension of their educational and vocational activities in the wake of the pandemic as most centres for special education in India are not equipped to provide their services through digital platforms or home-based interventions (Mahapatra and Sharma 2020). While the Indian Government as well as other State Governments have taken several initiatives to improve access to education by introducing various online platforms and repositories of educational resources such as DIKSHA and e-Pathshala, the accessibility of these e-resources to the lower segments of society needs to be addressed. To this end, there is a need to scale the technological infrastructure across all governmental education institutions (Mahapatra and Sharma 2020).

Among many things that India achieved post-Independence, one significant achievement has been the growth trajectory of higher education in terms of institutions, academic programmes, and enrolment (Bhoite 2009). A large network of universities, colleges, and research institutes have been established in India which has produced some globally recognised leaders and industry experts (Bhoite 2009). However, the problem of equity in terms of access to higher educational institutions in India has been often been highlighted for the underrepresentation of individuals hailing from underprivileged categories, castes, and classes (Bhoite 2009). Moreover, with the privatisation of professional education, the cost of professional education has skyrocketed and has increased beyond the paying capacity of students in the low-income brackets (Bhoite 2009). The National Sample Survey (NSS) of 2014 shows that the private expenditure on education for general courses has experienced a 175.8% increase from 2007 to 2014 and as many as 16.6% of males and 9.5% of female undergraduate students were found to be too poor to pursue higher education (Panigrahi and Singh 2016).

---

[63] Id. at 10.

[64] The Right to Education with Equity: Access and Quality Education for All in India, The UN Secretary-General's Global Initiate on Education, United Nations India, p. 8 (https://in.one.un.org/wp-content/uploads/2016/09/Right_to_Education_with_Equity.pdf).

[65] Alka Malvankar 2018, 13.

The disparity is also witnessed in private elementary schools, where despite having 25% reservation for children coming from poor socio-economic categories at entry levels mandated by the RTE Act, many seats reserved under these quotas have remained unfilled, with the reservation seat rates hovering between 20 and 26% since 2013.[66] Since India does not have a common national schooling system, the 25% quota system has been susceptible to inequalities at different levels including discriminatory behaviour faced by parents, difficulties experienced by students to blend in with a different socio-cultural environment and several implementation hurdles including financial allotments and reimbursements by State Governments.[67] Thus, despite guarantees to education for all, there are still constraints with respect to the delivery of high quality education, at all levels. The NEP 2020 aims to address this, in part, through training and up-skilling policies in education throughout the country.[68]

4.3 Foreign Universities in India

Foreign universities are currently permitted to collaborate with Indian institutions in several forms of permissible partnerships. In fact, such international collaborations are encouraged under the NEP 2020. Until recently, however, foreign universities and education institutions were not permitted to set up a campus in India in their own right. The NEP 2020 suggested an amendment to this policy. The policy within the 2020 NEP to permit foreign universities in India is not in itself a novel policy decision. In fact, in 2007 and 2010 the Central Government introduced two separate Bills in Parliament to permit entry of foreign universities into India. Neither of these Bills were passed. The latter Bill—The Foreign Educational Institutions (Regulation of Entry and Operations)—imposed strict requirements on foreign universities, including conditions on the repatriation of surplus funds raised in India.[69] Commentators argued that reforming the education sector to permit (and regulate) the entry of foreign education institutions would increase competition and benchmark quality within the system (Gawarikar and Pramanik 2015).

---

66 Sanchayan Bhattacharjee 2019 , 4.

67 Id. at 4–5.

68 *See* The National Education Policy 2020, Ministry of Human Resource Development, Government of India, pp. 7–30 (https://www.education.gov.in/sites/upload_files/mhrd/files/NEP_Final_English_0.pdf).

69 'See, https://prsindia.org/files/bills_acts/bills_parliament/2010/Foreign_Educational_Institutions_Regulation_of_Entry_and_Operations_Bill__2010.pdf; https://prsindia.org/billtrack/the-foreign-educational-institutions-regulation-of-entry-and-operations-bill-2010.'

Reform to promote internationalisation of the higher education sector took great strides under the NEP 2020, which stated:

> High performing Indian universities will be encouraged to set up campuses in other countries, and similarly, selected universities e.g., those from among the top 100 universities in the world will be facilitated to operate in India. A legislative framework facilitating such entry will be put in place, and such universities will be given special dispensation regarding regulatory, governance, and content norms on par with other autonomous institutions of India.[70]

Accordingly, there was clear intent to legislate to enable foreign universities to physically enter the Indian market. This intent manifested in 2023, with the Indian government permitting Foreign Higher Educational Institutions to set up in India, if certain eligibility and compliance criteria are complied with (see, University Grants Commission Notification, dated 7 November 2023). To be eligible, foreign universities are required to be ranked in the top 500 of a recognised global ranking system (either overall, or in a subject ranking). The University Grants Committee oversees the approval process for foreign universities wishing to set up a campus and award qualifications within India.

5 Conclusion

India has a population of more than 1.4 billion people, and more than half of this population is under the age of 25.[71] To meet the challenges of educating hundreds of millions of young people at any one time is no easy feat. To this end, Indian policymakers and other stakeholders in the education system have their work cut out for them. This is a significant challenge, but it is of utmost importance for the future of India, and indeed the world, that India's young students are properly educated. As a consequence, India's policy makers have been proactive, and at times innovative, exploring ways to ensure that education can reach the masses. This chapter has identified some of the regulatory structures and mechanisms adopted by India in creating and implementing education reform. It has also, however, explained some of the key challenges and opportunities faced by the education system currently and into the future. Policy intervention is needed at the highest level to ensure that quality education institutions continue to grow throughout the country. However, every stakeholder has an important role to play in India's education narrative—from Government, to scholars, to teachers, and students. Once new and improved education policies are created, Governments and institutions at all levels must ensure that they are properly implemented, such that *all* students have the opportunity to receive quality education.

[70] The National Education Policy 2020, p. 39.

[71] 'Press Trust of India, More than 50% of India's population 25 years or older: Survey, Livemint (3rd July 2020), https://www.livemint.com/news/india/more-than-50-of-india-s-population-25-yrs-or-older-survey-11593793054491.html.'

Appendix: Compulsory Education Acts presently in Force in States/Union Territories of India

S.No	State	Name of Legislation
1.	Andhra Pradesh	The Andhra Pradesh Right of Children to Free and Compulsory Education Rules 2010.
2.	Arunachal Pradesh	The Arunachal Pradesh Right of Children to Free and Compulsory Education Act 2009.
3.	Assam	The Assam Elementary Education Act 1968. The Assam Right of Children to Free and Compulsory Education Rules, 2011.
4.	Bihar	The Bihar State Free and Compulsory Education of Children Rules, 2011.
5.	Chhattisgarh	Chhattisgarh Primary Education Act, 1961. Chhattisgarh Right of Children to Free and Compulsory Education Rules, 2010.
6.	Delhi	The Delhi School Education Act & Rules 1973 Delhi Right of Children to Free and Compulsory Education Rules, 2011.
7.	Daman & Diu; Goa	Goa, Daman and Diu School Education Act, 1984. Goa, Daman and Diu School Education Rules 1986. Goa Right of Children to Free and Compulsory Education Rules, 2012.
8.	Gujarat	The Gujarat Secondary Education Act 1972 The Gujarat Right of Children to Free and Compulsory Education Rules 2012.
9.	Haryana	Haryana School Education Act 1995. Haryana Right of Children to Free and Compulsory Education Rules 2011.
10.	Himachal Pradesh	Himachal Pradesh Right of Children to Free and Compulsory Education Rules 2011.
11.	Jharkhand	Jharkhand Right of Children to Free and Compulsory Education Rules 2011.
12.	Karnataka	The Karnataka Education Act 1983. Karnataka Right of Children to Free and Compulsory Education Rules 2012.
13.	Kerala	The Kerala Education Act 1958. Kerala Right of Children to Free and Compulsory Education Rules 2010.
14.	Madhya Pradesh	Madhya Pradesh Right of Children to Free and Compulsory Education Rules 2011.
15.	Meghalay	The Meghalaya School Education Act 1981. Meghalaya Right of Children to Free and Compulsory Education Rules 2011.

(continued)

(continued)

S.No	State	Name of Legislation
16.	Maharashtra	The Maharashtra Primary Education Act 1947. Maharashtra Right of Children to Free and Compulsory Education Rules 2011.
17.	Manipur	Manipur Elementary & Secondary Education Act 1972. Manipur Right of Children to Free and Compulsory Education Rules 2010.
18.	Mizoram	Mizoram Education Act 2003. Mizoram Right of Children to Free and Compulsory Education Rules 2011.
19.	Nagaland	Nagaland Right of Children to Free and Compulsory Education Rules 2010.
20.	Odisha (erstwhile Orissa)	The Orissa Education Act 1969. The Orissa Right of Children to Free and Compulsory Education Rules 2010.
21.	Punjab	The Punjab Primary Education Act 1960. Punjab Right of Children to Free and Compulsory Education Rules 2011.
22.	Rajasthan	Rajasthan Right of Children to Free and Compulsory Education Rules 2011.
23.	Sikkim	Sikkim Primary Education Act 1960. Sikkim Right of Children to Free and Compulsory Education Rules 2010.
24.	Tamil Nadu	Tamil Nadu Right of Children to Free and Compulsory Education Rules 2011.
25.	Tripura	Tripura Right of Children to Free and Compulsory Education Rules 2011.
26.	Uttarakhand	The Uttaranchal School Education Act 2006. Uttarakhand Right of Children to Free and Compulsory Education Rules 2011.
27.	Uttar Pradesh	Uttar Pradesh Right of Children to Free and Compulsory Education Rules 2011.
28.	West Bengal	West Bengal Primary Education Act 1973. West Bengal Right of Children to Free and Compulsory Education Rules 2012.

References

Aggarwal JC (1993) Landmarks in the history of modern Indian education. Vikas Publishing House Pvt Ltd, New Delhi, p 194

All India Council for Technical Education (AICTE). Overview. https://www.aicte-india.org/about-us/overview. Accessed 31 Mar 2022

Altbach PG (2022) Indian higher education: twenty-first-century challenges. In: Kumar K (ed) The Routledge handbook of education in India. Taylor & Francis, p 220

Barooah VK, Dubey A, Iyer S (2007) The effectiveness of jobs reservation: caste, religion and economic status in India. Dev Chang 38(3):423–424

Basu A (1982) The origins and operations of Indian education system, 1757–1947. In: Essays in the history of Indian education. Concept. New Delhi

Bhattacharjee S (2019) Ten years of RTE act: revisiting achievements and examining gaps. In: Observer research foundation. ORF Issue Brief, No 304, p 2 https://www.orfonline.org/research/ten-years-of-rte-act-revisiting-achievements-and-examining-gaps-54066/. Accessed 31 Mar 2022

Bhoite UB (2009) Higher education in India: a system on the verge of chaos. Sociol Bull 58(2):147–149

Biswas A, Agrawal SP (1986) Development of education in India: a historical survey of educational documents before and after independence. Concept Publishing Company, New Delhi, p 71

British Council (2019) The school education system in India: an overview, p. 21. https://www.britishcouncil.in/sites/default/files/school_education_system_in_india_report_2019_final_web.pdf. Accessed 31 Mar 2022

Central Institute of Educational Technology (CIET) (2022) About CIET. https://ciet.nic.in/. Accessed 31 Mar 2022

Central Tibetan School Administration (CTSA), Department of School Education & Literacy, Government of India. https://dsel.education.gov.in/ctsa. Accessed 31 Mar 2022

Chalam K (1990) Caste reservations and equality of opportunity in Education. Econ Pol Wkly 25(42):2333

Council of Architecture (COA). About us. https://www.coa.gov.in/. Accessed 31 Mar 2022

Department of Higher Education, Ministry of Education, Government of India. Overview. https://www.education.gov.in/en/institutions. Accessed 31 Mar 2022

Department of Higher Education, Ministry of Education, Government of India. Apex level bodies. https://www.education.gov.in/en/apex-level-bodies. Accessed 31 Mar 2022

Department of School Education & Literacy, Ministry of Education, Government of India. Institutions. https://www.education.gov.in/en/autonomous_bodies. Accessed 31 Mar 2022

Deshpande S (2019) Reservation and the republic: one constitution, two amendments and seven decades. Social Change 49(3):512–514

Dewan H, Mehendale A (2015) Towards a new education policy: directions and consideration. Econ Polit Weekly 50(48):15

Editorial (2015) A tale of greed and cynicism: investigation into Madhya Pradesh's Vyapam scam must be completed quickly. Econ Polit Weekly 50(20):8

Education Department. Government of NCT of Delhi. http://edudel.nic.in/directorate.html. Accessed 31 Mar 2022

Encyclopaedia Britannica (2007) The Britannica guide to India, p 315

Eri, R et al (2021) Digital resilience in higher education in response to COVID-19 pandemic: student perceptions from Asia and Australia. J Univ Teach Learn Pract 18(5):1–20

Gawarikar V, Pramanik S (2015) Foreign education regulatory bill—a ray of hope or despair. IOSR J Hum Soc Sci 20(6):25–30. https://doi.org/10.9790/0837-20642530

Government of India (1980) Report of the backward classes commission, Vol I, p 58. http://www.ncbc.nic.in/Writereaddata/Mandal%20Commission%20Report%20of%20the%201st%20Part%20English635228715105764974.pdf. Accessed 31 Mar 2022

Higher Education Profile, Department of Higher Education, Ministry of Education, Government of India i, iii (2019–20). https://www.education.gov.in/sites/upload_files/mhrd/files/statistics-new/he_profile_1920.pdf. Accessed 31 Mar 2022

https://prsindia.org/billtrack/the-foreign-educational-institutions-regulation-of-entry-and-operations-bill-2010. Accessed 31 Mar 2022

https://prsindia.org/files/bills_acts/bills_parliament/2010/Foreign_Educational_Institutions_Regulation_of_Entry_and_Operations_Bill__2010.pdf. Accessed 31 Mar 2022

https://www.business-standard.com/article/current-affairs/available-but-unaffordable-story-of-higher-education-in-india-116123100779_1.html. Accessed 31 Mar 2022

https://www.business-standard.com/podcast/current-affairs/four-labour-codes-that-everyone-is-talking-about-121122900040_1.html#:~:text=The%20four%20labour%20codes%20%2D%2D,are%20in%20the%20unorganised%20sector. Accessed 29 Dec 2021

Indian Council of Historical Research. Aims & objectives. http://ichr.ac.in/content/innerpage/aims---objectives.php. Accessed 31 Mar 2022

Indian Council of Philosophical Research (ICPR). Aims and objectives. http://icpr.in/about.html. Accessed 31 Mar 2022

Indian Council of Social Sciences Research (ICSSR). ICSSR at a glance. https://icssr.org/icssr-glance

Jain R (2005) Minority rights in education: reflections on article 30 of the Indian constitution. Econ Pol Wkly 40(24):2430–2431

Jayaraman R, Simroth D (2015) The impact of school lunches on primary school enrolment: evidence from India's midday meal scheme. The Scandinavian J Econ 117(4):1176–1201

Kabir H (1957) Indian education since independence. The Phi Delta Kappan 39(3):104–107

Katiyar P (2019) PENCiL power: keeping victims of child labour in schools through attendance stipend. The Economic Times, 31 Aug 2019. https://economictimes.indiatimes.com/news/politics-and-nation/pencil-power-keeping-victims-of-child-labour-in-schools-through-attendance-stipend/articleshow/70926584.cms?from=mdr. Accessed 31 Mar 2022

Kaur R (2021) Estimating the impact of school feeding programs: evidence from mid-day meal scheme of India. Econ Educ Rev 84(1):1

Kaur N, Byard RW (2021) Prevalence and potential consequences of child labour in India and the possible impact of COVID-19—a contemporary overview. Med Sci Law 61(3):208

Kendriya Vidyalaya Sangathan (KVS), Ministry of Education, Government of India (2022) Vision and mission. https://kvsangathan.nic.in/. Accessed 31 Mar 2022

Khanna G (2020) Does affirmative action incentivize schooling? Evidence from India. Rev Econ Stat 102(2):219–221

Kingdon GG (2007) The progress of school education in India. Oxf Rev Econ Policy 23(2):168–171

Kumar A et al (2019) Right to education act: universalisation or entrenched exclusion. J Social Incl Stud 5(1):89–90

Kumar MJ (2020) National education policy: how does it affect higher education in India? IETE Tech Rev 37(4):327

Mahapatra A, Sharma P (2020) Education in times of Covid-19 pandemic: academic stress and its psychosocial impact on children and adolescents in India. Int J Social Psychiatry 67(4):397

Maheshwari SR (1997) Reservation policy in India: theory and practice. Indian J Public Admin 43(3):662–671

Malvankar A (2018) Elementary school education and the right to education act, 2009. Sociol Bull 67(2):1–2

Ministry of Education, Government of India. Overview. https://www.education.gov.in/en/about-moe. Accessed 25 Mar 2023

Mirta SK (2017) Politics in India: structure, process and policy. Routledge, New Delhi, p 77

Mosse D (2018) Caste and development: contemporary perspectives on a structure of discrimination and advantage. World Dev 110:422–424

Mukherjee M (2015) Indian Education at the crossroads of postcoloniality, globalization and the 21st century knowledge economy (Part I). Policy Fut Educ 13(2):165

Mukhopadhaya P et al (2012) Education for child labour: evaluating the national child labour policy in West Bengal, India. J Contemp Asia 42(4):651

Nariman FS (2006) India's legal system: can it be saved? Penguin Books, New Delhi, p 37

National Bal Bhavan. Overview. http://nationalbalbhavan.nic.in/aboutus/overview.html. Accessed 31 Mar 2022

National Council for Teacher Education (NCTE). Objective. https://ncte.gov.in/Website/about.aspx. Accessed 31 Mar 2022

National Council of Educational Research & Training (NCERT). About us. https://ncert.nic.in/about-us.php?ln. Accessed 31 Mar 2022

National Institute of Open Schooling (NIOS). Objective. https://www.nios.ac.in/. Accessed 31 Mar 2022

National Medical Commission. Introduction .https://www.nmc.org.in/about-nmc/introduction/. Accessed 31 Mar 2022

Naveen P (2021) Vyapam scam: CBI gets MP nod to prosecute top officials. The Times of India, 24 Dec 2021. https://timesofindia.indiatimes.com/india/vyapam-scam-cbi-gets-mp-nod-to-prosecute-top-officials/articleshow/88463126.cms. Accessed 31 Mar 2022

Navodaya Vidyalaya Samiti (NVA). Vision. https://navodaya.gov.in/nvs/en/Home1. Accessed 31 Mar 2022

Panigrahi S, Singh J (2016) Available but unaffordable: story of higher education in India. Business Standard, 31 Dec 2016

Press Trust of India (2020) More than 50% of India's population 25 years or older: survey. Livemint, 3 July 2020. https://www.livemint.com/news/india/more-than-50-of-india-s-population-25-yrs-or-older-survey-11593793054491.html. Accessed 31 Mar 2022

PRS Legislative Research. Demand for grants 2021–22 analysis: education. https://prsindia.org/budgets/parliament/demand-for-grants-2021-22-analysis-education. Accessed 31 Mar 2022

Ramachandran P (2019) School mid-day meal programme in India: past, present, and future. Indian J Paediatrics 86(6):542–543

Rameshwar Sarma V et al (1995) Impact of midday meal program on educational and nutritional status of school-going children in Andhra Pradesh, India. Asia Pacific J Public Health 8(1):48–50

Ray S, Saini S (2016) Efficacy of right-based approach to education: a comparative study of two states of India. Policy Futures in Educ 14(2):274–276

Srikrishna (2008) The Indian legal system. Int J Legal Inform 36(2):242

Star S (2021) The impact of COVID-19 on the right to education in India. In: Education law association, yearbook of education law

Star S, Bharadwaj A (2020) 'A comparative overview of constitutional human rights protections'. In: Tomar A (eds) Comparative reflections on the constitutional models of India and Australia. Bloomsbury Professional India, pp 5.1–5.16

Star S, Bharadwaj A (2021) Constitutional rights and guarantees: the contrasting approaches of Australia and India. Int J Human Rights 1:9.https://doi.org/10.1080/13642987.2021.1954618

The Bar Council of India. About the council. http://www.barcouncilofindia.org/about/about-the-bar-council-of-india/. Accessed 31 Mar 2022

Tierney WG, Sabharwal NS (2016) Analysing the culture of corruption in Indian Higher Education. Int High Educ 87:6–7

Tilak JBG (2015) How inclusive is higher education in India? Social Change 45(2):185–210

Unified District Information System For Education Plus (UDISE+). Department of School Education and Literacy, Ministry of Education, Government of India 1, 9 (2019–20) https://www.education.gov.in/sites/upload_files/mhrd/files/statistics-new/udise_201920.pdf. Accessed 31 Mar 2022

University Grants Commission (UGC). Genesis. https://www.ugc.ac.in/page/Genesis.aspx. Accessed 31 Mar 2022

Vaidyanatha Ayyar RV (2017) History of education policymaking in India, 1947–2016. Oxford University Press, London, p 37

Vanamali KV (2021) Four labour codes that everyone is talking about. Business Standard

Weisskopf TE (2004) Impact of reservation on admission to higher education in India. Econ Pol Wkly 39(39):4339

Whitehead C (2005) The historiography of British imperial education policy, Part I: India. History Educ 34(3):315–318

Zachariah M (1972) Positive discrimination in education for India's scheduled castes: a review of the problems. Comp Educ Rev 16(1):16–17

Educational Law in Japan

Koju Sasaki

1 Introduction

In Japan the rule of law as a modern nation was begun by the Meiji Restoration, since then the educational legal system related has being transformed and developed in the influence of political, economic, and international environment peculiar to Japan. After World War II, under the occupation policy by the General Headquarters of the Allied Forces (mainly United States of America), new democratic policies were implemented. And after the restoration of independence from the General Headquarters, the centralized educational legislation was back. From the 1950s administrative bureaucrats had power to lead the development of educational legislation during the period of political stability. At the beginning of twenty-first century, administrative and financial reforms occurred designed to decentralization and deregulation of the central government, the policy was triggered by the first full-scale change of government by the Democratic Party.

In recent years, under the percolation of the Convention on the Rights of the Child as a domestic law, laws focusing on issues facing school problems, such as bullying, poverty, school absenteeism and abuse, have been developed. On April 1, 2023, in order to comprehensively promote children's policies, the Act on the Establishment of the Agency for Child and Families will be established and the Basic Act on Children will be enforced. Cross-disciplinary legislation for welfare and medical care for "children" that are not limited to the "school" and "school age" is being formed.

In academia as well, the debate on educational law in Japan has taken a distinctive turn. Discussions on educational legislation and educational administration are being developed with the involvement of the state in education as a central research topic (Kaneko 1978). The background to this is that it has developed in close relationship

K. Sasaki (✉)
Tokyo Gakugei University, Koganei, Tokyo, Japan
e-mail: copyright@esph.com.cn

C. J. Russo and L. Ma (eds.), *A Comparative Analysis of Systems of Education Law*,
https://doi.org/10.1007/978-981-97-1052-2_8

with political and labor movements against the backdrop of the political confrontation between the left and the right that has intensified since the 1950s. In Japan, educational law research on education has flourished since the 1950s, and this issue has been discussed mainly through hermeneutics and sociological jurisprudence. In recent years, however, discussions in academia have shifted to focus on practical issues related to schools and education, such as the relationship between individualized and collaborative learning, the problem of child poverty and abuse, and the reform of teachers' work styles. Evidence-based policymaking and the active involvement of the state and government have become the main themes.

In this paper, we will give an overview of the characteristics of the educational legislation in Japan, the historical development of its educational legislation and educational trials, and the trends in educational law in recent years.

2 Characteristics of Japan Educational Legislation

In Japan, the Meiji Restoration (1868) began the construction of a modern state centered on the emperor and the creation of a system as a nation governed by the rule of law. In 1889, the first constitution in the Japan, the "Constitution of the Great Japan Empire" (Meiji Constitution), was promulgated, and politics and administration began to develop as a modern state with the constitution under the authority of the Emperor. In 1947 Japan then reached a major turning point at the end of World War II, under occupation by the General Headquarters of the Allied Forces, the democratic Japan constitution was enacted with popular sovereignty, respect for fundamental human rights, and pacifism as the pillars. In addition, the Fundamental Law of Education was enacted as a law closely related to the Constitution, and a democratic educational legislation embodying the constitutional philosophy was developed. The following is an overview of the characteristics of educational legislation in post-war Japan.

(1) **Legislation based on the Fundamental Law of Education**

A major feature of the Japan's educational legislation is that it is formed based on a law called the "Fundamental Law of Education." (Tanaka 1961) In Japan, the Fundamental Law of Education has two major meanings. These are the "Declaration of Education Meaning" that widely presents the basic principles of education to the public, and the "Constitutional Meaning of Education" that complements the provisions on education in the Constitution and provides basic principles and guidelines for the interpretation and application of other general laws and regulations. To add to the latter, the current Constitution was enacted in 1947, but the only article that directly stipulates education is Article 26 of the Constitution (which provides for the right to education and compulsory education), and the Fundamental Law of Education plays a role in embodying the principles and ideals that should be stipulated in the Constitution in education, and presenting principles that form the basis of education-related laws and regulations. Although the Fundamental Law of Education is a "act" in legal form, it has been given the status of a "constitution of education" as a "constitution of education" that provides basic principles and principles to education-related laws and as a standard for interpreting them.

Since the Fundamental Law of Education has a history of being regarded as one with the Constitution, both the Constitution has not been amended for a long time. However, more than half a century has passed since its enactment, and since the situation surrounding education has changed significantly, in March 2000, Prime Minister Obuchi Keizo established the National Council for Educational Reform as Prime Minister's private advisory body, held a comprehensive review of postwar education and discussed the basics of education, and under the next Prime Minister Mori Yoshiro, a report was made that it was necessary to review the Fundamental Law of Education and formulate a basic plan for the promotion of education suitable for the new era. In December 2006, under the first Cabinet of Abe Shinzo, the Fundamental Law of Education was amended entirely. The revised Fundamental Law of Education was enacted through major amendments and additions to the text, such as a large number of new philosophies that are considered important in light of today's situation, such as morality, autonomy, and public spirit, while inheriting the principles of the old Fundamental Law of Education. It is said that the revision greatly reduced the direct relationship between the Fundamental Law of Education and the Constitution, and on the other hand, the Fundamental Law of Education itself came to have the character of a "fundamental law of education," and strengthened its character as a basis for the enactment of education-related acts and regulations and as a standard for interpretation. In addition, the Fundamental Law of Education newly stipulates that the national and local governments should formulate a basic plan for the promotion of education, and the necessary budgets are taken in accordance with the comprehensive education plan formulated by the government, and various administrative measures are implemented. As a result, it can be said that the Fundamental Law of Education is not only a philosophy law that broadly provides educational principles and basic principles, but also strengthens its character as a policy basis law and a policy promotion law (Sasaki 2009).

The current Fundamental Law of Education (revised in 2006) after the amendment consists of a preamble and 18 articles. Chapter 1 (Purpose and Philosophy of Education) stipulates the purpose of education (Article 1), the goal of education (Article 2), the philosophy of lifelong learning (Article 3), and equal educational opportunity (Article 4). Chapter 2 (Basics of the Implementation of Education) stipulates compulsory education (Article 5), school education (Article 6), university (Article 7), private school (Article 8), teacher (Article 9), home education (Article 10), early childhood education (Article 11), social education (Article 12), cooperation and coordination among schools, families, and local residents (Article 13), political education (Article 14), and religious education (Article 15). Chapter 3 (Educational Administration) stipulates the administration of education (Article 16) and the Basic Plan for the Promotion of Education (Article 17), and Chapter 4 (Enactment of Laws and Regulations) stipulates the enactment of laws and regulations (Article 18).

(2) The relationship between the state and education as a major issue in education law

In Japanese education law, the relationship between the state and education has always been a major theme since the end of World War II. Reflecting on the pre-war nationalism and excessively centralized educational system, the relationship between the "state" and "education" has long been questioned in Japan. At the root of this is the idea that when the state is involved in education, special considerations different from those in other fields are necessary. The first reason for this is that education is an activity that directly affects the irreplaceable personality itself, and since it has a great influence on the formation of each person's way of being, individuality and personality, there is a belief that involvement in education by the state should be as restrained as possible. Second, education is an activity that directly affects the values and cultures related to the identity of individuals and groups, and if the state denies the basic values and cultures that support the existence of families and ethnic groups through education, there is a fear that they will lose their basis and raison d'être. The state and the laws mediating education have become points of contention, and specifically, the legal character of the national curriculum standards, the constitutionality of textbook examinations, and the constitutionality of national achievement survey (national achievement tests) have been disputed.

In particular, the question was asked who had the right to educate children. In this regard, the "theory of the right to education of the state," which holds that the state is involved in the content of education and has the authority to make decisions, and the "theory of the right to education of the people," which holds that the entire nation is centered on parents and teachers who have been entrusted to it, are at odds, and the location of the right to education has long been a point of contention. This issue was settled to a certain extent by the Supreme Court judgment of May 21, 1976 (Asahikawa National Achievement Test Case). The Supreme Court rejected the "theory of the right to education of the state" and the "theory of the right to education of the people" as "both extreme and unilateral" and held that the state could be involved in the content of education "to the extent deemed necessary and appropriate."

This judgment is outlined because it is an important lawsuit that has had a major impact on the state of education legislation in Japan. The Ministry of Education (the predecessor of the current Ministry of Education, Culture, Sports, Science and Technology) conducted the "National Junior High School Achievement Survey" (National Achievement Test) conducted in 1956–1965 for 2nd and 3rd grade students of junior high schools nationwide. Teachers who opposed the implementation of this test were charged with obstruction of the execution of official duties and other offenses because they tried to prevent the implementation of the test by force. In both the first trial (the Asahikawa District Court judgment on May 25, 1966) and the second trial (Sapporo High Court judgment of June 26, 1968), the defendant was found guilty of trespassing on a building, but was acquitted of the crime of obstructing the execution of official duties on the grounds that the national achievement test was illegal, and only the establishment of the crime of cooperative assault was recognized.

In response, the Supreme Court found the national achievement test to be legal and granted the defendant a suspended sentence of obstruction of the execution of official duties. The main issues in this case are (1) the ownership of permission to decide for children's education, (2) the existence of right to learning as constitutional right, and (3) the freedom of education of teachers. As for (1), as mentioned above, the eclectic theory is adopted because neither the "right to education of the state" nor the "right to education of the people" can be fully adopted. Although the right of parents to education is considered to be a natural right derived from the relationship between parents and children, the freedom of education of parents is regarded as limited as appearing mainly in the freedom of education and school choice outside of school, such as home education. Regarding (2), Article 26 of the Constitution passively expresses "the right to education," but the judgment confirms that behind this provision lies the inherent right to learn as a human right. With regard to (3), it was stated that teachers are allowed to exercise freedom of education to a certain extent on the basis of academic freedom and freedom required by the essential requirements of education, but are subject to restrictions due to the developmental stage of the student and the request to ensure a national standard. The Supreme Court's ruling in the Asahikawa Achievement Test Case has had a major impact on the future state of education legislation.

Article 16 of the Fundamental Law of Education, which stipulates educational administration, prohibits unjust rule over education. Here, "unjust rule" means something that harms the neutrality and impartiality of education, and it has been confirmed that even administrative organs authorized by law are entities that carry out unjust control depending on the content.

(3) **Educational legislation based on special laws**

The educational law in Japan is characterized by the fact that it is developed on the basis of special laws enacted separately from general laws in educational administration and public official legislation. In Japan, the legislation for politics and administration in local areas is implemented based on the Local Autonomy Act, which is a general law, while educational administration is implemented based on the "Act on the Organization and Operation of Local Educational Administration," which corresponds to a special law of the Local Autonomy Act. In the case of general administration, while the legislative system has been established in which the mayor of municipality elected by the public election of the residents has administrative authority and responsibility, in the case of educational administration, a collegial body of education is established and assigned to it in charge of educational administration, thereby preventing the concentration of authority on the mayor and implementing specialized administrative management related to education. Specifically, from the perspective of ensuring political neutrality, continuity, and stability in local educational administration, both at the prefectural and municipal levels, educational administration power is granted for the Board of Education, which is a collegial administrative committee independent from the mayor (consisting of one superintendent and four members, in principle). The superintendent and the four members are to be appointed by the mayor with the consent of Local councils and are to be independent of the general administration).

In addition, in the public service legislation, educational public servants, such as public school teachers, are not only subject to the Local Public Officials Act, which is a general law, but also to the "Special Act for Educational Public Officials," which corresponds to a special law of the Local Public Officials Act, in consideration of the characteristics of their duties and the special nature of their work styles. The Act provides for special treatment of educational public officials in a wide range of areas, including appointments, dismissals, quotas, salaries, discipline, service, training, and staff associations. Specifically, recruitment (including promotions, etc.) should be based on the process of "selection" rather than "competitive examination", opportunities for training such as training outside the place of work and long-term training within the range that does not interfere with classes are secured, restrictions on political acts are based on the process of national public officials, and the scope of the restriction extends not only to the area of work but also to the whole country, and for concurrent employment and concurrent work related to education. And the public school teachers can engage within the scope that the appointing authority deems that there is no hindrance to the main duties. In addition, the salary system for public school teachers is established in the "Act on Special Measures Concerning the Salaries of Educational Staff of Public Compulsory Education Schools" (Special Salary Act). In light of the peculiarities of teachers' duties and work patterns, which are difficult to measure in terms of working hours, unlike general public servants, holiday work allowances and overtime allowances are not paid, but instead a certain percentage of salaries are uniformly paid as adjustment amounts for teachers regardless of working hours (in recent years, it has been pointed out that this has become a hotbed of long working hours for teachers).

In this way, a major feature of the Japanese educational law is that special laws are applied to the educational administration legislation and the civil service legislation for public school teachers due to the characteristics of educational administration and teachers' duties.

(4) **Multi-layered legislation for the right to learning**

As a characteristic of the educational law in the Japan, it can be said that in the accumulation of various laws of the postwar education law, the three legal systems for guaranteeing the right to learning have been formed in a multilayered manner (Sasaki 2023).

One is legislation to guarantee the right to learning that is uniformly provided by nationwide common education-related acts and regulations enacted about half a century after the end of World War II. With regard to school education, especially compulsory education, in order to ensure equal opportunities and a nationwide standard of education in order for the national government to guarantee the right to education of the people nationwide, the development of basic legislation for the school system under the School Education Act, etc., the development of legislation that will serve as the basis for the allocation of teachers and financial measures for compulsory education expenses under the Act on the Burden of Compulsory Education Expenses of the National Treasury, etc., The educational legal system is formed mainly by acts and regulations at the national level as national standards, such as the development of legislation for teacher licensing to ensure the professionalism of teachers under the Educational Staff Licensing Act, etc. Many of the legislative acts in local governments have been enacted in a manner that is subject to the provisions of national laws and regulations, and it can be said that educational legislation has been formed mainly by national law in the form of individual act such as the Fundamental Law of Education, the School Education Act, and local delegation ordinances. It can be said that this legislation seeks to guarantee the right to learning in school education based on uniform nationwide standards.

Since then, progress has been made mainly in the 2000s with moves toward decentralization and deregulation from the national government. A major turning point in this process was the enactment of the Package of Acts for the Promotion of Decentralization in 1999. As a result of the revision of the law, the control of local governments by the national government became severely restricted, and the enactment and application of local laws unique to each region was promoted. The relationship between the national government and the local governments has changed from a hierarchical relationships to an equal partnership, the system of affairs delegated to agencies that allow local governments to handle the affairs of the state as a branch of the state has been abolished, the basic rules for the involvement of the national government in local areas have been established, and a legal system has been established to make decentralization that had been just formally institutionalized in the past. For example, in 2002, the Enforcement Order of the School Education Act was amended to introduce a system whereby students who fall under the school enrollment criteria and who are deemed to have special circumstances that allow them to receive appropriate education at elementary and junior high schools at the discretion of the municipal board of education to enroll in elementary and junior high schools in order to determine where to enroll students with disabilities. In addition, when the "Act on Special Zones for Structural Reform" was promulgated in 2002, measures that took advantage of regional characteristics were developed, such as the establishment of a new type of school utilizing the special provisions of the School Education Act (establishment of schools by joint-stock companies and NPOs), and elementary, junior high, and high school integrated education in English that flexibly applied the national curriculum standard. In this way, the discretion to guarantee children's right to learning was expanded by the decision of each region and each board of education.

What is currently progressing is the development of laws and regulations to address individual educational issues such as poverty, bullying, and school absenteeism. Specifically, the Act on the Securing of Educational Opportunities Equivalent to General Education at the Stage of Compulsory Education for dealing with students with school absenteeism problems, the Act on Promotion of Measures to Prevent Bullying to respond effectively to bullying problems, the Act on Promotion of Measures to Child Poverty to solve poverty, and the Act on Elimination of

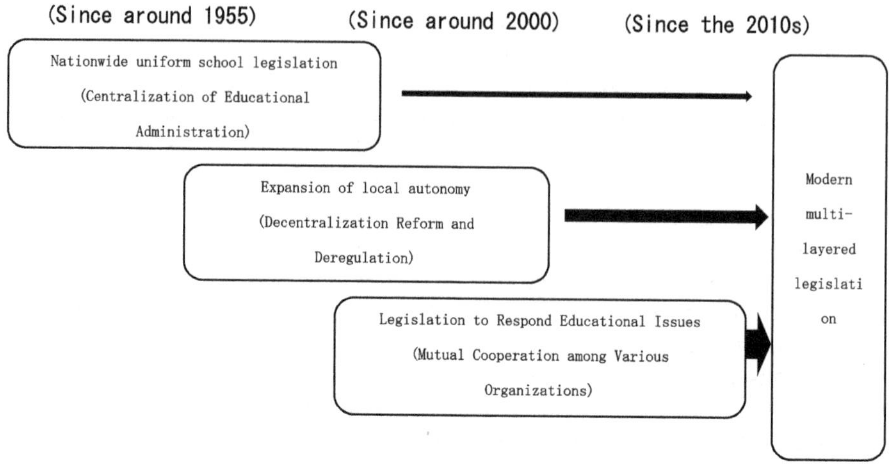

Fig. 1 Multi-layered educational legislation in modern times

Discrimination against Persons with Disabilities requiring "Reasonable Accommodation "for persons with disabilities, etc., in accordance with individual educational issues and individual circumstances, Legislation is being developed to make the guarantee of the right to learning substantive. Laws to respond to these educational issues are not limited to schools, but are based on the premise of linkages in a wide range of fields such as welfare, police, medical care, and NPOs, and differ from conventional legislation in that they assume mutual linkages between legal domains and the comprehensive development of legal systems.

In this way, it can be said that the current educational legislation is at the stage where school legislation to guarantee the right to learning uniformly throughout the country, legislation to promote the guarantee of children's right to learning based on the voluntary decisions of local governments, and legislation to respond to individual educational issues among the legal domains are coexisting in a multi-layered manner (Fig. 1).

3 Trends About Legislation and Court Cases

Next, with regard to the changes in the education law in the Japan, we will outline the legislative trends related to education and the trends of court cases in educational (Sasaki 2022).

(1) **Trends about Legislation**

<Phase 1: Establishment of Legislation based on the Constitution and the Fundamental Law of Education, which advanced under the GHQ occupation>

After the end of the war in 1945, Japan was occupied by the General Headquarters (GHQ). During the occupation, the Japanese government negotiated repeatedly based on the proposals presented by GHQ, and in 1947, a new constitution was enacted based on popular sovereignty, guarantee of fundamental human rights, and pacifism, and educational legislation based on the constitutional philosophy was developed based on the principles of separation of powers and the rule of law.

Before the war, important and basic matters concerning education were to be determined by the "Royal Decree" ordered by the Emperor, but Article 26 of the Constitution enacted in 1947 and Article 16 of the Fundamental Law of Education established the "legalism of education" that education is conducted in accordance with the provisions of laws enacted by the Diet composed of representatives of the people.

Under the new Constitution, the Fundamental Law of Education was enacted, which stipulates the basic principles concerning education. The Fundamental Law of Education has been given a special place in the educational legislation of Japan, as evidenced by the enactment of the Fundamental Law of Education as an annex to the Constitution to supply the provisions of the Constitution concerning education. The Fundamental Law of Education has become to provide a philosophy and principle in education-related laws as a "Constitution of Education" and has been given a position as an interpretation standard. During this period, under the Constitution and the Fundamental Law of Education, basic laws supporting public education, such as the School Education Act and the Private School Act, were developed. With regard to local educational administration, the Board of Education Act was enacted, and the Board of Education, consisting of members elected by the public election of residents, was to be in charge of local educational administration, and the board was given the right to submit mayor education-related budgets.

<Phase 2: Establishment of Centralized Legislation after the Independence—55 Regime>

Later, the GHQ occupation came to an end with the conclusion of the San Francisco Peace Treaty, and with the independence of the Japan, the educational legislation changed greatly in a centralized direction.

In 1951, the Act for the Organization and Operation of Local Educational Administration was enacted (Board of Education Act was abolished). The post-war democratization and decentralization policies shifted significantly to a centralized educational administration system, with the change about the board members from a system of public election by residents to an appointment system by the mayor, and the approval of the Minister of Education required for the appointment of the superintendent of education of local boards of education.

In 1955, the Liberal Democratic Party and the Socialist Party formed two major parties through the unification and reorganization of political parties, but the political situation in which the Liberal Democratic Party was dominant and in charge for the long term in power (this political situation is said to be the "55-Regime"). Under this political situation, the educational administrative system also took the form of decentralization outwardly, but in reality, a local educational administration was controlled by the national government, consisting of hierarchy as the Ministry of Education-prefectural boards of education- municipal boards of education- schools. In terms of educational legislation, the Constitution and the Fundamental Law of Education, which have a strong democratic and decentralized nature, remain unrevised, and it can be said that this was an era in which the government was able to develop a controlled and uniform legal system such as the enactment of the Act Concerning the Organization and Operation of Local Educational Administration (for example, strengthening textbook screening by the government, shift of board member election system from public election to appointment of mayor).

<Phase 3: Progress in decentralization and development of local government legislation>

In the phase 2, while taking the just form of decentralization, practically centralized educational legislation system had been formed and maintained. In response to this situation, it was strongly pointed out that it was necessary to comprehensively reforms to enhance the autonomy of local governments, transfer of authority and financial resources from the national government to local governments, and deregulation over local governments and private sectors. In response to this, the Package of Acts for Decentralization (enforced in 2000), which was enacted in 1999, restricted the involvement of the national government in local governments, promoted the transfer of authority and financial resources to local governments, and greatly revised the state of centralized administration, and strengthened the autonomy of local governments and private sectors. The background to this was the movement by the national government to relax restrictions on the private sectors and local areas that had been intermittently promoted since the 1980s, and the administrative and fiscal reform that was developed in the 2000s under the Koizumi Junichiro administration that used deregulation and decentralization as two wheels for the reform. In addition, a new school board system was launched with the revision of the Act Concerning the Organization and Operation of Local Educational Administration in 2015. In the new board system, the relationship between the mayor and the board of education was strengthened, the involvement of the mayor in the educational administration was strengthened, and in the local education administration, the integration between general administration and educational administration was promoted through the newly established General Education Council composed of the mayor and the board members.

In addition, against the backdrop of decentralization reform and deregulation movements, local governments (boards of education) are developing their own education policies. For example, unique initiatives are expanding in rural areas, such as the adoption of a school choice system by making school zones more flexible, the establishment of a new type of school for compulsory education schools, the introduction of the school management council system and the community school system, the development of distinctive operation through the utilization of Act on Special Zones for Structural Reform, and the establishment of new type community centers. With regard to compulsory education, to the response to student needs who have school absenteeism problem, each municipality has been developing its own measures, such as promoting initiatives in cooperation with social education facilities and NPOs, etc., and its own ordinances and rules have been enacted for this purpose.

<Phase 4: New system based on the revised Fundamental Law of Education>

The Fundamental Law of Education of 1947 contributed to the realization of equal opportunities in education and the improvement of the level of education, but responding to major changes society and the serious situation of educational issues, revisions to the Fundamental Law of Education were proposed. As mentioned above, the Fundamental Law of Education was revised totally in 2006. It is said that the revision of the Fundamental Law of Education has greatly transformed the educational legislation of Japan. First, the Fundamental Law of Education, which was enacted in 1947 as one with the Constitution and maintained its character as an annexed law to the Constitution, has been weakened because of becoming separate from the Constitution, and although it is subject to the constraints of the Constitution, the direct relationship between the Constitution and the new Fundamental Law of Education has been greatly reduced. Secondly, as a result, the new Fundamental Law of Education, which has lost its close relationship with the Constitution, has strengthened its character as a fundamental law of education-related acts and regulations, and a legal system headed by the new Fundamental Law of Education has been formed. In particular, the relationship with school education-related act and regulations, which have an organized and systematic character, is that a strong system has been formed, including delegated ordinances and rules in local governments. Third, Article 2 of the new Fundamental Law of Education stipulates the goals to be achieved in education, so that it has come to function not only as a system of educational institutions but also as a system of educational content through revisions to the national curriculum standards, textbook examination standards, guidelines for school administration, etc.

<Phase 5: Establishment of politically led legislation to responding to educational issues>

During this period, the deteriorating educational issues such as school absenteeism were recognized as serious problems that could not be solved by the conventional uniform educational legislation. In order to respond to this situation, progress has been made in recent years in the development of various acts and regulations to respond to individual educational issues. In particular, the full-fledged change of government by the Democratic Party in 2009 is recognized as the turning point of policy making, political parties and politicians have taken the lead in the development of legislation, and reform of the education legislation to solve educational issues such as bullying has come to be raised as an election campaign manifest list. Specifically, the enactment of the Act on Promotion of Measures to Prevent Bullying to settle bullying problems (2013), the enactment of the Act on Promotion of Measures to Child Poverty to deal with the problem of poverty of children and students (2013), the revision of the Child Welfare Act and the Child Abuse Prevention Act for the prevention of child abuse, and the development of legislation for persons with disabilities to address the problem of persons with disabilities were promoted mainly in the 2010s.

In order to deal with actual social problems, measures have been developed to promote cooperation among administrative agencies and the private sector across a wide range of fields such as school education, welfare, medical care, police, and the judiciary, and this means that interpenetration of the legal domain and the integration of legislation will advance toward the resolution of educational issues. In addition, in order to respond to educational issues that are difficult to resolve and increasingly complex disputes, laws are being revised in rapid succession, and it can be said that a situation is emerging in which the precedents formed in the stable period of educational administration can no longer be applied as they are.

(2) **Trends about court cases in education**

In exploring the status of education law, it is important to confirm trends in court cases in educational. This is because by confirming court cases in detail, it is possible to clarify legal issues in educational practice, school management, and policy making, and to objectively confirm the actual process of dispute formation through mutual claims in specific cases, and to confirm changes in the legal situation in schools and educational administration by examining court cases.

<What is the Education Trial>

In Japan, the term "educational trial" can be broadly understood as a trial case concerning education and educational activities (categorization from the viewpoint of factual involvement), or it can be regarded from a special viewpoint as a trial in which the legal logic of educational laws peculiar to the educational system is formed. Regarding the latter, Kaneko Masashi, who led the study of educational law at the time, stated, "The legal logic of 'educational law' peculiar to the education system was formed in such a way as to encourage education to be conducted well." In addition, Kaneko categorized educational trials into the "Autonomy Protective Educational Trial," which has the function of protecting the autonomy of education, the "Educational Condition Demanding Education Trial," which has the function of securing the external conditions of education, and the "Educational Corrective Education Trial," which has the function of improving education itself. This categorization and view of "education trials" is based on the knowledge accumulated at the time when discussions focused on the relationship between the state and education on the modalities of education-related acts and regulations. Recently, in order for the healthy growth and development of children and the resolution of educational issues, new ways of relationship between various related entities such as schools, families, governments, NPOs, and companies are being sought, not limited to the framework of the relationship between the state and education, and in addition, education, welfare, and the need for children who actually have problems of poverty and abuse are being sought. Mutual cooperation among stakeholders and related organizations that transcend administrative boundaries such as the police has become an important issue. In light of the situation in which children, education, and schools are placed recent years, it can be said that it is necessary to find useful perspectives from the analysis of educational trials with a broader understanding of the subject matter and to realize the happiness and benefits of children and to solve educational issues.

<The history of educational trials after WWII and perspectives on recent educational trials>

The historical development of educational trials in our country can be broadly categorized as follows due to the nature of legal disputes. (I) the transition period of educational legislation, (II) the period of political conflict, (III) the period of diversification in conflict. The first period is positioned as a turning point in the educational legislation after the enactment of the Constitution and the Fundamental Law of Education. This was the period when core laws such as the School Education Act and the Board of Education Act were put in place. This period was a period of transition from the edict-based principle of education to the principle of law, and although the basic acts and regulations were in place, the provisions concerning textbooks, staff councils, etc. were not sufficiently developed, and it can be said that it was a time when lawsuits were filed over the location of rights and authority and the interpretation of the law. The second period ranged from the so-called "55 Regime", when political confrontations between the left and right sides of the politics were conspicuous, to the period when the political confrontations subsided. During this period, educational disputes frequently broke out between policy sides and their counterparts under the legislative system centered on the Constitution and the Fundamental Law of Education, and under the long-term administration of the Liberal Democratic Party, in the background of political confrontations between the left and right. The third phase was a period in which the left–right confrontation settled since the 1990s had subsided and administrative and financial reforms centered on decentralization and deregulation from national government had been developed, and information disclosure had progressed, and disputes diversified over violations of educational human rights by schools, boards of education, etc., such as corporal punishment and bullying among children, parents, and citizens.

Various laws have been enacted and revised since the III period. In recent years, politically led educational legislation such as the Act on Promotion of Measures to Prevent Bullying has increasing sharply, and domestic legislation based on the Convention on the Rights of the Child and the Convention on the Rights of Persons with Disabilities has been developed. The following perspectives have been observed from recent educational court cases, and it is thought that it will have more important meaning in the future.

- It is necessary to review administrative interpretations formed under the so-called left–right political conflicts since the 1950s, such as voluntary training of teachers and political activities, in a contemporary context <the viewpoint of reviewing administrative interpretations accompanying changes in social conditions>
- In addition to systematic setup of guaranteeing the right to learning, it is necessary to have the viewpoint that a new framework has been formed for the guarantee of the right to learning in a separate and flexible manner in the legal system concerning school education <from the compound perspective of legislation for systematic guarantee of the right to learning and legislation for individual guarantee>

- There is a need to devise legal interpretation to meet the needs of modern educational practice and educational management, such as encouraging voluntary training of teachers and fostering a culture of donation in schools <the perspective of developing legal interpretation in light of contemporary educational practices and educational management needs>
- It is necessary to clarify the trend of trials based on the shift from a policy-based approach to a rights-based approach in education legislation and to consider the modalities of multiple legal processes <the viewpoint of creating legal logic based on the rights-based approach>
- It is necessary to pay attention to the creation of new functions of the law, such as the educational commitment promotion function of the "definition of bullying" based on the subjective judgment of the victim in the Act on Promotion of Measures to Prevent Bullying, and the social communication promotion function of "reasonable accommodation" that obliges the response of the request of persons with disabilities under the Act on Elimination of Discrimination for persons with disabilities <the new function of the law to deal with the problem>
- Actual educational issues are not limited to other areas of education such as school education, social education, and home education, but are also required to respond in a cross-sectional manner to realize the best interests of children, such as education, welfare, medical care, and the police <the perspective of comprehensive, complex efforts to realize the best interests of children>
- From the viewpoint of organizing legal theories concerning school accidents, including the improvement of educational activities <in addition to improving and devising educational activities and curricula, such as group gymnastics at athletic events and making martial arts compulsory due to the revision of the national curriculum standard, as well as the need to reconsider the doctrine of danger tolerance that has been accepted in school educational activities in the past>
- The need to review the modalities of responsibility in crisis management, such as proactive response to disasters that have not been anticipated in the past, such as the Great East Japan Earthquake <the perspective of organizing based on judicial precedents such as the responsibility for proactive response in crisis management>
- The need to consider legal interpretation and legislation based on the recent movement to introduce new principles in educational disputes, such as children's advocacy and restorative justice <the perspective of incorporating new philosophies for the resolution of educational disputes>
- In light of the current situation where lawyers are involved in educational disputes, it is necessary to pay attention to the fact that the involvement of lawyers affects the trend of trials <the viewpoint of evaluating the involvement of lawyers in cases>
- Based on the rapid development of ICT technology such as personal information protection, copyrights, and correspondence with providers, the development of a new legal system to enable schools and other institutions to develop effective educational activities in an appropriate and timely manner, and the operational ability of teachers, governments, etc. to respond to such legislation are required

<the viewpoint of developing acts and regulations that can respond promptly to changes in society and improving the ability to respond to on-site responses>

4 Recent Trends in Educational Law and Challenges for the Future

(1) Growing impact of the conventions on education and the rights-based approach

In 1989, the 44th session of the United Nations General Assembly adopted the Convention on the Rights of the Child, and Japan ratified the convention in 1994. At the time of ratification, the Japanese government indicated that it did not need to develop special domestic laws in accordance with ratification, and the impact of the Convention on the Rights of the Child on domestic legislation and policies was considered to be limited. However, in recent years, the Convention on the Rights of the Child has been gaining its position and influence as a convention that has a major impact on the development of domestic laws and educational measures.

Specifically, the Child Welfare Act amended in 2016 states that "all children shall be in accordance with the spirit of the Convention on the Rights of the Child" in Article 1, the Act on the Securing of Educational Opportunities Equivalent to General Education at the Stage of Compulsory Education enacted in the same year states that Article 1 (purpose) "in accordance with the spirit of the Fundamental Act on Education and the Convention on the Rights of the Child", and the Acts on Promotion of Measures to Child Poverty, which was amended in 2019, states that Article 1 (purpose) states that "in accordance with the spirit of the Convention on the Rights of the Child", and Article 1 (purpose) of the Act on Promotion of Support for the Development of Children and Young People, which was amended in 2015, stipulates that it is "in accordance with the principles of the Constitution of Japan country and the Convention on the Rights of the Child." Given these things, the Convention on the Rights of the Child is clearly positioned as an important basis for recent main educational acts.

As for the reason why the Convention on the Rights of the Child has become a basis for domestic law, it can be pointed out that, first, since the Japan ratified the Convention, the provisions of the Convention have become standards and guidelines for the interpretation and development of domestic laws, domestic measures in line with the intent of the Convention have been developed, and acts and regulations and measures have been revised on matters that may conflict with the Convention. Secondly, after ratification of the Convention, the government is required to submit a report on the measures taken to realize the rights under the Convention, and in response to this, the United Nations Committee on the Rights of the Child has made recommendations on matters of concern and improvement in the Japan, and in response to this, domestic laws and system revisions have been made. Although the recommendations of the Committee on the Rights of the Child are not legally binding in their own right, their recommendations have come to have a de facto impact on domestic legislation and institutional reforms, as they are often used as a basis for pursuing government education measures in the Diet. Third, after the ratification of the Convention on the Rights of the Child at the local and private levels, local governments have been actively developing policies and civic activities on the basis of the Convention on the Rights of the Child. A certain number of municipalities are promoting comprehensive efforts to guarantee children's rights, such as the enactment of the Children's Rights Ordinance as local governments. These are movements that are not based on national laws and are aimed directly by local governments to guarantee children's right to learning. In this way, there has been a marked movement in recent years to position each child as a human rights subject based on the Convention on the Rights of the Child, and legislation to guarantee children's right to learning individually is being developed.

As a result, school education was to be run on the basis of two legal systems. One is the educational legislation as a solid foundation formed by the School Education Act, the Educational Staff Licensing Act, etc., with the Fundamental Law of Education at the top. It can be said that the school education legislation, which is based on the Fundamental Law of Education, has exerted great power in systematically guaranteeing the right to enjoy general education at school. The other is legislation that is being developed in Japan on the basis of the Convention on the Rights of the Child and the Convention on the Rights of Persons with Disabilities, which seeks to guarantee the right of each child to learning. The revision of the Child Welfare Act and the enactment of the Act on the Elimination of Discrimination against Persons with Disabilities have given rise to a movement to flexibly and individually guarantee the right to learning in a comprehensive and diverse field such as education, welfare, and medical care. If the former legislation is a movement to guarantee the right to learning systematically in places such as schools (guaranteeing the right to learning through a policy-based approach), it can be said that the latter legislation is a movement to guarantee the right to learning individually according to the circumstances and needs of each person (guarantee of the right to learning by the rights-based approach). This suggests that the government is facing a major legislative change in that it has made a major shift in its approach to clarifying the rights of each individual and guaranteeing the right to learning based on the Convention on the Rights of the Child and the Convention on the Rights of Persons with Disabilities etc.

(2) Expansion of the legalization phenomenon at school and school lawyer system

In recent years, in response to the serious situation of educational issues and the growing awareness of the rights of students and their guardians, there has been an increase in the number of cases in Japan which parents and guardians make various requests to schools accompanied by lawyers. On the other hand, it is said that schools and boards of education are increasingly using lawyers to respond to excessive demands by parents and requests made through lawyers.

The background to this is the expansion of the "legalization phenomenon" in schools and other educational settings. "Legalization" can be said to be a phenomenon in which the scope and scope of legal treatment of social issues expands. In recent school education, the concrete legal phenomena that have become prominent are: (1) the movement to seek the resolution and adjustment of conflicts that have been entrusted to educational guidance within schools and internal rules for that purpose through the rules of general society outside the school has become conspicuous (expansion of the rules of general society into schools). (2) The fact that a situation has emerged in which a solution is required through the direct application of acts and regulations, As represented by the emergence of the Act on Promotion of Measures to Prevent Bullying, for educational issues that should basically be solved through education and guidance, such as responses to bullying, etc. (direct application of the law to educational issues), (3) Movements by local governments and the legal entity that manages the school to demand individual responsibility have emerged, such as the movement of local governments to demand that teachers bear water charges due to water spills caused by forgetting to close the pool faucet has become normal (movement to clarify individual responsibility), (4) Parents and guardians accompanying lawyers for troubles in schools are involved in various ways on the part of the school and the other student. It is said that it means a situation where the movement of legal experts to intervene in matters between parties, such as the movement to make such demands, has become conspicuous (increase in the involvement of legal experts).

From the perspective of students and parents, it has been pointed out that the involvement of lawyers and others in school education has the following effects: the resolution of educational problems is achieved by sorting out the issues from a legal perspective, the involvement of lawyers encourages the response of the school, the opinions of parents and students are appropriately reflected, and the involvement of lawyers alleviates emotional conflicts between the parties. However, on the other hand, there are also problems such as the atrophy of school guidance and the excessively defensive nature of schools, legal issues such as compensation for damages that do not necessarily lead to the realization of real interests and solution for the child, and the pursuit of unilateral interests on the part of the client by lawyers.

It has been pointed out that the use of lawyers has advantages for schools and boards of education, such as being able to organize problems legally and objectively, to respond with a crisis management outlook, to reduce the burden on administrators and teachers, and to prevent the development of legal disputes.

The Ministry of Education, Culture, Sports, Science and Technology (MEXT) has announced a policy to assign school lawyers to boards of education nationwide, and it is presumed that the involvement of legal experts such as lawyers in school matters will rapidly increase in the Japan in the future. In Japan, the idea of "school legal practice" is still immature. It is necessary to investigate the qualities and abilities required for legal professionals such as lawyers to be involved in educational issues, and what is the expertise in legal practice that is necessary for lawyers to be involved in school matters.

(3) **From "Educational Legislation" to "Child Legislation": flexibility, complexity, and comprehensiveness for the cases**

Currently, in order to respond to the educational issues that children face, such as poverty and abuse, it is necessary to develop legislation that can respond not only to bullying and school absenteeism, but also to cross-disciplinary and cross-institutional responses that encompass education, welfare, the judiciary, etc., according to "the child" and "the problem." On the other hand, with regard to Japanese legislation and administrative organizations, it has been pointed out that there are adverse effects of "horizontal barrier," which means the wall between the ministries and agencies in charge, "vertical barrier," which means the division of the country, prefectures, and municipalities, and "age barrier," which means a break in measures during the perinatal period, pregnancy and childbirth, and before and after schooling.

Based on this recognition, the Japan newly established the "Agency for Child and Family" under the Cabinet Office (the head is the Prime Minister) from 2023 in order to comprehensively promote measures targeting children and families across education, welfare, justice, etc. The Agency for Child and Family plays the role of a control tower for children's policies and is responsible for the comprehensive coordination of government departments such as the Ministry of Education, Culture, Sports, Science and Technology, which has jurisdiction over education, and the Ministry of Health, Labour and Welfare, which is in charge of welfare.

In addition, together with the Agency for Child and Family, the Fundamental Law for Child has been enacted by the Diet. The Fundamental Law for Child stipulates the principles of the Constitution and the Convention on the Rights of the Child as the basic principles for children's policies. The law stipulates the responsibilities of the national and local governments, as well as the obligations of business owners and citizens to make efforts, and the basic principles set forth in the law are the guidelines for all children's policies.

5 Summary

In Japan education legislation has undergone significant changes in response to social and political conditions and the educational challenges of the day. The education legislation that has evolved to the present day can be summarized as follows: the uniform national education legislation formed under "55-Regime"; the education legislation that encouraged autonomous efforts by local governments and schools amid the decentralization of power and deregulation that made significant progress in the 2000s; and the subsequent development of education legislation that enabled efforts that transcended the boundaries of education, welfare, medicine, and justice to address such educational issues as bullying, school absenteeism, abuse, poverty, and juvenile crime. Legislation has since been developed to enable efforts that transcend the boundaries of education, welfare, medical care, and the judiciary in order to address educational issues such as bullying, school absenteeism, abuse, poverty, and juvenile crime. Currently, laws with several of these characteristics overlap to form a multi-layered education law system.

And now, education law in Japan is moving toward the next stage. The Convention on the Rights of the Child is having a major impact on domestic law, lawyers are getting involved in school issues, the school lawyer system is starting to be established, and the Agency for Child and Family and he Fundamental Law for Child will be enacted in 2023. The legal framework surrounding education is being reconfigured from the framework of "schools" and "education" to that of "child" and "issue".

The framework of the Child Law that is currently being formed is expected to be developed in a flexible and comprehensive manner, transcending territorial, age, and institutional barriers. It is expected to be project-driven and developed under a certain level of political leadership in the development of measures related to education. In education law research as well, it is required to proceed across legal and administrative fields such as "education," "welfare," "justice," and "medical care," and to elucidate and continuously reconstruct the essence of legislation through understanding the dynamism behind the formation of legislation under social and political change.

References

Kaneko M (1978) Educational law, New ed. Yuhikaku, Tokyo

Sasaki K (2009) The revised fundamental law of education: the enactment process and issues of government interpretation. Nihonbunkyoshuppan, Tokyo

Sasaki K (2022) Educational trial casebook. Gakubunsha, Tokyo

Sasaki K (2023) School legal practice. Jidaisha, Tokyo

Tanaka K (1961) Theory of the fundamental law of education. Yuhikaku, Tokyo

Education Law and Administration in Hungary

Balázs Szabolcs Gerencsér and Boróka Luca Balla

1 Introduction

Hungary, with a population of almost 10 million[1] and a size of 93,000 km^2 (36,000 sq. miles), is a middle-sized Middle-European country. This country is located in the Carpathian Basin, east to the Alps and west to the Ural; its main river is the Danube, which connects ten countries from Germany to Romania. It lay south to the northern Hanseatic trading countries but north to the Adriatic Mediterranean culture. Its language (Hungarian, Magyar) is far from the neighboring countries' mainly Slavic families and has roots in the East; however, the main religions in the country are in connection with western Christianity. This geographical position had a close effect on the country's history as well: it was always at the stop and/or contact point of West and East.

The right to education was an integral part of the historic Hungarian Constitution, which was in force from the founding of the state (AD 1000). This so-called 'Historic Constitution' was often compared with the British Constitution in their legal tools and historical milestones.[2] Education, in and after the Middle Ages, was provided typically by the Church; later, Queen Maria Theresa (1740–1780) introduced public education (Ratio Educationis 1777), so the state has continuously and increasingly

[1] According to the 2022 census data the population of Hungary is 9.689 million.

[2] "Some states of the world have no written constitution even today. They have no single constitutional document but rather what is known as an unwritten or uncodified constitution, which embodies written and unwritten (common) sources adopted during certain levels of historical evolution in constitutional statutes enacted by the Parliament and also unwritten sources. England has such an uncodified constitution, but until the adoption of the written soviet-style Constitution in 1949, the Hungarian Constitution was also referred to as a historical, unwritten constitution." (Patyi and Téglási 2014, p. 203).

B. S. Gerencsér (✉) · B. L. Balla
Pázmány Péter Catholic University, Budapest, Hungary
e-mail: copyright@esph.com.cn

C. J. Russo and L. Ma (eds.), *A Comparative Analysis of Systems of Education Law*,
https://doi.org/10.1007/978-981-97-1052-2_9

taken over this task by the second World War. According to our topic, we must mention two main characters of the last two centuries, János Eötvös (nineteenth century) and Kunó Klebelsberg (twentieth century), who were the most influental professionals and politicians helping to approach modern public schooling in the pre-communist modern era. When the Second World War was ended, the Constitution of the Soviet dictatorship had taken place. After 1948 the communist dictatorship had nationalized all church schools, and all services were declared to be provided only by the state. Until 1989, the collapse of the dictatorship, church and private education almost did not exist, nor even religious education could occur. The state explicitly discriminated against the Church and its members, which is why the fall of the dictatorship brought a significant change, particularly in this area.

It is also worth mentioning that since its founding Hungary has been a multi-ethnic state. In the medieval Hungarian state, a significant number of minorities lived who could practice their own language to express their identity. A region inhabited by the minority could use their mother tongue in all private and public relations. In fact, at the end of the 1800s, more than half of schools did not teach in the majority (Hungarian) language but in a minority language. Today, 13 minorities are acknowledged legally in Hungary.

Article 59 of the communist constitution adopted in 1949[3] included the right to culture and education, amended in 1972 when modern terms in the Constitution replaced the Bolshevik vocabulary. This amendment was a milestone in the development of education, approaching the contemporary meaning. In 1989 the Constitution was amended[4] due to the democratic change in the political system; however, major provisions of the right to education remained the same with the previous text, and only clarification of the text has been made (Horváth 2009, p. 2595). By this, the Constitution contained real democratic provisions. A new constitutional framework was adopted in 2011 by the Fundamental Law of Hungary. The new constitution kept the previous democratic achievements.

2 Nature of the Legal System

2.1 Constitutional Framework of the Right to Education

2.1.1 Legislation and Sources of Law in Hungary

Building on democratic traditions, the Fundamental Law states in Article R para (1) that "The Fundamental Law shall be the foundation of the legal system of Hungary." and in Article R para (2) that "The Fundamental Law and the laws shall be binding

[3] Act XX of 1949. This new Constitution meant a great fracture in Hungary's constitutional development and turned on another direction, mainly determined by the Soviet interests.

[4] Act XX of 1949 on the Constitution of the Hungarian People's Republic. At the time of the regime change, its content was completely amended by Act XXXI of 1989.

on everyone." This makes a formal distinction between the Constitution and legislation since legislation is based on the Fundamental Law, and Article T para (3) states that "No law shall conflict with the Fundamental Law." According to Article T(1), "[g]enerally binding rules of conduct may be laid down in the Fundamental Law and in laws adopted by an organ having legislative competence specified in the Fundamental Law and promulgated in the official gazette." Since not only the legislation but also the Constitution lays down a generally binding rule of conduct, it can still be considered a law in substance (Csink and Mayer 2012, p. 19–20).

According to Article T para (2) of the Fundamental Law, there are two types of legislation: acts and regulations.[5] In terms of its adoption by Parliament, a law may be a cardinal act (i.e. it requires a qualified majority of two-thirds of the Members of Parliament to be adopted) or a simple act (i.e. it is adopted by a majority of the Members of Parliament). The scope of cardinal laws is defined in the Fundamental Law.

A simple act lays down the rules on the right to education and scientific life. There is a separate law for public education,[6] higher education,[7] vocational education[8] and adult education.[9]

The administrative aspects of education (running, controlling and organizing institutions) are governed by lower-level rules. For example, the government regulates by decree the administrative management of institutions,[10] the promotion of teachers,[11] and the general implementation of the Public Education Act.[12] Further detailed issues are regulated by ministerial decree on the basis of the law's authorization.

Control of education legislation and enforcement of rights is guaranteed by the courts and the special education ombudsman, which is discussed in more detail below in Sect. 3.3.1.

2.1.2 From Decentralization to Centralization—A Brief History of the Development of Education Law

In Hungary, the history of education is as old as the state. The first king, Saint Stephen (997–1038), established the Hungarian kingdom by embracing Christianity

[5] "Article T (2) The law, the Government Decree, the Prime Ministerial Decree, the Ministerial Decree, the Decree of the President of the National Bank of Hungary, the Decree of the head of the independent regulatory body and the Municipal Decree shall be the law".

[6] Act CXC of 2011 on National Public Education (hereinafter: Nkt.).

[7] Act CCIV of 2011 on National Higher Education.

[8] Act LXXX of 2019 on Vocational Education and Training.

[9] Act LXXVII of 2013 on Adult Education.

[10] 134/2016 (VI. 10.) of the Government Decree on the bodies participating in the performance of public education tasks as maintainers and on the Klebelsberg Centre.

[11] 326/2013 (VIII. 30.) of the Government Decree on the implementation of Act XXXIII of 1992 on the Career System of Teachers and the Status of Public Servants in Public Education Institutions.

[12] 229/2012 (VIII. 28.) of the Government Decree on the implementation of the Act on National Public Education.

and consolidating the church and state institutions, which remained stable despite the struggles of its first century. In the Middle Ages, the Church was responsible for education. The education organization was also adapted to the ecclesiastical administration: primary schools were mainly attached to parishes, while secondary schools were established in bishoprics, next to chapters and monasteries (Szalay and Baróti 1896). There were also separate schools for girls as early as the first royal dynasty (so-called "House of Árpád", eleventh–thirteenth centuries). The Hungarian kingdom made several attempts to establish a university,[13] but the first one to survive was founded in 1635 by Cardinal Peter Pázmány in Nagyszombat (now Trnava, Slovakia).[14]

From the eighteenth century onwards, royal legal and normative regulation centralized more and more public tasks in Hungary. The name of Maria Theresa (1740–1780) and her son Joseph II (1780–1790) is associated with significant centralization and rationalization in education. In 1777, Maria Theresa issued the educational decree *Ratio Educationis.* This made education a state responsibility and provided for compulsory education, which was not generally introduced until 1868. An important part of the document was the establishment of an education administration, which unified the previous education system and introduced centralized management. The Crown supervised education; at the same time, the territorial organs of governance were the 'school districts', which were atypical regional-level administrative units, not adapted to the typical county level. A second Ratio Educationis decree was issued by King Francis I in 1806, which partially reorganized the supervisory system but maintained centralized control.

Act XXVI on Religion of the years 1790/91 guaranteed, among other things, freedom of religious education, freedom of church schools (Catholic and Protestant) and the right of Protestant churches to exercise the rights of the Catholic Church. In this way, Parliament struck a balance between church-run schools. It stated that each area had the right to choose a headmaster or a curate according to its faith and the freedom to determine the teaching method while maintaining the royal right of supervision (5. §). It should be noted that the latter legislation was a law, a higher source of law than the royal decree.

---

[13] 1367: Pécs, 1395: Óbuda, 1467: Pozsony (now: Bratislava).

[14] This University was founded in 1635 by the Jesuit Cardinal Péter Pázmány. The period was also one of the booms in Jesuit education, as the Ratio atque Institutio Studiorum Societatis Iesu (Ratio Studiorum), characteristically separates public and higher education, had been published shortly before in 1599. In 1777, after the dissolution of the Jesuit order, the four-faculty university was transferred to Buda by Queen Maria Theresa, and in 1784, during the reign of Joseph II, it was moved to Pest. In 1950, during the first years of the communist dictatorship, it was nationalised (except for the Faculty of Religious Studies) and took the name Eötvös Loránd University (ELTE). In 1950, Decree No. 23/1950 of the Presidential Council of the Hungarian People's Republic decreed that the theological faculties should be separated from the universities and transferred to competent churches. After the regime change in 1989, the Catholic Church established the faculties of humanities, law and computer science and bionics, renamed Pázmány Péter Catholic University (PPKE) after the founder.

The first unified education law came into being with the Austro-Hungarian reconciliation and the consolidation of the monarchy.[15] It introduced compulsory education and stated that schools could be public or private. The state was obliged to establish a school in a municipality to the extent that a church did not do so. The administration and control of the school were vested in the municipalities through elected bodies ('school boards'), i.e. the inhabitants of the municipality were directly involved in the school's running.[16] The higher level of supervision was exercised by state bodies ('school district'). School administration moved from *decentralized* administration in the sixteenth century to a *deconcentrated* administration, i.e. a sector organized centrally but implemented by territorial authorities. Hungary lost the First World War and 2/3 of its territory in 1918 and 1920. The reforms of the 1920s also affected the education system, but the administrative system remained fundamentally intact and education law in the first half of the twentieth century continued to build on the achievements of the historical constitution.

The next big turning point was 1947–1948, when the communist takeover in Hungary, which had lost the Second World War, established a total dictatorship on the Soviet model. At the same time—from an administrative point of view—a period of complete *centralization and concentration* began, which also applied to education. Church and private schools were nationalised, and the previous territorially based administrative system was replaced by centralised management. The state, under the control of a communist party, not only transformed education administration but also determined its content. The 1950 curriculum was radically different from the previous one. It aimed to "educate our young pupils to become self-conscious, disciplined citizens of the People's Republic, loyal sons of the working people, builders of socialism …"(Curriculum 1950) "Education for 'disciplined citizenship' meant at that time nothing more than the development of a subordinate attitude that would meet the demands of a monolithic state power, a dictatorial command system." (Pukánszky and Németh 1996). The right to education was regulated by Article 48 of the first text of the Charta Constitution (based on Soviet law) introduced by Act XX of 1949 on the Constitution of the Hungarian People's Republic (the Constitution). Following the 1972 amendment of the Constitution, Article 59 of the Charter of the Hungarian People's Republic recognizes the right to education for all citizens (Horváth 2009, p. 2595). The Constitution then enshrines the right to education for all citizens by extending the right to public education and the elements of the right to education: free and compulsory primary education, secondary and higher education, further education, and financial support for those who receive an education (Oszlánczi 2018, p. 62–64).

---

[15] Act XXXVIII of 1868 on the subject of public school education.

[16] Today, the "school board" has retained its name but has taken on a completely different function: it has become a coordinating and consultative body within the school. According to Article 73 (2) of the National Act, "A school board may be formed to promote the cooperation of the teaching and educational work, the teaching staff, parents and pupils, the institution's administrators and other organizations interested in the operation of the institution.".

The regime change that began in 1989 brought a real democratic change. A multi-party system was established, and pluralism was introduced in education. The constitution, adopted in 1949 and modelled on the Soviet model, was amended in 1989 almost in its entirety.[17] The first law on public education, which gave substance to democratic constitutional rules, was adopted by parliament in 1993.[18] With the amendment of the Constitution, § 70/F now regulated the right to education, with essentially similar content to the previous texts. The concept of public education and the provision of multi-level education remain important constitutional elements. Concerning education, the text also contains clarifications: primary education is free and compulsory, while secondary and higher education is made accessible to all based on ability in constitutional arrangements. The text of the amended Constitution continues to recognize financial assistance (scholarships) as an essential part of the fundamental right.

In 2011, the Parliament of Hungary adopted the Fundamental Law of Hungary, which formally replaced the 1949 Constitution, but in terms of content, it built on the democratic traditions of 1989. The Fundamental Law continues the public law tradition outlined above. The text is identical to the earlier constitutional rules as regards the content of the fundamental right. The only change is about the financing of education: free education has been included in the text for secondary education, and the Fundamental Law allows for the possibility of making financial support for access to higher education subject to conditions limited in time and subject matter.[19]

From an administrative and regulatory point of view, the period of 2011–2022 has brought several changes. Whereas previously, the primary responsibility for running schools was with the local authorities, the new legislation in 2012 returned this responsibility to the state. The government set up a centralized management body (Klébelsberg Institutional Maintenance Centre—KLIK)[20], which was dysfunctional due to its excessive centralization. Therefore, the government changed the regulatory framework four years later and de-concentrated the tasks, thus re-establishing the "school districts" as the regional educational administrative bodies managed by the reorganised Klebelsberg Centre (K.K.) as the central administrative body.[21] The administrative arrangements are described in more detail in Sect. 2.3.2.

[17] Act XXXI of 1989 amending the Constitution.

[18] Act LXXIX of 1993 on Public Education.

[19] Article XI (2) and (3) of the Fundamental Law.

[20] 202/2012 (VII. 27.) of the Government Decree on the Klebelsberg Centre for the Maintenance of Institutions.

[21] 134/2016 (VI. 10.) of the Government Decree on the bodies participating in the performance of public education tasks as maintainers and on the Klebelsberg Centre.

2.2 The Broader Content of the Right to Education in Hungarian Law

2.2.1 Culture and Education in a Complex Fundamental Right

The right to education is a complex fundamental right. In the Hungarian legal terminology the English term "right to education" has two meanings. First, in a broader sense, it is a combination of the right to culture and education (közművelődéshez való jog). Secondly, in the narrower sense, it means education (oktatáshoz való jog). This means, it has a multi-element structure and is closely linked to other fundamental rights. The constitutional protection of each of its components may differ, given that different content may be regulated for different social groups (Balogh 2019, p. 335).

Within the right to education, we first distinguish the right of access to cultural values. In line with international treaties (e.g. ICESCR, ECHR), Hungarian constitutional law also emphasizes that culture is a universal value that is the property of the individual and that everyone should have access to it, either to cultivate it (active form) or to benefit from it (passive form).[22]

According to the Fundamental Law, Hungary "extends and generalizes community culture".[23] As a type of constitutional provision, this is a state objective which creates a long-term obligation for the State to take action. (Balogh 2019, p. 335) The Fundamental Law does not provide any further details in this regard. Still, from the twentieth century onwards, Hungarian regulatory history has known the most diverse types of national and local public cultural institutions, which form the basic system of cultural administration from local cultural centers to the most diverse public collections. Public education is always an opportunity for the individual to enrich himself with cultural values, never an obligation.[24]

On the subjective side, the right to education is open to all. The universality of the right to education in a broader sense presupposes that everyone has equal access to cultural values and learning. Equality implies a possibility of access for the subject and a differentiation obligation on the part of the State, whereby individuals with different abilities and skills are able to access these values in a way that suits them.

The Hungarian Fundamental Law—similarly to the previous constitutional rules—declares access to this fundamental right for Hungarian citizens, but this does not narrow down the scope of the subject since both the international treaties cited earlier and the international court practice[25] developed based on them clearly emphasize that this is a *universal human right*, i.e. a right guaranteed as an innate right to

[22] See Sect. 3.2 below.

[23] Article XI (2) of the Fundamental Law.

[24] See the parallel reasoning of János Zlinszky, Judge of the Constitutional Court, to the decision of AB 18/1994 (III.31.).

[25] See e.g. CJEU C-388/01 Commission v Italy (13 January 2003) or C-147/03 Commission v Austria (7 July 2005), in which the Court of Justice also held that the right to education must be enjoyed equally by all nationals of the Member States.

all people regardless of their nationality. Therefore this reference to nationality no longer appears at the level of the law under the constitutional arrangements.

Within the right to education, the primary source of sub-rights other than education is Article 15 of the ICESCR, which links education to two aspects of one's intellectual life: cultural and scientific life. This is the basis on which Hungary's present constitutional system is built.

Hungary recognizes the right of everyone to participate in *cultural life*. Culture is closely linked to art as the transmission of spiritual values. This means, first and foremost, according to the classical approach, creating the beauty and the beauty tangible through any intellectual expression (literature, music, song) or material (architecture, painting, sculpture, applied arts) (Révay and Varjú 1936). Art is as old as mankind (see cave paintings) and follows the evolution of man. The purpose and role of art and culture in society have changed considerably over the millennia.[26] Culture also plays a key role in developing emotional intelligence, enriching people's emotional lives through transmitting values. An emotionally and intellectually rich person can become more inclusive and more open to respecting others, which is ultimately a prerequisite for harmonious coexistence in small and large human communities. Therefore, participation in culture is valuable for both the individual and society and impacts the enjoyment of other fundamental rights.

This fundamental right can be achieved through active action by the state. In fulfilling its international obligations, the United Nations expects States to provide a legal environment that fully integrates access to culture. As with all fundamental rights, the right to education is subject to the requirement of adequate legal protection.[27]

The Hungarian Fundamental Law ensures that everyone enjoys the benefits of the progress of science and its application and that the moral and material interests of the authors of all scientific, literary or artistic works are protected. Regarding the freedom of scientific life, it provides protection for two main categories of subjects: (i) those who take part in the pursuit of science and (ii) those who enjoy the fruits of the results of science. Regarding the former, respect for the freedom essential to scientific research and creative activity is also a condition.

Both culture and science point outside themselves: their true purpose is in society. Thus, the state's obligation linked to this fundamental right extends to ensuring participation (cultivation) and free communication and access to the results. Regarding

[26] Antal Szerb, a twentieth century Hungarian writer and literary historian, uses the example of literature to show that while in the ancient world, the role of art was to convey the divine and to represent the supernatural, after the industrial revolutions, this was relegated to the every day and detached from the "supernatural". (Szerb 1981, p. 509–511).

[27] Committee on Economic, Social and Cultural Rights, Nineteenth session, Geneva, 16 November-4 December 1998 Agenda item 3. E/C.12/1998/24.

culture, international treaties[28] even specifically highlight the right and the state obligation to preserve and develop it (Láncos 2014, p. 45; Gerencsér 2015, p. 97).

2.2.2 The Right to Education in a Narrower Sense

Another major area of the examined fundamental right is the right to education. Education and upbringing,[29] i.e. the development of skills and social relations and the transfer of knowledge to children and young people, has been key issue in all ages, regardless of who was responsible for education. The harmonious spiritual, physical and intellectual development of children and young people, the development of their skills, abilities, knowledge, skills, emotional and volitional qualities and literacy, taking into account their age-specific characteristics, has been the basis for a system of education and training with a variety of tools and at different levels for centuries. In addition, in the second half of the twentieth century, the international legal community recognised it as a universal human right and it appeared in Hungarian constitutional law.

The Hungarian constitution distinguishes between three levels of education: primary, secondary and higher education. There is significant differentiation between them, as primary education is "free and compulsory". In contrast, secondary education is "free and accessible to all", and tertiary education is "accessible to all on the basis of ability."[30] The Constitution does not define types of institutions. Still, levels of education, so that within the levels, the state is free to decide to establish different types of educational institutions or forms of education.

The right to education is most closely linked to *human dignity*. Education, knowledge, and enrichment in spiritual values make a fuller human being. International and national constitutional rules tailor participation in education to the individual's own abilities but also require a minimum level (primary education). The requirement of compulsory education is important for society and promotes equal rights and individualizing the exercise of this fundamental right. Equality of access to education is therefore guaranteed for all, but it is adapted to each person's personality and abilities.

Academic and artistic freedom makes particular sense concerning higher education. Higher education has a specific autonomy beyond institutional and economic

[28] In addition to the ICESCR, the international treaties governing the right of minorities specifically emphasize the right to preserve culture. See, for example, Article 5 of the Council of Europe Framework Convention for the Protection of National Minorities: '1. The Parties undertake to promote the preservation and development of the culture of persons belonging to national minorities and the conditions for preserving of their identity, namely their religion, language, traditions and cultural heritage'.

[29] The English texts use the term "Right to Education", which covers education and upbringing in Hungarian. Considering that these two forms of activity have created their own institutional and methodological systems in Hungary, it is reasonable to use both terms when speaking about the fundamental right in a summarized way.

[30] Article XI (2) of the Fundamental Law.

autonomy: it also implies freedom of scientific and artistic life.[31] Freedom of academic and artistic life, alongside the autonomy of higher education institutions, also protects the autonomy of science, freedom of creation, freedom of research and freedom of teaching (Láncos 2009, p. 2611). The latter is also constitutionally protected as part of the right to education, as shown below.

Freedom of conscience and religion is a fundamental right closely linked to education. The provision of religious education in state institutions (content) and public services in educational institutions maintained by churches (form) have been included in the content of the right to education since the Ratio Educationis (Gerencsér and Csekő-Lengyel 2021). The communist-socialist dictatorship radically restricted the exercise of religious freedom. After the change of regime, there was a lively debate on the relationship between the state and the church in society in legal practice and jurisprudence, which has now resulted in the regulation of both the content and the form of the framework mentioned above (Schanda 2012, p. 122).

Finally, the right to education is also an enabler of several other fundamental rights. Therefore, Enikő Horváth considers it a so-called "key right" (Horváth 2009, p. 2596). The right to education plays an essential role in fulfilling all members of society, especially in the choice of work and occupation (Article XII of the Fundamental Law), which is closely linked to personal knowledge and skills. In addition, the former constitutional judge János Zlinszky underlines that "up to a certain level, it is also a guarantee of the functioning of the democratic rule of law. The rule of law and democracy in public life cannot be achieved if the politically empowered (adult) part of the citizenry is not capable of acquiring, understanding and evaluating the information necessary for the exercise of the law. Citizens must be empowered to choose and support political goals, exercise their rights, elect and monitor their representatives, and participate in public life. This requires a basic level of literacy."[32]

Social responsibility plays a significant role in the system of Fundamental Law. As mentioned above, compulsory basic education and the higher education that can be acquired in addition to it contribute to the proper exercise of this social responsibility (cf: social responsibility of property[33] and duty of care[34]).

In Hungarian constitutional thinking, we usually distinguish between the right to learning and the right to teaching in the content of the right to education. The right to *learning* (freedom of education) is first related to the right to access education. The constitutional rule places this right on a dual basis: primary and secondary education must be (a) accessible to all (b) 'on the basis of ability'. Of course, the State will establish educational institutions that are differentiated in certain respects precisely to ensure that all children, despite their different abilities, can receive the appropriate education. The right to education also implies the right to choose the educational establishment that corresponds to the ideological convictions of the parent and the

[31] Article X of the Fundamental Law.

[32] Parallel reasoning of János Zlinszky, Judge of the Constitutional Court, to the AB Decision 18/1994 (III.31.). See also Balogh 2019, p. 334.

[33] Article XIII of the Fundamental Law.

[34] Article XVI (3) and (4) of the Fundamental Law.

child. The right to education also means access to quality education, which means modern, high-quality and objective education.

The right to education is a more structured right that takes into account the education levels and the institution's educational profile. This right is particularly valued in the freedom of academic and artistic life. (Balogh 2019, p. 335) The right to education is also linked to the right to establish institutions, which allows non-state actors (national governments, churches, NGOs, etc.) to play a role alongside the state (Árva 2020, p. 860–861).

On the other hand, the right to education creates not only rights but also a civic obligation (*compulsory education*). In line with international documents (and Hungarian public law tradition), participation in primary education is an obligation for all. The purpose of compulsory primary education is to ensure equality and to support the development of an independent and responsible human being through the acquisition of elementary knowledge.

The compulsory nature of primary education is not an end in itself: it aims to enable children to develop their personalities to the fullest, to be able to lead independent lives and to make responsible choices.

From the point of view of fundamental rights protection, it should be stressed that a specific form of enforcement is *ombudsman control*, which may apply specifically to education rights. This is discussed in more detail in Sect. 3.3.1.

Regarding public education, the state has an obligation to provide services and maintain institutions which, like other social and cultural rights, are adapted to the state's economic capacity. Horváth calls it "progressive" tasking, as its implementation is gradual (Horváth 2009, p. 2597; Balogh 2019, p. 317). However, both in the field of public education and in the field of education law, it is the *activity of the State* and the obligation to provide services that must be emphasized. In the area of the right to education, there is no negative side, i.e. no action from which the state should refrain since the institutional protection side is clearly present in the provision of public services. Access to the fundamental right would not be possible if the state did not provide the institutional backing for it.

In the state's tasks in the enforcement of education law (education administration, i.e. the administration of public education and higher education), we can distinguish between two further elements: education as a *public service* and the *activities of the* education *authorities*. The latter is an explicitly public, even governmental, task, but the provision of public services is not exclusively open to the state. Given that the state's role in public education, in particular, emerged several hundred years later than that of non-state (ecclesiastical) education, non-state actors have traditionally been involved in this public service.[35] The public provision of education and training by state and non-state actors has established a pluralist educational system in Hungary (Balogh 2019, p. 335). The uniformity of the quality and standard of

[35] According to paragraph (3) of Article 2.3 of the current Nkt., "An institution of public education may be established and maintained by a) the state, and b) within the framework of this Act, ba) a national minority self-government, bb) a religious legal person, bc) a religious association or bd) another person or organization.

education and training (and, ultimately, the equality of rights for all legal entities) is guaranteed by a system of public control which uses a mix of contractual, regulatory and quality assurance instruments (see for example public education contracts, operating licences, accreditation, etc.).

Non-state institutions, mainly church-run, not only complement the provision of public services but also guarantee the exercise of freedom of conscience and religion (parental right to choose the upbringing and education of their children).[36] The state must establish ideologically neutral institutions, not religiously committed schools (Schanda 2012, p. 104). It does, however, provide subsidies for the maintenance of the latter: the public tasks taken on by the religious institution receive budgetary compensation from the state commensurate with the number of public tasks it takes on.[37]

Article XI of the Constitution continues to contain provisions on free movement and subsidies (Láncos 2009, p. 2625). International treaties also emphasize that primary education should be free of charge, in addition to being compulsory. Concerning free education, the Constitutional Court stresses both the subjective and the institutional aspects of the right to education: "the State has a constitutional obligation and parents and pupils a fundamental subjective right to free education."[38] The support system enshrined in the Fundamental Law (e.g. the setting of scholarship ceilings) is a constitutional guarantee that further broadens access to education and, thus, equal opportunities in society. However, financial support is not of a constitutional nature but is determined by the state according to its capacity to bear the burden.

2.3 Organizational and Administrative Aspects of Education Law

2.3.1 School Maintainers and Founders—Institutional Side

The Explanatory Memorandum of Act CXC of 2011 on National Public Education (hereinafter: Nkt.) underlines that the new educational legislation is intended to be a framework law.[39] The wording of the Nkt. is detailed and has been subject to several amendments over the last decade, so the depth of regulation in the text is not homogeneous. The Nkt. regulates first the main subjects: the institutional system, the order of operation, the pedagogical program, the different rules for religious, private and defense institutions, the rights and obligations of pupils and teachers, the representation and promotion of teachers, parents' organizations, and finally the

[36] See also 22/1997 (IV. 25.) AB Decision.

[37] 4/1993 (II. 12.) AB Decision.

[38] 22/1997 (IV. 25.) AB decision.

[39] Proposing legislation No. 4856 on the National Public Education. Available via https://www.parlament.hu/irom39/04856/04856.pdf p. 83.

government's and the maintenance authorities' tasks, controls and financing, and the supply of textbooks.

Regarding the right to education, the Constitution expects citizens to participate in the public education system. At the same time, the state is responsible for ensuring its attainment and high quality for all citizens. According to its explanatory memorandum,[40] the law guarantees the state's tasks primarily through the common definition of a minimum curriculum, national professional supervision, introducing a career model for teachers and, linked to this, sector-neutral central wage financing. At the same time, the law also ensures a certain degree of participation by local communities. It highlights the diversity of the Hungarian kindergarten and school structure, the circle of maintainers and the pedagogical culture as values.

As discussed in the previous chapters, the law in force has not decentralized (or only minimally deconcentrated) the education administration. The term 'local communities' is used here to refer primarily to the multi-stakeholder model of the school maintenance circle. According to Article 2 of the Public Education Act, public education institutions are primarily maintained by the state. In exceptional cases, the national minority self-government, a religious legal person, a religious association[41] or any other person or organization may establish and maintain an educational institution within the Act's framework if it has acquired the right to do so. Before 2012, local authorities were the main providers of education and health services. By then, however, significant funding difficulties had arisen, and the financial capacity of local authorities had been overstretched. In addition, there was tension between the government's responsibility for education and the municipalities' ability to use their independence to implement the law to make decisions that went against the government's wishes. The 2012 reform, therefore, opted for centralisation and gave municipalities powers in development policy decisions instead of education and health. Local governments may establish and maintain only kindergartens.

Non-state operators (i.e. minority self-governments, churches, religious associations and other foundations and enterprises) may establish and operate a school (or an equivalent institution under the law) if they meet the quality assurance requirements. The first step is establishing a contractual framework,[42] which the maintainer enters with the ministry to participate in the public education service. Through the public education contract, the non-state operator undertakes to fulfill the public functions, operate the institution under the same regulatory framework as the state schools, and receive the state subsidy that makes education free for pupils in such institutions. According to a specific rule for churches, if they have a framework contract for public human services, they may establish an educational institution by unilateral act (notification). In two cases, an international treaty regulates the framework for

---

[40] Proposing legislation No. 4856 on the National Public Education. Available via https://www.parlament.hu/irom39/04856/04856.pdf

[41] In Hungary, the parliament recognizes churches by law. All other churches operate as religious associations and are registered by the courts in a similar way to associations.

[42] This is the public education contract, see also Nkt. 31.§ (2) e). For detailed rules, see 229/2012 (VIII. 28.) of the Government Decree on the implementation of the National Public Education Act.

the provision of education. (i) The provision of education by the Catholic Church is governed by an international treaty between the Holy See and Hungary (Schanda 2015, para 75–76; Gerencsér 2017, p. 95–108). (ii) The establishment of a foreign educational institution may be based on an international treaty, but the Ministry will still register the educational institution. The established public education institution will receive an operating license from the authority, establishing the elements of its operation's legality.

2.3.2 Government Administration and Governance in Education

Until 2010, the Hungarian government typically had a ministry with a separate education portfolio. In 2010, the government placed the management of the main public human services (health, social services, sport, and education) under one ministry.[43] The year 2022 brought changes at all levels of education in Hungary. This year, these sectors were separated, the former ministry was abolished, and education came under the control of the Ministry of the Interior.[44] From 2018, the Ministry of Innovation and Technology was responsible for higher education and vocational training; from 2022, the Ministry of Culture and Innovation took over these areas.[45]

The minister manages the public sector, typically through state administration bodies. The management and control of Hungarian educational institutions are exercised by two main types of bodies: an administrative-authority body and a professional-administrative body.

(i) The administrative operation of schools is ensured by the *school district centers* [tankerületi központ], which is a network of administrative institutions organized on a regional basis.[46] The central body is the Klebelsberg Centre, which is managed by the Minister responsible for education. The school district center may propose, in addition to its operation, the reorganization, closure, change of core tasks and naming of any school, but the Minister decides on these matters. It supervises the management, carries out national and international measurements and studies in the field of public education, performs statistical tasks and prepares development plans. It has an advisory, consultative and advisory body. The centers of the school districts carry out some of the official tasks when the school takes decisions of the first instance, for example, on the establishment or termination of pupil status or disciplinary matters.[47]

(ii) The *Education Office* [Oktatási Hivatal] is a central administrative professional body for education headed by the Minister. Its main tasks are record-keeping and

[43] Ministry of Human Resources (EMMI).

[44] 182/2022 (V.24.) of the Government Decree 66. § (1).

[45] 182/2022 (24.V.24.) of the Government Decree 128. §

[46] See Regulation 134/2016 (VI. 10.) of the Government on the bodies participating as maintainers in the performance of public education tasks and on the Klebelsberg Centre.

[47] See Nkt. 37–38. §

data management concerning schools, the operation of national education information systems, the administration of school-leaving examinations and central admissions to higher education, textbook publishing, international professional relations, the preparation of vocational examinations for vocational training, and other tasks as defined by law, such as the development of teacher qualifications. In addition, it provides pedagogical-professional services and, in some cases, performs tasks of secondary authority.

3 Major Legal Developments

3.1 Main Legislation Affecting Education

3.1.1 Substantive Legal Framework

The Nkt. regulates the operation of public education, which the Minister manages. The purpose and rationale of the Act are to establish a system of public education, which it defines as a public service.[48] In this way, it fulfills its obligation under the Fundamental Law to provide free and compulsory primary education and secondary education and training for all.[49]

All children between the ages of 6 and 16 are compulsory school-age.[50] The Nkt. regulates the tasks of the institutions of the *public education* system, such as kindergartens, primary schools, secondary schools, vocational schools, vocational schools, and schools for skills development. It also provides for colleges, specialized pedagogical services and professional services, the pedagogical program, and determines the organization of the school year. It also sets out the rights and obligations of pupils, parents and teachers, the framework for rewarding pupils, disciplinary action and liability for damages, the rules for children with special educational needs and the status of pupils.

Higher education is currently regulated by Act CCIV of 2011. In addition to the Minister of Culture and Innovation, the Hungarian Higher Education Accreditation Commission (MAB) is linked to Hungarian higher education, which is responsible for quality control and its tasks are defined in the Higher Education Act[51] and Government Decree 69/2006 (28.III.2006) on the MAB. The tasks of the authority are performed by the Education Office, which is a central budgetary body operating as a central office under the authority of the Minister responsible for public education.[52] The National Doctoral Council, the Higher Education Planning Board, the

---

[48] Nkt. 1.§

[49] Article XI (2) of the Fundamental Law.

[50] Nkt. 45.§

[51] Act CCIV of 2011, 109-110. §

[52] 121/2013. (IV. 26.) of the Government Decree.

Dual Education Council, the Hungarian Rectors' Conference, the National Conference of Student Self-Governments and the National Association of Doctoral Students are responsible for the representation of interests.

Higher education comprises higher education vocational training, the interlocking bachelor's degree, master's degree, doctoral training and specialized continuing training. A bachelor's and master's program may be organized in a split or undivided organization according to the provisions of the legislation.[53] The Hungarian state may establish institutions of higher education, a national minority self-government, a religious legal entity, a business company with its registered office in Hungary, or a foundation, trust foundation, public foundation or religious association registered in Hungary.[54] In the academic year 2021/2022, there were 63 higher education institutions in Hungary. Studying at higher education institutions with a Hungarian state scholarship, partial scholarship, or self-financed study is possible. Higher education students can take advantage of the possibility of pursuing part-time studies related to their studies and establish a visiting student status with another higher education institution.

Vocational education and training is a partially separate subsystem of the education sector, governed by the Minister of Culture and Innovation and, since 2020, regulated by Act LXXX of 2019 on Vocational Education and Training. VET is "vocational education and *training preparing for a vocational qualification."*[55] The legal status of a vocational training institution is that of a legal entity established to perform a basic vocational training task. Currently, in Hungary, two types can be distinguished: technical and vocational schools. The "technicum" prepares the student for the general school-leaving examination and the vocational examination, whereas the vocational school only prepares the student for the vocational examination.[56] The State, a national minority municipality, a religious legal person, a company, a foundation or an association may run a vocational training establishment.[57] The school year is the same as that of a public education establishment, and the decisions of the vocational establishment and their review are subject to the procedures laid down for public education. In vocational training, a student status and an adult education status may be established, the latter being subject to the provisions of Act LXXVII of 2013 on Adult Education. Under the legislation in force, it is possible to acquire two professions free of charge.

3.1.2 Special Actors in Education

The Nkt. defines the children eligible for special treatment in the special subject area of public education. This group includes children with special educational needs,

[53] Act CCIV of 2011, 3. §

[54] Act CCIV of 2011, 4. §

[55] Act LXXX of 2019, 8. § (1).

[56] Act LXXX of 2019, 19-21. §

[57] Act LXXX of 2019, 22. §

children with difficulties in integration, learning and behavior, and particularly gifted or talented children.[58]

> "A child or pupil with special educational needs is a child or pupil requiring special treatment who, based on the expert opinion of the committee of experts, are handicapped or have perceptual, mental deficiency or speech disorder, or have multiple disabilities in case of the simultaneous occurrence of several deficiencies or have autism spectrum disorder or any other psychic disorder (serious disorder concerning learning or the control of attention or behavior)"[59]

According to the data of the Hungarian Central Statistical Office (KSH) for 2021, the number of children with special educational needs has been steadily increasing since 2013, and in the school year 2020/2021, 7.9% of pupils had special educational needs, which means 57.7 thousand pupils.

Children with integration, learning and behavioral difficulties include children and pupils with special needs who, according to the expert opinion of the expert committee, are significantly underachieving in relation to their age, have problems with social relationships, learning and behavioral deficits, and have difficulties in integrating into the community and personality development, but do not qualify as children with special educational needs.[60]

In accordance with the Fundamental Law, the Nkt. states that the special needs of children in the situations mentioned above requiring special attention should be taken into account as a priority task of public education.[61] Compulsory schooling also applies to children with special educational needs, from the age of six to sixteen, and may be extended to the age of 23 for children with special educational needs.[62]

The Nkt. also states the right of pupils with special educational needs to receive pedagogical, remedial or conductive educational care appropriate to their condition within the framework of special treatment, starting from the time when their eligibility for special treatment has been established[63] and provides additional rights in accordance with their needs.

The legislation refers to ten types of institutions where pupils with special educational needs have the opportunity to participate in public education. These are kindergartens, primary schools, secondary schools, vocational schools, vocational schools, primary art schools, special education establishments, educational establishments providing special education, educational establishments providing conductive education, colleges, specialized educational services, and establishments providing pedagogical-professional services. In addition, the Nkt. names the specialized vocational school, the unified institution for curative education, the specialized pedagogical services, the pedagogical-professional services, and organizes the services and

[58] Nkt. 4.§ 13.

[59] Nkt. 4.§ 25.

[60] Nkt. 4.§ 3.

[61] Nkt. 3.§ (6).

[62] Nkt. 43.§ (1).

[63] Nkt. 47.§ (1).

Table 1 Relevant rules for decisions in the public education system[65]

Decision-maker	Kindergarten, school, college		
	Decision of first instance		
Subject-matter of the application	Petitions submitted in reference to the **breach of law** Nkt. 37.§ (3) (a)	Petitions submitted in reference to **violation of interests** related to admission to or exclusion from a pre-school, the establishment or **termination** of **student status** or membership in a hall of residence, **or matters pertaining to student's discipline.** Nkt. Article 37.§ (3) b)	Claim made on the grounds of **breach of interests,** other than Nkt. 37.§ (3) b)
	Breach of the law	*Breach of interests*	
Decision-Maker	Maintainer or school district centers		School Board, or in the absence of a three-member committee
	Decision at second instance		
Subject of the application	Appeal against a decision on an application alleging a **breach of the law** Nkt. 38.§ (4)	Challenge to a decision on an application alleging a **breach of interests** Nkt. 38.§ (4)	
Decision-maker	Court in an administrative case		
	Decision of the Court		

the time frame. In addition, there are guidelines for pupils with special educational needs in pre-school and public education.

3.2 *Litigation or Dispute Resolution Concerning Education*

3.2.1 Traditional Legal Route

Table 1 lists the relevant rules for decisions in the public education system.[64]

3.2.2 First Instance

If an educational establishment makes a decision, takes a measure or fails to take a measure (hereinafter: decides) that affects a pupil, the pupil may appeal against

[64] Nkt. 37–38.§

[65] Own editing based on the Nkt.

it. The right to legal remedy is guaranteed by Article XXVII(7) of the Fundamental Law, which applies to *everyone*, including children.[66] The legal representation of the child is the responsibility of the parents who have parental authority, which is not only their right but also their duty.[67] Thus, they can appeal against a decision taken by the school. The form of how the decision is communicated does not affect the possibility of bringing proceedings (Szüdi 2012, p. 125).

The Nkt. lists the disciplinary sanctions that can be imposed on a student if he or she is guilty of a serious breach of duty. Disciplinary sanctions may only be imposed as a written decision during disciplinary proceedings. No disciplinary proceedings may be taken against a child under the age of ten who is necessarily of compulsory school age.[68] The scope of disciplinary measures and the arrangements for their application shall be laid down in the rules of the educational establishment.[69]

3.2.3 Second Instance

As shown in Table 1, if the parent, pupil or child does not claim breach of interest in their application, the decision in the second instance is made by the maintaining authority, thus removing the possibility of solving the problem from the school and the directly involved actors.

The state, national minority self-government, a religious legal entity, an organization carrying out religious activities, or any other person or organization may maintain a public education institution, provided it has been authorized to do so. The municipal government may also maintain a kindergarten (Report of the Commissioner for Education Rights 2015). The State Secretariat for Public Education within the Ministry of the Interior and the Education Office are responsible for the management of public education. Since 1 January 2017, the Klebelsberg Centre has been the central management body liable for the 60 school district centers.[70] These centers are responsible for the maintenance of state-run primary and secondary schools. As a result of the change in 2017, the school district centers have an autonomous budget. The Klebelsberg Centre does not control private, church-run and minority self-government-run schools and municipal kindergartens.[71] Thus, either the competent school district center under the Klebelsberg Centre or, in the case of church-run, private or minority-run institutions, which are independent of the Klebelsberg Centre is entitled to act as a second-tier provider.

---

[66] Article XXVIII (7) of the Fundamental Law.

[67] Act V of 2013 on the Civil Code 4:161. §

[68] Nkt. 58.§ (3)–(5).

[69] 20/2012 (VIII. 31.) of the Ministerial Decree on the operation of educational institutions and the naming of public educational institutions (hereinafter: Ministerial Decree 20/2012) 5. § (f).

[70] 134/2016 (VI. 10.) of the Government Decree on the bodies participating in the performance of public education tasks as maintainers and on the Klebelsberg Centre.

[71] 134/2016 (VI. 10.) of the Government Decree 1. §

At the end of its procedure, the maintainer may reject the appeal, change it or order the educational institution that has been tried in the first instance to make a new decision.[72] The discretion of the maintainer is within limits set by the law. The maintainer has a direct, subordinate relationship with the educational establishment.

3.2.4 Administrative Proceedings

The Nkt. regulates the legal remedy procedure against the decisions of educational institutions with a separate procedure. In the first instance, a decision taken by an educational establishment is not a decision of an administrative authority since by virtue of its legal status. Likewise, a decision taken by the maintainer in the second instance is not an administrative authority's decision (Szüdi 2012, p. 126–127). As in the case of private, ecclesiastical and national self-government institutions, the Klebelsberg Center, as a central budgetary body operating as a central office under the authority of the Minister responsible for education, is not an administrative authority.[73] Nevertheless, the legislator provides for the possibility of judicial review of a decision taken by the maintainer in the second instance. The application must be lodged with the court.[74] At the end of the procedure, a judicial decision is issued, which establishes obligations and settles the dispute as to its legality. However, as with the decision in the second instance, the source of the problem that caused the conflict is not identified, and the court decision does not give any guidance on how to prevent it in the future. The court is completely independent of the child, his parents, and the educational establishment.

Act I of 2017 on the Act on Public Administration Court Procedure (hereinafter: Kp.) allows for court mediation.[75] The previous legislation did not allow for this, but since 1 January 2018, parties may use it voluntarily. Given the nature of education disputes, one of the parties is usually a minor in a vulnerable situation due to his or her age. He or she is dependent on his or her parents and, in the educational institution, on his or her teachers. The Convention on the Rights of the Child[76] and, in line with this, Act XXXI of 1997 on the Protection of Children and Guardianship Administration declare that the best interests of the child must be the primary consideration in decisions affecting the child. It can hardly be doubted that the best interests of the child would not be better served if it were possible to have recourse to a mediation procedure where a decision is taken in accordance with the principles of interest-based dispute resolution and where the real interests of both parties are taken into account. The court decides on the application, within narrowly defined rules, on what is lawful. However, mediation aims to produce a settlement in which both parties

[72] Nkt. 38.§ (1).

[73] 61/2016. (XII. 29.) Ministerial Instruction on the Organizational and Operational Rules of the Klebelsberg Centre 1. § (1).

[74] Nkt. 38.§ (4).

[75] Act I of 2017 on Public Administration Court Procedure (hereinafter: Kp.) Part 2.

[76] Kp. Part 2.

agree (Bereczki 2020, p. 65–67). This does not mean, however, that the parties can reach an agreement on content contrary to the law. The court will examine whether the settlement conforms with the law before approving it, and only then will it issue an order.[77]

In mediation, the parties define the problem and have the opportunity to decide on issues that cannot be taken into account in court. Another important aspect of mediation is its preventive character. In addition to redressing past grievances, mediation can also lead to a settlement that explores the problem in sufficient depth to prevent similar situations from arising in the future. In contrast, the judicial process focuses exclusively on past events to establish the facts and reach a decision (Bereczki 2020, p. 68–69). Mediation is voluntary, unlike litigation, where one party is obliged to participate in the proceedings (Bereczki 2020, p. 70). The parties' decision to participate in mediation can be seen as a declaration of intent for the future, that they are interested in finding common ground to resolve the problem. In litigation, the parties face each other in court, whereas in mediation, they face the problem side by side. It is also important to highlight the sensitizing function and role of mediation. A sensitization is an essential tool for effective communication, consensus building and openness towards the other party. (Fehérpataky B et al. 2012, p. 78.)

Another advantage of mediation is its speed and cost-effectiveness. Speed is an extremely important factor in education disputes, as in many cases, the right to education of school-age children is violated, and a protracted dispute can have serious consequences for the student's academic progress. In the event of a successful mediation, the court will enter the settlement into a decree with the effect of a judgment, and in the absence of a settlement, the proceedings will continue.[78]

3.3 *Alternative Legal Instruments*

3.3.1 Commissioner for Educational Rights

The legal Commissioner for education rights institution is a rare but not unknown institution in Europe. Some countries have created a special ombudsman among the parliamentary commissioners for fundamental rights, specifically to oversee education rights.[79] In Hungary, a specialized ombudsman system was established in 1999, which placed the control of educational rights under the control of the Minister responsible for education (Education Rights Commissioner).[80] Any person involved in education (pupils, parents, teachers, students, researchers, lecturers and their associations) can turn to the Education Rights Commissioner if they believe their rights have been infringed or are at risk of being infringed. This is particularly the case

[77] Kp. 70.§ (3).

[78] Kp. 69–70. §

[79] Such as in Malta (Commissioner for Education—Kummissarju għall-Edukazzjoni).

[80] Nkt. 77.§.

where a decision or measure or lack of those infringe an educational right or creates an imminent threat of such infringement.

The Education Rights Commissioner is not an authority but rather a mediating body. If it finds something illegal, it reports it to the head of the educational establishment; if no progress is made, it reports it to the maintenance or supervisory body. The Education Rights Commissioner can also open an inquiry of his own motion if a law or measure or lack of action causes serious violations of rights or affects a large group of citizens.[81] The procedure of the specialized ombudsman is subject to two conditions: (i) The available remedies must be exhausted, except for judicial proceedings; (ii) In addition, an application must be submitted within one year of the date on which the decision adversely affecting the education system becomes final. The *ex officio* proceedings may be brought without a time limit. The Nkt. provides for the right of children, pupils, teachers and parents to apply to the Education Rights Commissioner in case of a violation or imminent threat of violation of their rights in education. Complaints may be made in writing, orally or in person. The Commissioner cannot act in the case of a final court decision or pending court proceedings.

The Office's tasks, status and operation are regulated by the Ministerial Decree 40/1999 (X. 8.). The Office operates as an autonomous internal department within the Ministry. The Minister responsible for education appoints and dismisses the Commissioner and exercises the Commissioner's powers as an employer.[82] The Commissioner is accountable only to the Minister. The Education Rights Commissioner heads the office. He may not be instructed in the performance or execution of his duties.

The Education Rights Commissioner will seek an agreement between the parties to remedy the situation. As a first step, it will contact the institution or individual concerned with a view to obtaining a statement on the complaint received. It then invites the parties to agree in writing and reconcile their positions. If this is unsuccessful, a personal meeting will be arranged. If the infringement persists, it shall take the initiative to bring it to an end by recommending it to the institution or individual concerned and its supervisory body.[83] Proceedings may also be initiated ex officio if there is a serious infringement or an imminent threat of a serious infringement affecting a large group of citizens.[84] The Commissioner will report annually on his/her activities, experience, the effectiveness of his/her recommendations, ex-officio and complaint procedures.

[81] The official website of the Office of the Hungarian Commissioner for Education Rights. Available via https://www.oktbiztos.hu.

[82] Nkt. 77.§.

[83] Office of the Commissioner for Education Rights—Our procedure. Available via https://www.oktbiztos.hu/mission/index.html.

[84] Ministerial Decree 40/1999 (X.8.) on the tasks and rules of operation of the Office of the Ministerial Commissioner for Education Rights 9. § (2).

3.3.2 Commissioner for Fundamental Rights

The provisions of the Commissioner for Fundamental Rights are contained in the Fundamental Law of Hungary and the Act CXI of 2011 on the Commissioner for Fundamental Rights.

The Commissioner for Fundamental Rights is the Parliament's control body to protect fundamental rights (Varga 2012, p. 127). Its task is to investigate "irregularities" that arise in connection with the proceedings of an administrative authority[85] that comes to its attention. The fundamental rights that affect education are the *right to education,*[86] *the right of children to protection and care,*[87] *the right to human dignity,*[88] *and the right to legal remedy.*[89] According to Article 18 (1) of the Act CXI of 2011, anyone who considers that a decision or failure to act by a public authority, in this case, a public service[90] infringes a fundamental right may apply to the Commissioner. In case No. AJB-860/2017[91], the Commissioner for Fundamental Rights, deduced that his jurisdiction also extends to schools and their maintainers. The Fundamental Law lays down the obligation to provide free, compulsory primary and universal secondary education[92] as a public service of the Hungarian state.[93] Thus, education stakeholders—pupils, teachers, and parents—can also turn to the Commissioner for Fundamental Rights if they have experienced or are at risk of violating fundamental rights. The Commissioner's procedure is subject to the condition that the petitioner has already exhausted the legal remedies available to him/her or that no final court decision or administrative action is pending. Complainants have one year from the date the administrative decision in question becomes final or enforceable to lodge a complaint.[94]

The Commissioner may take action to remedy the situation, which may include a recommendation, an initiative to the head of the body concerned to remedy the instance of maladministration, a request for a Constitutional Court proceeding, a request for prosecution, or a proposal for a change in the law.[95]

The Commissioner is elected by a two-thirds majority of the National Assembly on the proposal of the President of the Republic for a term of 6 years. He is required to

---

85 Act CXI of 2011 18. §.

86 Article XI (1)-(2) of the Fundamental Law.

87 Article XVI (1) of the Fundamental Law.

88 Article II of the Fundamental Law.

89 Article XXVIII (7) of the Fundamental Law.

90 Act CXI of 2011 18. § (2) paragraph.

91 Report of the Commissioner for Fundamental Rights AJB-860/2017.

92 Article XI of the Fundamental Law.

93 Nkt. 2. §.

94 Act CXI of 2011. 18. §.

95 Act CXI of 2011 11. Measures of the Commissioner for Fundamental Rights.

report annually to Parliament on his activities.[96] The Commissioner is independent, cannot be instructed and is subject only to the law.[97]

The Fundamental Rights Commissioner has the following tools at his disposal: he can ask the authorities for information and copies of documents, and he can ask the head of the authority concerned or its supervisory body to carry out an investigation, which the bodies concerned must do within the time limits set. They may also attend public hearings and carry out on-the-spot checks.[98]

For cases concerning education, as described above, anyone can apply to both the Commissioner for Education and the Commissioner for Fundamental Rights under almost similar conditions—exhaustion of remedies, one a year time limit. A significant difference is that the Commissioner for Fundamental Rights can act in cases of fundamental rights violations or threats thereof, whereas the Commissioner for Education can be approached for any kind of rights violation related to education. Both can make recommendations, but the Commissioner for Fundamental Rights has wider powers in terms of means. The Commissioner for Education aims to bring the parties' positions closer together and to facilitate a joint resolution of the situation and is specifically responsible for dealing with education matters. The Commissioner for Fundamental Rights, while seeking solutions to the situations complained of in individual complaints, draws attention to systemic shortcomings and problems, including those of a legislative nature. The annual reports of the Commissioner for Education provide a comprehensive picture of the current state of the education system, typical problems encountered in schools and the difficulties that currently need to be addressed. While the Commissioner for Education reports to the Minister responsible for education and works to remedy situations of non-compliance and promote the education system's positive development, the Commissioner for Fundamental Rights is responsible for protecting fundamental rights and promoting their unhindered and lawful exercise.

3.3.3 Alternative Dispute Resolution Methods in Public Education as Provided for by Law

In Hungary, there are three types of alternative dispute resolution options available to educational institutions for the resolution of educational conflicts, as specified in the legislation[99]: the conciliation procedure prior to disciplinary proceedings, the educational mediation procedure and the reparation mediation in the conciliation procedure.

Table 2 lists the options for alternative dispute resolution in the public education system.

---

[96] Article 30 of the Fundamental Law.

[97] Act CXI of 2011 11. §

[98] Act CXI of 2011 21. §

[99] 20/2012. (VIII. 31.) of the Ministerial Decree.

Table 2 Options for alternative dispute resolution in the public education system[100]

Disciplinary procedure Ministerial Decree 20/2012 53.§ (2)	**Education mediation procedure** Decree 20/2012 52.§
Optional	
Conciliation procedure prior to disciplinary proceedings Ministerial Decree 20/2012 53.§ (2)	
Optional	
Reparation mediation in the framework of the conciliation procedure Ministerial Decree 20/2012 62.§ (9)	

Ministerial Decree 20/2012 (VIII. 31.) on the operation of educational institutions and the naming of public educational institutions (hereinafter: Ministerial Decree 20/2012) provides that the detailed rules of disciplinary proceedings and the conciliation procedure preceding them must be defined in the organizational and operational rules of educational institutions.[101]

A pupil who culpably and seriously fails to comply with his/her obligations may be disciplined by a written decision based on disciplinary proceedings.[102] By contrast, the scope of disciplinary measures is not specified; the forms and principles of application must be laid down in the institution's rules of procedure.[103]

The legislation defines the conciliation procedure as an option with two objectives. On the one hand, to deal with the events and grievances that led to the misconduct and, on the other hand, to create an agreement between the two parties—the person who has suffered the harm and the person suspected of misconduct. Participation in the conciliation procedure is voluntary and only possible if the parties—in the case of minors, their parents or legal representatives—have agreed to it. Although the Decree regulates the conciliation procedure itself as an option, it establishes an obligation to notify.

The legislation also states that the disciplinary authority may refuse to apply the conciliation procedure if a third instance of misconduct occurs.[104] The Regulation does not specify which instances of misconduct should be taken into account when determining the third occasion. According to one piece of literature, "if the institution's rules of organization and operation do not provide for it, it is appropriate to take into account two instances of misconduct for which the pupil has already been the subject of a conciliation procedure or disciplinary proceedings." (Juhász 2015, p. 6). Thus, on this basis, in the case of a first or second disciplinary procedure, the

[100] Own editing based on the 20/2012. (VIII. 31.) of the Ministerial Decree.

[101] 20/2012. (VIII. 31.) of the Ministerial Decree 4. § (1) q).

[102] Nkt. 58.§ (3).

[103] 20/2012. (VIII. 31.) of the Ministerial Decree 5. § (1) f).

[104] 20/2012. (VIII. 31.) of the Ministerial Decree 53. § (4).

disciplinary authority would not have the possibility to reject the conciliation procedure. On the contrary, the Administrative and Labour Court of Eger, in its judgment No. 9.K.27.058/2016/12[105] concluded that the disciplinary authority had lawfully refused to hold the conciliation procedure. It reasoned that the repeated misconduct or disciplinary offense could be established on the basis of the nine warnings for minor misconduct, which dated from the past period, and the partial admission of the student concerned. The Curia confirmed the court's first instance reasoning in its precedent-setting decision no. Kfv.37827/2014/8.[106] The fact that more than three disciplinary offenses had been committed and that the achievement of the objective of the conciliation procedure, i.e. the remedying of the grievance and the conclusion of an agreement, could not have been envisaged in the case in question, justified the lawful dismissal of the proceedings. However, it must be concluded that, in calculating the third misconduct, an account may be taken not only of misconduct which has been the subject of a disciplinary or conciliation procedure but also of misconduct that, where appropriate, is a disciplinary offense for breach of the measures of the rules of conduct set by the school and which is embodied by a warning. On this basis, two disciplinary measures taken in response to a breach of the rules of conduct prior to the culpable and serious misconduct giving rise to the disciplinary procedure may be sufficient grounds for dismissing the conciliation procedure.

The second dispute resolution option in an educational establishment is the educational mediation procedure which can be used in two cases. It can be applied if the institution cannot eliminate the reasons that endanger the child or pupil by pedagogical means and if it is justified to protect the learning community. Thus, the school may seek help from the services to protect minors and family law or the educational mediation service.

In his 2018 report, the Commissioner for Education Rights pointed out that in the event of conflicts between students, the institution must fulfill its supervisory obligation under Article 25 (5) of the Nkt., and ensure the creation of healthy and safe conditions for education (Székely L et al 2019). However, there may not be an appropriate method in the teachers' pedagogical toolbox to fulfill the supervision obligation. In such cases, the educational mediation procedure provided for by the Regulation may be a solution. "Mediation is a conflict management and dispute resolution procedure to reach a mutual agreement between the parties involved in a dispute. With the involvement of a third party (mediator) who is not affected by the dispute, the parties reach an agreement to resolve the dispute." (Fehérvári 2013). The aim of the educational mediation procedure is also to reach an agreement. It is important to stress that education mediation emphasizes mutual understanding of the needs and interests of the parties (Juhász 2015, p. 6). Thus, since the agreement is based on consensus, the parties will be more motivated to comply. Therefore, it is of particular importance that the mediator does not influence the content of the decision but only the process (Fehérvári 2013, p. 4).

[105] Judgment of the Administrative and Labour Court of Egri. No. 9.K.27.058/2016/12.

[106] The Curia's precedent-setting decision No. Kfv.37827/2014/8.

The Ministerial Decree 20/2012 also allows reparation in conciliation procedure, optionally available in the conciliation procedure preceding disciplinary proceedings. Thus, reparation mediation differs from educational mediation or any other mediation procedure in that the parties are confronted as parties who have suffered harm and are suspected of misconduct. Thus, in this dispute resolution technique, the parties involved are not equal, and there is a meaningful role in reparation and restitution.

Instead of disciplinary proceedings, the conciliation procedure can be used, which offers the possibility to settle the conflict through reparation mediation. The conciliation procedure prior to disciplinary proceedings and reparation mediation differ in terms of the requirements concerning the identity of the mediator,[107] and, in the case of the latter, the agreement on reparation is a prerequisite for the agreement. Thus, victim protection and prevention play a key role in reparation mediation. The focus is not on sanctioning the wrongdoer but on reparation and reparation for the harm suffered by the victim.

4 Before and After Reforms: The Need for Strategy in Education

Education has been the state's responsibility for almost 250 years in Hungary. Education is a public service for which the state is primarily responsible, but its implementation is a multi-stakeholder model in which churches (and civil actors) have always had a prominent role. For two centuries, contemporary Hungarian education administration has been following a progressively centralized and deconcentrated model,[108] the advantages and disadvantages of which are not the aim of this study. Today in Hungary, the historical administrative achievements and the application of modern international tools are present at the same time. However, the application of the historical acquis is mostly only apparent: the "school board" [iskolaszék] and the "school district" [tankerület] are the same in name as they were in the eighteenth and nineteenth centuries, but their content has changed.

Since the regime change in 1989, educational reforms in Hungary have placed great emphasis on setting up the institutional system and the legal environment. In addition, international measurements and comparisons have had a major impact on the development of education. It is, therefore, instructive to take a brief look at where Hungarian education stands in major international comparisons.

Of the 79 countries participating in the OECD PISA 2018 survey, Hungary is in the middle of the field, ranked 29–38. The picture that Hungarian education is in the middle of the pack on most measures is supported by other surveys.

---

107 20/2012. (VIII. 31.) of the Ministerial Decree 54. § (2).

108 Deconcentration is used here in the sense that the provision of public services is carried out by regional state administration bodies under the direction of the Minister, which is currently the "school district centers".

The TIMSS (Trends in International Mathematics and Science Study) 2019 survey on mathematical competencies involved students from 64 countries. The survey also shows Hungary close to the international average. The survey shows that the home environment is more conducive to learning than the school environment. Teachers' teaching experience is significant (16 years on average, 24 years in Hungary), but this does not reflect the social prestige of teachers, but rather an aging teaching society (TIMSS 2019a, b).

The 2016 Progress in International Reading Literacy Study (PIRLS) a survey of reading literacy skills involved 50 countries. In this survey, Hungary ranked 9 out of 16, meaning that students scored substantially high in reading comprehension skills (PIRLS 2017, 2021).

The TALIS (Teaching and Learning International Survey) is the largest international questionnaire survey that asks teachers and school leaders about their teaching and learning conditions, attitudes towards teaching, teaching practices and the characteristics of school leadership. The 2018 survey showed that the Hungarian teaching profession is aging, with few young teachers and high average age (48), and that the social prestige of teaching is very low (TALIS 2018, 2019).

According to international surveys, the Hungarian education system is not outstanding, but it is not the last. Nevertheless, in 2022, teachers and students took to the streets of Budapest and major cities across the country to demonstrate a better education system and for the dignity of the teaching profession (Euronews 2022). In our view, the strong social pressure being felt as we write this paper points to a new—and, we hope, deeper—education reform than before.

Today's education legislation pays particular attention to administrative and institutional tasks. However, the experience of the international surveys shows that the means of improvement must be sought at a deeper level than the administrative level (teacher training, teacher careers, pedagogical tools, inclusive education). The development of education law does not necessarily mean the development of education.

From the above analysis, we can conclude that since the fall of the socialist dictatorship, institutional reforms have been the focus in Hungary. It is also clear from the above that a series of problems have accumulated since the change of regime in 1989, which came to light in the recent times. In comparison, however, the development of staff and training and the restoration of the prestige of the teaching profession in general has taken a back seat. In particular, the current government strategy sets out objectives geared to students' output requirements but does not address the system's weaknesses or teachers. We are aware that an education strategy is not a common tool in Europe, most of the EU member state countries do not have such (Public Education Strategy 2020). Nevertheless, in our view, the main challenge for the development of Hungarian education is to prepare a comprehensive strategy that does not address the current (basically well-functioning) administrative system but instead provides a realistic assessment of the situation from the perspective of all actors in education and sets targets based on this.

5 Conclusion

In 2022, Hungarian education appeared in the news more than once. The main reason teachers and students went on strike together was to raise awareness of the need to restore the prestige of the teaching profession, both morally and financially and fill in those gaps that were accumulated since the fall of the communism. Therefore, there is a strong social pressure to improve the education system further. In our view, the present study was born on the threshold of an era. Today's Hungarian education system draws on both the legacy of democratic change in 1989 and centuries of experience. Despite (or perhaps because of) the legal reforms in education over the last 30 years, Hungarian education is currently facing a new turning point.

In our study, we have presented the history of the development of educational administration and the cornerstones of today's education system. We have seen how, from 1777 onwards, the government has been responsible for education by involving churches and civil actors in public service. Today, we find in Hungary an administrative (management and legal guarantee) system that has been overhauled several times and which, overall, fulfils its function. The right to education can be asserted, and the law has created a system of legal protection with several levels and actors. The legislation protects vulnerable groups of society, particularly children and people with special educational needs and disabilities.

Further reforms are expected to improve teachers' financial and professional situation and the cooperation between the actors involved in education (teachers, students, parents, and administration), as well as to improve teacher training and reduce the administrative burden. A strategy based on a realistic assessment of the situation of education can be built on a modern needs-based strategy, the implementation of which is expected to lead to an improvement in the international benchmarks of Hungarian education.

References

Árva Zs (2020) The administrative foundations of public education. In: Lapsánszky A (ed) Közigazgatási jog—Szakigazgatásaink elmélete és működése [Public administration law—theory and operation of specialized agencies]. Wolters Kluwer, Budapest, p 860–861

Balogh Zs (2019) Social rights. In: Schanda B, Balogh Zs (eds) Alkotmányjog—Alapjogok [Constitution law—fundamental rights]. Pázmány Press, Budapest, p 317–335

Bereczki I (2020) A közigazgatási per során elrendelt közvetítői eljárás [Mediation ordered in the course of administrative proceedings]. Dissertation, University of Debrecen, p 65–70

Csink L, Mayer A (2012) Variations on regulation [Variációk a szabályozásra]. Institute of Media Studies, Budapest, p 19–20

Curriculum for primary schools. The Ministry of Religious and Public Education 1220–10/1950. of the Ministerial Decree (1950) Tankönyvkiadó, Budapest

Euronews: Thousands march of Hungary's parliament as teachers' crisis continues (2022) Available via https://www.euronews.com/2022/10/06/thousands-march-on-hungarys-parliament-as-teachers-crisis-continues. Accessed 26 Oct 2022

Fehérpataky B et al (2012) Contributors to the Alternatív Vitarendezési Projekt [Alternative dispute resolution project] In: Fehérpataky B et al (eds) Konfliktuskezelési iránytű [Conflict management compass]. Oktatáskutató és Fejlesztö Intézet, Budapest, p 78
Fehérvári A (2013) Bevezető [Introduction]. In: Ercsei K et al.: Az alternatív vitarendezés társadalmi környezete [The social environment of alternative dispute resolution]. Oktatáskutató és Fejlesztő Intézet, Budapest. Available via https://ofi.oh.gov.hu/sites/default/files/attachments/zarotanul many.pdf. Accessed 26 Oct 2022
Gerencsér BSz (2015) Nyelvében él… [Live in its language…] NSKI, Méry Ratio, Budapest, p 97
Gerencsér BSz (2017) State and church—education in Hungary: the content of a human right and the role of external instruments. In: De Groof J, Du Plessis G, Smirnova M (eds) Religion, law and education: tensions and perspectives. Wolf Legal Publishers, Oisterwijk, p 95–108
Gerencsér BSz, Csekő-Lengyel NZs (2021) Religion in the Hungarian education system—an overview. In: Russo CJ (ed) Law, education, and the place of religion in public schools: international perspectives. Routledge, Abingdon
Horváth E (2009) The right to education. In: Jakab A (ed) Commentary on the Hungarian constitution [Az Alkotmány kommentárja] 2nd edn. Századvég, Budapest, p 2595–2597
Juhász ÉA (2015) Az alternatív vitarendezés módszerei alkalmazásának jogi háttere az iskolai konfliktusokban [The legal background of the use of alternative dispute resolution methods in school conflicts]. Available via https://docplayer.hu/10110858-Az-alternativ-vitarendezes-mod szerei-alkalmazasanak-jogi-hattere-az-iskolai-konfliktusokban.html. Accessed 26 Oct 2022
KSH [Hungarian Central Statistical Office] Education in primary school in 2020/2021. Available via https://www.ksh.hu/docs/hun/xftp/idoszaki/oktat/alt-iskola2021/index.html#asajtosnevelsii gnytanulkszmasarnyatovbbemelkedett. Accessed 28 Oct 2022
KSH [Hungarian Central Statistical Office] Higher Education 1990–2022. Available via https://www.ksh.hu/stadat_files/okt/hu/okt0020.html. Accessed 26 Oct 2022
KSH [Hungarian Central Statistical Office] Census data the population of Hungary (2022) Available via https://www.ksh.hu/. Accessed 26 Oct 2022
Láncos PL (2009) Freedom of scientific and artistic life. In: Jakab A (ed) Commentary on the Hungarian constitution [Az Alkotmány kommentárja] 2nd edn. Századvég, Budapest, p 2611
Láncos PL (2014) Language policy and linguistic diversity in the European Union. Pázmány Press, Budapest, p 45
Oszlánczi T (2018) The history of the regulation of the right to learning and education in Hungary. In: Studies in education. Líceum, Eger, p 62–64
Patyi A, Téglási A (2014) The constitutional basis of Hungarian public administration. In: Patyi A, Rixer Á (eds) Hungarian public administration and administrative law. Schenk, Passau, p 203
PIRLS Progress in International Reading Literacy Study in 2016 (2017) Available via https://nces.ed.gov/surveys/pirls/. Accessed 26 Oct 2022
PIRLS (Progress in International Reading Literacy Study) (2021) Available via https://www.oktatas.hu/kozneveles/meresek/pirls. Accessed 26 Oct 2022
PISA (2018) Összefoglaló jelentés [PISA 2018 Summary report by the office of education] (2019) Available via https://www.oktatas.hu/pub_bin/dload/kozoktatas/nemzetkozi_meresek/pisa/PIS A2018_v6.pdf. Accessed 26 Oct 2022
Public Education Strategy 2021–2030 for the European Union (2020) Available via https://2015-2019.kormany.hu/download/d/2e/d1000/Köznevelési%20stratégia.pdf. Accessed 26 Oct 2022
Pukánszky B, Németh A (1996) Neveléstörténet [History of education]. Nemzeti Tankönyvkiadó, Budapest. Available via https://magyar-irodalom.elte.hu/nevelestortenet/
Report of the Commissioner for Education Rights: Maintenance management (2015) Available via https://www.oktbiztos.hu/ugyek/jelentes2015/fenntartoi.html. Accessed 16 Oct 2022
Révay MJ, Varjú E (1936) Encyclopedia of Révai. Révai Irodalmi Intézet, Budapest
Schanda B (2012) State Church law—religious freedom and religious communities in contemporary Hungarian law. Szent István Társulat, Budapest. p 104–122
Schanda B (2015) Religion and law in Hungary, 2nd edn. Wolters Kluwer, 2015, p 75–76

Szalay J, Baróti L (1896) A magyar nemzet története [The history of the Hungarian nation]. Lambel R., Budapest

Székely L et al (2019) Report on the activities of the Commissioner for Education Rights in 2018. Available via https://www.ajbh.hu/documents/10180/2937330/AJBH+beszámoló+2018.pdf/297b2860-f3b6-f554-d61a-3b3b092c1d10?version=1.0&t=1553600198068. Accessed 26 Oct 2022

Szerb A (1981) A világirodalom története [The history of global literature]. Magvető, Budapest

Szüdi J (2012) Kommentár a köznevelési törvényhez [Commentary on the education act]. CompLex, Budapest, p 125–127

TALIS—The OECD Teaching and Learning International Survey (2018) Available via https://www.oecd.org/education/talis/. Accessed 26 Oct 2022

TALIS 2018 Összefoglaló jelentés [TALIS 2018 Summary Report by the Office of Education] (2019) Available via https://www.oktatas.hu/pub_bin/dload/kozoktatas/meresek/talis/TALIS_jelentes_2018.pdf. Accessed 26 Oct 2022

TIMSS (Trends in International Mathematics and Science Study) (2019a) Available via https://nces.ed.gov/timss/. Accessed 26 Oct 2022

TIMSS (2019b) Összefoglaló jelentés [TIMSS 2019 Summary report by the office of education] (2020) Available via https://www.oktatas.hu/pub_bin/dload/kozoktatas/nemzetkozi_meresek/timss/TIMSS2019.pdf Accessed 26 Oct 2022

Varga ZsA (2012) Ombudsman, ügyész, magánjogi felelösség. Alternatív közigazgatási kontroll Magyarországon [Ombudsman, prosecutor, private liability. Alternative administrative control in Hungary.] Pázmány Press, Budapest, p 127

The Law and the Development of the Education System in Malaysia

Fatt-Hee Tie

1 Introduction

The development of the education system in Malaysia is regulated to a significant extent by the law. The development of the education system can be divided into four stages: (a) the pre-colonial period before 1824; (b) the education system under the British administration; (c) the pre-independence period 1951 to 1957; and (d) the period after independence in 1957.

At each stage, the law has gradually played an important role in charting the progress of the education system. During the pre-colonial period, schooling was non-formal in nature. Each of three major ethnic communities, namely the Malays, Chinese, and Indians organized its school system with its own curriculum and teaching pedagogy. The curriculum was imported from the country of their origin. The teachers did not receive any form of formal training. The subjects in school consists of religion, values, morality, martial arts, handicraft, agriculture, fishing, and hunting. The legal framework that governs the school system was almost non-existent.

During the second stage, the British colonial government allowed the establishment of four types of schools: English, Malay, Chinese, and Tamil schools. The schools were allowed to use their own medium of instruction and curriculum. The schools recruited their own teachers where most did not receive any form of formal training. At this stage, the law has a minimum influence on the education system.

F.-H. Tie (✉)
Faculty of Law, University Malaya, 50603 Kuala Lumpur, Malaysia

C. J. Russo and L. Ma (eds.), *A Comparative Analysis of Systems of Education Law*,
https://doi.org/10.1007/978-981-97-1052-2_10

The third stage of the development occurred between 1951 and 1957. The influence of the law on the development of the education system became more significant. During this stage, four committees were set up to examine and provide recommendations to improve the education system. These were the Barnes Committee, the Fenn-Wu Committee, the Razak Committee, and the Rahman Talib Committee. The committees' recommendations for the reform of the education system were contained in the following reports: The Barnes Report on Malay Education (1951); The Fenn-Wu Report on Chinese Education (1951); The Report of the Education Committee (1956) which is also commonly referred to as the Razak Report 1956; and The Report of the Education Committee (1956) also known as the Rahman Talib Report 1960.

The Education Review Committee presented its Report (the Rahman Talib Report of 1960) to the federal government in 1960. Parliament accepted the recommendations which were then incorporated in the Education Act of 1961.

In 1950, the government had established an education committee to examine and improve on the quality of the Malay schools. L. J Barnes, the director of Social Training at Oxford University, chaired the committee. The committee published a report called the Barnes Report on Malay Education (1951) or the Barnes Report 1951. It recommended a national school system that provides a six-year primary education. It also proposed that all Malay and English schools would be maintained and given priority. The Malay language would become the medium of instruction. It proposed that the Chinese and Tamil vernacular schools should be converted into national schools with Malay as the only language to be taught. It recommended the abolition of the Chinese and Tamil schools and the setting up of a common single type primary school for all the races. At the secondary school, the medium of instruction would be English. Free education was provided in the national schools. However, the Chinese and Indian communities rejected the recommendations. They insisted that the national education system should continue to protect the interests of the Chinese and Indian communities rather than eliminate the language and culture of both the communities.

Subsequently, an education committee was established to examine and improve on the quality of schooling in Chinese schools. The Fenn-Wu Report on Chinese Education (1951) recommended that the Malay, Chinese, and Tamil languages should be the medium of instruction in the school system. Both Chinese and Indian schools should be allowed to continue.

Both the Barnes Report and the Fenn-Wu Report represents a significant milestone in the development of the education system. It paved the way for the early legalization of the education system. The government adopted some of the recommendations of both reports and enact it into a law. Thus, the first piece of legislation related to education was passed. It became the Education Ordinance of 1952.

In 1955, the government conducted another study to further improve the education system. Tun Abdul Razak, the first Minister of Education and later, the second Prime Minister of Malaysia chaired the committee. The Federal Legislature Council accepted the recommendations of the Razak Report 1956. It acted as the basis of the Education Ordinance of 1957. The Razak Report 1956 endorsed the concept of a national education system with the Malay language, the national language, as the main medium of instruction. It recommended that the primary purpose of education is to foster national unity. It recommended the establishment of two types of secondary schools, that is: "national schools" and "national-type schools". The national schools would use Malay as the medium of instruction in Malay school while the national-type schools would use Chinese, Tamil, or English as the medium of instruction. At the primary school, the child's mother tongue would be the medium of instruction. Parents had a choice to choose any schools. There was a general consensus that students could learn English or Malay as a foreign language even though they are enrolled in the Chinese or Tamil primary schools.

The Razak Report 1956 proposed the establishment of a national system of education that is accepted by the citizens and at the same time, fulfilled the country's need to promote the cultural, social, economic, and political development of the country. It recognized the need to preserve and sustain the growth of the Chinese and Tamil culture and languages. This was incorporated into Sect. 3 of the Education Ordinance 1957.

Later, some of the recommendations in the Razak Report 1956 acted as the basis of the Education Ordinance of 1957. It was an important piece of legislation as for the first time, it sets out the national education policy of the country. Thus, the legalization of education has become more evident.

In 1960, Abdul Rahman Talib, the education minister chaired a committee to review the education policy. The Rahman Talib Report 1960 became the basis for the Education Act of 1961. The national language became a compulsory subject in primary and secondary schools. Students must pass the subject in order to receive the certificate for the public examination. Schools that used English as the medium of instruction gradually changed to the national language.

On 1 January 1962, the Education Act 1961 was implemented. Chinese schools that did not convert to national-type Chinese national secondary schools became Chinese independent high schools. These schools continued to use the Chinese language as the main medium of instruction. However, the government did not provide any financial aid to these schools.

On the other hand, Sect. 21(2) of the Education Act 1961 contained an infamous provision that empowered the Minister of Education to convert any national-type Chines and Tamil primary school to a national primary school. However, the Education Act 1996 has removed Sect. 21(2) of the Education Act 1961. Section 17 of the Education Act of 1996 provides that the national language shall be the main medium of instruction in all educational institutions except for a national-type school or any other educational institutions that have been exempted by the Minister of Education.

After independence in 1957, the national education policy was incorporated into the Education Act of 1961. The Education Act of 1961 further strengthened the legislative framework that governs the education system in Malaysia. Later, the Cabinet Committee Report of 1979 further strengthened the national education policy. There is a focus on science and technology in schools, emphasis on vocational education, and developing a holistic education system that considered the intellectual, spiritual, physical and emotional development of students.

2 Nature of the Legal System

2.1 Sources of Law

Article 160(2) of the Federal Constitution defined "law" to include three sources, namely: (a) written law; (b) the common law; and, (c) any custom that have the force of law. Thus, the sources of law in Malaysia may be from legislation, subsidiary legislation, judicial precedents, and recognized customs.

The most important source of law is from written law. It comprises the Federal Constitution, the State Constitution, legislation and subsidiary legislation. Article 4(1) of the Federal Constitution declared that the Federal Constitution is the supreme law in Malaysia. The Federal Constitution came into force in 1957. Laws that are passed after independence which are inconsistent with the Federal Constitution shall, to the extent of the inconsistency, be void. The Federal Constitution contains provisions that are related to education.

The Federation of Malaysia consists of thirteen states that have their own constitution. Parliament legislates the laws at the federal level. At the state level, it is the state legislative assemblies. Parliament enacts laws that are known as Ordinances. After independence, these laws are called Acts. The state legislative assemblies enact laws that are called Enactments. In the state of Sarawak, they are called Ordinances. Parliament and the state legislature enact laws according to the provisions set out in the Federal Constitution and the State Constitutions. In Malaysia, there are a lower house known as the House of Representatives and an upper house known as the Senate. Parliament exercises its power to make laws by passing Bills in both houses. A Bill may originate from either of the House.

Another source of law in Malaysia is the unwritten law. It consists of English law, judicial decisions, and customs. A part of Malaysian law is formed by English law that is found in the rules of equity and the English common law. The application of English common law is subject to two conditions, that is, the local statutes on a particular matter is absent; and, local circumstances allowed part of the English law.

Judicial decisions of the High Court, Court of Appeal, and the Federal Court are the decisions made by the judges. They are called judicial precedents as the courts have adopted the doctrine of binding judicial precedent. The courts have also recognized the validity of customary laws. In personal and family matters that are related to marriage, divorce, and inheritance, judges may make decisions based on local customs. On the other hand, if some of the customary laws are not acceptable, the courts would apply the principles of English law.

The third source of law is Islamic law. A separate court known as the Syariah court administers the law that relates to marriage, divorce, and family matters among the Muslims. The Federal Constitution expressed that the states have the power to administer Islamic law.

In Malaysia, the two primary pieces of legislations that played a significant role in governing the education system is the Federal Constitution and the Education Act of 1996. Both of these two legislations lay down the legal framework that regulates the education system as a whole. The states have the power to enact laws that are related to education at the state level. However, the states have not enacted such laws since the country achieved independence. The primary reason is that education is a federal matter. The federal government provides complete funding for all primary and secondary public schools. Consequently, the federal government exercise full control over the direction and policies of the national education system. The federal government has given the Ministry of Education the responsibility to plan and implement the various national education policies. The state education department and the district education department assist the Ministry of Education to ensure the smooth implementation of the education policies at the school level. Generally, the Ministry of Education is also accountable for the management and administration of the public schools.

Article 12(1) of the Federal Constitution expressed that all citizens have a right to education.

It also states that no citizens should be discriminated in terms of the right to education on the grounds of religion, race, descent, or place of birth, (a) in the administration of any educational institution maintained by a public authority and, in particular, the admission of pupils or the payment of fees; or (b) in providing out of the funds of a public authority financial aid for the maintenance or education of pupils or students in any educational institution, regardless of whether it is maintained by a public authority and whether within or outside the federation.

Article 12(2) of the Federal Constitution provides that every religious group has the right to establish and maintain institutions for the education of children in its own religion, and there shall be no discrimination on the ground only of religion in any law relating to such institutions or in the administration of any such law; but it shall be lawful for the Federation or a State to establish or maintain or assist in establishing or maintaining Islamic institutions or provide or assist in providing instruction in the religion of Islam and incur such expenditure as may be necessary for the purpose.

2.2 The Education Act of 1996

It is the primary legislation that governs the entire education system, in particular, public primary and secondary schools. The Education Act of 1996 is a comprehensive piece of legislation that covers fifteen major areas. Sections 3 to 9 of the Education Act 1996 sets out the areas as follow:

(a) the administration of the overall education system. It sets out the appointment and functions of the Minister of Education, the Director General of Education, State Directors of Education, Registrar General of Educational Institutions, the Chief Inspector of Schools, and the Director of Examinations;
(b) the National Education Advisory Council;
(c) the National Education System that consists of pre-school education, primary education, secondary education, post-secondary education, vocational colleges,

other educational institutions, technical education and polytechnics, special education, teacher education, religious teaching in educational institutions, the management of educational institutions, and the provision of facilities and services.

The six years of primary school education caters to children age 7 to 12. Section 29A(2) of the Education Act of 1996 requires all parents to send their children to primary school. Parents who failed to send their children to primary school are punished with a fine that does not exceed five thousand ringgit or imprisonment that does not exceed six months or both. Enrolment at the primary school is compulsory. The enrolment rate for primary education is almost 98% whereas the enrolment rate for secondary education is 90% in 2014.

The types of primary schools are: national primary schools, national-type primary schools, and special schools for the children with special needs. The medium of instruction is the national language for the national primary schools except for the national type Chinese and Tamil schools. The objective of primary schools is to teach children the basic skills of reading, writing, and arithmetic.

The five years of secondary school education can be divided into three years of lower secondary and two years of upper secondary education. There are six categories of schools at the secondary level, namely: regular, fully residential, vocational, technical, religious, and special schools. The type of education at the upper secondary education offers academic, technical, and vocational skills. At the end of the two years of upper secondary school, students sit for a common public examination, that is the Malaysian Certificate of Examination for the academic and technical students. Students from the vocational schools sit for the Malaysian Certificate of Examination (Vocational Examination).

Post-secondary education prepares students for entrance to the university. At the end of two years of post-secondary education, students sit for the Malaysian Higher School Certificate examination.

(d) Assessment and examination;
(e) Higher education;
(f) Private educational institutions;
(g) Registration of educational institutions. It includes the cancellation of registration, the registration of governors and employees, the registration of pupils, and the inspection of educational institutions by the Registrar General;
(h) Registration of teachers;
(i) The Inspectorate of Schools;
(j) Finance;
(k) Appeals;
(l) Regulations made by the Minister of Education;
(m) Offences and penalties;
(n) Miscellaneous such as the status of officers that are deemed to be public servants, requirements that are related to the premises, and the enrolment of pupils in the government and the government-aided educational institutions; and,

(o) Transitional and repeal such as changing the title of certain educational institutions, and the contributions towards religious teaching.

The Ministry of Education also issued administrative letters that governs the daily affairs of the school. These administrative letters include guidelines that are related to mandatory compliance with the national curriculum, the teaching hours for each subject, school uniform, school attendance, the rules and procedures related to disciplining pupils such as caning or corporal punishment, the types of punishment that can be meted out for the various categories of offences, and co-curricular activities.

The Ministry of Education sets out the education policies, plans and projects for the entire public education system. It controls the finance and expenditure together with the physical development of the public schools. It also formulates the school curriculum and determines the recruitment, training and posting of teachers.

Malaysia consists of 11 states. The Ministry of Education has established a state education department in each state. The state education department is accountable to the Ministry of Education. The Ministry of Education often issues administrative directives to the state education department. It then implements the instructions and all educational programs within the state. It also monitors and supervises all matters that are related to the school curriculum, schools, teachers, students, and funds from the Ministry of Education.

In 1982, the district education offices were established to assist the state education department. It supports the state education departments in managing the matters related to teachers, students, and the community. It is responsible for the supervision of public examinations and the maintenance of schools.

At the school level, secondary school principals and primary school headmasters or headmistress assist the state education department in implementing the Ministry of Education's programs. They also supervise and guide the teachers. Teachers, in turn, monitor and supervise students and liaise with parents and the community.

3 Major Legal Developments

3.1 The Challenge on the Constitutionality of Vernacular Schools

In the first case, on December 2021, the High Court in Kuala Lumpur ruled in favor of Malaysia's vernacular schools (Dzulkifly 2021). The Federation of Peninsular Malays Students, the Islamic Education Development Council, and the Confederation of Malaysian Writers' Association brought the lawsuit against the vernacular schools. The plaintiffs sought to abolish vernacular schools that use Chinese or Tamil as the medium of instruction. The plaintiffs claimed that the schools were unconstitutional and their existence violated Article 152(1) of the Federal Constitution that had declared the Malay language as the national language. It also claimed that Sects. 2, 17, and 28 of the Education Act 1996 were unconstitutional as they allowed the vernacular schools to conduct lessons in Chinese and Tamil. Further, they sought the court's approval to declare that vernacular schools had violated Article 5 (right to a dignified life), Article 8 (equality), Article 10 (freedom of speech, assembly and association), Article 11(freedom of religion), and Article 12 (rights in respect of education) of the Federal Constitution (Dzulkifly 2021).

In the case, there were two constitutional issues:

(a) Whether Sects. 2, 17, and 28 of the Education Act 1996 (that allow Chinese and Tamil schools to use the languages as the medium of instruction) are inconsistent with Article 152 of the Federal Constitution; and,
(b) Whether the establishment of these vernacular schools infringe Articles 5, 8, 10, 11, and 12 of the Federal Constitution.

Section 2 of the Education Act 1996 defines the various terms used in the act. Section 17 mandates the use of the national language in all educational institutions except national-type schools. On the other hand, Sect. 28 empowers the minister to establish national schools and national-type schools.

In addition, Article 152(1) of the Federal Constitution states that the national language shall be the Malay language and shall be in such script as Parliament may by law provide. There is a proviso in, paragraph (a) which states that no person shall be prohibited or prevented from using otherwise than for official purposes), or from teaching or learning, any other language.

Article 152(6) states that "official purpose" means any purpose of the government, whether federal or state; and includes any purpose of a public authority.

The Honorable Judge Nazlan held that vernacular schools were educational institutions under the Education Act of 1996. The vernacular schools were not public or statutory authorities. As such, they were not subject to the rule that the national language must be the medium of instruction. Article 152(1) of the Federal Constitution provides that languages other than the national language can be used as long as it is not for official purposes. The teaching and learning in languages other than the national language is protected under Article 152(1) (a) and (b) of the Federal Constitution. The plaintiffs had failed to show how vernacular schools had infringed upon their personal liberty under Articles 5, 8, 10, 11, and 12 of the Federal Constitution.

In the second case, on 30 May 2022, the High Court in Kota Baru dismissed a lawsuit by a Muslim teachers' group that sought to declare vernacular schools in Malaysia as unconstitutional (Yeong 2022). The court held that the constitutional requirement for the vernacular schools to use the national language must not be taken in isolation although vernacular schools were considered to be public authorities. Article 152 of the Federal Constitution guaranteed that vernacular schools can use Chinese or Tamil as the medium of instruction since it protects the use of the mother tongue in schools. Both the appellants then appealed to the Court of Appeal. The court dismissed the appeal. Subsequently, the appellants further appealed to the Federal Court, the apex court, in Malaysia. In *Mohd Zai Mustafa v. Menteri Pendidikan Malaysia & Ors and other appeals* (2024), the Federal Court dismissed the appeal. It affirmed that vernacular schools have the constitutional right to be established as well as the right to exist. In addition, the vernacular schools have the constitutional right to use Chinese and Tamil languages in the schools.

3.2 *Freedom of Religion in School*

In *Meor Atiqulrahman bin Ishak & others v. Fatimah bin Sihi & Others.*, (1994) three primary school pupils wore a religious headgear (also referred to as a 'serban' or a 'turban') to school. The religious attire represents the pupils' religion. The school regulation banned pupils from wearing a religious headgear to school. The school expelled the pupils for violating the regulation. The parents sought a court order to declare that the expulsion was null and void.

The High Court decided in favor of the plaintiffs. It held that the headmistress's decision to expel the pupils was *ultra vires*. The headmistress then appealed to the Court of Appeal. In *Fatimah bte Sihi & Ors. v. Meor Atiqulrahman & Ors.* (2005), the Court of Appeal held that the respondent parents must bear the burden of proof to show that the wearing of the headgear was mandatory in Islam. The parents failed to prove that the practice of wearing the type of religious attire was compulsory. The court also recognized that schools have the authority to decide on the dress code for the pupils. The parents then appealed to the Federal Court.

In *Meor Atiqulrahman bin Ishak & Ors. v. Fatimah bte Sihi & Ors.* (2006), the Federal Court upheld the decision of the Court of Appeal. It held that the school regulations did not impose a complete ban on the pupils as they were allowed to wear the headgear when they enter the school's prayer room. Schools have the freedom to introduce its own regulations on school uniform.

In this case, the court sought to strike a balance between the individual's right to freedom of religion and at the same time, recognizing the authority of schools to determine regulations related to school discipline. However, it is a difficult task to place religion outside the school gate as religion has been deeply entrenched in the school system in Malaysia.

4 Emerging Issues in Education Law

This section discusses 5 emerging issues in education law. These issues affect the right of the student to receive a proper education in school under a safe and conducive school climate. The 5 emerging issues are: (a) the rise of conservatism in Malaysian public schools; (b) teacher absenteeism; (c) students' safety; (d) concern over the quality of the education system; and, (e) the national education policy.

4.1 The Rise of Conservatism in Malaysian Public Schools

Many Muslim parents prefer to send their children to Islamic kindergartens and schools based on the belief that these schools provide a strong foundation in the faith. The schools tend to allocate more teaching time on three subjects: Islamic studies, Quranic studies, and individual recitals of the Quran. Students in some Islamic religious schools that are called "tahfiz" schools spend even longer hours to memorize the Quran. In some schools, Muslim students are required to take a fourth subject, that is, Arab language even though it is an elective subject.

There are three major concerns that have emerged. Firstly, there is less time allocated for teaching other subjects such as mathematics, science, and technology in these schools. The teaching of reading, writing, and arithmetic skills in most cases tend to be given less emphasis. Consequently, the curriculum promotes rigid rather than lateral thinking skills that is urgently needed in the present information technology era.

Secondly, the gradual indoctrination of Islam in schools. In some cases, the teachers imposed their own personal religious leaning on the students. The Chairman of the Parent Action Group, Noor Azimah Abdul Rahim has expressed her concern about this type of teachers' conduct. She expressed that the abuse and misuse by this group of teachers violates the good practices of the Islamic religion. Another example is the issuance of religious directives that are not from the Ministry of Education. These non-formal religious directives dictate the practice of Islam in schools. An example is the directive that relates to the mandatory requirement for primary school children to wear a head wear to cover the head or the "hijab."

Thirdly, the Islamization of the national education system. The indoctrination of Islamic values has gradually divided the national school system along ethnic lines. The increase in racial biasness, segregation, and radicalism may lead to tension and extremism in the long term. The threat to national security in the near future is indeed a challenge for the authorities. Siti Kassim, a human rights lawyer and activist, has described the national school system as "indoctrination factories" for Malay children. She has aptly described the numerous problems that would emerge due to the progressive institutionalized racism and Islamo-fascism from the primary school to the university.

4.2 Teacher Absenteeism

The culture of teacher absenteeism violates the right of a student to access education. It is a common problem in school. This can be a seasonal problem when teachers are instructed by the school principal to accompany students for sports competitions with no extra teachers to teach a particular subject. A teacher who takes over as a "relief" teacher may be asked to supervise the class. However, there may not be any teaching as the teacher may be a specialist in another subject. Sometimes, school prefects supervised the class. Under such circumstances, teaching and learning does not take place. In a worst-case scenario, students may be left to their own devices without any supervision. As such, some students prefer to stay away from school (Noor Azimah 2018). The Education Ministry must be serious in addressing the culture of teacher absenteeism with severe punishment, rather than merely transfer the teacher to another school.

In September 2022, the High Court heard a lawsuit that was filed against a teacher who did not turn up in class (Anjumin 2002). The plaintiff, a former student, claimed that the defendant had failed to turn up in class to teach English for seven months in 2015. The other defendants were the school principal, the district education officer, the state education director, the Director General of Education, and the government. They did not take action against the teacher despite the plaintiff's multiple complaints. The lawsuit was filed on 16 October 2018.

Another student filed a separate lawsuit against the same teacher in November 2020.

The plaintiff alleged that the defendants had breached their statutory duty under the Education Act of 1996 for the failure to ensure that the students were taught the English lessons. In addition, the action had violated her constitutional right for access to education. The court decided in favor of the plaintiffs. It held that the teacher had violated the plaintiffs' constitutional right to access in education (Anjumin 2023).

The case is a significant development in the area of education law as this was the first time that students had filed an action against an absentee teacher. Some questions that arose are: How did the teacher get away with it for seven months? Schools require teachers to record their daily attendance in school. School principals check the lesson plans every week. Schools have to follow the standard operating procedures with checks and balances at each stage. Yet, the teacher got away with it. Was the school principal in cahoots with the teacher or were the records fabricated? The teacher may have thought that the students come from poor families that are uneducated and that poor students would not have an opportunity to be heard (Noor Azimah 2018).

In the near future, cases related to teacher absenteeism may increase as parents and students become aware of their rights. Teachers are expected to enter and teach in class. Teachers are deemed to be a professional after completing training in teacher's colleges and the universities.

4.3 *Students' Safety*

Another emerging issue that relates to the law is the safety of students while in school. School bullying has a negative effect on students. The National Human Right Society report showed that school bullying continues to remain a cause of concern among parents and teachers (Wong 2018).

In one case, the victim of bullying suffered permanent ear damage as his eardrum was ruptured after being kicked and slapped by some bullies. The victim sued five of his bullies, the senior assistant for students' affairs, the school principal, the Ministry of Education and the government. The court allowed the plaintiff to succeed in a suit against the school.

The toxic culture of sexual harassment in schools was exposed when a student alleged that a male physical education teacher had made a joke during a class about rape. The teacher stated that the law protects minors from sexual abuse. However, he also expressed that boys should target women above 18 if they wanted to commit rape. A female student alleged that the rape jokes in class was made in a discussion on sexual harassment during the health and physical education lesson. The plaintiff student and her father took an action in tort for the intentional infliction of emotional distress over the rape joke.

There is another form of sexual harassment which is degrading. In Malaysia, some schools carry out "period spot checks" where female students were told to prove in a physical manner that they are having their periods. These embarrassing and humiliating acts forced students to prove that they are having menstruation. These acts include showing their blood-soaked sanitary pads, swabs being done on their vagina with either cotton buds, tissues or fingers, or even a teacher, warden or school prefect that pat down on the student's groin to feel if they are wearing a sanitary pad. These shameful and traumatic acts exist in the day schools, Islamic private schools, and residential schools.

Teachers demand "proof of menstruation" from girls who did not join the daily congregational prayers that are held in residential and religious schools The Islamic religion prohibits girls from performing their ritual prayers during their menstruation. Such ingrained belief which accepts the period spot checks resulted in the victims keeping quiet and suffering in silence even though their dignity and respect has been violated.

The recent "period check" scandal by sexual predators who are school administrators is a form of control of women and state-sanctioned sexual harassment against women. The sexual abuse, public humiliation, and mental torture has damaged the dignity and self-respect of the victims. The "period checks" does not have anything to do with religion. In Islam, a menstruating woman is not allowed to perform the ritual prayer nor fast. The religion does not force checks on people to see what is stopping them from praying. It does not force a believer to pray if he or she does not want to (Mariam Mokhtar 2021).

The duty of care expected of teachers and school principals is of a very high standard as parents trust that their children study in a safe environment. Section 31 of the Child Act 2001 states that it is a criminal offence if any person abuse, neglect, abandon or expose a child under his or her care to harm. If a staff member or the school management knew what was happening and did not do anything, they could be charged as an accessory (Ida Lim 2017). Section 29 of the Child Act 2001 states that the punishment could be a fine of RM50,000.00 or a maximum of 20 years imprisonment or both. Schools could face a civil or criminal action. Schools are also vicariously liable for all the acts and omissions of its staff.

4.4 Concern Over the Quality of the Education System

The 2018 Program for International Student Assessment (PISA) scores showed that Malaysian students performed below students from East Asia. The Organization for Economic Cooperation and Development (the OECD) conducts the PISA survey among 15-year-old students to measure their ability to apply their skills and knowledge to real-life problem-solving in reading, mathematics, and science.

The 2018 PISA results showed that Malaysian students continued to perform poorly below the OECD average. The score for reading was 415 compared to the OECD average of 487; in mathematics, 440 as against the OECD average of 489; and in science, 438 against the OECD average of 489.

The OECD cross-country surveys among 65 countries revealed that the quality of the education system in Malaysia is low. Malaysia's ranking for mathematics, reading and science were 52, 59 and 53, respectively (Wing 2019). The scores were almost similar to those of Thailand (50, 48 and 49), Chile (51, 48 and 47) and Mexico (53, 51 and 55). Generally, the Malaysian education system has failed to ensure that the average students are competent in the basic skills related to reading, mathematics and science.

A second problem faced is the politicization of the education system where the interests of politicians seem to have over-ride the interests of the student. The political interests and demands of the ruling party tend to dictate the direction of the national education system. There is limited time and resources spent on the teaching of mathematics, and science. Wing (2019:2–3) described the problem as follow:

> These politically-motivated courses promote recitation by students of state-set viewpoints rather than critical examination by students of these viewpoints. This politicization of the school curriculum means that the overall tone in Malaysian schools is conformity to 3/4 orthodoxy rather than creative thinking that produces knowledge-led growth. The education system underwent numerous systemic reforms in the 60-plus years of Barisan Nasional (the "National Front' government) rule. Every reform was a contentious affair and every reform failed to improve the performance of the average student. What usually went up after each systemic reform was the quantity of students in the education system but not the quality of the education"

4.5 The National Education Policy

The Preamble to the Education Act of 1996 states that the national education policy that is based on the national philosophy of education seeks to develop the potential of individuals in a holistic and integrated manner. It aimed at producing individuals who are intellectually, spiritually, emotionally and physically balanced and harmonious, based on a firm belief in and devotion to God. This effort is commendable as it is designed to produce Malaysian citizens who are knowledgeable and competent, who possess high moral standards, and who are responsible and capable of achieving a high level of personal well-being as well as being able to contribute to the betterment of the family, the society and the nation.

Both the objectives of national education policy and national philosophy of education sets a clear direction for the education system. Unfortunately, there is a lot of emphasis on passing examinations. Although two public examinations have been abolished at the primary school and the lower secondary school level, the examination-oriented school culture continue to create a lot of stress among students. The situation is aggravated by the implementation of a school ranking system. Schools are ranked according to their performance in the national examinations. Schools are now focused on the national ranking and see who is on top of the ranking. Students are becoming more stressed up, anxious, and even depressed in the competitive examination-oriented school climate. The focus on academic performance or on only dimension, that is, the intellectual development has undesirable effects. There is less time to consider the emotional, physical and spiritual development. This may limit the development of other skills such as, people and life skills. There is little time for students to reflect and learn life skills (Soo 2020).

5 Conclusion

The law has played a significant role in regulating the development of the education system. Before independence, more than 50% of the population did not any form of formal schooling (Malaysia Education Statistics 2017). About 6% had secondary-level schooling and less than 1% had post-secondary education. However, by 2011, the country had achieved almost 96% enrolment at the primary level, 91% enrolment at the lower-secondary level, and 81% enrolment at the upper-secondary level (Malaysia Education Statistics 2017).

On the other hand, the education system faced numerous challenges. The need to improve students' critical thinking skills, problem-solving skills, soft skills and the command of the English language remains a major concern. Strong measures are needed to avoid public schools being turned into indoctrination mills that produced a future unemployable and an unproductive workforce.

The post-Covid-19 economic era requires students to be equipped with the necessary skills rather than having a classroom-based qualification. Vocational education may help students to acquire a lifelong skill. This could help Malaysia's education system to realign with the needs of the society of tomorrow (Hunter 2022). Nevertheless, the law would continue to contribute towards the progress of the education system.

References

Anjumin E (2 Sept, 2022). English teacher sued for failing to turn up in class in Sabah. New Straits Times, p 2

Anjumin E (19 July, 2023). Former students win unprecedented suit over 'absent teacher' awarded RM150,000 in damages. New Straits Times. Available at www.nst.com.my/news/crime-courts/2023/07/932495/former-students-win-unprecedented-suit-over-absent-teacher. Accessed 7 April 2024

Dzulkifly D (29 Dec, 2021) Court rules vernacular schools constitutionally protected, throws out Malay-Muslim group's suit. Malay Mail. Available at www.malaymail.com/news/malaysia/2021/12/29/court-rules-vernacular-schools-constitutionally-protected-throws-out-malay/2031761. Accessed 27 Sept 2022

Fatimah bte Sihi & Ors. v. Meor Atiqulrahman bin Ishak & Ors (2005) 2 MLJ 25

Francis L (2019) How to reform Malaysia's ailing educational system. Aliran

Federation of Malaya (1952) Education ordinance 1952. Government Press, Kuala Lumpur

Federation of Malaya (1957) Education ordinance 1957. Government Press, Kuala Lumpur

Federation of Malaya (1956) The report of the education committee. Government Printers, Kuala Lumpur

Federation of Malaya (1951a) The Barnes report on Malaya education. Central Advisory Committee on Education, Kuala Lumpur

Federation of Malaya (1951b) The Fenn-Wu report on Chinese education. Central Advisory Committee on Education, Kuala Lumpur

Hunter M (2022) Turning Malaysia's failure in education into great success. Available at http://www.freemalaysiatoday.com/category/opinion/2022/04/26/reimagining-malaysian-higher-education. Accessed 16 Sept 2022

Ida Lim (3 May, 2017) Experts: Tahfiz school can be held responsible for student's death. Malay Mail, p 5. Available at http://www.malaymail.com/news/malaysia/2017/05/03/experts-tahfiz-school-can-be-held-responsible-for-students-death/1368631. Accessed 7 Sept 2022

Malaysia. Child act 2001. National Printers, Kuala Lumpur

Malaysia. Education act 1961. National Printers, Kuala Lumpur

Malaysia. Education act. 1996. National Printers, Kuala Lumpur

Malaysia. Federal constitution. National Printers, Kuala Lumpur

Malaysia. Ministry of Education. Report on the implementation of the recommendations of the education review committee 1960. Dewan Bahasa dan Pustaka, Kuala Lumpur

Mariam Mokhtar (23 April, 2021) The sexual predators whom we call school administrators. Malaysiakini. Available at www.malaysiakini.com/news/571826. Accessed 6 Sept 2022

Meor Atiqulrahman bin Ishak & Ors v. Fatimah bte Sihi & Ors (1994) 3 MLJ 61

Meor Atiqulrahman bin Ishak & Ors v. Fatimah bte Sihi & Ors. (2006) 4 CLJ 1Mohd Zai Mustafa v. Menteri Pendidikan & Ors. and other appeals [2024] 2 CLJ 753.

Noor Azimah AR (21 Nov 2018) Edu Nation: enforce exit policy for absent teachers, strip them of their pension. The Edge Weekly, p 10

Soo J (2020) Teachers reveal how much our school system has changed over the years, 4 Dec 2020. Available at http://www.cilsos.my. Accessed 18 Sept 2022

Wong KH (2018) How to deal with gender-based bullying in schools. Malaysiakini, 14 July 2018. Available at http://www.malaysiakini.com/news/434144. In 2014, there were 2825 cases of bullying in secondary schools. In 2015, the number of cases increased to 2968. However, the number increased to 3448 in 2016. Accessed 7 Sept 2022

Wing TW (2019). Decentralizing Malaysia's education system. Eastasiaforum. 27 Mar 2019

Yeong A (30 May, 2022) In latest case, High Court again finds vernacular schools constitutional. Available at http://www.malaymail.com/news/malaysia/2022/05/30/in-latest-case-high-court-again-finds-vernacular-schools-constitutional/9574.30. Malay Mail, p 15. Accessed 27 Sept 2022

Mexico. An Enduring Quest for the Elusive Idea of National Identity and Unity

Ricardo Lozano

1 Introduction

Education in Mexico, to our day, continues to be affected by its unresolved past and its enduring ethnic and class divisions. This unresolved history of ethnic, cultural, and social divisions can trace its origins to the role played by the Spanish Crown during the Colonial era. The first Spaniards arrived in Mexico in 1517, and a year later, reached the Gulf coast along what is now Veracruz. Hernán Cortez then landed in 1519 with eleven ships and 550 men and succeeded in conquering the Aztecs in three years. Once Montezuma II was captured, Cortez named this land the "New Spain" (Thomas 2013).

Spain, like all other major colonial powers, provided education mainly for the ruling aristocracy. The Spanish intended to annihilate the traditional ways and culture of the indigenous peoples of the New Spain; however, numerous elements of these traditions and customs survived, setting the stage for the unexpected emergence of the new mestizo culture with elements from both civilizations, but characterized by its distinct individuality (MacLachlan 2015). The unexpected emergence of this mestizo nation resulted in the internally conflicting culture and society characteristic of Mexico's identity to our day.

In the Spanish colonies, including Mexico, education was provided solely by the Catholic Church. Here, the upper class and clergy were educated in the classics, while the peons and mestizos remained ignorant. The Mayan and Aztec had their traditions trampled, for the most part, by the religious systems imposed by the Spanish Crown (Sheridan 1941).

R. Lozano (✉)
Associate Professor of Educational Leadership, Texas A&M International University, Laredo, TX, USA
e-mail: Ricardo.Lozano@tamiu.edu; Dr.Ricardo.Lozano@gmail.com

C. J. Russo and L. Ma (eds.), *A Comparative Analysis of Systems of Education Law*,
https://doi.org/10.1007/978-981-97-1052-2_11

Wary of the influence of the Crown and the Holy Roman Empire, the local Spanish attempted to establish their own plantation form of government in the New Spain, one that exploited both the Indians and peasants (Spielvogel 2007). The Spanish Crown, on the other hand, sought to establish a colonial system based on privilege formed and controlled through religious unification. The Catholic Church's intention was cultural genocide, often building their churches on sacred sites built by the original inhabitants of the land (Tucker and Janick 2018).

Missions and monasteries became the form of control over the local indigenous population. Rural estates called haciendas surrounded these missions, and monasteries functioned as self-sufficient centers of political and economic power. Within this system, Franciscans provided early education to natives and mestizo peasants, which consisted mainly of instruction in Catholicism (Turley 2016). The Jesuits and Augustinians, on the other hand, provided the more classical education for Spanish immigrants and the criollos (Mexican born individuals of pure Spanish descent) (Polzer and Polzer 1976). Vasco de Quiroga, a liberal catholic judge and Bishop, is credited with starting the first school for the natives, the hospital-school of Santa Fe established on the outskirts of Mexico City in 1531 (Weaver 2014). Viceroy Mendoza and Bishop Zumárraga established another school, the School of Santa Cruz de Tlatelolco, in 1536. With its focus on Latin, rhetoric, logic, philosophy, music, and native medicine, the school's student body comprised mainly the Spanish privileged class (Greenleaf 2018). During the colonial times in Mexico, the small group of well-educated Indians was still held to an inferior status even by the illiterate Spaniards (Melvin 2012).

In 1547, the Orphanage School of San Juan was opened for the education of both Indian and mestizo youth and, in 1548, the Caridad School was established for orphaned mestizos. This was the beginning of a limited number of schools providing education for the female peasant youth (The Catholic Encyclopedia 1913). Nonetheless, few natives or mestizos benefited from these schools, and most learned the Spanish language and customs informally. Soon, this level of education and understanding of the Spanish language among the native and mixed-bloods frightened the Spanish with fears that continued formal education would lead to rebellion, and thenceforth, the education of the natives and mestizos was deemed undesirable by the colonial rulers (Marlow-Ferguson 2002).

Alongside the education of the natives and mestizos being discussed by the Spanish rulers, the Royal and Pontifical University of Mexico opened in 1553, making it the first university in the New World. Its main purpose was to educate the criollos for the Catholic clergy. During the colonial period, nearly 30,000 bachelor's degrees and more than 1000 masters and doctorates were awarded, thus establishing the New Spain's educated elite (Huck 2017). In 1791, a second university was established in Guadalajara. Despite these advancements in education in the New World, by 1842, less than one percent of the Mexican population was educated and only about 33% of education was free (Manzanárez and French 2004).

Under the haciendas system, a number of major urban centers emerged—including Puebla, Guanajuato, Guadalajara, and Mexico City. Universities soon became established within these major urban trade centers. The Mexican born criollos' resentment of Spanish influence germinated the seeds of revolution resulting in the beginning of the war of independence in 1810. Mexico declared its independence from Spain in 1821, and in 1822, it proclaimed its own Emperor, Agustín I. The empire was overthrown a year later, and Mexico was declared a republic (Middleton 2015).

Following wars with the north, first with Texas (1836) and then with the United States (1846–1848), a civil war (War of Reform, 1858–1861), and the attempt to establish a Mexican empire under the Austrian prince, Maximilian, the liberals, under their Mexican leader, Benito Juárez, brought about substantial reforms creating educational and economic opportunities for all, and especially for the native and mestizo peasants (State University 2020).

The birth of an independent republic guaranteed educational and social benefits for all. A Constitution was produced in 1917—one based on anticlericalism, land reform, nationalism, workers' rights, and secular education. The hemisphere's first university, the Royal and Pontifical University, was then named the National Autonomous University of Mexico which was a multicampus facility throughout the country (Johnston 1956). The new constitution provided greater powers to the federal government over education, including its structure and curricula. Religious, or parochial, schools were separated from public schools. In 1921, the Secretariat of Public Education was created. At this time, a nationalistic theme was incorporated into all public schools in Mexico. This nationalistic theme was a major feature of the revolution, and was designed to obviate the foreign influence dictated by the catholic schools (Priestley 1920).

Marked changes occurred in Mexico following the revolution and World War I, which liberated the mestizos and Indians from their rural haciendas and pueblos, opening greater opportunities for their migration and integration into larger communities. Rural schools grew rapidly within these communities, thus providing greater educational opportunities for all Mexicans regardless of ethnicity or social class (State University 2020).

Post-World War II industrialization saw two avenues of growth in Mexican education. One was in the direction of adequate training for the new industrial workers, while the other was a focus on higher education. A major project of the institutionalized revolution era (1946–1958) was the construction of the new University City built to house the National Autonomous University of Mexico. Completed in 1952, the new campus of the National University of Mexico sits on three square miles and was, at the time, one of the most modern structures in the world. As a result, a new intellectual movement emerged, moving toward objective scholarship and learning (Miller 1989).

The educational efforts of the revolution of 1910 reduced illiteracy in Mexico from 77% in 1910 to less than 38% in 1960. Due to the rapidly growing Mexican population, this figure represented more than 13 million people (State University 2020). In its attack on illiteracy, the Mexican government established a network of rural schools comprised of prefabricated buildings. The government provided these buildings while the communities provided the land and labor, thereby increasing the cohesiveness of the local community and education, a process that continues to the present (Congressional Record 2020). At this time, the Mexican government established the ongoing policy of a national, uniform curriculum. Compulsory textbooks provided in public schools are selected by the federal government and are free to all students.

Today, education in Mexico consists of three levels: primary, secondary, and higher education. Formal basic, compulsory, education encompasses preschool, elementary, and secondary (K-12). Federal, state, and local schools provide 93% of basic education, while private schools provide about 7% of the education available in the country (Monroy 2020).

2 The Legal Foundation for Education in Mexico

2.1 The Federal Government

Mexico is a federal republic formed by 31 states. Governmental powers are divided constitutionally between the executive, legislative, and judicial branches. The constitution of 1917 guarantees personal freedoms and civil liberties and also establishes economic and political principles for the country.

The legislative branch is divided into an upper house, the Senate, and a lower house, the Chamber of Deputies. Senators serve six-year terms and deputies three-year terms; members of the legislature cannot be reelected for the immediately succeeding term. Three-fifths of the deputies are elected directly by popular vote, while the remainder is selected in proportion to the votes received by political parties in each of five large electoral regions. Popularly elected and limited to one six-year term, the president is empowered to select a cabinet, the attorney general, diplomats, high-ranking military officers, and Supreme Court justices (who serve life terms).

2.2 Local Government

The Constitution delegates several powers to the 31 states. The State Constitutions follow the model of the Federal Constitution in providing for three independent branches of government—executive, legislative, and judicial. Most states have a unicameral legislature called the Chamber of Deputies, whose members serve three-year terms. Governors are popularly elected to six-year terms and may not be reelected. Because of Mexico's tradition of a highly centralized government, state and local budgets are largely dependent on federally allocated funds, and although such centralized control is no longer generally accepted, Mexico's main political parties still maintain locally dominant power bases in various states and cities.

At its most basic level, local government is administered by more than 2000 units called municipios (municipalities), which may be entirely urban or consist of a town or central village and its surrounding communities. Members of municipio governments are typically elected for three-year terms.

2.3 Legal Foundations of Education in Mexico

Article Three of the Constitution provides the framework for the configuration and philosophy of education in the country:

> All people have the right of education. The State – Federation, States, and Municipalities – will provide preschool, elementary, middle and high school education. Preschool, elementary and middle educations are considered as basic education; these and the high school education will be mandatory.
>
> Education provided by the State shall develop harmoniously all human abilities and will stimulate in pupils the love for the country, respect for human rights and the principles of international solidarity, independence and justice.

Article Three also establishes the duty of the states to ensure the quality of compulsory education:

> The State will guarantee the quality in mandatory education, in a way that educational materials and methods, school organization, educational infrastructure and the suitability of teachers and principals ensure the highest learning achievement of students.

Section I of Article Three of the Mexican Constitution establishes the separation of public education from any religious doctrine.

I. According to the Article 24 regarding the freedom of religion, the education provided by the State shall be laical; therefore, state education shall be maintained entirely apart from any religious doctrine.

Section II of Article Three stresses the need for education to be science based, and also establishes education as the national guardian against ignorance, fanaticism, and prejudices:

II. The guiding principles for state education shall be based on scientific progress and shall fight against ignorance and its effects, servitude, fanaticism and prejudices.

Section II of Article Three also establishes that education shall:

> Contribute to a better human coexistence, in order to strengthen the appreciation and respect for cultural diversity, human dignity, the integrity of the family, the convictions over society's general interest, the fraternity and equality of rights ideals, avoiding privileges based on race, religion, group, sex or individual.

Section III determines the establishment of a national curriculum by the federal executive taking into consideration the views and opinions of the States, as well as civil society, namely, parents and teachers.

III. To fully comply with the provisions established in the second paragraph and under section II, the Federal Executive shall establish the syllabus for preschool, elementary and secondary education, as well as for teacher training colleges, to be applied throughout the country. To that end, the Federal Executive shall take into account the opinion of the States' and the Federal District's governments, as well as the opinions of civil society groups involved in education, teachers and parents, in accordance with the law.

Section VI addresses private versus public education: private persons may engage in education of all kinds and grades. But with regards to elementary, secondary, and normal education, they must previously obtain, in every case, the express authorization of the State. This section also requires that all private educational institutions conform to the provisions of Sections I and II and must be in harmony with official plans and programs.

VI. Private entities may provide all kinds of education. In accordance with the law, the State shall have powers to grant and cancel official accreditation to studies done at private institutions. In the case of pre-school, elementary and secondary education, as well as teacher training college, private schools must:

   a. Provide education in accordance with the same purposes and criteria established in paragraph second and section II, as well as to comply with the syllabus mentioned in section III; and
   b. Obtain a previous and explicit authorization from the authorities, under the terms provided by the Law.

Article Three of the Mexican Constitution concludes, despite the national scope of its centralized education system, by establishing the authority and responsibility of the States and Municipalities to establish appropriate funding and assurance of quality of education at the local level.

> The Congress of the Union, with a view to unifying and coordinating education throughout the Republic, shall issue the necessary laws for dividing the social function of education among the Federation, the States, and the Municipalities; for fixing the appropriate financial allocations for this public service; and for establishing the penalties applicable to officials who do not comply with or enforce the pertinent provisions.

3 The Protection for Freedom of Belief in Education

As stated above, in Mexico, public education operates under the principle of separation of church and state. Given this approach to public education in Mexico, the following section addresses the government's position on freedom of belief.

The constitution provides all persons with the right to exercise the religion of their choosing, or to not have a religion. This freedom includes the right to participate in ceremonies and acts of worship, so long as they do not constitute an offense otherwise prohibited by law. Philosophical freedoms of conscience and religion have equal treatment by the state. Congress may not dictate laws establishing or prohibiting any religion (Vargas 1998).

Notwithstanding the fact that the constitution requires public education to be secular and independent of religious doctrine, religious groups may operate private schools, teach religion, and hold religious ceremonies at their schools. Private schools affiliated with a particular religious group must be open to all students irrespective of their religious beliefs. Students in private schools are free to not participate in religious courses and activities if they are not associated with the school's religious group.

Despite the legal provision for the imparting of religious education through private schools endorsed by properly registered religious associations, a series of conflicts have arisen concerning the inclusion of topics deemed controversial in the national curriculum taught in schools throughout the country. These recent additions to the national curriculum have clashed with the views of conservative and religious groups. Among these additions to the national curriculum are the definition of what constitutes a family, the non-binary definition of gender, and same sex marriage. Private schools, as part of the national education system, must comply with the mandate to teach the national curriculum in its entirety, regardless of their affiliation with religious associations whose philosophies are in conflict with the teaching of these topics in their schools.

4 Judicial Analysis of the Freedom of Belief in Education

The Directorate of Religious Associations (DGAR) works with state and local officials to mediate conflicts involving religious intolerance. And although the majority of these cases are observed outside of context of public education, most of them concern entire families, thus affecting the freedom of school-aged children to attend schools and, therefore, continue to exercise their constitutional right to education.

In 2019, The Secretariat of the Interior (SEGOB) launched the National Strategy for the Promotion of Respect and Tolerance of Religious Diversity. According to government officials, the constitutionally established separation of church and state will not be impacted by this new strategy. The strategy is a combined effort by different elements of the government to work together and promote religious freedom. Actions included roundtables, workshops, and the combined efforts to develop and implement trainings for state-level officials, as well as courses for elementary school students with reference to religious freedom (SEGOB 2019).

Also in 2019, the Commission for Human Rights in Mexico City (CDHCM) held the First Gathering for Cultural Diversity. Present at the event were representatives from CONAPRED, the Federal Council to Prevent and Eliminate Discrimination in Mexico City, and the Secretariat of Public Education. During the event, it was acknowledged that religious minorities in the country faced prejudice at institutional levels. The participating institutions reiterated their commitment to eradicate discrimination and prejudices in the country. Religion was identified as one of the main causes of discrimination in Mexico, particularly in public settings and schools (CDHCM 2019).

5 Emerging Issues

In matters or freedom of belief, the challenges faced by the Mexican public education system are complex. Despite the official separation of church and state in public education, conflicting understandings on ethics, morals, and values are constantly at odds, especially among groups promoting opposing ideas with regards to controversial issues like same sex marriage, gender identity, abortion rights, and their inclusion, or not, in the national curriculum.

The fact that the education system in Mexico is centralized, and thus, uniform throughout the country, makes these debates even more heated, as any change in curriculum, as minute as it might be, has the enormous potential to impact the collective understanding of right and wrong, truth, and the cultural identity of an entire generation of children in the country.

In addition to the debates on issues regarding the content of the national curriculum, a piece of legislation being currently debated, concerns the rights of parents of children in public schools to decide whether their children can opt out of courses with contents contrary to their ethical, moral, or religious beliefs. The National Coalition of Parents (UNPF), and the National Front for the Family (FNF) have vehemently opposed the inclusion of a gender ideology that, from their perspective, promotes the liberation of sexuality in minors without legal consequences for anyone. UNPF and FNF have also expressed their unmistakable disapproval of these issues being presented in books and physical spaces funded by taxpayers (Siete24 2020).

Another issue regarding education in Mexico concerns the somewhat recent, and increasingly popular, idea of homeschooling. Parents whose ideology differs from that of the public education system, or even those who simply have confidence on their ability to provide their children with a holistic education with greater emphases on academics, athletics, the arts, or with a greater emphasis on their personal values, have discarded the public and private education systems in the country, and have opted for the idea of educating their children at home. Homeschooling is not closely monitored or regulated in Mexico; yet, homeschooling is mentioned in the General Education Law and in the recommendations for the validation of alternative models of basic education in the country. In both, it is stated that, according to article 31 of the

Constitution, the idea of homeschooling is not legal in Mexico. However, article 26 of the Universal Declaration of Human Rights establishes that parents have priority when choosing the kind of education that shall be given to their children. Mexico, as a supporter of the Universal Declaration of Human Rights, tolerates the idea of parents educating at home.

In order to validate the homeschooling of their children with the Secretariat of Public Education (SEP), parents in Mexico have two distinct alternatives. Families can take advantage of the different distance adult-education programs offered by SEP, have their children take their proficiency exams, and validate their studies; or they can transfer credits from a foreign education system accredited in a country where homeschooling is lawful (HSLDA 2020).

6 Conclusion

The foundation upon which Mexico was established as a nation, was imprinted by the clashing of cultures, classes, religions, and characterized by a sense of "them" and "us". Today, Mexico is not that different. The ongoing struggle for identity permeates virtually all layers of society and culture. Education is the stage where these struggles materialize and are unmistakably clear.

Religion, in particular, is one of the bases upon which Mexico's identity was founded. Some say that "to be a Mexican is to be a Catholic". Millions of non-Catholics in Mexico have lived under the shadow of the mantle of the religion of the majority; the religion which provides the country with a sense of identity and unity. Religious minorities, which have been an integral part of Mexico's history, culture, and even its economy, have always had to adjust to the social norms established by the religious majority. Nevertheless, the separation of church and state established by the Mexican Constitution provides a more leveled field where every Mexican can express his/her religion or non-religious preferences freely.

Private education is the provision by the Mexican legal system for religious associations to provide its adherents with access to an education aligned with their values. This is, in theory, the solution to the problem of families providing their children with an education aligned with their personal views and values.

Now, the challenge presents itself when the centralized education system in Mexico imposes a national curriculum that all schools in the country must adhere to. Private schools have found ways around this issue by simply displaying the books provided by the Public Secretariat of Education on shelves where they are visible to everyone, authorities included, but using the curriculum and materials of their preference, provided that they cover the basic academic requirements established by the national curriculum.

Families not able to afford the costs of private education, have no other option but to send their children to public schools. The challenge faced by these families presents itself when the national curriculum includes viewpoints opposed to theirs. Some of these are signified by the inclusion of sex education, the idea of same sex marriage, and the non-binary understanding of gender, in the national curriculum. Families, through the National Coalition of Parents and the National Front for the Family, have challenged the authority of the public education system to teach issues related to gender and sexuality to their children in public schools. The Public Secretariat of Education responds by stating that children should not be deprived from their right to a holistic approach to education, including sex education, through the public education system.

Parents not willing or able to send their children to private, religious schools, have recently embarked on the quest for independent education through several home-school models where their ethics, moral, and religious views are not compromised by the education received by their children.

The distinct public, private, and homeschool education systems present in Mexico today, are a clear representation of the challenges faced by the nation regarding its cultural, social, economic, and religious identity. These challenges have been present from the moment the original inhabitants of the land faced the arrival of European conquistadores in the 1500s. Mexico's struggle to define its identity continues to this day. Education is clearly only one of the many stages where Mexico, as a nation, continues the struggle for the elusive idea of national identity and unity.

References

CDHCM (2019) Instituciones Firman Compromiso a Favor de la Diversidad Cultural del País. https://cdhcm.org.mx/2019/10/instituciones-firman-compromiso-a-favor-de-la-diversidad-cultural-del-pais/. Accessed 17 June 2020

Congressional Record: Proceedings and Debates of the United States Congress (2020) US Government Printing Office, United States

Greenleaf RE (2018) Zumarraga and the Mexican Inquisition, 1536–1543. Papamoa Press, United Kingdom

HSLDA (2020) Legal status and resources on homeschooling in Mexico. https://hslda.org/post/mexico. Retrieved 2 July 2020

Huck JD (2017) Modern Mexico. ABC-CLIO, United States

Johnston MC (1956) Education in Mexico. US Department of Health, Education, and Welfare, Office of Education, United States

MacLachlan CM (2015) Imperialism and the origins of Mexican culture (n.p.), Harvard University Press

Manzanárez M, French L (2004) NAFTA & Neocolonialism: comparative criminal, human & social justice. University Press of America, United Kingdom

Marlow-Ferguson R (2002) World education encyclopedia: a survey of educational systems worldwide. Gale Group, Germany

Melvin K (2012) Building colonial cities of god: mendicant orders and urban culture in New Spain. Stanford University Press, United States

Middleton J (2015) World monarchies and dynasties. Taylor & Francis, United States

Miller RR (1989) Mexico: a history. University of Oklahoma Press, Japan

Monroy C (2020) Education in Mexico. https://wenr.wes.org/2019/05/education-in-mexico-2. Accessed 6 July 2020

Polzer CW, Polzer CW (1976) Rules and precepts of the Jesuit missions of Northwestern New Spain. University of Arizona Press, United States

Priestley HI (1920) Modern Mexican history. Institute of international education, United States
SEGOB (2019) Estrategia Nacional Para la Promoción del Respeto y la Tolerancia a la Diversidad Religiosa. https://www.gob.mx/segob/prensa/secretaria-de-gobernacion-presenta-estrategia-nacional-para-la-promocion-del-respeto-y-la-tolerancia-a-la-diversidad-religiosa-218341. Accessed 2 July 2020
Sheridan JD (1941) Education in the New Spain. The Irish Monthly, vol 69, no. 811, 1941, pp 5–11. JSTOR. www.jstor.org/stable/20514825. Accessed 3 June 2020
Siete24 (2020) El gobierno debe educar sexualidad de niños, no los padres de familia: SEGOB. https://siete24.mx/vida-y-familia/el-gobierno-debe-educar-sexualidad-de-ninos-no-los-padres-de-familia-segob/. Accessed 4 July 2020
Spielvogel J (2007) Western civilization: a brief history, volume II: since 1500. Cengage Learning, United States
State University (2020) Mexico, history and background. https://education.stateuniversity.com/pages/979/Mexico-HISTORY-BACKGROUND.html. Accessed 4 July 2020
The Catholic Encyclopedia (1913) An international work of reference on the constitution, doctrine, discipline, and history of the Catholic Church. Encyclopedia Press, United States
Thomas H (2013) Conquest: Cortes, Montezuma, and the fall of Old Mexico. Simon & Schuster, United States
Tucker AO, Janick J (2018) Unraveling the Voynich Codex. Springer International Publishing, Germany
Turley SE (2016) Franciscan spirituality and mission in New Spain, 1524–1599: conflict beneath the Sycamore Tree (Luke 19:1–10). Taylor & Francis, United Kingdom
Vargas JA (1998) Freedom or religion and public worship in Mexico: a legal commentary on 1992 Federal Act on religious matters. BUY Law Review 1998(2):420–481
Weaver J (2014) The Red Atlantic: American indigenes and the making of the modern world, 1000–1927. University of North Carolina Press, United States

The System of Educational Law in the Netherlands

Mark van den Hove and Stefan Philipsen

1 Introduction

The Dutch education system ranks among the best educational systems in the world. In addition to offering a high quality of education, the Dutch education system exhibits two predominant features that are closely intertwined with the legal framework it is based on. Firstly, the Dutch education system is highly diverse, and secondly, it involves substantial and early differentiation between various levels and types of education.

The diversity within the Dutch education system directly stems from the robust protection granted by the Dutch Constitution to the freedom to provide education according to one's own beliefs (freedom of education).[1] This freedom results in a right all Dutch citizens to establish a school.[2] Remarkably, these private schools are, in the majority of cases, fully funded by the government. This right to full government funding does not result in a loss of the schoolboard's constitutional freedom to structure education according to its own insights and beliefs.

The diversity is most pronounced in primary and secondary education. Parents have ample choices. These choices, first and foremost, involve the possibility to select between public or private schools. In contrast to many other countries, the majority of primary and secondary schools in the Netherlands are private schools in nature.

[1] The freedom of education should be distinguished from the right to education. Where the right to education offers protection to pupils, students and parents, the freedom of education offers protection to the providers of education and tot teachers.

[2] Philipsen (2017a).

They wrote this contribution in a personal capacity.

M. van den Hove · S. Philipsen (✉)
Ministry of Education, The Hague, The Netherlands
e-mail: s.philipsen@uu.nl

C. J. Russo and L. Ma (eds.), *A Comparative Analysis of Systems of Education Law*,
https://doi.org/10.1007/978-981-97-1052-2_12

This is directly linked to the possibility for private schools to receive full government funding while maintaining the freedom to shape education as they see fit. In primary education, around 60% of schools are private, while the rest of the schools are public. Besides the basic choice between public and private schools, both private and public schools offer a variety of pedagogical and didactic approaches. This includes methods such as Montessori, Dalton, the Rudolf Steiner concept, and approaches centered around personalized learning. Some schools heavily incorporate digitalization in their didactic approach. These schools are referred to as Steve Jobs schools or iPad schools. School boards have the autonomy, in collaboration with participation councils consisting of parents and teachers, to determine the pedagogical and didactic character of the school. This applies to both public and private school boards. Additionally, private schools may also have a distinct religious or philosophical foundation. The Dutch educational systems offers schools with Catholic, Protestant, Islamic, Jewish, or Hindu backgrounds.[3]

Not only does the Netherlands possess one of the most diverse education systems globally, but education in the Netherlands is also highly differentiated, and early selection is commonplace. Within primary education, there are four different forms of basic education. This encompasses of two types of basic education for children requiring additional support, primary schools where English is the language of instruction, and finally, basic education attended by children who don't fall into the aforementioned categories. Primary education caters to children aged around four to twelve years old (K-12). Towards the end of primary school, pupils receive a binding advice on the educational level they should continue their secondary education. Secondary education, designed for students aged twelve to eighteen, consists of seven different levels of education that differ in content and duration. The longest secondary education program lasts six years, while the shortest takes four years. Within each level of secondary education, there are various directions available that prepare pupils for further education. Within this further education—also referred to as tertiary education—three types of education exist: vocational education, higher professional education (HBO) provided by higher professional education institutions, and academic education provided by universities (WO).

Following this brief introduction to the Dutch education system, the subsequent sections will delve deeper into the legal regulation of education in the Netherlands. In Sect. 2, we will first explore the key characteristics of the Dutch legal system, focusing on the elements that play a role in the regulation of education. Section 3 will subsequently examine the most significant legal developments, concentrating on the main trends of the past decade. In Sect. 4, we will turn our attention to future developments. Ultimately, Sect. 5 will conclude with some summarizing observations.

[3] For a more detailed discussion on the role of religion in Dutch education, see: Huisman and Philipsen (2022).

2 Nature of the Legal System

In this section, we discuss the nature of the Dutch legal system. The Dutch legal system is a system of civil law.[4] Building on this observation, we will delve deeper into the various sources of law—particularly education law—that are used in the Netherlands. Following this, we will expand on the distinct position that international law has within the Dutch legal system. It will become apparent that international law holds significant importance and weight in the Dutch legal system, particularly in the field of education. In the ensuing section, we outline the system of adjudication by which disputes in education law are resolved. Finally, in Sect. 4 we discuss a phenomenon—which we will refer to as—the Dutch legal culture and the culture of Dutch education law in particular. We discuss the culture towards dealing with law and its application in the field of education.

2.1 Sources of Dutch Educational Law

Like all civil law systems, the Netherlands has a written constitution.[5] The Constitution establishes governmental bodies, confers powers upon these bodies, and delimits these powers. In relation to education, the Constitution particularly fulfills these latter two functions. The foundation of Dutch education law lies in the constitutional provision regarding education: Article 23 of the Constitution.[6] Article 23, first paragraph, of the Constitution assigns to the central government the responsibility for ensuring the quality the education. Through this provision, the Constitution expresses the idea that the Netherlands is a unitary state. It shows that there exists a close relationship between the organization of the education system, the content of the education that is provided, and notions of citizenship disseminated in and taught through education, which primarily aim to safeguard and promote national unity. An important objective of any education system is, in addition to the elevation of the individual and securing economic progress, is the promotion of national unity. This is the reason why Article 23, first paragraph states: Education shall be the constant concern of the central government. This specific paragraph was included in the Constitution at the formation of the Netherlands as an unitary state. Although the Netherlands has other governmental bodies alongside the central government to which the Constitution

---

[4] See for a detailed introduction in Dutch law: van den Herik et al. (2022).

[5] The Constitution of the Kingdom of the Netherlands 2018 is available on: https://www.government.nl/topics/constitution/documents/reports/2019/02/28/the-constitution-of-the-kingdom-of-the-netherlands.

[6] An extensive discussion on the scope and content of Article 23 can be found in the commentary on the constitutional provision regarding education by: D. Mentink, B.P. Vermeulen and P.J.J. Zoontjens: https://www.nederlandrechtsstaat.nl/grondwet/inleiding-bij-hoofdstuk-1-grondrechten/artikel-23-onderwijs/.

grants autonomous powers—these bodies are referred to as provinces and municipalities—these governmental bodies have either no (provinces) or only a limited role (municipalities) in the realm of education. The Constitution declares education a matter of the central government. In carrying out this task, the Constitution not only obliges the government to ensure the quality of education but also, as stated in Article 23, fourth paragraph, to ensure the establishment of a sufficient number of public schools that also should be publicly accessible (this is also known as the 'safeguard function' of public schools). There must always be a public school available and accessible for any pupil or student who wishes to attend such a school. In practice, at least in primary and secondary education, municipalities bear the responsibility for implementing this constitutional obligation within the legal framework set by the national legislator.

Based on the constitutional division of tasks, within the central government, the national legislator is responsible for formulating the legal framework within which education must be provided. This applies to primary, secondary, and tertiary education. This means that almost all educational regulations—and at least all regulations relating to the quality of education and the qualifications of teachers—are established by national legislation. The government oversees the implementation of these legal rules by schools through the Inspectorate of Education.

The governmental responsibility for the quality of education and for providing sufficient public schools is only one of the two pillars upon which the constitutional provision regarding education—Article 23—is based. In addition to defining the government's responsibility for the quality of all education and the obligation to offer sufficient public education, Article 23, second paragraph, also grants to every citizen in the Netherlands the freedom of education. The freedom of education actually sets limits on the government's powers in the field of education. Article 23, second paragraph, of the Constitution stipulates that everyone is free to provide education. This freedom encompasses both substantive autonomy (the religious ethos or the choice for a pedagogical and educational concept on which the school is based) and institutional or organizational autonomy (such as the hiring of teachers).[7] Furthermore, the Constitution states that private primary and secondary schools that meet the statutory quality requirements shall receive full public funding (Article 23, paragraph seven). This means that private schools must receive funding according to the same standards set for public schools. The Constitution determines that public and private education must be treated equally. Thereby offering practical meaning to the freedom of education. The constitutional legislator was of the opinion that the freedom of education only holds significance when private schools can compete with public schools on an equal footing. In this way, parents would be free to choose the school they prefer without having to worry about differences in quality or high tuition fees asked for by private schools. At the same time, the ability to establish funding requirements provides an important instrument for the legislator to guarantee the quality of private education.

[7] See on the scope of this freedom: Philipsen (2017b).

The Constitution not only stipulates that the legislator must treat public and private education equally. When establishing quality requirements, the legislator must also respect the freedom of education. If the legislator were able to establish any requirement, it could significantly curtail the freedom of fully subsidized private schools to provide education as they see fit. The Constitution provides that the legislator must always sufficiently respect the freedom of education when formulating funding requirements. Furthermore, the Constitution explicitly states that the legislator must in particular respect the freedom to provide education according to one's religious or non-religious beliefs. This implies in particular that the government cannot be overly prescriptive in matters related to ethical and moral questions. The legislator must allow room for the religious diversity that exists within society and the education system. Additionally, the government must also respect the freedom of private schools to choose their teaching materials and appoint teachers as they deem appropriate. This requirement particularly applies when schools select teachers and students based on the religious ethos of the school. Schools that are fully funded by the government maintain the freedom to consistently apply religious admission policies. This means that denominational private schools have the freedom to only admit students or only appoint teachers who live according to the religious principles of the school community.

The educational system that has emerged from Article 23 of the Constitution is also referred to as a dualistic educational system, in which both public and private education coexist on an equal footing. The dualistic characteristic of the education system is reflected throughout all levels of the official education (primary and secondary education, as well as higher education). Even at the university level, a distinction exists between public institutions and fully funded private institutions.

The dualistic nature of the education system is also reflected in the way it is regulated. Public education is considered to be an integral part of the government. Consequently, public education is regulated by public law, and public schools are directly bound by what is prescribed in the law. This is not the case for fully funded private schools. Fully funded private schools are exclusively bound by the legislation (on education) because of the funding they recieve. For these schools abiding by the legislation on education serves as a condition (a prerequisite) for receiving funding. Therefore, schools that do not receive funding are not bound by a significant portion of the requirements that apply to fully funded private and public schools.

An important consequence of the aforementioned framework and the constitutionally protected freedom of education is that the Minister of Education or the Inspectorate of Education does not possess any direct powers over private schools. This applies even to fully funded private schools. For instance, the Minister of Education does not have the authority to close fully funded private schools. This holds even when they fail to adhere to quality requirements set by law. However, such powers do exists concerning public schools. Within the Dutch system of quality supervision for fully funded private schools, the consequence of not adhering to quality requirements is in most cases a reduction of suspension of the schools funding. In extreme cases, funding can be ended altogether. In higher education, the authority to confer degrees can also be revoked if the quality of the higer education is lacking. Often, these measures result in private schools or private universities having to close their doors, as they cannot function without funding or the authority to issue official and recognized diplomas.

The quality requirements imposed on schools are outlined in a plethora of delegated regulations. Several Acts of Parliament, or Statutes are based on the Constitution. And based on these statues are other forms of delegated regulations. The most significant of these Statues or Acts of Parliament are known as the 'sector legislation'. These Acts provide the primary regulation for each educational sector. In the case of primary education, the most important national legislation is the Primary Education Act, while for secondary education, it is the Secondary Education Act 2020, which underwent substantial revision in 2020. Furthermore, there are two other 'sector Acts' for tertiary education. The Law on Education and Vocational Training regulates vocational education, and the Law on Higher Education and Scientific Research governs higher practical education and academic education.

In addition to the legislation tailored to specific educational sectors, there is the Compulsory Education Act, which serves as a generic law on educational covering many educational sectors. The Compulsory Education Act mandates that parents are obligated to enroll their children in a school and ensure their attendance until the age of sixteen. After reaching the age of sixteen, the students themselves are obligated to continue attending school until the age of eighteen. By way of compulsory education the legislator aimed to secure that most children eventually obtain a diploma enabling them to effectively participate in the job market and society.

2.2 *The Position of International Law in the Dutch Legal System*

The Dutch legal system assigns a significant weight to international law. This is primarily due to the provision in the Constitution that states that statutes (Acts of Parliament) shall not be applied if such application conflicts with provisions of international treaties. This applies at least to the extent that the outcome to be achieved by applying the obligation of international law is clearly and unconditionally stated by the treaty provision.[8] As such, international law constitutes an integral part of the Dutch legal system, and in cases of conflict, international law takes precedence over national law, even over the Constitution.

Hence, within the Dutch legal order, international law holds a notably strong position. This robust status is particularly evident in the realm of fundamental rights protection. In relation to fundamental rights, international law plays a significant complementary role by augmenting the protection already afforded by the Constitution. Education serves as a notable illustration of this. While the Dutch Constitution offers a strong protection to those who provide education, it does not contain a constitutionally guaranteed right to education. Article 23 of the Constitution primarily

[8] Philipsen and de Wit (2014).

emphasizes on the perspective of the providers of education which includes school-boards and the teachers. To safeguard their rights of education, students, pupils and parents must resort to international law.

The most significant source of international law for legal practice, especially in the context of adjudication, is the European Convention on Human Rights (hereinafter: ECHR).[9] The ECHR is an international treaty and should be considered the most important human rights instrument on the European continent. The importance of the ECHR is underscored by the existence of an independent and specialized court responsible for overseeing its application. Additionally, the International Covenant on Economic, Social and Cultural Rights is worth mentioning. Article 13 of this United Nations treaty contains the most extensive formulation of the right to education.

The importance of international law in the Dutch legal order is heightened further by Article 120 of the Constitution, which prohibits the judiciary from assessing the constitutionality of statutes (Acts of Parliament) and treaties. As a consequence, the judiciary is precluded from evaluating whether a statute violates Article 23 of the Constitution. That the Constitution assigns the responsibility for assessing the constitutionality of statues to the democratically elected legislature. When assessing the conformity of statutes with fundamental rights, it is often necessary to weigh moral considerations, and the framers of the Constitution assumed that such assessment would be best conducted by the democratically elected legislature.[10]

EU law plays a limited role within the system of primary, secondary and tertiary education. Article 165 of the Treaty on the Functioning of the European Union (hereinafter: TFEU) states that education remains a matter of the national jurisdictions of the member states. Thus, the European Union does not have a primary task or authority concerning the organization of the official education system. Nevertheless, the European Union has a role in linking the education systems of the member states. For instance, the European Union operates its own scholarship program to enhance the mobility of students and researchers. In addition it supports instruments that facilitate the comparability of diplomas. Additionally, EU-citizenship plays a role in ensuring and safeguarding the mobility of students and teachers. On the basis of EU law economically active students are admissible to Dutch institutions of higher education on an equal footing with Dutch students. This means that students from other EU countries pay the same tuition fees and are eligible for financial aid. The free movement of persons and services comes into play for private education that is not fully funded and cannot be placed within the official educational system of primary, secondary and tertiary education.

[9] C.f. Vermeulen et al. (2004).

[10] See extensively on this topic: Bovend'Eert et al. (2021).

2.3 The Dutch System of Legal Protection and Adjudication in Education

The structure of legal protection and adjudication within Dutch education law is notably intricate. Several reasons contribute to its complexity. The primary reason is probably the dualistic nature of the education system as such. This duality has also resulted in a bifurcated system of legal protection. The administrative courts adjudicate disputes on decisions taken within public schools. Civil courts on the other hand, preside over disputes in private schools. In the Netherlands, there is no supreme court that can issue a final judgment when the rulings of the administrative courts or the civil courts diverge. Instead, there are distinct highest courts for administrative matters (the Administrative Jurisdiction Division of the Council of State) and for civil matters (the Supreme Court). While the jurisdictions of these highest courts do not overlap, they are occasionally summoned to adjudicate similar types of disputes. For example, a dispute concerning the admission of a pupil to a public school is adjudicated in administrative court, whereas a dispute regarding admission to a private (fully funded) school is adjudicated in a civil court. In practice the highest courts prevent their rulings from deviating too far apart through the mutual appointment of judges. In cases involving issues transcending a specific legal area, both the Supreme Court and the Administrative Jurisdiction Division of the Council of State have the authority to establish a grand chamber in which members of the other courts participate. Furthermore, both highest courts have the ability to seek legal advice from an Advocate-General who can point to differences in the jurisprudence.

In addition to the formal route of adjudication by courts the legislation mandates that primary and secondary schools establish their own complaints committees. In practice, most schools have fulfilled this obligation by joining a nationwide complaints committee to which they are all affiliated. This national complaints committee functions as a quasi-judicial entity. Parties voluntarily subject themselves to the committee's advice, and its decisions carry authoritative weight. If either party disagrees with the committee's advice, there is always the option to pursue the regular route to a court.

Although, the system of adjudication in education is dualistic in nature, there is a significant exception to this rule. In 2010, the legislature deemed it necessary to establish an autonomous educational court for higher education disputes. All students (of both public and private higher education institutions) can appeal decisions made by examiners or examination boards. They first appeal to an examination appeals committee, which is appointed by the institution where the students are enrolled. The examination appeals committee consists of teachers (at least half of the committee) and students (typically the other half) from the institution. The chairperson must meet the qualifications for a judge's. The chair is often an external appointee. If a student is not satisfied with the committee's decision, they can subsequently appeal to the Appeals Board for Higher Education. This board acts as the initial and final court in disputes between students and institutions. This is particularly relevant for decisions regarding the assessment of the students' knowledge or skills. Starting from January

1, 2023, this specialized educational court has merged with the Administrative Jurisdiction Division of the Council of State. Since then, the highest administrative court has become the sole and highest court in student cases. This applies to both public and private (fully funded) institutions.

2.4 *The Dutch Legal Culture*[11]

The history of the regulation of education is closely intertwined with the history of the Netherlands as a unitary state. This history began in 1814.[12] One of the most significant political points of contention during those years was the extent to which there should be room for religious diversity within the official education system. Advocates for the establishment of denominational private schools sought to provide parents with a genuine opportunity to choose for denominational education. Until 1917, parents often found themselves compelled to send their children to public schools due to the high school fees associated with private schools. The necessity to offer parents a meaningful choice became more prominent as the debate on the introduction of compulsory education increased towards the end of the nineteenth century. If the government were to enforce compulsory education for children, then parents also needed the freedom to choose a school that aligned with their preferences and their conscience. The dispute over the role of religion within the education system escalated during periods of significant turmoil on the European continent. The freedom of education was constitutionally established in the revolutionary year of 1848, and equal funding for public and private education was added to the constitutional provision on education in the equally eventful year of 1917. The constitutional revision of 1917, in which the constitutional provision on education took its current shape, is known as 'the pacification'.[13] This marked the moment when political peace was restored. It was achieved through the political decision to peacefully accommodate the religious diversity that had always characterized the Netherlands. This choice resulted in a peaceful 'living apart together'. This political approach, characterized by compromise to maintain peace, has had a significant impact on education.[14] The Dutch legal culture, stemming from the aforementioned history, is known for its practice of compromise. It's a legal culture marked by pragmatism, tolerance, consensus-seeking, and tact.[15] This also means that regulations are rarely imposed from the top down. Instead, they are formulated collaboratively with those affected by the policies. Within the Dutch education system, there exists a well-established tradition of consultation, during which various interest groups provide input. Only after this input is provided definite decisions are made. Coercion is avoided whenever possible. The

[11] See for more details on the Dutch Legal Culture: Graaf (2023).

[12] Efthymiou (2019).

[13] Se extensively: Vermeulen (1999); See also: Lijphart (2007).

[14] Vermeulen (2010).

[15] Van Rossum (2016).

interest groups that play a major role in educational decision making comprise representatives from diverse sectors, various religious organizations, educators, parents, and students. Although the Constitution assumes that the regulation of education occurs entirely through acts of parliament and delegated legislation, in practice, much of the regulation takes place through soft law instruments, such as guidelines. And these soft law instruments often emerge through dialogue with stakeholders. Legally speaking, adherence to these instruments is based on voluntariness.

3 Major Legal Developments

In this section we discuss the most important legal developments in education in the last ten years.

3.1 *Citizenship*

Following the 9/11 attacks in the United States and religiously motivated attacks in the Netherlands in the years after 9/11, a discussion arose on the necessity of enhancing citizenship education, or civics in schools.[16] The initial step was taken in 2005 when the Acts on primary and secondary education stated that education should aim at promoting active citizenship and social integration.[17] Additionally it was determined that education should start form the assumption that pupils grow up in a diverse society. Therefore schools should ensure that pupils have knowledge of and are exposed to different backgrounds and cultures. Active citizenship referred not only to the transmission of knowledge but also to learning citizenship "by doing, by experiencing what it is and means to be a citizen in a multi-cultural society and, by forming actual social ties with each other within the school."[18] Initially, this obligation to ensure citizenship education in schools did not have to manifest itself through a separate course. Instead, it was meant as a general principle to permeate the entire school organization and, if necessary, the entire curriculum. It was intended as an underlying principle and as an objective of the primary and secondary education as such. To give schools a bit of direction the general obligation to ensure citizenship education was further elaborated in the 'learning outcomes'. Learning outcomes represent what students should achieve by the end of primary school, and school boards are obliged to gear the education towards these outcomes or goals. These goals are usually formulated in broad terms, allowing schoolboards and teachers ample room to determine the specific content of their teaching. All learning outcomes

[16] Zoontjens (2019).

[17] See for a justification of a role of government in de education of civics: Macmullen (2015).

[18] *Kamerstukken [Parlementairy documents] II* 2004/05, 29,959, nr. 3, p. 3, these documents are accessible via: https://zoek.officielebekendmakingen.nl/uitgebreidzoeken/parlementair.

together constitute the Dutch curriculum, which is characterized by a high level of abstraction. Regarding the obligation to contribute to active citizenship, the following learning outcomes were established:

> 43. The student learns about similarities, differences, and changes in culture and belief systems in the Netherlands, the student learns to relate their own and others' ways of life to these belief systems, understands the significance of respecting each other's opinions and lifestyles, and learns to handle and respect sexuality and diversity within society, including sexual diversity.
>
> 44. The student gains a general understanding of how the Dutch political system functions as a democracy and learns to recognize the various ways people can be involved in political processes.
>
> 45. The student grasps the meaning of European cooperation and the European Union for themselves, the Netherlands, and the world.

The main objection to this original citizenship obligation was that it was non-prescriptive or too broad. After 2006, there were several incidents in which doubts arose whether students at the respective schools were taught sufficient citizenship skills. However, the highest administrative court ruled that the citizenship obligation was primarily a duty of care.[19] If schools attempted to achieve the statutory goals, then they fulfilled their legal obligation. After various comparative international studies revealed that the citizenship knowledge of Dutch pupils lagged behind by their international peers, the government decided to initiate a change in legislation that would result in a more extensive citizenship obligation.

The proposed legislative change aimed to prescribe much more explicit what schools were obligated to teach. This should provide schools with more guidance in structuring their education and also offer the Inspectorate of Education more guidance in the supervision of schools. Since August 1, 2021, the citizenship obligation in primary and secondary education is as follows:

> 3 Education actively promotes active citizenship and social cohesion in a goal oriented and cohesive manner, in which education is recognizably focused on at least:
>
> a. instilling respect for and knowledge of the fundamental values of the rule of law [rechtsstaat], as anchored in the Constitution, and the universally applicable human rights and freedoms, and acting in accordance with these fundamental values in school;
>
> b. developing the social and societal competences that enable the student to be part of and contribute to the diverse, democratic Dutch society; and
>
> c. instilling knowledge of and respect for differences in religion, belief, political beliefs, origin, gender, disability, or sexual orientation, as well as the value of equality.
>
> 3a The schoolboard ensures a school culture that is in line with the values referred to in the third paragraph, subsection a, creates an environment in which students are encouraged to actively practice dealing with and acting in accordance with these values, and furthermore

[19] ABRvS [administrative jurisdiction division of the Council of State] 30 March 2011, ECLI:NL:RVS:2011:BP9541. The Dutch Case Law can be consulted with the ECLI-number at: www.rechtstraak.nl.

ensures an environment in which students and staff feel safe and accepted, regardless of the differences mentioned in the third paragraph, subsection c.

3.2 More Space for the Establishment of New Fully Funded Schools

On November 1, 2020, a new law came into effect altering the procedure school-boards have to follow if they wish to apply for funding of their school. The legislation was named: "More Space for New Schools".[20] Until November 2020, a private school could only qualify for full funding if it was based on a religious ethos. To determine whether a religious ethos existed, that is a religious ethos recognized by law—the belief or non-religious belief should be recognizable as such. This meant that the belief put forth as religious or non-religious belief had to have sufficient "cogency, seriousness, cohesion, and significance." An example of a belief not recognized as religious is Pastafarianism.[21] Furthermore, based on legislation and related jurisprudence, for a belief or non-religious belief to be considered a religious ethos under the law, it also had to be considered as a "movement that manifests itself as an observable movement within the Netherlands. Which means that it should also impact other areas of society." This requirement often demanded the existence of other societal organizations adhering to the same belief. Once it was established that there was a religious ethos upon which the school was founded, the demand for a new school with that specific religious ethos had to be assessed. This demand was calculated through a complex formula, considering elements such as: the number of children already attending a school with the specific religious ethos in question, projected student growth, and the number of students not yet enrolled in a school.

This system of funding application resulted in a system in which only schools affiliated with larger, established religious movements could get fully funded. New religious movements were not eligible for funding. Additionally, establishing schools solely based on a pedagogical-didactic approach was virtually impossible. As society became less religious and religion played a less prominent role in society, the question arose whether the existing funding system should be abandoned. In an effort to preserve the freedom to establish fully funded private schools even in a society that's becoming increasingly secular, the legislature decided to remove the requirement that schools could only qualify for funding if they were based on a religious ethos recognized by law. Since 2020, schools qualify for funding if they are able to collect

[20] Philipsen (2018).

[21] Pastafarianism is the religion of people belonging to the Church of the Flying Spaghetti Monster. It originated as a response to the teaching of intelligent design in schools in the United States of America. See on the ruling of the Jurisdiction division of the Council of State: https://www.raadvanstate.nl/@112547/pastafarisme/. See on the same question also the European Court of Human Rights (ECtHR) 9 November 2021, ECLI:CE:ECHR:2021:1109DEC000947619.

a sufficient number of signed declarations from parents declaring that they intend to send their child to the newly established school. The regulations on the funding of schools specify the number of signatures required. The required number of signatures varies by region and factors such as population density. This approach aims to create a supply of schools that better align with parental school choice motifs. The new system makes it easier, for example, to establish schools based solely on pedagogical or didactic approaches.

The classic funding system which reserved funding to schools based on a religious ethos, had a somewhat conservating effect. Schools could only be established if they had some connection to existing religious communities, which often held significant experience in running schools. The design of the new system raised questions on whether society had become so diverse that facilitating the establishment of new schools could potentially compromise the quality and the coherence of the education system. Consequently, with the expansion of possibilities to establish fully funded schools, government oversight was also extended. In the new system, the government evaluates, prior to funding decisions whether it is sufficiently likely that the newly established school will meet the quality requirements. An essential consideration in this assessment is whether the new school is expected to meet the new citizenship education requirements [as discussed above].

3.3 *Inclusive Education*

Since the beginning of this century, there has been an ongoing discussion in the Netherlands about how children with special needs can be provided with the most appropriate education. This discussion anticipates the larger question that will need to be addressed in the coming years on how to provide inclusive education to all children with disabilities. Inclusive education refers to the principle that children, regardless of the difficulties they face in learning, should be able to learn in regular schools.[22] Article 23, paragraph 2, of the Convention on the Rights of the Child states that member states: *'recognizing the special needs of a disabled child, assistance shall be provided free of charge, whenever possible, taking into account the financial resources of the parents or others caring for the child, and shall be designed to ensure that the disabled child has effective access to and receives education [...]'*. In addition, in 2016 the Netherlands ratified the Convention on the rights of persons with disabilities. Article 24, paragraph 1 of the Convention states: *'States Parties recognize the right of persons with disabilities to education. With a view to realizing this right without discrimination and on the basis of equal opportunity, States Parties shall ensure an inclusive education system at all levels and lifelong learning directed.'* Additionally paragraph 2, subsection a, states: *'in realizing this right, States Parties shall ensure that persons with disabilities are not excluded from the general education system on the basis of disability, and that children with disabilities are not excluded*

[22] See on the system of appropriate education: Huisman (2020).

from free and compulsory primary education, or from secondary education, on the basis of disability.'

In 2013, the system of 'suitable education', known as "passend onderwijs," was introduced in the Netherlands. Five years later, in 2018, this system was extensively evaluated. The evaluation showed that it is challenging for schools to organize timely support, especially in situations involving complex needs of care, while also considering the interests of all other parties involved. An extensive agenda for the improvement of suitable education has been proposed to address the key shortcomings of this system. Additionally, there's a forward-looking approach towards a future where the ideal remains to establish a system of inclusive education.

The central goal of the Dutch system of suitable education is to provide pupils who require extra support in the classroom with an appropriate educational setting that meets the required level of support. The guiding principle is to provide regular education when possible and special education in separate schools —which will also be maintained for the time being—when necessary. In broad terms, the system of appropriate education is structured as follows: Firstly, school boards are obligated to collaborate within territorially defined regions. This collaboration encompasses primary and secondary education, regular schools, and special education schools for children with specials needs that cannot be met in a regular school. Special education schools are established specifically to provide education for students with disabilities. Within the collaboration network, schoolboards have to reach an agreement on the type of support each school can offer. The support provided by schools must be tailored to the needs of the students. And within the region there should be a school for every type of need. When a student with special needs applies to a school, the school must first assess the nature of the support required. If the school concludes that it cannot provide the requested support, the schoolboard must actively search for another school that can offer the necessary and appropriate support. However, schoolboards cannot simply redirect a student to specialized special school to avoid the search for a regular school that is able to supply the support needed. Placement in special education is only possible if the collaboration network agrees to it and gives permission. The collaboration network independently assesses whether a student would genuinely be better off in regular school or a special school.

3.4 Administrative Tools to Guarantee the Quality of Education

In recent times, a clear trend seems to be emerging in Dutch education law. The education law seems to evolve towards more direct control by the Minister of Education. As of August 1, 2023, the "Law on Expansion of Administrative Tools in Education" has come into effect. This Act of Parliament is the government's response to irregularities in private education. As mentioned earlier, due to the freedom of education, the Minister of Education has very limited possibilities to directly control fully funded private schools. However, there seems to be a growing desire to intervene immediately and more directly in fully funded private schools in case irregularities within these schools arise. The justification for this need is the wish to safeguard the interests of students.

The new legislation introduces additional tools that strengthen the Minister of Education's position towards fully funded private schools. Henceforth, the Minister can intervene in urgent situations. An urgent situation arises when there is a substantial presumption that the public tasks of the schoolboard are being severely neglected, jeopardizing the interests of students involved. In such cases, the Minister can issue a directive to improve the situation. This directive can even result in the removal of members of the school board of a fully funded private school. These additional tools have been introduced in all education sectors, including higher education.

3.5 Participation

Dutch education has a long tradition of involving stakeholders in decision-making. This is part of the Dutch legal culture. Striking a balance between the "power" of the school board and the "counter-power" of participation is crucial for the functioning of the educational community. The most recent major change with regard to the regulation of participation in education occurred in 2017. The "Law on Strengthening Administrative Capacity" came into effect on September 1, 2017. This law granted various "extra" rights to participation bodies within educational institutions and schools. In all education sectors, participation councils were given the right to vote on the main aspects of the budget. By having more influence on how funds are allocated, the position of participation councils were strengthened. Participation bodies always consist of a combination of teachers and parents/students. Furthermore, in higher education, every curriculum or educational program is set by what is referred to as a 'program committee'. This also can be considered a form of participation. A program committee comprises of both students and teachers who contribute to the setting of the curriculum and the way in which the educational program is run. The program committee has the right to approve essential aspects of the program and curriculum, such as the number of exam opportunities.

3.6 Legal Protection for Students in Vocational Education

As mentioned earlier, all education sectors in the Netherlands consist of both fully funded private schools and publicly accessible public schools. In primary and secondary education, the majority of schools is private. An exception to this rule is the vocational education sector (hereinafter referred to as: MBO). The entire MBO sector is privately organized, meaning there are no public MBO institutions. However, private institutions are obligated by law to be publicly accessible if necessary. An important consequence of this organizational approach is that MBO students have recourse to the civil court. The legislator deemed it undesirable for MBO students to solely rely on the civil court, as such proceedings are costly and less accessible, according to the government. This prompted the government to propose legislation supporting the legal protection of MBO-students in a manner similar to that of students in higher education. This transformation holds significant implications in the fully privatized MBO sector. The law "Improvement of Legal Protection for MBO Students" came into effect on August 1, 2023. The key changes stemming from this legislation include the following:

- Where the legal relationship between students and educational institutions was initially governed entirely by an educational contract, it is now governed by public law. A student is enrolled by a unilateral decision of the educational institution. This decision is made after the student has submitted a request and meets the entry requirements.
- All MBO-institutions are required to establish internal mechanisms for dispute resolution. Students must have the option to file an internal appeal against a decision that is unfavorable to them.
- Starting from August 1, 2023, the Administrative Jurisdiction Division of the Council of State is the highest court for education matters in vocational education, higher professional education, and scientific education. The Administrative Jurisdiction Division of the Council of State aims to prioritize education cases and deliver decisions within 90 days.

With this framework, the complete alignment of the system of legal protection in higher education has been achieved. This means that a student who progresses from vocational (MBO-) education to higher education will encounter the same form of legal protection and have the same options for litigation.

3.7 Litigation

There is no recent national litigation concerning education that would require discussion in this contribution. Most educational disputes revolve around specific cases of admissions and expulsions, as well as disputes regarding assessment of the knowledge and skills of students (disputes about grades). However, there is substantial international jurisprudence that also impacts the Dutch legal system. This includes case law from the European Court of Human Rights (ECHR) and European Union Court of Justice. Below, we briefly discuss the two major recent developments.

European Union Law

In a judgment issued by the Court of Justice on September 7, 2022, the Court addressed a preliminary question on whether Member States are free to require educational institutions to provide education in the language of that Member State. This may appear to be a straightforward matter, given the fact that Article 165 TFEU grants Member States autonomy in structuring their education systems. However, the question is intriguing due to the general assumption that language requirements might hinder the ability of students and educators to move freely within other European Union. Therefore, the Court of Justice in its assessment of the case focused on the question whether language requirements in education limit free competition between educational providers by limiting the free movement of services. Language requirements might make it less appealing or less feasible for foreign providers to offer education in the country that has language requirements. In the specific case, Latvia imposed the requirement that education is offered in Latvian. The Latvian government's intention was to protect the national language, which can be assumed to be a legitimate goal in limiting the right to free movement of services.[23]

When a legitimate goal is established, the next step is to assess whether the proposed measure is proportionate in its effects.[24] The Court concludes that obliging education to be conducted in the national language is, in principle, permissible. However, the Court also appears to emphasize the importance of exceptions to this general rule. At the very least, the Court suggests that the possibility of collaborating at the European or international level using a different language should always be possible and allowed. Additionally, it should be possible to provide education in a different language for programs focused on that another language or on a different culture.

European Court of Human Rights (ECtHR)

One of the most significant jurisprudential developments in European (and thus in Dutch) education law pertains to the ECtHR's case law regarding the segregation of Roma pupils. People of Roma origin constitute the largest ethnic minority in Europe. Nevertheless, their societal and socio-economic status remains vulnerable in many European countries. This vulnerability is evident in the fact that Roma children do not always have equal access to the mainstream education system or regular schools. In many European countries, they are still placed in separate schools or classes.[25]

Based on the jurisprudence of the ECtHR, the member states have been bound for some time by a positive obligation to prevent segregation and to eliminate existing segregation. Segregation is almost never justifiable. This is probably also the case when the segregation occurres due to parents' school choice motives or from the composition of a neighborhood in which the school is located. Recently, it seems that the Court is broadening the scope of the positive obligation to counteract segregation by granting it a more general applicability. The Court stated:

[23] C.f. Groener/Ierland, C-379/87, ECLI:EU:C:1989:599.

[24] C.f. Commissie/Hongarije, C-66/18, ECLI:EU:C:2020:792 and more extensively: van den Hove (2022).

[25] P.W.A. Huisman and S. Philipsen, X e.a. t. Albanië (EHRM, 73,548/17 en 45,521/19)—Positieve verplichting: snelle en passende maatregelen tegen segregatie in het onderwijs [Positive obligation: prompt and appropriate action against segregation in education]; https://www.ehrc-updates.nl/commentaar/212236.

> It further reiterates that the coexistence of members of society free from racial segregation is a fundamental value of democratic societies (see, mutatis mutandis, Vona v. Hungary, no. 35943/10, § 57, ECHR 2013) and that inclusive education is the most appropriate means of guaranteeing the fundamental principles of universality and non-discrimination in the exercise of the right to education (see Çam v Turkey, no. 51500/08, § 64, 23 February 2016). Having regard to these principles, the Court considers that measures to be taken in the context of the present case must ensure the end of the segregation of Roma pupils at the Jókai Mór school and, more generally, develop a policy against segregation in education and take steps to eliminate it as recommended by [the European Commission against Racism and Intolerance].[26]

The question rising from this consideration is whether the ECtHR is interpreting a general obligation to counteract segregation and, if necessary, implement anti-segregation measures. Even when no Roma pupils are involved, for example the segregation of minority students who do not share the same highly vulnerable history as the Roma population.

4 Outlook of Future Developments and Emerging Issues in Dutch Education Law

Below, we discuss some of the most significant developments in Dutch education law. These are often topics for which preparatory steps have been taken to introduce new legislation in the near future.

4.1 Student Safety

In the Netherlands, there is an increasing focus on the safety of students and pupils in schools. This focus was primarily spurred by a number of deeply impactful incidents, wherein bullied students, for instance, tragically took their own lives. Since 2005, the legislation on education contains a duty of care for schoolboards to ensure the social, psychological, and physical safety of students, and to establish policies guaranteeing their safety. Evaluations of this legislation reveal that still not all students feel safe, especially those belonging to the LHBTIQ+ community. For this reason, the Minister of Education has prepared a legislative proposal aimed at clarifying the obligations that schoolboards have to meet in this regard. A component of this proposed legislation mandates schools to immediately report certain serious safety incidents explicitly defined in the law to the Inspectorate of education. When such

[26] P.W.A. Huisman and S. Philipsen, Szolcsán t. Hongarije (EHRM, nr. 24408/16)—Overplaatsing als desegregatiemaatregel [Szolcsan t. Hungary (ECtHR, no. 24408/16)—Transfer of a pupil as a desegregation measure]: Szolcsan t. Hungary (ECtHR, no. 24408/16); https://www.ehrc-updates.nl/commentaar/212236.

a report is received by the Inspectorate of Education, it can promptly and immediately investigate the school and its safety policies. Additionally, school boards are required to promptly notify the Inspectorate of Education if teachers are found guilty of sexual misconduct. Previously, a report was only necessary if there was suspicion of committing a sexual offense. The proposed legislation, titled "Freedom and Safety in Education," suggests expanding this threshold to include instances of sexual harassment as well.

4.2 Knowledge Security

In the Netherlands, there are several highly regarded programs in which technology is employed for various 'beneficial' purposes. However, the same knowledge could also be employed for 'harmful' activities. This pertains, for instance, to so-called dual-use technology, which can be used to produce medicines as well as weapons. It is essential that this knowledge is disseminated within education. Nonetheless, it is crucial that such knowledge does not fall into the wrong hands. In this context, the government intends to introduce a 'knowledge security assessment'. In certain high-risk sectors, it might be necessary to assess the reliability of students and researchers. The government is working on a legislative proposal to implement such assessments. This is aimed at safeguarding the freedom of scientific research as well as (national) security.

4.3 Citizenship Requirements in Vocational Education

Whereas in 2022 the citizenship education requirements in primary and secondary education underwent significant changes, the focus shortly after shifted to vocational education. The Minister of Education has already shared his plans regarding citizenship education in vocational education with the Dutch Parliament.[27] The minister has expressed the intention to clearly define what students in vocational education should know when it comes to citizenship education (civics). The current guidelines are deemed insufficiently clear concerning the content and minimum quality of civic education in vocational education. Students often lack a clear understanding of what is expected from them. The requirements will be specified, encompassing aspects such as citizenship in a digital society and critical thinking. In this context, an advisory committee has presented a preliminary outline for citizenship education in the realm of vocational education.[28]

---

[27] https://www.rijksoverheid.nl/documenten/kamerstukken/2022/07/01/versterking-burgerschapsonderwijs-in-het-mbo.

[28] https://www.government.nl/latest/news/2023/07/14/online-consultation-starts-on-proposed-legislation-concerning-internationalisation-of-higher-education.

4.4 Adjustment of Binding Study Advice

Institutions of higher education in the Netherlands have the possibility to give students a 'binding study advice.' The binding study advice serves as a tool through which institutions of higher education can send students away which in their assessment are not suitable for the program for which they have enrolled. This assessment of suitability is typically based on the number of credits a student has earned in the first year of study. Educational institutions have the authority to determine the minimum number of credits a student must reach. If a student does not obtain the number of credits set by the institution, they are withdrawn from the program and cannot re-enroll in the same institution for the same program. Some institutions remove students from the program if they have not earned all the first year credits by the end of the first year, while others allow students to continue their studies if at least 3/4 of the first year credits have been earned.

The government recognizes that the enforcement of these often stringent standards has a negative impact on students' well-being. Furthermore, research indicates that some of the students who are dismissed from a program continue that same program at another educational institution and subsequently are successful. To provide students with more flexibility, the government intends to make significant changes to the regulations surrounding the binding study advice. The proposed changes aim to allow institutions to only remove students from a program if they have clearly demonstrated insufficient progress. The government is considering a threshold of thirty credits, which is half the total credits a student can obtain in the first year.[29] However, institutions will also be granted the flexibility to assess whether a student is suitable for the program at the end of the second year of study. In that case, a student must have achieved a minimum of 60 credits; otherwise, the institution is permitted to terminate the enrollment.[30] These new regulations should take effect starting from the academic year 2025/2026.

4.5 Balancing Internationalization

Recently, on July 14, 2023, the Minister of Education announced new legislation that aims at regulating the influx of international students.[31] The majority of Master degree programs in the Netherlands is conducted entirely in English. Additionally, a significant portion of Bachelor degree programs education is also provided in English. This makes the Netherlands an attractive country for foreign students. However, negative effects resulting from this anglicization can also be identified. The Dutch language

[29] https://www.rijksoverheid.nl/actueel/nieuws/2023/05/08/verbeteren-van-welzijn-studenten-door-aanpassen-bsa.

[30] An academic year comprises 60 credits for all higher education programs in the Netherlands.

[31] https://www.government.nl/latest/news/2023/07/14/online-consultation-starts-on-proposed-legislation-concerning-internationalisation-of-higher-education.

as an academic language is at risk of disappearing. This may result in the overall declining language proficiency, despite Dutch remaining an important language in the business and society at large. In addition, the education in the English-language attracts a large number of international students. This has the potential to lead to displacement of Dutch students. The resources allocated to higher education are not infinite. The government is questioning the efficiency of offering so much non-Dutch education when there is not a significant demand for English-speaking professionals in the Dutch labor market. Additionally, a substantial portion of the international student population tends to leave the Netherlands shortly after graduating. The number of incoming and outgoing students is imbalanced. For these reasons, the Minister of Education has announced several measures. Bachelor's programs may only be offered entirely in a different language after acquiring the permission of the Minister of Education. The Minister of Education will assess whether there are valid reasons to do so. If a program is allowed to be offered in a different language, there is an obligation to enhance the Dutch language proficiency of all students. This is justified by the fact that proficiency in the Dutch language is important for societal participation. The aim of this proposed policy is also to increase the chances that foreign students stay in the Netherlands, and to or improve their prospects in the labor market.

Universities will also have the option to reserve capacity specifically for European students in programs with limited capacity. This reflects the acknowledgment that Europe constitutes a distinct legal order, and the Netherlands has a special responsibility towards EU citizens compared to students from outside the EU. It will also be possible to implement specific capacity limitations for certain tracks within a program, such as an alternative language track. This allows for targeted restriction of enrollments where capacity is limited. Through these measures, the government hopes to bring balance to internationalization.

5 Concluding Observations

The Netherlands possesses an educational system that has historically been distinguished by a significant degree of freedom for schoolboards and teachers. This freedom remains constitutionally safeguarded to the present day. Simultaneously, it must be acknowledged that the freedom of education was established in a society that was moderately pluralistic. While there existed some religious diversity, the diversity remained limited to the Christian tradition. The contemporary Dutch society is radically diverse. This diversity consequently prompts a quest for a shared foundation within education, and results in: an increased emphasis on citizenship, language, and enhanced oversight. At the same time, society has also become more individualized. This has resulted in: a stronger protection of the individual student and pupil, manifesting in aspects such as social safety and the restructuring of legal protection mechanisms within education. Dutch education law is a dynamic system of law, and the recently proposed legislation indicates that this dynamics is likely to persist in the foreseeable future.

References

Bovend'Eert PPT et al (2021) Constitutioneel recht [Constitutional law]. Kluwer, Deventer, pp 88–89

Efthymiou NS (2019) De Grondwet van 1814 en de Grondwet van 1815 [The constitution of 1814 and the constitution of 1815]. TvCR 2019/2 [Dutch journal on Constituional Law]. pp 24–50

Graaf N (2023) An introduction to Dutch legal culture. In: Koch S, Kjølstad MM (eds) Handbook on legal cultures. Springer, pp 327–326

Huisman PWA (ed) (2020) Basisboek onderwijsrecht [Introduction to education law]. Sdu, Den Haag, pp 229–254

Huisman P, Philipsen S (2022) Law, education, and the place of religion in Dutch public schools, Chap. 10. In: Russo C (ed) Law, education, and the place of religion in public schools. Routledge

Lijphart A (2007) Verzuiling, pacificatie en kentering in de Nederlandse politiek [in English: The politics of accommodation: pluralism and democracy in the Netherlands], 9th edn. Amsterdam University Press

Macmullen I (2015) Civics beyond critics. Oxford University Press, pp 1–42

Philipsen S (2017a) De vrijheid van schoolstichting [The freedom to establish schools]. Rotterdam

Philipsen S (2017b) The Netherlands—two landmark decisions regarding religious, philosophical and ideological convictions in education. In: Cereceda PM, de Groof J (eds) Religious and ideological rights in education. Judicial perspectives from 32 legal systems. Wolf, Oisterwijk, pp 203–216

Philipsen S (2018) Meer ruimte voor nieuwe scholen? [More space for new schools?]. Tijdschrift voor Religie, Recht en Beleid [Journal of Religion, Law and Policy] 62–75

Philipsen S, de Wit JC (2014) Het spoorwegstakingsarrest: achterhaald of actueel? [The railway strike ruling: outdated or up to date?]. TvCR 2014/4 [Dutch Journal on Constitutional Law], pp 4–26

van den Herik L, Hondius E, Voermans W (2022) Introduction to Dutch law. Kluwer, Deventer

van den Hove MSP (2022) Onderwijs in de officiële taal van het land, een inbreuk op het Unierecht of een vrijheid van lidstaten [Education in the official language of the country, a breach of European Union Law or belonging tot de descrecion of Member States]. NTOR 2022/31 [Dutch Journal on Education Law]

van Rossum WM (2016) Dutch legal culture. In: Chorus J, Hondius E, Voermans W (eds) Introduction to Dutch law. Kluwer, Deventer

Vermeulen BP (1999) Constituioneel onderwijsrecht [Constitutional education law]. Elsevier, Den Haag, pp 13–18

Vermeulen B (2010) On freedom, equality and citizenship. In: Foblets G, Renteln D (eds) The response of state law to the expression of cultural diversity. Brussels

Vermeulen BP, Mentink D, Zoontjens PJJ (2004) The European convention on human rights and the Dutch education system. In: de Groof J, Lauwers G (eds) No person shall be denied the right to education. Wolf, Nijmegen, pp 375–381

Zoontjens PJJ (2019) De weg naar burgerschap [The road to citizenship]. Tilburg University

Emerging Issues in Polish Education Law

Boguslaw Przywora and Maria Moulin-Stozek

1 Introduction

The purpose of this piece is to synthetically present emerging legal problems in of the education system in Poland. It should be noted that the Polish system is grounded in various legal acts, while the right to education plays a pivotal role in the Polish system. The realization of the right to education under pandemic and during the war in Ukraine has put the Polish authorities in a difficult situation. On one hand, there was a need to continue teaching in a remote mode, and on the other hand to ensure efficient communication between children and teachers, including children of different ethnic and religious backgrounds. This chapter shows how preserving rights in these circumstances was a challenge for relevant public bodies. This right in Poland has both a cultural and an economic human rights dimension (Banaszak 2012), which is also reflected in many modern constitutions (e.g. Belgium, Denmark, Sweden, Switzerland, Italy), as well as in international documents (e.g. the International Covenant on Economic, Social and Cultural Rights of December 19, 1966; Convention for the Protection of Human Rights and Fundamental Freedoms of November 4, 1950, European Convention of Human Rights, or in the Convention on the Rights of the Children[1] (Derlatka and Garlicki 2016; Królikowski and Szczucki 2016). Similarly, the Polish Constitution of April 2, 1997[2] includes the right to education stipulated

[1] The Convention on the Rights of the Child adopted by the United Nations General Assembly on November 20, 1989 (Journal of Laws of 1991 Nr 120, item 526 as amended).

[2] Constitution of the Republic of Poland of April 2, 1997, Dz. U. Nr 78, item 483 as amended.

B. Przywora (✉) · M. Moulin-Stozek
The Interdisciplinary Research Centre On Deradicalization, Jan Dlugosz University in Czestochowa, Częstochowa, Poland
e-mail: b.przywora@ujd.edu.pl

M. Moulin-Stozek
e-mail: m.moulin-stozek@ujd.edu.pl

C. J. Russo and L. Ma (eds.), *A Comparative Analysis of Systems of Education Law*,
https://doi.org/10.1007/978-981-97-1052-2_13

in the Article 70, which establishes besides the right to education also the accompanying obligation—compulsory education for persons under the age of 18. How is compulsory education carried out is determined by the relevant laws (Stożek and Ponikowska 2018).

In addition, the Articles 70(2)-(5) of the Polish Constitution stipulate:

1. free education in public schools, although the law may allow some educational services to be provided by public higher education institutions for a fee (Sect. 2).
2. the freedom of parents to choose schools other than public schools for their children, as well as the right of citizens and institutions to establish primary, secondary and higher education schools and educational institutions (the conditions for the establishment and operation of nonpublic schools and the participation of public authorities in their financing and the principles of pedagogical supervision of schools and educational institutions are regulated by law).
3. the obligation of public authorities to provide citizens with universal and equal access to education through systems of individual financial and organizational assistance to pupils and students (the conditions for providing assistance are defined by law).
4. autonomy of higher education institutions.

Also closely related to these provisions is the freedom of teaching and scientific research (Article 73 of the Polish Constitution), the principle of neutrality of public authority (including schools) in matters of religious, philosophical and ideological beliefs (Article 25(2) of the Polish Constitution). Within the framework of this issue, the right of parents to ensure their children's moral and religious upbringing and instruction in accordance with their beliefs is of vital importance (Article 53(3) of the Polish Constitution). This is supported by the state's assertion of freedom of conscience and religion (Article 54 of the Polish Constitution). It should be emphasized that freedom of religion includes the freedom to profess or adopt a religion of one's choice and to externalize one's religion individually or with others, publicly or privately, through worship, prayer, participation in rituals, practice and teaching (Article 54(2) of the Polish Constitution). The religion of a church or other religious association with a regulated legal situation may be the subject of instruction at school, without violating the freedom of conscience and religion of others[3] (Stożek and Ponikowska 2018; Przywora and Ponikowska-Stejskal 2021).

Polish education law system is regulated in various legal acts, for example the Law of December 14, 2016 Education Act[4] or the Law of September 7, 1991, on the educational system[5] (Piszko 2018; Pilich 2021). The rights and duties of teachers in

[3] Article 54(4) of the Constitution.

[4] See Law of December 14, 2016 Education Act, Journal of Laws of 2021 item 1082 as amended.

[5] See Law of September 7, 1991, on the educational system Journal of Laws of 2021 item 1915 as amended.

kindergartens, schools, and institutions are defined by the Law of January 26, 1982, Teachers' Charter (Lisowski and Stradomski 2021).[6]

The preamble to this law emphasizes that education in Poland is the common good of the whole society; education is guided by the principles contained in the Constitution, as well as the Universal Declaration of Human Rights, the International Covenant on Civil and Political Rights and the Convention on the Rights of the Child. In addition, it was emphasized that education and upbringing—while respecting the Christian system of values—take are based on the universal principles of ethics. Education and upbringing serve to develop in young people a sense of responsibility, love of the homeland, and respect for the Polish cultural heritage while opening up to the values of European and world cultures. At the same time, special importance is attributed to the school, which should provide each student with the conditions necessary for their development, and prepare them to fulfill family and civic duties based on the principles of solidarity, democracy, tolerance, justice, and freedom.

These principles in education were particularly important during the COVID-19 pandemic when the educational system was reorganized and the right to education was implemented regardless of the difficult circumstances (Moulin-Stozek 2020). In this difficult time, a series of restrictions caused by the epidemic were necessary to be implemented and new models in education, including the system of remote education were developed (Dobrzeniecki and Przywora 2021; Syryt et al. 2022). At that time, the Ordinance of the Minister of Education of March 20, 2020, on special arrangements during the period of temporary restriction of the operation of units of the educational system in connection with the prevention, counteraction, and eradication of COVID-19 was in force (Moulin-Stozek 2020).[7] Other acts that discuss education law is the Law of July 20, 2018 Law on Higher Education and Science, as well as the Law of March 12, 2022 on Assistance to Citizens of Ukraine in Connection with the Armed Conflict in the Territory of Ukraine[8] as far as the incoming students from Ukraine who join the Polish education system are concerned.

2 Nature of the Legal System

The jurisprudence of the Polish Constitutional Court has emphasized the importance of the Article 70 of the Constitution. On one hand, this Article establishes the state's numerous tasks in the field of education and science, which, however, do not entail

[6] See Law of January 26, 1982, Teachers' Charter, Journal of Laws of 2021 item 1762 as amended.

[7] Ordinance of the Minister of Education of March 20, 2020, on special arrangements during the period of temporary restriction of the operation of units of the educational system in connection with the prevention, counteraction, and eradication of COVID-19, Journal of Laws, item 493 as amended.

[8] Law of March 12, 2022 on Assistance to Citizens of Ukraine in Connection with the Armed Conflict in the Territory of Ukraine, Journal of Laws, item 583 as amended.

the possibility of making claims for their enforcement by an individual. The implementation of these tasks, on the other hand, constitutes an institutional guarantee for the subjective right to education, which is covered by the second set of norms in the Article 70 of the Constitution. In the first sentence of the Article 70(4) of the Constitution 'universal and equal access to education' is regulated as a subjective constitutional right—among other rights (Judgment of the Constitutional Court 2007 U 5/06). The Constitutional Court shared the Commissioner for Human Rights' position on the universality of access to education, that it cannot be understood that it guarantees everyone (regardless of skills and knowledge), access to every level of education. On the other hand, compensatory measures carried out by public authorities should specifically address inequalities and barriers (including financial ones), rather than educational results themselves, which, by definition, reflect a person's actual stock of knowledge and skills. It is fundamental to create real educational opportunities for an individual at different educational levels, including in higher education. Thus, it is important to ensure equality of opportunity, not universal access to educational outcomes. In the opinion of the Constitutional Court, the right to education must be viewed as an individual value on one hand, and basic social good on the other. The realization of this right is an indispensable condition for the development of society and the full participation of an individual in the social life. Education is recognized by the Constitutional Court as universal in terms of the most important engine of economic and civilizational development in the modern world (Judgment of the Constitutional Court 2007 U 5/06; Judgment of the Constitutional Court 2000 SK 18/99).

A similar position was taken by the Constitutional Court in a judgment dealing with the issue of the right to education and universal and equal access to education juxtaposed with the generally understood imperative of free tuition in public higher education institutions (Judgment of the Constitutional Court 2014 K 35/11). The Court noted that the purpose and essence of this right is to create real opportunities for an individual to receive education at various levels of education (including higher education). In turn, the forms of realization of this right, as a rule, take a complex form and do not exhaust themselves in instruments and solutions belonging to one category of measures. In addition to supporting or developing the system of public schools, subsidized directly from budgetary sources, commonly used instruments of accessibility to study and equalization of opportunities for various groups of society are systems of social assistance and scholarships, organizing adequate financial infrastructure by creating a system of bank loans and tax solutions, as well as various forms of support for private educational institutions, including universities.

3 Major Legal Developments

The jurisprudence of the Constitutional Court has had a great impact on the shape of regulations concerning the education system in Poland. For example, the judgment of the Constitutional Court from December 2, 2009 (Judgment of the Constitutional

Court 2009 U 10/07) was another statement by the Court on the relationship between the state and churches and other religious associations in the Republic of Poland. The Court stressed that the legal-constitutional status of the Roman Catholic Church should be read in principle only in the context of Article 25(4) of the Constitution, which constitutes a 'peculiar' *lex specialis* to the other provisions of Article 25 of the Constitution (Białogłowski 2022).

Worth noting is the implementation of compulsory education in a state of pandemonium and the risks associated with it. These issues were raised by the Commissioner for Human Rights (Commissioner for Human Rights 2021, 225). In the wake of the decision to return elementary school students in grades I–III and special education students to school from remote learning, several issues occupied the attention of those with a special interest in how the education system is organized and how the right to education is realized.

One of the most serious issues was the legitimate fear of teachers and other school employees of being infected with the coronavirus. As the experience of schools has shown, the risk of teachers contracting the disease was higher than in other professional groups. This has negative consequences for the organization of school work and, by extension, for society as a whole. Therefore, the Commissioner for Human Rights supported the demand to ensure prompt access to vaccinations for employees of the education system, on whom the smooth functioning of this key public service depends. This also applied to teachers and employees of nurseries and kindergartens, who have repeatedly complained to the Commissioner for Human Rights about unequal treatment. Many found incomprehensible the decision to exclude them from coronavirus testing, the refusal to reduce the size of kindergarten groups as the epidemic unfolded, and the establishment of guidelines that differed from those used in schools and other institutions. The Commissioner for Human Rights drew attention to the situation students, for whom the organization of learning forced by the epidemic meant unfavorable changes. This is especially true for students who have not participated in remote education again in recent months. Experts warn that the long-term social impact on student's educational achievements, as well as on the condition of teachers and parents, could be felt for years.

Another problem identified by social organizations is the deterioration of mental health of children and adolescents (lowered mood, anxiety, suicidal thoughts, addiction to electronic equipment). The school has largely lost the ability to respond to disturbing signals, so the question of what is being done at the central level to provide students with the psychological support they need remains relevant. Among the negative phenomena mentioned were ongoing uncertainty, lack of understanding of the solutions being introduced, organizational difficulties, including the need to organize replacements for absent teachers, and overloading teachers with a large number of working hours (Commissioner for Human Rights 2021, 226).

It is also important to emphasize the problems associated with the education of children and young people with disabilities during the pandemic. Each student has individual needs, which, according to recommendations for special education needs, should be adequately addressed. Unfortunately, due to the reintroduction of distance learning for most of the students, some of them remained excluded from the education and upbringing system. Complaints received by the Commissioner for Human Rights office indicated that students with special educational needs, including children and adolescents with disabilities, were in a particularly difficult situation (Commissioner for Human Rights 2021, 227).

4 Outlook on Future Developments

What should be deemed important is a comprehensive development of the strategy and explanation to citizens of the reasons for specific decisions about restrictions of individual rights, to gain greater public acceptance (Commissioner for Human Rights 2021, 226). In particular, the functioning of online mental health clinics should be highlighted. To some extent, this is a response to the threats posed by the pandemic and the need to increase accessibility to obtaining specialized psychological assistance for students, alumni, parents, and teachers at schools and educational institutions (in particular in Cracow). One of the problems is the provision of adequate teaching staff. This was particularly noticeable during the pandemic period. A further decline in interest in working in schools could affect the realization of the right to education. The Supreme Audit Office report on the organization of teachers in public schools, announced on September 2, 2021, provides important information on this. It shows that between 2018 and 2021 nearly half of the head teachers reported difficulties in hiring teachers with appropriate qualifications (Information on the activities of the Commissioner for Human Rights 2021, 230). Efforts should be made to improve the conditions and organization of teachers' work in schools. In this regard, the proposals of the Supreme Audit Office are justified (Supreme Audit Office 2021):

(1) finalize the work on updating the solutions to organizational standards and the socio-economic status of the teacher in cooperation with the stakeholders of the educational environment;
(2) to take legislative action to determine, for the sake of the didactic and educational process, how extracurricular activities should be organized;
(3) analyze the regularity and adequacy of the organization of extracurricular activities and take possible measures for their better use by schools in the didactic-educational and welfare process;
(4) to analyze and evaluate the identified barriers and opportunities during the implementation of remote education and use them in the process of organizing and improving the teaching and educational process;
(5) to take measures, in cooperation with the leading authority, to create organizational conditions conducive to the implementation of tasks by teachers, also taking into account the need for teachers to carry out their tasks remotely, through, among other things, proper organization of work, retrofitting of workstations and ensuring occupational health and safety;

(6) support (among other things: financial), school principals in the creation of organizational conditions conducive to the implementation of tasks by teachers (also taking into account the need for teachers to implement tasks remotely).

It is also legitimate to debate changes in the process of empowerment of alumni leaving various types of institutions upon reaching adulthood. In particular, the issue of combining or eliminating classes in schools raises many doubts. This is also pointed out by the Children Rights Commissioner (Commissioner for Children's Rights 2021, 262). There is also a need, in particular, to intensify efforts to ensure that children with disabilities fully realize their constitutional right to an education. It should also be considered important to discuss effective solutions in the area of pedagogical supervision. Moreover, the curricula should include more content that promotes human rights and forms of deradicalisation. (see e.g. Moulin-Stozek 2021).

5 Conclusion

It is the duty of public authorities to implement the provisions of the Constitution of the Republic of Poland, including its Article 70(1) regarding the right to education and the accompanying obligations—with respect to persons who have not reached the age of 18—compulsory education. The realization of these rights under pandemic and war in Ukraine has put the authorities in Poland in a challenging situation to which it responded by enacting relevant legistlation.

As the Constitution has left quite far-reaching freedom in the realization of this right by prescribing the manner of exercising compulsory education by law, it is important to ensure that, as a rule, education in public schools is free of charge (although the law may allow certain educational services to be provided by public higher education institutions for a fee) and students are provided with universal and equal access to education through systems of individual financial and organizational assistance.

References

Banaszak B (2012) Konstytucja Rzeczypospolitej Polskiej Komentarz. Warszawa, 415

Białogłowski W (2022) "Konstytucyjna moc" Konkordatu? In: Przywora B, Rogacka-Łukasik A, Skotnicki K (eds) Z prawem ustrojowym porównawczym przez ponad półwiecze. Księga jubileuszowa Profesora Mariana Grzybowskiego z okazji 55-lecia pracy naukowej. Częstochowa

Commissioner for Children's Rights (2021). Informacja o działalności Rzecznika Praw Dziecka za rok 2021. Access 8 Sept 2022, https://brpd.gov.pl/wp-content/uploads/2022/03/Informacja-o-działalności-Rzecznika-Praw-Dziecka-za-rok-2021

Commissioner for Human Rights (2021), Information on the activities of the Ombudsman in 2021 and on the state of play of human and civil freedoms and rights. Access https://bip.brpo.gov.pl/sites/default/files/2022-07/Informacja%20RPO_wersja%20elektroniczna.pdf

Derlatka M, Garlicki L (2016) Komentarz do art. 70. In: Garlicki L, Zubik M (eds) Konstytucja Rzeczypospolitej Polskiej. Komentarz. t. II, Warszawa, 746
Dobrzeniecki K, Przywora B (2021) Legal basic for introducing restrictions on human rights and freedoms during the first wave of the COVID-19 pandemic. Review of European and Comparative Law 46(3):43–65
Królikowski M, Szczucki K (2016) Komentarz do art. 70. In: Safjan M, Bosek J (eds) Konstytucja RP. T. I. Komentarz. Art. 1-86. Warszawa, 1578
Lisowski K, Stradomski K (2021) Teachers' charter. Commentary, Warszawa
Moulin-Stozek M (2020) Polish education law: evaluation of its response to COVID-19. In: Russo C (ed) Yearbook of education law. Education Law Association, University of Virginia Press, pp 303–310
Moulin-Stozek M. (2021): De-radicalization and Integration. Legal and Policy Framework. D4 Country Report. Horizon 2020 project 'De-Radicalisation in Europe and Beyond: Detect, Resolve, Re-integrate' (959198)
Pilich M (eds) (2021) Prawo oświatowe. Komentarz. Warszawa
Piszko A (2018) Ustawa o systemie oświaty. Komentarz. Warszawa
Przywora B , Ponikowska-Stejskal M. (2021) A legal framework for teaching religion and ethics in the Polish education system, In: Russo CJ (ed) Law, education, and the place of religion in public school. International perspectives. Routledge
Stożek M, Ponikowska M (2018) Governance, constitutional rights and emerging issues in Polish Education Law. In: Russo C (ed) Handbook of comparative education law. Rowman and Littlefield
Supreme Audit Office (2021). Information of the Supreme Audit Office on the results of the audit: Organisation of teachers' work in public schools KNO.430.013.2020 Ref.no.122/2021/P/20/027/KNO, s. 20. Access https://www.nik.gov.pl/plik/id,24597,vp,27344.pdf, 3 Sept 2022
Syryt A, Przywora B, Dobrzeniecki K (2022) Freedom of assembly in the COVID-19 pandemic and the limits of its restraints in the context of the experiences of the republic of Poland and the United States of America, Bialystok Legal Studies, vol 27, no 2, pp 55–73. http://bsp.uwb.edu.pl/wp-content/uploads/2022/06/Book-BSP-27-nr-2.pdf; 8 Sept 2022

Judgments of the Constitutional Court

Judgment of the Constitutional Court from 16.01.2007, U 5/06, OTK-A 2007, no. 1, item 3
Judgment of the Constitutional Court from 5.06.2014, K 35/11, OTK-A 2014, no. 6, item 61
Judgment of the Constitutional Court from 2.12.2009, U 10/07 OTK ZU 11A/2009, item 163
Judgment of the Constitutional Court from 8.11.2000, file ref.no.SK 18/99, OTK ZU no. 7/2000, item 258

Legislation

Constitution of the Republic of Poland of April 2, 1997, Dz. U. Nr 78, item 483 as amended
Convention for the Protection of Human Rights and Fundamental Freedoms drawn up in Rome on November 4, 1950, subsequently amended by Protocols Nos. 3, 5, and 8 and supplemented by Protocol No. 2 (Journal of Laws of 1993 r. Nr 61, item 284 as amended)
International Covenant on Civil and Political Rights opened for signature in New York on December 19, 1966
Law of December 14, 2016 Education Act, Journal of Laws of 2021 item 1082 as amended
Law of September 7, 1991, on the educational system Journal of Laws of 2021 item 1915 as amended

Law of January 26, 1982, Teachers' charter, Journal of Laws of 2021 item 1762 as amended
Law of March 12, 2022 on Assistance to Citizens of Ukraine in Connection with the Armed Conflict in the Territory of Ukraine, Journal of Laws, item 583 as amended
Ordinance of the Minister of Education of March 20, 2020, on special arrangements during the period of temporary restriction of the operation of units of the educational system in connection with the prevention, counteraction, and eradication of COVID-19, Journal of Laws, item 493 as amended
The Convention on the Rights of the Child adopted by the United Nations General Assembly on November 20, 1989 (Journal of Laws of 1991 Nr 120, item 526 as amended)

Russian Education Law

Olga Seliverstova

1 Introduction

An inseparable feature of the education system is the continuous change of social relationships related to the realization of the right to education, ensuring that the state guarantees human rights and freedoms in the field of education, and creating conditions for the realization of the right to education. Since the adoption of the Russian Federation Education Law No. 273-FZ (hereinafter referred to as the "Education Law") on December 29, 2012, the modernization of the modern education system in the Russian Federation and the process of improving public relations legislation in the field of education have been actively developed.

Over the past decade, there have been many changes in the characteristics of the development of legal norms in the field of education, including revisions to the normative legal basis to abolish technically outdated normative legal acts, as well as those related to education, which greatly increases the bureaucratic burden on educational institutions and teachers.

This is the so-called "legal guillotine" mechanism, which aims to abolish existing normative legal acts, departmental orders, letters, and directives in the field of control and supervision of educational institutions (Ladnushkin and Postyliakov 2021).

According to the message given by the Russian President to the Federal Parliament, the Russian Federation government is required to abolish all normative legal documents established for national management and control (supervision) from January 1, 2021. At the same time, the new regulations formulated based on the risk-oriented approach and development level of modern technology were enabled (Item 3 of the "Task List for Achieving the President's Message to the Federal Parliament" approved by the President of the Russian Federation on February 27, 2019).

O. Seliverstova (✉)
Faculty of Teacher Education, Lomonosov Moscow State University, Moscow, Russia
e-mail: o-seliverstova@yandex.ru

C. J. Russo and L. Ma (eds.), *A Comparative Analysis of Systems of Education Law*,
https://doi.org/10.1007/978-981-97-1052-2_14

At present, it can be said that the education legislation of the Russian Federation has gone through a difficult path of formation and development. In the modern era, it is generally in line with the development level of relations in the field of education in Russia, while considering international integration.

An important and indivisible component of educational legislation is the regulation of effective mechanisms to realize the subjective rights of participants in educational relationships and to appropriately fulfill their legal obligations (Radko et al. 2018). This mechanism is a set of legal means that can completely or partially eliminate the impact of negative factors on specific educational legal relationships, and includes effective procedures for resolving legal conflicts between participants in educational relationships. Therefore, in order to ensure the popularization and compulsory nature of basic general education, current legislation requires national and municipal education management institutions to establish a wide network of general education institutions, enabling citizens' right to choose general education institutions (Seliverstova 2016). At the same time, it is stipulated that general educational institutions have an obligation to ensure the reception of all citizens who reside in the covered areas and have the right to receive corresponding levels of education. Another legal provision to guarantee students' right to education in rural general education institutions is that rural preschool or general education institutions can only be dissolved with the consent of the residents' assembly served by the institution. The effective legal guarantees for safeguarding students' right to education include the right to receive education in accordance with the national education plan, the right to free access to libraries and information resources of educational institutions, and the right to participate in the management of educational institutions. In the origin of educational relations, social protection measures for students implemented by national or local autonomous institutions are crucial. However, the complexity of the legal regulatory mechanism lies not only in the different legal means established for each participant in educational relations, but also in the particularity of fitting for various levels of educational relations.

2 The Nature of the Legal System

The national education policy is the sum of various measures, actions, and decisions taken by national institutions, with the common goal of promoting the sustainable development of education in Russia. When determining national education policies as the goal of national education development activities, it must be understood that one of the main directions of such activities is to regulate the relationships that arise in the field of education.

The diversity of relationships in the field of education has led to a complex and multifaceted normative legal documents adjustment system, consisting of four levels: federal level, Russian Federation subject level, local autonomous institutions, and educational organizations. According to the Education Law, the main legal sources in the field of education are the Constitution of the Russian Federation, the Education Law, other federal laws, subsidiary normative acts of the Russian Federation, subject laws of the Russian Federation, and other normative acts, which contain rules regulating the relationship in the education field.

The Constitution of the Russian Federation and the federal laws on education passed by the State Duma of the Russian Federation are the foundation of the normative legal system for education at all levels.

The President of the Russian Federation exercises the power to set standards in the field of education by using the powers conferred by the Constitution to determine the basic principles of national science and education policies. The orders issued by the President involve the most important aspects of national education policy, national education management, and the protection of citizens' constitutional rights to education The President of the Russian Federation issues orders and directives in this field, where orders are of normative nature, while directives are generally not legal norms.

In order to promote the exercise of the power of the head of state in the fields of education and science, the Office of the President of the Russian Federation established the Science and Education Policy Bureau within its institutional framework. The President of the Russian Federation. According to the Regulations of the Office of the President of the Russian Federation for Science and Education Policy approved by Presidential Decree No. 882 of June 25, 2012, the main responsibility of this office is to participate in the drafting of orders, directives, and tasks of the President of the Russian Federation on science and education issues.

In order to develop science and education in the Russian Federation and improve national management in this field, the Science and Education Commission of the President of the Russian Federation has been established, which is a deliberative body formed under the leadership of the Head of State aimed at ensuring cooperation between federal state power institutions. The main bodies of state power, local autonomous institutions, public associations, and scientific and educational organizations on the issues related to the development of science and education, and formulate recommendations and practical issues raised to the President of the Russian Federation regarding national policies in the fields of scientific and technological development and education. The activities of this committee are regulated by Presidential Decree No. 1059 of July 28, 2012. On the Presidential Science and Education Commission of the Russian Federation. One of the main tasks of the committee is to make recommendations to the President of the Russian Federation to determine the priority directions and mechanisms for the development of science and education in the Russian Federation, as well as measures aimed at implementing national policies in the field of science and education.

The government of the Russian Federation has considerable legislative power in the field of education. The Education Law clearly stipulates that the Russian Federation government has an obligation to formulate any subsidiary normative legal documents. For example, according to Article 11 of the Education Law, the Russian Federation government approves the procedures for developing, approving, and modifying federal national education standards. According to Article 46 of the Education Law, the government of the Russian Federation has the authority to approve the naming law for educators and leaders of educational institutions engaged in educational activities, and according to Article 54, it has the right to approve rules for providing paid educational services.

A series of government orders from the Russian Federation government, as sources of education law, are passed in accordance with the provisions of other legislative acts other than the Education Law (Kozyrin 2019). For example, Resolution No. 796 of the Government of the Russian Federation issued on August 5, 2015, on the approval of the rules passed by the Committee on Minors' Affairs and Protection of Their Rights established by the highest executive body of the state power of the Russian Federation, and the decision on allowing or disallowing individuals with criminal records to engage in teaching activities, Entrepreneurship and/or labor activities in the fields of education, education, the development of minors, organizing their rest and health, healthcare, social protection and services, sports for children and adolescents, culture and the arts, etc., Article 11 of Federal Law No. 120-FZ of June 24, 1999, "Basic Principles for the Prevention of Negligence and Crime by Minors" stipulates the form and form of this decision.

The Ministry of Science, High Technology and Education, established within the institutional structure of the Russian Federation government, is responsible for ensuring the government's activities on issues within its jurisdiction and cooperating with federal administrative agencies, other national institutions and organizations in the corresponding fields (Article 12 of the Regulations on Government Institutions of the Russian Federation approved by Resolution No. 260 of the Russian Federation Government on June 1, 2004). One of its responsibilities is to draft based on decisions made by the Russian Federation government.

In addition, the Russian Federation government submits an annual report to the Russian Federation Parliament on the implementation of national education policies to ensure the implementation of unified national policies in the field of education, and publishes it on the official website of the Russian Federation government.

The most extensive secondary regulation passed at the federal level to regulate educational relations should be the orders from the federal administrative department. Central administrative agencies—Federal departments and agencies can issue orders, directives, guidelines, and regulations in the field of education. The normative legal documents they issue can be departmental documents, which take effect within specific ministerial systems, or have universal binding force.

These federal administrative agencies include the Ministry of Education and Science of the Russian Federation, the Ministry of Education of the Russian Federation, and the Federal Bureau of Education and Science Supervision.

The Ministry of Science and Higher Education of the Russian Federation as a federal administrative authority, is responsible for formulating and implementing national policies and regulations in the fields of higher education and related supplementary vocational education, science and technology education, the development of science, technology, and innovation activities, nanotechnology, federal science and technology centers, national science centers, and science cities, intellectual property right (Excluding laws and regulations regarding the control, supervision, and provision of public services to protect inventions, utility models, industrial designs, computer programs, integrated circuit databases and topologies, trademarks, service marks, geographical indications, location names, etc.), student social support, social protection and youth policy areas. In addition, it is responsible for providing public services and managing national property in the fields of higher education and related supplementary vocational education, science, technology, and innovation activities (including the Federal Science and High Technology Center, the National Science Center, unique science booths and facilities, the Federal Public Center, leading science schools, the next-generation National Research Computer Network, and information support for science, technology, and innovation activities).

According to the Resolution No. 682 of the Government of the Russian Federation on June 15, 2018, on the Approval of Regulations of the Ministry of Science and Higher Education of the Russian Federation and the Recognition of the Invalidation of Certain Acts of the Government of the Russian Federation, the Ministry of Science and Higher Education of the Russian Federation submitted a project to the Government of the Russian Federation Federal laws, normative legal acts of the President and Government of the Russian Federation, and other documents that require the Government of the Russian Federation to make decisions on the following issues: The goal of the organization is to ensure national scientific certification and award of doctoral and doctoral degrees.

According to and implementing the Constitution of the Russian Federation, the Federal Constitution, federal laws, the President of the Russian Federation, and bills of the Russian Federation government, the Russian Ministry of Education is responsible for formulating the following normative legal documents: The organization and implementation procedures for educational activities in accordance with the teaching syllabus of higher education—bachelor's degree courses, professional courses, master's courses, internship courses; The formation and operational procedures of innovative infrastructure in the education system; List of indicators, standards, and frequency of evaluating the effectiveness of national research university development plans; Federal Higher Education National Education Standards and many other standards (Barabanova 2015). At present, the legal documents issued by the Russian Ministry of Education and Science cover more than 70 directions.

Special attention should be paid to the legislative direction of the Russian Ministry of Education regarding the status of foreign students. The Ministry specifically stipulates that:

The procedure for selecting foreign citizens to study within the quota range set by the Russian Federation government and the requirements for them;

The procedures and standards for selecting federal state educational institutions, where foreign citizens in the preparatory and preparatory departments have the right to study supplementary general education courses within the quota range set by the Russian Federation government, Ensure that foreign citizens master Russian language professional education courses on the basis of federal budget allocation, and list the above-mentioned educational institutions;

The requirements for foreign citizens to master the supplementary general education courses and provide preparation are aimed at ensuring that foreign citizens can master the vocational education curriculum in a Russian-speaking environment.

The Russian Ministry of Education and Science has summarized the application of Russian federal legislation in established areas of activity, analyzed the implementation of national policies, and proposed suggestions for improving Russian federal legislation.

The Ministry of Education of the Russian Federation (MFE) is a federal administrative authority that performs the functions of formulating and implementing national policies and normative legal provisions in the fields of general education, secondary vocational education, and corresponding supplementary vocational education, vocational training, supplementary education for children and adults, education, guardianship and guardianship of underage citizens, social support and protection for students, as well as the functions of providing public services and managing national property in the field of general education, Secondary vocational education and corresponding supplementary vocational education, vocational training, supplementary education for children and adults, education.

According to Resolution No. 884 of the Government of the Russian Federation on July 28, 2018, approving regulations of the Ministry of Education of the Russian Federation and recognizing certain actions of the Russian Federation government as invalid, the Ministry of Education of the Russian Federation serves as the national client for federal target plans and projects and coordinates the activities of federal state institutions, administrative power institutions of the Russian Federation, and other entities within the established scope of authority; The Ministry of Education is also responsible for formulating national education standards for federal general education and secondary vocational education, setting general standard indicators for evaluating the quality to measure the implementation of educational activities by institutions in accordance with major general education outline, secondary vocational education outline, and major vocational training outline, supplementary general education programs, etc.

The Minister of Education and Science and the Minister of Education are personally responsible for fulfilling the fulfillment of their duties and the implementation of national policies within their respective responsibilities by the Ministry of Science and Higher Education of the Russian Federation and the Ministry of Education of the Russian Federation.

The third national agency, the Federal Bureau of Education and Science Supervision (Rosobrnadzor) serves as the federal administrative authority responsible for regulatory legal adjustments in the following areas: The national regulation of educational activities, as well as federal state control (supervision) of foreign citizens' participation in foreign Russian language, Russian history, and the legislative foundation of the Russian Federation, and their certificate issuance procedures (whether they comply with mandatory requirements). The Supervisory Bureau is also responsible for controlling and monitoring the fields of education and science, foreign citizens' participation in foreign Russian language, Russian history and basic knowledge of

Russian Federation legislation and their certification, as well as protecting children from information harmful to their health and/or development.

According to the regulations of the Russian Federation Government's Decision No. 885 of July 28, 2018, on the Approval of the Regulations of the Federal Education and Scientific Supervision Agency and the Recognition of Certain Acts of the Russian Federation Government as Invalid, Rosobrnadzor has issued normative legal acts on the implementation of the main body of state power in the Russian Federation. The transfer of power in the field of education and in the confirmation of degree and academic title documents in the Russian Federation, including administrative regulations on the provision of public services in the authorized field of education and administrative regulations on the provision of public services to confirm degree and academic title documents, and Stipulate the target prediction indicators for the exercise of delegated powers in the field of education by the Russian Federation and the power of the Russian Federation to confirm degree and professional title documents. In addition, Rosobrandzor is also responsible for organizing the establishment and maintenance of a national education supervision information system; The control (supervision) of the state over the exercise of power by the main administrative authority of the Russian Federation in the field of education; Proposing to the government of the Russian Federation to revoke the power of the Russian Federation delegated by the main administrative organs of the Russian Federation in the field of education and the confirmation of degrees and academic title documents transferred by the main body of state power in the Russian Federation.

These three public power institutions are interrelated at the federal level, and their functions and powers in the field of public education policy often overlap and complement each other. Everyone is an independent unit with a clear area of activity.

In educational legislation, as well as in other departments legislative regulation is jointly completed by the Russian Federation and its subjects, as stipulated in the Constitution of the Russian Federation. Similarly, the concept of "legislation" is combined with the constituent parts of the Federation, it also includes the laws of the regional components—the main body of the Russian Federation, as well as secondary legislation passed under these laws for the main body of the Russian Federation, regional governments, and heads of regional education management institutions (Putilo 2019).

The Education Law stipulates the powers of the main state power institutions of the Russian Federation in the field of education, as well as the powers of the Russian Federation in the field of education. The power transferred to the main state authority of the Russian Federation (understood as: 1) the control (supervision) of the federal state over organizations engaged in educational activities in the field of education; (2) The state controls (supervises) the exercise of power by local autonomous institutions in the field of education; (3) Issuance of educational activity permits; (4) National certification of educational activities; (5) Confirm education and/or qualification documents.

In addition, the principle of consistency between regional legislation and the Education Law has been established:

- The rules regarding the relationship in the field of education contained in the laws and other normative legal documents of the various entities of the Russian Federation should comply with the Education Law, and should not limit rights or lower the level of the standards of protection provided, but should match the level of protection provided by the Education Law;
- If the provisions of the Regional Education Law are inconsistent with the provisions of the Education Law, the provisions of the Education Law shall apply.

The laws of the main body of the Russian Federation on education issues are formulated in accordance with the Constitution of the Russian Federation, the Constitution of the Main Body of the Russian Federation (Charter), and the Education Law. All other actions of the subject of the Russian Federation, including those passed by local autonomous institutions, shall not conflict with it. The secondary legislation of the main body of the Russian Federation can be distinguished from: the decrees and decisions of the highest officials of the main body of the Russian Federation, the decisions of the main government of the Russian Federation, and the orders and orders of the administrative power organs of the main body of the Russian Federation.

The next level is the normative legal actions adopted by local autonomous institutions on various education issues at the local level, such as the decisions and orders of local administrative heads on practical issues in the field of education, and the orders and orders of local administrative officials.

One of the main tasks of regulating the relationship in the field of education by law is the division of power among the federal state power institutions, the main state power institutions of the Russian Federation, and local autonomous institutions in the field of education.

According to the Constitution of the Russian Federation, social relations in the field of education are the common responsibility of the Federation and the subjects. Therefore, each subject in the Russian Federation has the right to regulate the relations in the field of education through normative laws, to develop and concretize the normative provisions of federal legislation to adapt to the specific regional characteristics and conditions (born in 2019).

So far, the legislative bodies of the main body of the Russian Federation do not have a unified method to address the issue of aligning the regional legislative foundation with the Education Law. There are at least three ways for the main body of the Russian Federation to form educational legislation: (1) to pass a special law that specifies the specific basis for legal regulation in the field of regional education; (2) to pass laws on certain educational issues; (3) to revise previous laws and regulations.

Regional laws with the same name as federal laws include Moscow State Education Law No. 94/2013-OZ of July 27, 2013, St. Petersburg Education Law No. 461-83 of July 17, 2013, and Arkhangelsk State Education Law No. 712-41-OZ of July 2, 2013. Sverdlovsk State Education Law No. 78-OZ of July 15, 2013, etc. The following are provided as examples of aligning regional education legislation with the Education Law by passing laws at all levels or fields of education: The Irkutsk Region Law No. 91-OZ of July 10, 2014, on Certain Issues Concerning Education in the Irkutsk Region, The Law No. 1569-OZ of July 18, 2013 on the Management of Relations in the Education Field of the Omsk Region, and the Law No. 361-OZ of July 5, 2013 on the Management of Relations in the Education Field of the Novosibirsk Region.

Although federal rules do not require the subject of the Russian Federation to pass laws to specify the basic education law on topics jointly governed by the Russian Federation and its subjects, the logical premise for forming a series of normative legal acts is through such a law. This conclusion is based on the assumption that the systematization of the regulatory foundation of federal law ensures the logical consistency of normative materials in relevant legal institutions in the legal field, without duplication or contradictions, and allows clear language to organically establish and consolidate legal regulatory mechanisms.

Some researchers in the field of Russian education law believe that every subject of the Russian Federation, including cities with federal significance such as Moscow, should have their own education law, which is a unified whole (the Moscow education law system), and correspondingly, it is also improve and supplement federal education laws. However, taking the current education legislation system in Moscow as an example, it is still a fragmented set of legal acts.

In the system of regional legal sources, the education law of the subject of the Russian Federation should clearly play the same role as the education law at the federal legislative level, which serves as the basis for regional education legislative norms and can ensure the effective implementation of federal general norms based on economic, ethnic, cultural, geographical, and other conditions of the relevant region.

In the process of concretizing federal legislation, the laws of the main body of the Russian Federation aim to address three main tasks: (1) establishing additional rights and benefits for participants in education relations at the regional level, including scholarships and other benefits, salary levels, transportation barriers, and catering organizations for employees in the education field; (2) Filling certain gaps in federal legislation; (3) Standardizing the individual procedures of the education process within its scope of authority and determining supplementary means for legal regulatory mechanisms, to simplify the process of relationships in the field of education.

3 Major Legislative Developments

The main tasks of legal norms in the field of education relations are:

(1) Safeguarding and protecting the constitutional right of citizens of the Russian Federation to education;
(2) Creating legal, economic, and financial conditions for the free operation and development of the education system in the Russian Federation;
(3) Establishing legal protection to coordinate the interests of all parties involved in the field of education;
(4) Determining the legal status of all parties involved in the field of education;

(5) Creating conditions for foreign citizens and stateless individuals to receive education in the Russian Federation;
(6) Defining the scope of power in the field of education among the federal state power institutions, the main state power institutions of the Russian Federation, and local autonomous institutions.

The purpose of federal education legislation is to provide basic and main principles and norms for legal relations in the field of education, consisting of three interrelated legal sources: (1) the Constitution and Education Law of the Russian Federation, which stipulate the basic and main norms and principles of education law and legislation; (2) Federal laws passed to regulate individual institutions and the field of education law; (3) The main theme of federal law is to regulate the relationship between other branches of law, while also encompassing comprehensive institutions on education law issues.

The fundamental principle of the Education Law is written in Article 43 of the Constitution of the Russian Federation, which states that everyone has the right to education.

The Education Law of the Russian Federation passed in 2012, is the fundamental law for all education legislation. The law stipulates that:

- Established the legal, organizational, and economic foundation of education in the Russian Federation;
- Established the basic principles of the national policy in the field of education in the Russian Federation;
- Established general rules for the operation of the education system and the conduct of educational activities;
- The legal status of participants in the relationship in the field of education has been determined.

It is worth noting that legislators have found in the Education Law the possibility of expanding the scope of universal education and free education, giving citizens of the Russian Federation the right to receive free secondary general education (i.e. 11th grade). Compared to the Constitution of the Russian Federation, which only provides for the right to free education in the ninth grade, it provides higher guarantees for the right to receive this level of education. This does not constitute a conflict as it does not violate the provisions of the Constitution of the Russian Federation. On the contrary, the state guarantees that all individuals receive general secondary education in national and municipal educational institutions, thereby greatly strengthening constitutional provisions.

This is not the case in secondary vocational education. Although the Constitution of the Russian Federation and the Education Law stipulates that everyone has the right to receive free secondary vocational education in national or municipal educational institutions and enterprises, many of these educational institutions recruit students on a paid basis.

The Education Law is a comprehensive legal instrument aimed at regulating social relations in the field of education, determining the type, level, and form of education, and regulating the relationships between educational activity subjects. The fundamental importance of the Education Law in the education law system is twofold. Firstly, make its provisions have the highest legal effect. If other federal laws and normative legal acts of the Russian Federation, laws and normative legal acts of Russian Federation entities, and legal acts of local autonomous institutions are inconsistent with the norms of the Education Law, the provisions of the Education Law shall apply. Secondly, the Education Law contains 224 provisions granting federal administrative agencies and the main bodies of the Russian Federation the right to adopt normative legal actions on issues related to education law; Among them, 60 directives are aimed at the government of the Russian Federation, 85 are aimed at federal administrative agencies and other federal administrative agencies that fulfill the functions of formulating national policies and regulating the field of education, and 79 are aimed at national institutions of the main body of the Russian Federation. According to The Education Law, this legal body is responsible for establishing normative legal actions on specific issues related to legal norms, thus laying a solid and effective foundation for the unity of its legislative activities. Its purpose is to achieve high-quality and effective norms, Organic connection with all other institutions and educational laws and regulations.

The Education Law has received high praise from the national scientific and educational community (Seliverstova 2013). For example, in the main positive trends of the law, scientists mentioned financial security regulations in the field of education, providing new guarantees for increasing the salaries of teachers in municipal education institutions, increasing budget quotas for students to simplify their access to free education, and formulating regulations to improve funding for small schools. We also actively evaluated the introduction of a network format for implementing educational plans, which provides students with opportunities to learn educational plans and/or individual learning subjects, courses, disciplines (modules), practices, and other components specified in educational plans (including different types, levels, and/or directions) by utilizing the resources of several organizations engaged in educational activities, including foreign organizations.

The Education Law legally guarantees the realization of the triple task of Russian education: (1) upholding constitutional norms and ensuring that Russian citizens receive preschool education, general education, secondary education, vocational education, and higher education on a competitive basis; (2) Ensuring teachers' and students' right at the aspects of social and professional, which helps promote their self-development and achieve comprehensive and comprehensive creativity in teaching activities and teaching; (3) Introducing innovative mechanisms for the development of the entire education system. People realize that the new Education Law has made more comprehensive legal provisions for social relations in the field of education, and has made some provisions that were not previously regulated by law into norms.

Most of the changes involve students' education and social support (Kurov 2008). A national social scholarship has been established for students who have lost both or single parents during their studies. This regulation stipulates that if the care and care of children in organizations carrying out educational activities are paid by the founder, no parental fees will be charged. It is stipulated that the cost of parental guardianship and child care in national and municipal educational institutions shall not exceed the maximum amount set by the normative laws of the Russian Federation for each municipal entity on its territory, depending on the conditions of guardianship and child care. There have been changes in the rules regarding the control of enrollment rates for federal budget allocations, the Russian Federation's main budget, and local budget funding. A new law prohibits individuals who are not allowed to engage in teaching activities or are suspended from work under labor laws from engaging in educational activities as individual entrepreneurs.

As a follow-up to the Education Law, federal laws were passed to regulate certain norms and institutions of the Education Law. It's like federal law Measures taken specifically to regulate educational relations For example, Federal Law No. 259-FZ of November 10, 2009 "On the Moscow State University and St. Petersburg State University Named after M.V. Lomonosov", and Federal Law No. 84-FZ of May 5, 2014 "On the Special Nature of Legal Regulation of Relations in the Education Field Related to the Accession of the Crimean Republic to the Russian Federation and the Ministry of Education of the Russian Federation" The federalization of important cities in the Crimean Republic and Sevastopol Federation, as well as amendments to the Federal Law on "Education in the Russian Federation", as well as a large number of "non core" laws, are the new subjects.

Non core laws have been passed to regulate various relationships and contain separate provisions on education and educational activities.

These laws can be divided into several groups:

- Federal laws that regulate the basic issues of educational organizations include the Russian Law on Ethnic Languages, the Law on Freedom of Conscience and Religious Associations, and the Law on Ethnic Cultural Autonomy;
- Federal laws containing special education norms: military education—laws on military service obligations and conscription; sports training—laws on sports in the Russian Federation; vocational education for individuals deprived of their liberty—Criminal Code of the Russian Federation;
- Federal laws providing welfare for participants in educational relations: "Supplementary guarantees for social support for orphans and children without parental care", "Social protection for persons with disabilities in the Russian Federation", and other laws;
- Federal laws governing labor relations and determining social security procedures for participants in educational relations: the Russian Federation Labor Law, the Russian Federation Scholarship and Social Assistance Amount Determination Procedure Law;
- Federal laws governing relations in the fields of economy, finance, and education: the Civil Code of the Russian Federation, the Tax Law of the Russian Federation, the Budget Law of the Russian Federation, and the Federal Law on "Autonomous Institutions";

- Federal laws that stipulate criminal and administrative responsibility for illegal acts in the field of education include the Criminal Code of the Russian Federation and the Code of Administrative Violations.

An important component of Russian education legislation is the federal state education standards. The Russian government has the normative capacity to develop procedures for the development of the Global Environment Facility, and its approval and implementation are carried out by orders from relevant ministries such as the Russian Ministry of Education and the Russian Ministry of Education.

The federal national education standards, along with education standards and federal national requirements, are the essential content of the education process.

The legislative definitions of these concepts are as follows:

The Federal State Education Standards—The sum of mandatory requirements for a certain level of education and/or vocational, professional, and training direction approved by the Ministry of Education or the Ministry of Higher Education and Science of the Russian Federation based on educational level;

Education Standards—The sum of mandatory requirements for various majors and training directions in higher education (bachelor's degree, associate's degree, master's degree, internship program, and teaching assistant internship program for higher qualified personnel training), which are approved by higher education institutions recognized by the Education Law or Presidential Decree of the Russian Federation;

Federal state requirements—The mandatory requirements for graduate school (associate degree) science and education personnel training programs, as well as supplementary career programs authorized by federal administrative authorities.

The federal national education standards and federal national requirements aim to ensure:

(1) Unification of educational space in the Russian Federation;
(2) Continuity of basic education programs;
(3) The possibility of developing basic vocational education courses with different levels of difficulty, overview, and direction based on students' educational needs and abilities, as well as the needs of society and the country for qualified personnel;
(4) Provide national guarantees for the level and quality of education based on unified mandatory requirements for the implementation conditions and results of basic education programs.

Federal National Education Standards and educational standards are of particular importance in organizing education processes, as they serve as the foundation for national and municipal education institutions to develop core education programs, courses teaching outlines, testing and measurement materials, textbooks, national (final) and mid-term assessments of students, and assessments of teachers and administrative personnel.

They are used as the basis for controlling and supervising the field of education, forming an internal monitoring system for educational quality, and developing financial support standards for educational institutions (Marchenko 2017).

In order to achieve each Federal National Education Standard, educational organizations have developed an education plan, which is a synthesis of the basic characteristics of education (scope, content, planned outcomes), organizational and teaching conditions, and certification forms, Teaching calendar, work plans for each subject, course, subject (module), and other components, as well as evaluation and methodological materials. According to the levels of general and vocational education, basic education programs have been implemented in vocational training, and supplementary education programs have been implemented in supplementary education.

Requirements for Federal National Education Standards:

(1) The structure and scope of the basic education plan (including the proportion of the mandatory part of the basic education plan to the part formed by the participants in the education relationship);
(2) The conditions for implementing the basic education plan, including personnel, financial, material and technical conditions;
(3) Achievements of major educational projects.

In addition, in the federal national education standards, the length of education for general and vocational education is also specified, taking into account different forms of learning, educational technology, and the unique characteristics of specific categories of students.

The federal national education standards for general education are formulated according to educational levels:

- Preschool education: Order of the Russian Ministry of Education on October 17, 2013 No. 1155 "On the Approval of Federal National Preschool Education Standards";
- Initial: Order of the Russian Ministry of Education on October 6, 2009 No. 373 "On the Approval and Implementation of Federal National Standards for Primary General Education";
- Main: Order of the Russian Ministry of Defense on December 17, 2010 No. 1897 "On the Approval of Federal National Basic General Education Standards";
- Secondary: Order of the Russian Ministry of Education on May 17, 2012 No. 413 "On the Approval of Federal State Secondary General Education Standards".

Federal National Education Standards for vocational education can also be formulated according to the requirements of different levels of vocational education, including secondary vocational education, higher education bachelor's degree, higher education professional education, master's degree, higher education higher education higher skill training, and different professions, majors, and training directions.

Let's give a few examples.

Federal National Education Standards for Secondary Vocational Education:

Professional—Order No. 692 of the Russian Ministry of Education on October 4, 2021 "Regarding the Approval of the Federal State Education Standards for Secondary Vocational Education in the Construction Industry 07.02.01";

Vocational—Order No. 697 of the Russian Ministry of Education on October 6, 2021 "Regarding the approval of the Federal State Education Standards for Vocational Secondary Vocational Education for Firefighters 20.01.01";

Higher Education—Federal National Education Standards for Bachelor's Degree:

In the training direction—Order No. 512 of the Russian Ministry of Education on June 8, 2017, regarding the approval of Federal State Higher Education Standards - Advertising and Public Relations for Bachelor's Degree 42.03.01 in Training Direction;

Higher Education—Federal National Education Standards for experts:

In the training direction—Order No. 953 of the Russian Ministry of Education on August 12, 2020, "Regarding the approval of the national education standards for federal higher education—majors in Applied Geology 21.05.02";

Higher Education—Federal National Education Standards for Master's degree:

In the training direction—Order No. 1451 of the Russian Ministry of Education on November 25, 2020, "Regarding the approval of the national education standards for federal higher education—Master's degree in the legal training direction of 40.04.01";

Higher Education—Federal National Education Standards for cultivating high-quality talents:

- In the training direction (associate Ph.D. student): Order from the Russian Ministry of Education on July 30, 2014. No. 902 "On the Approval of National Education Standards for Federal Higher Education in the Training Direction 44.06.01 Education and Educational Science (Training high-quality talents)";

Higher Education—Federal National Education Standards for cultivating high-quality talents:

Major (Hospitalization)—Order No. 275 of the Russian Ministry of Education on March 22, 2016, approving the federal higher education standards for 52.09.07 drama major (high-level talent cultivation level).

The development of Federal National Education Standards for Vocational Education takes into account the provisions of relevant occupational standards, which refer to the qualifications required for employees to engage in a certain profession.

The power to formulate and approve educational standards for higher education at all levels is delegated to:

- Lomonosov Moscow State University and St. Petersburg State University;
- Higher education institutions, classified as "federal universities" (Siberian Federal University, Southern Federal University, Far Eastern Federal University, etc.);

- Higher education institutions classified as "national research-oriented universities" (Moscow Institute of Physics and Technology, Novosibirsk State University, Higher Economic College, etc.);
- Higher education institutions conducting educational activities on the territory of Skolkovo Innovation Center and Innovation Technology Center;
- Federal higher education institutions approved by the Presidential Decree of the Russian Federation. According to Presidential Decree No. 405 of the Russian Federation on July 5, 2021, "List of Federal State Higher Education Institutions with the Power to Develop and Approve Educational Standards for Higher Education Projects", The National Economic and Administrative College of the President of the Russian Federation, and the Military Academy of the General Staff of the Russian Armed Forces are defined as such educational institutions.

Although there is no case law in Russia, judicial practice is considered a source of educational law and used as a reference for law enforcement practice (Shebanov 1965). Of particular importance is the decision of the Constitutional Court of the Russian Federation, which is the Supreme Court responsible for evaluating whether legal norms comply with the Constitution of the Russian Federation.

As of March 2023, the most important legal positions of the Constitutional Court of the Russian Federation on various issues related to the right to education can be listed in chronological order.

According to ruling No. 167-O/2004 of the Constitutional Court of the Russian Federation on April 8, 2004, "the right to education is declared as one of the fundamental constitutional rights, which predetermined the obligations of the state, According to the important goal stipulated in the Constitution, which is to ensure the widest possible access of citizens to higher education (based on equality and everyone's abilities), and take necessary measures to fully realize this right, including creating socio-economic conditions, and providing legal guarantees for the free operation and development of the education system, so that citizens can not only receive basic general and secondary vocational education, but also higher education".

According to Resolution 5-P/2006 of the Constitutional Court of the Russian Federation on May 15, 2006, "The most important function of the Russian Federation as a social state is to guarantee the right of everyone to education, including the right to preschool education". According to the principle of legal equality stipulated in the Constitution, the universality and free access to public or municipal educational institutions are guaranteed. The right to universal free preschool education stipulated in the Constitution is systematically linked to the principle of equality stipulated in the Constitution, which means that every child has equal opportunities to develop their personality, regardless of their social background, place of residence, or other circumstances. Equal educational opportunities mean equal access to existing national or municipal educational institutions.

On December 8, 2011, the Constitutional Court of the Russian Federation ruled No. 1696-O-O/2011, stating: "According to Article 43 of the Constitution of the Russian Federation, parents (who replace parents) and relevant state institutions have an obligation to ensure that their children only receive basic general education. Everyone who receives higher education in national or municipal educational institutions has the right to receive free education through competition". On the issue of the right to free higher education on a competitive basis, which is one of the elements in safeguarding the right to education, The Constitution of the Russian Federation clearly stipulates a system to guarantee this right, which is only implemented in national or municipal educational institutions.

The possibility of realizing the constitutional right to education in non-state educational institutions, although not explicitly guaranteed by the Constitution, is stipulated by the Constitution. Therefore, citizens are free to choose the form, educational institution, and training direction of higher education, including choosing public or private educational institutions.

The main conclusion of the Constitutional Court of the Russian Federation's ruling No. 1345-O/2012 of July 17, 2012, is as follows: the state guarantees citizens universal access to free primary general education, basic general education, and secondary (full) general education, as well as free secondary vocational education, higher vocational education and graduate vocational education on a competitive basis. In national and municipal educational institutions.

In addition to receiving secondary vocational education in educational institutions through the corresponding budget of the Russian Federation budget system (on a competitive basis), it is also allowed to recruit students at their own expense based on contracts signed with natural and/or legal persons. This legal provision stipulates the procedures for public secondary vocational education institutions to attract additional funds when the enrollment target exceeds the funding provided by the founder, intended to ensure the accessibility and diversity of secondary vocational education conditions.

The Constitutional Court of the Russian Federation, in its judgment No. 1141-O/2014 of May 29, 2014, stipulated that the Education Law provides objective reasons for refusing admission to national or municipal education organizations—there are no vacancies. In this case, the administrative authorities of the Russian Federation that implement state management in the field of education have an obligation to assist in the placement of children in another general education organization.

Resolution No. 18-P/2017 of the Constitutional Court of the Russian Federation on July 5, 2017 states: "According to the provisions of the Constitution of the Russian Federation on the right of everyone to education, equality before the law and the courts, regardless of place of residence, The standards that limit the rights and freedoms of individuals and citizens, as well as the principles based on these principles stipulated in public policies and laws in the field of education, including the right of everyone to choose educational forms and organize educational activities as stipulated in the Education Law, This law does not allow the refusal of admission to municipal educational institutions that provide basic general education programs solely on the grounds that children reside outside the designated territory of the educational institution". Therefore, in the legal norms for the enrollment relationship of municipal education organizations, the interests of children play a decisive role—when choosing educational institutions for children to attend, on the one hand, priority should be given to children residing in designated areas. On the other hand, it is necessary to ensure the territorial availability of educational institutions.

Resolution 15-P/2018 of the Constitutional Court of the Russian Federation on April 17, 2018 states: "The Constitution of the Russian Federation lists the right of everyone to education as one of the fundamental constitutional rights, and includes the right of everyone to receive free higher education in national or municipal educational institutions and enterprises on a competitive basis as an integral part of it". The state not only has the obligation to create necessary socio-economic conditions, but also has the obligation to legally guarantee the free operation and development of the education system, so that citizens not only have the obligation to obtain basic general and secondary vocational education, but also have the obligation (on an equal basis, according to each person's abilities) to receive higher education.

Based on this, the Education Law establishes the goal of higher education, which is to cultivate high-quality talents in all major fields of public service in accordance with the needs of society and the state, meet the needs of individuals in terms of intellectual, cultural, and moral development, deepen and expand the demand for education and scientific education qualifications, and determine its level—bachelor's degree; experts, master's degree; high-quality talents cultivation; People with a secondary general education degree can pursue a bachelor's or expert program, while those with higher education degree at any level can pursue a master's programs.

In Resolution 19-P/2018 of May 22, 2018, the Constitutional Court of the Russian Federation ruled that "delaying conscription while studying in organizations engaged in educational activities is stipulated by the legal protection of the constitutional right to education". At the same time, as pointed out by the Constitutional Court of the Russian Federation in Judgment No. 13-P of October 21, 1999, this is also an integral part of the legal procedure for fulfilling the constitutional obligation of military service for certain categories of citizens. Granting an extension does not necessarily mean exemption from military service. In addition, The system of delaying military service related to education established by federal legislators means that citizens have the opportunity to receive full-time education in accordance with the nationally recognized vocational training programs that include secondary vocational programs or bachelor's and master's programs in higher education immediately after completing general secondary education.

Resolution No. 39-P/2020 of the Constitutional Court of the Russian Federation on July 23, 2020, stipulates: "The state power institutions of various entities in the Russian Federation, in accordance with the Education Law, have the right to ensure that the state guarantees the realization of the rights to universal and free primary general education, basic general education, primary general education, and primary general education in organizations that provide general education in municipal and national educational institutions of the Russian Federation and develop conditions and procedures for independent selection of organizations". When implementing normative regulations, it is an obligation to balance the interests of students who wish to continue developing general education courses according to the comprehensive basic curriculum of secondary general education, and students who prefer to study according to the general secondary school education curriculum in general education institutions, which delves into certain specific subjects.

These decisions not only contribute to the more effective implementation of education laws, but also affect further legislative activities in the field of education.

4 Prospects for Future Development/Emerging Issues in the Field of the Right to Education

The analysis of Russian education legislation indicates that considering the scope and nature of the amendments already made, further modifications to existing education legislation are no longer effective. In this regard, it is necessary to develop a new education legislation development strategy to ensure the establishment of a unified and effective legal regulatory system for education and related relationships.

To improve legal norms in the field of education, it is necessary to fundamentally reconsider the relationship between legislation and secondary norms. This requires the development of a division of the legislative and secondary legislative levels to increase the proportion of legislative norms, and ensure that Norms with a secondary legislative nature and more legally effective norms, first and foremost, are laws (Kashanina 2014).

The modern development of the Russian education system aims to ensure the high quality of Russian education to meet the constantly changing needs of the population and ensure its competitiveness in the world education market. This has also brought about some issues that have not yet been clearly resolved, but that need to be addressed under modern conditions are being updated:

- The coordination of the normative legal document system in the field of education;
- Effective national management in the education system, taking into account the coordination of administrative power;
- In the context of increasingly digital education, the coordination of the legal status between participants in educational relations (educational organizations, students);
- The general issue of educational immigration, especially the issue of foreign students' education in the Russian Federation in modern reality.

Education law can become an effective means of coordinating in the field of education when it meets the necessary conditions for its own (at least all its major parts) coordination and unification. Therefore, the coordination of educational law is the primary task of legal science and legal practice, and its resolution largely depends on whether the Russian jurists have the willingness and ability to break away from the outdated dogmas and viewpoints of the last century, recognize the fact that education law exists as an independent department, and codify existing legal provisions related to education issues.

The majority of conflicts between federal legislation and the main laws of the Russian Federation on education issues arise from the provisions of the Education Law, which stipulates the material and financial obligations of the main administrative authorities of the Russian Federation towards participants in educational relations (2020 basket). For example, despite federal and case law, the Law No. 32 of June 29, 2005, on "Vocational Education in Moscow City" guarantees that citizens have the right to receive free secondary vocational education on a competitive basis at Moscow State Vocational Education Institutions. This conflicts with the Constitution of the Russian Federation, which ensures that everyone has universal and free access to this level of education at national and municipal educational institutions.

The Russian Federation Model Law on Subject Education, written by high-quality experts under the guidance of central administrative agencies, can be seen as an effective means of successfully coordinating education legislation in the Russian Federation. It not only unifies the basic content of regional legislation, but also greatly simplifies its formation process.

At the federal level, despite the Basic Education Law, legal conflicts provide a legal basis for many conflicts between parties in legal relationships, as each party has the opportunity to understand their rights and obligations from the perspective of a rule that prioritizes the rights of the other party. We only need to review the controversies and lawsuits arising from the conflicting provisions on the right of full-time college students to postpone military service. At that time, the Education Law granted this right to all students of licensed universities, and the Federal Law of March 28, 1998, No. 53-FZ "On Military Service and Military Service" only granted this right to students with national certification from higher education institutions.

The repetition of legal rules in several laws and other normative documents does not help improve the interpretation and application of legal rules. On the contrary, the use of this legislative technique unnecessarily increases legal texts, making it difficult to find original norms and misleading law enforcement personnel, giving the illusion that there are "redundant norms" in legislation that can be ignored in specific legal relationships. Legislative theory and practice only know the most effective way to address the diversity of legal acts, duplication and contradictions of legal norms, and loopholes—codification (Kechekyan 1946). It is departmental compilation that enables us to analyze all the main normative materials of the legislative branch corresponding to the same name legal branch, and ensure the interconnectivity of the normative documents contained therein, thus enabling us to discuss the broader legal framework of departmental compilation. It has a greater impact on the organic and complete nature of the legislative system itself. Therefore, the formulation and adoption of the Education Law of the Russian Federation may be the main measure to improve the quality of education legislation.

Of course, the code must include legal rules for regulating the digitization of education, which are currently forming a circular legal framework. The increasing digitization means significant changes in education and related relationships. The legal supervision of the digital process of education means that national power institutions, local autonomous institutions, organizations, and citizens must strive to organize legal supervision to provide necessary conditions, including providing the possibility of using digital infrastructure in educational institutions and forming digital literacy to ensure flexibility in management.

At present, Russia is forming a complete and complex digital legal regulatory system, including various sources of digital legal regulation in education, from international agreements to local education institution bills. It is still too early to say the integrity of this system.

However, an analysis of the emerging legal regulatory system for digital education indicates that at this stage, some of its characteristics have been emphasized. Especially, we can talk about the Constitution of the Russian Federation, the special role of soft legal acts, the diversity and multi-level nature of regulatory sources, and the abundance of technical normative legal acts. At present, the role of law in ensuring the digitization process is not only to provide appropriate guarantees for participants in educational relationships, including eliminating the negative effects of digitization, but also to provide appropriate forms for the digitization process of education (Aleksandrov 2019). At the same time, the emerging digital legal supervision system for education is a circular legal system that includes norms for different legal branches such as civil, financial, labor, and administrative legislation.

The explosive growth of digitalization in general education has also brought challenges to the legal supervision of digitalization in schools. Among these issues, it should first be mentioned that legal norms are chaotic and unsystematic, with loopholes. The so-called "manual" management mechanism plays a significant role and lacks appropriate mechanisms, which can ensure that participants in educational relationships receive the necessary legal protection when they are negatively affected by digitization.

As a digital object, educational relationships include various participants, each of them with their own legal status. This applies not only to educational institutions, but also to their employees, students, and parents.

In the context of digitalization, the transformation of the status of educational institutions mainly develops in two aspects:

- The first direction is to create conditions to achieve educational plans to meet the digital requirements, including the possibility of providing electronic learning and distance education technologies. This direction requires equipping educational institutions with electronic information and educational resources, as well as digital services, introducing digital educational content, information and telecommunications technology, and technological means, to ensure that students can fully grasp the educational curriculum, regardless of where they reside;
- The second direction involves digitizing the internal and external management processes of educational organizations (Zenin 2020).

Both aspects require the establishment of appropriate legal norms. An important aspect of the digital transformation of educational institutions is the transformation of the legal status of teachers and other employees (mainly administrative personnel).

This transformation has developed in three aspects:

- According to the requirements of the external environment, improving the qualification requirements of teachers;
- The emergence of new professions in the field of education;
- The changes in organizational conditions of teachers' professional activities within the framework of educational relations.

In each of these areas, there is a need to reform or expand the existing mechanisms for supplementing vocational education with teachers and administrators.

Many issues remain unresolved, such as the status of remote work teachers. This leads to a problem of calculating and allocating the time teachers spend on remote (remote) work. In this regard, it is particularly important to provide guarantees for the staff of educational institutions to prevent their situation from deteriorating in response to the transition to remote mode.

The legal supervision of the impact mechanism of digitization on the legal supervision of student status is very urgent. The increasing diversity of educational forms is almost immediately changing, which is also the result of the digitalization of educational relationships and requires a special legal regulatory method. Among the main educational trends in today's period, emphasis can be placed on cloud learning, the use of social media in teaching, large-scale open online courses, virtual reality and augmented reality technologies, digital communication technologies, and big data formation analysis.

In this regard, the digital environment of educational institutions, including typical information solutions, new information content and the functions of open and public information resources, as well as corresponding technical support, requires continuous improvement of students' skills, and continuously improving the skills of educational institution staff. COVID-19 has greatly increased the spread of distance education technology around the world, especially in Russia. Furthermore, the further development of the socio-economic system means that the application of digital technology in educational relations will only be strengthened.

In this regard, an obvious task of legal regulation is to improve the legal status of students and teachers as participants in educational relations.

5 Conclusion

The conclusion drawn from this study is that consistency and coordination among all components of the education field are particularly important. Activities in the field of education should comply with existing social and political conditions as well as the goals set by society and the state. In this process, the law holds special significance as it is a means of bringing millions of people together in a fair manner and striving to successfully master the knowledge accumulated by humanity through specific norms, and guide people to effectively utilize this knowledge to further promote the progress and development of society and the country.

Today, it is necessary to form a new branch of Russian law and an independent branch of scientific knowledge—educational law. There are at least four basic directions for coordinating education laws.

Firstly, it is particularly urgent to coordinate Russian education legislation with international law and ensure that Russian laws fully comply with international legal norms and international treaties on education in the Russian Federation. So far, the differences between these legal sources have hindered students and other subjects of educational relations from realizing a series of rights and freedoms at the level of international legal standards, and have also caused certain difficulties for other countries to recognize Russian educational documents.

Secondly, it is necessary to further coordinate the relationship between federal legislation and the legislative documents of the President of the Russian Federation, the Russian Federation Government, and other federal administrative agencies, in order to eliminate the gaps, contradictions, and contradictions that still exist in the current federal normative legal action system. This greatly reduces the overall efficiency of the legal regulatory mechanism for educational relations. It is important to comprehensively and extensively systematize existing normative regulations to identify and abolish outdated, invalid, and conflicting legal norms, which will inevitably lead to the codification of all norms of education law and legislation.

Thirdly, the relationship between the federal education law and the main legislation of the Russian Federation should be better. In the process of coordinating this relationship, it is first necessary to eliminate normative provisions in federal legislation that limit the initiative and autonomy of Russian Federation entities in seeking and implementing measures that meet specific regional conditions. The next step should be to systematically align regional legislation with federal legislation. Recent legal research in Russia has shown that there are still gaps and inconsistencies between these two levels of legislation. It is not uncommon to see examples of serious contradictions between regional legislation and federal institutions, and we also know examples of our own broad interpretation of federal regulations (such as those related to teaching languages in different regions of the Russian Federation). It should be emphasized once again that citizens, regardless of their residence in any region, must have a genuine opportunity to exercise the constitutional right to education in accordance with the standards prescribed by federal law.

Fourthly, coordination must be achieved at the level of specific types of educational legal relationships that constantly arise, change, develop, and terminate. At the same time, the essence of this direction cannot be limited to strengthening the legitimacy of educational institution activities, although legitimacy is undoubtedly a key priority principle. The ultimate goal of coordination is to establish an educational organizational system that ensures the popularization of education and enables everyone to meet their needs for quality general and vocational education in the most effective and acceptable way. As is well known, reality is the standard for testing the authenticity of theoretical viewpoints and transforming them into normative provisions of practice. Therefore, the entire complex process of legislative coordination can only be justified if a system can be formed to achieve specific legal relationships in the field of education, thereby fully ensuring that the rights of all subjects in the legal relationship of education are truly and effectively respected.

References

Alexandrov AY (2019) Discusses the digitization of Russian education space in the context of constitutional protection of the right to education. Russian Journal of Higher Education 10:73–82

Barabanova SV (2015) Practical issues in legal support for educational activities: theory and practice of secondary regulation. Yearbook of Russian Education Legislation 10:4–24. ISSN 1997-7549

Chekha VV, Terpugov AE, Seliverstova OI (2022) Digitalization of Russian schools: legal issues. Moscow, Federal Education Legislative Center, 144 p. https://doi.org/10.51285/978-5-88045-527-0

Kashanina TV (2014) Legal structure. Moscow, Street, 580 p. ISBN 978-5-392-12356-8

Kechekyan SF (1946) On the concept of legal sources: works of the legal department. Moscow State University Press, Moscow, pp 3–25

Knyaginina MV (2016) Legal provisions of the education system at the federal, regional, and municipal levels in the Russian Federation. Yearbook of Russian Education Legislation, 11174-190. ISSN 1997-7549

Kozyrin AN (2019) Russian education law: textbooks and practice. Moscow, Higher School of Economics Press, p 799. ISBN 978-5-7598-1186-2

Kurov SV (2008) The social value and effectiveness of protecting the rights of subjects in the field of education. Law and Education 11:13–25

Ladnushkina NM, Postyliakov SP (2021) Collective monograph chapter: modern methods for legalizing social relations in the field of education. Moscow, Federal Education Legislative Center, 87–111. https://doi.org/10.51285/978-88045-488-4

Marchenko MN (2017) Legal source: training manual. Moscow, Main Street, p 759. ISBN 978-5-392-24634-2

Putilo NV (2019) Collective monograph chapter: coordination of Russian education law: theoretical and practical issues. Moscow, Federal Education Legislative Center, 491–514. ISBN 978-5-6042680-3-3

Radko TN, Azmi DM, Golovina AA (2018) Legal system: history, modernity, prospects. Moscow, Street, 256 p. ISBN 978-5-392-21923-0

Seliverstova OI (2013) "Education law of the Russian federation": positive trends in legal regulation. Yearbook of Russian Education Legislation, 8, 64–75. ISSN 1997-7549

Seliverstova OI (2016) Legal issues related to the exercise of state power in the field of general education. Yearbook of Russian Education Legislation, 11113-125. ISSN 1997-7549

Shebanov AA (1965) On the concept of legal sources and legal forms. Journal of Law 4:23–33

Zenin SS (2020) Legal creation under the condition of legal algorithm. LEXRUSSIA 7(164):97–104. ISSN 1729-5920

Education Law in South Africa

Marius Smit

1 Introduction

This chapter provides an account of the effect that Education law and transformative constitutionalism have had on education in post-apartheid South Africa. In 1994 the negotiated settlement between former political antagonists resulted in the transference of political power to the African majority. The constitutional structure of South Africa changed from a Westminster system of government based on parliamentary sovereignty, to a constitutional democracy with a supreme constitution and justiciable Bill of Rights. Most scholars have high regard for the progressive, modern content and format of the Constitution of South Africa of 1996, which inter-alia entrenches socio-economic rights such as the right to education, housing, health care and a safe environment.[1] Prior to its inclusion in the Bill of Rights the political, legal, and academic discourse questioned the enforceability of such rights in view of the separation of powers-doctrine and the classical notion that judges should interpret. Education has been at the centre of a transformation process as the previous racially segregated system was replaced by a unified (non-segregated) education system that aims to provide equal opportunities to all. The Constitution and Bill of Rights has ostensibly been designed to protect individual rights, not group or collective rights that was the norm under Apartheid.

South Africa presents a case where, on the one hand, comprehensive statutory and policy reforms have resulted in some advances in the education system, but on the other hand, the government's failure to implement the reforms in a competent and sustainable manner has contributed to the dysfunctionality of the system. As a result,

[1] Liebenberg (2010).

M. Smit (✉)
Faculty of Education Sciences, North-West University (NWU), Potchefstroom, South Africa
e-mail: copyright@esph.com.cn

Faculty of Education, North-West University, Potchefstroom, South Africa

C. J. Russo and L. Ma (eds.), *A Comparative Analysis of Systems of Education Law*,
https://doi.org/10.1007/978-981-97-1052-2_15

South Africa is very high on the index of failing states (Fund for Peace 2021). South Africa is a particularly complex society composed of a heterogeneous amalgam of ethnic, cultural, language, ideological and religious groups. The provision of quality education for most learners from impoverished socio-economic backgrounds, and the pervasive activism and negative influence of the dominant teachers' union, are themes that may resonate with other countries.

The discussion in this chapter sheds light on the justiciability and legal enforcement of the fundamental right to education, analyses developments in the education and legal systems, and evaluates the effect of progressivism or transformative constitutionalism on education in South Africa.

2 Nature of the Legal System

The South African common law is Roman-Dutch law, which is the substratum and framework of the basic concepts, structure and legal principles underpinning the legal system (Hosten et al. 1995). Contrary to the Civil law systems of the countries of mainland Europe (such as France, Germany, Netherlands, Italy, Spain, etc.) classical Roman-Dutch law of the sixteenth and eighteenth centuries was never codified. During the colonial era the British Colonial office determined that the inherent justice, clarity of legal principles and systematic structure of Roman-Dutch law was more suitable to govern the Southern-African colonies and thus Roman-Dutch law eventually became the common law of the Cape, Natal, Transvaal, Free State, Southern Rhodesia (present day Zimbabwe), Lesotho, Botswana, Swaziland and South-West Africa (Namibia) colonies and protectorates (Fund for Peace 2021). Although classical Roman-Dutch law is Romanist-oriented, it did not remain static but evolved and was modified by English law, new statutes (legislation), case law precedents and recently the Constitution of South Africa. The South African law is therefore a modernised hybrid legal system based on Roman-Dutch law combined with English Common law features such as the precedent system of adjudication, accusatorial (adversarial) court procedure, the principles of English Law of Evidence and most aspects of English commercial law.

The Constitution implicitly acknowledges the reality that not only the legislative branch of the state, but also the judiciary make law. One of the innovations of South African law is that Sections 39(2) and 8(3) (the so-called development clauses) of the Constitution confer significant powers and responsibilities upon South African courts to renew common and customary law to promote the spirit and values of the Constitution (Davis and Klare 2010).

The sources of Education Law in South Africa are legislation, the common law and case law.[2] The first decade after 1994 was characterised by the fervent development of new education policies and education specific statutes such as the National Education Policy Act, the South African Quality Assurance Act, the South African

[2] Oosthuizen and Smit (2020).

Schools Act ("Schools Act"), the Further Education and Training Colleges Act, the Employment of Educators Act, the South African Council of Educators Act and the Higher Education Act to regulate the education system.[3] The establishment of a unified education system thus saw the introduction a slew of new legislation and policies, regular cycles of curriculum reform, and the restructuring of school and higher education.

In terms of Section 49(1) of the Constitution, government is constituted as national, provincial and local spheres of government, which are distinct, interdependent and interrelated.[4] Section 41 of the Constitution inter alia provides that different spheres of government and organs of state should not assume any power or function except those conferred on them in terms of the Constitution. This pre-supposes co-operation between organs of state and impels power-sharing in education. The state departments and functionaries must exercise their powers and perform their functions in a manner that does not encroach on the geographical, functional or institutional integrity of government in another sphere; and should co-operate with one another in mutual trust and good faith by fostering friendly relations; assisting and supporting one another; informing one another of, and consulting one another on, matters of common interest; co-ordinating their actions and legislation with one another.

The complex system of co-responsibility and co-operation between the national and provincial departments of education, school principals and school governing bodies exist regarding the determination of national policies, the execution of administrative functions and the local governance and management of public schools. In terms of Schedule 4 of the Constitution of South Africa the provincial legislatures share concurrent legislative competence with the National Parliament in the functional field of primary and secondary education. Tertiary education is the sole responsibility of the national Minister of Higher Education. The national government is given overall responsibility for ensuring that other spheres of government carry out their obligations under the Constitution. Where a province cannot or does not fulfil an executive obligation in terms of legislation or the Constitution, the national executive may intervene by either issuing directives or by assuming responsibility for the relevant obligation in that province.

In terms of Section 3(4) of the National Education Policy Act the national Minister of Basic Education (the "Minister") must determine national policy for the planning, provision, financing, staffing, co-ordination, management, governance, programmes, monitoring, evaluation, and well-being of the school education system. In terms of Section 61 of the Schools Act the Minister is responsible for policy and regulations on safety measures at public and independent schools; the national curriculum statement, with the minimum core outcomes or standards applicable to public and independent

[3] National Education Policy Act No. 27 of 1996; South African Quality Assurance Act, South African Schools Act No. 84 of 1996; Higher Education Act no. 101 of 1997; Employment of Educators Act No. 76 of 1998; Skills Development Act No. 79 of 1998; South African Council of Educators Act No. 31 of 2000; Further Education and Training Colleges Act No. 16 of 2006.

[4] Constitution of South Africa Act 108 of 1996.

schools[5]; the assessment, monitoring and evaluation of education in public and independent schools; drafting regulations regarding initiation practices at schools; the age norm per grade; norms and minimum standards for school funding; minimum uniform norms and standards for school infrastructure, the admission capacity of a school; the provision of learning and teaching support material[6]; norms and standards for the school funds[7]; the ages of compulsory attendance at schools for learners with special education needs[8]; the testing devices to test for the suspected use of illegal drugs[9]; equitable criteria and procedures for exemption of parents who are unable to pay school fees; and the annual determination of the national quintiles for public schools.

The Premier of a province assigns powers and functions regarding the provision of education in the province to the provincial Member of the Executive Council ("the MEC"). The provincial Members of Executive Council (MECs) are the executive officials leading the nine provincial education departments respectively and are supported by the provincial Heads of the Education Department ("the HED") responsible for implementing government policy. The provincial government acts through the MEC for Education who bears the responsibility to establish and provide public schools and, together with the Head of the Provincial Department of Education, exercises executive control of a public schools by oversight and management of school principals and educators employed by the department of education. The HEDs have administrative and executive duties in terms of the School Act including managing and leading the department, approval of school policies, appointment of school personnel based on valid recommendations by a school governing body, oversight over school principals and governing bodies, allocation of funds for school programmes, approval (or denial) of additional functions for a school governing body in terms of Section 21 of the Schools Act, as well as the removal or suspension of functions of school governing bodies.[10]

3 Transformation of the Education System

The South African education system has its roots in the Western educational traditions of the Dutch and British colonial powers and Christian missionary schools, but also underwent a series of fundamental changes. Research on school safety that was conducted among students in forty countries by the South African Institute of Race Relations (SAIRR, 2008) ranked South African schools as the most dangerous of those sampled in the survey. South Africa is categorised as a middle-income

---

[5] Section 6A(1)(a).

[6] Section 5A(1).

[7] Section 20 (11).

[8] Section 3(2).

[9] Section 8(11).

[10] South African Schools Act—Section 9, 16, 16A, 19.

developing country. It is a multicultural society comprised of a complex interdependent social order, that was historically shaped by colonialism and apartheid, largely determined along racial, class and cultural lines. It has a two-tiered economy, one developed, largely white, and Asian (Indian), and the other a developing economy, largely African (black), with relatively low levels of productivity and pre-industrial technology. The racial composition of the population of 55.9 million people is approximately 80.1% black, 8.8% coloured (mixed race), 8.1% white (European), and 2.5% Indian.

The matter of *Matukane v Laerskool Potgietersrus*[11] is the watershed case in South Africa which dealt with a public school's refusal to admit African students by virtue of their race and culture. The High Court held that although differentiation based on culture and language is not unconstitutional per se, the admission policy of the public school in question was unconstitutional because it unfairly discriminated against black students based on race. The Court rejected the argument that the state has a duty to provide a minority with its own public schools where minority children could be educated in their mother-tongue and according to their own religion and culture. The Court held that the refusal to admit black learners was unfair discrimination and ordered the school to admit the learners. Following this verdict, the process of deracialisation of public schools commenced in earnest as all previously segregated schools amended their admission policies to eliminate unfair discrimination based on race, ethnicity, colour, religion, and culture.

One of the first policy changes that the education department made was to amend the school choice and access policy by doing away with strict geographic zoning requirements (feeding areas) for public schools. In terms of Section 34(b) of the regulations to the National Education Policy Act "a learner who lives outside the feeder zone is not precluded from seeking admission at whichever school he or she chooses". The effect of this provision has been that all the children of parents who live and work within a school zone had been accommodated, any other child—irrespective of parental domicile or the place of a parent's employment—may apply for admission to the school. This had far-reaching consequences and led to large-scale migration of learners from dysfunctional rural schools to more functional village, urban, suburban schools (Smit 2020). Quasi-markets developed for well-functioning public and independent schools, and home schooling showed strong growth. Elite sports schools also thrived because of the open school choice policy because talented learners from the far reaches of the country could gain admission to these schools.

[11] *Matukane v Laerskool Potgietersrus* [1997] JOL 102 (T).

4 Enforcing the Constitutional Right to Education

While the constitutions of older democracies such as the United States of America and Canada do not contain the right to education, the modern constitution of South Africa expressly establishes the fundamental right to basic and further education (Russo 2012).

Section 29 of the Constitution of South Africa provides as follows:

Education

(1) Everyone has the right-

   (a) to a basic education, including adult basic education; and
   (b) to further education, which the state, through reasonable measures, must make progressively available and accessible.

(2) Everyone has the right to receive education in the official language or languages of their choice in public educational institutions where that education is reasonably practicable. In order to ensure the effective access to, and implementation of, this right, the state must consider all reasonable educational alternatives, including single medium institutions, taking into account-

   (a) equity;
   (b) practicability; and
   (c) the need to redress the results of past racially discriminatory laws and practices.

(3) Everyone has the right to establish and maintain, at their own expense, independent educational institutions that-

   (a) do not discriminate on the basis of race;
   (b) are registered with the state; and
   (c) maintain standards that are not inferior to standards at comparable public educational institutions.

The efficacy of litigation as a means of enforcing socio-economic rights, including the right to education, is contentious. One of the concerns relates to whether courts have the capacity to assess how much money the executive arm of the state should allocate to provide such services. In view of the separation of powers doctrine, courts are generally reluctant to wade in and make orders that bind the state in situations where polycentric issues and policy decisions are at stake (Skelton 2015).

The Constitutional Court's seminal decision on the enforceability of socio-economic rights is the matter of *Government of the Republic of South Africa v Grootboom.*[12] Although the provision of housing for homeless persons was at issue in *Grootboom,* the principles expounded by the Constitutional Court apply to other socio-economic rights as well. In accordance with the separation of powers-doctrine the courts will defer to the executive branch of government's discretion regarding

[12] *Government of the Republic of South Africa v Grootboom* 2000 (11) BCLR 1169 (CC).

the measures adopted or the manner in which the public money had been spent. However, in *Grootboom* the court held that the design, adoption and implementation of government policy and action to realise socio-economic rights should be adjudicated by the standard of reasonableness. The mere adoption of policy or legislative measures is not enough. *Grootboom* confirmed that the egalitarian and remedial design of the Constitution requires progressive achievement of substantive equality and the protection of human dignity for the vulnerable and weakest. Therefore, in the education context, *Grootboom* establishes the principle that even when resources are scarce, the standard of reasonableness requires the design, adoption and implementation of an inclusive education policy to afford students that experience barriers to learning the right to basic education.

In the matter of *Governing Body of the Juma Musjid Primary School v Essay N.O.* a public school was housed on private property owned by a Trust.[13] As a result of the Department of Education, KwaZulu-Natal province's failure to pay the rent in terms of the lease agreement for this property, a High Court eviction order was obtained by the Trust. On appeal the Constitutional Court confirmed the eviction order and held that there was no obligation on the Trust to continue accommodating the school. The primary positive obligation to provide basic education in rests on the Member of Executive Council ("MEC") of the provincial Department of Education. The Trust was entitled to compensation and the MEC was obliged to immediately secure an alternative place for the school. Unlike other socio-economic rights such as health care, housing and a safe environment, which are merely progressively realisable subject to available state funding, the Constitutional Court determined that right to basic education is immediately realisable.[14]

An important question to be determined is the scope and meaning that should be ascribed to the term 'basic education'. Malherbe is of the opinion that basic education entails that the state must provide education to a level of literacy and numeracy that enables all individuals to exercise and comply with their rights and duties of citizenship (Malherb 2004). In the case of *Phillips v Manser*, which addressed the legal question whether a Grade 11 learner (17 year old) could be expelled from school, the High Court held that the right to basic education extends only to the level of compulsory education, i.e. until grade 9 or when the learner reaches the age of 15 years, whichever is the first to occur.[15] Accordingly, the court held that the learner, *Phillips,* was not entitled to insist on continued attendance of the school as his right to basic education had come to an end when he reached 15 years of age. However, in the recent case of *Moko v Acting Principal of Malusi Secondary School* a Grade 12 learner was prohibited by the acting school principal from writing the matriculation examination, because he had not attended supplementary classes during the school year.[16] The learner applied for urgent relief, but the High Court held that the matter was not urgent and refused to hear the application. The plaintiff appealed directly to

[13] *Governing Body of the Juma Musjid Primary School v Essay N.O.* (2011) ZACC 13.

[14] See note 13 at 8.

[15] *Phillips v Manser* [1999] 1 All SA 198 (SE).

[16] Moko v Acting Principal of Malusi Secondary School 2021 (3) SA 323 (CC).

the Constitutional Court thus side-stepping the normal hierarchy of superior courts. The Constitutional Court was willing to hear the matter and held that the High Court had erred in respect of urgency. Justice Khampepe (unanimous decision) held that the scope of the "right to basic education" extended to Grade 12. The Constitutional Court ordered that Moko had to be granted an opportunity to write the examination of the subject Business Studies during January 2021 supplementary examination period.

An aspect of South African jurisprudence that is worthwhile taking note of is the array of legal remedies that have been developed by the courts, inter alia including compensatory relief, injunctive order (compulsory mandamus), dialogic remedial process, supervisory directive order (follow-up supervisory role of court), individual supervisory order and systemic supervisory orders, in adjudicating and enforcing socio-economic rights.

5 State Funding of School Education—The National Quintile System

In terms of Section 34(1) of the Schools Act the state must fund public schools from public taxation revenue on an equitable basis to provide education and to redress past inequalities. Section 34(2) also provides that the state must, on an annual basis, provide sufficient information to public schools regarding the funding to enable the schools to prepare the budgets for the next financial year. Section 48 of the Schools Act provides that the Minister may grant subsidies to independent schools.

In terms of Section 35(1) of the Schools Act the national Minister of Basic education must determine national quintiles for public schools and *National Norms and Standards for School Funding* after consultation with the Council of Education Ministers (i.e. the provincial MEC's) and the Minister of Finance.[17] The *National Norms and Standards for School Funding* set out criteria for the distribution of state funding to all public schools in a fair and equitable manner [s.35(2)(a)]. The national quintile system of funding places public schools into quintiles according to the financial means and socio-economic circumstances of the school community in which the public school is situated.

In terms of the national quintile system of funding the most indigent public schools that are situated in impoverished school communities are categorised as Quintile 1 schools. The Quintile 1–3 are so-called No-fee schools which means that the parents are not obliged to pay any school fees. Although the No-fee schools may raise additional funds voluntarily, in practice it seldom occurs, and these schools are funded for the most part by the state. In practice, however, the degree of funding by the state correlates inversely with the degree of participation by parents, i.e. the less the state contributes by way of funding, the more the parents work to do fund-raising and provide voluntary services. According to Crouch, Gustaffson and Lavado public

[17] Department of Education (2006) Government Notice 869. *Government Gazette* No. 29179.

expenditure on education became ten times more equal in post-apartheid South Africa and achieved full equity by 2004 as measured by the Concentration Index of Public Expenditure on education (Crouch et al. 2009).

6 The State's Duty to Provide Education at an Acceptable Standard and Quality

The duty of the state to provide textbooks and learning material, school furniture and safe school buildings was challenges in a series of cases. In the matter of in *Centre for Child Law and Seven Others v Government of the Eastern Cape Province* (the 'mud schools' case) a civil society organisation took the Eastern Cape Department of Education to court to compel the provincial government to address the severe infrastructure backlogs.[18] The case was settled out of court, and the state pledged to spend R 8.2 billion towards infrastructure upgrades over three years. In the matter of *Section 27 v Minister of Education* the High Court held that the failure to provide textbooks at some schools was a violation of the learners' right to basic education.[19] In a follow-up case *Basic Education for All v Minister of Basic Education*, another voluntary organisation, and the school governing bodies of the affected schools filed an urgent application to compel the Department of Basic Education to provide textbooks to learners.[20] The court ordered a structured interdict that directed the Departments to provide monthly reports about the delivery of the textbooks within 90 days. In another example concerning the provision of school supplies, *Madzodzo v Minister of Basic Education,* it was held that the national Department of Basic Education, alternatively the provincial Department of Education of Eastern Cape, were in breach of the constitutional right of learners to basic education by failing to provide adequate, age and grade appropriate furniture (tables, chairs etc.) for each learner to have his or her own reading and writing space.[21] The court ordered a structured supervisory interdict and directed the Department to compile an audit within 90 days and to deliver the school furniture to all the identified schools within 90 days after the audit. In the watershed case of *Nyathi v Minister of Health,* the Constitutional Court determined that the State Liability Act of 1957, which had prohibited the attachment of state property (e.g. funds, movables, and fixed property) to settle state debts or to compel compliance with court orders, was unconstitutional.[22] Accordingly, the state was no longer immune against execution of court orders. In matters where state departments failed to comply with court orders, the vehicles, furniture and other movables were

[18] *Centre for Child Law and 7 others v Government of the Eastern Cape Province* Eastern Cape High Court, Bhisho, Case no 504/10.

[19] *Section 27 v Minister of Education* [2012] 3 All SA 579 (GNP).

[20] *Basic Education for All v Minister of Basic Education* 2014 (9) BCLR 1039 (GP).

[21] *Madzodzo obo Parents of Learners at Mpimbo Junior Secondary School v Minister of Basic Education* [2014] 2 All SA 339 (ECM).

[22] *Nyathi v MEC for Health, Gauteng* 2005 (5) SA 94 (CC).

on occasion attached to be sold in execution. This usually had the desired effect to jolt Heads of Department and MEC's into action to comply with the court orders.

7 Educator Rights

The main statutory instrument regulating the education profession is the Employment of Educators Act.[23] This Act stipulates the conditions of service (such as salaries, duties and terms of service); the appointment procedures (including promotions and transfers); the termination of service provision (which includes retirement, discharge or resignation) and the disciplinary procedure to be followed.

The national Minister of Education determines the salaries and other conditions of service of educators according to their ranks and grades. However, such determination takes place in accordance with the collective negotiation procedures prescribes by the Labour Relations Act.[24] This Act codified the labour rights of all workers (including educators) which include collective rights such as right to organise as unions, to negotiate employment conditions by collective bargaining, to resolve disputes, and the right to ultimately take recourse to strike action. Collective bargaining on behalf of the educators that are employed by the State, takes place annually when the Education Labour Relations Council (ELRC) confers with the Minister of Education as well as other cabinet ministers such as the Minister of Public Service and Minister of Finance by virtue of their responsibilities. Other educators employed by school governing bodies or independent schools must negotiate the terms of their employment on an individual basis. For educators that negotiate their contracts on an individual basis, the Basic Conditions of Employment Act regulates and standardizes the minimum conditions for fair employment of any worker, which includes stipulations with regard to working time, leave, particulars of remuneration and ancillary matters.

In terms of the National Policy Framework for Teacher Education a four-year Bachelor of Education degree, which includes the equivalent of one full-time year of supervised practical teaching experience in schools, is the standard qualification for students wishing to teach in any learning area, subject and phase (Department of Education 2006). For students with an appropriate first degree in another field of study, either an Advanced Diploma in Education or a Post Graduate Certificate in Education or a Higher Diploma in Education would be the qualification required to teach in any learning area, subject or phase. The minimum qualification required to teach is a three-year teaching Diploma.

In terms of the South African Council of Educators Act ('SACE'), it is compulsory for every qualified educator to register with the Council of Educators and no person may be employed as an educator by any employer unless the person is registered with the council.[25] In South Africa, education is regarded as a profession (Oosthuizen and

[23] Employment of Educators Act 76 of 1998.

[24] Labour Relations Act 66 of 1995.

[25] Section 21 of the South African Council for Educators, Act 31of 2000.

Smit 2020). The term 'educator', (the South African term for teacher) denotes more than an obligation to teach; it signifies the duty and calling to provide a broad and encompassing education over and above the teaching of the learning area outcomes. In this regard, educators are reminded to be role models, mentors, life-coaches as well as teachers. In keeping with their professional status, the discipline, work ethic and conduct of educators is regulated by SACE.

8 Democracy in South African Schools

The right to education vests in the recipient, i.e. the learner, student, or trainee as the subject of the right. A well-established legal principle at common law and international law, as affirmed in legislation and case law, is that parents are the primary educators of their children and that the state should be a supportive institution that provides public education for children at the behest of parents or legal guardians.[26] Accordingly, the state has the *ex lege* duty to support parents and to provide public education.

However, modern states have become immensely powerful in their ability to rule people. The twentieth century saw the emergence of the benefactor state and a great expansion of public power into what were formerly thought to be areas of private life, such as family relationships. The growth of the state is most apparent in the increase of government agencies; the development of state bureaucracy, the intensification of taxation, legislation, and programmes; and the expansion of government control over the economy. One such state program in South Africa is the expansion of public education to include compulsory primary, secondary, and, to some extent pre-primary and further education as well. However, neither the rights of parents nor the duties of the state are absolute.

In order to restructure and transform the education system the government appointed the Bertelsman Commission in 1995 to undertake an extensive public consultation process and eventually draft a negotiated South African Schools Act (the "Schools Act") based on the principles of participatory management, democracy, and a statutory partnership between the state, schools and parents (Bertelsmann 2018). This process resulted in the Schools Act which incorporated the following features: a system of local school governance with imbedded organisational democracy characteristics, a tripartite partnership between the state, parents and schools,

[26] Voet *Commentarius ad pandectas* 25.3.6; Van Leeuwen *Censura forensis* 1.1.101 1.13.7; Spiro 1985 *The Law of parent and child* 297; Van Heerden et al. (1999); Article 20(1) of the African Charter on Human and People's Rights provides that '[p]arents or other persons responsible for the child shall have the primary responsibility of the upbringing and development the child and shall have the duty'; Article 4(d) of the United Nations Convention on the Rights of the Child ("CRC") provides that: "[It] is the right of every child to a standard of living adequate for the child's physical, mental, spiritual, moral and social development. The primary responsibility to ensure this lies with the parents or other persons responsible for the child. The state's duty is to (within the means available) assist the parents with this responsibility…".

juristic personality for public schools, the quintile funding system, and the separation of functions (i.e. administration, management and governance).

The Constitutional Court affirmed the democratic design of the South African Schools Act ("Schools Act") in the matter of *Head of Department Mpumalanga Education Department v Ermelo High School* by stating:

> A governing body is democratically composed and is intended to function in a democratic manner. Its primary function is to look after the interest of the school and its learners. It is meant to be a beacon of grassroots democracy in the local affairs of the school. Ordinarily, the representatives of parents of learners and of the local community are better qualified to determine the medium best suited to impart education and all the formative, utilitarian and cultural goodness that comes with it.[27]

Elections of members of School Governing Bodies take place every three years at schools across South Africa, which makes these elections as significant as the national, provincial, and local government elections. Every high school must have a representative council of learners. Parents, learners, educators, and school personnel may participate in the elections. These provisions establish a form of representative democracy in schools (Smit 2013). Democratic principles such as accountability, transparency and openness are implied by the provisions of the Schools Act that require auditing of financial records, annual approval of the school's budget, due performance of governing body functions and regular elections of members of school governing bodies.[28] The principles of participative and deliberative democracy are apparent from the provisions that require approval of the financial governance by an annual meeting of the parents and participation of interested stakeholders either as members of the governing body or as members of committees serving under the governing bodies. Most well-functioning school governing bodies have committees that attend to matters such as finances, learner discipline, marketing, infrastructure, academic standards, culture, leadership, hostels, sport, and parent liaison to name a few.

The values of human dignity, equality and freedom enumerated in Section 7(1) of the Constitution are species of a generic value: democracy (Woolman and Fleisch 2009). The essential condition of democracy is foundational to the establishment of a mature constitutional democracy in South Africa. Fundamental rights do not stand in opposition to democracy but are constitutive elements of democracy. Education is probably the most important instrument for cultivating a human rights culture and establishing a consolidated and substantive democracy. Learners must be prepared for their future responsibilities as citizens of a democratic society. As learners are not born with an understanding of the principles of democracy, public schools function as the nurseries of democracy. Democratic values and principles cannot successfully be affirmed and transmitted to learners if an education system is bureaucratic or displays autocratic values and principles. If a school is run by autocrats, it is not

[27] *Head of Department, Mpumalanga Education Department v Ermelo High School* 2010 (2) SA 415 (CC) at para 57 & 79.

[28] SA Schools Act—Section 11; 23; 24; 36; 37; 38(2); 39(1); 42; 43.

likely to produce democratically minded citizens. The nature and practice of democracy in societal institutions, such as schools, must be congruent with the education that citizens receive; otherwise, the educative force of the real environment would counteract the effects of early schooling.[29]

9 School Leadership: Professional Management by School Principals and Governance by School Governing Bodies

In terms of the Schools Act the governance of every public school is vested in the local school governing body that is comprised of triennially elected representative members of the parents, educators, and learners of a school. School governing bodies are responsible for the strategic planning, the development of policies, overseeing financial governance, involvement to a limited extent in human resource governance, and promoting quality education in schools.[30] In addition, functions allocated in terms of Section 21 include the maintenance and improvement of a school's property and buildings, determining the extra-mural curriculum and choice subject options, and the purchasing of textbooks, educational materials, or equipment for the school, and payment of services provided for schools.

In terms of Sectsion 16(3) and 16A(2) of the Schools Act, the school principal is responsible for the professional management of a public school, which traditionally consisted of performing sound pedagogical practices, maintaining strong cohesion amongst the teaching staff, and running the daily affairs of a school. The school principal must implement all the educational programs and curriculum activities, manage all educators and support staff, manage the use of learning support material and other equipment, keep all school records safe, implement education policy and legislation, attend and participate in all meetings of the governing body, assist the governing body in disciplinary matters for learners, assist the Head of Department in disciplinary matters of educators and support staff, inform the governing body about policy and legislation, provide accurate data and reports to the Head of Department, assist the governing body with the management of the school funds, take all reasonable steps to prevent any financial maladministration, serve on the finance committee of the governing body in order to manage the finances of the school, and report any maladministration of financial matters to the governing body and to the Head of Department.

Although the demarcation of roles and functions between the school principal and the school governing body functions seems clear, tensions arise from time to time between these role players. Many principals hark back to the era of authoritarian school leadership before 1996 and the assume their responsibilities in an extensive controlling manner. On the other hand, it also happens that newly elected and inexperienced school governing body members overestimate or misunderstand their roles

[29] Smit (2013).

[30] SA Schools Act—Section 20.

and functions. The conflict came to the fore in a series of cases between Scheepers (the school principal) and the school governing body of Grey College, Bloemfontein, which is an elite boys-only sport school known for producing Springbok rugby players and other sportsmen.[31] The salient facts were that educators, learners and parents had complained about the way the newly appointed school principal had been managing the school. The provincial department of education investigated the complaints but took no remedial steps. Eventually the school governing body became frustrated and took matters in their own hands by removing the "delegated" functions of the principal. Scheepers took the matter to court and averred that the meeting with the governing body was procedurally unfair and that the decisions were unlawful. The department of education as well as the teacher's union (SAOU) to which the principal belonged, sided with the principal. The series of cases eventually resulted in the decision by the Supreme Court of Appeal declaring that the governing body had acted unlawfully because the school principal's functions were not delegated but were statutorily determined. In a follow-up case of *Büchner v Head of Department of Education, Free State*, the court held that the steps by the Head of Department of Education to dismiss the governing body in terms of Section 22 of the Schools Act were lawful.[32] However, these judgments have caused legal uncertainty about the role and legal footing of school governing bodies, and the court's restrictive interpretation of the functions of governing bodies to a confined role of policy makers (akin to the legislature of a school) is problematic (Smit 2022). A proper understanding of the role of a school governing body is that it is a *sui generis* organ of a public school that governs and performs managerial or executive functions in accordance with the functions specified in the Schools Act. According to Smit oversimplification of the roles and functions of the school governing body in the *Scheepers* judgment misinterprets the structure of the Schools Act and discounts the statutory partnership in education.

10 Religious Observances in Public Schools

The right to freedom of religion, belief and opinion, the right to believe or not to believe, and to act or not to act according to one's beliefs or non-beliefs, is one of the key ingredients of any person's dignity. In terms of Section 15(2) of the Constitution of South Africa,[33] everyone has the right to freedom of religion, belief, conscience, thought, and opinion. Religious observances may be conducted at state and state-aided institutions such as public schools, colleges, and universities in South Africa, in terms of Section 15(2). This section places three conditional requirements on the way religious observances may be conducted at state or state-aided institutions,

---

[31] *School Governing Body Grey College, Bloemfontein v Scheepers and another (Federation of Governing Bodies of South African Schools as amicus curiae)* [2020] 3 All SA 704 (SCA).

[32] *Büchner and others v Head of Department of Education, Free State* [2021] JOL 50888 (FB).

[33] Act 104 of 1996.

namely that the religious observances must follow the rules made by the appropriate public authorities (e.g. the school governing body), the observances are conducted on an equitable basis, and attendance should be free and voluntary. Section 7 of the South African Schools Act[34] specifically provides that religious observances may be conducted at public schools and echoes the conditions of the Constitution. In terms of the "Co-operative Model," which is applied in South Africa, the state does not establish or favour a particular religion. Rather, the state co-operates with religious communities by permitting religious observances at state and state-aided institutions, subject to the specified constitutional provisos (Department of Basic Education 2003). In order for the Co-operative Model to function optimally, a measure of tolerance and resilience among diverse religious and nonreligious communities and individuals are required.

Most public schools in South Africa have an ethos that is religious in orientation and thus they allow for religious observances to be conducted on fair and equitable bases. A core aspect of the Co-operative Model is that attendance at and participation in religious observances at public schools must be free and voluntary based on the rules (policy) of the school. The requirement of "free and voluntary" goes hand in hand with the prohibition of indoctrination or coercive inculcation of a specific worldview or religious doctrine.

In order to avoid indoctrination and proselytization, the National Policy on Religion and Education distinguishes between the following concepts: Religious training (or religious instruction)—Instruction in a particular religion or worldview with the view to establish belief, to convert, or proselytize a person to a particular religion or to strengthen that belief by way of upbringing; Religion education—a school subject that is part of a curriculum or course to study different religions, their holy or sacred texts, special days, beliefs and rituals; Religious observances—the practice of customs, rites, and traditions of religious character manifesting belief such as prayer, reading of sacred texts, meditation, praise and worship, witnessing, fasting and other dietary observances, dress, observance religious calendar days of significance, gathering of adherents and religious rituals; and Religious orientation—the ethos, life- and worldview, directional choice or foundation of beliefs. Ethos is the characteristic belief system and spirit of a person, community, culture, or era as manifested in its attitudes and aspirations, the prevailing character of an institution. Based on these distinctions it follows that religious instruction or religious training, evangelizing, or proselytizing by educators or other school personnel is not allowed in public school or in classrooms.[35]

The policies regarding religious observances at public schools were contested in the case of *Organisasie vir Godsdienste Onderrig en Demokrasie v Randhart Primary School.*[36] Unlike America and other secular countries there is no strict separation of

---

[34] Act 84 of 1996.

[35] Smit (2019).

[36] *Organisasie vir Godsdienste Onderrig en Demokrasie v Laërskool Randhart and others (Council for the Advancement of the South African Constitution and others as amici curiae)* [2017] 3 All SA 943 (GJ).

church and state in South Africa and religious observances are allowed at public institutions in so far as it complies with the Constitution and the South African Schools Act. In this case the "Organisation" (a voluntary association) applied to court for 71 interdicts against four specific public schools (and for good measure included a plea against all the schools in South Africa) inter-alia to prohibit various religious activities such as conducting religious observances during school programs, subscribing to a Christian ethos and values in a school's vision and mission statement, reading and praying to a specific deity during assembly or closure of a school, providing Christian books in school libraries, distributing Bibles at schools, using Christian biblical slogans as a school motto and teaching creationism in conjunction with evolutionism at schools.

However, the evidence submitted by all the respondent public schools indicated that the public schools had satisfactorily managed to arrange fair and equitable school religious policies that accommodated various religions in multicultural school. The respondent schools also provided evidence that the Co-operative Model, which allows for free and voluntary participation in religious observances according to the rules of the school governing body, had functioned very well without complaints or any perceptible unhappiness among the parents and learners for more than two decades. In terms of the South Africa's co-operative model towards accommodating religious freedom at public institutions, the state should remain impartial and not simply favour the "secular" approach but should allow each school governing body to consult with the parent and learner community when formulating an appropriate religious policy for each school.

The High Court of Gauteng (opinion of Van der Linde J) unanimously refused the Organisation's application for 71 interdicts. The Court indicated that the Applicant had followed the incorrect legal procedure by solely basing its case on the Constitution and the Schools Act. In accordance with the legal principle of subsidiarity, school policies also had to comply with provincial legislation and regulations and had to be approved by the MEC of the Department of Education. In circumstances where individuals, parents or learners felt aggrieved by the content or implementation of a school's religious policy, the appropriate procedure would have been to firstly apply to the MEC of Education to review the school's policy and thereafter to approach a court is the initial review was ineffective. The subsidiarity principle therefore requires disputes to be settled, in so far as possible, at local or grass-roots level between the aggrieved disputants and the responsible decision-making authority. This approach accords with the participatory design of the Schools Act that favours negotiations and democratic deliberations between all stakeholders in the school community. The Court avoided deciding on the merits of each complaint by the Applicant and indicated that the Applicant had provided insufficient evidence to justify each claim.

However, the Court held that it offends Section 7 of the Schools Act (which requires the free, voluntary and fair practice of religious observances according to the rules of the school governing body), for a public school to promote or allow its staff to promote only one or predominantly only one religion to the exclusion of others. In view of the multi-religious and diverse nature of the South African population, public schools should promote and accommodate religious diversity. Two important implications of the Randhart-case are that firstly, the Court refused to centralise decision-making about religious policies at schools and secondly, the Court maintained that South Africa is not a secular society and that religious freedom includes the right to conduct religious observances (e.g. prayer, reading holy scripture, singing hymns and religious songs, et cetera) at schools.

11 Language and Admission Policies

There has been an abundance of legal disputes because of provincial departments' attempts to compel Afrikaans single medium schools to change their language policies to English. The most recent case in this continuing saga is *Governing Body, Hoërskool Overvaal v Head of Department of Education Gauteng Province* (Overvaal-case) in which the District Director (Ms. Moloi) of the Gauteng Education Department instructed an Afrikaans single medium high school to admit 55 English-speaking Grade 8 learners to the school.[37] This order would have effectively sounded the death-knell of Afrikaans as a language of instruction at the school because the hegemonic position of English would overwhelm the minority language. The school is in a district in which there were five other high schools in relatively close proximity to each other. The school approached the High Court of Gauteng for urgent relief and applied for the decision of the education officials to be declared unlawful (*ultra vires*).

One of the main areas of dispute related to the capacity of the school to accommodate the English students, relative to the capacity of other schools in the district. In terms of the admission regulations relating in terms of the Gauteng Schools Education Act,[38] provided that the Head of Department had to consider the proximity of the schools to learners' places of residence to determine placement. The Court (opinion by Prinsloo J) held that language policy and admission policy of a school may be determined by the school's governing body and concluded, on the overwhelming weight of the evidence that the school had no capacity to receive the 55 students in question. By contrast, the neighbouring English medium school had sufficient capacity to accommodate those students. The Court held that the Head of Department (and the officials from the department) had acted in conflict with the constitutional principle of legality, the impugned instruction was unlawful and was set aside.

Even though Hoërskool Overvaal had an integrated student body comprised of various races that chose to receive education in Afrikaans, the MEC's point of departure was to equate the continued separation of languages of instruction at public schools as an indication of underlying racism. The court gave a punitive cost order

[37] *Governing Body, Hoërskool Overvaal v Head of Department of Education Gauteng Province* [2018] JOL 39440 (GP).

[38] Act 6 of 1995.

against the respondents because of the politicized manner in which the state chose to litigate this case. The Gauteng Department of Education appealed this decision and approached the Constitutional Court directly. However, the Constitutional Court dismissed the appeal with costs on the grounds that there was no prospect of success. The reasons provided were that the Head of Department had not taken the neighbouring English schools, which fall in the same feeder zone and had capacity to admit the students, into account and that single-medium Afrikaans instruction is not an indication of inherent racism at the school. The outcome of these judgments is a welcome affirmation that the law provides protection to minority learners who choose to receive education in another language (*in casu* Afrikaans).

12 The Rights of Learners (Students), Equality, Freedom of Expression and School Discipline

Corporal punishment was prohibited in terms of Section 10 of the Schools Act in 1997. The constitutionality of this section was contested on grounds of religious freedom of parents to discipline their children in accordance with their beliefs in the matter of *Christian Education South Africa v Minister of Education*.[39] However, the Constitutional Court unanimously held that corporal punishment is a form of cruel and degrading punishment that violates a person's human dignity and thus infringes Section 12(1)(e) of the Constitution. Sachs J explained the reason for the prohibition of corporal punishment at schools as follows:

> It had a principled and symbolic function, manifestly intended to promote respect for the dignity and physical and emotional integrity of all children.

Since the abolition of corporal punishment learner discipline has become a serious problem in South African schools (Wolhuter et al. 2010). A number of empirical studies about school-based violence confirmed many media reports and complaints by educators that violence in many South African schools had reached alarming proportions.[40] School-based violence in South Africa is a multidimensional phenomenon and depends on the context in which it arises. Bullying, gender-based violence, discrimination and violence, sexual violence and harassment, physical violence and psychological violence, describe some of the most prevalent forms that were identified in the studies (De Wet and Jacobs 2013). In the case of *Jacobs v Chairman, Governing Body, Rhodes High School* a 15 year old boy seriously assaulted a female educator by repeatedly striking her in the face and on her

[39] *Christian Education South Africa v Minister of Education* [2000] JOL 7320 (CC. Section10 of the South African Schools Act prohibits corporal punishment by anyone at a school.

[40] Vally et al. (1999); South African Human Rights Commission (SAHRC) 2008 *Report on school-based violence* 1; Van der Merwe (2009); South African Council for Educators 2011 School-based violence report: An overview of school-based violence in South Africa, Retrieved from http://sace.org.za/assets/documents/uploads/saceReport-2011.pdf; Makota and Leoschut (2016); Le Roux (2011); Davids and Waghid (2016); Grobler (2018).

body with a hammer.[41] She almost succumbed to her injuries and was never able to return to the teaching profession as a result of the severe trauma she experienced. The learner was convicted of attempted murder and sent to a reform school for juvenile delinquents. The Department of Education was held partially liable for the damages that Ms Jacobs incurred. Although human rights advocates are loathe to admit it, it seems undeniable that serious forms of violence (e.g. assault and murder) committed by learners against educators has increased markedly since the abolition of corporal punishment (Botha 2021). Murder and assault of educators by learners was unheard of before the ban on corporal punishment. It seems that the ban on moderate and just (reasonable) corporal punishment has had the opposite effect than intended in that schools have become more violent and unsafe. As a result, many educators resign their positions and blame the parlous state of poor discipline in many schools on the fact that educators no longer have an effective deterrent to correct ill-discipline or misconduct (Mahome 2019).

Generally the courts hold the perpetrators of violence or serious misconduct at schools accountable for their deeds.[42] In *Western Cape Residents' Association obo Williams v Parow High School* the parents of a Grade 12 girl, B, applied for an urgent interdict to compel the school to allow her to attend the matric farewell function.[43] The school had refused Williams permission as a result of her continued ill-discipline during the course of the year. In determining whether a rule should be developed to give effect to the Constitution, the court considered the arguments that the learner's dignity, equality and freedom of expression had been infringed by the school's refusal. The court considered the interests of the school, the other learners versus those of B and determined on balance that:

> Two of the important lessons that a school must teach its learners are discipline and respect for authority. The granting of privilege as a reward for good behaviour is one tool that may be used to teach such lessons. The withholding of such privilege can therefore not be claimed as an infringement of a right to equality or to dignity. Indeed, the granting of the privilege in the absence of its having been earned may well constitute an infringement on the rights to equality and dignity of those who have merited the privilege. The right to freedom of expression, of course, does not equate to a right to be ill-disciplined or rude. The system of rewards for good behaviour permeates all walks of life and to learn the system at an early age can only benefit the learner later on in his or her life.[44]

In casu there was no statutory provision or common law rule that granted the learner a right to attend the matric farewell function. Thus, the Court held that the attendance of a matric farewell function was a social activity and, as such, was a privilege and not an enforceable right. It is a misconception to regard democratic schools as places where unmitigated freedom or anarchy prevails. On the contrary, orderly

[41] *Jacobs v Chairman, Governing Body, Rhodes High School* 2011 (1) SA 160 (WCC).

[42] *Phillips v Manser* [1999] 1 All SA 198 (SE); *Le Roux v Dey (Freedom of Expression Institute & another as amici curiae)* [2011] JOL 27031 (CC).

[43] *Western Cape Residents' Association obo Williams v Parow High School* 2006 (3) SA 542 (C).

[44] Ibid at *p. 545 par.* B-C.

and well-disciplined schools can function democratically. Any democratic organisation or institution, such as a school, should per definition be orderly organisations governed by democratically confirmed rules and policies.

13 Endemic Dysfunctionality at Most Public Schools in South Africa

The outcomes and results of South Africa's performance in the education sector are very poor in any comparative terms, despite high levels of spending. Nationally, 72% of all Grade 6 learners failed the Annual National Assessment literacy test in 2011. In mathematics, the figure is substantially higher, with 88% of all Grade 6 learners failing to achieve the curriculum standard. Data from international evaluations affirm this outcome and indicate that the mean score of the Trends in Mathematics and Science Study (TIMSS) places South African Grade 8 learners at the very bottom of the 50 participating countries (Martin et al. 2020). Similar trends are evident in other cross-national studies of quality such as SACMEQ IV and PIRLS, where the average South African learner perform very poorly compared to a number of much poorer countries.[45] Given the centrality of reading, writing and arithmetic not only to all further learning, but also to most jobs in the information economy, the poor performance of South Africa's primary schools in providing basic education is one of the country's most urgent problems. South Africa's levels of inequality are revealed by cross-country testing programmes (Annual National Assessments) to be the highest by a large margin among participating countries.

Soobramoney, the former Director-General of the Department of Basic Education, candidly admitted that even though the national and provincial departments of education had introduced numerous interventions with the best intentions and based on reasonable theory, these measures have had a limited effect on improving education quality. Almost three decades of activity, increased financial investment, introduction of new reforms and providing schools with new resources, has been met by a stubborn unresponsiveness of system performance to management efforts and reform policies. Although some noteworthy measures by education departments, such as the Annual National Assessments, pro-poor public spending, the National Nutrition programme, introduction of no-fee schools, whole school evaluation, assistance and mentoring by subject specialists, and incentives to improve work performance (such as the National Teacher Awards, Best School awards, Dinaledi schools programme) have yielded some successes, the overall quality of education of the majority of schools remains dismally low. Spaull attributes the persistent dysfunctionality of South Africa's school system to two factors[46]:

---

[45] Taylor et al. (2007).

[46] Spaull (2012).

- Firstly, a weak capacity throughout the civil service—teachers, principals, and system level officials are incompetent as they simply don't have the skills to do their jobs.
- Secondly, a culture of patronage which permeates almost all areas of the civil service, with few departmental and, to a limited extent, one or two provincial exceptions.

These two factors are evident as ANC party membership, cadre deployment and union nepotism results in the appointment of unsuitable personnel, which further weakens government capacity.[47] The situation drives officials and principals, in the absence of professional skills and ability, to entrench their positions by building their own patronage networks. A derivative of these two factors is the political activism and influence of the dominant teachers' union, the South African Democratic Teachers Union (SADTU), has a stranglehold on the efficient functioning of the national and provincial departments of education.

14 The Outlook of Future Developments and Emerging Issues in Education Law

Diverse global influences, values, norms, and traditions ranging from Western philosophy and African thought patterns, belief systems of all the major religions, as well as divergent economic and political ideologies and new technologies continue to sway events in South Africa. In this regard, contemporary issues that dominate the cultural, political, educational, social, and religious landscape in South Africa are matters such as neo-liberalism, progressive secularism, woke ideology, decolonisation of education, free or affordable tertiary education, affirmative action and employment equity, political correctness, legalisation of marijuana, social justice, abortion on demand, and gender equity.

It seems that lessons learnt during the COVID pandemic and hard lockdown regulations provide possible outcomes for the South African dilemmas. Minority learners can be accommodated by providing home language education by means of alternative modes of education including blended learning, i.e. a combination of contact, virtual or distance education and state subsidized independent schools. The provision of quality teaching–learning and improved pedagogy can also be optimized by providing widespread virtual and blended learning public education to learners situated in poor socio-economic areas or impoverished circumstances by means of internet technology, mobile phone technology and the appropriate use of social media. Furthermore, the substantive issue of pedagogical quality in view of the influx or migration of learners to functional (higher quality) schools with limited spatial capacity has also not yet been resolved. Although virtual technology cannot completely annul the need for contact teaching or replace the classroom educator,

[47] Volmink et al. (2016).

virtual education is emerging as a viable solution for future developments in education in South Africa.

15 Conclusion

Although post-modernism and secular liberalism have substantively displaced modernism as the dominant philosophical paradigms during the last decades of the twentieth century,[48] legal positivism remains the preferred philosophical approach of the courts in South African law. Davis attributes the juridical practice of applying legal positivism as method to the pre-1994 tradition of formalistic interpretation in accordance with the Westminster constitutional model. Davis and Clare contend that the legal culture in South Africa does not have a well-developed tradition of critical jurisprudence (as is the case in the United States of America) and that the inbred formalism stultifies efforts to renovate the legal infrastructure in the manner envisaged by the Constitution (Davis and Klare 2010). Of course, the law plays a powerful part in determining the values of society, by virtue of its coercive nature and the ability to enforce compliance by legal sanction.[49] A priori philosophical points of departure, worldviews, religious or irreligious convictions, presuppositions and assumptions all play a role in science and judicial practice. Hosten et al. remind that legal theory includes a concern with moral values, as well as political values (such as the democratic tenets of equality, freedom, and human dignity), legal values (such as justice, fairness, righteousness, reasonableness, equity and impartiality) and administrative values (Hosten et al. 1995).

Although the moral, democratic and legal values correspond to a large extent, inconsistencies, unjust court decisions, erroneous judgments in South African jurisprudence have occurred at the periphery of these categories. The initial optimistic expectations have been confounded and many challenges regarding the provision of quality education persist especially in majority African (Black) schools. Striking a balance between equal access to education while maintaining quality of education at public schools remains a dilemma in South Africa. In the multilingual context of South Africa, the question whether equality in education should ideally be accomplished by assimilation of all languages of instruction into a homogenous system of monolingual (English) education or by the advancement of pluralism through a system of multilingual and single-medium mother tongue education is not yet settled.

South Africa thus presents an interesting case where some educational reforms such as local school governance, equitable school admission policies, and pro-poor school funding policies have contributed to the maintenance of quality education at functional schools despite an increasingly dysfunctional educational system and the failing state. The overlap and connectedness between education and the law has yielded meaningful results particularly regarding the judicial enforceability of

[48] Van der Walt (2002).

[49] Radbruch *Rechtsphilosophie* (*Studienausgabe*) translation from Alexy (2002) 6.

concrete aspects (such as provision of schools, infrastructure, facilities, furniture and learning material) of the constitutional right to education. The unique co-operative model of allowing fair and voluntary religious observances at multi-cultural public schools has accommodated religious freedom and respectful school cultures.

However, the South African experience also contains the dire warning that the wide-ranging revision of legislation, transformation of the legal system and the casuistic enforcement of the individual's right to education is not sufficient to improve the quality of a dysfunctional education system overall. The dedication of competent political leaders, the proper implementation of government policies as well as the widespread commitment by the whole educator corps to provide quality teaching are essential components for an effective, valuable, and meaningful education system.

References

Bertelsmann (2018) Drafting the South African Schools Act 84 of 1996. In: De Waal (ed) Pathways to successful schooling, Cape Town, p 1

Botha (2021) Onderwysers as slagoffers van geweld deur leerders in Suid-Afrikaanse skole. LitNet Akademies 18(3):21

Crouch L, Gustaffson M, Lavado P (2009) Measuring educational inequality in South Africa and Peru. In: Inequality in education: comparative and international perspectives, vol 24, Cape Town, pp 461–484

Davids N, Waghid Y (2016) Responding to violence in post-apartheid schools. Educ Change 20(1):28–42

Davis DM, Klare K (2010) Transformative constitutionalism and common and customary law. South African Journal on Human Rights 26(3):403–509

Department of Basic Education (2003) National policy on religion and education policy, para. 3–4

Department of Education (2006) National policy framework for teacher education and development in South Africa. Government Gazette No. 29832. Government Printer, Pretoria, Cape Town, pp 13–15

De Wet C, Jacobs L (2013) South African teachers' exposure to workplace bullying. Journal for Transdisciplinary Research in Southern Africa 9(3):446–464

Fund for Peace (2021) Fragile state index. South Africa is categorized as an "Elevated Warning" state. Available at https://fragilestatesindex.org/wp-content/uploads/2021/05/fsi2021-report.pdf. Accessed 20 May 2021

Grobler GW (2018) Narratives of teachers' experiences of school violence and ethics of care. M.Ed Education Psychology, University of Stellenbosch

Hosten WJ et al (1995) Introduction to South African law and legal theory. Butterworth, Durban, pp 220–237

Le Roux CS (2011) The persistence of violence in South Africa's schools: in search of solutions. Africa Education Review 8(2):318–335

Liebenberg S (2010) Socio-economic rights: adjudication under a transformative constitution. Juta, Claremont

Mahome MM (2019) The prevalence of learner-on-teacher school-based violence: a qualitative study. Acta Criminologica: African Journal of Criminology & Victimology 32(2):89

Malherb R (2004) The constitutional framework for pursuing equal opportunities in education. Perspect Educ 22(3):15

Makota G, Leoschut L (2016) The national school safety framework: a framework for preventing violence in South African schools. Afr Saf Promot 14(2):18–23

Martin MO, Mullis IVS, Foy P, Kelly D & Fishbein B. (2020). *TIMSS 2019 international results in mathematics and science*. Chestnut Hill, MA: TIMSS & PIRLS International Study Center, Boston College.

Oosthuizen, Smit (eds) (2020) Aspects of education law, 5th edn. Van Schaik, Pretoria, pp 105–106

Russo (2012) Reutter's the law of public education, 8th edn. Foundation Press, New York, p 8

Skelton (2015) Leveraging funds for school infrastructure: the South African 'mud schools' case study. Int J Educ Dev 39:59–63

Smit (2013) Fundamentals of human rights and democracy in education—a South African perspective. Cape Town, pp 339–341

Smit (2019) Religion in South African public schools—ORED v Randhart Primary School. IJLE 22:49–63

Smit (2020) School choice and school funding reform in South Africa. Journal for Contemporary Roman Dutch Law 83(2):264

Smit (2022) Conflict between school governing body and school principal: Scheepers v School Governing Body of Grey College—the "partnership" in education in tatters. In: Tydskrif vir Hedendaagse Romeins-Hollandse Reg (Journal for Contemporary Roman-Dutch Law) 85(1):91–107

Spaull (2012) Education in SA—a tale of two systems, Politicsweb. Available at: https://www.politicsweb.co.za/news-and-analysis/education-in-sa-a-tale-of-two-systems. Accessed 26 Sept 2022

Taylor N, Fleisch B, Schindler J (2007) Education scenarios for 2019. Paper prepared for the key driving forces scenarios 16 18 20

Vally S, Dolimbisa Y, Porteus K (1999) Violence in South African schools. Current Issues in Comparative Education 2(1):80–90

Van der Merwe (2009) Implementation of a school-based socio-emotional programme as strategy against crime and violence. MA Psychology dissertation, University of South Africa

Van der Walt H (2002) Scholarship in a Changing Intellectual Climate 27

Van Heerden et al (eds) (1999) Boberg's. Law of Persons and the Family 313–316

Volmink J, Gardiner M, Msimang S, Nel P, Moleta A, Scholtz G, Prins T (2016) Report of the ministerial task team appointed by minister Angie Motshekga to investigate allegations into the selling of posts of educators by members of Teachers Unions and Departmental Officials in Provincial Education Departments ('Volmink-Report'). Available at https://nicspaull.files.wordpress.com/dbe-2016-volmink-report.pdf. Date of use 12 Oct 2022. Accessed 26 Sept 2022

Wolhuter CC et al (2010) Skoolfase/Leerderouderdom as Faktor in Leerderdissipline in Suid-Afrikaanse Skole. Tydskrif Vir Christelike Wetenskap 40(1):169–186

Woolman S, Fleisch B (2009) The Constitution in the classroom—law and education in South Africa 1994–2008. Cape Town, p 174

Right to Education in Spain

Santiago Cañamares Arribas

1 Introduction

The Spanish Constitution (1978) in its first article identifies equality, liberty, and political pluralism as fundamental values of the constitutional system. The approval of the Constitution signified the transition from dictatorship to democracy (Martínez-Torrón 2013). This transformation required both the recognition of fundamental and universal rights, in accordance with the provisions of the international human rights instruments which Spain would subsequently ratify, and the adoption of new basic principles to inspire the actions of public authorities in political, social, and religious contexts.

Within the catalogue of fundamental rights recognized by Chapter II of the Spanish Constitution (hereinafter CE), those concerning education are included in art. 27. For a proper understanding of the content and limitations of this basic right, it must be born in mind that according to art. 10.2 CE, 'the laws concerning fundamental rights and freedoms recognized by the Constitution, must be interpreted according to the Universal Declaration of Human Rights and the international agreements and treaties on these subjects, which have been ratified by Spain.'

Within this framework, the European Convention on Human Rights is a significant factor, given its binding legal nature and the continuing oversight exercised by the European Court of Human Rights. Furthermore, a number of articles are particularly relevant to upholding the right to education and instruction. Art. 9 ECHR, covers religious and ideological freedom and art. 2 of its First Additional Protocol, recognizes both the right to education and the right of parents to choose for their children the instruction that is in accordance with their own ideological convictions. In addition, the International Covenant on Economic, Social and Cultural Rights (1966) is also

S. C. Arribas (✉)
Complutense University of Madrid, Madrid, Spain
e-mail: copyright@esph.com.cn

C. J. Russo and L. Ma (eds.), *A Comparative Analysis of Systems of Education Law*,
https://doi.org/10.1007/978-981-97-1052-2_16

relevant for interpretative purposes, as well as the Charter of Fundamental Rights of the European Union, which is also applicable when European Law is at issue.[1]

2 Nature of the Legal System

Art. 27 CE proclaims both the right to education and freedom of teaching. While the former corresponds to the obligation of the State to provide all individuals with a free place to attend the compulsory levels of education, the latter encompasses a set of provisions aimed at enabling parents to ensure that their children receive an education that is in accordance with their own worldview.

2.1 *Right to Education*

Historically, the right to education was conceived of in terms of the duty on the part of the State to provide to all citizens the elementary education completely free of charge through the establishment of state schools, which were ideologically neutral. Once the programme of the movement known as Illustration was implemented in the eighteen century, it was made clear that education had to be provided without taking the role of religious communities into account. Consequently, this crucial task was to be carried out by the State through a 'secularising' programme which aimed at ending the pre-eminence of religion in both the cultural and social life of the people.

Nowadays, the right to education is considered an individual right which guarantees a place in state educational institutions to all students. The provision of this service is guaranteed, as the Spanish Constitution acknowledges in art. 27.5 through general education programming, with the effective participation of all parties concerned and the setting up of educational centres.[2] Likewise, the creation of educational institutions by the State, proclaimed in the same article, is regarded as a mean to guarantee this right, as well as the public financing of those educational institutions which meet the criteria recognised by the legal framework.

The right to education is considered universal which means that it is refers to both Spanish citizens and others, irrespective of their legal status. Consequently, it is so recognized in the Organic Law 4/2000, on the rights and liberties of foreigners in Spain and their social integration (Spanish Offcial Bulletin 2000). Interestingly, this

[1] The right to education is shrined in art. 14 of the European Charter of Fundamental Rights, which reads as follows: (1) Everyone has the right to education and to have access to vocational and continuing training. (2) This right includes the possibility to receive free compulsory education. (3) The freedom to found educational establishments with due respect for democratic principles and the right of parents to ensure the education and teaching of their children in conformity with their religious, philosophical and pedagogical convictions shall be respected, in accordance with the national laws governing the exercise of such freedom and right.

[2] See Constitutional Court Judgement 86/1985, 10th July, *Fundamento jurídico tercero.*

norm was modified, in compliance with the doctrine set out by the Constitutional Court in its Judgment 236/2007, 7th November[3] where it acknowledged the right of all minors to enjoy the benefits accorded to Spanish citizens and legal residents from other jurisdictions in respect of compulsory and post-compulsory levels of teaching.[4]

It must be pointed out that the right to education effectively amounts to a right to be provided with a service. Although the State is required to guarantee a place for pupils during the compulsory stages of education, the Constitution does not establish any sort of correlation between the right to free basic education and the freedom of teaching insofar as there is no right to obtain a free place in one's favoured educational institution. Freedom of teaching is a freedom strictly speaking, which means is not a right to be provided with a service, and therefore there is no constitutional right to demand financial support from the State in order to attend a private teaching institution with a particular ethos.[5]

Finally, it should be highlighted that article 27.2 CE states that education shall aim at the full development of the human character in relation to the democratic principles of coexistence along with the fundamental rights and freedoms.

2.2 *Freedom of Teaching*

The freedom of teaching has been always conceived as the right of both citizens and social groups to create teaching institutions because it was considered that the function of the State in this respect was meant to be subsidiary.

More precisely, the Constitutional Court in its Judgment 5/1981, 13th February gave freedom of teaching a broad interpretation. According to this decision, this freedom includes the right of parents to choose religious and moral education for their children in accord with their convictions under art. 27.3 CE.[6] It is widely accepted that this recognition paved the way to the incorporation of religious teaching in state teaching institutions.[7]

---

[3] Fundamento jurídico octavo.

[4] Article 9 of this Organic Law reads as follows: Foreigners under the age of sixteen have the right and duty to education, which includes access to basic, free and compulsory education. Foreigners under eighteen years of age also have the right to post-compulsory education.

[5] Constitutional Court Judgment 86/1985, 10th July 1985. The Supreme Court took this same approach in its Judgment of 20th January 1987.

[6] Art. 27.3 CE reads as follows: The public authorities guarantee the right of parents to ensure that their children receive religious and moral instruction that is in accordance with their own convictions.

[7] This chapter uses the term 'state' rather than 'public' in order to refer to schools owned by public authorities. We opted to avoid the term public as it has the potential to generate confusion for readers in the United Kingdom, where it is used to describe privately funded educational establishments. Further, it should be borne in mind that education is a devolved matter in Spain, and therefore 'state' as an adjective has been used to refer to both the State and the regional authorities.

Consequentially to this content, this freedom also includes scope to create educational institutions as recognised in art. 27.6 CE and support the idea that private bodies may be supported by public funds, and in such cases, teachers, parents and, where appropriate, pupils, shall share in the control and management of the teaching centre.

It cannot be ignored that intimately related to the freedom in teaching is freedom of religion or belief that is recognised in art. 16 CE. This freedom encompasses both the individual and collective right to manifest religious and ideological beliefs, which cannot be limited beyond what it is strictly necessary for the protection of public order. The content of this provision was developed by the Organic Law[8] (Ley Orgánica) 7/1980, on Religious Freedom (State Official Bulletin 1980) which refers in art. 2 to some faculties that are inherent to this basic freedom, like the right to receive and to deliver religious teaching, whether orally, written, or through any other means, as well as the right to choose for oneself and for minor children, inside and outside of school settings, education in accordance with one's religious convictions.

Equally, from a collective perspective, this law also acknowledges the right of religious denominations to disseminate their own doctrine. In order to apply these rights properly and effectively, public authorities must adopt whatever measures are necessary to facilitate religious education within state educational institutions. At the same time, religious denominations, in common with all other legal persons, are recognised as having the right to fund their own teaching institutions, provided they act in conformity with constitutional principles.

The Organic Law on Education (State Official Bulletin 2006) (hereinafter LOE) in its second Additional Provision establishes that religious education will be tailored to the content of the cooperation agreements signed with the various religious denominations, viz, the Catholic Church, and the Protestant churches, the Jewish community and the Muslims.

Finally, it is also provided that "In the regulatory framework for Primary Education and Compulsory Secondary Education, non-denominational teaching on the culture of religions may be established."

As far as the Catholic Church is concerned, Article II of the Agreement on Teaching and Cultural Affairs between Spain and the Holy See (1979)[9] declares that in the different educational levels, excluding universities, the teaching of Catholic religion will be provided in all schools and must be offered in similar conditions to the other fundamental subjects. It is also agreed that such education will not have a compulsory character for students but they are guaranteed the right to receive it. On the other hand, the Agreements with minority religions in their respective article 10 guarantees, at all different teaching levels, the right of parents and students in state

[8] The *leyes orgánicas* are superior to ordinary laws in the juridical hierarchy and regulate, among other subjects, the development of fundamental rights and public freedoms, as set out in Art. 81 of the Constitution.

[9] Agreement on Teaching and Cultural Affairs, 3rd January 1979, available at http://spcp.prf.cuni.cz/dokument/esp4a.htm (Last visit 23 January 2023).

and publicly-funded private schools to received religious education, as long as the exercise of this right does not contravene an institution's own nature.

On some occasions, the parents' right to choose religious and moral education for their children in compliance with their convictions has not enjoyed the same level of protection as set out by the Strasbourg Court in Folgero[10] and Zengin.[11]

Another important aspect of freedom of teaching is the academic freedom (the so-called *libertad de cátedra*), which refers to the freedom of expression of teachers and lecturers in their academic positions. This freedom is not contained in art. 27 CE, but in art. 20 CE, alongside the right to freedom of expression and information.[12] This article states that its exercise must respect fundamental rights of others and particularly the protection of youth and childhood, amongst other rights. While the content of this right has not been developed through a specific legal instrument (Ley Orgánica), its coverage and limits have been clarified by the Constitutional Court.

This freedom, in its original understanding, is derived from the need to protect freedom of expression of university lecturers before any state coercion in light of their relationship with the State in the public teaching sector. Therefore, initially the only holders of this right were university lecturers.

The Constitutional Court, in its Judgment 5/1981, defined the academic freedom (libertad de cátedra) as follows: 'it is a freedom against public authorities, the content of which is defined by the specific characteristics of the teaching post or *cátedra,* and such a position entitles the teacher to enjoy such a freedom.' As the Court observed later on in its Judgment 179/1996, *libertad de cátedra* is undoubtedly a continuation of the ideological freedom of teachers and their right to convey, freely, their thoughts, ideas, and opinions in relation to the subjects which are the scope of their teaching.

The Constitution of 1931 first recognised in article 48 the academic freedom which led to its application to all teachers in the state educational sector. However, this freedom currently refers to all teachers, irrespective of their levels of teaching, and regardless of the relationships between their teaching and research.

In any event, the exercise of this right depends on both the level of teaching and the nature of educational institutions as state or private, as recognised by the Constitutional Court in its Judgment 5/1981. Consequently, in state schools, this freedom has a negative dimension which empowers teachers to reject any attempt to teach in accord with particular ideological stances. From this point of view, "libertad de cátedra" is incompatible with an official faith or ideological position.

In private educational institutions, the aforementioned Judgment of the Constitutional Court declared that the existence of an ethos does not obligate teachers to

[10] ECtHR Judgment (GC) Folgero v. Norway, 29 June, 2007. Available at http://hudoc.echr.coe.int/eng?i=001-81356

[11] ECtHR Judgment Zengin v. Turkey, 9 October 2007. Available at http://hudoc.echr.coe.int/eng?i=001-82580.

[12] Article 20 of the Spanish Constitution reads, in relevant part, as follows: "1. The following rights are recognised and protected: [...] the right to Libertad de cátedra (academic freedom)[...] These freedoms are limited by respect for the rights recognised in this Title, by the legal provisions implementing it, and especially by the right to honour, to privacy, to personal reputation and to the protection of youth and childhood."

promote it actively or to teach with a view toward indoctrination. Further, teachers are not expected to subordinate scientific rigor to a particular ethos. However, such exercise must be compatible with the freedom of a school with a particular ethos and from that point of view any direct or indirect attacks to such an ethos is not acceptable. In this context, the Court considered that teachers in general can carry out their activities in the way they deem appropriate.[13]

The academic freedom also has a positive dimension which refers to the determination of the content of teaching and its methodology. This freedom is wider in higher education, because in the lower levels of schooling educators must respect the minimal content of teaching as established by relevant educational authorities.

In any event, the positive content is not that generous to allow these professionals to teach in a manner which is completely in accordance with their convictions and subject to no limitation. More precisely, in state schools, the teaching activities must respect the principle of state neutrality which requires the rejection of ideological indoctrination because this is the only possible way to respect the freedom of families who have decided to provide their children with a non-biased education and therefore have chosen not to send their children to schools with particular ideological stances. Conversely, in private centres the academic freedom is as complete as the freedom of teachers in state schools but its boundaries has set by the school's ethos. The Constitutional Court in its Judgment 5/1981, rightly acknowledged that 'the limiting factor of the ethos will be more significant in relation to purely educational and formative aspects of the teaching, and less relevant with regard to the mere transmission of knowledge, which is obviously an area in which the legitimate demands of teaching provide very limited room for different ethos.'

2.3 Constitutional Inspiring Principles in Education

Setting this aside, a reference should be made to some general principles of the Spanish constitutional system that have a direct impact on the exercise of some education rights. In particular, the principle of religious neutrality must be highlighted. This principle is recognized by Article 16.3 CE, which states that no religious denomination may have an official status. As a result, the traditional model of Catholic confessionalism was abandoned and in its place a positively separatist system was set up. Such a framework prohibits any intermingling of religious and State functions and when it comes to education rights it requires State to abstain from supporting any religious belief in the providing education.

As indicated in its Judgment 5/1981, the Constitutional Court wrote that in a juridical and political system based on pluralism, ideological, and religious freedom of individuals and the non-confessional nature of the State, all public institutions, but in particular those focused on teaching, must necessarily be ideologically neutral. This neutrality does not prevent these schools from supporting religious activities in

[13] See Fundamento jurídico 10.

order to enable parents to choose religious and formal education for their children in conformity with their own convictions according to art. 27.3 CE.

Consequently, neutrality must be observed by all teachers working in state schools. This requirement imposes a duty on teachers to renounce any type of ideological indoctrination because this is the only possible way to make teaching compatible with the freedom of families who have chosen not to send their children to schools with explicit ideological stances.

In relation to state schools, religious neutrality is not in itself an ideology. The exercise of the religious freedom of employees is shaped by both the safeguard of the legitimate aims of education as well as the respect for the right to religious and ideological freedom enjoyed by the members of the educational community. Among the members of the community, pupils, who should never be subject to any sort of ideological indoctrination by their teachers, must receive proper attention. Consequently, the observance of specified religious practices is possible as long as these do not involve unfair or excessive inconvenience for educational centres, particularly in their internal running and organisation.

3 Major Legal Developments

Both the right to education and freedom of teaching have been developed by different Organic Laws which have been successively enacted as a result of changes within Government and Parliament.

3.1 Freedom to Establish Teaching Centres

The Spanish Constitution recognizes in article 27.6 the free establishment of teaching centres applicable to both natural and juridical persons as long as they respect constitutional principles. This provision was developed by article 21 of the Organic Law 8/1985 on the right to education (hereinafter LODE) (State Official Bulletin 1985) which recognises that all natural or juridical persons of private nature and Spanish nationality have the freedom to create private teaching institutions within the parameters recognised by both the Spanish Constitution and the remaining legal framework.

From this background article 108 of the Organic Law 2/2006, on Education (State Official Bulletin 2020a, b) (hereinafter LOE) distinguishes three different types of educational institutions: state institutions, the holders of which are public administrations; private schools, which belong to natural or juridical persons; and publicly-subsidised private schools, which are private, but are under the umbrella of legal agreements with public administrations (Guardia Hernández 2019).

With regard to the freedom to create teaching centres, it the Organic Law 5/1980, on the statute of teaching centres (LOECE) (State Official Bulletin 1980), repealed is also crucial. The Constitutional Court confirmed in its Judgement 5/1981, 13th July that it is constitutionally appropriate for a private educational institution to maintain a particular ethos while clarifying the extent to which public authorities can intervene in the administration of institutions funded by public authorities. The Court went on saying that the possibility of adopting a particular ethos is a faculty which goes certainly far beyond the freedom of enterprise which is recognised in article 38 of the Spanish Constitution.[14] At the same time, the Constitutional Court clarified that the terms 'own character,' and 'ethos' are synonymous. However, it did not provide a definition of them, although it highlighted that it is the expression of the ideological character of a school which also comprises the pedagogical and educational aspects of a particular institution.

Consequently, it can be affirmed that both fully private and publicly subsidised private schools are entitled to establish their own ethos as a direct consequence of their freedom of establishment. Even though this faculty is not explicitly mentioned in the Constitution, it is a right with direct constitutional protection because an ethos is nothing different from the practical expression of the freedom of teaching, and it is a necessary tool which facilitates educational pluralism. The LOE recognizes in article 115 that the holders of private institutions, irrespective of being financially subsidised, are entitled to establish their "own character".

In any event, setting up an educational ethos has a double dimension: a positive and a negative one. The positive dimension facilitates the freedom of teaching while enabling parents to choose for their children a school the ethos of which is in accordance with their personal convictions. The negative dimension becomes a limit to the fundamental rights of others members of the educational community, particularly to the so called "Libertad de cátedra" of the teacher. The limitations that are derivative from the ethos are more significant in relation to the purely educational aspects of teaching and less relevant in relation to other aspects related to the mere transmission of knowledge (Rebato Peño 2021).

Article 27.7 CE states that teachers, parents and students, when appropriate, will take part in the management of those educational institutions which are financially supported by public administrations, in compliance with the relevant legal provisions. In consequence, insofar as they are financially supported, there is an entitlement on the part of the community to be involved in their control and administration. This right clearly gives rise to limitations on the holder of the centre in the governance of these schools and stands in stark contrast to the position of schools which are completely private. These rights to participate are implemented through two different governing bodies: a School Board and a Council of Teachers (art. 54 LODE).

The School Boards are composed of the school's director, three representatives of the holders of the institution, four teacher representatives, four parent representatives, two student representatives, and a representative of the support staff.

[14] Article 38 of the Spanish Constitution reads as follows: "Free enterprise is recognised within the framework of a market economy. The public authorities shall guarantee and protect its exercise and the safeguarding of productivity in accordance with the demands of the economy in general and, as the case may be, of its planning."

The functions of School Boards are those embedded in art. 57 of the LODE, including amongst others, to take part in the appointment of the director of the school as well as in the selection of teachers and in the process of admission of students; to approve the budget of the educational institution in accordance with the funds allocated by the public administration; to propose, to the relevant public administration, an authorisation to charge some families for complementary activities; etc.

It is important to highlight that the School Board cannot alter the ethos of an educational institution. In this regard, the Constitutional Court, in its Judgment 77/1985, 27th June declared that respect for the ethos is within the core of the right of the holder to establish and govern an educational center.[15] Consequently, whatever the circumstances are, and whatever use is made of the powers of the various branches of the educational community, this fundamental content can never be set aside.

3.2 *Teaching of Religion*

The unique position of teachers of religion in state schools must be highlighted. Following art. 27.3 of the Spanish Constitution, the religion can be taught within the state school system; this has been implemented via the establishment of agreements of cooperation between the State and some religious denominations: the Catholic Church, and three other communities: Protestants, Jewish and Muslims.

The legal position of teachers of religion in public schools is developed by the Third Additional Provision of the LOE, according to which 'teachers, who without being civil servants, are in charge of the teaching of religion in state schools, will be subject to Employment Law, and their status will be according to the Workers' Statute. The selection of these teachers is based on objective criteria, namely: equality, merit, and capacity. They will receive equivalent salaries to those subject to temporary working arrangements at the same educational levels.

In any event, although the employer will be the public administration, the appointment will come from the religious authorities and will be automatically renewed every year. Spanish case law has regarded the employment position of these teachers as a special one because the signatures of the contracts by relevant administrations who will be responsible for the payment of the salary and social security contribution, require the prior appointment by relevant religious authorities. Contracts, either on full or a part-time bases, depending on a school's specific needs, are to be determined by the relevant public administration. Any retraction of the appointment by the religious authorities must be done in accordance with the law.

The contracts of these teachers are indefinite, but they can be terminated, if the relevant religious authorities revoke the declarations of suitability. Such revocations must necessarily be in accord with the law and due process.

The removal of some teachers of the Roman Catholic faith by the relevant ecclesiastical authorities because their private lives were not in accordance with Catholic

[15] Fundamento Jurídico Noveno.

doctrine (Otaduy 2013) has been particularly problematic. The most well-known case involved a priest, a celibate, whose bishop withdrew his appointment after a regional newspaper published a report of him having a wife and five children. In the write up, the priest made statements completely incompatible with the doctrine of the Catholic Church, particularly in terms of sexual morality and contraception.

The Constitutional Court, in its Judgment 128/2007, 4th June, declared that the actions of ecclesiastical authorities are subject to jurisdictional control where they impact on the fundamental rights of teachers. The Court found that the bishop's retraction of the priest's proposal, as a teacher of Catholic religion, did not constitute a disproportionate breach of his fundamental rights to religious freedom and ideological freedom in connection with the freedom of expression. The Court added that the priest's removal was justified out of respect for the religious freedom of the Catholic Church, on the one hand, and the rights of parents to the religious education of their children on the other.

As the Constitutional Court affirmed 'it would be simply unreasonable if the teaching of religion in schools were carried out without taking into consideration, as a criterion in the process of selection of the teachers, the religious convictions of those people who put themselves forward to attain one of these positions, as this is a conscious guarantee of the right of religious freedom, in both its external and collective dimension.'[16]

This case was finally decided by the Grand Chamber of the European Court of Human Rights in Fernández Martínez v Spain (Valero 2014). In rejecting the applicant's appeal, the Strasbourg Court decided that the dismissal of the teacher of Catholic religion was not a disproportionate restriction of his private life. In fact, the Court explained that the teacher was subject to particular obligations of loyalty due to his membership in the Church he voluntarily embraced and which should have been manifested through a coherent connection between his classroom teaching and life style.

The Court concluded that the breach of these obligations entitled the Church, in the exercise of its right to autonomy, to dismiss the applicant as a teacher of religion in order to avoid the risk of scandal and maintain the—credibility of the Catholic Church.

In relation to the position of teachers of religion in educational institutions, there have been controversies about it in terms of their right to vote and to be elected for a School Board, as well as their entitlement to be eligible as directors of a school. The Supreme Court resolved the first question in its Judgment of 1st February 1990, recognising the teachers' right to the full participation in the designation of the members of the School Boards. Later, the Ministerial Order of 21st November 1993 accepted the right of religion teachers to participate in the governing bodies of particular schools.

Yet, as far as their entitlements to be elected as directors of educational institutions, both the Supreme Court's Judgment of 13th October 1987 and the Order

[16] Fundamento jurídico quinto.

of the Constitutional Court 47/1990, 20th March, acknowledged the constitutional legitimacy of non-eligibility, due to the temporary status of their working agreement. Still, from the enactment of the *Decreto 696/2007*, the employment relationship of teachers within public administrations has been accorded permanent status, and, as a result, people in such positions are now eligible to become directors (State Official Bulletin 2007).

3.3 Teachers' Equality and Non-Discrimination on Religious Grounds

Article 14 of the Constitution proclaims the equality of all Spanish citizens before the law, while declaring that discrimination on the grounds of race, sex, opinion, or religion, is unconstitutional. Following the decisions of the Spanish Constitutional Court, equality does not mean uniformity. In other words, differences in treatment are legitimate when they have objective and reasonable justifications and are proportionate to the aims they pursue.

In state schools, teachers are civil servants who are appointed on merit and capacity basis. The Royal Legislative Decree 5/2015, on the basic legal framework of civil servants (State Official Bulletin 2015a, b), recognises the rights and obligations of public employees. In contrast, in private schools, irrespective of being publicly subsidised, teachers are subject to the Worker's Statute and specific collective agreements (State Official Bulletin 2015a, b).

The teachers of both state and private educational institutions are entitled to religious freedom which allows them to profess religious beliefs and to hold them before third parties while rejecting interference by the State and any other social groups. However, the exercise of this freedom in education is conditioned by two elements.

First and foremost, its exercise must be compatible with the general aims of education, as affirmed by art. 27.2 CE. Second, it depends on the nature of an educational institution, whether state or private, since the exercise of religious freedom must be weighted with neutrality of state schools and the respect for the ethos of private educational institutions.

It must be pointed out that schools with a particular ethos are regarded as "empresas de tendencia"[17] which enjoy a wider degree of protection to guarantee that they can fulfil their goals when developing their activities. In consequence their holders are entitled to subject their employees to specific duties of loyalty that in case of contravention can lead to the dismissal of the teacher.

Moreover, officials in these schools are entitled to hire or to dismiss employees according to their religious beliefs without receiving the risk of sanction for employment discrimination. In this context, a mention must be made of the content of

[17] See Constitutional Court Judgment 38/2007, 15th February, *fundamento jurídico 10*; Constitutional Court Judgment 106/1996, 12th June, *fundamento jurídico tercero.*

European Directive 2000/78 by virtue of which religious denominations and faith-based organizations may take into account the religion of a worker as a legitimate and justified professional requirement, by reason of the nature of their activities or the context in which they are carried out.

In this way, a school with a religious ethos may require its teachers to profess the faith with which it identifies. They may opt to refrain from hiring those who belong to other religions or who have no religion, provided that the religious belief has a direct bearing on the activity that they are required to undertake.

In any case, the provisions of EU Directive 2000/78 allow religious denominations and ethos-based organizations to subject their workers to obligations of loyalty as long as they are proportionate to the fulfillment of the purposes that inspire the activity of the employer. In other words, in order to be acceptable such obligations must operate as an essential, legitimate and justified professional requirements in view of the nature of the activity performed or the context in which it is provided. Needless to say that the EU Directive 2000/78 applies to the educational sector, which means that denominational schools are considered as ethos-based organizations (*empresas de tendencia)* that are entitled to discriminate against employees by subjecting them to heightened duties or loyalty with respect to their doctrine or ethos.

In this context it is important to make reference to a remarkable Judgment of the European Court of Justice: IR v. JQ (2018) (Cañamares Arribas 2018). In this case the Court decided a preliminary ruling raised by a German court in the context of a labour procedure initiated by a physician, head of the internal medicine service at a Catholic hospital who was dismissed for not having respected the indissolubility of canonical marriage as he celebrated a second civil marriage after being divorce from his previous canonical marriage before the civil courts. The Court of Justice considered that the dismissal was discriminatory since adherence to the notion of marriage advocated by the Catholic Church does not appear to be necessary for the promotion of the employer's ethos due to the importance of the occupational activities carried out by the physician, namely the provision of medical advice and care in a hospital setting.

As to this issue, the European Court of Human Rights in *Siebenhaar v. Germany* (2011)[18] decided on the possible discrimination suffered by a nursery school teacher who was fired for belonging to a different religious denomination from that of the employer. The Court stressed that teachers in schools with a particular ethos are subject to obligations of loyalty which are more demanding than those that can be imposed on professionals working in other contexts. The Court explained that in this case the duties of loyalty were acceptable as long as they were proportionate to the aims pursed by the employer according to his ethos. In this case, the fact that a kindergarten teacher who belonged to a Protestant Church was, at the same time, a member of another denomination, was regarded as a sufficiently powerful reason to justify her dismissal on the basis that this diminished her credibility in the eyes of the parents of students and the wider general public.

[18] Judgment Siebenhaar v. Germany, 3 February 2011. Available (only in French) at: https://hudoc.echr.coe.int/eng#{"itemid":["001-103236"]}.

From this point of view, the main difference is that the teacher that works in a private centre is obliged to respect the ethos of the school meanwhile those who work in a public institution are bound by the principle of state religious neutrality. Explicit and implicit attacks on such ethos are prohibited and such conduct could lead to the dismissal of teachers.[19]

Finally, in the Spanish experience there have been situations in which the holders of educational institutions have exceeded their power and have gone beyond legitimate requirements in relation to the religious profiles of their employees. The decision of the Supreme Court of Justice of Valencia, on 30th July 2015[20] should be highlighted. In this case, the Court considered the dismissal of a teacher of Spanish Language and Literature as void because the reasons offered by school officials had only a weak link with the defence and promotion of the institution's ethos.

4 Emerging Issues in Education Law

4.1 Funding for Public and Non-public Schools

Closely related to the right to establish educational institutions and to the parent's rights to choose the religious and moral education of their children the state funding of private institutions, mentioned by article 27.9 CE, is also a key element of the framework, as it enables those citizens who could not afford private education to provide their children a religious or moral education that cannot be obtain in public schools because of the principle of religious neutrality.[21]

However, the Constitutional Court, in its judgment 77/1985, 27th June, warned that this constitutional disposition cannot be interpreted in a manner which grants the legislature a broad range of discretion as far as the financial support is concerned. Further, neither can the Constitution be read as there is a general constitutional duty to support every single educational institution since the legislative delegation implies that such financial support must be qualified in light of the constitutional principles and values contained in it.

Developing this constitutional provision, the LODE established a system of financial agreements (so-called conciertos) which could be adopted by private educational institutions meeting a list of requirements. Moreover, the LODE declares that the conditions and limits of the financial support must be articulated by giving due weight to educational rights and freedoms as well as the principle of equality.

The basic elements of the system of financial agreements are currently contained in the LOE that have been recently amended by the Organic Law 3/2020 (hereinafter LOMLOE) (State Official Bulletin 2020a, b). In accordance with its article 116, all

---

[19] Constitutional Court Judgment 47/1985, 27th March.

[20] Judgment of the Superior Court of Justice of Valencia, 30 July 2015.

[21] Article 27.9 CE reads as follows: "The public authorities shall give aid to teaching establishments which meet the requirements to be laid down by the law."

private centres can join this system as long as they satisfy the schooling needs of a certain area. This reference, added by the LOMLOE involves an important limitation on the possibility of making financial agreements, since authorities will deny this possibility when there are places available in public centres. In consequence, the new regulation presents a significant impact on freedom of education as it will not allow parents to send their children to a private subsidized school when there are places available in a public centre.

Apart from these considerations, this article provides a list of preferential criteria for the establishment of such agreements, that includes the following: those that serve school populations in economically deprived communities, those whose work contributes particular pedagogical interest for the educational system, those that promote local schooling and those that are constituted and operate under a cooperative regime.

As a counterpart to the signing of a financial agreement with the educational administration, the LOE establishes in its art. 88 that "to guarantee the possibility of enrolling all students without discrimination for socioeconomic reasons, in no case may public or private but subsidized institutions take funds from families receiving free education, impose on families the obligation to make contributions to foundations or associations or establish mandatory services, associated with education, that require financial contributions from the families of the students."

However, in light of the provisions of art. 51 LODE, extracurricular activities and school services are excluded from these express prohibitions, as these will be voluntary in any case. Conversely activities that are considered *necessary* for educational development must be scheduled and carried out in such a way that does not impose discrimination for economic reasons.[22]

Financial agreements, though, brings about a number of obligations for schools in relation to the admission of pupils, the composition and functions of a School Board (art. 54 LODE), and the selection of the teachers which must respect the principles of merit and capacity (art. 60 LODE). The establishment of agreements does not prevent private schools from adopting an educational ethos, but such ethos cannot not be incompatible with the respect for freedom of conscience, which in case of religious inspired institutions means that any confessional activity must have an elective nature.

In relation to the renewal or termination of a financial agreement, once its allotted term has expired, it can be renewed at the discretion of the school. Consequently, such a renovation is a right of the institution and cannot be denied by the public administration as long as it meets the relevant requirements, provided that school authorities have not acted in a way justifying its termination, as set out in art. 62 LODE. In this regard, it is important to consider that according to the LOMLOE the administration can terminate the agreements with private schools when there are places available in public centers in a certain area.

[22] The decision of the Superior Court of Justice of Andalucía of 17th October 2013, which confirms the sanction imposed to a publicly-funded private school because of its request of a donation of 20 euros every three months, is particularly interesting in this field.

In any case, in situations in which these agreements are terminated, educational administrations are bound to take the necessary actions in order to provide for students who wish to continue under a free system of provision (art. 63 LODE).

4.2 Students Admission in Publicly-Subsidised Centres

Article 84.3 LOE declares that when it comes to the admission of students there should be no discrimination on grounds of birth, race, sex, religion, opinion, or any other condition or personal or social circumstance. In this regard is important to make reference to the Organic Law 8/2013, on the improvement of the quality of education (hereinafter LOMCE) (State Official Bulletin 2013) which modified that article by declaring that the division of teaching by genders was not discriminatory (Carazo Liébana 2022) 'as long as the teaching is delivered in accordance with Article 2 of the Convention against Discrimination in Education 1960.'

This disposition added that under no circumstances the election of one gender education could give rise to a less favourable treatment of families, students, and educational institutions, or a disadvantage in terms of agreements with educational authorities about any other aspects of schooling.

The Constitutional Court declared this model of education fully constitutional in its Judgment 31/2018, 10th April, by saying "From a strictly literal perspective, the separation of students by gender during the schooling process constitutes a legal differentiation between boys and girls, specifically in terms of access to an educational establishment. However, this practice corresponds to a pedagogical model or method flowing from certain ideals that conceive that this approach is more effective than others. Given that the Constitution recognizes the freedom of education (art. 27.1 CE), any educational model that aims at the full development of the human personality and respect for the principles and fundamental rights and freedoms that recognizes the art. 27.2 CE must be deemed lawful."

The Court continued that single sex education is a pedagogical approach voluntarily adopted by the educational establishments, and is the free choice of parents opting for such institutions, and, in some instances, also by the students attending. As such, it is part of the ethos or educational character of the schools that opt for such an educational formula. At this point, it recalled that, according to the doctrine established in its Judgment 5/1981, the right to establish an ethos is not limited to religious and moral aspects of the educational process, and could therefore logically include establishing single sex education.

Aware that the right to set a particular ethos is not absolute, the Court maintained that it is clear that "it would not be acceptable if its content is incompatible with fundamental rights or if, even without a direct violation of such protections, any policy fails to comply with the obligation, derived from art. 27.2 of the Constitution, to ensure that the education provided has as its core objective the full development of the human personality, including respect for democratic principles, social harmony and coexistence, as well as fundamental rights and freedoms." Finally, the

Court considered that it was not the case of an ethos of single sex education, as this model of education is not per se discriminatory, provided that, as set out in the 1960 Convention, the conditions and teachings within schools for each gender were equal and comparable. It therefore concluded that "if any undue difference in treatment existed, it would only be attributable to the school in which it occurred, and would not be attributable to the model itself. Therefore, the premise from which the appellants start, that single sex education implies discrimination, is not fulfilled." (Báez Serrano 2019).

Although, as affirmed, the Court declared this model fully compatible with the Spanish Constitution, the modification introduced by the LOMLOE has meant that not only has any reference to single sex education in art. 84.3 LOE been removed, also, it has also been indirectly declared prohibited, as the new law states that the regulations governing access to public and private but subsidized institutions: "will have the necessary measures to avoid the segregation of students for socioeconomic reasons or any other nature". This sweeping ban on segregation undoubtedly includes divisions between male and female students. The consequence, therefore, is that the financial agreements with those private institutions that have opted for a single sex education will be terminated.

4.3 Students' Free Exercise of Religion

Article 8 of the *Organic Law 1/1996*, of Juridical Protection of Minors, recognises that minors have a right to freedom of expression allowing them to publish and disseminate their opinions (State Official Bulletin 1996). The exercise of this right can be subjected to the restrictions contemplated by the law in order to guarantee the respect for the rights of others and the protection of security, health, moral and public order. Further, this right faces a specific limit in the protection of intimacy and images of the minors.

In the educational sector, the right to freedom of speech can be exercised as long as it does not harm the rights of the other members of the educational community; there must also be assurances that the expression does not breach the due institutional respect in conformity with the constitutional principles and rights. It must be pointed out that in publicly-subsidised private schools, pupils are bound to respect the ethos of their schools, and defamatory or insulting statements against such ethos are unacceptable.

In relation to religious dress, educational legislation does not prohibit the use of religious symbols by students. There have been some conflicts triggered by the use of the Islamic veil that, in general, have been decided at the administrative level. The only judicial pronouncement so far has been the Judgmente 35/2012, 25th January, of the *Juzgado de lo Contencioso-Administrativo de Madrid.* In this case, parents of a Muslim student unsuccessfully challenged the actions of educational authorities of the Region of Madrid upholding the decision of different secondary schools that forbade the use of this attire in their premises. The regional authorities decided to move the Muslim student from one school to another within this region in order to avoid any prohibition adopted by the School Board.

The Superior Court of Justice of Madrid, in a widely criticised decision (Cañamares 2012), based on previous decisions of the Court of Strasbourg, found that the prohibition to wear the Islamic veil did not amount to a breach of the girl's religious freedom. The Court reached this conclusion because authorities met the requirements established by the European Convention on Human Rights: the prohibition was recognised in the internal regulations of the school and it was necessary to protect the safety and fundamental rights of others in the school premises.

With regard to dietary requirements the Agreement with the Islamic Commission of Spain, declares in article 14 that 'the food [...] of Muslim pupils in state and publicly-funded private schools, who request it, will be adapted to the Islamic religious precepts, as well as fasting dietary requirements.'

Such accommodation is required from the public administration unless it causes harm or undue pressures on the general delivery of the food. Despite the fact that all other Agreements do not refer to this question, in order to respect the religious freedom of the students of all other faiths, the same response would have been expected.

Some controversies have emerged over observance of dietary requirements of a particular faith. An example of such a situation was present in the decision of the Superior Court of Justice of Madrid of 16 June 2015 which rejected the request of a Muslim student for due protection of his religious beliefs in the school dining room. The Court declared that this service was voluntary and that the student was free to look for another school which was more responsive to his requests.

5 Conclusion

The division of competences between the State and regional authorities in Spain, as acknowledged by the 1978 Constitution, requires the State to approve the basic norms for the development of educational rights, while regional authorities are in charge of the development of the applicable legislation within their respective territories. This has given rise to situations in which the implementation of national rules has not been homogeneous throughout Spain.

At times, required legislation from regional authorities has been subject to delays for a variety of reasons, including political friction, a situation bound to continue unless the underpinning national legislation is the result of a strong parliamentary consensus. Apart from these issues, the exercise of educational rights by different bodies has been controversial. As a result, teachers have been subjected to indirect discrimination on religious or ideological grounds when school authorities have gone beyond their entitlements in expecting their employees to conform with the ethos in their schools.

To sum up, generally speaking, the exercise of educational rights is in good health in Spain. However, the new Organic Law 3/2020 has proved quite controversial due to its significant impact on some aspects of freedom of teaching. In particular, because it unnecessarily limits the possibility of private centers to establish financial agreements, by making them conditional upon the absence of schooling needs in a certain area. Secondly, because it leads to the termination of financial agreements with those educational institutions which segregate on the basis of sex, with the consequence that students are forced to be transferred to a private but subsidized institution, or if there are no places available, to attend a public school.

Yet, selected aspects of these freedoms still must be carefully examined, particularly in relation to the exercise of religious and ideological convictions of schools. Some of the conflicts which have been described in this chapter come from the wording of Acts of Parliament which were approved by different political parties in recent years, with little parliamentary consensus, and worryingly, without a proper understanding of the needs of minorities. On other occasions, problems were generated by the poor application of the rules by the relevant educational authorities. This misguided approach to the real and effective exercise of freedoms in the educational field is ironic insofar as this arena is one in which it is important learn to respect the exercise of fundamental rights by others.

Acknowledgements The author is extremely grateful to Prof Javier Garcia Oliva, at the University of Manchester, for his generous help in editing the final version of this work. Any remaining infelicities are of course entirely my own.

References

Agreement on Teaching and Cultural Affairs, 3rd January 1979, http://spcp.prf.cuni.cz/dokument/esp4a.html. Accessed 23 Jan 2023

Báez Serrano R (2019) Hacia la consolidación de la constitucionalidad de la educación diferenciada. A propósito de la sentencia del Tribunal Constitucional 31/2018. Revista De Derecho Politico 105:251–278

Cañamares S (2012) La inclusión de los otros: la simbología religiosa en el espacio público. La inclusión de los otros: símbolos y espacios de la multiculturalidad, Ed. Comares, 99–120.M

Cañamares Arribas S (2009) El control jurisdiccional de la autonomía de la Iglesia católica en la designación de los profesores de religion. In: Revista Española de Derecho Canónico, vol 66. Madrid, pp 275–292

Cañamares Arribas S (2018) Obligaciones de lealtad y discriminación religiosa de los trabajadores de las confesiones religiosas y empresas de tendencia: Sentencia del Tribunal de Justicia de la Unión Europea de 11 de septiembre de 2018, asunto C–68/17: IR v. JQ.La Ley Unión Europea 64

Carazo Liébana MJ (2022) La educación diferenciada por sexos: ¿discriminación o libertad de enseñanza.In:Revista General de Derecho Canónico y Derecho Eclesiástico del Estado, vol 58, Madrid, p 89

CEF (2022) Legal: Revista práctica de derecho. Comentarios y Casos Prácticos 255:81–110

ECJ Sentence IR v. JQ Case C-68/17 (2018) Available at https://www.curia.europa.eu. Accessed 23 Jan 2023

ECtHR Judgment (GC) Folgero v. Norway, 29 June 2007. http://hudoc.echr.coe.int/eng?i=001-81356. Accessed 23 Jan 2023

ECtHR Judgment Zengin v. Turkey, 9 October 2007. http://hudoc.echr.coe.int/eng?i=001-82580. Accessed 23 Jan 2023
Guardia Hernández JJ (2019) "Marco constitucional de la enseñanza privada española sostenida con fondos públicos: recorrido histórico y perspectivas a futuro" Estudios constitucionales. Revista Del Centro De Estudios Constitucionales, Año 17(1):321–362
Judgment Siebenhaar v. Germany, 3 February 2011. https://hudoc.echr.coe.int/eng#{"itemid": ["001-103236"]}. Accessed 23 Jan 2023
López-Sidro A (2007) Dimensión colectiva del derecho de libertad religiosa en los centros docentes públicos: la designación de los profesores de religion. Revista General de Derecho Canónico y Eclesiástico del Estado14:90. http://www.iustel.com. Accessed 23 Jan 2023
Martínez-Torrón J (2009) La cuestión del velo islámico en la jurisprudencia de Estrasburgo. Derecho y Religión, pp 87–109
Martínez-Torrón J (2013) Religion and law in Spain. International encyclopaedia of laws: religion. Wolters Kluwert, Madrid, pp 17–33
Otaduy J (2013) La idoneidad de los profesores de religión católica y su desarrollo jurisprudencial en España. Estudios Eclesiásticos 88(347):849–871
Puppinck G (2012) El "principio de autonomía" de la Iglesia Católica ante el Tribunal Europeo de Derechos Humanos. El caso Fernández Martínez contra España.Revista General de Derecho Canónico y de Derecho Eclesiástico del Estado 28. http://www.iustel.com. Accessed 23 Jan 2023
Rebato Peño ME (2021) Los límites del ideario o carácter propio de los centros educativos de titularidad privada en el marco de la libertad de enseñanza. In: Revorio D, Vidal Prado C (eds) Enseñar la constitución, educar en democracia / coord. F. J. pp 29–56
State Official Bulletin (1980) de Libertad Religiosa, Ley Orgánica 7/1980. https://www.boe.es/diario_boe/. Accessed 10 Dec 2022
Spanish Offcial Bulletin (1980) De junio, por la que se regula el Estatuto de Centros Escolares. Ley Orgánica 5/1980, de 19
Spanish Offcial Bulletin (1985) Reguladora del Derecho a la Educación. Ley Orgánica 8/1985, de 3 de julio
Spanish Offcial Bulletin (1996) De enero, de protección jurídica del menor, de modificación del Código Civil y de la Ley de Enjuiciamiento Civil. Ley Orgánica 1/1996, de 15
Spanish Offcial Bulletin (2000) sobre derechos y libertades de los extranjeros en España y su integración social.Ley Orgánica 4/2000, de 11 de enero
Spanish Offcial Bulletin (2006) Ley Orgánica 2/2006, del Derecho a la Educación
Spanish Offcial Bulletin (2007) De junio, por el que se regula la relación laboral de los profesores de religión prevista en la disposición adicional tercera de la Ley Orgánica 2/2006, de 3 de mayo, de Educación. Real Decreto 696/2007, de 1
Spanish Offcial Bulletin (2013) De 9 de diciembre, para la mejora de la calidad educative.Ley Orgánica 8/2013
Spanish Offcial Bulletin (2015) De octubre, por el que se aprueba el texto refundido de la Ley del Estatuto Básico del Empleado Público. Real Decreto Legislativo 5/2015, de 30
Spanish Offcial Bulletin (2015) Por el que se aprueba el texto refundido de la Ley del Estatuto de los Trabajadores. Real Decreto Legislativo 2/2015, 23 Oct
Spanish Offcial Bulletin (2020) De diciembre, por la que se modifica la Ley Orgánica 2/2006, de 3 de mayo, de Educación. Ley Orgánica 3/2020, de 29.
Spanish Offcial Bulletin (2020) De diciembre, por la que se modifica la Ley Orgánica 2/2006, de 3 de mayo, de Educación.Ley Orgánica 3/2020, de 29
Valero MJ (2014) Autonomía institucional de las confesiones religiosas y derecho al respeto de la vida privada y familiar en Estrasburgo: la sentencia de la Gran Sala del TEDH Fernández Martínez c. España, Revista General de Derecho Canónico y de Derecho Eclesiástico del Estado 36

The Right to Education in Sweden

David Ryffé

1 A Brief Introduction to Rights as a Theoretical Framework

The following chapter deals with the *right to education* in a Swedish context; the system, the rules of law and also touching upon the pedagogical outcome. Regarding rights in general, however, there is a reluctance to clarify what one de facto mean by a *right* and how these rights differ from other legal rules (Dworkin 1975). Since the concept of rights is central in the following account, a brief introduction to rights follows below.

Most fundamental rights in Sweden follow from the constitution, which gives them a special hierarchical status among legal rules.[1] With regard to the right to education, the provision in the constitution is supplemented with provisions in the European Convention of Human Rights (ECHR), as well as with other international convention texts, and a clarification and development in the Education Act.[2] This gives the right to education a special status also among rights.

However, a right differs from a common legal rule on several levels. Although all legislation, at least within the *rechtsstaat*, has a strong connection to the political dimension in that political assemblies decide on the origin of the law, the right has an even more politicized position. One can argue that a right is an expression of political will in legal form, or as Foucault has put it: "...a right in its real effects is much more linked to attitudes and patterns of behavior than to legal formulations." (Foucault

[1] See Instrument of Government (1974, 152), Chap. 2, Sect. 1–25.

[2] Instrument of Government (1974, 152), Chap. 2, Sect. 18, European Convention on Human Rights, first additional protocol, Art. 2, Convention on the Rights of the Child, Art 26, Education Act (2010, 800), Chap. 7, Sect. 3.

D. Ryffé (✉)
University of Gothenburg, Gothenburg, Sweden
e-mail: david.ryffe@law.gu.se

C. J. Russo and L. Ma (eds.), *A Comparative Analysis of Systems of Education Law*,
https://doi.org/10.1007/978-981-97-1052-2_17

1997, p. 157). According to Foucault, a right thus also goes beyond the political sphere since the emergence of rights is usually based on the people's demand for an overriding principle to be able to rely on (Foucault 1994, 1997). The first thing to consider when it comes to rights is thus that rights are not only a form of legislation, but also a political expression of will, or aspiration, which in turn is linked to human behavior.

Another aspect of rights one must take into consideration, which relates to both the legal and the political, is the impact of a right when brought up as an argument for why someone should receive the benefit stated by the right. Within the legal sphere, which is mainly represented by courts, although other authorities also have a substantial influence on the right to education in the Swedish context, a right is not always the most fruitful argument. Rights tend to be imprecise, and it is therefore not always possible to predict how a court will interpret the right in a specific case. The Swedish legal philosopher Axel Hägerström (1868–1939), who had a great influence on the legal development of Swedish society, went even further and argued that rights per se are a form of "metaphysics" because they de facto do not "exist" (Olivecrona 1940). The fact that the legislator uses rights, said Hägerström, is partly a tool for duping the masses and it would be more honest to instead establish more precise legal provisions if the intention actually is to achieve what is promised by the state, as concrete legal rules can be more easily applied in court (Glavå and Petrusson 2002).

Another significant element in the characteristics of rights originated from the American lawyer and legal philosopher Wesley Newcomb Hohfeld (1879–1918). Hohfeldt argued that a right is not in fact a right for the individual if it does not correspond to a correlating obligation for the public, or for another individual (Hohfeldt 1917, p. 717). That a legal rule is referred to as a "right" is thus not sufficient, since there must be a responsible party who is obliged to secure the right (Hohfeldt 1917). Rights also have an effect outside the legal sphere and can be understood as a form of political endeavor which legal rules and court decisions must aim at, but both Hägerström and Hohfeldt argues that a right is only to be understood as a de facto right if it grants a benefit and is constituted by law.

When it comes to how the right to education is perceived and practiced by Swedish courts and authorities, the right is rather imprecise since neither the constitution, nor any other legal source, clarify what is included in the right. That is, how *education* is to be understood. But still, as a positive right granted by the state, it is though understood as fundamental one alongside the negative rights (freedoms of opinion).[3] How the right to education is to be interpreted in the Swedish context can to some extent be deduced from the school constitutions as a whole, from the rulings of the courts and from the decisions of the authorities.

[3] Instrument of Government (1974, 152), Chap. 2, Sect. 1.

2 The Nature of the Swedish Legal System in Education

2.1 The "Chain of Command" and the School Authorities

The Swedish school system, from preschool to high school, is managed as a chain where the different links are given different responsibilities. At the top of the chain is the state in the capacity of legislator, but also through the state authorities that issue regulations, carry out inspections, decide cases and provide advice and guidance. In addition, the state also holds real influence by the fact that the state universities control both the teacher and the headmasters training.

The next link in the chain is the principles, who are either municipalities or private entities and who both are financed by public funds and governed by common legislation.[4]

The principal's primary task is to organize the activities overall and give the headmasters the conditions they need to be able to carry out their tasks.[5] The municipalities have very limited standard-setting capacity, but in reality, have great influence over education through their role as employers. It is also the principals who have the overall responsibility for compulsory school pupils completing their schooling and for guaranteeing everyone's right to education.[6]

The headmaster, the third link in the chain, has many of his tasks specified directly in the Education Act and in its supplementary regulations. The headmaster is the educational leader and controls the internal organization and decision making of his unit, but risks being caught between the legislator and the principal in cases where their respective governance does not agree (Svensson 2019).[7] In case of an inspection by the School Inspectorate, the law however always takes precedence over municipality guidelines, through the principle of legality, but going against one's employer can also have consequences, albeit more so for one's personal career.

The fourth link in the chain consists of the teachers, whose mission is primarily educational. What the teachers must teach, i.e., what the right to education actually includes, is governed by course plans and curricula issued by the government and The National Education Agency.

Higher education, in the form of universities and colleges, is more autonomous and regulated by different legislation.[8]

A significant part of the state management of the Swedish school system takes place through various authorities. In terms of legal governance, there are three authorities besides the courts that take a special position in the matter of the school system and, furthermore, what concerns the activities of the universities. The National Education Agency issues regulations in the form of course- and lesson plans and contributes

[4] The Education Act (2010, 800), Chap. 2, Sects. 2 and 5.

[5] The Education Act (2010, 800), Chap. 2, Sects. 8 and 8b.

[6] The Education Act (2010, 800), Chap. 7, Sect. 19a.

[7] The Education Act (2010, 800), Chap. 2, Sect. 10.

[8] The Higher Education Act (1992, 1434) and The Higher Education Ordinance (1993, 100).

to the curricula which are formally issued by the government, and which regulate the content of the various forms of schooling. The Swedish National Agency for Education also issues guidance in the form of, among other things, general advice and comments that indicate how laws and regulations can and should be understood and implemented in practical pedagogy.[9] Even though these general advices are not formally binding, they do in reality have a great impact on how education is organized and how the rules are interpreted (Statsrådsberedningen 1998).

The School Inspectorate has a reviewing role and carries out regular inspections of various preschools, schools, and high schools. The agency is also receiving and following up on reports from guardians and from the public, as well as issue permits for private actors. Since the Education Act states that many issues and decisions within the school cannot be appealed to the court, the School Inspectorate, through its decisions, has a strong normative role regarding how the law is to be interpreted. The School Inspectorate has a counterpart in terms of higher education in the form of the University Chancellor's Office (UKÄ), which has the task of reviewing that universities and colleges comply with legislation and maintain satisfactory quality in education and research.

Another important authority in terms of the state management of the school system is The School System Appeals Board (ÖKN), which takes on the role of a semi-court with a mandate to make decisions on appeals of various forms of decisions made by schools or principals, such as reception in a certain form of school or decisions on special support.[10]

2.2 Preschool

The Swedish preschool has a long tradition but has only in recent years become a pronounced part of the Swedish education system. Preschool can be run either under municipal or private auspices and from having primarily been an "equality institution", in terms of women with younger children being given the opportunity to work on equal terms with men, a curriculum for preschool was introduced in connection with the new Education Act in the year 2011.[11] The activities therefore came to include stated goals in terms of education and teaching, the content of which is specified in the preschool curriculum, which constitutes a binding regulation issued by the government even though de facto authored by the National Board of Education. The curriculum applies equally to all preschools, regardless of whether the preschool is run privately or publicly, and compliance with it is reviewed by the state School Inspectorate and by the municipalities themselves.[12]

---

[9] Ordinance (2015, 1047) with instructions for the National Agency for Education.

[10] The Education Act (2010, 800), Chap. 27, Sects. 1–3.

[11] Curriculum for preschool (Lpfö 18).

[12] The School Inspectorate inspects the municipal (public) preschools in accordance with Chap. 26. Section 3 of the Education Act (2010, 800) and the municipality inspect preschools with private principals according to Chap. 26. Section 4 of the Education Act (2010, 800).

According to the curriculum, education in preschool must lay the foundation for lifelong learning and be based on a holistic view of children and their needs, where care, development and learning form a whole. Furthermore, it is stated that the teaching should stimulate and challenge the children with the curriculum's goals as a point of departure and direction and be based on content that is planned or arises spontaneously because children's development and learning take place all the time.[13] The stated goals in the curriculum aim at language development, mathematics, science and technology, as well as the use of digital tools.[14]

In terms of rights, the Education Act states that children who are resident in Sweden and who have not started any education to fulfill compulsory schooling must be offered pre-school for a minimum of 525 h per year.[15] The main rule is, however, that children from the age of one must be offered pre-school to the extent necessary, taking into account the parents' gainful employment or studies or if the child has a special need due to the family's situation in general.[16] The right to education, if it is at all possible to speak of such a right regarding preschool, therefore accrues primarily to the child's guardian, since preschool is not compulsory. According to the Swedish National Agency for Education's statistics, approximately 86% of all children between the ages of one and five went to preschool in 2021 (The National Education Agency 2022a).

One reason why children do not attend preschool may be that the parents are not gainfully employed or studying, or that, on ideological grounds, one chooses to have their children at home up to the mandatory start of school, which happens the year in which the child turns six.[17]

Even in cases where the guardians do not work or study, there is an option to have the child in preschool for 15 h per week, which can be seen as a right that accrues to both the child and the guardians.[18] A child who is in "education" in preschool and has a social context should not therefore have to be uprooted from that context and miss out on the educational progression just because he or she gets a sibling or the parents lose their jobs (Imsen 2006). In addition, it is stated that the child must be offered preschool even to a greater extent than the minimum limit of 15 h if, due to physical, mental, or other reasons, the child needs special support in his development in the form of preschool.[19] That investigation and assessment is made by the municipality where the preschool is located.

In addition to the fact that the preschool must cover a certain number of hours, and also to some extent consist of planned teaching, the preschool must also compensate for developmental difficulties that a child may have. It is stated that if a child is judged to have a need for special support, the child must also be given such support,

[13] Curriculum for preschool (Lpfö 18), p. 7.

[14] Id. at p. 18.

[15] The Education Act (2010, 800), Chap. 10, Sects. 37 and 39.

[16] The Education Act (2010, 800), Chap. 8, Sect. 5.

[17] The Education Act (2010, 800), Chap. 7, Sects. 4and 10.

[18] The Education Act (2010, 800), Chap. 8, Sect. 6.

[19] The Education Act (2010, 800), Chap. 8, Sect. 7.

without specifying in more detail what the support can consist of or what it must compensate for.[20] As there are stated subjects that the preschool must work on, it is reasonable to assume that if the difficulties are linked to learning, linguistically or otherwise, the preschool must put in the support needed so that the child, in the same way as other children, should receive as good a preparation as possible for the compulsory school system.

2.3 The Compulsory School System

As mentioned at the beginning of this chapter, the right to education is stated in the constitution.[21] It stipulates that "all children who are subject to compulsory public schooling have the right to free basic education in public schools". Thus, there is a distinct statement regarding a right to education, even if it is not clear what the right de facto means with *basic education*, or who is covered by compulsory schooling. Since Sweden joined the European Convention for the Protection of Human Rights (ECHR), which functions as domestic law with a special status because no other rules may contradict the convention, the constitutional right is supplemented by the provision that "no one may be denied the right to education".[22] How this is to be interpreted ("denied") is partly unclear as the wording can mean either that it is first required that such a right has been given to the individual, or that the right is to be understood as part of natural law and is thus both universal and absolute.

The Swedish school system includes five compulsory forms of schooling, where the first year consists of a "preschool class"—a bridge between the preschool's more play- and care-oriented education to the school's structure with clear learning goals.[23] After preschool class, as a general rule, nine years of education takes place in primary school, but for children and students with various forms of intellectual disabilities or impairment in terms of hearing or language ability, there are two forms of special schools.[24] For the Sami indigenous population, there is also the opportunity to complete the first six years of compulsory schooling in the Sami school, which primarily takes into account linguistic and cultural features in the curriculum (Belančić 2020).[25]

The compulsory school system is regulated in the Education Act and is supplemented by curricula for the respective school forms, which in turn are specified

---

[20] The Education Act (2010, 800), Chap. 8, Sect. 9.

[21] Instrument of Government (1974, 152), Chap. 2, Sect. 18.

[22] The European Convention for the Protection of Human Rights, First Additional Protocol, Article 2. *See* also domestic Law (1994, 1219) on the European Convention on the Protection of Human Rights and Fundamental Freedoms and The Instrument of Government (1974, 152), Chap. 2, Sect. 19.

[23] The Education Act (2010, 800), Chap. 9, Sect. 2.

[24] The Education Act (2010, 800), Chap. 7, Sect. 4.

[25] The Education Act (2010, 800), Chap. 13, Sects. 3–4.

through course and timetables for the various subjects, issued by the National Board of Education. Decisions that the school makes towards an individual, for example regarding support measures, disciplinary measures or the reception of an individual at a certain school unit, can be appealed either to a court or to the School Education Appeals Board (ÖKN), depending on what the issue concerns.[26] That both public and independent principals fulfill their duties in accordance with the legislation and the curricula is reviewed by the state School Inspectorate, which also receives and investigates reports from the public. The fact that the authority's decision as a general rule cannot be appealed means that the authority in the individual case takes on a role almost similar to a court to the extent that the authority's interpretation of the meaning of the law becomes indicative. In the case of onerous sanctions against a certain school unit, such as a revoked permission to operate a school, temporary closure or fines, the decisions can always be appealed to an administrative court for reasons of legal certainty.[27]

The right to education is, as mentioned before, not specified at the constitutional level, but gets its actual meaning in quantitative and qualitative terms from the Education Act and from the course- and lesson plans. Furthermore, the Education Act specifies who is to be considered covered by compulsory schooling and who is thus covered by the right, namely children who are resident in Sweden.[28] Compulsory schooling, however, does not apply to children who are permanently staying abroad or whose circumstances are such that the child obviously cannot be asked to go to school.[29]

Quantitatively, all children have the right to a total teaching time in primary school corresponding to at least 6890 h and the teaching is distributed across the various school subjects through the timetables.[30] Furthermore, it is stated as a limitation regarding the distribution that the compulsory activities may not exceed 190 days per academic year and eight hours or, in the preschool class and the two lowest grades, six hours per day. Such activities may also not be held on Saturdays, Sundays, or other holidays.[31]

In terms of quality, there are general requirements for teachers' qualifications and basic quality in teaching, partly specific requirements for extra adaptations and special support if a pupil is feared not to meet the knowledge requirements or has other difficulties in his school situation. For students who are considered to have an extensive need for special support, which conceptually is not specified in the legislation, an independent principal can apply for a so-called additional amount if the measures they intend to take can be considered extraordinary.[32] In reality,

---

[26] *See* The Education Act (2010, 800), Chap. 28 for rules of appeal in matters regarding mandatory education.

[27] The Education Act (2010, 800), Chap. 28, Sect. 2.

[28] The Education Act (2010, 800), Chap. 7, Sect. 2.

[29] The Education Act (2010, 800), Chap. 7, Sect. 2, part 2.

[30] The Education Act (2010, 800), Chap. 10, Sect. 5.

[31] The Education Act (2010, 800), Chap. 7, Sect. 17.

[32] The Education Act (2010, 800), Chap. 10, Sects. 37 and 39.

such extraordinary measures means remodeling of the premises, special technical equipment or a student assistant dedicated to an individual student (The government's bill 2008/09:171 2008).

As there is normally a duty to attend school, schools are also required to deliver education adapted to the needs of each student.[33] If a guardian does not believe that the school delivers education adapted to the student, they can make a report to the School Inspectorate or appeal decisions about what they believe are deficient action programs to The School System Appeals Board. This, in turn, has resulted in a school where those who assert their right are more likely to receive the adaptations they are entitled to, while families with lesser resources do not take advantage of that right because they lack knowledge of the system. Even though the primary school has a stated requirement in the Education Act to be equal for all students, the system of *required rights*, which were added from a "legal certainty perspective", creates an imbalance between children from different socio-economic backgrounds, i.e., the opposite of what the legislation was designed to achieve (Ryffé 2017).

In summary, the right to education is strongest when it comes to compulsory school, as it rests on a constitutional basis and is supplemented by provisions both in the Education Act and in international treaties. The scope and content are regulated in the Education Act and in associated regulations, as well as the qualitative aspects of what students are expected to learn and what right they have to individual adaptation.

2.4 The High School

Education in the upper secondary school (high school) is free of charge and must build on the knowledge the students have acquired in primary school or in equivalent education.[34] It is further specified that the education in upper secondary school consists of national programs that are either vocational programs or university preparatory programs.[35] A national program extends over three years, but whoever is in charge of the education can grant an extension of one year for students who, for various reasons, do not complete the education within the allotted time.[36] Anyone who has passed grades after completing primary school is eligible for a national program at upper secondary school, which restricts the right to a narrower circle of students. In 2021, approximately 85.6 % of the students leaving primary school were eligible for such a national program (The National Education Agency 2022b).

Students who do not have eligibility for a national program have the opportunity to study at an introductory program, which can aim to either give eligibility for further studies or provide conditions for employment on the labor market.[37] Within

[33] The Education Act (2010, 800), Chap. 3, Sects. 5 and 7–12.

[34] The Education Act (2010, 800), Chap. 15, Sect. 2.

[35] The Education Act (2010, 800), Chap. 15, Sect. 7.

[36] The Education Act (2010, 800), Chap. 16, Sect. 15.

[37] The Education Act (2010, 800), Chap. 17, Sect. 3.

the framework of the introductory programs, there is also a language introduction for students who come from other countries and have not yet achieved passing grades and have not learned sufficient Swedish to be able to study further.[38]

Regarding the rights aspect, it applies that a student who has started an education on a high school program has the right to complete his or her education on that program or the current specialization or variant.[39] Exceptions to that rule apply, among other things, if a student has started an education and then without notification has been absent from the education for more than one month in a row, without this having been due to illness or granted leave, the student shall be considered to have left/completed the education.[40]

Furthermore, it is possible to suspend a student for a longer period of time at the upper secondary school due to disciplinary reasons, which can also be considered to in some way restrict the right to education.[41] Decisions on suspension may not last longer than two weeks during a calendar semester, unless it is deemed necessary with regard to the student's behavior. However, a decision on suspension may never cover a longer period than the remainder of the current calendar half-year and three further calendar half-years.[42] In a way this means that a student's behavior can cause one to lose the right to education.

Based on the idea of progression in the Swedish school system, the student is charged with increasing personal responsibility based on age and maturity.[43] In high school, which is voluntary, it is thus up to the student himself to be responsible for his attendance, his behavior, and his study results to a greater extent than in the previous forms of schooling which are covered by a stated duty to attend. A consequence of this is that the special support offered to students who, for various reasons, show difficulties in their schoolwork often comes more in the form of an offer of support of a certain kind, than in the previous school forms where the support is individually adapted to a greater extent. Formally, the legal requirements are the same as for the mandatory school and are based on the same regulations, but the School Inspectorate's inspections of high schools have identified that the support work is lacking to a greater extent in the upper secondary school than in other forms of school (The School Inspectorate 2021).

The right to education that exists in upper secondary school is, in light of what has been stated above, not as strong as in primary school. There is no constitutional protection, but instead the right is based on the sum of various legal rules in the Education Act. The right is voluntary and puts higher demands on the individual to actually draw an advantage of the right. The education is still free of charge, even if occasional elements of lesser fees are allowed, but in high school there is not, in

[38] The Education Act (2010, 800), Chap. 17, Sect. 12.

[39] The Education Act (2010, 800), Chap. 4, Sect. 37 and Chap. 5, Sect. 15.

[40] The High School Ordinance (2010, 2039), Chap. 12, Sect. 4a.

[41] The Education Act (2010, 800), Chap. 5, Sect. 17.

[42] The Education Act (2010, 800), Chap. 5, Sect. 18.

[43] The Education Act (2010, 800), Chap. 1, Sect. 10.

the same way as in the primary school, a requirement to provide the students with school food, although in principle all principals still provide it ex gracia.[44]

2.5 Higher Education

Education at universities and colleges is regulated in the Higher Education Act, the Higher Education Ordinance, as well as by regulations from the University and College Council. That the universities comply with the legal regulations and maintain required quality is then reviewed by the state authority University Chancellor's Office, whose activities are regulated in an instruction from the government.[45] Most universities are run under state auspices and financed with state funds, although some of the most prestigious institutions of higher learning are run in the form of foundations or non-profit associations, that are not subject to the same legislation.[46]

To a certain extent, even studies at universities and colleges can be said to be covered by "some form" of right to education. This is based on the premise that the education is free of charge and that admission takes place on a non-discriminatory basis, based on criteria set by the university itself.[47] Since the education at basic university level, according to the Higher Education Act, builds on the knowledge that the students acquired during their upper secondary school studies, the grades from upper secondary school are used for selection where the students compete based on merit points.[48] For educations with a special focus, such as artistic activities, other selection grounds may also be required on top of the basic eligibility requirements. In addition, there is a special exam, "the college exam" (högskoleprovet), which is organized annually and can serve as a supplementary selection basis instead of upper secondary school grades.[49]

The right to education is thus dependent on having grades in the subjects required for a certain education, and that the grades, or the result on the college exam, are high enough to stand up to the competition in terms of selection. Once a student has been admitted to a course at a university or college, however, it is up to the student himself to pass the exams that test the course's various learning objectives. For students who have various forms of physical or cognitive difficulties, but who stand out in the competition regarding selection for admission, it is up to the universities to adapt the education to a certain extent so that the students are not discriminated against because of their disabilities.[50]

---

[44] The Education Act (2010, 800), Chap. 15, Sect. 17.

[45] *See* Ordinance (2012, 810) with instructions for the University Chancellor's Office.

[46] Two examples are Chalmers tekniska högskola (CTH) and Stockholm school of economics that are both run as foundations.

[47] The Higher Education Act (1994, 1434), Chap. 4, Sect. 2.

[48] The Higher Education Act (1994, 1434), Chap. 1, Sect. 8.

[49] The Higher Education Ordinance (1993, 100), Chap. 7, Sect. 12 § 20.

[50] The Discrimination Act (2008, 567), Chap. 2, Sect. 5.

All students originating from an EU-country or within the EEA-area have the same right to study grants and preferential student loans via the government authority The Swedish Board of Student Finance (CSN), provided that they have a residence permit in Sweden.[51] The grant and the loan are intended to enable the students to focus on their studies on equal terms, so that students from less well-off backgrounds do not have to work in parallel with their studies. The fact that the right can be understood as a "freedom from fees" is thus also supplemented with a "right" to financial resources, unless the student has a substantive income, provided that the student is able to complete his or her studies.[52] Otherwise, both the grant and the loan may be withdrawn until the student has passed his or her exams. For students with disabilities, full compensation may be paid, even if the student is not studying full-time. This works as a compensatory measure to enable studies even for those who, due to their disability, cannot complete university studies at the same pace as otherwise required.

In summary, there is not a legally stated right to education in terms of higher education studies, but the system has nevertheless been designed in such a way that a certain right can still be discerned through the equivalent requirements that are set through the selection criteria, the quality requirements that apply equally to all institutions of higher education and the compensatory measures, both in educational and financial terms, which should enable all students to take part in higher education on equal terms.

3 Major Legal Developments Concerning the Right to Education

3.1 The Freedom from Fees Opens up the "Right" for Everyone

As far as the preschool is concerned it is unusual for any cases to be dealt with in court. One case bearing on the right to education, however, is the "diaper case" that drew a lot of attention in Sweden. A municipality directed an injunction coupled with an administrative fine against an independent principal because the preschool asked parents with small children to provide diapers for their children themselves. The preschool is not covered by total freedom of fees but is based on a so-called "maximum fee" which is an upper limit for what a family may have to pay to have their child at the preschool.[53] Those with no income do not have to pay at all, while those with a high income for the year 2022 had to pay SEK 1572 (approx. USD

---

[51] The Student Support Act (1999, 1395), Chap. 1, Sect. 4.

[52] The Student Support Ordinance (2000, 655), Chap. 3, Sect. 16–17.

[53] Ordinance (2001, 160) on state grants to municipalities that apply maximum rates in preschool and after-school care.

140) per month. In addition to this fee, however, the preschool has no possibility of charging additional fees, which should be seen as part of making preschool available to everyone and thereby guaranteeing all children's right to education even in preschool.[54]

The administrative fine issued by the municipality was appealed to the administrative court, which ruled that there was no legal basis to demand compensation for children at the preschool in addition to the maximum rate, which was indirectly an admission that the preschool itself should be responsible for diapers for the smaller children.[55] Since this meant a substantial increase in costs for smaller businesses such as a private preschool, the judgment was appealed to the Court of Appeal, which however ruled in the same direction.[56] When the Supreme Administrative Court decided not to take the case up for review, the verdict was confirmed. However, the assessment of what this meant differed.

Sweden's municipalities and regions (SKR) is an employer- and lobby organization that acts on behalf of the municipalities vis-à-vis the state, among other things. Through their advice and guidelines, they have an extensive impact on how legal rules and judgments are interpreted in within the public school system run by the municipalities, even if SKR formally lack normative capacity and represent a certain interest. In their interpretation of the judgment and of the fact that the Supreme Administrative Court had nothing to object to, and therefore did not take the matter up for consideration, it was believed that the judgment should be interpreted *in casu* and had no real effect on how other preschools in Sweden should behave on the matter.

The court case is of particular interest because it puts the finger on the Swedish model where the right to education is strictly associated with freedom from fees, that is to say that the financial capacity of the guardians must not constitute an obstacle to the child's individual right to take part in the education system.

3.2 The Right to the Correct Form of School

Another issue of great importance for the Swedish model is that the students' right to education within the compulsory school system is dependent on that the school form where the child is received is the best form to meet the students' needs.

A student who has a confirmed intellectual developmental disability has the right to be admitted to the *primary special school*, a form of school adapted specifically for these students since they can hardly meet the requirements set in the more comprehensive elementary school.[57] However, it is the student's guardian who must normally allow the student to be admitted to the primary special school, even if in certain cases

[54] The Education Act (2010, 800), Chap. 8, Sect. 16.

[55] Stockholm Administrative Court, case no. 16898-18.

[56] Stockholm Court of Appeal, case no. 10160-18.

[57] The Education Act (2010, 800), Chap. 11, Sect. 2.

there is the possibility of placing a student in the primary special school against the guardian's wishes, taking into account the best interests of the child.[58]

In a case that was tried by the School System's Appeals Board it was a question of a student who was accepted in a primary special school, but who received his education in a primary school as a so-called integrated student.[59] This means that you study towards different goals according to a different curriculum than your classmates and must have the teaching adapted, but that you can continue in your regular class.[60] Often this is justified based on social considerations but can prove difficult when the students get older and the demands are higher.

In the case in question, the municipality decided that the integration was no longer functional, and that the student would transfer to a purely elementary primary special school. The guardians objected that in that case they would take the student out of the school form, the elementary special school, so that the student could continue in the same class as before. The municipality then chose to apply the exception rule that forces a student to fulfill compulsory schooling within the special school, which was appealed to the board by the student represented by his guardians.

The board's investigation showed that the student did not have the conditions to reach the primary school's goals and therefore believed that, considering the child's best interests, which must be taken into account in all decisions concerning children and students, there were such extraordinary reasons as the law requires.

The decision, which is one of several dealing with the same kind of issue, shows that the right to education includes the "right" education for the student in terms of adaptations, regardless of what the guardians believe or wish. It also shows that the right to education lies with the individual student and not with the guardians, which harmonizes with the very idea behind the Convention on the Rights of the Child, which emphasizes the child as an individual bearer of rights.

Even the opposite scenario can, however, raise questions about which form of school a student is entitled to, taking into account the overall right to education. Another notable court case concerned two brothers who, at a young age, were believed to have an intellectual disability and were therefore admitted to the elementary special school after examination.[61]

As the brothers grew older, however, questions were raised among the teachers as to whether the students were really being educated in the right school format, and renewed psychological examinations showed that there was no intellectual disability. The brothers had then basically completed their entire schooling in the "wrong" school form—a form of schooling that does not entitle them to higher studies or provides a good basis for an establishment on the labor market. Against this background, the brothers sued the municipality with claims for damages due to errors and negligence in the exercise of authority in connection with their admission to the primary special school. In addition, damages were also claimed because the

[58] The Education Act (2010, 800), Chap. 7, Sect. 5.

[59] The School System's Appeal Board decision, Dnr: 2018:1034, October 10th of 2018.

[60] *See* The Education Act (2010, 800), Chap. 7, Sect. 9.

[61] Malmö District Court judgment in case T 79-10, May 10th of 2011.

municipality violated the European Convention's (ECHR) provision on the right to education. As it was a question of financial claims, the case was decided in the general court, which is unusual as school-related issues are mainly dealt with in the administrative courts.

The District Court, as well as the Court of Appeal later, determined that there was a basis for damages due to errors and negligence in the exercise of authority, but rejected the claim based on the provisions of the European Convention. The latter states that "no one may be denied education" and as the two brothers had received education, albeit in the wrong form of school. The municipality had therefor not denied them the right as it is expressed in the text of the convention. The Supreme Court chose not to hear the case.

The court cases show, in the same way as above, that the right to education according to Swedish law includes that one is received in the right school form, but that the right as it is expressed in the European Convention has a partly different meaning—at least as interpreted by national courts.

That students are given education in the right school form and with the right adaptation to needs was also made clear in a case from the Supreme Administrative Court in 2017.[62] As mentioned earlier, as a basic rule, it is not possible to appeal against the School Inspectorate's decisions, but in cases where the inspection authority wants an administrative fine imposed, this must be tried by court. Thus, there is an opportunity for the party who has become the subject of the authority's decision to have the entire case tried.

Linköping municipality had opened a number of "resource schools" for children with various forms of special needs. Since 2011, the Education Act has included an explicit rule that allowed such resource schools for private principals, without there being a corresponding rule for public principals. The School Inspectorate had interpreted this against the background of another provision which states that a student must be placed at the municipality's school unit where the student's guardian wishes the student to go, as long as there is a vacant seat. The interpretation meant that even such a resource school organized by Linköping municipality would be open to all students and not only to the students with special needs or diagnoses that the municipality had in mind.

The municipality of Linköping was of a different opinion and believed that the municipality's task is to meet the needs of the municipality's residents/members and that there was no explicit prohibition in the Education Act. In a submission to the court the Swedish Education Agency spoke out in favor of the municipality's position, which meant that two school authorities representing the state took opposite sides in the case. In the first two instances it was ruled in favor of the School Inspectorate, but the Supreme Administrative Court found that, just as the municipality stated, there is no explicit prohibition in the Education Act. Furthermore, an equal treatment reason is given as there is a rule that allows resource schools for independent principals.

From the legal case, it can be concluded that the court adopts a pragmatic approach to the issue of schools adapted for students with special needs, so far as the openness

[62] Supreme Administrative Court judgment, case no. HFD 2017:50.

requirement that characterizes Swedish schools must not stand in the way of children who are obliged to attend school to exercise their right to education in a school environment adapted to their needs.

3.3 Rights in Conflict—Education Versus Religion

A recurring question regarding how the concept of "need" should be interpreted is when compulsory schooling and the right to education are set against religious considerations. Freedom of religion is enshrined in the Swedish constitution and supplemented by a provision in the European Convention.[63] Together, they provide a relatively strong protection for the individual in terms of belief and practice of religious rites and expressions, but in practice, freedom of religion has come to be seen in many ways as a sole concern of the individual, which only may conflict with the individual's interaction with the surrounding society to a certain extent.

A series of legal cases, that got a lot of attention and that concerned the right to education in relation to freedom of religion, has dealt with an Orthodox Jewish family in Gothenburg who wished to home-school their children in accordance with their religious beliefs. According to Swedish law, there is limited scope for home schooling as physical integration is considered to promote social development, which is one of the school's various missions.[64] At the same time freedom of religion does not mean that religion trumps other areas of law but is primarily to be seen in the individual's personal affairs. The Swedish position can, somewhat naively it may seem, be said to be that religion is something that the individual can practice in his or her "free time".

The parents had home-schooled their children for several years, first in the form of a "school" in their own home and later, when the permission was withdrawn, through exceptions in the older Education Act (1985, 1100). When the new Education Act (2010, 800) came into force in 2011, however, the conditions for home schooling were changed, which led to the municipality ordering the family to ensure the children's compulsory schooling so that they could thereby secure their right to "correct" education. The parents appealed the decision and argued that it constituted a violation of Article 9 of the European Convention regarding freedom of religion, which The Administrative Court disagreed with.[65] In the Court of Appeal, on the other hand, the assessment was made that, with the support of the Education Act, there was room to grant home schooling, as the children's clothing and religious behavior deviated so much from the behavior of other children.[66] However, the municipality appealed the decision to the Supreme Administrative Court, which ruled partly that

---

[63] Instrument of Government (1974, 152), Chap. 2, Sect. 1 and The European Convention for the Protection of Human Rights, Article 9.

[64] *See* the"portal paragraph" in The Education Act (2010, 800), Chap. 1, Sect. 4.

[65] Gothenburg Administrative Court judgment, case no. 7728-1 I.

[66] Gothenburg Court of Appeal judgment, case no. 76-12.

the education the children received at home could actually be considered satisfactory from a learning point of view, and partly that education at home, on the other hand, could not be seen as compatible with the social goals stated in the Education Act and associated curricula.[67] Against the background of the latter argument, the court ruled in favor of the municipality, which meant that the children would immediately begin their schooling in the public school. However, the family continued to refuse to send their children to school, which is why the municipality's substantial administrative fine could be imposed in order to secure the children's right to education through financial pressure.

The case is interesting because it establishes that the student's right to education also includes social goals that indirectly prohibit teaching in contexts that are "too small". Since differences are considered enriching in that respect, the possibilities has also shrunk when it comes to establishing schools with a more strict religious profile that is not in line with the values expressed in the curricula.

The question of the right to education in relation to religious beliefs also appears in other school forms. In a case with the Discrimination Ombudsman, it was examined whether the denial of a request for time off from school on Fridays, for a young practicing Muslim at High school, in order to prepare for and join during the prayer, could be seen as discrimination.[68] The Discrimination Ombudsman is certainly not a court, but is the state social body tasked with countering discrimination and investigating reports. Their statements in various cases also have a great impact on a possible court process, which is why most instances follow their statements.

In the current case, the student's teacher had initially taken a positive view of granting recurring leave. However, the headmaster made a new decision that did not allow any recurring time off, as he considered that the student is subject to "compulsory attendance"—which, however, should not be confused with the compulsory schooling that applies to the compulsory forms of school.

The Discrimination Ombudsman said that it ultimately becomes a matter of a proportionality assessment, as freedom of religion is supported in both the constitution and the European Convention, while the duty to attend is only enshrined in national law. At the time of the authority's review, however, the issue of exemption from teaching for reasons related to religion had recently been brought up in the European Court of Human Rights.[69]

The case concerned the question of whether a decision to refuse two parents' request that their children be exempted from compulsory swimming lessons constituted a violation of the parents' right to freedom of religion. In its judgment, the European Court of Human Rights found that the children's compulsory attendance at the swimming lessons did constitute an interference with the parents' freedom of religion, but that this interference was not contrary to the requirements of Article 9, second paragraph. The students' duty to attend was supported by law, and the

---

[67] Supreme Administrative Court judgement in case HFD 2013 ref 49.

[68] Discrimination Ombudsman, case no. GRA 2016/31.

[69] European Court of Human Rights' judgment in the case *Osmanoğlu and Kocabaş v. Switzerland*, application no 29086/12.

decision in question had, among other things, the purpose of maintaining respect for compulsory schooling, the effective implementation of teaching and to protect foreign students from social exclusion. According to the European Court of Human Rights, the measure was thus aimed at maintaining public order as well as the freedoms and rights of others.

In the light of that case, even though it was now a question of a high school student who was not bound by school duty in the same way, the Discrimination Ombudsman announced that there was no discrimination as the student was not given time off to participate in the prayer, since the duty to attend was also supported by law.

3.4 A Right for Whom?

A fundamental question when dealing with a right is who is covered by the right. Is the right individual, civic or universal? As mentioned above, the right to education in Swedish legislation is based on the constitution, which states that all students covered by compulsory schooling also have the right to free basic education. It is clear from the provisions of the Education Act that anyone who is permanently resident in the country is also obliged to attend school, which also includes citizens other than Swedish, who can be considered to reside in the country more or less permanently. That group includes, among other things, children of compulsory school age who hold a residence permit or who stay in the country because their parents work in Sweden. In addition to these groups, children who were brought into the country illegally are also included, as children should not be punished for their parents' choices or lack of upbringning. In that respect, the right can be seen as universal—but there is one glaring exception.

If a child staying in Sweden comes from another EU country, they are covered by the right of residence, which extends for three months.[70] This also applies if the guardians lack housing, financial means or work, as long as one holds a passport or a EU identification card. Only if a EU citizen exceeds his or her stay for more than three months one can be considered to be staying "illegally" in Sweden. In that case one would be covered by the special rules in the Education Act that give a right to education without requiring compulsory schooling.[71]

Since each EU country is considered to meet the requirements to ensure its own citizens' right to education, Swedish principals, at least for the first three months, have no obligation to provide education. Or do they?

The legal issue has been unclear for a long time and Sweden's municipalities and regions (SKR) have interpreted the law in their circulars so that there is no need to provide education to children from the EU who stay in the country because their parents, for example, beg or take short-term jobs on the black labor market (SKR

[70] Directive 2004/58/EC of The European Parliament and of The Council ("the mobility directive"), Article 9.

[71] The Education Act (2010, 800), Chap. 29, Sect. 2.

2022). The same has been expressed by the national coordinator for vulnerable EU citizens who in 2016 in a report, on very loose legal grounds, determined that children of EU citizens are not covered by any right to education in Sweden (SOU 2016:6, p. 54). As support for the claim, reference was made, among other things, to a decision by the Swedish Education Agency's appeals board concerning a Bulgarian family who made a living by begging.[72] When their request to the municipality for education for the children was rejected, they appealed the decision, but the board stated that the family lacked a right of residence according to the provisions of the EU Mobility Directive and that any right to education could not be based on Article 10 of Regulation 492/2011 either, as none of the guardians had employment in Sweden.

The matter includes that the board rejected the request according to the Education Act, Chap. 29. Sect. 2, third point, but did not take a position on the fifth point in the provision, which specifically concerns children who are staying in the country illegally, i.e., "without the support of an authority decision or constitution".

Another school authority representing the state, the School Inspectorate, had come to the opposite conclusion less than a month earlier in a similar case, precisely against the background of the fifth point of the provision mentioned above.[73] The family in that case were EU citizens and had bought an apartment in Sweden because the father expected to find work. The municipality considered that the family lacked the right of residence and rejected a request for education for the child, without further specifying how they came to that conclusion. After reporting to the School Inspectorate, it was found that the child was "resident" in the country according to the law and thus considered undocumented or illegal. For that reason, the child was also considered to have a right to education in Sweden.

The fact that two government authorities have come to the opposite conclusion is problematic as it is these two decisions which, in the absence of guiding judgments by the courts, constitute legal practice. Authorities in Sweden must act independently, which means that none of the authorities has come to conform to the other.[74] However, the fact that it was only the School Inspectorate that tested and applied the fifth point in the provision concerning the children who are staying illegally in the country suggests that children from other EU countries should also be considered covered by the right to education—at least after three months when they reside in the country illegally.

3.5 The Matter of Satisfying Quality and Fees in Higher Education

As mentioned at the beginning of this chapter, the starting point is that university studies should be free of charge. According to the Higher Education Act, this applies

[72] The School System's Appeal Board decision, Dnr: 2014:556, February 2nd of 2016.

[73] The School Inspectorate decision, Dnr 41-2015:8526, January 13th of 2016.

[74] Instrument of Government (1974, 152), Chap. 12, Sect. 2.

to EU citizens and citizens who are part of the EEA agreement, who according to the Student Support Act are also entitled to study grants and favorable low-interest loans. For students outside the EU, however, a fee is charged. For those who meet the criteria and also have sufficient grades in the required subjects, there is thus a form of right to begin studies at a Swedish university free of charge. In order to complete the education, however, there may be various forms of "barriers", i.e., elements that the student must complete, and that the student may lose his right through disciplinary sanctions or due to criminal activity. The number of legal cases concerning these issues are very few, but in a case that began in the Swedish courts in 2013, it can be deduced that the right to education regarding the university includes minimum quality requirements for the "right" to be considered fulfilled by the party who must satisfy the right (the college or university).

The American student Connie Dickinson began a bachelor's degree at Mälardalen College but was disappointed with the quality of the education and therefore dropped out. Because of her nationality, she had paid for her education and when the examining authority, the University Chancellor's Office, criticized the college for lack of quality in the education, she turned to the court for a refund of her paid semester fees, which amounted to SEK 170,812 (approximately $16,000).[75] However, the college claimed that it would not refund the fee.

The main legal question did not primarily concern the right to education, but whether there was a mutually binding agreement and whether there were deficiencies in the education that would justify liability. This has an indirect bearing on the rights aspect because a court opinion on repayment would mean that there are qualitative aspects that must be met.

The case was tried by all instances until it reached the Swedish Supreme Court, which ruled in the student's favor, but reduced the required amount by two-thirds of the tuition fee plus court costs.[76] A reduced amount was considered justified as the education was not "completely worthless", since the student had nevertheless been able to earn a number of university credits.

What was not tried in the case was whether, in addition to the reimbursement, there could also be grounds for compensation for wasted time in education that did not live up to the quality requirements. Such a claim could probably have been used to an even greater extent as justification for setting qualitative demands linked to a presumptive "right" to education even at universities and colleges.

[75] Västmanland District Court judgment in case TR T 1806-15, June 14th of 2016.

[76] Supreme Court judgment in case T 2196-17, April 17th of 2018.

4 Emerging and Present Issues in Education Law

4.1 A Major Problem for Swedish Schools

The biggest problem for Swedish schools is that as many as 14.4% of all students leave ninth grade of elementary school without complete grades and thus lack eligibility for a national program at high school (The National Education Agency 2022a). The development has taken place gradually since the beginning of the 2000s but accelerated with the large wave of refugees that began in 2015, among other things as a result of the war in Syria. Children who came to Sweden without knowing the language or understanding the social structure naturally had significantly worse conditions to pass school, which is completely understandable. The challenge lies in meeting the needs that arise and the consequential effects that are visible far outside the domains of the school.

Although it is a sensitive issue, figures have been produced that show that if you only measure Swedish-born children, with Swedish-born parents, only 9% of the students do not achieve passing grades after grade nine, which is still a little higher than as the Swedish school's glory days during the 1980s and early 1990s (SOU 2017:54).[77] The questions that become relevant given the right to education are in the same way as explained above, *who* holds the right and *what* it is worth if the school is unable to meet the needs that exist. It is also to a large extent children with an immigrant background that do not go to the Swedish preschool and are therefore not as prepared for compulsory school either—neither socially, nor linguistically (The governments' bill 2021/22:132 2021).[78] The problem with the lack of adaptation for students with a foreign background is not only purely educational but contributes to an increasing polarization in society through social segregation and a feeling of exclusion, which in turn, among other things, leads to increased crime and thereby increases the polarization even further in an ongoing downward spiral.

Linked to the issue of education quality and adaptability is another concern. There is a shortage of teachers in Sweden and since the requirement for eligibility was tightened through a teacher's ID 2011, there is a shortage of trained pedagogues in several subjects.[79] This leads to situations where no one with knowledge of and qualifications in the subject, which is, among other things, required to be able to grade students, can teach. Teacher training is becoming less and less popular among students who choose higher education and universities have been forced to lower the entry requirements for admission in order to fill the training places as much

[77] It was 91% of the students who were born in Sweden who became eligible for the upper secondary school national program in the spring term of 2016. The proportion of newly immigrated1 students who were eligible was 30%.

[78] Among the children who do not go to preschool are children from a weak socio-economic background and children with a foreign background overrepresented. Children who are born abroad has the lowest participation.

[79] *See* Ordinance (2011, 326) on eligibility and identification for teachers and preschool teachers.

as possible.[80] This in turn risks deteriorating the quality of the next generation of teachers, which also endangers the right to a quality education.

Among the legislative politicians, there is still a belief that several of the school system's problems linked to the right to education can be solved by legal or financial means. Regarding the economy, however, according to the OECD, Sweden is already among the countries that spends most money on schools in the world, converted to GDP, which is why more financial contributions do not seem to be a viable path (OECD 2015).

In terms of legislation, certain measures and steps have been taken to try to meet the educational problems that the increasing immigration has led to. Study guidance in the mother tongue, also via distance learning online, is one such initiative.[81] In addition, rules have been introduced to the effect that students who fear that they will not reach the national goals or grading criteria in year 8 or 9 must attend a preparatory school during school holidays, and that each school must offer at least two hours of extra study time a week to even out the socio-economic injustices that result from that some children get help with school work and homework at home, while others do not.[82] However, both initiatives can be criticized for being naive. More time for things that didn't work in the first place is hardly a solution to a pedagogical problem, and since both the holiday school and the extra study time are voluntary, the probability is high that it is already committed children who take advantage of the opportunities, while children from homes with no study habit opt out of these opportunities. Both the Swedish National Agency for Education and the Government have held discussions about making vocational school compulsory for students who did not pass full grades but have put the work on hold because it is considered "complicated" taking into account the right to education and compulsory schooling (The governments' bill 2021/22:111 2021).

4.2 Ban on Religious Free Schools

Another issue that also concerns the right to education in relation to the emergence of an even more multicultural society, is the issue of religious free schools. A majority of the political parties in the Parliament are behind a ban on the establishment of new schools with a religious focus, and the possibility of withdrawing permits for already existing schools is also being discussed.[83]

The Swedish school, regardless of whether it is run under public or private auspices, must rest on democratic foundations of, among other things, equality

[80] *See* University and College Council press release April 27th of 2022, Fewer people want to start teacher training this autumn: The number of people who applied for teacher training in the fall has decreased by 13% compared to last fall semester.

[81] The Education Act (2010, 800), Chap. 3, Sects. 11a and 13i.

[82] The Education Act (2010, 800), Chap. 10, Sects. 5a and 23a–23f.

[83] *See* Committee Directive, Dir. 2022:102.

between the sexes, as well as rest on research and proven experience.[84] Freedom of religion has in several cases in both courts and with the authorities had to stand back for the right to education, but the practice of the European Court is not clear, why a total ban could be in conflict with the European Convention of Human Rights, Article 9. The arguments from the legislative politicians who are for a total ban are currently that public funds pay for schools that do not follow the curricula, differentiate between boys and girls, and seem to indoctrinate in a direction away from Swedish values. Against this, however, it can be argued that the purpose of freedom of religion is precisely to ensure a right for the minority to live in accordance with their faith or outlook on life and that a ban, even if it were to take place on good grounds, undermines one right in order to strengthen another.

In addition, the issue of religious free schools has become a major political issue, which is in reality mainly aimed at Muslim free schools. The number of independent schools with a religious orientation is few in Sweden and most also have a Christian profile, but to only act with legislation towards schools associated with but a specific religion would definitely be in conflict with the foundations of the Discrimination Act and would probably not be accepted by the European Court either. Thus, there is a risk of "throwing the baby out with the bathwater" if the proposals for a total ban gain traction and results in that several well-functioning schools, of which many do not have a Muslim profile, are forced to close for no other reason than as part of the current political opinion.

By introducing new and tougher requirements for competence in the ownership and management circle, which includes the board that constitutes the principal of the school, as well as requirements for financial conditions to maintain the business in the long term, the state, through the inspection authority and the courts, has to some extent found religious schools that misbehaved (SOU 2019:64). The problem is that even the schools that had no objections are now subjected to even tougher scrutiny that puts them in the spotlight.

4.3 An Increase in "Adapted Course of Study"

A third problem that relates directly to the right to education, but which concerns more of the students' individual right, is an increasing number of students who either have their study time reduced through the "adapted course of study" measure, or who do not come to school at all (The National Education Agency 2020). This may be due to an experience among children and young people of an extensive set of demands which they are unable to meet, and which also extend outside the sphere of school, but the research is not clear-cut (Lundell 2021).

Adapted course of study is a special support measure that was originally aimed at students who, for various reasons, were judged to need to reduce their time at school in favor of other activities. Legally, it is a question of a change to the student's

[84] The Education Act (2010, 800), Chap. 1, Sects. 4 and 9.

timetable, which affects the right to education in quantitative terms.[85] In practice, this could mean that a student had their school day or week reduced and instead put the scheduled time outside of school into practice at a workplace to prepare for working life. The measure was then used so that language-impaired students would not learn a second language (English) in grade four, but instead spend that time consolidating Swedish. The measure is not intended to be permanent but should work as supportive measure during a transitional period and requires a concrete decision by the headmaster. The decisions shall only extend over a short period of time to be evaluated continuously.

The number of decisions on adapted courses of study has increased throughout the 2000s, mainly as a result of the increase in the proportion of students who are judged to be depressed or have other mental difficulties (The National Education Agency 2020). For that group of students, adapted study has been used as a way to shorten the student's school days, with the justification that it is better for the student to come to school part of the day than not at all. In a way, however, through the headmasters' decisions, the schools have legitimized the students' absence instead of addressing the student's well-being, which is the underlying factor. In other words, the schools have focused on the symptoms, because it is significantly easier.

Decisions on adapted course of study that reduce a student's hours in various subjects also reduce compulsory schooling. Given that it is a support measure specified in the Education Act, it must be possible to justify how the measure promotes the student's school performance, which can be difficult when the measure runs for a longer period of time.[86] The decision also means that the student's right to education is weakened, because neither in qualitative nor quantitative terms does the student receive an education corresponding to the one they are entitled to according to the course plans and timetables.

5 Conclusion

The present chapter shows that there is no given picture of how the right to education *should* be understood. Instead, it becomes a question of how the right *can* be understood, which to some extent politicizes the issue. This in turn can be seen as completely natural given that a right, which was stated at the beginning of this chapter, can be seen both as a political goal and as a legal rule.

The "chain of command" which is supposed to ensure the right to education, however, creates some problems through double and sometimes contradictory governance. Thus, the organization of the school system itself can be seen as a factor behind the lack of clarity of the right, and voices have been put forward in the political arena that the school system as a whole should be nationalized to avoid different municipalities acting differently and thus undermining equality.

[85] The Education Act (2010, 800), Chap. 3, Sect. 12.

[86] Administration Act (2017, 900), Sect. 32.

That so few legal issues reach the courts, because the legislation is constructed in such a way, leaves a lot of room for the state school authorities to chisel out the meaning regarding the right to education in different issues as well as other underlying issues concerning preschool, school, and higher studies. The fact that the authorities, as shown in some of the examples highlighted in the chapter, in some cases come to directly opposite conclusions reinforces the image that the right to education is not "precise" in its meaning. An important part of the meaning of the right, which is in fact clearly expressed in the wording of the rule in the constitution, is the demand for freedom from fees regarding the primary school which is covered by compulsory schooling. The provision is not absolute, as the Education Act allows for smaller costs in connection with, for example, study visits and the like, but it is not possible to pay for a "better" education and thereby segregate the school system on socio-economic grounds even more than it already is due to segregation. Although the right to education in the strict sense does not include other forms of schooling than the compulsory, ten-year primary school and its equivalents adapted for children of Sami origin or children with special needs, as a general rule, freedom from fees applies from preschool up to university. The *formal* conditions for everyone to acquire a higher education and thereby meet the increasing demands of the future are therefore good.

At least for Swedish children, whoever they are considered to be.

References

Belančić K (2020) Language policy and sámi education in Sweden: ideological and implementational spaces for Sámi language use, University of Umeå

Dworkin R (1975) Hard cases. 88 Harvard law review

Foucault M (1994) Power. Faubion JD (ed). The New Press, New York, p 109

Foucault M (1997) Ethics, subjectivity and truth. Rabinow P (ed). The New Press, New York, p 158

Glavå M, Petrusson U (2002) Illusionen om rätten – Juristprofessionen och ansvaret för rättskonstruktionerna. In: Askeland B, Bernt JF (ed) Erkjennelse og engasjement : minneseminar for David Roland Doublet, Fagbokforlaget, Bergen, pp 18–20

Hohfeldt WN (1917) Fundamental legal conceptions as applied in judicial reasoning. The Yale Law Journal 26(8)

Imsen G (2006) Elevens värld: Introduktion till pedagogisk psykologi. Studentlitteratur, Lund

Lundell S (2021) Allt fler unga blir hemmasittare när den psykiska ohälsan ökar, 11 March 2021, Arbetsvärlden

OECD (2015) Improving schools in Sweden: an OECD perspective, p 27

Olivecrona K (1940) Om lagen och staten. Gleerup, København, p. 60–61

Ryffé D (2017) Likvärdighet genom särskilt stöd. Sverker Scheutz (ed) En likvärdig skola för alla, Iustus förlag, Uppsala, pp 190–191

SKR (2022) Några juridiska frågor gällande utsatta EU-medborgare, p. 9

SOU 2016:6 (2016) Framtid sökes — Slutredovisning från den nationella samordnaren för utsatta EU-medborgare

SOU 2017:54 (2017) Fler nyanlända elever ska uppnå behörighet till gymnasiet, p. 16

SOU 2019:64 (2019) Nya regler för skolor med konfessionell inriktning

Statsrådsberedningen (1998) Myndigheternas föreskrifter – Handbok i författningsskrivning. Ds 1998:43

Svensson S (2019) Systemskiftet – när skolan gick från gemensam till privat. Arenaidé, p 18
The government's bill 2008/09:171 (2008) Public grants on equal terms, p 42
The government's bill 2021/22:132 (2021) Preschool for more children, p. 8
The government's bill 2021/22:111 (2021) More time for learning—extra study time and extended holiday school, p 48
The National Education Agency (2020) Descriptive statistics, p 1
The National Education Agency (2022a) Statistics on children and staff in preschool 2021
The National Education Agency (2022b) Eligibility for upper secondary school is increasing in all student groups, p 1
The School Inspectorate (2021) Arbetet med individuella stödinsatser i gymnasieskolan – Fokus på skyndsamhet, helhetsperspektiv och elevdelaktighet, pp 5–7

Education Law in the United States

Charles J. Russo

1 Introduction

The United States Supreme Court's ruling in *Brown v. Board of Education* (*Brown*, invalidated racial segregation in elementary and secondary public schools, the focus of this chapter,[1] violated students' rights to equal protection under the Fourteenth Amendment to the Constitution, is its most important case on education. *Brown*, which involved disputes from Kansas, Delaware, South Carolina, and Virginia not only initiated an era of equal educational opportunities for children who were African-American but served as the impetus for the Civil Rights Movement that resulted in federal laws protecting the educational rights of females as well as students with disabilities, topics discussed later in this chapter.

This chapter begins with a brief overview of the legal system in the United States with a focus on federal, rather than state, law because it is the background against which most major developments emerged. The second section reviews key institutional issues starting with school governance and compulsory attendance before examining faculty and student rights. The final substantive section briefly highlights two emerging topics, technology in schools and issues involving students who are transgender. The chapter rounds out with a brief conclusion. In reviewing cases, it is important to note that as litigious as Americans are, there are more cases on elementary and secondary education, or most other topics for that matter, in one year in the United States than at least a decade or longer elsewhere. Thus, while the footnotes often identify just one case, most can be replaced with multiple citations.

[1] This chapter does not address the voluminous body of law involving higher education.

C. J. Russo (✉)
University of Dayton, Dayton, USA
e-mail: copyright@esph.com.cn

C. J. Russo and L. Ma (eds.), *A Comparative Analysis of Systems of Education Law*,
https://doi.org/10.1007/978-981-97-1052-2_18

2 The Legal System

Because major developments in education involve the legal system, it is a logical starting place for this chapter. The United States Constitution, the primary source of American law, provides the framework within which the legal, and school, systems operate. As such, enactments of federal, state, and local governments, including state constitutions, statutes, regulations, and common law, are subject to the Constitution as interpreted by the Supreme Court and lower courts. However, as a democratic republic, meaning one in which citizens elect representatives to enact laws on their behalf, in areas not covered under their federal counterpart, particularly many topics impacting education such as criteria for serving on school boards and teacher qualifications, state constitutions are supreme in their jurisdictions.

As important as education is, it is not mentioned in the United States Constitution. Under the Tenth Amendment, according to which "[t]he powers not delegated to the United States by the Constitution, nor prohibited by it to the States, are reserved to the States respectively, or to the people," education is primarily the concern of individual states. To this end, in *San Antonio Independent School District v. Rodriguez*, its only case on financing public education, in which the Court refused to intervene, the Justices declared that "[e]ducation, of course, is not among the rights afforded explicit protection under our Federal Constitution. Nor do we find any basis for saying it is implicitly so protected."[2]

The United States does have a Federal Department of Education and a growing body of federal statutes regulating elementary and secondary schooling. Yet, unlike most nations, there is not a centralized national body or ministry establishing educational policy for the entire nation. Rather, because each state has its own educational system, and is divided into independent school districts governed by boards, most of which are elected by a vote of local citizens, they work together in establishing policies for schools, their faculties, and students.

Federal courts have the authority to intervene in educational disputes if a statutory or constitutional right is at issue such as in *Brown*.[3] The Court had the authority to intervene because once states provide benefits such as schooling to residents, under the equal protection clause of the Fourteenth Amendment to the Federal Constitution, they must make them available to all children on an equal basis, thereby preventing discrimination as here, based on race.

In addition to identifying the rights of Americans, the Federal Constitution establishes three coequal branches of government. The legislative, executive, and judicial branches of government give rise to the three other sources of law. The legislative branch "makes the law." Once bills complete the legislative process, they are signed into law by a Chief Executive such as a President or Governor with the authority to enforce them by carrying out their full effect by means of promulgating regulations written by personnel at administrative agencies who are experts in their fields.

---

[2] 411 U.S. 1, 35 (1973).

[3] 347 U.S. 483 (1954).

Statutes set broad legislative parameters in such areas as compulsory attendance. As such, regulations permit administrative agencies such as individual state Departments of education to flesh the intent of statutes by adding necessary details concerning, for example, the amount of time children must be in class and the subject matter they need to study in order to satisfy the law. Regulations are thus presumptively valid.

The fourth and final source of law is judge-made or common law. Common law requires judges to "interpret the law," examining issues that may have been overlooked in the legislative or regulatory process or that may not have been anticipated when statutes were enacted. Common law involves precedent, the concept that a majority ruling of the highest court in a given jurisdiction is binding on lower courts within its purview. An order of the United States Supreme Court is thus binding throughout the nation, while decisions of state supreme court apply only in their jurisdictions.

The federal judiciary and most state court systems have three levels: trial courts, intermediate appellate courts, and courts of last resort. In the federal system, trial courts are known as federal district courts; state trial courts use a variety of names. Each state has at least one federal district court while densely populated states, such as California and New York, have as many as four.

Trial courts typically involve a judge and a jury. The role of the judge, as trier of law, is to apply the law by determining, for instance, whether evidence is admissible while providing direction for juries on how to apply the law to the facts of the specific cases they are examining. There are thirteen federal intermediate appellate courts known as Circuit Courts of Appeal; state intermediate appellate courts employ a variety of names. The highest court in the United States is the nine-member Supreme Court; although most states refer to their high courts as supreme courts, jurisdictions use various titles.

3 Institutional Issues

3.1 Compulsory Attendance and School Governance

Massachusetts was the first jurisdiction in the United States to enact a compulsory attendance law when it did so in 1852.[4] When Mississippi adopted its compulsory attendance law in 1918, it became the last existing jurisdiction at that time to adopt such a statute.[5]

Parents typically have the right to send their children to the public schools, which, outside of a few large cities, governed by popularly elected boards, communities as long as they satisfy legitimate residence requirements, an issue the Supreme Court has

[4] MASS. GEN. LAWS ANN. 76 § 1 (historical notes St. 1852, c. 240, §§ 1, 2, 4).

[5] Michael S. Katz, A History of Compulsory Attendance Laws 18 1976.

addressed in a pair of cases from Texas, both of which are relevant in today's disputes over immigration. In *Plyler v. Doe*[6] the Supreme Court affirmed that Texas could not deny a free public school education to children whose parents were undocumented residents. Acknowledging the importance of education, coupled with the fact that the children had no say over the legal status of their parents, the Court invalidated a law denying these students the opportunity to attend public schools.

A year later, in *Martinez v. Bynum*, the Supreme Court rejected a challenge to the constitutionality of Texas' residency law. A student, a citizen of the United States who lived apart from his parents because they remained in Mexico while lived with his sister as his custodian rather than legal guardian, sought to attend public school. The law obligated students to live with their parents or legal guardians and be in districts not simply to obtain a free education. Upholding the constitutionality of the statute, the Court held that "[a] bona fide residence requirement, appropriately defined and uniformly applied, furthers the substantial state interest in assuring that services provided for its residents are enjoyed only by residents."[7]

3.2 Funding for Public Education

Financing public education is ordinarily a joint activity of state and local officials because, as noted in *San Antonio Independent School District v. Rodriguez*,[8] the Supreme Court reasoned that funding public schools is not a matter for the federal judiciary. Other than litigation over funding formulas, few finance cases concern state-level issues.

Finance cases typically examine state constitutional mandates and legislative limits on how resources to pay for public education are raised and/or allocated, often resulting in the creation of new funding plans. In the process, school finance cases seem to take on lives of their own, often going through multiple rounds of litigation before returning to legislatures.

3.3 Charter Schools

As parents desired greater options as to where their children can receive public educations, the charter schools movement that emerged in 1991 when Minnesota enacted the first statute authorizing their creation.[9] Forty-five jurisdictions plus the District of Columbia, Guam, and Puerto Rico currently have adopted laws permitting

---

[6] 457 U.S. 202 (1982), *reh'g denied*, 458 U.S. 1131 (1982).

[7] 461 U.S. 321, 328 (1983).

[8] 411 U.S. 1 (1973).

[9] MINN. STAT. ANN. § 124D.10.

the creation of charter schools,[10] public schools of choice, that cannot be operated by faith-based organizations, largely exempted from state curricular laws and requiring them to hire certificated teachers.

In exchange for being exempt from many state standards, charter schools are accountable for the academic achievement of their students and can lose their charters if pupils are not successful. Charters vary in duration, typically from three to five years in length. When contracts expire, depending on state law, charters can be renewed or terminated. Other public school options available to parents include on-line and vocational schools wherein students can learn trades such as mechanics and plumbing.

3.4 Exceptions from Compulsory Attendance

Parents who choose not to send their children to public schools must provide them with equivalent instruction elsewhere either by having them educated in non-public schools or via home schooling.

3.5 Faith-Based Schools

The Supreme Court upheld the right of parents to send their children to non-public schools, most of which are faith-based, in *Pierce v. Society of the Sisters of the Holy Names of Jesus and Mary* (*Pierce*).[11] In so doing, the Court invalidated a law from Oregon which would have required children, other than those who today would be described as needing special education, between the ages of eight and sixteen to attend public schools.

Pierce was filed by officials in two non-public schools, one religiously affiliated, the other a military academy, who sought to avoid having their schools forced out of business, relying on their property rights under the Fourteenth Amendment. Ruling in favor of the school officials, the Supreme Court found that because parents had the right to direct the upbringing of their children, they could satisfy the compulsory attendance law by sending their young to non-public schools.[12]

Wisconsin v. Yoder (*Yoder*)[13] is perhaps the most significant exception to compulsory attendance laws. In *Yoder*, the Supreme Court ruled in favor of Amish parents

[10] Charter School Data Dashboard, (2023), https://data.publiccharters.org.

[11] 268 U.S. 510 (1925).

[12] *See also Farrington v. Tokushige*, 273 U.S. 284 (1927) (confirming the parental right to send their children to non-public schools, rejecting attempts by state officials to regulate foreign language schools in Hawaii, most of which were Japanese, who alleged that the schools did not serve the public interest).

[13] 406 U.S. 205 (1972).

who challenged the denial of their request to have their children excused from formal public education beyond eighth because they would have received all of the preparation they needed for life in their home communities. Relying on the First Amendment's Free Exercise Clause, the Court agreed that the community's then almost 300-year way of life would have been endangered, if not destroyed, by forcing the parents to comply with the law. Following *Yoder*, few, if any, religions groups can meet its test for being excused from compulsory education requirements as courts consistently deny religion-based applications for exemptions to substantial or material parts of compulsory education requirements such as home schooling.[14]

3.6 Home Schooling

The home schooling movement largely began in the early 1980s, is now legal throughout in the United States for parents to educate their children on their own or with groups of other parents. Courts have review various issues associated with home schooling such as teacher qualifications and curricular content, both of which are largely inapplicable to parents.

As to state oversight of home schooling, courts recognize the right of public officials to ensure that students who are home schooled are progressing whether by means of standardized tests[15] or measures such as portfolios[16] and annual reports.[17] Parents who home school have had limited success over whether their children can participate in extracurricular activities. Yet, parents have had a fair degree of success seeking change legislatively as a growing number of jurisdictions allow students who are home schooled to participate in extracurricular activities, including sports. Conversely, parents who engage in home schooling have had little success in seeking to enroll their children in public schools on part-time bases.

3.7 Aid to Faith-Based Schools

The Supreme Court enunciated what is referred to as the Child Benefit Test, a term the Justices have not actually used, starting in a 1947 case from New Jersey, *Everson v. Board of Education*,[18] wherein they permitted public transportation for children to and from their faith-based schools. Later, in 1968, in *Board of Education of*

[14] *Johnnson v. Charles City Cmty. Schs. Bd. of Educ.*, 368 N.W.2d 74 (Iowa 1985), *cert. denied sub nom.* Pruessner v. Benton, 474 U.S. 1033 (1985).

[15] *Murphy v. State of Ark.*, 852 F.2d 1039 (8th Cir. 1988).

[16] *Stobaugh v. Wallace*, 757 F. Supp. 653 (W.D. Pa. 1990).

[17] *State v. Rivera*, 497 N.W.2d 878 (Iowa 1993), *reh'g denied* (1993).

[18] 330 U.S. 1 (1947), *reh'g denied*, 330 U.S. 855 (1947).

Central School District v. Allen,[19] the Supreme Court upheld a statute from New York directing local boards to loan textbooks for secular instruction to all students regardless of where they attended classes because doing so benefitted the children rather than their religiously-affiliated schools.

Starting with *Lemon v. Kurtzman*, a 1971 case involving disputes from Pennsylvania and Rhode Island, the Supreme Court placed significant limits on aid to students and their faith-based schools, basically refusing to extend aid beyond transportation and textbooks. Under *Lemon's* now repudiated tripartite test, as discussed below, interactions between the governmental and religious institutions had to "[f]irst have a secular legislative purpose; second, its principal or primary effect must be one that neither advances nor inhibits religion; finally, the statute must not foster 'an excessive government entanglement with religion,'".[20]

In a dramatic shift, in 1997 in *Agostini v. Felton*.[21] the Supreme Court expanded the limits of aid by permitting the on-site delivery of Title I services to eligible students in their faith-based schools in New York City because they qualified due to the low socio-economic status of their parents and education needs. Five years later, in *Zelman v, Simmons Harris*,[22] the Justices upheld a voucher program in Cleveland, Ohio, that allowed parents to move their children from failing public schools and place them in mostly Catholic schools. The Court was satisfied that the program passed constitution muster both because the students were the primary beneficiaries and their parents placed their children in these schools as a matter of their own free choices, not because the law obligated them to do so.

Continuing the trend it initiated in *Agostini*, the Supreme Court's three most recent cases on aid expanded the reach of the Child Benefit Test. *Trinity Lutheran Church of Columbia v. Comer*, from 2017, began when officials in a year-round faith-based preschool and daycare center in Missouri challenged their being denied a state grant to obtain aid to install a new surface in its playground to make it safer for children. After lower federal courts rejected the application solely due to the center's religious nature, the Supreme Court reversed in their favor because the Free Exercise Clause does not allow states to single out faith-based institutions, and/or believers, to be denied generally available benefits simply because they are religious. Writing for the Court, Chief Justice Roberts emphasized that "the exclusion of Trinity Lutheran Church from a public benefit for which it is otherwise qualified, solely because it is a church, is odious to our Constitution all the same, and cannot stand."

Three years later, in *Espinoza v. Montana Department of Revenue*, mothers challenged an order invalidating a tax credit program for contributions to student scholarship organizations under the state constitutional prohibition of public funds to aid "sectarian" schools. Holding in favor of the three mothers, the Supreme Court explained that because the program was permissible under the Establishment Clause, the state's no-aid provision discriminated based on religion. The Justices concluded

---

[19] 392 U.S. 236 (1968).

[20] 403 U.S. 602, 612–613 (1971).

[21] 521 U.S. 203 (1997).

[22] 536 U.S. 639, 649 (2002).

that while the state constitution sought to separate church and state more strictly than the Federal constitution, it violated the Federal constitutional insofar as it lacked a compelling interest to invalidate the program.

At issue in *Carson v. Makin*, a 2023 case from Maine, was a statute that denied tuition payments to parents in districts lacking their own secondary schools unless they sent their children to nonsectarian schools. The Supreme Court invalidated the program's nonsectarian requirement as violating the Free Exercise Clause because it was neither neutral toward religion nor afforded parents the opportunity to send their children to the schools of their choice.

Also in 2022, in *Kennedy v. Bremerton School District*, the Supreme Court upheld the right of a football coach in a public high school in Washington to engage in silent prayer on the field at the end of games. Although not involving aid, *Kennedy* is crucial because, recognizing that it "long ago abandoned *Lemon* ..." the Court held that "the Establishment Clause must be interpreted by 'reference to historical practices and understandings,'" ushering a new era and test in its First Amendment jurisprudence. It remains to be seen how the Court applies this new standard in future litigation.

4 Faculty Rights

State laws provide the primary source of regulating the employment rights of teachers. Even so, federal law, especially in the area of anti-discrimination, has a major impact on the rights of teachers in public schools.

4.1 Certification/Tenure

All jurisdictions require teachers in public school to be certified or licensed ordinarily based on having completed professional preparation programs along with passing competency examinations and criminal background checks. If candidates meet the legal standards for certification, including successful completion of examinations,[23] state agencies may not arbitrarily reject their applications[24] or impose new conditions such as age requirements. Once employed, teachers are evaluated regularly, usually on multiple occasions during their three to four year probationary periods.

Once teachers earn tenure, called continuing contract status in some states, they are typically evaluated annually, often pursuant to provisions in their collective bargaining agreements. The benefits of tenure is that it confers substantive due

---

[23] Courts typically reject challenges to teacher competence examinations. *See, e.g.*, *Allen v. Alabama State Bd. of Educ.*, 164 F.3d 1347 (11th Cir. 1999), *vacated*, 216 F.3d 1263 (11th Cir. 2000); *Association of Mexican-American Educators v. State of Cal.*, 231 F.3d 572 (9th Cir. 2000).

[24] *Keller v. Hewitt*, 41 P. 871 (Cal.1895); *State ex rel. Hopkins v. Wooster*, 208 P. 656 (Kan.1922).

process rights on teachers, but usually not administrators because they are managerial employees such that they cannot be dismissed without receiving procedural due process, a topic discussed below.

4.2 Statutory Protections

Title VII of the Civil Rights Act of 1964 (Title VII),[25] the most significant federal anti-discrimination statute addressing employment, both before and after hiring reads.

"It shall be an unlawful employment practice for an employer:

(1) to fail or refuse to hire or to discharge any individual, or otherwise to discriminate against any individual with respect to his compensation, terms, conditions, or privileges of employment, because of such individual's race, color, religion, sex, or national origin[26];

Three other major federal laws forbid workplace discrimination. The Age Discrimination in Employment Act[27] protects workers forty or over. The Americans with Disabilities Act (ADA),[28] mirroring Section 504, requires employers in the private sector to make reasonable accommodation for employees who are otherwise qualified to work. The Family and Medical Leave Act[29] provides protections for employees who need to take time off to care for family members or themselves needing medical attention.

4.3 Dismissals and Due Process

Because public school teachers can lose their jobs under two broad categories, not for cause, and for cause, this section examines dismissals.

4.4 Dismissal not for Cause

Most states have statutes on the dismissal of teachers or others in schools without fault, a practice commonly known as reduction-in-force (RIF). The grounds for RIF, the order in which employees are released, can "bump" others from their jobs, and

---

[25] 42 U.S.C. §§ 2000 *et seq.*

[26] 42 U.S.C. § 2000e–2(a).

[27] 29 U.S.C. §§ 621 *et seq.*

[28] 42 U.S.C. §§ 12101 *et seq.*

[29] 29 U.S.C. §§ 2611 *et seq.*

call-back rights are matters of state law subject to modifications by board policies and/ or collective bargaining agreements.

State laws typically permit RIFs due to declines in student enrollments, financial exigencies, elimination of jobs or programs, and board discretion. While courts ordinarily defer to the discretion of school boards on the need for RIFs, if challenged, officials must demonstrate that RIFs complied with state laws, board policies and/ or collective bargaining contracts.

Once school boards decide to RIF staff, they must establish the order of release. Insofar as RIFs are ordinarily based on seniority, courts typically treat it as a rational, but not exclusive, factor in selecting employees for RIFs. Courts place the burden of proving that positions are unnecessary on school officials when boards RIF employees. In evaluating seniority, absent modifications based on board polices or collective bargaining agreements, the first criterion is years of full-time service in schools systems. Beyond that, the methods that boards rely on must be reasonable and not prohibited by state or federal law such as dismissing individuals in such protected categories as race or gender.

When tenured staff members are dismissed pursuant to RIFs, non-tenured employees usually can neither be retained nor granted tenure. The upshot is that current employees who are about to have their jobs eliminated as part of RIFs are entitled to "bump" less senior staff members. "Bumping" is a term of art that makes it possible for employees with more seniority, and at least the same credentials, to retain the jobs for which they were certificated even if those positions are occupied by equally qualified staff members with less seniority.

4.5 Dismissal for Cause

Because tenure statutes permit teacher contracts to continue without the express need for renewals, boards must follow specified procedures when they wish to dismiss tenured teachers. There are three basic elements in due process are timely notice of a possible dismissal, specification of charges, and an opportunity to respond at fair and impartial hearings at which allegations are examined and judgments rendered on the records regarding teachers' future employment. Most statutes also include provisions for appeals often resulting in judicial review.

State laws typically provide that tenured teachers may be dismissed only for specified grounds because, as discussed above, they have substantive due process property rights in their jobs entitling them to procedural due process, a topic reviewed below. Teachers who have not earned tenure can have their employment terminated for any lawful reason[30] without hearings.[31]

[30] *Haviland v. Yonkers Pub. Schs.*, 800 N.Y.S.2d 578 (N.Y. App. Div. 2005).

[31] *Von Gizycki v. Levy*, 771 N.Y.S.2d 174 (N.Y. App. Div. 2004).

Conceding that states use a variety of terms for the same topics, the three sometimes overlapping grounds for which teachers can be dismissed for cause are insubordination, which occurs when teachers intentionally fail to comply with legitimate orders of supervisors or with valid rules and regulations of which they were, or reasonably should have been, aware; conduct unbecoming a professional, which increasingly has dealt with misconduct involving students; and incompetence, perhaps the most difficult of the three grounds to prove because it can be so difficult to measure teacher performance.

4.6 *Procedural Due Process*

Tenure statutes, local board policies, and collective bargaining agreements often require school officials to warn teachers before they initiate disciplinary actions for remediable offenses. Absent specific remediation provisions, boards are under no obligation to warn teachers and to offer them opportunities to correct their behavior.[32]

In *Cleveland Board of Education v. Loudermill* (*Loudermill*),[33] a dispute from Ohio, its most important case in this arena, the Supreme Court explained that absent unusual circumstances, wherein they can be suspended with pay, the Fourteenth Amendment requires school boards to provide educators who have property interests in their jobs, whether through tenure or unexpired contracts, to procedural due process, beginning with notice. Depending on state law, tenured teachers are not necessarily entitled to full hearings as long as they are afforded opportunities to have hearings after they are dismissed.

The heart of procedural due process is notice and a hearing at which employees have the chance to address the charges they face. Initial hearings are usually conducted by local school boards, hearing officers, or state administrative agencies. While hearings need not meet strict judicial processes, evidence that might not be admitted in courts may be admissible as long as it does not violate the fundamentals of fairness. Once hearings are done, dissatisfied parties can seek judicial review.

4.7 *Free Speech Rights*

Beginning with *Pickering v. Board of Education of Township High School District* (*Pickering*),[34] the Supreme Court handed down four major cases, two involving

[32] *Roberts v. Lincoln Cnty. Sch. Dist. No. One*, 676 P.2d 577 (Wyo. 1984).

[33] 470 U.S. 532 (1985), *on remand*, 763 F.2d 202 (6th Cir. 1985), *on remand*, 651 F. Supp. 92 (N.D. Ohio 1986), *aff'd*, 844 F.2d 304 (6th Cir.1988), *cert. denied*, 488 U.S. 941 (1988), *cert. denied*, 488 U.S. 946 (1988).

[34] 391 U.S. 563 (1968).

teachers, about the First Amendment rights of teachers and other public employees, to freedom of speech.

Pickering concerned the attempt of a school board in Illinois to dismiss a teacher for writing a letter to a local newspaper criticizing it over a bond issue and the use of financial resources for its athletic programs. Along with recognizing that the teacher had the right to speak out on a legitimate matter of public concern as a private citizen, the Supreme Court was of the opinion that he could not be dismissed did not have a close working relationship with those he criticized, his letter did not have a detrimental impact on the district's administration, and it did not negatively affect his regular duties.

In *Mt. Healthy City Board of Education v. Doyle*,[35] a case from Ohio, the Supreme Court considered the effect of including a constitutionally protected right as a factor in not renewing the contract of a teacher who placed the call to a radio talk show in which he was criticized his board. The Court thought that where a teacher shows that protected conduct about a school matter was a substantial or motivating factor when board choose not to renew a contract, it must be given the opportunity to show that it would have chosen not to re-employ in the absence of the protected conduct. On remand, the Sixth Circuit upheld the board's a claim that that it would not have renewed the teacher's contract regardless of whether he made the call.[36]

At issue in *Connick v. Myers* (*Connick*),[37] a non-school case from Louisiana, was whether *Pickering* protects individuals who communicate their views about workplace matters to peers. A former assistant district attorney failed in challenging her dismissal for circulating a questionnaire about office operations among staff. The Supreme Court established a two-step test to evaluate whether speech is entitled to First Amendment protections. First, the Court stated that the judiciary must consider whether the speech involved a matter of public concern by examining its content and form along with the context within which it was expressed. Second, the Court commented that if speech deals with a matter of public concern, the judiciary must balance employees' interests as citizens in speaking out on such matters against those of public employers in promoting effective and efficient services.

In *Garcetti v. Ceballos* (*Garcetti*),[38] again not involving a school, the Supreme Court affirmed that because a deputy district attorney's complaints about supervisors in California were not on matters of public concern, his speech was not entitled to First Amendment protection. The Court wrote that because public employees who speak out pursuant to their official duties are not doing so as citizens for First Amendment purposes, the Constitution is unavailable to protect their communications from employer discipline.

---

[35] 429 U.S. 274 (1977).

[36] *Doyle v. Mt. Healthy City Sch. Dist. Bd. of Educ.*, 670 F.2d 59 (6th Cir.1982).

[37] 461 U.S. 138 (1983).

[38] 547 U.S. 410 (2006).

4.8 Freedom of Religion

Teachers in public schools are free to believe as they wish but may not proselytize or actively practice their faiths in ways that might otherwise influence students or peers to share their beliefs. In a related vein, courts agree that educators cannot wear distinctively religious dress to work[39] but may be able to wear small, unobtrusive religious items.[40]

In two successive years the Supreme Court reached major decisions expanding the religious rights of public employees. First, in 2022, in *Kennedy v. Bremerton School District*, the Supreme Court upheld the right of a football coach in a public high school in Washington to engage in silent prayer by kneeling on the field at the end of games. Reversing earlier judgments in favor of the board, in a major change in its jurisprudence, the Court pointed out that it violated the coach's First Amendment rights under the Free Exercise and Free Speech Clauses.

A year later, in *Groff v. DeJoy*,[41] the Supreme Court, a non-school case, ruled in favor of a postal worker in Pennsylvania, a professed Evangelical Christian, who quit his job and sued the United States Postal Service alleging its officials failed to accommodate his religious obligation not to work on Sundays. The Court remarked that Title VII's requiring employers to make "reasonable accommodations" for the religious beliefs and practices of their employees means that before they seek to be excused from doing so due to undue hardships, they must now demonstrate that when employees need to take time off for religious reasons, granting such requests would result in substantial, rather than minimal, increased costs and inconveniences.

On another matter, the Supreme Court has upheld provisions in Title VII allowing religious employers alone to decide who qualifies for positions deemed ministerial, including teachers.[42] In such situations, the burden of proof is on officials to prove that staff members engage in activities such teaching that is so integrally related to promoting the spiritual and pastoral missions of their schools that their duties can be treated as ministerial. If such matters are addressed in teacher contracts, school officials generally prevail.[43]

---

[39] *See, e.g.*, *Cooper v. Eugene Sch. Dist. No. 4J*, 723 P.2d 298 (Or. 1986), *appeal dismissed*, 480 U.S. 942 (1987).

[40] *Nichol v. ARIN Intermediate Unit 28*, 268 F. Supp.2d 536 (W.D. Pa. 2003) (enjoining a board policy under which an employee was suspended for refusing to remove or conceal a small cross she wore on a necklace as viewpoint discrimination because it only forbade religious items).

[41] 143 2279 S. Ct. (2023).

[42] *See, e.g.*, *Hosanna-Tabor Evangelical Lutheran Church and School v. Equal Employment Opportunities Commission*, 563 U.S. 903 (2011), *rev'g*, 597 F.3d 769 (6th Cir. 2010), *reh'g and reh'g en banc denied* (2010); *Our Lady of Guadalupe School v. Morrissey-Berru and St. James School v. Biel*, 140 S. Ct. 2049 (2020).

[43] See, e.g., *Crisitello v. St. Theresa Sch.*, 2023 WL 5185586 (N.J. 2023).

4.9 Freedom of Association-Unionization

Collective bargaining in public education allows school boards, teachers, and other employees to negotiate over terms and conditions of employment. The extent to which boards may engage in bargaining varies from one jurisdiction to the next. While the First Amendment does not require boards to recognize or bargain with unions, it does protect teachers who join labor organizations and cannot discipline them for doing so or for engaging in protected union activities.

Before they can negotiate with their school boards, employee unions must organize bargaining units that are recognized as the exclusive bargaining agents of their members.[44] Once boards recognize unions, bargaining is limited to sessions with these exclusive bargaining agents.[45] In return, unions have the duty to represent all employees in good faith[46] during bargaining, even individuals who are not members who must pay so-called agency or representation fees.[47]

In a significant limitation on unions, in *Janus v. American Federation of State, County, and Municipal Employees Council 31*,[48] a non-school case, the Supreme Court rejected plan in Illinois as unconstitutional because it violated the free speech rights of nonunion members by compelling them to subsidize private speech on matters of substantial public concerns with which they might not agree.

5 Student Rights

5.1 Discrimination-Free Schooling

The enactment of compulsory education laws in the mid-nineteenth century, starting In Massachusetts,[49] changed the face of American public schooling. As school systems evolved to meet the needs of their students, the Supreme Court opened schools to children who were African American. As noted earlier, *Brown* was the catalyst leading to fundamental changes in American education resulting in the enactment of Title IX of the Education Amendments of 1972 (Title IX) which was designed to provide gender equity in athletics but was leater extended to prevent

---

[44] *Appeal of Londonderry Sch. Dist.*, 707 A.2d 137 (N.H.1998).

[45] *Independence-Nat'l Educ. Ass'n v. Independence Sch. Dist.*, 162 S.W.3d 18 (Mo. Ct. App. 2005), *transfer denied* (2005), *on subsequent appeal*, 223 S.W.3d 131 (Mo. 2007).

[46] *See, e.g., Leer v. Washington Educ. Ass'n*, 172 F.R.D. 439 (W.D. Wash.1997); *Fratus v. Marion Community Schools Bd. of Trustees*, 749 N.E.2d 40 (Ind. 2001).

[47] *O'Brien v. City of Springfield*, 319 F. Supp.2d 90 (D. Mass. 2003).

[48] ___U.S. ___, 138 S. Ct. 2448 (2018).

[49] MASS. GEN. LAWS ANN. 76 § 1 (historical notes St. 1852, c. 240, §§ 1, 2, 4).

sexual harassment of students.[50] Section 504 of the Rehabilitation Act of 1973[51] (Section 504).[52]In 1975, Congress enacted Education for All Handicapped Children Act, now the Individuals with Disabilities Education Act (IDEA),[53] discussed later in this chapter.

According to Title IX, "[n]o person in the United States shall, on the basis of sex, be excluded from participation in, be denied the benefits of, or be subjected to discrimination under any education program or activity receiving Federal financial assistance."[54] The Supreme Court first relied on Title IX in resolving disputes over sexual harassment in schools with *Franklin v. Gwinnett County Public Schools*,[55] a case from Georgia. Although not setting evidentiary standards, *Franklin* is important because it was the initial dispute in which the Court ruled in favor of a student who had been sexually harassed by a teacher, allowing her claim to proceed.

The Supreme Court clarified the circumstances under which school boards can be liable for teacher sexual harassment of students in *Gebser v. Lago Vista Independent School District*,[56] a dispute from Texas. The Justices refused to impose liability on boards unless an official who, at a minimum, with the authority to institute corrective measures, has actual notice of, and acts with deliberate indifferent to, sexual misconduct by a teacher or other school employee.

In *Davis v. Monroe County Board of Education,*[57] another dispute from Georgia, the Justices addressed peer-to-peer sexual harassment in an order in favor of a female who was harassed by a male classmate and her parents. The Supreme Court began by indicating that damages are limited "to circumstances wherein the recipient exercises substantial control over both the harasser and the context in which the known harassment occurs."[58] The Justices asserted that school boards, as recipients of federal financial assistance, "are properly held liable in damages only when they are deliberately indifferent to sexual harassment, of which they have actual knowledge, that is so severe, pervasive, and objectively offensive that it can be said to deprive the victims of access to the educational opportunities or benefits provided by the school."[59] The Court stressed that while boards may be accountable if officials are deliberately indifferent, this does not allow them to avoid liability only by eliminating actionable peer-harassment claims or taking specified disciplinary steps because they must take proactive steps to prevent such situations from occurring such as adopting

---

[50] 20 U.S.C. § 1681. Employees are protected by Title VII on the Civil Rights Act of 1964.

[51] 29 U.S.C. § 794(a).

[52] As noted, the ADA, 42 U.S.C. §§ 12101 *et seq.*, extends similar protections to individuals in the private sector.

[53] 20 U.S.C. §§ 1400 *et seq.*

[54] 20 U.S.C. § 1681.

[55] 503 U.S. 60 (1992), *on remand*, 969 F.2d 1022 (11th Cir. 1992).

[56] 524 U.S. 274 (1998).

[57] 526 U.S. 629 (1999), *on remand*, 206 F.3d 1377 (11th Cir. 2000).

[58] *Id.* at 645.

[59] *Id.* at 650.

anti-harassment policies and educating students and staff about how they must treat others.

5.2 Due Process in Discipline

It is well established that courts ordinarily grant educational officials "wide discretion in school discipline matters"[60] to adopt reasonable policies and procedures overseeing student conduct. School board policies on discipline are presumptively valid. Accordingly, the burden of challenging rules rests on students and their parents. Even so, the more rules impact the constitutional rights of students, the greater the need for educational officials to justify them, even in light of the broad discretion afforded educators, pupils do not shed their constitutional rights at the schoolhouse gate.

Courts vitiate rules lacking rational relationships to legitimate educational objectives, are too vague in describing what they forbid, and/or are over-broad insofar as they prohibit constitutionally protected activities along with matters subject to discipline. As the severity of punishments increases, courts take closer looks at school rules and procedures.

Whether all rules are written is immaterial if offenses such as cheating are punishable under general norms of school behavior. Because courts concede that educators cannot develop written rules for all possible student infractions, jurists typically defer to the authority of school officials as long as their actions in imposing discipline meet the requirements of due process.

Consequently, when students know, or reasonably should know, school rules and punishments are appropriate to their offenses, courts ordinarily do not interfere as long as educators treat similarly situated students similarly when applying sanctions.

Two Supreme Court cases stand out in the area of student discipline. *Goss v. Lopez*[61] was a dispute from Ohio wherein students who did not receive a hearing challenged their suspensions for allegedly disruptive conduct. Ruling in favor of the students, the Justices held that due process requires they be given "oral or written notice of the charges against [them] and, if [they] den[y] them, an explanation of the evidence the authorities have and an opportunity to present [their] side of the story."[62] The Court found no need for a delay between when officials give students notice and the time of their hearings, conceding that in most cases disciplinarians may well have informally discussed alleged acts of misconduct with them shortly after they occurred.

In *Goss* the Supreme Court explained that if the presence of students in schools constitute threats of disruption, they may be removed immediately with the due process requirements to be fulfilled as soon as practicable. The Court expressly

---

[60] *DMP v. Fay Sch. ex rel. Bd. of Trs.*, 933 F. Supp.2d 214, 222 (D. Mass. 2013) (internal citations omitted).

[61] 419 U.S. 565 (1975).

[62] *Id.* at 581.

rejected the claim that students should be represented by counsel, be able to present witnesses, and be able to confront and cross-examine witnesses when facing short-term exclusions.

In non-binding *dicta* the *Goss* Court noted that "[l]onger suspensions or expulsions for the remainder of the school term, or permanently, may require more formal procedures ... [and that] in unusual situations, although involving only a short suspension, something more than the rudimentary procedures will be required."[63] Jurisdictions have followed the Court's suggestion and developed statutory guidelines when students are subject to long-term suspensions and/or expulsions.

Two years after *Goss*, *Ingraham v. Wright*,[64] a case from Florida, the Supreme Court upheld the constitutionality of corporal punishment as a valid exercise of school board authority. Most jurisdictions now ban corporal punishment with courts penalizing educators who use it if their behavior is conscience-shocking.

5.3 *Search and Seizure/Drug Testing*

The spread of violence and the presence of contraband such as weapons and drugs in schools has led to significant amounts of litigation over the Fourth Amendment[65] as educators search students and their property in strive to maintain safe and orderly learning environments.

The Supreme Court first examined the Fourth Amendment in a school context in *New Jersey v. T.L.O.* (*T.L.O.*).[66] When a fourteen-year-old, first-year high school student, identified as T.L.O., and a friend were accused of violating school rules by smoking in a lavatory, because the latter admitted to smoking, she was not brought to the office for a search. When T.L.O. denied smoking and claimed she did not smoke at all, the teacher brought her to the Assistant Principal's (AP) office.

On opening T.L.O.'s purse, when the AP saw her cigarettes "in plain view," a term of art borrowed from criminal law, he removed them and accused her of lying. Continuing with the search, the AP discovered cigarette rolling papers, a small amount of marijuana, a pipe, a number of plastic bags, a substantial quantity of one-dollar bills, an index card apparently identifying a list of students who owed T.L.O. money, and two letters implicating her in dealing marijuana.

After T.L.O. confessed to selling marijuana at her high school, a state trial court refused to suppress the evidence, adjudicated her delinquent, and sentenced her to a year on probation.[67] An appellate court affirmed the denial of the motion to suppress the search of T.L.O.'s purse but vacated and remanded because it was

[63] *Id*. at 584.

[64] 430 U.S. 651 (1977).

[65] Under the Fourth Amendment, "[t]he right of the people to be secure in their persons, houses, papers, and effects, against unreasonable searches and seizures, shall not be violated....".

[66] 469 U.S. 325 (1985).

[67] *In re T.L.O.*, 428 A.2d 1327 (N.J. Juv. & Dom. Rel. Ct. 1980).

unclear whether she knowingly and voluntarily waived her Fifth Amendment rights before confessing.[68] The Supreme Court of New Jersey invalidated the search as a violation of the Fourth Amendment.[69]

On further review in *New Jersey v. T.L.O.*, the Supreme Court reversed in favor of the State. Applying the Fourth Amendment's prohibition against unreasonable searches and seizures in public schools, the Justices devised a two-part test to evaluate the legality of searches by school officials: "[f]irst, one must consider 'whether the … action was justified at its inception;' second, one must determine whether the search as actually conducted 'was reasonably related in scope to the circumstances which justified the interference in the first place.'"[70] The Court added that "a search will be permissible in its scope when the measures adopted are reasonably related to the objectives of the search and not excessively intrusive in light of the age and sex of the student and the nature of the infraction."[71]

In *T.L.O.* the Supreme Court explained that a search is justified at its inception "when there are reasonable grounds for suspecting that the search will turn up evidence that the student has violated or is violating either the law or the rules of the school."[72] A subjective measure based on specific facts that must be more than a mere hunch, reasonable suspicion for searches is significantly less than the probable cause standard applicable to the police; "[p]robable cause exists when there is a fair probability that … evidence of a crime will be found in a particular place."[73] Because school, also known as administrative, searches are designed to ensure safety where there are usually large numbers of students and relatively few adults present, educators need only articulable justification in order to proceed. The Court later invalidating strip searches in *Safford Unified School District No. 1* v. *Redding*.[74]

The Supreme Court twice upheld the use of suspicionless drug testing of student-athletes in *Vernonia School District 47J v. Acton*[75] and *Board of Education of Independent School District No. 92 of Pottawatomie v. Earls* (*Earls*), cases from Washington and Oklahoma, respectively.[76] In *Earls* the Court modified the third part of the test it created in *Action*. First, the Court examined the nature of the student-athletes' alleged privacy interest, noting that they are limited both due to the need of officials to preserve discipline and safety plus because those taking part in extracurricular activities voluntarily subject themselves to greater intrusions on their privacy than

---

[68] *In re T.L.O.*, 448 A.2d 493 (N.J. Super. Ct. App. Div. 1982).

[69] *In re T.L.O.*, 463 A.2d 934 (N.J. 1983).

[70] *New Jersey v. T.L.O.*, 469 U.S. 325, 341, (1985).

[71] *Id.* at 342.

[72] *Id.*

[73] *Evans v. Chalmers*, 703 F.3d 636, 653 (4th Cir. 2012), *cert. denied*, 571 U.S. 822 (2013) (internal citations omitted).

[74] 557 U.S. 364 (2009).

[75] 515 U.S. 646 (1995), *on remand*, 66 F.3d 217 (9th Cir. 1995).

[76] 536 U.S. 822 (2002), *on remand*, 300 F.3d 1222 (10th Cir. 2002).

their non-participating peers. Second, the Court reviewed the character of the intrusion, finding that the protections officials adopted in collecting and analyzing urine samples protected students' interests.

Turning to the third part of the test, the nature and immediacy of the board's concerns and the policy's efficacy in meeting them, the Supreme Court acknowledged the importance of governmental interest in preventing drug use, a problem that had not abated since *Acton*. As such, the Justices rejected the students' claims that drug use was not a problem at the school by relying on evidence to the contrary from board officials. The Justices posited that it did not require schools to have particularized or pervasive drug problems before permitting educators to conduct suspicionless testing.

5.4 Freedom of Religion

While students in public schools are free to believe as they wish, there has been a great deal of controversy over such issues as prayer and Bible study clubs among other issues. Even so, the religious freedom rights of students are greater than those of teachers except that while students are certainly free to believe as they wish, when conflicts arise In between student beliefs and curricular control, courts ordinarily uphold the actions of school officials if they are able to demonstrate their reliance on legitimate pedagogical reasons. In such a case, the Sixth Circuit affirmed that a student in Tennessee could not write a biography about Jesus as a historical figure because she failed to follow her teacher's directions in completing the assignment.[77]

The Supreme Court consistently banned school-sponsored prayer[78] before invalidating a school board policy that would have allowed student led prayers before high school football games in *Santa Fe Independent School District v. Doe*.[79] The Court affirmed an earlier order that a board policy in Texas allowing student-led prayers prior to the start of high school football games violated the Establishment Clause because permitting prayer at football games was an impermissible governmental approval or endorsement of religion rather than a form of psychological coercion. Interestingly, because the Court chose not to address the related question of student prayer at graduation, the issue is unsettled. At present, officials can prevent student

---

[77] *Settle v. Dickson Cnty. Sch. Bd.*, 53 F.3d 152 (6th Cir. 1995), *cert. denied*, 516 U.S. 989 (1995).

[78] See, e.g., *Engel v. Vitale*, 370 U.S. 421 (1962) (banning a prayer composed by the New York State Board of Regents for suggested use in public schools to inculcate moral and spiritual values in students); *School Dist, of Abington Twp. v. Schempp & Murray v. Curlett*, 374 U.S. 203 (1963) (forbidding Bible reading and prayer before school in Pennsylvania and Maryland; *Lee v. Weisman*, 505 U.S. 577 (1992) (invalidating school-sponsored graduation prayer in Rhode Island).

[79] 530 U.S. 290 (2000).

led graduation prayer in the Third,[80] Tenth,[81] and Ninth[82] Circuits, can be used if it is non-sectarian and non-proselytizing in the Fifth Circuit,[83] and is permitted in the Eleventh Circuit.[84]

At the same time, in *Board of Education of Westside Community Schools v. Mergens*,[85] the Supreme Court did uphold the rights of high school students in public schools in Missouri to organize prayer and Bible study under the Equal Access Act clubs as long as other groups are allowed to meet during instructional time. The law specifies that "on the basis of the religious, political, philosophical, or other content of the speech at such meetings."[86] The Act does allow officials to exclude groups if their meetings "materially and substantially interfere with the orderly conduct of educational activities within the school."[87]

Lower courts have extended the scope of the Equal Access Act to allow students to chose leaders who meet this religious standards[88]; gather at lunch time[89] and during a morning activity period during which attendance was taken[90]; access to funding, fund-raising activities, a school yearbook, public address system, bulletin board, school supplies, school vehicles, and audio-visual equipment[91]; and broadcast a video promoting a club during morning announcements.[92] Courts have further extended the reach of the Act in largely agreeing that educational officials could not deny Gay/Straight Alliance clubs the opportunity to use school facilities.[93]

[80] *American Civil Liberties Union of N.J. v. Black Horse Pike Reg'l Bd. of Educ.*, 84 F.3d 1471 (3d Cir. 1996).

[81] *Corder v. Lewis Palmer Sch. Dist. No. 38*, 566 F.3d 1219 (10th Cir. 2009), *cert. denied*, 558 U.S. 1048 (2009).

[82] *Lassonde v. Pleasanton Unified Sch. Dist.*, 320 F.3d 979 (9th Cir. 2003).

[83] *Doe v. Santa Fe Indep. Sch. Dist.*, 168 F.3d 806 (5th Cir. 1999).

[84] *Adler v. Duval Cnty. Sch. Bd.*, 250 F.3d 1330 (11th Cir. 2001), *cert. denied*, 534 U.S. 1065 (200.1).

[85] 496 U.S. 226 (1990).

[86] 20 U.S.C. § 4071(a).

[87] 20 U.S.C. § 4071(c)(4).

[88] *Hsu v. Roslyn Union Free Sch. Dist.*, 85 F.3d 839 (2d Cir. 1996), *cert. denied*, 519 U.S. 1040, (1996).

[89] *Ceniceros v. Board of Trs. of the San Diego Unified Sch. Dist.*, 106 F.3d 878 (9th Cir. 1997).

[90] *Donovan ex rel. Donovan v. Punxsutawney Area Sch. Bd.*, 336 F.3d 211 (3d Cir. 2003).

[91] *Prince v. Jacoby*, 303 F.3d 1074 (9th Cir. 2002), *cert. denied*, 540 U.S. 813 (2003).

[92] Krestan v. Deer Valley Unified Sch. Dist. No. 97, of Maricopa Cnty., 561 F. Supp.2d 1078 (D. Ariz. 2008).

[93] See, e.g., *Straights and Gays for Equality v. Osseo Area Schs.-Dist. No. 279*, 540 F.3d 911 (8th Cir. 2008); *Colin ex rel. Colin v. Orange Unified Sch. Dist.*, 83 F. Supp.2d 1135 (C.D. Cal. 2000); *Gay-Straight Alliance of Yulee High Sch. v. School Bd. of Nassau Cnty.*, 602 F. Supp.2d 1233 (M.D. Fla. 2009).

5.5 Freedom of Speech

Tinker v. Des Moines Independent Community School District (*Tinker*)[94] was a watershed dispute over student rights as the first case in which the Supreme Court recognized the free speech rights of students in public schools in Iowa, upholding their right to wear black armbands in a protest over American activity in Viet Nam. The Justices limited student expressive activity in *Bethel School District No. 403 v. Fraser*,[95] finding that school officials in Washingtom could restrict student speech that is vulgar or lewd.

Hazelwood School District v. Kuhlmeier[96] dealt with the content of a school-sponsored newspaper that students prepared as part of a journalism class in Missouri. The Supreme Court held that "educators do not offend the First Amendment by exercising editorial control over the style and content of student speech in school-sponsored expressive activities so long as their actions are reasonably related to legitimate pedagogical concerns."[97] Finally, in *Morse v. Frederick*,[98] The Court upheld a principal's authority to order a student stop displaying a sign at a school-supervised activity because its message could reasonably have been interpreted as supporting the use of illegal drugs.

Most recently, the Supreme Court addressed its first dispute over student use of social media in a case involving off-campus speech. In *Mahanoy Area School District v. B. L. by and Through Levy*, the Justices maintained that when educational officials in Pennsylvania suspended a high school student from the cheerleading team for posting a photograph of herself making an obscene gesture and using vulgarity on Snapchat, they violated her right to free expression because she was not under their control insofar as she did so off-campus on a Saturday.[99]

On a related matter, courts uphold dress code policies if they are narrowly drawn, are rationally related to legitimate pedagogical concerns in support of schools' educational missions,[100] and are neither vague nor over-broad.[101] When dealing with religious dress, courts seemingly agree that educators must devise less restrictive alternatives to preventing students from wearing religious garb to schools.

---

[94] 393 U.S. 503 (1969).

[95] 478 U.S. 675 (1986).

[96] 484 U.S. 260 (1988).

[97] *Id.* at 273.

[98] 551 U.S. 393 (2007).

[99] 141 S. Ct. 2038 (2021).

[100] *Blau v. Fort Thomas Pub. Sch. Dist.*, 401 F.3d 381 (6th Cir. 2005); *Dempsey v. Alston*, 966 A.2d 1 (N.J. Super. Ct. App. Div. 2009), *cert. denied*, 973 A.2d 386 (N.J. 2009).

[101] *See, e.g., Canady v. Bossier Parish Sch. Bd.*, 240 F.3d 437 (5th Cir. 2001).

5.6 Students with Special Needs

Two federal statutes identified earlier, Section 504[102] and the IDEA,[103] are the primary laws protecting the educational rights of students with disabilities. These two laws provide varying degrees of protection to eligible persons. The ADA,[104] mentioned earlier, which mirrors Section 504, requires officials in non-public schools to make reasonable accommodation for students who are otherwise qualified.

There are eight significant differences between Section 504 and the IDEA. First, while Section 504 applies to school systems receiving federal financial assistance such as free lunches, it does not provide additional funds to serve qualified children. Second, Section 504 protects individuals under the broader notion of impairment rather than the IDEA's statutory definitions of disabilities. Third, while the IDEA covers primarily students from the ages of three to twenty-one there, are no age limits under Section 504. Fourth, Section 504 covers students, employees, and others, including parents while the IDEA is limited to students.

Fifth, the IDEA places an affirmative obligation on states, through local school boards, to identify, assess, and serve students with disabilities.[105] Those seeking help under Section 504 must request accommodations and may have to submit proof they are qualified if there are differences of opinion. Sixth, the IDEA contains more extensive due process protections than Section 504. Seventh, Section 504, unlike the IDEA does not require parental consent when making accommodations for students. Eighth, unlike the IDEA's zero-reject approach, educators can rely on Section 504's three defenses to avoid being charged with noncompliance.

Section 504 was the initial comprehensive federal law addressing the needs of the disabled. According to Section 504, "[n]o otherwise qualified individual with a disability in the United States … shall, solely by reason of her or his disability, be excluded from the participation in, be denied the benefits of, or be subjected to discrimination under any program or activity receiving [f]ederal financial assistance…."[106] Once officials identify children as "otherwise qualified" to receive assistance under Section 504, they must decide what accommodations they are willing, and/or able, to provide. Reasonable accommodations may involve minor adjustments such as permitting different children to have a service dog[107] and hearing interpreter[108] at school.

---

[102] 29 U.S.C. § 794(a).

[103] 20 U.S.C. §§ 1400 *et seq.*

[104] 42 U.S.C. §§ 12101 *et seq.*

[105] 20 U.S.C. § 1412(a)(3).

[106] 29 U.S.C. § 794(a).

[107] *Alboniga v. School Bd. of Broward Cnty.*, 87 F. Supp.3d 1319 (S.D. Fla. 2015).

[108] *Jones v. Illinois Dep't of Rehab. Servs.*, 689 F.2d 724 (7th Cir. 1982).

Even if children or teachers appear to be "otherwise qualified" under Section 504, school officials can rely on one of three defenses to avoid being charged with noncompliance. First, need not make accommodations resulting in "a fundamental alteration in the nature of [a] program."[109] Second, officials can avoid making changes resulting in "undue financial burden[s]."[110] Third, "otherwise qualified" students can be excluded from programs if their presence creates a substantial risk of injury to themselves or others such as possibly not allowing a student with poor hand eye coordination to work in around heavy machinery in a shop class.[111]

The IDEA was last revised in 2004, effective July 1, 2005; it has now gone the longest time in its history without being updated. Four eligibility requirements apply before students can receive IDEA services. First, students must be between the ages of three and twenty-one. However, local boards are not required to provide special education to persons between the ages of eighteen through twenty-one who are incarcerated in adult facilities if they were not previously identified as disabled and lacked Individualized Education Programs (IEPs) when they were incarcerated[112] or graduated from high school with regular diplomas.[113] Unless state laws dictate otherwise, courts interpret the IDEA as obligating officials to treat students as being twenty-one until the end of the academic years in which they reach the age limit.

Second, children must have specifically identified disabilities.[114] Third, students must require special education,[115] meaning they need a free appropriate public education[116] in the least restrictive environments[117] directed by the contents of their IEPs.[118] Fourth, children must need related services such as transportation or speech therapy.[119] Although a detailed review is beyond the scope of this chapter, the IDEA continues to generated significant amounts of litigation over such issues as the level of services school boards must provide to children with disabilities,[120] the rights of

---

109 *Southeastern Cmty. Coll. v. Davis*, 442 U.S. 397 (1979).

110 *Id.* at 412.

111 *See School Bd. of Nassau Cnty. v. Arline*, 480 U.S. 273, 287–288, (1987).

112 20 U.S.C. § 1412(a)(1)(B)(ii).

113 34 C.F.R. § 300.102(a)(2)(B).

114 20 U.S.C. § 1401(3)(A)(I). According to this section:

The term "child with a disability" means a child:

(I) with intellectual disabilities, hearing impairments (including deafness), speech or language impairments, visual impairments (including blindness), serious emotional disturbance (referred to in this chapter as "emotional disturbance"), orthopedic impairments, autism, traumatic brain injury, other health impairments, or specific learning disabilities....

115 20 U.S.C. § 1401(3)(A)(ii).

116 20 U.S.C. § 1401(9).

117 20 U.S.C. § 1412(a)(5).

118 20 U.S.C. §§ 1401(14), 1414(d)(1)(A).

119 20 U.S.C. § 1401(3)(A)(ii).

120 *Endrew F. v. Douglas Cnty. Sch. Dist. RE-1*, 580 U.S. 386, 399 (2017) (ruling that "[t]o meet its substantive obligation under the IDEA, a school must offer an IEP reasonably calculated to enable a child to make progress appropriate in light of the child's circumstances").

parents to litigate claims relating to their children in their own names,[121] and whether parents can be reimbursed for expert witness and other fees,[122] most of it in federal courts.

6 Emerging Issues

Two emerging issues have created controversy in recent years. First, as technology continues to become increasingly important in schools, it is not surprising that the resulting litigation reflects how courts reach markedly different outcomes over the extent to which educators can punish students for breaking school rules, particularly when they are on social media, especially when they raise claims that their being disciplined violates their First Amendment rights to free speech. If courts are satisfied that student messages on the internet are true threats, they uphold the authority of school officials to discipline them for such behavior.[123] In light of how rapidly technology advances, and the difficulty courts have keeping pace, it is likely to take some time before the judiciary devises clear ruled for educators to follow.

The second issue deals with the rights of students who are transgender. Because, for example, courts disagree whether students who are transgender should have access to school restrooms and/or be able to participate in sports with others that are different from their sexes at birth, suffice it to say that this is an emerging issue that will take years to resolve.

7 Conclusion

One of the few things that can be certain when dealing with American schools is that change is a constant. That is, while some issues such as school governance, as well as the rights of students and school staff, because new issues are almost always on the legal horizon, the law will continue to evolve to meet the needs of all in public education.

---

[121] *Arlington Cent. Sch. Dist. v. Murphy,* 548 U.S. 291 (2006) (denying reimbursement to parents for the services of expert witnesses or consultants who assisted in their disagreements with their boards because the IDEA does not explicitly allow for such recovery).

[122] *Winkelman v. Parma City Sch. Dist.*, 570 U.S. 516 (2007) (deciding that because non-attorney parents have rights separate and apart from those of their children, they can proceed *pro se* in judicial actions challenging the IEPs of their children).

[123] See. e.g., *Riehm v. Engelking*, 538 F.3d 952 (8th Cir. 2008); *D.J.M. ex rel. D.M. v. Hannibal Pub. Sch. Dist. No. 60*, 647 F.3d 754 (8th Cir. 2011) (upholding punishments for threats). But see *J.S. v. Manheim Twp Sch. Dist.*, 263 A.3d 295 (Pa. 2021); *C1.G on behalf of C.G. v. Siegfried*, 38 F.4th 1270 (10th Cir. 2022) (rejecting punishments in finding that postings were not true threats).

Global Development of Education Law

Lanlan Liu

1 Introduction

After experiencing the COVID pandemic, which is unprecedented in human history, people appreciate more the important role that education plays in responding to the daunting challenges of human society, and at the same time we also see the fragility and uncertainty of education during the process of fighting against huge disasters. In 2021, the United Nations Educational, Scientific and Cultural Organization (UNESCO) released an important global report, Reimagining Our Future Together: Towards a New Social Contract for Education, emphasizing the fundamental role that education plays in the renewal and transformation of our societies, which helps us to navigate an ever- changing and unpredictable world, connect and unity people from all over the world to work together to build 'a more inclusive social environment, a more just economic environment, and a sustainable ecological environment' (UNESCO 2021). Despite marked increases in the coverage of education since the beginning of the twenty-first century, there is still a considerable gap between the global education situation and the goals of the Sustainable Development Goals (SDGs). As pointed out by the UN Secretary-General in his 2022 report, the pandemic has left billions of children severely out of school, more than 100 million children have reading and other academic skills below the minimum ability level, and school closures have severely affected children's access to knowledge and education (UN 2022). Governments should establish a governance model for education with the guarantee of human rights as the goal. The UN Special Rapporteur on the right to education has also stressed that, in order to achieve the education goals of the sustainable development agenda, states should establish a "rights-based approach to

L. Liu (✉)
College of Political Science and Law, Capital Normal University, Beijing, China
e-mail: liuaa@cnu.edu.cn

C. J. Russo and L. Ma (eds.), *A Comparative Analysis of Systems of Education Law*,
https://doi.org/10.1007/978-981-97-1052-2_19

education governance" (UN 2018), mainstream human rights guarantees—in particular the right to education—in education governance, formulate legally binding guarantee standards, and implement these standards in the laws and policies regarding on education, institution establishment, administrative law enforcement, judicial remedies and accountability mechanisms, so as to promote the development of the rule of law in education governance.

This paper analyzes education governance from two perspectives: human rights and development. The human rights perspective focuses on the human rights protection in the field of education with the right to education as the core, and the development perspective focuses on the education legislation and policy implementation as the means of the rule of law.

2 A Global Framework for the Rule of Law in Education

In order to achieve the global development goals in education, the United Nations has led to establish a global framework for the rule of law in education, which guides governments to develop their national education policies and laws and monitors the implementation of states' obligations under this framework to guarantee the realization of the right to education. From the perspective of the global rule of law in education, the responsibility to implement the right to education rests with governments. When formulating education laws and policies, states first turn to the international human rights treaties to which they have acceded or the advocacy plans launched by the international organizations that they have participated in. The sets of international rules not only constitute international standards guaranteeing the right to education, but also embody a global framework for education governance characterized by universality, inclusiveness, non-discrimination and the provision of quality education.

(i) **The right to education is a fundamental human right universally recognized around the world**

Education itself is a human right and an indispensable means of realizing other human rights. On the one hand, education serves as a fundamental tool that enables economically and socially marginalized adults and children to escape poverty and acquire the means to fully participate in the life of their communities; on the other hand, it promotes the dissemination of human rights and democratic values, enhances an inclusive understanding of a diverse world, and makes important impacts for the achievement of social harmony and stability (UNESCO 2021).

The 1948 Universal Declaration of Human Rights affirms that education is an inalienable right of everyone (Article 26), which sets a basic framework for the subsequent human rights conventions to endow the right to education with specific normative content. Articles 13 and 14 of the International Covenant on Economic, Social and Cultural Rights (ICESCR) of 1966 provide the normative content of the right to education, among which Article 13 is the most extensive and comprehensive provision on the right to education in the international human rights law. The UN Committee on Economic, Social and Cultural Rights has established a framework for evaluating the right to education based on the four features, namely, availability, accessibility, acceptability and adaptability (UNESC 1999). Articles 28 and 29 of the Convention on the Rights of the Child of 1989 clarify the obligations of States to guarantee the child as a fundamental subject of the right to education and emphasize that the purpose of education is to develop the child to his or her full potential and to promote human rights and fundamental freedoms (CRC 2001). Article 24 of the Convention on the Rights of Persons with Disabilities (CRPD) of 2008 requires an inclusive education system at all levels of education. This is the first international legal instrument with binding effect which puts forward the concept of "inclusive education," specifying its essential elements and standards for the protection of human rights (CRPD 2018). Not only the core United Nations human rights treaties provide the general framework for the protection of the right to education, but other international human rights law regulating the right to education includes the First Protocol to the European Convention on Human Rights and the Protection of Fundamental Freedoms (Article 2),[1] the Additional Protocol to the American Convention on Human Rights in the area of Economic, Social and Cultural Rights (Article 13),[2] the African Charter on Human and Peoples' Rights (Article 17),[3]the African Charter on the Rights and Welfare of the Child (Article 11)[4]and the Convention against Discrimination in Education.[5]

In addition to the above legally binding international human rights law, the right to education is also embodied in two far-reaching international frameworks for action, one is the Education for All (EFA) initiative of the United Nations Educational, Scientific and Cultural Organization (UNESCO), the other is the Sustainable Development Goals (SDGs) advocated by the United Nations (UN).

The idea of "EFA" originated at the 1990 UNESCO World Conference on Education For All, held in Jomtien, Thailand. The final document of the Conference, the World Declaration on EFA (also called the "Jomtien Declaration") emphasized the importance of the EFA goals for individual and social development (UNESCO 1990a, b). To realize the EFA goals. In 1994, UNESCO launched the global initiative for "Inclusive Education" at the World Congress on Special Needs Education, held in Salamanca, Spain (UNESCO 1994). At the beginning of the first decade of the twenty-first century, political leaders at the World Education Forum reaffirmed their commitment to the goals of Education for All and developed an action framework, the Dakar Framework for Action, Education for All: Realizing Our Collective Promise (UNESCO 2000). Turning into the second decade of the twenty-first

[1] Protocol No. 1 to European Convention for the Protection of Human Rights and Fundamental Freedoms (1952), Article 2.

[2] Addition Protocol to the American Convention on Human Rights in the Area of Economic, Social and Cultural Rights (1988), Article 13.

[3] African Charter on Human and People's Rights (1981), Article 17 (1).

[4] African Charter on the Rights and Welfare of the Child (1990), Article 11.

[5] UNESCO, Convention Against Discrimination in Education (1960), ED/2003/CONV/H/1.

century, representatives of more than 100 countries at the World Education Forum in Incheon, South Korea, reaffirmed that the primary responsibility for implementing the goals of inclusive and equitable education rests with national governments, and adopted Education 2030: Towards Inclusive and Equitable Quality Education for All and Lifelong Learning (the "Incheon Declaration") (UNESCO 2015), committing collectively to develop legal and political frameworks that promote accountability and transparency, participatory governance as well as partnership.

The Sustainable Development Goals (SDGs) are part of the 2030 Agenda for Sustainable Development, launched in 2015, at the United Nations' seventieth anniversary, as a global initiative for concerted action to end poverty, protect the planet, and improve the lives and futures of all people (UN 2015). All UN member states achieve a consensus to set up 17 Sustainable Development Goals (SDGs) in economic, social, and environmental areas that are important to human society, and set specific targets for each of these goals, which charted the way for the world to achieve these goals in the next 15 years. Education is the fourth goal of the SDGs, meaning 'to ensure inclusive and equitable quality education and lifelong learning opportunities for all',[6] which particularly is essential to achieve many of the other SDGs. Since the cycle of poverty cannot be broken without access to quality education, accessing to quality education and learning opportunities for all helps to reduce inequalities, enables people to have healthier and more sustainable lives, and promotes harmonious social development.

(ii) **Inclusive education plays a means to realize other basic human rights**

The concept of inclusive education dates back to the initiative of 'Education for All' established at the 1990 World Conference on Education for All (UNESCO 1990a, b). In 2005, UNESCO defined "inclusive education" as an education system that responds to the diverse learning needs of all learners, reduces the exclusion of certain categories of children from the education system, and ensures that all students, including those with disabilities, enjoy the right to education without discrimination and on an equal footing with others.[7] In 2006, the UN Convention on the Rights of Persons with Disabilities adopted the concept of inclusive education, and incorporated the legislative philosophy of "inclusiveness" into Article 24, which explicitly states that inclusive education is a human right. It rejects the medicalized perception of individuals with disabilities as less than fully competent actors, whereby persons with disabilities are placed in special education schools or institutions (Ballard 1997).

[6] See UN 'sustainable development' website, https://www.un.org/sustainabledevelopment/zh/education (last visit on 2023, July 20).

[7] UNESCO, Guideline of Inclusive Education: Make sure Education for All. The Chinese translation of 'inclusive education' differs among international organization. The governing Chinese version of the UN Convention on the Rights of Persons with Disabilities is translated as 'bao rong xing jiao yu (包容性教育)', while the Chinese version of the UNESCO document is translated as 'quan na jiao yu (全纳教育)'. From the perspective of legislative authority, the document issued by UNESCO is a political advocacy declaration, rather than a legally binding instrument. Therefore, in order to be consistent with the letter of the UN human rights treaties, this paper adopts the Chinese translation of inclusive education as '包容性教育'.

The Convention on the Rights of Persons with Disabilities clearly opposes this stereotypical perception of persons with disabilities as objects of social welfare, and notes that "disability" is an evolving concept that results from the interaction of persons with disabilities and the attitudinal and environmental barriers that prevent their full and meaningful participation in society on an equal basis with others. The United Nations Committee on the Rights of Persons with Disabilities has also emphasized that disability is a social model and disagreed the view of persons with disabilities as mere welfare recipients. The philosophy of social model emphasizes that persons with disabilities are subjects of rights and holders of fundamental human rights, including the right to education, and that the diversity of persons with disabilities must be taken into account when formulating laws and policies regarding the education for people with special education needs (CRPD 2018).

Education should be available to all. Inclusive education not only develops the enjoyment of the right to education by persons with disabilities, but also broadens the realistic ways for everyone to receive education. As noted by the United Nations Committee on Economic, Social and Cultural Rights, the right to education is a primary means for persons with disabilities to escape from poverty, participate fully in the life of their community and be free from exploitation (UN ESC 1999). Inclusive education is a prerequisite for persons with disabilities to exercise their other rights in the economy and society. Numerous research data indicate that persons with disabilities face relatively more discriminatory treatment in the labour market. Apart from negative representation of persons with disabilities in society and entrenched urban architecture, low educational attainment and the lack of necessary vocational training opportunities are also important barriers that prevent persons with disabilities from being employed or promoted (UN HRC 2012b). Studies by the International Labour Organization indicate that low educational attainment affects the productivity of persons with disabilities. Inclusive education helps persons with disabilities to acquire the skills of employment, thereby increasing the employment rate (Buckup 2009). It is evident that inclusive education not only provides persons with disabilities with basic survival skills for independent living and employment, but also promotes they actively integrate into society and thus realize individual economic value (Lanlan 2022).

Moreover, inclusive education aims to promote mutual respect and the appreciation of all learners, and strives to uphold the values of inclusion and respect for diversity in the educational process, curricula and school culture (CRPD 2016). It provides a reliable platform to combat segregation and discrimination, because each learner's personality and contribution can be valued despite the fact that different learners possess different capacities for inclusion. This will facilitate the gradual elimination of prejudices against minorities, the removal of barriers that prevent persons with disabilities and other minorities from exercising other basic rights, and the building of an inclusive society based on mutual respect and understanding.

(iii) **Eliminating discrimination in education and achieving equality in education**

Equality in education is the global political commitment made by the international community to the goal of Education for All at the World Education Forum in 2000. At the United Nations Millennium Development Summit in the same year, political leaders adopted the Millennium Development Goals (UN 2000) to address the eight most pressing challenges of the new millennium. The important concerns on education include the appeal to States to ensure that all children complete primary education, to eliminate the gender gap in primary and secondary education and to fully respect equal educational opportunity in the design, implementation and evaluation of education policies (Liu 2014). The global political commitment to promoting equality in education is also reflected in the Durban Declaration and Programme of Action, adopted at the World Conference against Racism, Racial Discrimination, Xenophobia and Related Intolerance. The Declaration and Programme urged States to ensure access to education for all without discrimination, to remove barriers to access to education, to ensure quality education, to monitor the educational achievements of children belonging to disadvantaged groups and to allocate resources to address inequalities in children's educational outcomes (Durban 2001). Moreover, with regard to equal access to education for women and men, the Beijing Platform for Action, adopted at the Fourth World Conference on Women in 1995, identified women and education as one of its 12 key areas of concern, recognizing, inter alia, that "only when women have equal access to education and access to academic qualifications will more women become agents of change" (Beijing 1995).

The promotion of equality in education lies in guaranteeing that this right is enjoyed equally by everyone. This principle of non-discrimination forms a core principle of all international human rights treaties. No one shall be subjected to discrimination to the right to education on the grounds of race, sex, disability, religion, ethnicity or language. Article 13 of the International Covenant on Economic, Social and Cultural Rights (ICESCR) explicitly provides that everyone has the right to free primary education and that the State has the responsibility to progressively make it available to all and to guarantee equal access to higher education in accordance with abilities. The United Nations Committee on Economic, Social and Cultural Rights has emphasized that the "accessibility" of the right to education includes access to educational institutions and resources for all without discrimination (UN ESC 1999). The Convention against Discrimination in Education, adopted by UNESCO in 1960, is an important instrument on equality in education, as it expounds the principles of non-discrimination and equal opportunities in education. The Convention seeks not only to eliminate discrimination in education, but also to take positive measures to promote equality of opportunity and treatment. Article 4 of the Convention specifically provides that States have the obligation to adopt, develop and implement national policies to promote equality of opportunity and equality of treatment in education.

As for the meaning of the principles of non-discrimination and equality in education, the United Nations Committee on Economic, Social and Cultural Rights has explicitly stated that the prohibition of discrimination in education should apply immediately to all aspects and components of education and that the scope of the prohibition of discrimination includes those grounds of discrimination that are prohibited in international treaties. While the prohibition of discrimination aims at achieving substantive equality, special measures adopted in particular cases to promote and achieve equality should not be regarded as the violation of the principle of non-discrimination. For example, in order to change the disadvantaged situation of girls in education, the educational institutions established and maintained separately for girls and boys shall provide equal educational opportunities, employ the same qualified teachers, use the same school buildings and equipment with the same quality requirements, and provide the opportunities to attend the same courses. As a further example, separate educational institutions may be established or maintained on religious or linguistic grounds to safeguard equal access of educatees with different educational needs, on the basis of respect for freedom of education. The provision of educational content or curricula that meet standards set by the authorities is also a means of promoting equality in education.

(iv) **Quality education is the goal of sustainable development in education**

While significant progress has been made towards the goal of universal primary education since the World Education Forum in Dakar, the issue of quality of education has not been effectively addressed. The lack of resources for quality education and the uneven development have attracted widespread attention and prompted the international community to put forward several initiatives. The right to quality education plays the key role to move forward the Education for All agenda and accelerate the process of achieving sustainable development goal four.

"Quality education" is a conceptual framework for assessing the quality of education in terms of knowledge, skills and abilities (Sobhi et al. 2012). It ensures education service to meet basic learning needs and it has become a priority in national education development strategies. According to the report on quality education of the United Nations Special Rapporteur on the Right to Education, the comprehensive conceptual framework of quality education comprises the following elements: (i) Minimum standards for the acquisition of the knowledge, values, skills and abilities that constitute the basic learning needs of educatees as an important component of basic education as well as a priority in improving and assessing the quality of education. Moreover, the universally recognized value of human is one of the criteria of quality education. Education is unparalleled in its value in promoting the development of values of a culture of peace, mutual understanding and international solidarity; (ii) An adequate school infrastructure, facilities and environment, without which quality of education cannot be improved unless there is adequate financial investment in education; (iii) A qualified and adequate pool of teachers, quality teachers with the requisite capacity to impart knowledge, values and skills; and (iv) Schools that are open to all, particularly students, parents and communities. Moreover, the universally recognized value of humanism is one of the criteria of quality education. (i) Education is unparalleled in its value in promoting the development of values of a culture of peace, mutual understanding and international solidarity; (ii) An adequate school infrastructure, facilities and environment, which the quality of education cannot be improved unless there is adequate financial investment in education; (iii) A qualified and adequate pool of teachers, quality teachers with the requisite capacity to impart knowledge, values and skills; and (iv) Schools that are open to all, particularly students, parents and communities.

The Universal Declaration of Human Rights, the International Covenant on Economic, Social and Cultural Rights and the Convention on the Rights of the Child constitute the international normative framework for quality education. Article 26 of the Universal Declaration of Human Rights makes it clear that the purpose of education is to develop fully the human personality and to strengthen respect for human rights and fundamental freedoms. Article 13 of the International Covenant on Economic, Social and Cultural Rights provides that education shall enable all people to participate effectively in a free society and shall promote understanding, tolerance and usefulness among peoples and among racial, ethnical or religious groups and shall further put forward the activities of the United Nations for the maintenance of peace. Article 29 of the Convention on the Rights of the Child also provides that education shall cultivate the respect for human rights, for the children and their parents' cultural identity, language and values, as well as for the values and cultures different from those of nations. Quality education thus contributes to the full development of the human person and his or her dignity.

Moreover, women have the right to quality education. Article 10 of Convention on the Elimination of All Forms of Discrimination against Women provides that States parties shall ensure, on the basis of equality of women and men, equal rights of women to education with regard to access to schooling, conditions of schools, vocational training, curriculum content, quality of teachers and quality of school buildings and facilities. The Convention against Discrimination in Education, adopted by UNESCO, also reinforces States' obligations to ensure the quality of education by establishing an obligation to develop a uniform framework of standards for measuring and evaluating education throughout the country.

3 Protection of the Rights Concerned by Education Law

Under the global framework of the rule of law in education, members of the international community not only shoulder the political mission to achieve the goal of sustainable development in education, but also have the obligation to protect the various rights to education within their own legal systems. According to the national rule of law system, education is an important field under the legal system of each country. Some countries have established a complete system of education laws, while others have passed separate legislations to regulate the rights and obligations of education subjects. The protection of the rights concerned by education law is mainly reflected in the following aspects:

(i) The right to education is a fundamental constitutional right

Since the right to education was first included in the Weimar Constitution of Germany, it has been reaffirmed as a fundamental civil right by most modern countries in the world (Wen 2008). The constitutions of China, Japan, Russia, Argentina, Hungary, Spain and other countries explicitly provide that citizens have the right to education. The right to education is established as a fundamental right in national constitutions, especially in the provisions on the aims of education and the mature of the right, which embodies the important value of education as a means to realize human dignity and freedom.

The expressions of the aims of education in national constitutions have distinct national characteristics, and also reflect some common values. For example, all countries generally agree with the people-oriented philosophy, the rights-based theory and the respect for human development. All countries agree with the concept stated in the second paragraph of the Universal Declaration of Human Rights, "The aim of education is to fully develop the human personality and to strengthen the respect for human rights and fundamental freedoms," and protect the right to education in the form of their own fundamental laws. The provisions of the right to education in national constitutions emphasize that the purpose of education is the full development of human personality, the respect for human dignity and the realization of the comprehensive human development. For example, the Spanish Constitution stipulates that the purpose of education is the full development of human personality, within the context of respect for democracy and the fundamental rights and freedoms.

In addition, the right to education articles in national constitutions also stipulate the nature of education. For example, the Russian and Portuguese Constitutions both clearly provide that citizens have the right to education, which is a fundamental right and freedom of citizens. In some constitutions, education is considered as both a right and a duty. For example, the Japanese Constitution states that all citizens have the right to education according to their ability as prescribed by law; all citizens have the duty to ensure their children to receive general education as prescribed by law. The Basic Law of Germany stipulates that childrearing and education is inalienable right and primary duty of parents, which under supervision by the State. Article 46 of the Constitution of China stipulates that citizens have the right and duty to receive education. Most scholars in China think that the right to education is a fundamental right with the attributes of both social right and freedom right (Wen 2003). As a social right, the right to education pursues equal value, and requires the State to fulfill its positive obligation to protect citizens to equally access to education (Zheng 2007). As a freedom right, the right to education is manifested as the freedom to choose education, which means an individual can make decision on content of education and the way to receive education by his or her own action without external compulsion (Lao 2021). Some scholars also think that the constitutional provisions of the right to education are constitutional norms in which rights and obligations coincide (Lì 2002), which embodies the right to education is the combination and unity of rights and obligations. If we discuss the right to education without involving the obligation of education, we cannot understand the complete meaning of the right to education.

(ii) **Equality in education and equal rights in education**

From the perspective of the realization of the right to education, the education legislation of all countries is based on equality in education, attaches importance to the legal obligation of prohibition of discrimination required by international human rights treaties, and guarantees equal opportunities in education through their constitutions and equality laws or anti-discrimination laws. Many countries have guaranteed equal opportunities and equal access to education in their constitutions. The constitutions of all countries embody such concepts as equality and full opportunity, equal right to free compulsory education, etc. This provides sufficient legal basis for state actions at the national level, not only enacting education laws, but also making policies and programmes to ensure equal opportunities to education for all.

Equality in education is the ultimate goal of the right to education, and also the main value of education development. Countries apply various guarantee systems protecting equal rights in education. Usually, civil law system countries stipulate the equal right to education by formulating special education laws, while common law system countries pay more attention to provide the relief for the right to education through case law. For example, in Japan, the Basic Law on Education is the fundamental law on education, and its Article IV specifies that all citizens have equal opportunities to education. Later, Japan promulgated a series of separate laws on education, such as the School Education Act, the Act on the Promotion of Life-long Learning, the Act on the Organization and Function of Local Education Administration, etc. In order to promote and facilitate equal access to education for persons with disabilities, the United States has enacted such education laws as the Education of All Children with Disabilities Act (1975), the Individuals with Disabilities Education Act (1990) and the Disability Education Promotion Act (2004). These laws have specific objectives to eliminate the discrimination faced by persons with disabilities in education and pursue substantive equality in education.

In addition to statutory laws, case law develops the jurisprudence of human rights protection, and further improves the quality of education legislations. For example, Article 41 of the Constitution of India provides for free and compulsory education for children as a guiding principle of national policy (Vashist 2010). By engaging in a series of influential constitutional lawsuits,[8] in 1993 the Supreme Court of India recognized that the free and compulsory primary education is a fundamental right of every child in India, which derives from the constitutional right to life and personal liberty. To ensure the full and effective realization of this right, the Union Parliament enacted a constitutional amendment by adding that "children between the ages of six and fourteen shall have the fundamental right to free and compulsory primary education" (Article 21A of the Constitution of India). In 2009, India formulates the Right of Children to Free and Compulsory Education Act, which provides a legal and regulatory framework for the implementation of the fundamental right to free and compulsory education, and it recognizes and implements the fundamental right to primary education in India.

---

[8] Mohini Jain v. State of Karnataka, AIR 1992 SC 1858, Unni Kirshnan, J.P. and Ors v. State of Andhra Pradesh and Ors. 1993 AIR 2178.

(iii) **Freedom of education**

Education freedom is one of dimensions of the right to education as a human right. According to the United Nations Committee on Economic, Social and Cultural Rights in its general comment on the right to education, the right to freedom of education has twofolds. First, parents and guardians are free to choose the religious and moral education for their children in accordance with their own convictions; and second, parents and guardians are free to choose private schools for their children (UN ESC 1999). The first allows public schools to offer courses in religion and ethics on the condition that teaching a particular religion or belief must be conducted in an objective, unprejudiced manner; the second requires private educational institutions to meet minimum educational standards or approved by the State, which may relate to admission, quality of courses, validation of certificates, etc. The content of these freedoms of education can be embodied in the domestic law of each country as freedom of religion, academic freedom, or right to home education, etc.

In domestic practice, freedom of education often closely links to the fundamental freedom of religion or belief. For example, Article 27 of the Spanish Constitution provides that parents have the right to choose the religious and moral education of their children in accordance with their convictions and that the State has a duty to guarantee religious education, including access to its financial resources and the right of communities to practice their religion in accordance with their creeds. Moreover, freedom of education can also closely connect to the expression of thoughts and behaviors, particularly with regard to academic freedom and the exercise of cultural rights. Academic freedom is one of the fundamental rights of freedom of expression established by constitution, because it derives from the protection of freedom of expression for teachers and students, but the exercise of this right depends on could be effected or limited by particular policies by educational institutions. In public schools, this freedom is restricted by national policy, because teaching and learning must respect the principle of State neutrality which rejects ideological indoctrination. In private schools, by contrast, the boundaries of academic freedom are determined by the private schools themselves, which is the freedom of the sponsor of education.

As for the legal status and regulation of home schooling, the legislations generally either oppose or support home schooling. The former one stipulates that home schooling during the period of compulsory education is illegal, while the other one grants home education legitimacy and stipulates detailed regulations on it. For example, Article 11 of China's Compulsory Education Law provides that all children aged six or over must attend school and receive compulsory education. The Chinese Ministry of Education has clarified that where a child needs to postpone school due to health or other reasons, his/her parents or other guardians should apply to the relevant education authorities for deferment of school. Once the application has been approved, they may postpone school, but must not substitute home schooling for compulsory education (Ministry of Education 2017). Therefore, according to China's education law, home schooling is illegal, and every school-age child must attend a primary school or middle school to receive compulsory education. The main considerations in such laws are, first, whether the quality of home schooling meets the minimum national education standards; and, second, whether home schooling leads to children dropping out of school, affecting the realization of the child's right to education, and thus putting the child's growth at great risk (Chu et al. 2017). Different from China's legislative practice, in countries such as Australia and the United Kingdom, home education is regarded as the result of parents' or guardians' choosing education and therefore it is recognized as legitimate. On the issue of compulsory school attendance, laws in all Australian states oblige parents or guardians to ensure that children attend school and receive school education. They may also choose home schooling, but the curriculum, quality and implementation of home education must be regulated by each state's education department, in order to ensure that children receive a high-quality education, furthermore, parents are required to submit annual reports on their child's progress in home schooling.[9] The United Kingdom, on the other hand, adopts a very liberal system of home education. In the United Kingdom, parents or guardians are allowed to choose alternatives to schooling for their children, but there are no clear and specific requirements on curriculum standards, learning assessment and teaching staff for home education, and the law does not provide for regular inspections by education administrations (UK 2018). The quite liberal and flexible home schooling system in UK remains much debate on whether home schooling ensure the quality of education. In the absence of clear standards and effective regulation for the quality of home education, children may not be acquiring knowledge and skills that meet national standards or societal expectations.

(iv) **Quality of education**

The quality of education always has attracted great attention in reforms of national education systems, including the adoption of education laws and decrees that establish specific rules and regulations to improve the quality of education. The right to quality education is enshrined in the legislation of many countries, effectively showing how international obligations are reflected in the domestic legal order.

The right to quality education is a constitutional right in some countries. In order to improve the academic achievement in schools, the United States enacted the No Child Left Behind Act, stipulating national standards for education quality and establishing measurable objectives on quality of education. In Brazil, based on the "minimum standards for equality of educational opportunity and quality" enshrined in the Constitution, the National Education Act specifies education quality standards, such as national curricula for basic and secondary education, and teacher requirements. Indian Right of Children to Free and Compulsory Education Act (2009) provides for compulsory education to "ensure good quality of basic education". Indonesian National Education System Act (2003) imposes state with the obligation to provide quality basic education to all. This law establishes the minimum national standards to be attained by all schools in the country.

---

[9] School Education Act 1999 (WA), ss 47-48; Education Act 1990 (NSW), ss 72-73, Education (General Provisions) Act 2006 (QLD) s 217.

The quality of education is not only concerned by education legislation in various countries, but also an important part of education policy reform. For example, Article 3 of Chinese Compulsory Education Act stipulates that compulsory education must comply with the country's education policies, implement quality education and improve the quality of education. In 2020, the Chinese Government issued the Outline of the National Medium- and Long-term Plan for Education Reform and Development (2010–2020), which made improvement of the quality of education as the core task of education reform and development. Subsequently, in 2021, the Ministry of Education issued two key policies, the Guidelines for Quality Evaluation of Compulsory Education and the Implementation Plan for Auditing and Evaluating Undergraduate Education in General Institutions of Higher Learning (2021–2025). In 2022 the policies regarding on assessment of education quality extended to the senior secondary schools and kindergartens, which established a national quality standard system covering the entire school cycle of education.

National standards on quality education address the following aspects: campus learning environment, teacher-student ratio, teacher qualification and in-service training, course content, teaching supervision and inspection, etc. First, the full realization of the right to education requires a healthy, hygienic and safe learning environment, which includes, on one hand, a physical environment with basic amenities (UN HRC 2012a), such as clean sanitation, adequate barrier-free access, uncontaminated student playing fields, and well-equipped classrooms and school buildings, and on the other hand, a cultural environment that respects and accommodates students' individual freedoms (CRPD 2014), such as individualized lesson plans, inclusive learning environments and reasonable accommodation for specific groups of people. Second, the teacher-student ratio is another important indicator of education quality. In many developing countries, crowded classrooms do not guarantee the quality of teaching and learning, and smaller class sizes can help teachers to reach out to their students as much as possible and to individualize their teaching and learning. Third, the shortage of qualified teachers is particularly acute in underdeveloped countries (Mulkeen 2010). As a profession, it is necessary to set minimum standards of qualification for the teaching personnel. The State is required to, on the one hand, legally clarify teachers' working conditions and welfare, enhance the social recognition of the teaching profession, and on the other hand, increase investment in teacher training, teacher qualification and in-service training. Fourth, national laws and policies require public schools to implement uniform national curriculum standards to ensure the quality of education. For example, in Australia, the local education legislations provide that the Minister for Education who is also responsible for setting and monitoring teaching and learning standards in public schools, has the power to determine the curriculum framework for public schools,[10] and that the implementation of school curricula in each state is monitored and evaluated by an independent

[10] Education (General Provisions) Act (QLD), s. 21; Education and Children Services Act 2019 (SA), s. 8 (1) (a); School Education Act 1999 (WA), s. 61.

regulator.[11] Moreover, regardless of how standards of quality in education are set, the State needs to strengthen monitoring and oversight to check and guide policies on the implementation of education quality indicators. The regulator should ensure effective implementation of education quality standards, and provide oversight and accountability for situations and personnel that do not conform to standards.

4 New Challenges in Education in the Digital Age

In an era of digital technologies, generative artificial intelligence technologies like ChatGPT are changing the traditional function of education and affecting daily lives of educators and educatees. For instance, information and communications technologies applied in accessing digital content, online educational materials and courses, e-textbooks, and course video and audio files on the Internet are revolutionizing the way education is delivered (OECD 2005). Moreover, in the context of the global pandemic, massive open online courses, such as MOOCs, provide an alternative route to higher education, and many people have accessed information and knowledge using open educational resources on the Internet (UNESCO 2012). On the other hand, digitization of education has created a huge "digital divide," especially in developing and underdeveloped countries.[12] Accessing to education in a digitized context requires necessary may marginalize poverty families, children in remote areas, persons with disabilities, etc., and impact their enjoyment of the right to education. How to embrace digital technologies while guaranteeing the realization of the right to education is a major challenge facing the ongoing digital revolution in education (UN HRC 2016). These challenges are represented by:

(i) **Exacerbation of the digital divide in education**

Reliance on digital education, particularly distance-access digital education, may exacerbate inequalities that already existed in education (UN HRC 2020). Students have unequal access to Internet services, appropriate hardware and qualified teachers with digital skills, and teachers' proficiency in the use of digital technologies is also uneven. When the digital approaches applied into education, it is worth to pay attention to the rights of the marginalized people. Many factors such as gender, religion, ethnicity, social class, disability, etc., may influence students' and teachers' experiences on digitization. The digital technology potentially exacerbates rather

[11] Victorian Curriculum and Assessment Authority established under the Victorian Curriculum and Assessment Authority Act 2000 (Vic), and the Western Australia School Curriculum and Standards Authority established under the School curriculum and Standards Authority Act 1997 (WA).

[12] According to International Telecommunication Union (ITU) statistics, the global average of household internet access is 43 and 80% in developed countries, while the percentage of households in developing countries is 34% and in underdeveloped countries is only 7%. See ITU, The world in 2015: Facts and Figures, https://www.itu.int/en/ITU-D/Statistics/Documents/facts/ICTFactsFigures2015.pdf (last visit on 2023, July 20).

than mitigates digital inequalities in a variety of ways. Biases embedded in algorithms applied to educational APPs and platforms also need to be addressed (UN HRC 2022).

(ii) **The infringement on privacy by digitization of education information**

Digital technologies in education have generated a large and growing amount of personal data of actors in schooling, including students and teachers. There is a clear imbalance in power, awareness and knowledge between those owning the decision-making power over technology and the internet users, which runs counter to the human-rights principles of freedom, equality, autonomy and participation. The ways in which data are collected and used in education, in some cases keep complete secrecy and do not respect the right to privacy and the principle of effective informed consent, which impose huge risk on students' privacy (CRC 2021). Although some countries have adopted specific legislation to protect children's online privacy,[13] most countries have no specific rules on the protection of children' data to protect children's privacy in a complex cyber environment.

(iii) **Illegal and criminal acts caused by abuse of digital technology**

Cyberspace is not a law vacuum zone. Illegal and criminal acts involving the misuse of technologies, such as cyberbullying, leaking of personal information and even terrorism, will seriously affect students' right to education. The Committee on the Rights of the Child (CRC) emphasized the need to protect children from the harmful effects of harmful information on the Internet, such as information that is aggressive, violent, hateful, prejudiced, racist, pornographic, inappropriate and misleading. States must take measures to protect children from online harassment, while at the same time ensuring that children are not involved in law-breaking and terrorism (CRC 2011).

(iv) **Using digital technologies to achieve lawful knowledge sharing**

In 2020, with the COVID-19 pandemic sweeping through the world, the Internet has become the main platform for work, life and study of people all over the world. During the epidemic period, in the field of education, both the daily courses provided for students in schools and the skill training for employed people have almost changed to online mode, and the online education industry has experienced explosive growth in recent two years (China Internet Network Information Center 2021). These open online courses are not only public education resources, but also intellectual property of teaching staff. All forms of intellectual property are protected by the Copyright Law, but under certain conditions, these learning materials are also permitted to be used free of charge for teaching purposes.[14] In the digital age, how to strike a

[13] In the United States, the laws that specifically protect privacy in education include the Family Educational Rights and privacy Act, The Children's Internet Protection Act and the Children's Online Protection Act. In China, the law that specifically protect minors include the Protection of Minors Law, and in addition, the Children's Personal Information Network Protection and the Provisions on the Protection of Minors in Schools have also been formulated to particularly protect minor's online privacy.

[14] Berne Convention for the Protection of Literary and Artistic Works (1971), Article 3 and Article 10.

balance between the rights of copyright owners and the public interest of knowledge sharing, puts forward higher requirements for the Copyright Law. After the birth of ChatGPT, generative AI technologies can not only cope with vocational examinations (Choi et al. 2023), assist teaching (Cui et al. 2023), but also lead to cheating in examinations,[15] and academic ethics and integrity (Jiao et al. 2023). Thus, the wide application of digital technology in the field of education has both positive and negative effects. Educational legislation and policy should take into account the "double-edged sword" effect of science and technology and make good use of digital technology to help knowledge sharing.

5 Legal and Policy Responses to the Digitization of Education

In the process of the digital transformation of education, laws and policies should balance values of freedom and fairness to ensure people enjoy the freedom of education and the fair access to quality education. Specifically:

First, education legislation should make it clear that the use of digital technologies must assist to fulfill the right to education and promote educational fairness, rather than expand educational gaps. Education legislation takes the "rights-based" approaches as the guide and strengthen the protection of the equal right of education for the minority groups and marginalized groups. For example, the laws of the education for persons with disabilities incorporate the concept of "inclusive education" embodied in the Convention on the Rights of Persons with Disabilities; and the ideas of establishing the barrier-free accessibility and reasonable accommodations in educational institutions. This accessibility includes both physical facilities and services such as sign language interpretation and braille readers. The laws of education for disabled people aim to eliminate the social barriers against persons with disabilities to education.

Second, digital technologies not only develop the tools of teaching and learning, but also create tremendous learning resources for generating and connecting knowledge and information. Therefore, in order to make open educational resources (OER) available and effective, education law and policy should promote and encourage the empowerment of digital technologies for education. For example, education policies facilitate the sharing of open educational resources and multiple and continuous interaction among teachers, students, educators and others, which ensure digital technologies to enhance, rather than replace, the traditional classroom pedagogical approaches and educational content.

Thirdly, in order to take full advantage of OER and e-learning, education legislation should explicitly stipulate the rules of monitoring and supervision for online

[15] A number of universities from different countries have explicitly declared that students are not allowed to use generative artificial intelligence tools to complete examinations. See https://m.thepaper.cn/baijiahao_21973100 (last visit on 2023, July 20).

education. Education policies can adopt specific criteria to determine the teaching qualification, content of online courses and quality of online education. Regulatory frameworks are extremely important in establishing requirements for responsibility and accountability. States have the primary responsibility to respect and protect the right to education and must ensure that educational institutions remain essential public services. In the view that the application of digital technologies brings both opportunities and risks to the education sector, it is necessary to put the digital technology under an effective regulatory framework by government to supervise the digitization of education and promote the improvement and optimization of the quality of education.

References

Ballard K (1997) Researching disability and inclusive education: participation, construction and interpretation. Int J Incl Educ 243:244

Beijing (1995) World conference on women, Beijing declaration and platform for action. A/CONF.177/20. http://hrlibrary.umn.edu/instree/bejingdec.htm

Buckup (2009) Sebastian the price of exclusion: the economic consequences of excluding people with disabilities from the world of work. International Labour Organization

China Internet Network Information Centre (CINIC), 47th China's internet development statistical report. Available at http://www.cac.gov.cn/2021-02/03/c_1613923423079314.htm. Accessed on 1 March 2024

Choi HJ, Hickman EK, Monahan A, Schwarcz BD (2023) ChatGPT goes to law school. Minnesota Legal Studies Research Paper No. 23-03. https://ssrn.com/abstract=4335905

Chu C, Xiong B, Wang J (2017) "Home schooling" remains unsolved legal issue (in Chinese "在家上学" 尚有法律问题待解). Legal Daily, 2017-03-02(005)

Committee on the Rights of the Child (CRC) (2001) General Comment No. 1. CRC/GC/2001/1

Committee on the Rights of the Child (CRC) (2011), General Comment No. 13. CRC/C/GC/13

Committee on the Rights of the Child (CRC) (2021) General Comment No. 25. CRC/C/GC/25

Committee on the Rights of Persons with Disabilities (CRPD) (2014) General Comment No. 2. CRPD/C/GC/2

Committee on the Rights of Persons with Disabilities (CRPD) (2016) General Comment No. 4. CRPD/C/GC/4

Committee on the Rights of Persons with Disabilities (CRPD) (2018) General Comment No. 6. CRPD/C/GC/6

Cui Y, Bai F, Zhang R (2023) Application, risks and countermeasures of ChatGPT in the field of higher education (in Chinese ChatGPT 在高等教育领域的应用、风险及应对). J Chongqing Univ Sci Technol (Soc Sci) 05:1–17

Durban (2001) World conference against racism, racial discrimination, xenophobia and related intolerance. A/CONF.189/12

UN Economic and Social Council (UN ESC) (2022) Report of the secretary-general on progress towards the sustainable development goals. E/2022/55

UN Human Rights Council (UN HRC) (2012a) Report of the special rapporteur on the right to education on normative action for quality education. A/HRC/20/21

UN Human Rights Council (UN HRC) (2012b). Report of the office of the United Nations high commissioner for human rights on the work and employment of persons with disabilities. A/HRC/22/25

UN Human Rights Council (UN HRC) (2016) Report of the special rapporteur on the right to education on issues and challenges to the right to education in the digital age. A/HRC/32/37

UN Human Rights Council (UN HRC) (2018) Report of the special rapporteur on the right to education on governance and the right to education. A/HRC/38/32

UN Human Rights Council (UN HRC) (2020) Report of the special rapporteur on the right to education on impact of the coronavirus disease crisis on the right to education. A/HRC/C/44/39

UN Human Rights Council (UN HRC) (2022) Report of the special rapporteur on the right to education on the impact of the digitalization of education on the right to education. A/HRC/50/32

Jiao J, Chen L, Wu W (2023) Educational issues triggered by ChatGPT: possible impacts and counter measure (in Chinese 由ChatGPT引发的教育之问: 可能影响与应对之策). China's Educ Inform 29(03):19–32

Liu, L (2014) Taking basic education in China forward: a study of the enjoyment of the right to education in the PRC in international and domestic law. LAP Lambert Academic Publishing

Liu, L (2022) What is inclusive education? Reflections on the right to education for people with disabilities (in Chinese 何谓包容性教育? 对残疾人受教育权的再思考). Chin J Hum Rights 8(01):102–124

Lao K (2021) New views on the right to education (in Chinese 受教育权新论). Educ Res 42(08):23–34

Lì Y (2002) Research on basic theory on right to education (in Chinese 受教育权利的基本理论问题探讨). China Educ Legal Rev 2002(00):345–356

Ministry of Education (2017) Notice on compulsory education enrollment in 2017 (in Chinese 关于做好2017年义务教育招生入学工作的通知)

Mulkeen A (2010) Teachers in Anglophone Africa: issues in teacher supply, training and management, World Bank. https://openknowledge.worldbank.org/server/api/core/bitstreams/f173aac1-09dc-542c-8291-80b53161103f/content

OECD, Centre for Educational Research and Innovation (2005) E-learning in tertiary education: where do we stand. https://www.oecd-ilibrary.org/docserver/9789264009219-en.pdf?expires=1683179908&id=id&accname=guest&checksum=815367D4D56902702E3DF741C12C9F2A

Sobhi T et al (2012) Beyond the conceptual maze: the notion of quality in education. UNESCO ERF Thematic paper, No. 2. https://unesdoc.unesco.org/ark:/48223/pf0000217519

UK, Department for Education (2018) Elective home education. https://consult.education.gov.uk/school-frameworks/home-education-call-for-evidence-and-revised-dfe-a/supporting_documents/Elective%20home%20educationGuide%20for%20LAs.pdf

UN General Assembly Resolution (UN 2015), Transforming our world: the 2030 Agenda for Sustainable Development (2015), A/RES/70/1

UNESCO (1990a) World declaration on education for all, framework for action meeting basic learning needs: guidelines for implementing world declaration on education for all

UNESCO (1990b) World declaration on education for all: meeting basic learning needs

UNESCO (1994) The Salamanca statement and framework for action on special needs education

UNESCO (2000) Dakar framework for action: education for all: meeting our collective commitment

UNESCO (2015) Incheon declaration: education 2030: towards inclusive and equitable quality education and lifelong learning for all. ED/WEF2015/MD/3

UNESCO (2012) World open education resources congress. https://en.unesco.org/courier/julio-septiembre-2017/sharing-legally-and-freely-better-learning

UNESCO (2021) Reimaging our futures together: a new social contract for education. UNESCO, Paris

UN Economic and Social Council (UN ESC) (1999) General Comment No. 13. E/C.12/1999/10

United Nations Millennium Declaration (UN 2000) A/RES/55/2

Vashist L (2010) Enlivening directive principles: an attempt to save their vanishing present. LIL Law Review 1(2):205–226

Wen H (2003) Research on the right to education in constitution (in Chinese 受教育权入宪研究). Peking University Press, Beijing

Wen H (2008) Constitutional analysis of the education (in Chinese 教育的宪法学解读). J Natl Prosecutor's Coll 76(04):101–106

Zheng X (2007) Study on basic rights (in Chinese 基本权利研究). China Democracy and Law Press, Beijing

www.ingramcontent.com/pod-product-compliance
Lightning Source LLC
Chambersburg PA
CBHW060452240325
23959CB00003B/124
9789819710515